COMMAND

COMMAND

A Historical Dictionary
of
MILITARY LEADERS

General Editor
JAMES LUCAS

MILITARY PRESS
NEW YORK

Military Press
New York

This 1988 edition published by Military Press, distributed by Crown Publishers Inc., 225 Park Avenue South, New York, New York 10003

Typeset in Britain by SX Composing Ltd
Originated, printed and bound in Singapore by Toppan Printing Co (Singapore) Pte Ltd.

This book was edited, designed and produced by The Paul Press Ltd, 41-42 Berners Street, London W1P 3AA

General Editor: James Lucas
Contributing Editors: Tim Newark, G. D. Sheffield
Editorial: Michael Brook
Design: Jerry Goldie, Lester Cheeseman
Indexer: Lyn Greenwood
Cartography: Map Consultants
Picture Research: Helen Fickling
Production: Nicky Bowden

Art Director: Stephen McCurdy
Editorial Director: Jeremy Harwood

ISBN 0-517-64791-5

h g f e d c b a

CONTENTS

THE EVOLUTION OF COMMAND

The evolution of military command through the ages is the story of a concept that has been moulded and shaped by changing historical, social and economic circumstances. At its root lies the basic fact that aggression is a natural human characteristic, despite all claims – or hopes – to the contrary and that, as far as recorded history shows, warfare is an endemic part of life.

The first commanders

Organized battles, of whatever description, demand commanders. From earliest times, ancient heroes and the battles they fought were commemorated. The first written record of a battle is of Megiddo in 1469 BC; this shows that the victorious Egyptian army, led by the warrior pharaoh Tuthmosis, not only made use of efficient fighting tactics, but also possessed a reliable communications system to pass orders during the general melée.

The next step was an interesting diversification, with the evolution of the warrior-ruler into a sacred priest-king. The latter was too precious to be risked in combat, so the result was that the ruler appointed a substitute battlefield commander from among his relatives, or close friends. These, in turn, started to delegate battlefield responsibility, as they, in turn, became too important to put at risk.

The consequences of this were as follows. Where these new deputies lacked the necessary command skills, they were taught them in the world's first military academies, where a thorough grounding was given in the rules and the art of war. As a result, officers were being trained along common lines – a step that logically led to the development of a staff system.

Fighting for land and loot

Though empires rose and fell, this pattern – that of an organized force which could make use of sophisticated tactics and possessed a communications network, an excellent logistical organization and a staff system – set the framework in which commanders operated up until the declining years of Rome's empire. Paradoxically, it was the very success of its armies that indirectly destroyed imperial Rome. The population of the Italian homeland was too small to maintain the large army needed to garrison the territories that Rome controlled. The men needed to fill the ranks of the legions would not come forward voluntarily, while attempts to introduce conscription also failed. The alternative was to recruit foreigners, who had neither the mystic loyalty to Rome nor the stern discipline of the old legions and who broke under the attacks of the barbarian hordes. The empire fragmented and Europe entered the so-called Dark Ages.

The turmoil of that period of history obviously affected contemporary armies and their commanders. Living in an almost lawless society, they concerned themselves more with skirmishing for land and loot, rather than with national aims and policies. Even when the European continent was threatened with physical conquest by the expanding might of militant Islam, the warrior-rulers of the day could not agree on a united policy of defence. The same thing happened in the Crusades, when the leaders of the Crusader armies frequently spent more time disputing among themselves than in fighting the Saracens.

There were military professionals, of course. These were the mounted knights, who formed the core of the medieval fighting force. But the expense of summoning the feudal host was such that the armies of the day tended to be rag-bag collections of fighting men, hastily assembled when the occasion warranted. Even by the end of the 17th century, very few countries had a large, standing army. Such forces as existed were considered to be royal toys, paid for by the crown and which the monarch still led personally in the field. The idea of the warrior-king was still a potent force. What was different was the impact of mercenaries and mercenary commanders on the military scene (many of the great commanders of the time served as mercenaries during some stage of their careers).

The new nationalism

With the centralization of power in the new nation states of the 17th and 18th centuries, the idea of a professional national army revived. In 18th century Prussia, for instance, the army's importance was such that all matters of state policy were governed by its needs. It found its natural leader in *Frederick the Great*, who revolutionized battlefield strategy and military tactics; as a leader who understood the intimate link between politics and war, he also anticipated the theory that "war is the extension of diplomacy."

However, truly "national" armies – in the sense of the "nation in arms" – did not emerge until the time of the French Revolution. Now, a new breed of fighting force needed a new type of commander and this the French found in *Napoleon* – undeniably one of the greatest military geniuses of all time – and his marshals, many of whom would not have risen to prominence in the royal professional armies of the time.

Mass armies and modern war

From the Napoleonic period onwards, the move towards a modern mass army continued, aided by the impact of the Industrial Revolution and the inventions it spawned. In the wars Prussia waged in pursuit of German unity, for example, both the telegraph and railway were fully exploited. Mobilization plans were activated by a single telegraphed message, upon receipt of which conscript armies were moved up to the front separately at speed, then concentrating to strike together. Much the same phenomenon had been seen slightly earlier in the United States Civil War, where both the Federals and Confederates produced other innovations that forecast the future development of warfare. Here, too, the importance of material resources was realized for the first time. Despite their initial setbacks in the field, the Federals possessed far greater industrial resources than those of the Confederacy. Thus, they could stand a long-term struggle. The Confederacy could not.

This truth was even more apparent in both world wars, where industrial output, rather than the outstanding ability of particular commanders on either side, played a major part in determining the final victors. Here, too, political involvement with the process of command decision became important, leading to political, rather than military, factors being the dominant influence on the conduct of campaigns in places as far removed as Algeria and Vietnam.

The nature of command

In considering warfare today, the question must be asked as to whether any future war will produce another military genius – another great commander? For as long as warfare remains the kind of guerrilla conflict familiar to us from the Middle East and Africa, the answer must be in the negative. Local military heroes, of course, may arise, but these will lack the panache, the genius and, above all, the opportunities enjoyed by the great commanders of the past. In the confrontation between the forces of NATO and the Warsaw Pact, where the fear of mutual nuclear destruction threatens both sides, the answer must be that no atomic war could produce a great military leader. The remaining option of a major conventional war on a continent outside Europe is an unlikely possibility, as the superpowers would probably become involved.

Tomorrow's wars

Wars, therefore, are now more than likely to be third-world affairs. In them, states outside the main power blocs will fight on a largely conventional basis, seeking support in terms of military hardware, so-called "advisers", or funding. The other type of war will be guerrilla-style conflicts, in which, again, the guerrillas seek support from outside, but not direct armed support.

Great power involvement is unlikely, since the evidence of Afghanistan and, above all, Vietnam shows that this is likely to be counter-productive to the interests of the great powers themselves. What is apparent is that the nature of command as a general concept has been transformed as a result of the changing emphasis in warfare. This is a fairly recent phenomenon. As this book shows, not only does command, as a military concept, date back to earliest times, but that the idea of the great commander – the "man on horseback" – flourished over the centuries, becoming more and more important as time went by up to and including the great battles and campaigns of the Second World War. Would the exploits of the Afrika Korps, for instance, be so memorable had the Germans not had a "desert fox" in the person of Rommel to lead it? Or, to take a further example, is it Patton – or the army he commanded with such dash from 1942 onwards – that is better known?

Today, however, with the changing ways in which warfare is waged, the face of command has also been transformed. Gone are the flamboyant figures of yesteryear – there are no more Rommels, Pattons, MacArthurs or even Eisenhowers. With the exception of the Israelis, who could be argued to be fighting an old-style war, their place has been largely taken by back-room generals, who lead from their desks rather than from their tanks.

The Vietnam experience

Take, for example, the most prolonged conflict that the United States of America has been involved in since 1945 – and the first war in United States history in which the United States of America met defeat. The Vietnamese War was the first "modern" war in which a western super-power became involved (the Korean War was an old-style conflict, reminiscent in many of its aspects of the 1943 Italian campaign). Here was a situation in which there was no front line, no clearly defined positions to assault and capture. In short, there was no quick way of winning the war by conventional military means.

This view, albeit one formed with the advantage of hindsight, was not shared by many American politicians and commanders at the start of the United States involvement, however. What they believed was that United States technological superiority and traditional military might would inevitably lead to a decisive , quick victory. What they failed to realize was that they were fighting a revolutionary, not a conventional, war. The sheer weight of firepower employed itself mitigated against ultimate success, because the peasants of the south – whom, it is important to remember, were in the main on no one's side, but simply seeking survival – inevitably suffered.

What this meant was simple. The key battle – the battle for the "hearts and minds" of the South Vietnamese population – was lost by the United States of America and so the war became impossible to win. The United States might have its short-term military successes – indeed United States and South Vietnamese forces were more than a match for the *Viet Cong* and North Vietnamese regulars in the field, as set-piece actions such as the siege of Khe Sanh showed. This was a protracted siege – the action lasted from 21 January to 7 April 1968 – of a fortified United States "combat base" in the province of Quang Tri in the north of South Vietnam. In it, around 6,000 United States Marines and South Vietnamese Rangers held out for 77 days against an estimated 20,000 North Vietnamese regulars. The base was part of a chain of such fortifications set up in an attempt to block North Vietnamese infiltration of the south.

The Americans had learnt from the fate of the French at Dien Bien Phu and set up their defences accordingly. Unlike the French, they would hold the surrounding hilltops so as to prevent a close siege of Khe Sanh itself and its vital airstrip. What they also possessed – unlike the French – was the ability to call upon a helicopter fleet for resupply and air support, both of which became vital factors when the siege began in earnest.

At the time, Khe Sanh was important in more ways than one. The American high command decided to fight for it not just because of its strategic importance – it dominated Route 9, the main road to the coast – but also to demonstrate to the South Vietnamese that they could count on United States support. However, what Khe Sanh also showed was that though American airmobility and firepower could have a devastating effect, this was only so provided that it could be deployed in a conventional way. This was not the way in which the war was being fought; in addition, the United States success was defensive, rather than offensive.

The generals' argument

Many United States' commanders – notably General William Westmoreland, the supreme commander of United States forces in Vietnam from 1964 to 1968 – have always argued that they could have won the Vietnam War, had it not been for the constraints imposed on them by Washington. Their argument is that, for political reasons – the need President Johnson felt to limit United States involvement – they were forced on to the defensive from the start, adopting a policy of containment and response, rather than one of offensive aggression. Even the bombing of North Vietnam that Johnson eventually sanctioned was, they felt, a sign of weakness rather than strength, since it was not a policy that was executed with strength and determination, but with weakness and uncertainty. They point to the later success of President Nixon's decision to bomb the North Vietnamese into meaningful negotiations in Paris as an example of what could have been achieved earlier – to win the war, rather than to speed disengagement.

The three problem

What supporters of this line of argument fail to take into account is the fact that the battle for the support of the South Vietnamese population was effectively lost even before United States troops – as opposed to "advisers" – were committed. As early as 1963 junior United States officers in Saigon began leaking information to the press in an attempt to cut through official optimism, with talk of the success of the fortified hamlet policy, "kill ratio" statistics and estimates of the population now "pacified". As one unstable government followed another in the wake of the coup which overthrew President Diem and as the *Viet Cong* seemed to become ever stronger, the choice was clear – increased involvement or withdrawal. On 4 March 1965, United States marines hit the beaches at Da

Nang ready for action. By January 1969, 359,800 United States army troops, plus 144,100 personnel from the other United States services, had been committed.

This massive war effort, however, did not affect the basic dilemma facing the United States commanders on the spot and the generals and politicians at home in Washington. What needed to be resolved were the following questions. How could a highly-developed, technologically-advanced power best support an underdeveloped, technologically backward society, under threat from revolutionary warfare? How could United States armed forces, though undoubtedly strong, fight effectively in a counter-insurgency campaign in the light of their training for a different type of warfare? How could a consensus of support be maintained on the home front, given the fact that the war was being fought thousands of miles away, with the American people unconvinced that vital national interests were involved?

Revolutionary warfare
What the North Vietnamese grasped – though United States politicians did not, until after the event – was that the struggle for Vietnam could be decided by breaking the will of the American people to continue their support of United States involvement. The North Vietnamese profited from the teachings of Sun Tzu, an ancient Chinese philosopher of war, who advised as follows: "Break the will of the enemy to fight and you accomplish the true objective of war. Cover the enemy's traditions with ridicule. Stir up the young against the old. The supreme excellence is to defeat the armies of your enemies without ever having to fight them."

Here, in the view of the United States commanders on the spot, the role of the media must be called into question. The Vietnam War was the first television war, in which "live" coverage of the day's events was beamed into every United States living room – often with critical comment. As the war dragged on – largely due to the lack of political resolution in Washington – and the casualty lists mounted, active opposition to United States involvement in the war mounted.

The Tet offensive is undoubtedly a prime example of this. This was a co-ordinated series of attacks, launched by the North Vietnamese army and the *Viet Cong* against a series of key targets throughout South Vietnam. In the campaign's early stages, the most dramatic events undoubtedly took place in Saigon itself, where up to 4,000 Communists seized control of key areas while a 15-man suicide squad even managed to penetrate part of the United States' embassy compound. But the real struggle took place in Hué, the one-time imperial capital of Annam, where the Communists succeeded in infiltrating the Old City. It was to take bitter fighting to liberate the citadel in the Old City's centre, where the red, blue and gold *Viet Cong* banner fluttered from 31 January to 25 February, and the human cost was equally high.

The road to withdrawal
Militarily, Tet failed in its prime objective, which was to destroy the Saigon regime by triggering off a popular uprising, but the effects of the attacks on United States public opinion were far reaching. Although the North Vietnamese and the *Viet Cong* were undoubtedly badly hurt militarily as a result of their abortive guerrilla strikes – it is estimated that their joint casualties amounted to 30,000 men – this was not the picture presented to the American people on their television screens. What they saw was an apparently endless war, which, by now, was seriously dividing the nation. Official spokesmen might argue that the more aggressive search and destroy missions the United States forces and their South Vietnamese allies had by now instituted were turning the tide, but their previous optimism rebounded on them and they were simply not believed. Johnson's decision not to stand for re-election, the subsequent succession to the presidency of Richard Nixon, with his policy of "Vietnamizing" the war – withdrawing United States fighting forces and supporting the South Vietnamese with war material and credits – were steps along the road to an inevitable withdrawal and loss of prestige.

This took place in 1973, after the Paris peace agreement had imposed a cease-fire on both sides, which was to be monitored by an international commission. However, though the United States of American had assured the South Vietnamese that they would receive economic and military aid, changing political circumstances in Washington – notably the resignation of Nixon as a result of the Watergate scandal – meant that this came to a stop. Thus, though the South Vietnamese had over a million men under arms, they were short of the defence hardware they needed – and, even more importantly, were constricted by the tactical doctrines they had inherited from the Americans, which were now impossible for them to put into practice. The result was collapse.

What Vietnam also demonstrated is that it is now difficult – if not impossible – for commanders of democratic countries to fight a drawn-out conflict far from home, without the whole-hearted backing of the people, especially when conscript, as opposed to regular, forces are involved. This takes us back to the start of our story.

Ancient, Classical and Medieval Command

The qualities of command in the ancient world were many and various, with, at times, a strong injection of the supernatural. The Celts believed a dazzling light arose above the head of a hero, the appearance of this halo indicating his ability to transform himself from an ordinary human being into a raging, fighting animal. When Cuchulainn, the ancient Irish warlord, prepared himself for battle, for instance, it was a frightening transformation, according to legend. Beneath his leather armor, his very form twisted and shook, great balls of muscle throbbed beneath his skin, his veins dilated, and his face grew red and angry, until the heroic light finally shone above his forehead. These were the qualities of a great leader and his warriors, frightened as much by Cuchulainn's violence as the enemy, followed in his wake. When the Romans came against the Celts, they were impressed by the swagger and bravado of their tribal commanders. But once they heard the tale of the heroic halo, they used it against them. Around 130 AD, a centurion strode into battle with a glowing coal attached to his helmet. The Moesi fled before him.

Qualities of greatness

Logical and realistic as they might seem, the Romans were not without their own belief in the special, superhuman qualities of great military commanders. Augustus, victor of the civil war between the triumvirs and first Roman emperor, believed that a divine radiance shone from his eyes and was particularly pleased when anyone he glanced at dropped their head as though dazzled by the sun. This is only one of many examples, however. Today, the superhuman quality that the followers of great commanders throughout the ancient and medieval periods believed in is best understood as charisma. It brought the best out of warriors, who often won battles on the strength of it. Following a visit to a shrine in Egypt, *Alexander the Great* was convinced of his own divinity. Birds had mysteriously guided his expedition across the Egyptian desert and when he arrived there, the high priest recognized him as the son of the god Ammon. Combined with his reputation in battle for invincibility, such tales enhanced his leadership, although as Plutarch writes: "Alexander did not allow himself to become vain or foolishly conceited because of his belief in his divinity, but rather used it to assert his authority over others." Alexander was the perfect example of a commander whose personal leadership in battle was often the key to his victories. Frequently outnumbered by his Persian adversaries, Alexander turned defeat into triumph by leading his élite cavalry in a direct charge against the enemy commander, knowing full well that if the Persians saw their leader retreat then they would also break.

Command and good fortune

Alexander's model of a divine command in the midst of battle was embraced by many military cultures, especially that of the Romans. Julius *Caesar* was a keen believer in personal presence among his warriors and often seized hold of a sword to lead them personally out of difficult situations. But Caesar realized also the nature of warfare was a great gamble. "Fortune," he wrote, "has great influence on affairs generally and especially in war." This maxim is as true today as it was in Caesar's time. No matter how well prepared and trained an army is, or whatever cunning tactics are employed, there can be no guarantee of victory.

The history of great commanders, therefore, is also the history of men on whom fortune smiled. That being appreciated, the history of warfare, of course, also revolved around the constant search of people for an edge over their adversaries, whether it be superior weapons, organization, or indeed, leadership. The initial step in this development came with the emergence of a society in which specialization of tasks and skills took place. This was civilization. In the military sphere, what this meant was a development from the temporarily armed tribe to the standing professional army. The greatest empires of antiquity – including those of Persia, Macedonia, Carthage, and Rome – all possessed regular armies, in which specialization allowed the growth of sophisticated networks of command, from a single general through a host of professional captains and officers.

Organization and command

The Roman military system was based on the legion and its sub-divisions. Six centuries of 80 made up one cohort; ten cohorts made a legion, whose total strength averaged around 5,000 men. Centurions

ALEXANDER THE GREAT
Alexander's charisma helped him lead his warriors to Middle Eastern empire.

were usually veterans, promoted from the ranks, who often commanded cohorts and sometimes even led legions in the field. They were the seasoned professionals of the Roman army.

The next rank of officers, the tribunes, were not career soldiers, however. They were drawn from the aristocracy and held their posts as one step in a political or administrative career in civilian life. Similarly, the legate, holding overall command of the legion, and even the emperor, or general, of the army, came from the civilian upper classes, whose ultimate ambitions were to become senators or consuls. The weakness of this system became apparent when amateur commanders precipitated disastrous defeats. But civilian experience in politics, administration, and finance could also be highly useful in the management of war and Julius Caesar's civilian career in his 20s and 30s must have made its contribution to his phenomenal strategic and tactical success.

Aristocrats in command

Throughout antiquity, great commanders came in the main from aristocratic backgrounds. Undoubtedly, this gave them the immediate authority to lead men of a socially inferior rank and contributed to their charisma; it also gave them the leisure to study the martial arts and the money with which to fund their ambitions. This was true among the Romans and Greeks and continued to be so in the Middle Ages – for, as far as military leadership is concerned, the celebrated break between antiquity and the medieval period, grandly entitled the fall of the Roman empire, is misleading. The characteristic medieval image of a nobleman surrounded by his knights was very much part of the same tradition as Alexander the Great being supported by his "Companion" cavalry and the Roman emperors by the Praetorian Guard. Both *Belisarius* and *Flavius Aetius*, Byzantine and late Roman commanders respectively, who both lived at the time of the fall of the

Roman empire, possessed private armies of élite retainers, and then recruited additional forces by recruiting mercenaries, or calling on the services of landowners, who owed military service as part of their social obligations. This remained true throughout the so-called feudal period. Indeed, many medieval warlords modeled themselves on Roman commanders and called themselves imperator.

Ancient and medieval

The main difference between ancient and medieval commanders is a result of the Germanization of the martial élite, following the barbarian invasions of western Europe. Commanders continued to divide their lives between their civilian and military duties, but their culture was now dominated by Germanic concepts of manhood. This showed itself most clearly in their attitude to firepower. Whereas Roman commanders were happy to make use of oriental mounted archers, medieval knights believed that killing a man in close combat was a greater demonstration of male virtue than shooting him down with a bow and arrow. Misguided by this noble prejudice, many medieval commanders arranged their order of battle according to social caste, with peasant footsoldiers leading the way to be sacrificed at the beginning to soften up the enemy before the final charge of lance- and sword-bearing knights. The more intelligent medieval commanders, such as the English kings *Richard I* and *Edward I*, did not succumb to this foolish snobbery, however, and utilized all arms available to them equally.

The qualities of a war lord

The barbarian invasions brought about the break-up of the Roman empire, but the concept of a united western Europe remained in the form of Christendom, with the pope replacing the emperor as its spiritual – rather then secular – head. Roman provinces became the basis for Germanic kingdoms, while Germanic concepts of leadership and ideal warrior merged with the Latin tradi-

tion the Romans had established. Wealth, courage, and intelligence remained important attributes, but less weighty, almost exhibitionist, talents also impressed a warband.

In the early Middle Ages, there was a definite division between the bounds of decorum expected from leaders of Mediterranean soldiers and those of Germanic warriors. Indeed, the further north one went, the less were the limits of dignity. Running, rowing, skiing and swimming were all noble demonstrations of prowess among the Scandinavians. Their commanders even considered it worthy to make their own weapons – hence the inclusion of many details of weapon manufacture in Nordic literature. As far as Scandinavian nobles were concerned, the only pursuits that were not considered seemly for men of their rank to undertake were commercial and agricultural skills.

Such a prejudice against mastering the art of earning a living outside the fields of pillaged or inherited wealth continued among European aristocracy throughout the Middle Ages. The more outlandish pursuits of Germanic nobles were tempered by their adoption of Latin *gravitas*. By the time the Vikings became absorbed as Normans into the mainstream of medieval culture, a sense of civilized dignity had overcome the antics of the warband. Germanic heroism fused with the classical heritage, so that medieval European warriors took their exemplars of military leadership from a variety of cultures. In late medieval French court art, for instance, the "Nine Worthies" of all time included Celtic and Jewish heroes alongside Roman and German ones – they included Hector, Alexander, Caesar, Joshua, Judas Maccabeus, Arthur, Charlemagne, and the contemporary *Guesclin*.

China, Central Asia and India

Just as Germanic influences transformed European culture, so the barbarian impact on Asian societies was marked. Chinese civilization had long been under threat from Turkish and Mongolian raiders from the north and west. One answer had been to build barriers against the barbarians, but, as the Romans realized in Europe, static defences could never be relied on totally in the face of swift, mobile invaders. The solution the T'ang dynasty came to was to recruit large numbers of horsemen from Central Asia and Mongolia to compensate for their weakness in this field and then carry the war to the raiders.

The policy was initially successful, but the dependence of the T'ang on their barbarian auxiliaries increased the power of individual Turkish generals and one of them – An Lu-shan – almost destroyed the dynasty in his rebellion of AD 755. The military superiority of horsemen armed with bows led by imaginative cavalry commanders was again demonstrated by the Mongols. Rather than conquering from within the Chinese empire, *Genghis Khan* openly challenged the ruling dynasty for control of northern China and Central Asia with his Mongol hordes. His supreme ability to delegate command to talented subordinates and native administrators made his the greatest of the steppe empires, stretching from the Pacific to the Black Sea.

There is a tendency in history to regard the barbarian descent on settled civilizations as a culturally destructive event. As the majority of historical records have been produced by the civilizations so assaulted, this is not surprising. But, as we have seen in Europe, the Germanic intention was not to destroy the sophisticated culture they found, but to adopt and adapt it, adding layers of their own esperience. So it was in Asia.

When the Mongols invaded China and India, they established dynasties that refined the venerable civilizations they had conquered. And when they were too worn out to provide adequate defences, so new invaders established their regimes, such as the Manchu in northern China. In both western and eastern history, barbarian invasions resulted in periods of reinvigoration for a tired culture. It is the

talent of great commander to seize upon this weakness, just as Alexander and his Macedonian barbarians did with the Persian Empire.

Dawn of a new age

Though gunpowder and guns were to revolutionize warfare in Europe, for the first two centuries after their introduction to the battlefield, little in fact changed. The late Middle Ages was characterized by a renewed interest in footsoldiers, Swiss pikemen and British archers both winning spectacular victories in the 14th and 15th centuries. Much has been made of this. In truth, the Swiss pikemen were little different to the phalanxes of Greece, while dismounted archers had always been useful conveyors of firepower. It did little to question the inherent superiority of the horse-borne martial élite. Commanders still came from the aristocratic families of Europe and the knight remained a potent military presence. With political centralization, however, and the emergence of European superpowers, armies increased in size with a balanced array of cavalry, infantry and artillery. The development of the matchlock arquebus, standardized cannon and ocean-going sailing ships, set the seal on what has been aptly termed the "gunpowder revolution". It was the 16th century that witnessed this remarkable leap forward in technology and Spain was its chief beneficiary.

In the series of wars Spain waged against France in Italy, the Spanish commander *Gonzalo* de Cordoba transformed land tactics by using gun-carrying footsoldiers as his main striking force, protecting them against cavalry with earthworks and contingents of pikemen. By the end of the century, the *tercio*, or Spanish square, a mutually supportive combination of pikemen and musketeers, dominated European warfare. Gonzalo has also been credited as being the inspirational force behind the creation of a regular Spanish army, consisting of *colunelas* (columns), similar to the Roman cohort. The commander of these Spanish formations was called a

colonel and charged with their maintenance both during and after battle.

Other changes in command procedure were equally far reaching. European monarchs continued to command armies in the field, but increasingly this task was delegated, to their chief military adviser, or constable. It was a mark of Spanish military confidence that their kings rarely became involved in battlefield command, although this did not stop them from making political decisions that could undermine a general's strategy. Philip II's appallingly misjudged withdrawal of Alexander *Farnese* from the Netherlands, for instance, eventually lost him his Dutch territories. At sea, the Spanish galleon swiftly ensured Spain's conquest of the New World and further increased its economic and political power. It was an Englishman, however, Francis *Drake*, who best understood the new naval tactics that sail and cannon made essential. His long-range raids on the Spanish empire in the New World helped Elizabethan England resist the aggression of the Catholic superpower.

Even in an age of rapid technological advancement, however, the dazzling light of personal leadership still mattered. During the campaign of *Garigliano*, Gonzalo camped among his soldiers and visited their frontline trenches daily despite appalling weather. His French adversaries were less diligent – their commanders abandoned their men for comfortable quarters in nearby villages. French morale collapsed and before a determined Spanish assault the French army gave way in confusion.

Similarly, Hernando *Cortes'* conquest of Mexico was not the result of the superiority of his guns or the presence of horses, but because he possessed an inspiring endurance that prevented his followers being overwhelmed by vastly numerous Indians. The ability of excellent personal leadership to determine battles and campaigns is an abiding truth that has continued into modern warfare.

The Age of the Horse Warrior

At the battle of Marathon in 490 BC, the Greek warrior taking part in this memorable action fought on foot as hoplites. When it came to commemorating them on the Parthenon frieze, however, all of the 192 dead heroes were represented on horseback, for, in death, they were to be accorded the highest social status. From earliest recorded times, the horse has been a symbol of power, wealth, and privilege, and accordingly all great land commanders, have been portrayed on horseback until the final eclipse of cavalry in the 20th century. In the ancient and medieval worlds, the élite nature of horsemanship is a vital key to the understanding of developments in warfare.

The supreme horsemen
In Europe, throughout the thousand years before the birth of Christ, the Celts were the supreme horsemen, their talent for fighting on horseback enabling them to spread their culture from central Europe to northern Italy, Spain, France and Britain. The extent to which the Celts owed their conquests to their mounts is visually demonstrated in southern Britain, where they carved giant white horses in the chalk soil of the hillsides – a testament to their superior horsemanship that was visible to natives for miles. Their talent for riding ultimately came from their ancient origin among the steppe peoples of Eurasia. It was from them that the Celts derived their famed passion for chariots. In the forests of Europe, however, a more agriculturally-based economy superceded the pastoral ways of the steppes and there were less horses available for warfare. It was then that the horse, an expensive commodity, became a special symbol of social and military dominance.

Superb horsemanship, without stirrups
The Romans were not noted horsemen and preferred to hire mercenary cavalry. *Caesar, Scipio* and *Hannibal* admired Celtic horse warriors; as the Roman empire expanded to include the Near East, oriental horse-archers were employed in the late imperial armies of *Flavius Aetius* and *Belisarius*. The oriental horse archer was perhaps the most potent force in ancient and medieval warfare, combining mobility with supreme striking power. The pastoral herdsmen of the Eurasian steppe and the plains of Central Asia were brought up from childhood in the knowledge of horsemanship and archery. To them it was second nature and the greater number of horses available enabled them to form formidable armies, in which cavalry far outnumbered footsoldiers. It was with these horsemen that *Genghis Khan* and *Saladin* both carved out their impressive territorial conquests.

The impact of the stirrup on medieval horsemanship has been greatly overrated. Originating in the Far East,

the stirrup was only slowly adopted, many horsemen considering its use as an insult to their riding skills. It had very little effect on the development of horse archery, while heavy cavalry, wielding long lances, had already been a vital element of oriental and western armies long before its advent. Its main influence in the west was to encourage a stiff-legged riding posture, rather than one in which legs were bent to clutch a horse. It did not enable an armored lance-wielding horseman to charge into a group of footsoldiers. A horse will not charge into a static object, such as a wall of shield-bearing men; the lance is best employed in single combat against another horseman, or when pursuing an already broken formation of fleeing, disorganized infantry.

In Europe, after the disintegration of the Roman Empire, Germanic concepts of horsemanship dominated medieval warfare. As with the Celts, from whom they drew much of their military heritage, the Germanic peoples of western Europe viewed horsemen as a social and martial élite around which an army was raised. Added to this was an aristocratic prejudice best expressed by a French poet of the 13th century: "Cursed be the first man who became an archer. He was afraid and did not dare approach." The most noble Germanic warriors considered it beneath their dignity to kill a man from afar. True martial distinction could only be obtained in close combat with lance, sword, or mace. It was for this cultural reason that medieval knights never used the bow from horseback.

Such a prejudice had disastrous consequences when western horsemen confronted Mongol or Saracen horse-archers. *Richard I*'s answer, however, was not to adopt the methods of the infidel, but to enforce discipline among his vulnerable knights and use crossbowmen on foot to keep the Saracens at a distance.

Always the élite
Although their social status dictated that knights and their men-at-arms fought as heavily armored shock troops throughout the Middle Ages, these aristocratic warriors were not slow to employ socially-inferior soldiers, especially mercenaries, armed with bows, pikes, and firearms. Following the military crisis of the 14th century, when English bowmen and Swiss pikemen inflicted surprise defeats on heavy cavalry, knights recognized that their role was to be one part of an army alongside light cavalry, artillery, and infantry. Far from being a decadent hangover of past glories, the knights of the 15th and 16th centuries were a vital core, around which every late medieval army was formed. There were several reasons for this. They provided the command hierarchy and money for arms,

·HHΛRTOJΛN·VON·OWE·

**THE WARRIOR
KNIGHT** *Mounted
warriors played an important
role in armies across the
world from early times, but it
was in the battles of the
Middle Ages that the heavily
armored mounted knight
came into his own. The
knights of medieval times
were the social and martial
élite, around which the armies
of the day were formed.*

**THE ISLAMIC
VERSION** *Mounted
warriors were an extremely
important constituent of the
Muslim armies of the period,
as the Crusaders were to
discover. They were horse-
archers, combining fire-power
with a high degree of mobility.*

while, at the climax of a battle, they could launch the
deciding blow, both in the power of their arms and
expert horsemanship, and in the psychological impact
of their presence. That is why, as late as 1494, over
half the French army that invaded Italy were composed
of heavily-armored horsemen. "It was the gendarmerie
which was always the strength of the army," wrote
Gabriel Daniel in his 18th-century history of French
cavalry, "as much by the goodness of its arms as by the
strength of its warhorses."

The development of firearms consolidated the
identity of heavy cavalry on the battlefield. Still
armored well into the 17th century, the social
structures of knights and men-at-arms continued to
dominate the performance of heavy cavalry. Irregular
cavalry and dragoons provided mounted fire-power,
while socially-superior horsemen bearing sabre and
lance pursued the glamour of the charge. By
understanding the élite nature of these horsemen and
their impact on other warriors, great commanders long
after the Middle Ages employed them to best effect as a
powerful battlefield force.

The Development of Firepower

Over the centuries, new technology combined with the needs of armies to create weapons capable of causing considerable devastation on the battlefield. Chief among these was the oriental composite bow, the most deadly missile weapon of the ancient and the medieval worlds. This was the chief weapon of victory for such great leaders as *Genghis Khan* and *Saladin*, capable of outdistancing all other wooden bows, including the so-called longbow. Its power derived from the combined strength of several materials used in its construction; a wooden core was backed with layers of sinew and reinforced on the inside with strips of horn. All these materials were then sandwiched together with animal glue. The combination of wood, sinew, and horn produced a highly flexible bow, allowing a far longer draw than was possible from a wooden equivalent. This flexibility made it particularly easy to use from horseback and its design reached perfection among the encampments of the nomadic horsemen of the Central Asian steppes.

Crossbows and longbows

The crossbow was the European version of the composite bow. Much underrated by British historians, because of its supposedly unsuccessful use in the French armies of the Hundred Years' War, the crossbow could hurl a bolt more than 300 yards, as against an average range of 200 yards from the wooden longbow. At this extreme range, the crossbow was not aimed from the shoulder, but held at a 45° angle, so as to deliver its steel-tipped bolts like an artillery barrage. As for the much repeated criticism that it was slow to use, modern research has proved it possible for two men to shoot

two crossbows in rapid succession, provided that one man specializes in drawing the strings and then hands them to a shooter, who concentrates on aiming. Thus a team of two men can keep up a hail of crossbow bolts long after the muscle fatigue of the solitary longbowman has begun to slow his rate of fire. Records show that it was exactly this system that was employed during the Third Crusade, when *Richard I*'s crossbowmen indeed were employed in pairs – one to load, one to shoot. Only through this were Richard's archers able to match the lethal archery of their Saracen adversaries.

Despite its historical renown, the famed English longbow was in fact a very ordinary weapon of no great power; it was considerably inferior in design to that of contemporary continental reflex and composite bows, as well as the much maligned crossbow. To begin with, the word "longbow" did not exist in the medieval vocabulary. The weapon commonly thought of as a "longbow" is a Victorian invention. What is clear to historians is that the typical 14th-century English bow, as far as it can be reconstructed, was a simple, often inefficient weapon. The success of its use at *Crécy* and Poitiers stemmed from the English tactical employment of archers in massed formations in a strong defensive position, thus delivering an artillery shock to the French who had allowed themselves to be provoked into attacking at a disadvantage. French incompetence on these occasions was the decisive factor.

CROSSBOW TO MUSKET *The crossbow (left) could out-range the longbow, while teams of two – one loading, the other shooting – could keep up a fast rate of fire. The weapon's true replacement was the musket (right), but this took time to develop. The version here dates from 1586.*

The first firearms

A recent discovery in a Buddhist cave in south-west China has brought forward the invention of the gun by at least 150 years. A sculpted figure, dating from around 1128, holds a gun called an ox-jar, similar in shape to the first guns employed in Europe 200 years later. The length of time it took for the invention to reach Europe is indicative of the fact that, at this stage, gunpowder was not regarded as a major revolution factor in warfare, but more a novelty – useful for creating frightening sound and visual effects. It was not until the early 15th century that European chemists invented a method of producing effective gunpowder.

The development of "wet-mix" gunpowder allowed saltpetre to dissolve in water and percolate into charcoal. On drying, the active ingredients resided within the charcoal, rather than separately as they had before, and so produced a finer mixture which ignited immediately. When dried and squeezed through sieves to produce a powder of uniform grain size, this ensured a more consistent reaction. Recent firing tests with simulated medieval guns have revealed that a gun using 14th-century "dry-mix" powder misfired one time out of every ten. Firing a steel bullet at steel armor, one-tenth of an inch thick, a "wet-mix" gun penetrated five times out of eight, whereas a "dry-mix" gun did not penetrate at all. As a result, the use of firearms increased rapidly in the early 15th century. Some 3,000 handguns were in use among the Hussites, for instance; their leader, Jan *Zizka*, demolished several feudal armies by placing guns behind his wagon laager.

From bows to firearms

By the end of the 15th century, therefore, firearms had superceded bows, even though many oriental composite bows could still out-range them. The primitive hand cannon of earlier decades had been replaced by a barrel with a wooden butt, which meant that the gun could be held against the shoulder and actually aimed. This improvement was initiated by the introduction of the matchlock, an S-shaped mechanism attached to the side of the gun which brought a flaming match into contact with the priming powder by means of a trigger. The new gun became known as the arquebus.

Similar improvements were made in battlefield artillery, notably by the French. Their new cannon brought the Hundred Years' War to a rapid end; when Charles VIII invaded Italy in 1494, his many light cannon were mounted on gun carriages pulled by horses, had trunnions to elevate and aim the barrel, and were cast in bronze with iron cannon balls.

New tactics for a new age

It was the Spanish, however, who developed improved tactics to make the best battlefield use of footsoldiers and their matchlock firearms. *Gonzalo* Fernandez de Cordoba, the Spanish commander confronting Charles VIII in Italy, increased their number and protected them as they reloaded by placing them behind fieldworks, or attaching them to companies of pikemen. The new pike and shot tactics gave greater emphasis to the development of more powerful firearms. By the end of the 16th century, the heavier musket with longer range displaced the arquebus and wheel-lock pistols were invented for cavalrymen.

The development of artillery had just as profound effect on the nature of naval warfare as it did on the conduct of land battles. It brought the era of oar-propelled galleys and the use of ramming as the chief tactic to an end, introducing an age of long-range gunnery. After 200 years, the gun at last dominated all forms of warfare.

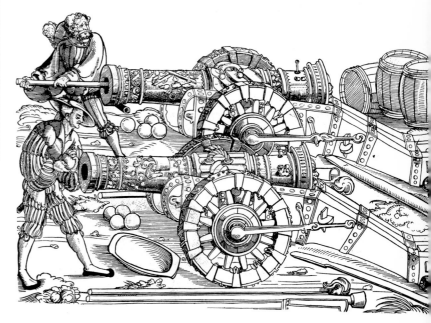

THE FIRST CANNON *Artillery was introduced into European armies as early as the 1300s; the cannon (above) was used by the English in 1327. The first bombards, as they were known, were inefficient and used more for show than for effect; the cannon of the 16th century (right) were far more deadly battlefield weapons, in addition possessing the extra element of mobility.*

331 BC

ARBELA:
Alexander's greatest victory

The battle of Arbela, or Guagamela as it is sometimes called, was Alexander the Great's culminating victory against the Persian Emperor, Darius. Before it, Persia stubbornly defied the Greek threat. After it – and the murder of Darius – the vast Persian Empire lay open to Macedonian conquest.

Arbela was the third major combat between Alexander and the Persians. The previous two years had seen him conquer Asia Minor, Syria, Palestine, and Egypt, but, crossing the Syrian desert into Mesopotamia in the summer of 331 BC, Alexander was resolved to put his fortunes to the ultimate test. Earlier Greek activities in Persia, such as the formidable march of Xenophon's "Ten Thousand", had demonstrated that the Persian Empire was not as invulnerable as it appeared. In Mesopotamia, Alexander's target was Babylon and he advanced southwards along the east bank of the Tigris. On a plain between Arbela and Guagamela, he was confronted by a huge army led by Darius in person.

As Alexander surveyed the Persian line of battle, he noted that it was composed largely of cavalry with a screen of chariots stretching along its entire length. In all, it was said to number some 200,000 soldiers, drawn from all parts of the Persian Empire. Although this figure is certainly exaggerated, the number of troops at Darius' disposal was certainly far greater than Alexander's 47,000 men. Parmenio, Alexander's second-in-command, had urged a delay, not only to rest their troops further, but to give the Macedonians time to reconnoiter the area. Darius had chosen the battlefield well. At Issus, the rugged terrain had prevented him from exploiting his superior numbers, so, at Arbela, he chose a flat plain from which bushes and other natural obstacles had been removed to facilitate the movements of his cavalry and chariots.

The night before the battle was spent by the Persians under arms. They feared a night attack and Parmenio had indeed recommended this, but Alexander proclaimed "I do not steal victory". He trusted in his own generalship and wanted to defeat the Persians openly and decisively so as to finish off Darius once and for all.

The opening stages
Alexander's line of battle took its usual echelon formation. On his right wing, advancing before the rest of the army, were his élite "Companion" cavalry and the *hypaspists*, his finest footsoldiers. To their left rear in the center was the main Macedonian phalanx. The left wing behind them was formed of Greek and Thessalian cavalry, led by Parmenio. Overall, the Macedonians were outflanked by the greater frontage of the Persians. To combat this, Alexander placed reserves of footsoldiers and cavalry behind both right and left wings. They could thus hold any outflanking maneuver by Darius. Predictably, Darius opened the battle with his chariots, rolling forward with razor-sharp scythes flashing on their wheels. Alexander's light infantry pelted the chariots with javelins and arrows. The hurtling machines were thrown into confusion and their advance came to nothing against the ranks of Alexander's "Companions" and his *hypaspists*.

When the Macedonians advanced in their turn, they drifted obliquely to the right. To counter this, Darius launched his Persian cavalry, including Scythian and Bactrian auxiliaries, against Alexander's right wing. The Persian horsemen swept around the Macedonian flank, but were met by Alexander's wing reserve, placed there for that very purpose. The fighting grew in intensity and Alexander had to send reinforcements to his right flank.

As the Persians sent forward more horsemen, however, Alexander observed their cavalry movements had created a gap in the Persian line left of center. This was the chance for which he had been waiting. Leading his "Companions" in a charge, Alexander penetrated the Persian line, splitting the enemy army in two. As at Issus, the fighting grew more furious around Darius and again he lost his nerve and fled in his chariot. The whole of the Persian center and left wing disintegrated before the combined thrusts of the "Companions", *hypaspists*, and phalanx.

The final clashes
Elsewhere on the plain, the Macedonian left wing was hard pressed by the Persians. The pressure of a reserve enabled the Greeks to hold the enemy, but their inability to keep up with the advance of the phalanx left a gap in the center through which a contingent of Persian and Indian cavalry dashed to loot the Macedonian camp. They were stopped by a further reserve of Greeks and Thracians, but as they retreated in good order they met Alexander, who had been dissuaded from pursuing the broken Persian army by Parmenio's call for assistance on the Greek left.

Alexander had led his "Companions" in the bloodiest encounter

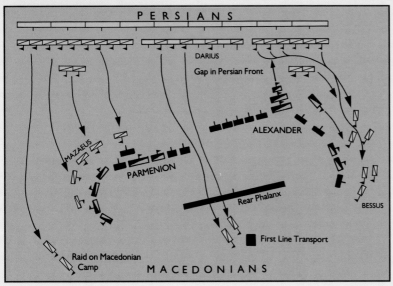

PERSIANS

DARIUS

Gap in Persian Front

MAZAEUS

ALEXANDER

PARMENION

Rear Phalanx

BESSUS

First Line Transport

Raid on Macedonian
Camp

MACEDONIANS

FIGHTING THE PERSIANS

*Alexander the Great's first clash
with the Persian Empire of Darius
came at the battle of Issus (above),
in which his Macedonian forces put
into practice the same tactics he
later employed against Darius at
Arbela. Though the Persians far
outnumbered the Greeks,
Alexander's imaginative tactical
innovations, including his
deployment of the Greek phalanx
formation, brought him victory in
both battles. As the map (left)
shows, the key moment at Arbela
came when, ignoring local Persian
success on the left wing, Alexander
seized the opportunity to launch his
élite troops in a charge through a
gap that had opened in the Persian
battle line to the left of the center.*

of the day. The Macedonians were
desperate to help their comrades on
the left wing, while the Indians and
Persians wished only to disengage
and save their lives. Eventually,
both Parmenio and Alexander

triumphed over their opponents and
the Macedonians claimed victory
having slaughtered some 50,000
Persians and losing only 500 men.

The battle of Arbela marked the
end of Darius' power and within the

year he was dead – murdered by his
own generals. Alexander was lord of
Asia. He had also demonstrated a
masterly use of tactical reserves in
defeating a numerically superior
opponent.

202 BC

ZAMA:
Scipio versus Hannibal

At the battle of Zama, wrote the Roman historian Livy, "the two most famous generals and the two mightiest armies of the two wealthiest nations in the world advanced in battle, doomed either to crown or destroy the many triumphs each had won in the past." *Hannibal* commanded 45,000 Carthaginian footsoldiers and 3,000 cavalry. *Scipio* led 34,000 Roman footsoldiers and 9,000 cavalry. They met on a plain in north Africa in the autumn of 202 BC, five day's march south-west of Carthage. Scipio had spent the previous weeks attacking towns in the North African interior, so as to reduce the supplies reaching Carthage. The action provoked Hannibal into pursuing him. Scipio avoided conflict until he had joined forces with the Numidian chieftain Masinissa, who was to provide him with the cavalry reinforcements he needed. Having made the link-up, Scipio went on the offensive.

Prelude to battle
The battleground chosen by Scipio was scrubland between two hills, close to a river that served the Roman camp better than the Carthaginian one. On the day before battle, Hannibal asked to meet Scipio between the two armies. The former was concerned about his lack of cavalry and the number of untrained raw recruits in the Carthaginian ranks. Accordingly, he proposed peace, but Scipio was uninterested and, after satisfying each other's curiosity, the two commanders returned to their lines. Hannibal made up for his shortage of cavalry by employing 80 terrifying war elephants in his vanguard. Behind these were a variety of newly recruited auxiliaries from all parts of the Mediterranean – Ligurians,

Gauls, Balaerics, and Moors. A second line comprised Carthaginians and Africans, while his third line contained his veteran soldiers from Italy – the backbone of his army. His few Carthaginian and Numidian horsemen were stationed on the wings. The cosmopolitan nature of Hannibal's army precipitated severe problems in command and communication. "Different words of encouragement were required in such an army," wrote Livy, "for the soldiers had nothing in common. Neither language, nor customs, not arms, nor dress, and least of all, motive."

Scipio commanded an essentially Roman army. The Senate had been reluctant to see him embark on the African invasion and assigned him only those legionaries banished to Sicily for their poor performance at Cannae. These veterans were eager to redeem themselves and embraced the rigorous tactical training Scipio insisted on wholeheartedly. At Zama, Scipio deployed them in *maniples* in three lines, but placed considerable intervals between the *maniples*. These gaps were created to combat the threat posed by the Carthaginian elephants.

When the elephants charged, the *velites*, or light infantry, were instructed to guide the animals through the gaps and so prevent the break-up of the Roman formations. Once in the gaps, the *velites* could then retire among the *maniples* and create a shooting ground in which the beasts could be slaughtered by the Roman javelins. On the left wing, Scipio placed his Italian cavalry and on the right his Numidian horsemen. Each wing was under a separate commander – the Italians led by a second-in-command, Laelius, and the Numidians

by Masinissa. This meant that while Scipio dealt with the main body of Carthaginian footsoldiers, the cavalry could act independently and carry out flank attacks.

The decisive blow
Before battle commenced, each commander addressed his troops. Hannibal reminded the Carthaginians of their 16 years of success on Italian soil and of all the Roman generals they had slain. Scipio inspired his men by recalling the conquest of Spain and their recent African victories. While Hannibal was still speaking to his men, Scipio began the battle. The Roman war trumpets blared out in a prearranged attempt to incite the Carthaginian war elephants. As expected, the trumpeting elephants charged into action. Some were panicked by the noise and trampled on their own troops. Those animals that did reach the Roman lines were guided by the *velites* as planned through the Roman columns to be pelted by spears. The assault drove the elephants back towards their own lines and broke up Hannibal's cavalry on his right wing. In the meantime, Masinissa had taken advantage of the confusion and launched an independent attack on Hannibal's left wing cavalry, putting them into headlong flight.

In the center, Scipio's Roman legionaries broke the first line of mixed Carthaginian recruits. The second line collapsed as the terrified auxiliaries fell back on it in rout. Only the third Carthaginian line held firm, battling its own fleeing soldiers as well as the advancing Roman legionaries.

In the excitement of the slaughter, the Roman frontline – the *hastati* – broke up to form irreg-

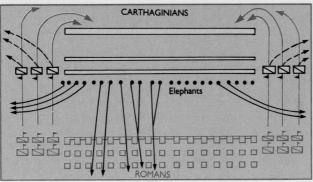

CARTHAGINIANS

Elephants

ROMANS

THE CAPTAINS MEET
Hannibal rides forward to meet Scipio in a vain attempt to propose peace before the Carthaginian and Roman armies clashed at Zama. The battlefield skill of Scipio's well-trained forces enabled the Romans to break the main body of the Carthaginian foot, while Scipio's cavalry attacked the flanks (left).

ular groups pursuing the fleeing Carthaginians. Scipio saw this was affecting the formation of his second line – the *principes* – and ordered the recall to be sounded. He then reformed his second and third lines in the center, with the exhausted *hastati* on the wings. It was a remarkable demonstration of discipline at the hardest period of the combat – veterans against veterans. Both sides had equal experience, skill, and courage, but the Romans were numerically superior.

The decisive moment came with the return of the Roman and Numidian cavalry from pursuing the routed Carthaginian horsemen and their plunge into the rear of Hannibal's veterans. The Carthaginian formations were shattered, surrounded by triumphant horsemen and slaughtered where they stood.

Those that escaped were hunted across the plain until they fell. Over 20,000 Carthaginians died with about the same number captured. The Romans, according to Livy, lost only 1,500 men and 4,000 wounded. Hannibal managed to escape with a handful of horsemen. It was the last battle of the Carthaginians' war against Rome and soon afterwards, Hannibal accepted peace terms.

Much has been made of the fact that Hannibal was hamstrung at Zama by his inferiority in cavalry and the inexperience of many of his troops. But Hannibal expertly compensated for his deficiencies with a formidable array of war elephants. By placing his auxiliaries in the first line, he not only ensured their fighting performance but intended to use them to exhaust the Romans before

his finest warriors could deliver the coup de grâce. As for his African and Carthaginian veterans, they were among the best soldiers in the ancient world. But, though Hannibal commanded well, Scipio commanded better. His imaginative legionary formation defeated the much feared elephants, while the influence of his discipline ensured that his troops maintained their battle formations despite the temptation of pursuing the fleeing Carthaginians. Above all, it was Scipio's ability to delegate command of his wings to able subordinates that gave them the opportunity of taking independent action to deliver the final blow. Hannibal was unable to do this. The flexibility that had enabled the Carthaginians to devastate the Romans at Cannae had now become Scipio's preserve.

58 BC-51 BC

THE GALLIC WARS:
Caesar's conquest of Gaul

Caesar's talents as politician, soldier, and writer were all amply demonstrated in his conquest of Gaul. Also revealed was his brutality. In 55 BC, near Maastricht, he massacred two entire German tribes, said to number 430,000. The barbarity sickened the citizens of Rome, who ordered an enquiry, but Caesar's military success overcame all criticism. Between 58 and 51 BC, he conquered the whole of Gaul, an area twice the size of Italy and far more populous than Spain. The province became a vital part of the western Roman Empire for half a millennium and its conquest established Caesar's legend for centuries afterwards. He himself commemorated his achievements in his *De Bello Gallico* ("Gallic Wars"), a year-by-year account of his campaigns from 58 to 52 BC.

The first steps
Caesar's conquest of Gaul began in 58 BC. Having received the governorship of the Roman province of Narbonese Gaul in southern France as part of the bargain that set up the First Triumvirate, he was well placed to intervene in Celtic politics. When the Gallic tribe of the Aedui asked him for assistance in defeating the invading Helvetii from Switzerland, Caesar made the most of the opportunity. With an army of Roman legionaries and Gallic cavalry, he defeated the Helvetii, slaughtered several thousands of them, and drove the rest back to their Alpine homeland. Such ruthless strength impressed the Celtic chieftains of central France and they asked for his assistance against invading Germans from the east. Caesar followed up the Celtic requests and threw the Germans back across the Rhine. In return, he annexed the land of the Aedui and their neighbors, the Sequani.

Conflict with the Belgae
While Caesar quartered his legionaries at Besancon for the winter, the Belgic tribesmen in northern France realized the error of their Celtic kinsmen. Caesar was not an ally, but a conqueror. Forming a powerful Germano-Gallic army, they were determined to resist the Roman invaders. Hearing news of their aggression, Caesar raised two more legions to add to his six in Gaul and rapidly advanced on Belgic territory. The speed of Caesar's move surprised the Remi, the nearest of the Belgic tribes, and they swiftly came to terms, offering him aid.

The ferocious reputation of the rest of the Belgae discouraged Caesar from confronting them in battle, however. Protecting the majority of his army behind earthworks and marshes, he tested the stamina of the Celts with several cavalry skirmishes, while as the Belgae failed to entice the Romans into battle, their supplies began to run out. When they heard reports of Caesar's Aeduan allies raiding their own territory, the Belgic horde disintegrated. Thus Caesar reduced the Belgic confederation tribe by tribe with a Romano-Gallic force, in which mounted Celtic auxiliaries played a vital part.

From invasion to conquest
So far, in Caesar's march through Gaul, he had good excuses for his invasion – the invitations of the Aedui, the aggression of the Belgae. But in 57 BC he sent a detachment of legionaries to the Atlantic coast. Their reduction of this peaceful area was unprovoked and clearly revealed Caesar's intention to con-

quer the whole of Gaul. The next year, recovering from the shock of Roman conquest, the Celts of Brittany, led by the Veneti, took up arms. The Veneti were a maritime power and fortified remote strongholds on headlands and islands. To defeat them, Caesar again called on the assistance of Gallic auxiliaries. Local Celts presented him with a fleet, which the Romans used to break the Veneti in a sea battle in the Loire estuary.

Over the next two years, Caesar consolidated his hold over northern Gaul by suppressing rebellions. Two expeditions were made to Britain on the pretext of quelling tribes who assisted the Veneti. Here, however, the Celts maintained a united front and kept the Romans out.

Throughout his Gallic campaign, Caesar had so far restricted himself to securing a ring of conquests around western central Gaul without venturing into the interior. As he prepared for this next stage of his conquest, the Celts rebelled with a vengeance on a massive scale. Led by an Avernian chieftain called Vercingetorix, the Gallic tribesmen savaged the Romans at the hill-fort of Gergovia. Caesar's aura of invincibility was shattered, even the Aedui throwing in their lot with Vercingetorix. Ceasar was forced to reinforce his cavalry with German auxiliaries. The final confrontation took place at the siege of Alesia in 52 BC, near Dijon.

The siege of Alesia
Sited high on a hill, the fortified city of Alesia defied immediate assault, while the Romans were also outnumbered – Vercingetorix commanding 90,000 men to Caesar's 55,000. The latter ordered the construction of palisades and earth-

works in a 10-mile long encircling wall to prevent the Gauls assaulting the main siegeworks; a 20-feet wide trench was dug some way in front of it. Wooden towers were placed at intervals of 130 yards along the entire circuit of fortifications.

To protect the Romans from the risk of another Gallic army coming to the relief of the city, Caesar had another 14-mile long line of earthworks constructed facing outwards. The wisdom of this great engineering feat was soon proved when a massive army of Gauls, said to number 250,000, arrived to besiege the besiegers. A cavalry skirmish was followed by a night assault in which the Celts moved silently towards the Roman lines with scaling ladders and grappling hooks. The alarm was given and the Romans hastily manned their defences, pelting the attackers with rocks and huge arrows from their *ballistae* (military catapults). Vercingetorix simultaneously assaulted the inner side of the Roman lines. Delayed by the trenches and treacherous pit traps filled with stakes, the Celtic onslaught was broken. Under a heavy Roman barrage, the relieving force retreated and Vercingetorix returned to Alesia.

Caesar's fortifications had more than achieved their purpose. Several more days of Gallic attacks came to nothing. Eventually, Caesar, clad in a distinctive scarlet cloak, led a cavalry counter-attack from his fortifications and charged the rear of the Gauls as they struggled to clamber over the ramparts. Only the exhaustion of the Romans prevented a greater slaughter. The next day, rather than let his people starve, Vercingetorix conceded defeat. "Here I am," he said to Caesar. "You, O most strong, have conquered the strong." The defeat of the most able of the Gallic leaders marked the submission of the entire region, though it took a further year for Caesar to mop up the surviving pockets of resistance.

The conquest of Gaul was the turning point in Caesar's career. It provided him with the army and the experience to defeat Pompey in the following civil war and achieve supreme power in Rome. His conquest was also a potent demonstration of the maxim "divide and conquer". In the absence of the intense internecine rivalry of the Gallic Celts, Caesar might have been forced out of Gaul as he was out of Britain. It was his political skill as much as his military talent that enabled him to survive.

THE CONQUEST OF GAUL *Caesar's campaigns to establish Roman rule in Gaul were a turning point in his career. His most determined opponent was the Avernian chieftain Vercingetorix, who managed to unite the Gauls and raise a revolt against Roman rule. However, the gallant Vercingetorix met his match at the siege of Alesia, after which he was forced to capitulate (above). The map (right) shows how carefully Caesar planned his campaigns of conquest.*

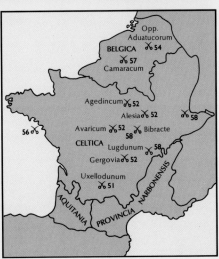

23

1219-1221

GENGHIS KHAN STRIKES:
The Conquest of Central Asia

Genghis Khan's conquest of Central Asia was his most remarkable achievement. Through it, he established the Mongol Empire as a threat not only to the ruling Chin dynasty of China, but to Persia, the Near East, Russia and eastern Europe as well. Following his conquest of northern and western China, Genghis Khan initially had hoped to open peaceful trade contacts with the Muslim Khwarizmian kingdom in the region now known as Soviet Central Asia, but Genghis Khan's trade mission was imprisoned and then executed at Utrar. This seemingly rash action by the governor of the region may have been justified, for Genghis Khan frequently sent spies alongside merchants to gather information on areas that he hoped to conquer. Whatever the truth, Genghis seized upon the insult as providing reason to invade the realm of Khwarizm. In 1218, the Mongol ruler assembled a horde said to number 200,000 Mongols, together with their Turkic allies. The horde was divided into three armies commanded by Genghis and his sons Jochi, Chagatai, and Ogedei. The overall number was probably an exaggeration, as Mongol armies usually consisted of two *touman* – that is, 20,000 warriors.

The following year the first Mongol army, led by Jochi, entered Khwarizm via the Ferghana Valley, but, at the battle of Jand, they were fought to a draw by the larger army of Muhammad Shah, ruler of Khwarizm. Early in 1220, however, this probing attack was followed by a broad advance by all three Mongol armies. Jochi continued along the Ferghana Valley to besiege Khojend, while Chagatai and Ogedei crossed the Irtysh river in the north and attacked Utrar, the scene of the

murder of the Mongol envoys. When the city fell, the Khwarizmian governor responsible for the outrage had molten gold poured down his throat. Genghis Khan himself crossed the Irtysh and then launched a wide sweep through the Kyzulkum desert to attack Bukhara.

The lack of resistance met by the Mongols was due largely to the speed of their movements. Also their three-pronged attack made it impossible to concentrate a substantial defending field army at any one point. At Bukhara, the Turkic garrison tried to break out, but the citizens wisely surrendered and so were spared the wrath of the Mongols. Carrying on to Samarkand, the other jewel of the Central Asian desert, Genghis Khan was joined by Chagatai and Ogedei. In a typical display of Mongol cunning, prisoners seized at Bukhara were paraded before the walls of Samarkand to give the appearance of an even greater Mongol army – this is an indication that Genghis Khan's soldiers were not as numerous as the chroniclers suggest. Having seen the apparent Mongol display of strength, Samarkand capitulated after only five days.

Into the Caucasus
Terrified by the sudden collapse of his kingdom, Muhammad Shah fled westwards. While Genghis Khan consolidated his hold over the key cities of Khwarizm, Jebe and Subedei, two of his most talented captains, were sent in hot pursuit. Although the capture of Muhammad Shah was the purpose of this expedition, it soon became clear that it was also intended to gather information on territory beyond the Caspian Sea. It was a demonstration of the flexibility and strength of

Genghis Khan's command structure that he could entrust captains to execute such a far-flung expedition and return with valuable intelligence. Pursued as far as the southern shores of the Caspian Sea, the exhausted Muhammad Shah died before the Mongols could reach him. Jebe and Subedei continued into the Caucasus and the Christian kingdom of Georgia, breaking all armies before them. On the steppes north of the Caucasus, the duo defeated a mixed army of Alans, Cherkes, and Kipchak Turks. From there, they defeated a Russian army on the shore of the sea of Azov and stormed a Genoese trading post in the Crimea. Advancing northwards into the Ukraine, they crushed an army of Bulgars and only then did they return eastwards via the northern coast of the Caspian Sea. The information they gathered on the weakness of Russia inspired the later Mongol conquest of the region.

The siege of Gurganj
In the meantime, Genghis Khan had advanced westwards. Using Chinese and Islamic engineers, he laid siege to the formidable fortress of Gurganj. Seven months passed before it fell and it paid the ultimate price for resistance. The city was completely destroyed and its citizens slaughtered. Turning south into Persian territory, the combined Mongol armies took town after town and inflicted terrible slaughters on their citizens. It was these acts, reported by outraged Islamic chroniclers, that made the civilized world tremble. Undoubtedly, Genghis Khan used his reputation of invincibility and terror to increase the speed of his conquests. Towards the end of 1221, Muhammad Shah's son, Jalal ad-Din, was desperately

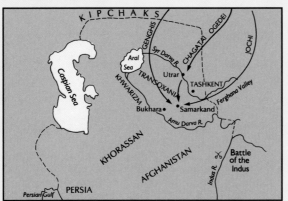

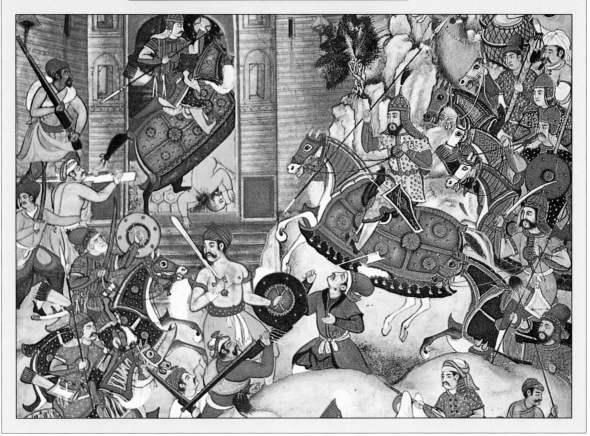

THE GREAT KHAN *The Mongol chieftain Genghis Khan was a brilliant fighting general. He gave his toumans the ability to embark on siege warfare (below) by enlisting engineers and artisans into his ranks, but it was the mobility of his celebrated cavalry that allowed him to wage his carefully-prepared campaigns in China and in Central Asia (left).*

trying to raise a fresh army to stem the Mongol advance. Near Kabul in Afghanistan, Jalal succeeded in breaking a Mongol vanguard. It was the first and only defeat suffered by Genghis Khan in the entire campaign and led to uprisings in several Central Asian cities. Fearing the punishment of Genghis Khan, Jalal retreated to northern India. Genghis rode hard after him.

On the banks of the river Indus, Jalal took a strong defensive position protected by mountains and the bend of the river. Initially, the Turks savaged the Mongol horsemen, but Genghis rallied his troops and sent a *touman* along a mountain track to attack Jalal in the flank. Threatened from two directions, Jalal admitted defeat and rode his horse over a cliff into the river and escaped. Genghis sent a few horsemen after him, but wisely decided

against an invasion of India, preferring to consolidate his hold over Central Asia. Combining armed strength with political reconciliation, Genghis used local administrators and the Muslim priests to subdue the Turkic population. Such was the complete success of his military and civil settlement that Central Asia remained a key province of the Mongol Empire he had created for 200 years.

AUGUST 1346

CRECY

English bowman defeat the flower of French chivalry

The battle of Crécy, fought on a wet August evening in 1346, did more than mark the end of the first stage of the Hundred Years War between England and France; it has been seen as a turning point in the story of medieval warfare, marking the start of the decline of the armored knight's effectiveness on the battlefield, when confronted with the devastating firepower of English longbowmen. However, as far as Edward III himself was concerned, the battle took place by accident, rather than design. Indeed, Edward did not intend to fight a major battle at all at the outset of his 1346 campaign.

Previously, Edward had launched two offensives in France, the first in Gascony, where the French were caught off guard, and the second in Brittany, which was also successful. With a large part of the French feudal host pinned down in the south-west – where Duke John of Normandy was besieging the Earl of Derby at Aiguillan – Edward now decided to open up a third front.

The road to Crécy
Having landed his army at La Hogue, on the north of the Cherbourg peninsula, what Edward intended was a *chevauchée* (a raid) through the rich countryside of the Cotentin and on into Normandy. The aim was plunder and destruction, rather than finite conquest. Having captured and sacked Caen, the English marched towards Paris, which, however, Edward had no intention of attacking, and then retreated northwards, their aim being to reach the safety of a Channel port.

On reaching the Seine, however, Edward found that the French had cut the bridges and, by this time,

Philip of France was close at his heels. He managed to repair a bridge at Poissy, only to find himself faced with the same problem when he reached the Somme. Here, he eventually forced a crossing over a ford near Abbeville, with the main French army under Phillip VI closing in behind him.

A perfect position
Having crossed the Somme, Edward drew his men up in a perfect position, on rising ground. His right flank was protected by a small river, the Maie, and some marshy ground, while a damp and reedy hollow, the Val aux Clercs, lay to his front. The downward slope gave his archers – 7,000 of his 11,000-strong army – a clear field of fire.

Edward's men set to work to strengthen what was already a strong position by digging pits in front of a hedge which ran through it to further increase its defensive value. They then formed up in three divisions – the Black Prince in command of the right, the Earls of Northampton and Arundel on the left and Edward in the center. Here, he set up a command post at a windmill, which was conveniently situated on high ground, so giving the king an over-view of the entire battlefield.

Meanwhile, Philip had ridden out of Abbeville en route for the battlefield. The French king should have felt confident, since his army outnumbered Edward's by nearly three to one, but, unfortunately, the French forces were still arriving on the scene. The cautious king decided to send four of his knights to reconnoiter the English positions. They advised Philip that the English were ready for battle and that his best move would be to wait until the

following morning before starting his attack. Accordingly, the king gave orders for his troops to halt and make camp.

Longbows versus crossbows
By now, however, the flower of French chivalry was out of control. Though the advance guard tried to obey their orders to halt, the ranks behind pressed forward, so forcing the entire army onwards towards the English positions. Eventually, Philip, recognizing he had lost control of his troops, ordered the attack to go ahead. By then, it was evening and the sun was starting to set.

The Genoese crossbowmen led the way, but, as they struggled into their best firing position in the aftermath of a short, but violent, thunderstorm, the English longbowmen discharged a hail of arrows at them. In the face of this devastating fire, the Genoese managed to fire only three volleys before falling back in confusion. Now, the Count of Alecon took a hand. Shouting to his fellow knights to "ride down this rabble who block our advance", he ordered his men-at-arms forward in a disorganized charge. The French knights accordingly pressed forward, riding through and over the hapless foot in their eagerness to get to grips with their enemy.

A welter of confusion
The English stood their ground and waited as the French horses slowed in the muddy terrain. Then, Edward's longbowmen loosed their shafts, bringing down the proud French knights and their mounts in a cycle of ever-growing confusion. The French charged 15 times – with the same result, the last attacks being launched in pitch darkness. Many died bravely, but useless, in

KNIGHTS AND BOWMEN *Crécy was the first major land battle of the Hundred Years War and in it the flower of France's mounted chivalry met their match when confronted by the arrow storm unleashed by Edward III's valiant longbowmen. However, the illustration (above) is idealized and inaccurate; in reality, Edward carefully positioned his army in a strong defensive position and let the French do the attacking (right).*

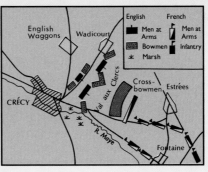

the gathering gloom – those few, like the blind King John of Bohemia, who managed to reach the English battle line being hacked down with axes and swords. Philip himself, while preparing to lead one last assault, was persuaded to flee the field, leaving his stricken army behind him.

Edward had won one of the great victories of medieval history. Tactically and technologically, the battle marked the triumph of the longbow over the armored knight. The French, hitherto regarded as the foremost warriors of Europe, had been defeated piecemeal, losing some 4,000 knights (including 1,500 nobles) in the process. The battle established Edward's reputation as a great commander, though he was in no position to exploit his victory. With his tired troops, he resumed his march to the sea – and safety.

DECEMBER 1503

GARIGLIANO:
The "great captain" triumphs

Gonzalo Fernández de Córdoba's most remarkable victory during the Italian wars was won at Garigliano in 1503. It put an end to the French claim to the kingdom of Naples and demonstrated Gonzalo's mastery of 16th-century warfare.

Following his victory at Cerignola, Gonzalo captured Naples on 26 April 1503 and advanced towards Gaeta. French and allied Italian reinforcements prevented Gonzalo from taking the strategically important port, but, following the numerically superior French army along the coast road of Via Appia, Gonzalo outmaneuvered it and took up position on the eastern bank of the river Garigliano, blocking the French route towards Naples. It was fall and the river was swollen with mountain rain. The banks were a morass and the Spanish had to work hard to build solid earthworks out of the mud.

The commander of the French army was an Italian *condottiere*, Gonzago, Marquis of Mantua. His forces numbered about 23,000 French, Italian, and Swiss troops; Gonzalo had about 15,000 Spanish, Italian, and German soldiers under his command. In October, the French tried to span the river Garigliano with a pontoon bridge. Spanish arquebusiers harassed the bridge builders, but French cannon kept them at a distance. On 6 November, the bridge was completed and the French advanced across it. They were met by the Spanish emerging from a trench on the eastern bank. The French cannon ceased to support the attack for fear of hitting their own men. A fierce hand-to-hand combat followed in which the Spanish proved the more determined fighters. Jammed on the narrow bridge, the French became confused. Reinforcements could not reach them and the fragile structure broke up under their weight. Spanish cannon completed the destruction and many French were drowned in the river as they tried to swim back to safety. A second French assault across a second pontoon bridge met a similar fate.

Bogged down in mud

By mid-November, the weather on the Garigliano had grown worse. Soldiers walked up to their knees in mud and had to construct paths out of plaited sticks. Despite the advice of his officers, Gonzalo refused to give up the position. Once the French were over the river, he reasoned, their superior numbers could not be stopped. To raise the morale of his wet and hungry troops, Gonzalo visited the frontline every day and lived in a modest hut only a mile from the trenches. In contrast, the French officers retired to the comfort of nearby villages, leaving their troops to suffer. Even the Marquis of Mantua lost interest in the dismal campaign and handed over command to Ludovico, Marquis of Saluzzo. For six weeks, the Spanish and French armies glared at each other across the river Garigliano.

Towards the end of December, Gonazlo's scouts confirmed the general deterioration of the French army. A great many had deserted and, because they believed the Spanish must be in a similarly dire situation, they were becoming complacent, believing that only a madman would launch an attack in the middle of a winter that was so severe. However, this was exactly what Gonzalo had in mind. Several miles behind his frontline, his chief engineer was constructing a pontoon bridge. While the French enjoyed a two-day truce over Christmas, Gonzalo moved the bridge and the majority of his army to the northern end of his position. Just before dawn on 29 December, through a torrent of rain, Bartolome de Albiano led the Spanish vanguard of 3,000 soldiers across the pontoon bridge. Only a few contingents of French cavalry stood in their way and they were not even equipped for battle. Their officers had yet to return after the Christmas celebrations.

Gonzalo commanded the main battle and followed Albiano across the bridge. His rearguard remained in trenches opposite the majority of the French army camped downstream. The Spanish completely overran the French quarters, forcing Saluzzo to order a general retreat to a defile near the village of Formia several miles west of Garigliano. Sensing complete victory, Gonzalo's rearguard leapt from their trenches and crossed the river to capture the French artillery before it could be removed.

By nightfall, Gonzalo was encamped on the west bank, but he could not rest with the French reforming near Formia. Through the night he sent *Genitor* light cavalry to harass them. The following day, Gonzalo led his vanguard towards the pass between mountain and sea, where Saluzzo was determined to make a stand. For an hour, Gonzalo's Spanish and German footsoldiers fought a bitter battle with the French cavalry. Eventually, the French gave way and fell back through the pass. In the meantime, a further Spanish contingent had ridden through the mountains to arrive behind the French at the junction of the Via Appia leading to

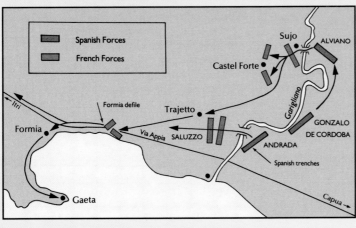

BATTLE AT THE BRIDGE
This romanticized view of the French and Spanish in action at the key bridge over the Garigliano in December 1503 (above) does little justice to the careful way in which Gonzalo, the Spanish commander, planned the battle. The contrast between the way in which the two sides fought is vividly demonstrated by the French failure to force the river crossing and Spanish success (left).

Gaeta. With their retreat completely blocked, most of the French army surrendered. They had lost about 3,000 men and all their baggage and cannon.

With little delay, the Spanish cavalry pressed on to the walls of Gaeta. On 1 January 1504 the city surrendered. The remains of the French garrison were allowed to sail from the city, provided that all fighting by the French in Italy came to an end. Gonzalo had won the war against the French and became the Spanish viceroy of the kingdom of Naples. The brilliant victory at Garigliano was Gonzalo's last campaign and sealed his reputation.

ALEXANDER THE GREAT
(356-323 BC)
MACEDONIAN KING
Wars in Greece and Asia

Alexander was the first great *conquistador* of world history. Inspired by a vision of conquests on a scale never before paralleled, he defeated one of the greatest empires in the ancient world and, as explorer and soldier, carried Greek culture throughout Persia to Central Asia and India. He remains one of the greatest commanders of all time, not so much for his last achievements, which barely survived his death, but for the extravagance of his dream to unite east and west, Europe and Asia.

All this was achieved before Alexander reached the age of 33. That he achieved so much in such a short time was due largely to his father, Philip II, King of Macedonia. Before his assassination, Philip bequeathed to his son both the idea of conquest and the means of executing it. Having subdued the tribes of northern Greece, Philip proceeded to defeat an army of allied Greek states in 338 BC at the battle of Chaeronea. Alexander fought with his father and witnessed the creation of a united Greece under Macedonian leadership. The basis of Philip's power came from a reformed Macedonian army. He fused the aristocratic horsemanship of northern Greece with the *hoplite* and phalanx warfare of the southern city states. It made the most of individual martial prowess, capitalizing

ALEXANDER IN INDIA *Alexander the Great's defeat of the Indian king Porus was his last triumph in his march east.*

on the mobility and impact of élite horsemen, but underpinned with the steady, disciplined ranks of the phalanx armed with 14-foot pikes – the *sarissa* – almost twice as long as the Greek spears. Light infantry and cavalry added flexibility in battle, while a corps of engineers increased its strategic ability.

A rift grew between Alexander and his father when Philip married for a second time. Alexander feared for his position as legitimate heir and expressed his contempt for his father's failing leadership. At a party, Philip tried to silence his son's complaints, but was drunk and tripped before he could reach him. "There," sneered Alexander, "lies the man who is preparing to cross from Europe to Asia, and he cannot even pass from one couch to another!" In 336 BC, Philip was stabbed to death and Alexander became King of Macedonia. Immediately, he quelled the rebellion that broke throughout Greece and secured the submission of all the city states. He was determined to follow his father's plans to invade Asia Minor and challenge the might of the Persian Empire.

The invasion of Asia Minor
With 30,000 footsoldiers and 5,000 cavalry, Alexander landed near the plains of Troy in Asia Minor (present-day Turkey). He was passionately devoted to the tales of the *Iliad* and may have conceived himself as a heroic warrior capable of superhuman acts. At the battle of Granicus, Alexander had his first brush with the mighty armies of the Persian emperor, Darius. Personally leading his élite

"Companion" cavalry to victory, Alexander followed this by a lightning advance across Asia Minor. To combat the threat posed by the Persian fleet, Alexander decided not to fight the Persians at sea, where his navy would prove inferior, but to capture and blockade key ports along the Mediterranean coast.

The battle of Issus
In Syria, at the battle of Issus in 333 BC, the Persian emperor in person confronted the impudent Greek. With an army of 100,000, Darius crossed Alexander's supply lines and threatened his rear. By this action, the Persians cramped themselves into a narrow position between land and sea, losing any opportunity of outflanking the Greeks. Alexander led his army in the usual oblique advance, perfected by Philip and *Epaminondas* before him. His "Companion" cavalry were in front on the right wing, with his phalanx in the center as support. The weakness of this maneuver was soon revealed. Alexander's cavalry were too keen to rush against the Persians and, although they scattered the left wing, a gap was created between them and their slower moving phalanx with the result that Darius' Greek mercenaries broke in between them.

At this point, the battle could have ended in disaster for Alexander, but fortunately for him the Macedonian leader grasped the simplest rule of warfare and made straight for the Persian ruler. By sheer hard fighting, the Macedonians closed in on Darius and forced him to flee the field. Although successful elsewhere, once the Persians saw their leader depart, they, too, fled.

Issus was a close-run, but key, victory, for, as a result, the whole of Syria, Palestine, and Egypt lay open to Alexander. Some of the richest coastal cities in the Mediterranean were there for the taking and Alexander demonstrated his skill at siege warfare. The toughest siege was that of Tyre, where the city was sited on a rock half a mile from the shore with a 150-foot high stone wall protecting it. Following the advice of his chief engineer, Alexander had a causeway built from the shore to the island. He then erected huge siege towers to deal with the wall, but Tyrian fire-ships destroyed them.

Alexander then attacked by land and sea, his triremes carrying rams to the base of the Tyrian walls. After seven months, a breech was finally made, Tyre fell and the triumphant Macedonians massacred its stubborn citizens. The conquest of the Near East was completed by the invasion of Egypt. There, Alexander met with little opposition and the Persian navy was denied its last bases.

The greatest test
This had been the limit of Philip's plans, but Alexander was impatient for more. In 331, he moved swiftly across the Syrian desert to Mesopotamia. Here, Darius sought to defeat Alexander once and for all. Between Arbela and Guagamela he assembled a huge force drawn from all parts of his empire. It was Alexander's greatest test, but with characteristic audacity he led the attack and won a remarkable victory. In the pursuit, Darius was killed by

his own subordinate commanders. From Babylon to Susa to Persepolis, Alexander occupied all the great cities of Persia. He was now master of a vast Asian empire. With a reduced, but dedicated army, he secured his hold over his new subjects by exploring his conquest's easternmost limits. For six years, he travelled and campaigned across Persia, through the mountains of Afghanistan to Central Asia, and to the river Hydaspes where he fought with the Indian King Porus. Employing yet again his oblique tactics, leading with the "Companion" cavalry, Alexander defeated the Indian army, his phalanx having the terrible task of battling 200 war elephants.

Realizing that the endurance of his men was finally exhausted, Alexander returned westwards. Wishing to unite east with west, he took a Persian wife and conducted a mass marriage between 10,000 Macedonian soldiers and Persian women. But his dream was short-lived. In 323 he died from fever at Babylon and almost immediately his empire broke up into numerous warring successor states. Although supreme in his imagination, the great weakness of Alexander's success was its dependence on his leadership. Without him, there was no substance to his conquests.

BELISARIUS
(c.505-565)
BYZANTINE GENERAL
Wars in Persia, North Africa, and Italy

Belisarius was the commander chosen by the Byzantine emperor Justinian to spearhead a series of remarkable counterattacks against the barbarians in the 6th century; these were so successful that they very nearly succeeded in re-establishing the Roman empire. Belisarius' achievement was all the more extraordinary, for his victories were won in the face of constant undersupply and underfunding from his jealous emperor.

VICTIM *Belisarius's success in war aroused imperial suspicion.*

Coming from the Balkan province of Illyria, Belisarius was commissioned into the imperial bodyguard and saw his first major active service on campaign against the Persians between 529 and 531. Combining skill at the art of long-range raiding with an ability to win set-piece battles, he successfully stemmed the Persian advance into Asia Minor and Syria. Two years later, after showing his loyalty by bloodily suppressing rioting in Constantinople, Belisarius was chosen by Justinian to lead an expedition to North Africa against the Vandals. Though he was given only 15,000 men, he completely outwitted his foes, despite their greater numbers. Exploiting the weakness of the Vandal cavalry, which only used the sword and lance in combat, he employed the horse-archery of his Byzantine and Hun cavalry to murderous effect. In two battles, the Vandals were overwhelmed and Carthage captured.

The reconquest of Italy

With such a competent general at his disposal, Justinian now conceived an even greater scheme – the reconquest of Italy from the Ostrogoths. This time, with even fewer troops under command – a mere 8,000 men – Belisarius landed in Sicily in 535 and proceeded to scatter the barbarians before him as he marched on Naples and on to Rome. Besieged there by a greatly superior Visigoth army, Belisarius resisted their assaults for a year until the Visigoths finally fell back on Ravenna. They then offered to make Belisarius emperor if he would give up his campaign, but Belisarius refused and went on to capture their king in 539.

Victim of jealousy

Recalled several times by an emperor fearful of his power, Belisarius was never given sufficient soldiers or support to deal with the barbarian threat once and for all. Subsequently, the Byzantine war in Italy dragged on for another 14 years without any lasting achievement.

Fighting briefly in Syria and Mesopotamia between 542 and 544, Belisarius again repulsed the Persians, while in 559 he defeated a Bulgar assault on Constantinople itself. But these victories and his devotion to duty were not enough to allay Justinian's suspicions; in 562 Belisarius was stripped of his wealth and honors and imprisoned. A year later, however, he was released and allowed to live in retirement until his death in 565.

CAESAR
Julius (100-44 BC)
ROMAN GENERAL
Wars in Gaul and the Mediterranean

Unlike Alexander, Scipio, or Hannibal, Caesar was not touched with young military genius. Throughout his 20s and 30s, he devoted himself to political ambition. It was not until he was 41, that Caesar began his famous conquest of Gaul and he was in his 50s when he won his decisive victories in the Civil War. Many military authorities have criticized his lack of innovation and military expertise, yet his achievements are far greater and long lasting than those of any other major commander of the classical Mediterranean world. His conquests created the power-bases from which the Roman Empire expanded to its greatest extent for a century and more afterwards. If Caesar lacked youthful inspiration, it is because he had a realistic understanding of war as part of politics. If he

HAIL CAESAR! *A politician turned soldier, Caesar's military triumphs won him the support of the legions on his road to supreme power in the Roman state.*

lacked the tactical precision of the text-book general, it is because he recognized the role of luck. "Fortune which has great influence on affairs generally and especially in war," wrote Caesar, "produces by a slight disturbance of balance important changes in human affairs."

The Gallic Wars

Caesar's earliest experience of command came against the Celtiberians in Spain in 61 BC. Prior to this, the patrician-born politician had served only briefly in Asia Minor. In 59 BC, he formed the First Triumvirate with Pompey and Crassus, an informal alliance in which these three leading Roman politicians obtained greater power for each other in opposition to the Senate. Each of the triumvirs had their own spheres of influence in the empire; Pompey ruled in Rome, Crassus fought in the east, and Caesar was governor of Cisalpine Gaul (northern Italy), Illyricum (Yugoslavia), and Narbonese Gaul (southern France). Realizing that the Celtic tribes of France would not present a common front against Roman intervention, Caesar began his conquest of the remainder of Gaul in 58 BC. In seven years, he subdued the entire region as far as the Rhine and the English Channel, the process culminating in his defeat of the Gallic chieftain Vercingetorix at Alesia.

Caesar owed his rise to political power partly to his considerable skills as an orator and demagogue. Once transferred to the military environment, his force of personality produced a commander of great charisma. That Caesar himself considered his leadership a primary reason for success is revealed in his *Commentaries* on the Gallic War. Describing himself in the third person, he recalls: "The situation was critical and as no reserves were available, Caesar seized a shield from a soldier in the rear and made his way to the frontline. He addressed each centurion by name and shouted encouragement to the rest of the troops, ordering them to push forward and open out their ranks so they could use their swords more easily. His coming gave them fresh heart and hope. Each man wanted to do his best under the eyes of his commander despite the peril."

Crossing the Rubicon

Caesar's successes in Gaul led to the collapse of the Triumvirate. Supported by an army of loyal Gallic veterans, he crossed the River Rubicon into Italy in 49 BC. Pompey and the Senate were already fearful of Caesar's power after his success in Gaul and this was the signal that the former allies were at war. Pompey had more legions under his command, but they were scattered throughout the Mediterranean and, not trusting popular support in Italy, he retreated to Greece. It was now that Caesar demonstrated his mastery of strategy. Rather than pursue Pompey, Caesar chose to defeat the threat to his rear posed by Pompey's legions in Spain. "I set forth to fight an army without a leader," he said, "so as later to fight a leader without an army." At Ilerda, through skilful maneuvering, Caesar cut off the retreat of the Spanish army and secured its surrender. Back in Rome, he was appointed dictator, but resigned the post, being content to exercise power through his consulship.

At the end of 49 BC, Caesar took the civil war to Pompey in Greece. Despite the latter's dominance of the sea, Caesar transported seven legions across the Adriatic to Dyrrhachium. Endeavoring to besiege Pompey's camp with a line of fortifications like those he had employed against the Gauls at Alesia, Caesar nevertheless failed to cut off Pompey's access to the sea. With the help of his fleet and twice as many soldiers, Pompey easily broke through Caesar's lines and forced him into retreat.

The decisive clash of the civil war was now to follow near Pharsalus in 48 BC, where the two commanders fought the crucial battle that was to decide the fate of the Roman republic. Pompey's army numbered some 40,000 soldiers, while Caesar's was only 22,000 strong. Both sides were organized in the orthodox manner of three lines of cohorts, but Pompey's cavalry far outnumbered Caesar's and he planned to send them against Caesar's right wing, so turning his flank. Extending his thin lines to match Pompey's frontage, Caesar noted the threat and placed a reserve of six cohorts to guard his right flank behind his few cavalry.

The battle of Pharsalus

The battle of Pharsalus began according to Pompey's plan. The opposing infantry lines clashed and Pompey's cavalry charged Caesar's inferior horsemen. These fought stubbornly, but could not resist Pompey's superior numbers. It was then that Caesar ordered his reserve to cover the flank. The legionary charge broke Pompey's cavalry – Caesar had ordered the footsoldiers to use their javelins as pikes, rather than throwing them as missiles. The reserve pressed on to attack Pompey's left flank. Caesar personally led his third line of legionaries through the other two and with these fresh warriors delivered the final blow to Pompey's army. For the cost of not more than 1,200 men, Caesar had killed 6,000 Pompeians and captured the remainder of Pompey's army.

Pompey fled to Egypt. Caesar followed him there, but, on his arrival learned that the luckless Pompey had already been assassinated. The surviving Pompeians, however, roused the Egyptians against him and, besieged in Alexandria, Caesar had to call on the assistance of Mithridates of Pergamum before he could claim victory. He then formed his celebrated liaison with the Egyptian queen, Cleopatra.

From Egypt, Caesar sailed to Asia Minor. There, he defeated King Pharnaces at the battle of Zela and is alleged to have expressed his contempt for the enemy by saying "Veni, vidi, vici" – "I came, I saw, I conquered".

The Ides of March

For two years, Caesar continued to campaign against the remnants of the Pompeian threat in Africa and Spain. When he returned to Rome in 45 BC, he was the undisputed master of its empire, but he held supreme power for only a single year. Hostility towards him increased when his dictatorship was converted into a lifelong office and, on 15 March 44 BC, he was assassinated. It was too late, however, to stop the process that Caesar had begun. The precedent of autocracy he had set brought an end to the Roman Republic and led directly to the proclamation of Augustus as the first Roman Emperor in 27 BC, an office of supreme power with which Caesar's name was ever afterwards synonymous.

CÓRDOBA
Gonzalo Fernández de (1453-1515)
SPANISH GENERAL
Wars in Spain and Italy

Defeat was the making of Gonzalo Fernández de Córdoba. After losing the battle of Seminara in Italy to a smaller French army in 1495, he revised his battlefield tactics and the military system that emerged as a result was the prototype that set the pattern for future pike and shot warfare. Giving priority to footsoldiers armed with firearms, Gonzalo proceeded to defeat the French in a string of victories, conquering the entire kingdom of Naples, and revolutionized the nature of warfare in 16th-century Europe.

Gonzalo's military career began during Spain's final campaign to rid itself of Moorish occupation. The son of a noble family in Montilla, Granada, he was brought up on the frontline, his family holding their estates on condition that they defended the kingdom of Castile against Moorish raiders. His early education was gained at the court of Isabella of Castile, for whom he acted as page. By the time he left her service in 1473, he was well connected with the Spanish royal house and thoroughly practiced in the martial arts. When the call to arms was raised in 1482, Gonzalo eagerly rode to the banner of Castile at the head of 60 lances. A decade of war ensued in which the newly united Castilians and Aragonese pushed the Moors further and further towards their last toe-hold of Granada. In 1492 the city fell and Spain was free of Muslim occupation after 800 years of struggle.

Lessons from the "reconquista"
The lesson gained by Gonzalo and the Spanish army in the Moorish wars were invaluable. Isabella, too, had a strong influence on the professional conduct of the campaigns. She commissioned the construction of a powerful artillery arm, enlarged the navy to stop Moorish reinforcements reaching Granada from Africa, raised the spirits of her men by appearing in the frontline, established hospitals and proper military bases, and supervised the construction of roads to transport supplies. On the battlefield, Gonzalo was impressed by the Spanish light cavalry raised to counter the Moorish horsemen. They were called *Genitors*, armed with javelins, and fought as skirmishers. The Spanish also hired several companies of mercenary Swiss pikemen and Gonzalo must have spent time noting the strengths and weaknesses of their battle formation. If he was ever to lead men against a European army, he would have to deal with their famous, supposedly invincible pike phalanxes.

Gonzalo's relationship with Isabella remained close throughout the war, and despite rumors of a more intimate friendship, Gonzalo emerged with increased royal patronage and the reputation of being a competent commander. At the siege of Montefrio, he won the admiration of the rank and file by personally leading an assault on the walls, reaching the battlements at the head of a scaling ladder and slaying several Moors. After the conquest of Granada, Gonzalo's material rewards included a new armory and several Moorish silk farms.

War in Italy
In 1494, Charles VIII of France invaded Italy. On the pretext of launching a crusade against the Turks from Naples, he marched the length of the peninsula, occupying Florence and Rome along the way. The kingdom of Naples and Sicily had formerly been Aragonese possessions and retained close links with the Spanish crown. As the king of France added the throne of Naples to his possessions, the ousted Neapolitan rulers called on Spain to defend its interests. Several distinguished veterans from the Moorish war were ambitious for command of the expedition, but Gonzalo's close connection with Isabella won through. On 26 May 1495 he landed at Calabria at the head of a Spanish army.

Charles VIII retreated northwards to defend his rear against a coalition of Italian states, leaving Naples under the command of Marshal Everard d'Aubigny. The French and Spanish met in battle on 28 June at Seminara. Gonzalo commanded a force of 8,000 men (including Neapolitan soldiers led by the exiled king of Naples). Gonzalo began by employing his *Genitors* against the French as he had against the Moors in Granada, but their skirmishing tactics and false retreats confused his Neapolitan allies as much as the French themselves and the former broke before a determined charge of heavier French men-at-arms. However, this was Gonzalo's first and last defeat. Over the following years, he avoided any major confrontation and resorted to the pattern of guerilla warfare he had learnt in Spain. This strategy wore down the French, whose lines of supply and command from northern Italy were vastly over-extended. In 1498, they completely withdrew from Naples and Gonzalo returned to Spain.

The following year, however, civil war in Naples encouraged the French to invade Italy again. A treaty was signed with Spain to divide the Neapolitan kingdom, but war nevertheless broke out and Gonzalo seized Taranto in March 1502. The French dominated most of Naples and blockaded Gonzalo in the port of Barletta.

It was during this campaign that Gonzalo perfected his celebrated military system. He replaced his crossbowmen with arquebusiers. He positioned his men armed with swords and shields among his pikemen, so that, when opposing phalanxes became locked in combat, the swordsmen could dash among the soldiers handicapped with long pikes and inflict close-quarter slaughter. The most significant development, however, was demonstrated at Cerignola, just outside Barletta, on 26 April 1503.

Fire-arms to the fore
At Cerignola, Gonzalo confronted the French Duke of Nemours, both commanding roughly equal forces of about 8,000 troops each. Gonzalo chose a defensive position on a hillside. At the foot of the hill was a dry stream bed. The Spanish made the ditch deeper, throwing up a rampart behind them with earth they had excavated. Behind the earthworks, Gonzalo placed his artillery and arquebusiers as part of a master plan to defeat the Swiss pikemen in the French service.

Harassed by Gonzalo's *Genitors*, the French were unable to make a proper reconnaissance of the position. The Swiss pikemen and French men-at-arms assaulted the front of the hillside earthworks. Brought to a halt by the ditch, they were raked mercilessly by the Spanish firearms. The Swiss endeavored to cross the earthworks, but were beaten back by the arquebusiers. Finally, Gonzalo led his army forward in a general rout of the shattered French army. Nemours died in the action from an arquebus bullet, and 4,000 French dead were counted. Cerignola has been termed the first battle in world history to be won completely by firearms.

The war continued with Gonzalo capturing the city of Naples and then besieging Gaeta. French reinforcements compelled him to retreat to the *Garigliano* river, but it was there that Gonzalo won his most ingenious victory. On 1

January 1504, Gaeta fell to Gonzalo and the French admitted defeat. The kingdom of Naples became part of the Spanish Empire and Gonzalo its first viceroy.

In 1507, the Spanish monarchy, fearing his powerful hold over Naples, recalled Gonzalo; he spent the rest of his life in retirement on his estates in Granada. Gonzalo's tactical innovations transformed the character of warfare in the 16th century and set Spain on the road to European military supremacy, his military system being copied and refined by subsequent Spanish commanders. At the battle of Biocca in 1522, Prosper Colonna placed his artillery and arquebusiers behind ramparts and inflicted such a crushing defeat on the Swiss mercenaries in their pike phalanxes that they ceased to be an important factor in European warfare from that time onwards.

CORTÉS
Hernando (1485-1547)
SPANISH GENERAL
Wars in Mexico

With just 550 Spaniards, 250 Indians, 15 horses and ten brass cannon, Cortés embarked on his conquest of Mexico. Some historians have put down his remarkable success to the superiority of European arms, but he had few of these and those that he possessed were no more effective than a good bow and arrow. Other historians say he succeeded because his appearance – mounted on horse-back and carrying firearms – terrorized the Aztecs, but they soon recovered from this. As he fought battle after battle against overwhelming odds, it was Cortés' endurance and steady nerve that won him victory over a mighty empire in a strange land.

The adventure in the New World
Coming from a noble Spanish family in Estremadura, Cortés sailed to the New World in the company of Diego de Velazquez. In 1518, Velazquez gave Cortés command of a small army and ordered him to explore the Mexican mainland. Almost immediately, Cortés ignored his orders, which strictly limited his objective, instead embarking on his own career of conquest, starting with the Indian state of Tabasco. He founded Vera Cruz and conquered the Indians of Tlaxcala.

It was then that Cortés received messengers from Montezuma, ruler of the Aztecs, but, despite these friendly overtures, the Spanish were ambushed as they marched towards the Aztec capital of Tenochtitlan. Cortés, however, was a supreme realist. When he saw the mighty city, he realized how greatly outnumbered he was and that his recourse must be reliance on deception and bluff.

Cortés took Montezuma captive and managed to hold the Aztecs at bay, while he pillaged their treasures. After six months, however, the Aztecs were becoming rebellious, while Cortés heard that an army had been sent by Velazquez to deal with him for his insubordination.

AZTEC CONQUEST *A contemporary Mexican view of Cortes in action, putting his Aztec opponents to flight.*

Cortés left his second-in-command at Tenochtitlan and marched against the punitive force. Defeating the Spaniards, he enrolled the survivors in his own army and returned to the Aztec capital, which now rebelled against him. Montezuma was slain and Cortés forced to fight a damaging withdrawal. In 1520, at the battle of Otumba, a desperate stand was made and although Cortés lost more of his men, he emerged victorious.

Reorganizing his army and recruiting more warriors, Cortés returned to Tenochtitlan and in 1521 laid siege to it. Using brigantines armed with cannon and infantry carrying arquebuses, Cortés launched an amphibious attack on the island city, finally breaking Aztec resistance. Destroying the ancient settlement, Cortés founded Mexico City nearby. Appointed governor, he continued his conquest of Mexico, but eventually he was replaced and returned to Spain in 1540.

CYRUS THE GREAT
(c.585-529 BC)
PERSIAN EMPEROR
Wars in Asia

Founder of the first superpower of the ancient world, Cyrus was the first great commander of whom any reliable records survive. Within 30 years of his death, the empire he established stretched from Macedonia and Egypt in the west to Central Asia and the River Indus in the east. Of noble Iranian birth, Cyrus first made his mark on history by leading a revolt against Astyages, his Median overlord. He deposed the latter and made himself lord of the Medes and Persians. The successful revolt marked the establishment of a vigorous new dynasty – the Achaemenids – a fact of great consequence for the Middle East.

Croesus, king of Lydia in Asia Minor, was the first ruler to test Cyrus' military ability. Seeking to restore his brother-in-law Astyages to power in Persia, Croesus crossed the River Halys and invaded the Cappadocian province of the Median-Persian Empire. Cyrus responded by fighting the Lydians to a stalemate, forcing them to withdraw to Croesus' capital at Sardis. In 546, Cyrus led a counter-invasion and on the plain of Thymbra, the two armies met. Cyrus had fewer warriors under command than Croesus and so drew his troops into a square to defend himself against the risk of envelopment. As the Lydians proceeded to attempt to encircle Cyrus, his Persian archers within the square raked the enemy ranks. Then, seeing that the Lydian formations were stretched in their attempt to literally swallow the Persians, Cyrus ordered his cavalry into action against the gaps that developed in their formations, eventually smashing the Lydian wings and scattering the rest of Croesus' army.

Cyrus pursued Croesus to Sardis and stormed the city. In a gesture characteristic of Cyrus and the Persian imperial system, he spared his opponent's life and set up a provincial government under a trusted general, or *satrap*. Cyrus' policy of moderation ensured that his subject people remained loyal and many formed important contingents in the vast Persian army.

Following his conquest of Asia Minor, Cyrus went on to subjugate Parthia, Sogdiana, Bactria, and the whole of eastern Iran. In 539, he entered Babylon unopposed and assumed the title of "King of Babel, Sumer, Accad, and the four quarters of the world." He next campaigned along the River Indus and penetrated Central Asia. It was while fighting the Queen of the Massagetai that he met his death. The Amazon ruler cut off his head and placed it in an animal skin full of blood, declaring that he now had as much blood as he wanted. His body was returned to Persia and his son continued his planned conquests by seizing Egypt. In 511, the Persians invaded Greece and Europe faced the threat of the mighty power that Cyrus the Great had created.

DRAKE
Sir Francis (c.1540-1596)
ENGLISH SAILOR
Wars in the Caribbean and Atlantic

The revolution in naval warfare of the 16th century meant that new tactics and strategies had to be devised to make full use of the new technology. Francis Drake was one of the seamen who grasped this idea wholeheartedly, with a full tactical and strategical understanding of the new power the galleon and the cannon could provide in combination. The temptation of wealth was also a major factor in his ambitions. In the 1560s, Spanish dominance of the Caribbean and the coasts of the New World was bringing it the wealth to support its role as the dominant European power. In 1565, Drake left his North Sea

TUDOR HERO *Sir Francis Drake played a key role in Elizabethan England's maritime war against Spain.*

coastal-trading business and sailed to the Caribbean in search of his own fortune. Several expeditions later, he had gained a reputation as an able and fearless captain, spearheading the Elizabethan assault on the riches the Spanish were drawing from the New World. This privateering was at first regarded as individual adventuring, but, soon – with concealed royal backing – it became a vital strategic step in the growing conflict between England and Spain.

"Singeing the King of Spain's beard"
In 1577, Drake sailed his *Golden Hind* in an extended campaign of ravaging Spanish ports and ships that resulted in his circumnavigation of the world. When he returned, he was knighted by Elizabeth I. This was taken by the Spanish as an official sanction for his acts and when England followed by openly supporting the Protestant Dutch in their revolt against Spain, war formally broke out between the two powers.

In 1586, Spain organized the mighty Armada to sail against England. Drake tried to pre-empt the attack with a long-range raid against the Spanish port of Cadiz, sinking at least 33 ships while they lay at anchor. It was a brilliant display of naval strategy, but was not enough to prevent the actual sailing of the Armada in 1588.

As the Spanish passed through the English Channel, Drake refused to be drawn into close-quarter combat in the old style of sea warfare. Instead, the English used the superior sailing qualities of their vessels to avoid close-quarter action and pounded away with long-range gunnery. Battered and unable to best the superior seamanship of their adversaries, the Spanish found themselves forced onwards by bad weather, suffering more losses from storm and shipwreck. It was a decisive victory, denoting the start of the eclipse of Spanish sea-power. Drake then continued his career of privateering, eventually dying in the West Indies from dysentery.

EDWARD I
(1239-1307)
ENGLISH KING
Wars in England, Wales, and Scotland

Edward I is generally regarded as the greatest warrior king of medieval England. He first demonstrated his considerable strategic skills in defence of his father, Henry III. Having initially been defeated by rebel barons led by Simon de Montfort, Edward led a royalist counter-attack in 1265, but, caught between the armies of Simon and his son, he found himself outnumbered two to one. The obvious strategic necessity was to prevent the two enemy armies joining.

Force-marching his soldiers rapidly eastwards against Simon's son's army, he took the rebels completely by surprise when he attacked at dawn and routed them. He immediately marched back westwards to meet Simon de Montfort's smaller army near Evesham, where by swift maneuvering, he trapped Simon in a loop of the River Avon. Victory there brought the rebellion to an end. The confidence and skill with which Edward had defeated the two armies, one after the other, ensured his rise to supreme power. In 1272, he became King of England.

The Welsh campaign
Wales, however, refused to pay homage to the new king, so in 1277 Edward led an invading army into the country in what, for its time, was a remarkably well equipped and planned expedition. Literally cutting a path through the Welsh forests, Edward drove through North Wales, ordering the building of a castle wherever he camped. Employing ships from the Cinque Ports – England's chief sea-ports along the south-east coast – he cut the Welsh supply lines from the grain-rich island of Anglesey and, through hunger plus the sheer professionalism of Edward's army, the Welsh were forced to admit defeat. A subsequent rebellion was also crushed and Wales became English. During these campaigns, Edward had been impressed by the fighting qualities of the Welsh and employed many of their bowmen on his next major campaign. By relying on the payment of professional soldiers, rather than depending on his barons and the feudal host, Edward established a more efficient army.

Attack on Scotland
A succession crisis in Scotland encouraged Edward to invade the country in 1296. Though he was already involved in war in France, he nevertheless conducted the subsequent campaign with great panache. Following the storming of Berwick and the defeat of the Scots at Dunbar, he proclaimed himself king of Scotland. A rebellion in 1297 led by William Wallace was crushed the next year at Falkirk. Here, Edward used his Welsh bowmen to break the stubborn Scots phalanx of spearmen. It was a demonstration of firepower that was to be developed by his grandson, Edward III.

In 1306, the Scots again revolted – this time under the leadership of Robert Bruce. An elderly Edward prepared to confront him, but died before the campaign got underway. His last wish was that his remains should be carried before his army, but his son failed to live up to his father's hopes and was beaten at Bannockburn.

EDWARD III
(1312-1377)
ENGLISH KING
Wars in Scotland and France

Edward III's reputation largely rests on his victory over the French at *Crécy* in 1346 – a battle that established English dominance in the first phase of the Hundred Years' War and created the legend of the longbow.

Succeeding to the English throne in 1327, Edward gained his first military experience against the Scots at Halidon Hill in 1333. The action was a triumph of defensive tactics. Dismounting his men-at-arms, Edward placed archers on their wings. When the Scots engaged the heavily armored troops in the center, Edward's archers punished them with their arrows and the Scots fled before a determined counter-charge. These were the self-same tactics that Edward was to use against the French to such effect.

The Crécy campaign
In order to defend his French lands, Edward led an invasion in 1346 (a French invasion fleet had been shattered at Sluys in 1340). In a display of strategic thoughtfulness, for which he has often been underrated, Edward prepared for war by supporting conflicts elsewhere in France – notably a civil war in Brittany and fighting in Gascony.

Landing near Cherbourg, Edward advanced rapidly through Normandy and captured Caen. He then followed the River Seine eastwards, but, hearing of a French army gathering near Paris, he crossed the river to the north to provide an open line of retreat to Flanders, if this proved necessary. Maneuvering further north across the River Somme with the French in pursuit, Edward finally felt secure enough to face the enemy army. Accordingly on 26 August 1346, he took up position near the village of Crécy and carefully prepared for the anticipated battle.

The English right flank was protected by a river, its left being covered by a forest and the earthworks that Edward had ordered his soldiers to dig. He himself took up position at a windmill on a ridge behind his main forces – a position which gave him a good overview of the battlefield. He ordered his men-at-arms to dismount, placing contingents of archers among them, while, in front, pitfalls and more earthworks were dug to break the French assault. Behind this main line, Edward placed reserves of mounted men-at-arms, ready for a counter-attack. The French, led by their king, failed to realize the extent and care of Edward's preparations and fell into his trap. They advanced on a broad front towards the English position, their crossbowmen leading, fol-

AGAINST THE FRENCH
Edward III, victor of Crécy.

lowed by mounted men-at-arms. Though the French forces outnumbered Edward's by almost three to one, they soon became disorganized when faced with the hail of English arrows and, despite several charges, were unable to drive the English from their well-protected position. As a result of the battle, Edward was master of northwestern France; he proceeded to lay siege to and capture Calais.

In 1356, Edward III's son, the Black Prince, took over his father's role and successfully repeated his defensive tactics at Poitiers. Neither of these victories, however, brought lasting victory. The prize of the French crown eluded Edward and his fortunes thereafter began to decline with the success of *Bertrand du Guesclin*.

EPAMINONDAS
(c. 410-362 BC)
THEBAN GENERAL
Wars in Greece

Until his defeat of Sparta at Leuctra in 371 BC, Epaminondas was best known as a private citizen involved in the fringe of Theban politics. After the battle, however, he was recognized as one of the greatest of Greek generals.

Well into his 40s when the city-state of Thebes rebelled against Spartan hegemony, Epaminondas had until then been noted as a man of broad cultural interests, devoting as much time to playing the lyre and the flute as to physical exercise in the gymnasium. Contemporaries observed that he knew much, but spoke little. The revolt of his city against Sparta ignited his patriotism and, despite his disinclination towards taking a prominent role in public affairs, he led a delegation of Theban patriots to discuss a settlement. The Spartans were not interested

in negotiation, however, their response being to invade Theban territory in 371.

Defeating the might of Sparta
At this time, Sparta was the greatest military power in Greece. Its hoplites, fighting in phalanxes of spear-carrying warriors, were famous throughout the Greek world for their ferocity and fighting strength. When Epaminondas confronted the Spartan army at Leuctra that summer, he must have cursed his bad luck. Not only were the Spartans superior fighters, but they outnumbered his Theban forces by 11,000 to 6,000.

Epaminondas, however, had a plan to deal with this. Recognizing his weakness, he responded by placing the majority of his hoplites on his left wing in a column 50 deep. The remaining warriors were echeloned to his right rear in thin lines screened by cavalry. The Spartans were organized in the traditional line of phalanxes. As soon as Epaminondas led his left wing against the Spartan right, its shallow lines began to break under the determined weight of the Theban thrust. At the same time, the rest of the Theban cavalry and footsoldiers advanced slowly, capturing the attention of the Spartans in the center and to the left, but refusing to engage them. Thus, the Theban left wing could concentrate on scattering the Spartan right and then turn on the flank of the remaining Spartans, completely defeating them.

This was the first known use of what is technically termed the deep column attack with oblique refused flank and it shattered Spartan power in Greece. Epaminondas continued to lead his warriors on successful campaigns, but his political skills failed to match his military talents. When he fell in battle at Mantinea, Theban power collapsed as quickly as it had risen.

FARNESE
Alexander, Duke of Parma (1546-1592)
ITALIAN GENERAL
Wars in the Mediterranean, France and the Netherlands

Towards the end of the 16th century, the Italian-born general Alexander Farnese was the greatest Spanish commander in Europe. If he had not been frustrated by the incompetent strategy of his superiors, he would have crushed the Protestant Dutch revolt and might even have invaded England to overthrow Elizabeth I.

Farnese first gained a

PHILIP'S VICEROY
Farnese led Spanish troops to victory over the Dutch.

reputation during the campaign following the Christian defeat of the Turks at Lepanto in 1571. Serving under *Don John* of Austria, he led a land assault against the Turks in Greece. When Don John became Spanish viceroy of the Netherlands, Farnese followed him and, in 1578, joined his superior at the battle of Gembloux, where his speedy pursuit of the defeated Dutch completely devastated the enemy. Later that year, on the death of Don John, Farnese succeeded him as viceroy. Over the next decade, he systematically conquered city after city in the southern Netherlands. His mastery of siege warfare and the latest engineering innovations was awesome. In 1585, during a siege of Antwerp that lasted for over a year, Farnese had a fortified bridge of ships built across the mouth of the Scheldt to cut off the city's access to the sea.

Foiled by his superiors

In 1586, Farnese succeeded to his family's title of Duke of Parma. A year later, he wasted time preparing an army of 25,000 to link up with the Spanish Armada, but the order to invade England never came. Instead, Farnese was ordered to France to assist the French Catholics against Henry of Navarre. The strategy was a mistaken reflection of Philip of Spain's overconfidence in his hold over the Netherlands following Farnese's victories there. While Farnese was embroiled in France, the Dutch fought back against the Spanish under the brilliant leadership of Maurice of Nassau.

Farnese's military skills were tested to their limit against Henry of Navarre. In a war of maneuver, his army was trapped in a loop of the Seine, but Farnese used his superior ingenuity to escape by building a bridge during the night. He was then ordered to return to the Netherlands, but before he could get to grips with Maurice, he was back in France again. The frustration of never being allowed to deal decisively with one enemy or the other was the destruction of Farnese's strategy and the Spanish position in northern Europe. Maurice continued his reconquest of the Netherlands, while Farnese himself died of wounds sustained during his French campaign.

FLAVIUS
Aetius (c. 390-454)
ROMAN GENERAL
Wars in France and Italy

Flavius Aetius was the last great Roman general. For more than 25 years, he was the supreme military power in western Europe, stemming the barbarian invasions by means of a combination of military victories and political settlements.

The son of a Scythian soldier and a Roman noblewoman, Aetius spent his early years as an imperial hostage among the Visigoths and Huns. During this time, the young Aetius came to understand barbarian ways, so establishing an understanding that was to be of vital im-

BARBARIAN ALLIANCE *Flavius Aetius's understanding of the barbarians within the empire enabled him to form a coalition powerful enough to defeat Attila's Huns.*

portance in the future. A favorite of the Emperor Valentinian and his formidable mother Placidia, his first major military task was the policing of Gaul. Here, his tasks were twofold. Not only did he have to defend the province's frontiers against external threats; he was also called upon to control the Visigoths who had settled in southern France and deal with rebellious peasants. In Gaul, Aetius learned the realities of imperial politics and the need to balance enemies.

Burgundians and Huns

In 437, the Burgundians posed a threat to Gaul's southern Rhine border. Aetius' response was typical of his strategic skills. He called on his friends among the Huns to come to his aid and between them they annihilated the German tribe. This was the last time that Aetius could form such a coalition, however, for in 445, he ceased to have any influence over his former allies. The Huns were now ruled by Attila, who was ambitious for conquests within the Roman Empire, and accordingly his armies crossed the border into northern Gaul in 451. A new coalition had to be formed. While Aetius readied his own Roman army, he also negotiated with the Franks and Visigoths, explaining to them the necessity of forming an effective defensive alliance if they were to preserve their settlements against the threat of an external invader. His political arguments were convincing and at *locus Mauriacus* (the Mauriac Plain), now present-day Châlons, Aetius led a combined barbarian-Roman army to victory.

Attila, however, survived this defeat, his next step being to march into northern Italy in 452. Unable to call upon his barbarian allies in this instance, Aetius deliberately chose a strategy of evasion, sacrificing the cities of northern Italy in order to allow the Huns to exhaust themselves. With his forces disintegrating through famine and disease, Attila then faced the approach of the Romans in force. Negotiations followed, as a result of which, Attila was compelled to retreat northwards out of the empire. A year later the Hun was dead.

Aetius did not survive to enjoy the rewards of his success, however. He now stood unchallenged in the western empire, but Valentinian could no longer bear being overshadowed by him. Although Aetius proclaimed his loyalty, the suspicious emperor stabbed him to death in 454. One shocked courtier commented: "the Emperor has cut off his right hand with his left". The following year, Valentinian was murdered in revenge.

GUESCLIN
Bertrand du (c.1320-1380)
CONSTABLE OF FRANCE
Wars in France and Spain

Guesclin became famous for his strategy of evasion and guerilla warfare, which deprived the English of the conquests they had made earlier in the Hundred Years' War, but he began his career with orthodox battle victories. Having captured several towns from the English following the French defeat at Poitiers in 1356, he won his first major victory against the Navarrese at Cocherel in 1364. First and foremost a mercenary for hire, he was next employed to support the French in the Breton civil war, but was captured at Auray. Ransomed by the French king, Charles V, Guesclin was then sent to Spain at the head of an army of mercenaries to defend French interests against the English-backed Peter of Castile.

In Spain, Guesclin was at first successful, but at the battle of Najera in 1367, he was again captured by the English. Ransomed for a second time the next year by Charles V, Guesclin resumed his defence of French interests in Spain and defeated Peter of Castile at Montiel.

War against the English
The cost of the Spanish campaign bankrupted the English in France and in 1370, Charles V took advantage of this to relaunch the war to rid his land of their presence. Guesclin was made Constable of France to execute his king's plans and captured Poitiers, Rochelle, much of English-held Aquitaine and several towns in Brittany. The English response was prompt; in 1373, Edward III sent an army to Calais. Here, however, Guesclin demonstrated his true mastery of strategy – employing his own version of the tactics the Romans had once used against the Carthaginians. The English march through France went unopposed. At a conference in Paris, Guesclin explained his strategy: "I do not say that the English should not be fought, but I want it to be executed from a position of advantage. That is what the English did at Poitiers and Crécy." According to the chronicler Froissart, Charles confirmed this sensible course of action: "I have no intention of marching out and hazarding my knights and my kingdom in one encounter for a piece of farmland."

Closely trailing and harassing the English, Guesclin kept them on the defensive, preventing them from foraging. The English baggage train was ambushed and any raiding parties annihilated. By the time they reached Aquitaine, they were hungry and exhausted, allowing Guesclin to counter-attack and win back yet more French territory. In 1375, a truce was agreed.

When he died, Guesclin was buried at Saint Denis next to the tomb of his king in recognition of his great service to France. Throughout French court art and literature, Guesclin was ranked alongside the so-called "nine worthies," which included *Alexander, Caesar,* Arthur, and Charlemagne.

HANNIBAL
(247-183 BC)
CARTHAGINIAN GENERAL
Wars in Italy and North Africa

Hannibal's celebrated crossing of the Alps and his victory over the Romans at Cannae have long been considered sufficient to place him high in the pantheon of military geniuses. However, romantic though these twin achievements were, cool modern analysis has cast doubts as to whether he possessed supreme military ability – according to some commentators at least. "Hannibal's strategy in Italy was a failure," wrote Field Marshal Montgomery, while on "the only occasion when Scipio and Hannibal faced each other in battle, Scipio won."

Hannibal was 29 when he led a Carthaginian army across the Alps into Italy in 218 BC. His father, Hamilcar Barca, was the chief Carthaginian warlord of Spain and had won his son a generalship four years previously. The Barca family had a strong tradition of military success and it was probably this inbred confidence that led to Hannibal's audacious plan to invade the Roman heartland via the land route. However, though his arrival in northern Italy gave him the initiative, it cost him dear. Of about 40,000 troops he led into the Alps, only 26,000 survived the journey. It was a serious strategic misjudgement.

Campaigning in Italy
Despite these severe losses, the army Hannibal led was highly disciplined, well trained, and devoted to its charismatic leader. It was these factors that won him three battles in succession against the Romans – at Ticinus, Trebia, and Lake Trasimere. His most celebrated victory came in 216 at Cannae in southern Italy. In it, Hannibal made classic use of enveloping tactics. Drawing the massed Roman center forward, the Carthaginian foot-

win back control of the land. Roman maritime supremacy meant that Hannibal received few reinforcements from Africa and became increasingly isolated. Roman victories in Spain further weakened the Carthaginian position, so that when *Scipio* invaded Africa, Hannibal was forced to abandon his Italian campaign and return to defend Carthage itself.

Not only had Hannibal's strategic ability been wanting from the beginning, but now his tactical flair had deserted him; at the battle of *Zama* in 202, he was defeated by Scipio's imaginative tactics. After his defeat, the Carthaginian leader concentrated on reviving the political fortunes of Carthage. Following the settlement of the Second Punic War, however, the Romans accused him of breaking the peace and he was forced to flee to Ephesus and then Bithynia in Asia Minor. While in exile, he committed suicide by taking poison.

Hannibal was the perfect romantic hero, a young, bold general of brilliance whose career ended in failure and tragedy. It is this that best explains his enduring appeal.

HUNYADI
Janos (c.1387-1456)
HUNGARIAN GENERAL
Wars in the Balkans

Janos Hunyadi was the greatest Crusader warlord of the late Middle Ages, his victories in the Balkans delaying the Ottoman advance into Central Europe for half a century. A nobleman of Wallachian origin, Hunyadi first served under the Emperor Sigismund against *Zizka* and the Hussites. He made a careful study of their defensive tactics, later making use of war wagons and firearms in the same way and even recruited Bohemian veterans into his ranks.

In 1441, Hunyadi began the first of his campaigns against the Turks in the Balkans. During the winter of 1443-4, he led an army of Hungarians, Romanians, Poles, Serbs, Bulgarians, and Bohemians across the Danube to occupy Nis and Sofia. Through speed and expert organization, Hunyadi stopped the Ottoman armies from uniting against him and defeated their individual components in detail in a series of battles. By the end of the campaign, Ottoman power north of Greece had been shattered and Sultan Murad II was forced to accept peace.

Advance on Varna
In 1444, Hunyadi hoped to push the Turks out of Europe completely and so led an international Crusading army towards the Black Sea port of Varna. His aim was to break the Turkish ring around Constantinople, but a Venetian-Burgundian fleet failed to prevent Ottoman reinforcements crossing the Dardanelles and Hunyadi was confronted by a massive army. In the ensuing battle, excited Hungarian knights rashly charged the retreating Turks, only to be annihilated in a counter-attack. Four years

ACROSS THE ALPS *Leading a Carthaginian army over the Alps was a tactical triumph, but a strategic mistake.*

soldiers withdrew in good order until the Romans were trapped within a concave formation. The wing contingents of Hannibal's army then outflanked the Romans, his cavalry completing the encirclement by striking the enemy in the rear. The Romans lost 60,000 dead in the most shattering defeat they had ever sustained.

Many feared Hannibal would follow up this success by marching on Rome, but Hannibal's forces were not strong enough to undertake the major siege this move would have made necessary. The cost of his march across the Alps had also denied him the manpower reserves he needed to capitalize on his success in the field. Instead, by establishing a power base in the countryside of southern Italy, he hoped to wrest Rome's Italian allies away from their allegiance to Rome. It was another misjudgement. The majority of Italian cities remained loyal to their alliances with the Romans, while the time Hannibal wasted in Campania on fruitless campaigning allowed Rome to gather its forces.

The Roman revival
Avoiding major confrontations, the Romans managed to keep Hannibal occupied in southern Italy and gradually

later, Hunyadi sought revenge for Varna at the battle of Kosovo. He placed German and Bohemian handgunners behind war wagons and earthworks. The battle lasted two days and both sides suffered heavily. The Turks claimed victory, but gained little material advantage.

In 1453, however, Sultan Mehmed II succeeded in storming Constantinople. It was a low point for Hungary, but Hunyadi rallied his followers and pre-empted a Turkish invasion by defeating a Turkish fleet on the Danube and then forcing the Ottoman army back from its siege of Belgrade. Planning to carry the war on to Turkish territory, Hunyadi fell victim to disease in his camp. His death marked the end of the last major resistance to Turkish occupation of eastern Europe.

DON JOHN OF AUSTRIA
(1547-1578)
SPANISH GENERAL
Wars in the Mediterranean

Don John of Austria was the author of the greatest Christian victory over the Turks in the 16th century. The son of the Emperor Charles V, he was the half-brother of Philip II of Spain and began his military career on land, driving the Moors out of Granada; he was then made commander of an allied Christian navy in 1571. A Turkish attack on Cyprus had stimulated the Papacy to create a Holy League of Italian, Venetian, and Spanish naval forces and, that September, the allied navy set sail in search of the Turkish fleet. On 7 October, the Turks were sighted in the Gulf of Patras near the Greek port of Lepanto and Don John deployed his fleet for battle.

Battle at Lepanto
The Turkish fleet consisted of some 250 galleys and other smaller ships. Both fleets had not changed much since the ancient days of oar and ram warfare, though, in addition to his 200 galleys, Don John possessed six galleasses, a larger version of the galley, carrying batteries of up to 70 guns. It was ramming and boarding, however, that were to determine the battle.

Both fleets rowed towards each other in long lines. Stretched along a five-mile front, the ships met in a series of close-quarter actions. The Christian galleasses broke the Turkish line, but there were not enough of them to exploit the gap. By sheer hard fighting, the Christian galleys forced back the Turkish right wing and center and eventually the Turkish left wing joined them in rout. The result was a major victory, dealing a major blow to the Turkish advance in the Mediterranean – even though the Christians retired to Italy for the winter and failed to follow it up.

Lepanto was the last great battle between galleys. The following year, Don John scored another victory against the Turks by recapturing Tunis. Thereafter, however, he incurred the suspicion of Philip II, who made him viceroy of the Netherlands to remove him from the center of power. He died at Bouges, perhaps the victim of poison.

KHAN
Genghis (1162-1227)
MONGOL EMPEROR
Wars in China and Central Asia

Renowned as one of the great barbarian leaders of world history, Genghis Khan achieved his victories not through the untamed fury of his hordes, but through careful planning and organization. Every campaign proceeded on information gathered by an army of spies. This intelligence was passed by horsemen riding along routes provided with rest-houses and replacement horses and disseminated to trusted and talented captains subordinate to the great khan. Only then would Genghis embark on his conquests. When his enemies ascribed his decisive victories to the vast numbers of his hordes, they were seeking to excuse their own failure and surprise at his sudden, expertly planned movements.

MIGHTY KHAN *Genghis Khan's ruthless military skills created the Mongol empire.*

Born into a noble Mongol family, the young Genghis was known as Temujin after a Tatar chieftain captured by his father. He was brought up along the banks of the Onon river in central Mongolia and, in common with all tribesmen, learnt to ride and shoot a bow at an early age. When Genghis' father died, however, the tribe refused to be ruled by a nine-year-old boy and he was forced into exile together with his mother. These difficult years taught the young Mongol the skills of survival and he emerged from the steppes hardened and keen for the power that was his by birth. Showing an early political aptitude, Genghis renewed the bond with his father's former ally, Toghril, and established a following of his own. Soon, the strength of this friendship was tested. Retaliating against a tribe that had kidnapped his wife, Genghis called upon Toghril and another childhood friend, Jamuka, to support him. Both arrived with thousands of tribesmen and Genghis won his first campaign.

The "universal Khan"
Temujin's reputation won him the respect of many Mongol tribal leaders and in 1194 he was proclaimed Genghis Khan, meaning "universal khan". This position enabled him to pay back the debt of friendship he owed Toghril by

helping him to retain power against a rebellion. Hearing of the new Mongol leadership, the Chin dynasty at Peking asked the Mongols to help them against the damaging raids of the Turkic Tatars. As Toghril was the elder, he became the senior commander, but Genghis seemed content to campaign against the Tatars as his subordinate. In 1202, a devastating victory over the Tatars extended Genghis' rule over the western lands of Mongolia.

Eventually, however, Genghis fell out with Toghril and Jamuka. A savage civil war followed, but in 1206 he emerged triumphant.

The Mongol war-machine

By the end of this struggle for supreme power, Genghis Khan's war-machine had emerged. He surrounded himself with talented captains, including his sons Jochi, Chagatai and Ogedei, as well as the remarkable Subedei, who later led an invasion of Europe. His army was composed almost exclusively of horsemen – light cavalry armed with the deadly composite bow and heavy cavalry with leather armor, saber, and lance – excelling in stamina, mobility, and striking power.

With such an army assembled and his position in Mongolia unchallenged, Genghis Khan looked further afield for new conquests. Remember the weakness of the Chin at Peking who had called on him for help, Genghis now turned against them and invaded the northern provinces of China. At first, the Mongols were successful against the field armies of the Chinese, but the great cities remained defiant. Always open to new military ideas, Genghis recruited Chinese engineers to improve his ability at siege-warfare. Thereafter, foreign engineers and craftsmen always accompanied the Mongol armies in the field. In 1215, Genghis captured Peking.

From Peking, Genghis turned his attention to the western Chinese lands as far as the Tien Shan and Altai mountains (now Xinjiang). A former Mongol enemy, Kuchlug, had set himself up as ruler of the Muslim Turkic people in this region, but he persecuted the Muslim population, who called upon Genghis Khan to help them. Sending an army of 20,000 horsemen into western China under the command of his general Jebe, Genghis Khan oversaw the death of Kuchlug in 1218 and added another realm to his growing empire.

This conquest brought Genghis to the foothills of the mighty Tien Shan, separating western China from Central Asia. Beyond the mountains lay the Khwarizmian kingdom, a realm of mountains and deserts centered around the prosperous trade centers of Samarkand, Bukhara, and other oasis cities. At first, Genghis wanted to establish trade relations with the ruler of Khwarizm, but a Mongol mission was murdered by a suspicious governor of the region and Genghis declared war.

Conquest of Central Asia

In a rapid campaign, Genghis Khan captured and sacked Bukhara and Samarkand in 1220. While two of his captains pursued the ruler of Khwarizm to the shores of the Caspian Sea, Genghis wintered in Central Asia. As in China, he placed native-born administrators in charge of his new conquests, partly because he did not trust governors from his own horde and partly because such men were obviously more acceptable to the local population. Genghis further strengthened his hold over the Muslim Turks of Central Asia by allowing them to follow their faith and exempting their priests from taxation. Such good sense, however, was accompanied by frightening brutality. Genghis slaughtered entire city populations that resisted.

The battle of the Yellow River

Having consolidated his conquest of Central Asia, Genghis Khan returned to Mongolia in 1224. In China, the Chin dynasty was far from subdued and to the west of them the Tangut kingdom of Hsi-Hsia scorned Genghis Khan's sovereignty. For a year, Genghis prepared his soldiers and in 1226 he struck. Choosing winter as the best time to cross the frozen waterways of Hsi-Hsia, the Mongols met the Tanguts at the battle of the Yellow River. Enticing the Tanguts across the ice, Genghis Khan directed his archers to shatter their cavalry and then followed through with his armored horsemen.

Genghis Khan was now over 60 and aware that he had not much longer to live, named Ogedei as his successor. While campaigning in Hsi-Hsia, Genghis died the following summer. His body was returned to Mongolia and buried in a secret tomb. Ning-hsia fell shortly afterwards and, in accordance with the dead khan's wishes, the entire population was put to the sword. It is a sign of the awesome authority that Genghis Khan had established that, after his death, Ogedei succeeded peacefully and simply continued the Mongol conquests.

RICHARD I
(1157-1199)
ENGLISH KING
Wars in Palestine and France

The fact that Richard I ever became king of England at all was purely coincidental as far as his military career was concerned. He was born and lived the life of a French Norman warlord. Like the greatest of his Norman forefathers, he travelled far and wide to pursue his love of campaigning, but, unlike many of them, he possessed the wit to adapt his methods of warfare to the varying circumstances of each individual campaign. From this grew his reputa-

THE LIONHEART
Richard's tactics in Palestine won him victory at Arsouf.

tion as one of the greatest of European Crusaders.

The third son of Henry II and Eleanor of Aquitaine, Richard spent his youth in France under the influence of his powerful mother. In 1173, he joined with her and his elder brothers in a rebellion to wrest his father's French possessions away from him. The rebellion failed and his mother was imprisoned, but Richard was allowed to continue ruling the duchy of Aquitaine. When he came to the English throne in 1189, Eleanor was released and she deputized for him while he sailed to the Holy Land. In all, Richard spent barely a year in England as king.

Richard on Crusade

In the company of Philip Augustus, king of France, Richard landed at Acre in Palestine in 1191, where the Crusaders already had the Muslim garrison under siege. Driving off a relieving Muslim army, Richard took the city and began his march to liberate the holy city of Jerusalem. Imposing a sense of common direction and purpose on the international collection of knights and freebooters that made up the Crusader forces, he molded them into a unified, disciplined army. As the Crusaders marched along the coast from Acre to Jaffa, *Saladin* sent Muslim horse-archers against them to harass their ranks and hopefully break up their formation. Richard, however, refused to be drawn, but protected his men against the raids by ordering them to march in battle order, the Crusaders being deployed in three divisions of three columns each, and using crossbowmen to defend his vulnerable mounted men-at-arms. Keeping close to the shore, Richard ensured that his fleet sailed parallel to him, so keeping his men well supplied. Failing to provoke the Crusaders by his hit-and-run tactics, Saladin launched an all-out assault on them near the town of Arsouf. This move suited Richard well. For most of the day, the Crusaders stood on the defensive as Richard had planned, repelling attack after attack. The decisive moment came when the Master of the Knights Hospitaller, commanding the Crusader rearguard, led his knights into the charge and Richard followed by ordering the whole Christian battleline forward in a surging advance. This took Saladin and his weary army completely by surprise and ended with their complete defeat. His armored horsemen decisively defeated the Muslim light cavalry, but his strict discipline enabled him to recall them before they fell victim to the temptation to pursue the defeated Muslims into a potentially dangerous chase across the desert.

Tactically, Richard had had the better of Saladin, but the Muslim leader had one further card to play. He laid waste the land between Arsouf and Jerusalem. By this, he denied the Crusaders, who now had to turn inland away from their fleet, any source of supply and so forced Richard to give up his advance. In 1192, the two leaders signed a peace treaty, which gave access to Christian pilgrims to the Holy City, but ultimately Richard had failed in his grand design. On his return home, he was faced with war and rebellion and died in France while besieging the castle of Chaluz.

SALADIN
(1137-1193)
KURDISH SULTAN
Wars in Egypt, Syria and Palestine

Renowned for his chivalry and culture, Saladin was the most formidable Muslim adversary the European Crusaders had to face in the Holy Land. The son of a Kurdish governor, he entered the service of Nur-eddin, Emir of Syria, and, in the war between Nur-eddin and the Fatimid caliph of Egypt was given command of the Syrian expedition to Egypt that overthrew the caliph. Nominally subject to Nur-eddin and the Syrian emirate, Saladin declared himself Caliph of Egypt on his overlord's death in 1174 and founded the Ayyubid dynasty. He then embarked on a career of conquest, establishing his rule over Syria, Mesopotamia, and some of the Seljuk tribes of Asia Minor. It was the Turkish warriors in his army – these were mainly highly-mobile horse-archers – that gave Saladin the military muscle he needed for his conquests.

The conquest of the Holy Land

Having encircled the Crusader states of Palestine, Saladin proclaimed a Holy War against them in 1187. In reply, Guy de Lusignan withdrew the garrisons from all the Crusader castles to form a concentrated Christian army to face the threat in battle at Hattin. Saladin hid among the dry hills of Galilee and drew the Crusaders onwards with bands of skirmishing horse-archers shooting and then breaking away before the Christians could make contact with them. For a day, Saladin kept the Crusaders under attack, so that by nightfall they were exhausted and short of supplies.

The next morning, Saladin sent more horse-archers against the Crusaders until they completely disintegrated, with the knights making rash, useless charges, leaving the footsoldiers isolated. Saladin then ordered his heavier armed horsemen to advance and surround the Crusader army, virtually annihilating them and capturing Guy, plus the splinters of the True Cross the Christians had carried into battle. Guy himself was released on parole, but broke his word not to continue fighting.

Saladin's victory at Hattin cracked open the Crusader states. Their castles, left defenceless by Guy, were easily captured, the Muslims taking Tiberias, Acre, and Ascalon at little or no cost. In October 1187, Saladin rode into Jerusalem. However, the capture of the Holy City provoked the Third Crusade in 1189 and battle with *Richard I* in 1191.

At first, Saladin was taken unawares by Richard's tactical ability, but his superior strategy of laying waste the land to deny the Crusaders any source of food or water on their march to Jerusalem won him the campaign. Richard was forced to retreat without retaking the city. A year later, however, Saladin was dead and his empire began to disintegrate.

PUNIC VICTOR *Scipio Africanus triumphs at Zama – and Hannibal's defeated Carthaginians flee in rout.*

SCIPIO
Africanus (237-183 BC)
ROMAN GENERAL
Wars in Spain and North Africa

When *Hannibal* confronted Scipio in the climactic battle of the Punic Wars between Rome and Carthage on the plains of Zama, "a master of war had met a greater master", wrote Basil Liddell Hart. Later, Field-Marshal Montgomery also placed Scipio ahead of Hannibal in tactical imagination and strategic brilliance. These views are not universal, however, for, ever since the 3rd century BC, many other military historians and soldiers have been impressed by the romance of Hannibal's military career to the detriment to that of Scipio. But on the one and only occasion when the two commanders met in battle, it was the Roman who triumphed.

The most important military experience of Scipio's youth was his presence at the disastrous battle of Cannae. At 21, he witnessed the complete destruction of a Roman army by Hannibal's smaller force. It was a terrible experience, but one which determined him to reform and revive the Roman war machine. Scipio came from a noble military family, his father and uncle having won several battles against the Carthaginians in Spain. In 211 BC, however, they suffered crippling desertions by their Celtiberian allies and were defeated by Hannibal's brother, Hasdrubal, both dying leading their men in the fighting. This second great blow convinced Scipio that the best way to avenge his country and his family was to beat the Carthaginians in the field. Influenced by his angry determination and the military skill of his father, the Senate sent Scipio to Spain.

Scipio in Spain

In Spain, Scipio wasted little time. Reports of dissension among the three Carthaginian armies that confronted the Romans encouraged him to march swiftly on the port of New Carthage. He believed it more vital to strike at an enemy's base rather than to slowly overcome his armies in the field. The Carthaginian armies were more than ten days march away from the port, giving Scipio time to assault the city by land and sea and his capture of the port immediately gave him the strategic advantage. The Carthaginians were denied their base and a valuable port for receiving reinforcements from Africa. They also lost a major arsenal, control of the local silver mines, and the local Spanish chieftains they had held as hostages for the good behavior of the native population.

Scipio spent the winter of 209-208 training his soldiers in the tactics he had learned from a study of Hannibal's methods. He taught his officers to act independently on the battlefield so as to accomplish more ambitious maneuvers. Formerly, Roman battle formations had consisted of three lines of maniples in quincunx order, so that gaps in the frontline could be filled by warriors in the second line. Such a formation relied on strength rather than intelligence and could not execute a successful flanking movement. The Romans had suffered for this at Cannae and Scipio was determined it would not happen again. Instead, he placed his light infantry and some legionaries in the center, with his most dependable veterans on the wings. To this tactical innovation, he added intensive training in discipline and weapon handling. He provided his legionaries with the finest Spanish swords.

Battle at Baecula

By the spring, Scipio was ready to try his new tactics in the field. At Baecula, the Roman center remained intact while his wings advanced to attack the flanks of Hasdrubal's Carthaginians. However, Scipio's lightly armed soldiers in the center were not strong enough to hold the opposing Carthaginians, so Hasdrubal managed to withdraw from the trap and retreat. Scipio's victory may not have been complete, but his success demonstrated the potential of his reforms. At the end of the battle, Scipio's troops hailed him as *imperator*, the first time this honor was accorded to a Roman general.

Following his defeat, Hasdrubal believed he would be more usefully employed in Italy, supporting his brother. Scipio allowed him to leave the country, for his absence gave the Roman commander a greater opportunity for conquest. In 206, after a series of successful sieges, Scipio confronted the remaining Carthaginian army at Ilipa, near Seville. The situation did not favor Roman success, for Scipio commanded 10,000 fewer men than the Carthaginian army, which was over 50,000 strong. To compensate for this, Scipio spread out his line of battle, placing his Spanish allies in the middle with Roman legionaries and cavalry on the flanks. An early morning attack on the Carthaginian camp lessened the enemy's advantage further. The Carthaginians placed their finest African troops in the center with their less dependable Spanish allies on the flanks.

Scipio exploited this weakness by ordering both his flanks to move forward. While his Spanish troops held the Carthaginians in the center, the Roman wings executed a complicated double-flanking movement that allowed them to envelop the longer Carthaginian lines at two points on each wing. The maneuver demanded first-class discipline and training and its success was a tribute to Scipio's generalship. Before the determined attack on both wings, the Carthaginian army crumbled, leaving Scipio absolute master of Spain.

Attacking Carthage

In 204, Scipio invaded North Africa. By threatening the homeland of the Carthaginians, he hoped to draw Hannibal away from Italy. He prepared for the campaign by training a Roman army in Sicily and by securing an alliance with a native Numidian chief, Masinissa. The Numidians would provide the excellent cavalry he needed to complete his outflanking maneuver. At first, Scipio was held by a powerful Carthaginian force, but by using the pretence of peace negotiations as a cover for a surprise attack, he broke the stalemate. At the battle of Bagbrades, near Utica, Scipio refined his tactics and used the *hastati* frontline of his legionaries as a screen behind which the second and third lines of *principes* and *triarii* acted independently as a reserve to follow up the success of the Roman and Numidian cavalry on the wings. This victory forced the recall of Hannibal.

The two great rivals met at the battle of *Zama* in 202. Scipio's subsequent victory brought an end to the war against Carthage. Hannibal agreed to peace and Scipio, now given the title of Africanus, emerged as military master of the Mediterranean. Scipio's adaption of the techniques of outflanking gave the Roman army a new confidence, while his dedication to training and discipline ensured his troops' ability to carry it out. He was by far the most influential Roman general before Caesar and his reforms had lasting influence.

SULEIMAN THE MAGNIFICENT
(1494-1566)
TURKISH SULTAN
Wars in Europe and Asia

Suleiman was one of a long line of brilliant Ottoman conquerors. His father, grandfather, and great-grandfather had succeeded in spreading Turkish rule from Asia Minor to Greece, the Balkans, Syria, and Egypt. The Turkish military system was at its peak, combining a strong artillery and engineering corps with dedicated, élite Janissary footsoldiers and Spahi cavalry. Above all, Suleiman's personal command was rewarded by the loyalty of his finest troops, who served as his private bodyguard. As one European observer commented: "The Turks surpass our soldiers for three reasons: they obey their commanders promptly; they never show the least concern for their lives in battle; they can live a long time without bread and

SVLEYMAN·IMPERATOR·TVR

De grote turc keyser va costant

OTTOMAN LEADER
Suleiman, a military genius.

wine, content with barley and water." With such an army, Suleiman was able to expand Ottoman power to its broadest limits.

Suleiman had one further advantage when he began his reign in 1520 – the services of an outstanding vizier, Ibrahim Pasha. Ibrahim's administrative competence left Suleiman free to lead his army in the field; accordingly in the following year, he began his career of conquest with the invasion of Hungary and the capture of Belgrade, a key city on the River Danube. His supply lines to Asia Minor were threatened, however, by Christian possession of the islands of Rhodes, Crete, and Cyprus and he therefore delayed his Balkans advance to concentrate on the reduction of the powerful fortress held by the Christian Knights Hospitalers at Rhodes.

For seven months in 1522, the Turks and the Christians fought a desperate battle for the island. Even using the finest artillery and the most ingenious engineers available to him, Suleiman could not crack the valiant Christian defence. In the end, he knew that his superior numbers would tell, but he did not want to waste future time and effort and so decided to open negotiations. By offering generous terms, including the evacuation of the Knights, Suleiman secured the island.

Advance on Vienna

Suleiman used the same tactic of negotiation before resuming his invasion of Hungary in 1526, securing his flank against the possibility of attack by Poland through a treaty. With an 80,000-strong army, he confronted a Christian force at Mohacs. Turkish discipline withstood the initial Christian onslaught; through a combination of calculated use of artillery and dashing Janissary counter-attacks, Suleiman triumphed. He went on to capture Budapest. In 1529, Suleiman followed up his success by invading Austria itself, advancing on Vienna. However, the city withstood his siege and the onset of winter forced his withdrawal. Rather than resume the offensive, he now concluded a treaty with the Hapsburg emperor, which sealed his conquest of Hungary.

The peace allowed Suleiman to turn his attention to Persia. In 1534 and 1548, he invaded and conquered Mesopotamia and Armenia. For the rest of his reign, Suleiman concentrated on establishing Turkish dominance in the Mediterranean proper, expanding the Ottoman presence along northern Africa. Finally, he turned to Austria again, but while launching another invasion, he died at the siege of Szigetvar. This was a lucky escape for Europe, for subsequent sultans were never to recapture his military genius.

ZIZKA
Jan (c.1360-1424)
HUSSITE GENERAL
Wars in Czechoslovakia

Zizka's charismatic skills as a commander enabled a collection of poorly armed peasants to defeat a succession of professional medieval armies. In achieving this, he laid the foundations for a new form of warfare, in which laagers of war wagons formed solid bases for the deployment of battlefield firepower.

A semi-retired veteran of Slavic wars against the Teutonic Knights, Zizka was half-blind and well into his 50s when he took on the military leadership of the Hussite revolution. Swept up in the spirit of religious and nationalist fervor that engulfed Prague in 1419, Zizka was a man of deep faith, believing in the purity and righteousness of the Hussite revolt against the decadence of the Catholic establishment. Elected as the Hussite leader in the field, Zizka had to organize and train his peasant followers rapidly in the art of war, for within the year the Emperor Sigismund led an international army of mercenaries on a Catholic crusade against the heretical Hussite rebels.

The Hussite army
Tabor in southern Bohemia became the base of Zizka's army and through a combination of religious fanaticism and rigorous training, the Hussites soon gained a fiercesome reputation. This was fully demonstrated in 1420, when Sigismund laid siege to Prague. What started as a skirmish on a hill outside the walls developed into a battle, in which Zizka's hymn-singing, flail-wielding Taborite warriors routed the Catholic army. Zizka followed up this victory by marching across Bohemia, consolidating the Hussite position. In a siege during this march, he lost the sight of his second eye, but, though now completely blind, he nevertheless continued to lead his warriors against the Catholics.

Victory at Kutna Hora
In 1421, Sigismund led a second major offensive against the Hussites at Kutna Hora. Fighting in the winter snow, Zizka had his war wagons chained together to resist the relentless charges of the Catholic cavalry, blasting at them with handguns and crossbows until they were forced to retire. In the meantime, however, the Catholics had overwhelmed the Hussite garrison in the nearby town, leaving Zizka isolated in his camp.

Zizka's solution was to unlimber his wagons and turn them into a mobile fortress. Under cover of night, he smashed through the Catholic ranks and reformed a short distance away. The Catholics mistakenly assumed that this move was an admission of defeat, but Zizka was merely awaiting reinforcements. As the Catholic army broke up to go into their winter quarters, Zizka launched a surprise attack and drove them in rout back to Hungary.

In 1423, however, politics led to a split between the moderate and radical Hussites, with Zizka leading the extreme Orebite community in a civil war against Prague. His subsequent victory reunited the Hussites. His plan was to invade Moravia on the border of Hungary, but, just as the campaign was launched, he died.

HUSSITE REBELLION *Ziska's imaginative use of war wagons helped him win victory over his Catholic opponents.*

Three Centuries of Warfare

The three centuries from 1560 to 1860 are one of the most significant periods in the development of warfare. In Europe, the end of the 16th century marks the transition between traditional quasi-medieval warfare, fought between kings and princes with mercenary armies for traditional objectives (such as rights of succession and property), and a recognizably modern type of conflict. The 17th century saw a revolution not only in tactics and strategy and, to a lesser extent, in weaponry, but also in the nature of warfare itself.

Society and warfare

To understand fully the nature of warfare in this period, it is essential to relate military developments to social ones. The replacement of mercenary forces in the 17th century by a regular standing army, for instance, was of enormous importance in making possible the development of royal absolutism in France, while the fact that wars came to be fought between states and nations for reasons of policy and patriotism, rather than as a means of resolving dynastic quarrels has political as well as military significance. Thus the story of warfare in this turbulent period involves more than the history of battles and generals, or strategy and tactics: it is also the story of the societies that were involved and were in turn changed by war.

As far as the 17th century is concerned, there is a clear dichotomy in the nature of warfare as far as the first and second parts of the period are concerned. The enormously destructive Thirty Years' War in Germany (1618-48) was followed by

ARMING THE CAVALRY Pistol *drill, as shown in 1630 military instructions, was essential training.*

wars of a consciously limited variety, fought between the new regular, professional armies of the time. These "cabinet" wars, as they were termed, were limited in objective and in the areas over which they were fought, though to the long-suffering populations concerned, these campaigns must have seemed anything but limited. Warfare continued to be endemic in Europe; in addition, as European nations carved out colonial empires, they fought not only the natives but each other. In particular, the British and French were involved in a whole series of wars lasting off and on from 1689 to 1815 and fought in India, North America and on the high seas as well as in Europe.

The nature of warfare again changed after 1789 as a result of the outbreak of the French Revolution – as did the nature of society. The overthrow of the French monarchy led to nearly all of the monarchical states of Europe taking up arms against the regicide French republic and the world moved abruptly into a

new era of warfare. The deliberately imposed limitations of the previous decades were thrown aside. In order to survive, the French raised a mass army – the "nation in arms". Campaigns now had as their objectives the destruction of the enemy's army in the field, the conquest of his territory, and the overthrow of his political system. Inspired by the genius of Napoleon, France achieved control of a large part of continental Europe by military conquest. Though the 50 years that followed saw no more wars on the scale of those of the revolutionary and Napoleonic eras, revolutions in weaponry (the basic weapons of the Napoleonic period differed little from those used by Marlborough's armies a century earlier), the Industrial Revolution had brought warfare to the very brink of the modern era by 1860.

Sieges and battles

War in the 16th century consisted primarily of sieges. There were relatively few pitched battles; indeed, by the middle of the century, the era of the armored horseman and the archer had come to an end as far as battlefield dominance was concerned. Infantry armies took their place, in which, though men armed with firearms had their place, the dominant factor was the massed phalanx of pikemen. Battles, indeed, were usually decided by "push of pike" – hand-to-hand combat between rival phalanxes.

The dominant military formation of the later 16th century was the 3,000-strong Spanish *tercio*, which attempted to combine shock action with firepower, though with only limited success. Nevertheless, commanders came to place increasing

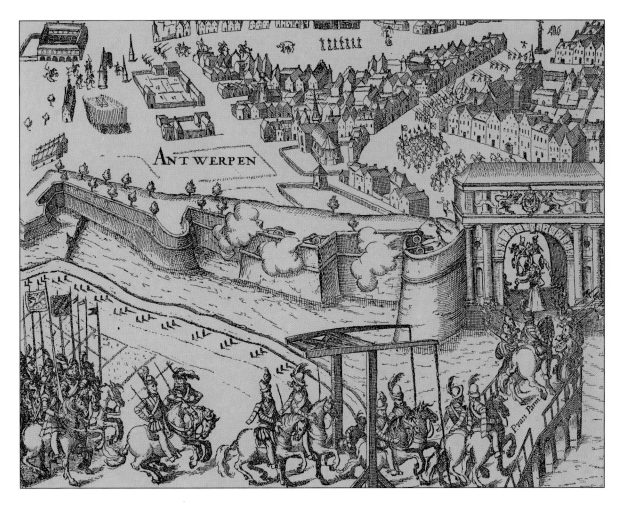

ANTWERPEN

reliance on their musketeers – the result, curiously enough, making battles less, rather than more, decisive, being reduced to firefights between twin sets of relatively inefficient weapons. The most extreme effect of this was seen in the cavalry maneuver known as the *caracole*. In this, rank after rank of cavalry rode up to the enemy to discharge their pistols at close range. Following the initial volley, the first rank would ride to the rear of the formation and the second rank repeated the process. The result was to reduce the feared shock weapon of former days to virtual impotence.

The new armies

Mercenary armies had served their purpose well, allowing Renaissance monarchs to break the power of their feudal underlings by freeing them from the necessity of offering a *quid pro quo* in return for military aid

THE SIEGE OF ANTWERP *Siege warfare was a predominant feature of warfare during much of this period.*

when this was needed. Such armies, however, were expensive – and liable to desert, or mutiny, if payment was slow. It was primarily the expense of mercenary war that led to warfare becoming increasingly static and indecisive, with commanders seeking to avoid battles in favor of siege operations.

It was the Dutch, under Maurice of Nassau (1567-1625), who made the first serious attempt to find a way out of the impasse. Maurice was inspired by the military writers of antiquity, such as Vegetius, and by his former teacher Justus Lipsius, who argued that discipline was the essential element in achieving military success. He accordingly set out to create a disciplined professional army. Although many of the

soldiers who served under him were foreign rather than Dutch, they were not mercenaries in the traditional sense of the word. They were permanently employed by the Dutch, who were in the fortunate position of being able to offer regular pay. As a result Maurice was an employer, rather than a contractor, and could thus force acceptance of his ideas on tactics and discipline; in short, Maurice's army actually had to obey his orders.

Maurice was therefore able to build the formidable fortifications that were to protect the Netherlands throughout the 17th century, and to introduce new tactics. The latter, however, were not uniformly successful. The *caracole* was retained, for instance, while although his tactical units were only 550-strong – and thus more flexible than the rival *tercio* – they lacked the firepower to compensate for the loss of striking power brought about by this reduction in number. Indeed, the new Dutch armies were by no means invincible when pitched against the Spanish in their *tercios*, which were halved in size to increase maneuverability, although Maurice's defeat of a Spanish force at Nieuport (2 July 1600) brought his system to the attention of Europe.

The role of Gustavus Adolphus

Thus, it is important not to exaggerate the importance of Maurice's reforms. He did, however, set an example – and one that was followed by the most revolutionary military leader of the 17th century. This was *Gustavus Adolphus*, the Protestant ruler of Sweden.

When Gustavus came to the throne in 1611, the strategic situation of Sweden was parlous. The country was surrounded by stronger enemies – Poland, Russia, and Denmark – and its army was of poor quality, suffering from low morale and poor discipline. Following Maurice of Nassau's example, Gustavus moved away from the concept of hiring mercenaries, establishing a truly national army, partly made up of conscripts. To create this force, Gustavus built on the basis of the army he had inherited, which was a species of national militia, itself a military oddity in the Europe of the day. Many of the problems inherent in the hiring of mercenaries were overcome. The troops were bound by an oath of loyalty to the king, not simply by money, while Gustavus, for his part, was able to impose his own ideas without having to battle against the vested interests of mercenaries. Though the Swedes were the first to introduce the concept of a national, standing army, which had become the norm throughout Europe by 1700, the "national" nature of Gustavus' army should not be exaggerated. About one out of every 10 Swedes of military age were called upon to hold themselves ready to serve under the colors for 20 years, but the force always contained a large number of foreigners. The Swedish element, the most reli-

able part of the army, was usually kept out of harm's way to guard rear areas, leaving the foreigners to do the bulk of the fighting; in 1632 in Germany, only 10 per cent of Gustavus' army of 120,000 men were native Swedes. Similarly, the impact of the "administrative revolution" in military affairs commonly attributed to Gustavus should not be overestimated. It did not prevent discipline from breaking down, and Swedish armies from sacking and looting. Nevertheless, Gustavus' army offered a model for the future.

Tactical innovations

Whatever limitations military historians might note about the recruitment and administration of the Swedish army, there is no denying the enormous impact that Gustavus' tactical innovations made on 17th-century warfare. He had studied both the *tercio* and the methods of Maurice, and his tactics were in the main a development of those employed by the Dutch leader. Gustavus' great achievement was to combine successfully shock action with effective firepower. He forbade his cavalry to use the *caracole*, and instead taught them to regard the sword as their main weapon. The dense formations of the *caracole* were reduced to six ranks for the charge. Although his attempt to integrate musketeers into cavalry formations to provide fire support was not successful, the Swedish pattern of shock tactics were adopted universally. During the English Civil War, both Oliver *Cromwell* and Prince *Rupert* of the Rhine used "Swedish" cavalry tactics to great effect. The cavalry charge, remained standard practice until the late 19th century.

Infantry tactics underwent a transformation under Gustavus as

well. He retained a high proportion of pikes to firearms, but reduced the size of the basic tactical infantry unit to a maneuverable 500 foot soldiers. The number of ranks were similarly reduced from ten to six, while Gustavus also developed the concept of volley fire to great effect. The role of the large numbers of pikemen the Swedes employed now became more defensive, their task being to protect the musketeers while the latter reloaded their cumbersome pieces. Once the muskets had been discharged, however, the pikemen took up an offensive role, advancing to inflict more damage upon the enemy and then withdrawing. This sequence was repeated until the enemy gave way. In the words of Professor Michael Roberts, the foremost authority on the Swedish army of the period, Gustavus "transformed the whole nature of infantry fighting from something essentially defensive to something essentially aggressive; and he solved the problem which had baffled all his predecessors, of how to combine shot and pike without sacrificing the essential military characteristics of each".

The Swedes also developed light, mobile artillery pieces, which enabled the infantry to be supported by 3-pounder guns, drawn by two horses in place of the 24 previously required. Finally, the Swedish tactical revolution was knitted together by the evolution of a more sophisticated form of command, in which horse, foot and artillery were integrated into an overall structure, instead of fighting a series of more or less separate battles. The twin arts of command and control were still in a more or less primitive state, but the

GUSTAVUS'S ARTILLERY *The new light cannon that Gustavus Adolphus introduced gave his artillery much-needed battlefield mobility.*

Swedes were more advanced than their contemporaries in this respect. Gustavus' strategy in Germany in 1630-32 was also based on sound principles. He paid careful attention to the problems of logistics, securing base areas in northern Germany before starting his 1631 campaign.

The era of "limited" war

The Thirty Years' War came to an end in 1648; with the Peace of Westphalia, Europe entered into a new period of warfare, which was to last until the wars of the French Revolution. Wars in this interim period were "limited". Battles were few, but bloody, and campaigns were generally confined to limited areas. They tended to revolve around complex series of maneuvers to seek a tactical advantage, and the reduction of fortresses. Only a handful of generals – exceptional commanders, such as *Condé, Marlborough, Charles XII* of Sweden and *Frederick the Great* of Prussia were renowned for seeking decisive battles, in the sense that Gustavus, and later *Napoleon*, would have understood them.

The reasons underlying the almost universal adoption of a policy of deliberate restraint in warfare were complex. European societies, of which, of course, armies were a part, suffered a natural reaction to the excesses of the Thirty Years' War, as a result of which the population of Germany had fallen by as much as a third. Perhaps eight million died as a result of that war. Such a scale of destruction threatened the survival of the existing social order, a fact that the ruling classes had to take into full consideration. The events in England between 1640 and 1660 had been a terrible portent of the dangers of unlimited war. The English Civil War had led to the breakdown of political and social order and the specter of lower-class unrest had raised its head. The oft-repeated example of Lawrence Sterne, the English author who successfully travelled to France without a passport during the Seven Years' War, neatly summarizes attitudes to

THE GREAT DUKE *Lille falls to Marlborough. In the era of "limited war," he was one of the few generals to seek decisive actions.*

war during the period of the Enlightenment. Hatred for an enemy seemed to be a barbaric relic of a less pleasant age. Naturally enough, there were other, more prosaic, reasons for the limitation of war, such as problems of logistics and recruiting and the sheer expense of armies. The campaigning season was limited to the period between late spring and October by the difficulties of living off the land. The alternative was to stock magazines, which was an expensive and time consuming process, and which further limited the mobility of armies. As in the 16th century, the strength of fortifications ensured that static warfare loomed large in 18th-century campaigns.

The reasons for war

The states of Europe still found reasons to fight, however. The wars of the 16th and 17th centuries had had a strongly religious flavor, overlayed with nationalism and pure power politics. The revolt of the Netherlands had been in part the struggle of a Protestant people against a Catholic colonial power. The Thirty Years' War was not only the culmination of the struggle between Reformation and Counter-Reformation for the soul of Germany. It was also a struggle between Catholic France and the Catholic Hapsburg dynasty, with Germany as the battlefield. The late 17th century was a period in which secular motives for war triumphed over religious ones. In the 1650s, the staunchly Protestant, regicide English Republic allied itself with Catholic, monarchical France and troops from the two states fought alongside one another against Catholic, monarchical Spain.

Some wars in this period were fought for avowedly economic motives. The universally-held economic doctrine of mercantilism stated that wealth was finite, and that prosperity was attained by seizing trade from rivals and wrecking their economies. Thus war brought profit. The English general, Monck is alleged to have bluntly summarized the causes of the Anglo-Dutch wars of the 17th century thus: "What we want is more of the trade that the Dutch now have". In the late 17th and 18th centuries the English and the French were to fight a series of wars in which trade rivalry was an important, although not the sole, motive.

It is generally recognized that the Peace of Westphalia brought about the creation of a European patchwork of nation states that was to last well into the 18th century. The 18th century thus saw a series of limited-scale wars fought for limited finite objectives. Wars might be fought to gain provinces or colonies; thus Frederick the Great fought two wars to acquire Silesia from Austria, while Canada was taken from the French by the British in the mid-18th century. While states at various times strove for European hegemony (Louis XIV's France, for instance, fought a sequence of wars lasting 40 years in an attempt both to expand France's frontiers and make the French the predominant European power), only in the case of Poland did this result in the total obliteration of a state as an independent entity. Such wars tended to be fought over the same ground again and again. The Low Countries earned a reputation as being the "cockpit of Europe", while northern Italy was another much fought over area. The growth of colonial empires meant that European wars sometimes spilled over on to other continents, but the forces employed were generally small as in the Franco-British struggle in India.

Vauban and fortification

The art of the siege dominated warfare in this period. The advent of gunpowder had brought to an end the useful life of the traditional medieval castle. High walls, which were vulnerable to gunfire, became liabilities, rather than assets, so a new type of fortification was devised, which relied on low defences, carefully planned to allow enfilade fire. Under the French Marshal Sebastien le Prestre de Vauban (1633-1707), the science of fortification reached its peak. Vauban designed fortresses that were complex and indeed beautiful. A typical fortress would be star shaped, with gun emplacements (bastions), arranged to give mutual supporting fire, plus outlying defences, such as miniature forts, ditches, and a glacis (a tract of land in front of the walls cleared of obstacles to create a "killing ground" that could be swept by musketry and gunfire).

Such formidable defences could not be simply ignored. They had to be masked by large bodies of troops, stormed, or invested. Thus they had the effect of making generals think cautiously and so acted as a restraining influence on the way in which wars were waged. To take a fortress, an attacker had to first surround it and then begin digging trenches, gradually working forward to get the siege guns within effective range so that they could batter a breach in the walls. Vauban, indeed, was as great a siegemaster as he was a builder of fortifications; and in the course of the 53 successful sieges he conducted, he refined his methods to such an extent that he was able to outline a 48-day timetable, at the end of which all the stages of an average siege would be complete. Operations did not always conclude with the storming of the fortress; on the 48th day it was considered acceptable for a defender to surrender without any loss of honor.

The importance of fortresses lessened during the Revolutionary and Napoleonic Wars, but on occasion they continued to play an important role. The sieges of the Spanish city of Saragossa in 1808-9 saw some of the most savage fighting of the entire Peninsular War. The conventions of 18th-century siege warfare had broken down, and the French were forced to fight their way through the city in the face of fanatical resistance. This was urban warfare of the most difficult kind. The total casualties amounted to 10,000 Frenchmen and 54,000 Spaniards. By comparison some 25,000 died in the sacking of Magdeburg in 1631, one of the worst atrocities of the Thiry Years' War.

Life was sometimes as unpleasant in the trenches of the besieging army as it was for the garrison. At the siege of Sebastapol (1854-55) in the Crimean War, the Anglo-French army suffered heavy casualties through sickness, cold, and shortage of food. In 1871, the capital of France, Paris, was besieged by the Germans, an event which caused widespread suffering and provoked the Communard rising. Thus it can be seen that the importance of the fortress long survived the so-called "Golden Age" of siege warfare in the 18th century.

Battlefield technology

By the end of the 17th century, technology affected the battlefield in two major respects. The heavy musket of the early part of the century, which needed a wooden prop to support it, was progressively lightened to make it a truly man-portable weapon. The old matchlock, fired by means of a slow-burning match, was replaced around 1700 by the lighter and more efficient flintlock. With the latter's faster rate of fire, the firepower of the infantry was substantially increased. The British and Dutch practice of deploying infantry in three lines maximized the firepower available, while the British practice of firing by platoons made their battalions more flexible than their French counterparts. The French used formations up to five lines deep, thus wasting the fire of the rear ranks, and fired in unwieldy company or battalion volleys.

The other advance was the replacement of the pike by the bayonet. This was an essentially simple device; a blade was fixed on to the end of a musket, thus allowing it to serve as a skewer. The first version was the plug bayonet, which prevented the musket from firing when fixed. This led to a disaster for a British force in battle against rebel Scots at Killiecrankie in 1689. The plug was superceded by the ring bayonet, and finally by the socket

bayonet. By 1700 the pike had lost its place in western warfare.

There were no major advances in the use of cavalry, however, where the methods of Gustavus Adolphus reigned supreme. Dragoons, useful mounted infantrymen trained to fight dismounted, transformed themselves into "horse" or charge-orientated cavalrymen, while "light dragoons" were raised in the mid-18th century for scouting purposes.

The professional army

No less important than technological development was the revolution in administration that occurred in the second half of the 17th century. Armies began to acquire a degree of professionalism becoming servants of the state, according to the pattern set by Gustavus Adolphus. As ever, the effects of this process should not be exaggerated, but it is possible to discern real differences between mid- and late 17th-century armies.

The leader in this field was Louis XIV's France. The growth of the French army accompanied the growth of royal absolutism, and the former's enlargement (from 72,000 men in 1660 to nearly 300,000 50 years later) was the essential precondition for Louis' grandiose foreign policy. Louis himself wrote in 1688 that "to extend one's territory is the pleasantest and most worthy occupation of a king", and virtually all of the period of his personal rule,

UNIFORMITY *Standard uniforms were gradually adopted in this period. From left to right, English, French and German examples.*

which lasted from 1661 to 1715, was spent in the pursuit of that objective.

As part of the general reform of the French administrative system that Louis initiated, two great ministers set about tackling the army. The father-and-son team of Michel Le Tellier and the Marquis de Louvois reformed the recruitment system and began to reduce the power of individual colonels to recruit regiments, thus increasing the grip of the state over the army. To oversee administration, supervise discipline and training, and to stamp out corrupt practices, *intendents de l'armée*, including the infamous M. Martinet, were appointed. In order to encourage and promote professionalism, officer training colleges were established, and limits were placed on the amount of money for which a commission could be sold in an attempt to allow the promotion of poor, but efficient, officers. This process of bringing the army under the control of the state was followed in other countries, notably in Brandenburg-Prussia and England, where in 1660 a royal standing army was raised to replace the New Model army of the Commonwealth period. Thus by

1700, the armies of Europe, generally speaking, were standing, professional armies whose loyalty was to the state. They were no longer mercenaries who owed loyalty only to themselves.

National uniforms

A tangible sign of the changing nature of armies was the development of military costume. Though soldiers tended to wear similar costumes at the beginning of the 17th century, armies were not clothed uniformly. "Uniforms" were a mid-century innovation, when they were adopted by the new standing armies. They were little more than adaptions of civilian dress, but they represented a major step forward. Previously a "field sign", such as a leaf or feather, had been used to make identification of friend from foe easier, while sometimes items of dress were worn in common; Swedish troops in the Thirty Years' War wore blue sashes, for example.

The adoption of uniform symbolized the "taming" of armies. No longer were they mercenaries, free to sell their services to the highest bidder. Their dress now made them recognizable as servants of the state. In addition, the adoption of uniforms helped to instill discipline, by ironing out individual characteristics and making each soldier part of a uniformly-clad military machine. By the end of the century, a basic coat color had been adopted by all armies. The red of the New Model army in England was retained by the Restoration army; France chose white; Russian chose green and so on.

In the 18th century uniforms grew more elaborate, until, by Napoleonic times, they had reached the heights of sartorial splendor. By varying the facing colors and by incorporating slight differences in their uniforms, individual regimental loyalties could be asserted, which had a beneficial impact on *esprit de corps*.

The rise of Prussia
The transformation of the small, weak Electorate of Brandenburg – Prussia into the most formidable military power in Europe took place over little more than a century. Frederick William, the "Great Elector", created a standing army in 1653 and he, and his successors, used it to expand their power within Brandenburg, which became the kingdom of Prussia in 1700. What this meant was that, in Prussia, the usual process of political development was inverted. As Professor Sir Michael Howard has written, ". . . the Prussian state was called into being to provide for the needs of the King of Prussia's army". When Frederick II succeeded to the Prussian throne in 1740, he inherited an 80,000-strong army, with the necessary state bureaucracy to support it. Frederick – known to posterity as "the Great" – expanded this army to a strength of 160,000 men and with it waged some of the most brilliant campaigns the world has seen.

Frederick the Great was the most important military figure to emerge between the death of Gustavus Adolphus and the rise of Napoleon. He was the greatest practitioner of warfare in the age of limited wars, and yet his methods looked forward to those of the post-1792 era. Frederick's army was a faithful reflection of his absolute state. His men were strictly disciplined, being trained to act as part of a machine. Their role was not to think, but to obey orders. Indeed, Frederick's management of

troops in roles which demanded a degree of initiative and self discipline – skirmishing light infantry, or light cavalry for outpost work, for instance – was poor. Although Frederick treated his soldiers as unthinking, bovine animals, the initiative taken by Frederick's subordinate commanders was of vital importance in battles such as *Leuthen*.

The Prussian army, a force which could be guaranteed to carry out orders rigidly, proved the perfect instrument for Frederick, who was one of the greatest tacticians of all time. He was no mere theorist. His Oblique Order was an efficient and practical response to the problems he faced of having almost invariably to fight enemies who were numerically superior. The Oblique Order called for use of a small force as a diversion, while the remainder of the troops maneuvered to achieve local battlefield superiority. By striking at a flank, Frederick could roll up the line of the opposing army. The attacking formation was staggered, so that units were held back from the fray to provide Frederick with a reserve with which he could respond to unforeseen crises. Thus time after time Frederick was able to beat a larger force.

Frederick was a man of his time, however, and paid due regard to the importance of establishing supply magazines and building fortifications. In the early period of his career he preached and practiced the need for rapid campaigns culminating in a conclusive battle. This strategy was forced upon Frederick because Prussia's army was outnumbered by the enemies that surrounded her, and only by moving rapidly and defeating his enemies in detail could Frederick hope to survive. As he grew older, however, Frederick paid increasing attention to permanent fortifications, which he described as "the mighty nails which hold a ruler's provinces together." It is ironical that, as the Revolutionary wars drew closer, the ageing Frederick reaffirmed the values of a style of warfare that was about to be rendered obsolete by the armies of the French Revolution.

Revolutionary war
The French Revolution began in 1789. Among its victims were the political order of the Ancien Regime, which was overturned, and Louis XVI, who was guillotined. As an act of monarchical solidarity, and to prevent the infection of revolution spreading to their own states, most of the other European powers went to war with Revolutionary France. Thus began a cycle of conflict that was to last from 1792 to 1815.

ON THE MARCH *Napoleon's army crosses the Danube to meet the Austrians at Wagram in 1809.*

To the surprise of all, the Revolution was not crushed by its conservative opponents. Having survived the initial period of greatest danger, the armies of the Revolution moved on to the offensive, achieving victories in Germany, Italy and the Low Countries that not only ensured the Revolution's survival, but made France the most powerful military power in Europe. By 1800, the worst excesses of the Revolution were over. From the ranks of junior officers forced up the ladder of pro-

motion by circumstance, Napoleon Bonaparte now emerged to become military dictator of France. What these years had shown was that the Revolutionary army was the guarantor of the survival of the Revolution. In fighting the wars which first saved France and then expanded the nation's borders, the army had also brought about a trans-

formation in the nature of warfare.

The "nation in arms"
In 1792 the borders of the French Republic were threatened by enemies approaching from every direction, while France itself was torn by a bitter civil war. At this juncture, the fledgling republic was fortunate to have Lazare Carnot (1753-1823) as its minister of war. Carnot attempted a feat that no other government had even contemplated – the mobilization of the

entire nation for war. His concept of a "nation in arms" represented a radical break with the theory and practice of the previous 150 years. On 23 August 1793 he proclaimed the *levée en masse*: "The young men will fight; the married men shall forge weapons and transport supplies; the women will make tents and clothes and will serve in the hospitals; the children will make up old linen into lint; the old men will have themselves carried into the public squares and rouse the courage of the fighting men . . . " This produced an army of a million men. Carnot's attempt to harness the economy of France to what a later generation would call the "war effort" was outstandingly successful, given the limits of a pre-Industrial Revolution society. Price controls were established; a form of industrial conscription of workers to man the munitions factories was introduced; and French society was thoroughly militarized. The next attempt to produce a society and economy geared for "total war" did not occur until the 20th century. Carnot well deserved his title of the "Organizer of Victory".

The Revolution on campaign

The French Republic's army scorned the attitudes to warfare that had prevailed since 1648. Carnot believed that France's dire military situation demanded the abandonment of conventional restraint. Logistical problems, for instance, were solved by encouraging the armies of the republic to forage in conquered territories – living off the land became official policy. Not only did this relieve the burden on the French treasury. It also freed the French from reliance on supply depots and magazines, and thus made war more economic and more mobile.

The rejection of conventional attitudes was not confined to logistics. Carnot ordered that the destruction of enemy forces in battle was to be the aim of the Revolutionary armies – not mere jostling for territorial advantage. In practice, victory in battle was often followed

by the imposition of a new political system on the enemy state. These strategic aims were a far cry from those of Marlborough, de Saxe or Frederick the Great. Interestingly, the type of army and war produced by Revolutionary France had been predicted in 1772 by de Guibert, an influential French theorist of war. He called for a mass army which would be supplied by foraging, thus making war mobile once again. However, by 1779 he had changed his mind. In that year, he wrote another work in which amounted to a refutation of his previous ideas, which he dismissed as the product of youthful inexperience.

The victories of the Revolutionary army were not achieved by the use of remarkable new technology, however. The weapons of 1793-1815 were very similar to those used by Marlborough's army: flintlock musket with socket bayonet, cavalry armed with a sword, and muzzle-loading smoothbore cannon. In the two decades prior to the revolution, the reform of the French artillery by Jean Baptiste de Gribeauval had produced more mobile guns though the introduction of lighter gun carriages. These made the creation of the Horse Artillery of the Napoleonic Wars possible. Similarly, the tactics the French armies employed should not have come as a great surprise to their enemies, for they were not particularly revolutionary. It is sometimes claimed, for instance, that columns were introduced to harness the élan and spirit of the French on the battlefield; in fact, it was the inability to march in line that promoted the column's adoption. The standard of training of the early Revolutionary armies was very low; the French volunteers and conscripts proved simply incapable of performing the complex drill necessary to carry out maneuvers in line, the standard formation of all pre-Revolutionary armies. Instead, the inexperienced French were sent forward in columns, covered by swarms of skirmishers. The relative merits of column and line had been debated by pre-Revolutionary armies, while

the use of light infantry as skirmishers was common to all armies, although this was to become more widespread after 1793.

How, then, were the Revolutionary victories achieved? The answer lies in the high morale and motivation of the army. Included in the army created by the *levée en masse* was a good proportion of soldiers and officers of the old Royalist forces, who received rapid promotion. Thus, the junior leadership of the army was generally of good quality, while commanders of higher formations were also often men who had been junior officers or NCOs in the Royalist army. Napoleon himself and many of his future marshals reached ranks in the Republican army that it would have been foolish to aspire to under the *Ancien Regime*. For the ordinary soldier, the French style of fighting meant a move away from the Frederician reliance on the military automaton, allowing more individuality. The army offered him the chance of promotion and of plunder.

It is worth remembering, however, that the Revolutionary armies were by no means invincible: at the beginning of the war, many inexperienced French units fought poorly. Even after the great Revolutionary victories of 1793-7, the allies put France under great pressure during the War of the Second Coalition (1798-1801), temporarily retaking many of France's earlier gains, and Napoleon himself only avoided defeat at Marengo (1800) through the timely intervention of Desaix. It was only through hard fighting and a fair measure of luck that the French avoided defeat.

The role of Napoleon

Napoleon Bonaparte was far more than just a soldier; however, it is his contribution to the story of warfare that will be considered here. As warlord and head of the French state from 1799 onwards, he was able to integrate political, economic, diplomatic and military considerations into his strategy. He was to invade both Portugal and Russia in an attempt to destroy the economy of Britain, for example, having tried and failed to exclude British goods from the continent by diplomatic means. When he lost sight of the primacy of political objectives and military strategy became divorced from political reality, as in the 1814 campaign, Napoleon was doomed. At the bottom he remained a Corsican adventurer. Having failed to legitimize himself, he had to win every battle, or face the loss of everything he had achieved. By refusing the allied terms for a compromise peace in 1813 and 1814, he condemned himself to fight a campaign that he could not possibly win. Perhaps he had come to believe in the legend of his own invincibility.

As a general, Napoleon was not an innovator. He used the French army and his knowledge of the methods of men like de Saxe and Frederick the Great to fashion his own style of warfare. In essence, his ideas were not very different from any of his contemporaries; he was simply better at putting them into practice. As he himself said, Napoleon's strategy was simple. It was to achieve superiority at a key single point in the enemy line, attack it, and win a decisive battle. He stuck to this basic principle throughout his career, and it served him well. In this, Napoleon was aided by the development of the corps system. Introduced into the French army in 1799, the army corps was an all-arms formation, ranging in size from two divisions upwards. One of their chief merits was that they allowed the use of several different axes of advance.

At the beginning of a campaign, a number of corps would be dispersed over a wide front. The whole army would then advance towards the enemy, aiming to concentrate at a pre-determined point. This gave Napoleon the flexibility to execute flanking attacks, to launch diversions and feints, to threaten the enemy rear and, if opposed by two or more forces, to defeat his enemies in detail. When the time came for the decisive battle, the corps would converge to form the concentration

of force that Napoleon required.

Napoleon was by no means perfect, however. Though he was still performing brilliant strategical feats at the end of his career – the defensive campaign of 1814 and the initial stages of the *Waterloo* campaign are two of the finest examples of his strategic skill – his battles from 1809 onwards deteriorated into crudely attritional slogging matches. Napoleon, in fact, was an uninspired tactician; his contribution to the art of war was at the higher level of strategy.

Impact of industrialization

The immediate impact of the Industrial Revolution upon the conduct of warfare is covered elsewhere (*see Railways and the Telegraph*). At the same time, industrial and technological advances meant that the armies of the mid-19th century could be armed with weapons that were rather more efficient than those of the Napoleonic era. The old smoothbore flintlock musket of Waterloo and Austerlitz had been replaced by more accurate rifled firearms; in a similar fashion, the smoothbore cannon had been replaced by a muzzle-loading rifled gun. By 1860, the first breech-loading rifle, the Prussian Dreyse "needle gun", had been introduced. The ancestor of the machine gun, the French *mitrailleuse*, was invented in 1851, although it was not adopted by the army until 1867.

However, the Industrial Revolution's impact was social as well as technological. Industrialization forced millions away from the land into the expanding towns and cities. This had the effect of making the ruling classes rightly nervous about the possibility of a proletarian revolution. As a result, armies spent as much time watching for signs of unrest in the cities as they did guarding against foreign invasion.

The Industrial Revolution was also accompanied by a European population explosion. The population of Europe grew from 187 million in 1800, to 266 million 50 years later. This vast reservoir of recruits did not remain untapped. Napoleon

had deployed 650,000 men for his campaign in Russia in 1812, but Prussia and its allies put 1.2 million men into the field against France in 1870. Thus, the Industrial Revolution made possible the creation of mass armies that could be rapidly moved and supplied by railway. To handle such vast masses of men, military administration had to be overhauled. Napoleon had relied on a small staff, led by Marshal Berthier, but, when faced with the problem of handling armies of the size of the one that was used to invade Russia, the Napoleonic system was less effective.

General staffs and war theorists

It was the Prussians who tackled this problem most effectively, with the creation of a modern general staff system, other armies eventually following their example. Historically, Prussian chiefs of staff, such as Scharnhorst and Gneisenau in the Napoleonic Wars, had been of greater importance than men of similar rank in other armies. Thus staff work was taken seriously by the Prussians, and *Moltke*, one of the 19th-century's most influential soldiers, assumed the post of chief of the general staff in 1857. It was superior staff work, as much as anything else, that brought the Prussians victory in the wars of German unification.

The Napoleonic Wars also spawned some serious analytical works that had an enormous impact on the theory and conduct of war in the late 19th and early 20th centuries. Prime examples include Baron Jomini (1779-1869), a Swiss soldier who served for some time on Ney's staff and Carl von Clausewitz (1780-1831), a Prussian who was to produce the most profound analysis of the Napoleonic experience.

In the long term, though Napoleon's influence was to long survive his death in 1821, it was the Prussian system that was to dominate the future. By 1860, the French army was no longer the paramount force of the Napoleonic era. Berlin, not Paris, was now the center of military excellence.

AUGUST 1704

BLENHEIM:
Marlborough's boldest stroke

At the beginning of 1704, the delicate balance of alliances that marked the War of the Spanish Succession seemed as if it was about to tilt decisively in favor of Louis XIV of France. Although Britain and its allies had an undoubted advantage at sea, elsewhere Louis had the upper hand, and appeared to be about to land a knockout blow on the eastern front. His ally, the Elector of Bavaria and the French commander, Marsin, were poised to capture the imperial capital of Vienna; the forces opposing them, under Count Styrum, were badly in need of prompt reinforcement.

Marlborough, as allied commander-in-chief, knew that if Vienna fell, the war there would be over. He therefore decided on the risky strategy of a march across Europe to the Danube. He would join forces with his allies, the Margrave of Baden (situated on the upper Rhine) and Prince *Eugene of Savoy*. Together, they would bring the enemy to battle and defeat them.

Courage and deception
This highly risky plan demanded considerable moral courage, as well as a degree of duplicity. The march across southern Germany would expose his army to attack by both Villeroi's French army in the Low Countries, and Tallard's force watching the Margrave of Baden. In carrying out such a plan, Marlborough was flying in the face of military orthodoxy, which regarded the necessity of keeping one's army intact as the primary responsibility of the general. Marlborough's greatness lay in his disregard for these conventions and his readiness to play for high stakes by taking a calculated risk. Marlborough based his

hopes of success on deception – not only of his enemies but also of his Dutch allies. The Dutch States-General were notoriously pusillanimous and would be unlikely to relish the prospect of their troops being marched deep into central Europe, 250 miles away from their home base in the Netherlands.

Marlborough's march from Bedburg began on 19 May 1704. His ultimate destination was known only to a few; it was part of his strategy to keep both friends and enemies guessing as to his true course until the last possible moment. The allied army grew stronger as it advanced; 5,000 Prussians, for instance, joined Marlborough at Coblenz. The possibility that he was about to commence operations on the Moselle was dispelled on 27 May, when he crossed to the right bank of the Rhine, but now it seemed as if he was heading for Alsace. However, when Marlborough struck out across the River Necker, it became clear where his army was marching. Uniting with Baden on 22 June at Stolhofen, on 2 July the joint forces stormed and took the Schellenburg, a fortress guarding the important town of Donauworth. The Elector of Bavaria refused either to fight or come to terms, despite the systematic harrying of his land, and the advance continued.

On 5 August, Marshal Tallard's French army reinforced the Elector at Ulm. Marlborough's plan of defeating the Bavarians before substantial reinforcements arrived had therefore failed. He was now in a precarious situation, and sought to force the issue in a battle. That battle was fought on 13 August 1704, at the village of Blindheim, which has become famous by its Anglicized name – Blenheim.

Weakness of the cavalry "hinge"
The task facing Marlborough and Eugene (who had arrived on the Danube on 6 August) was formidable. The Franco-Bavarians were 60,000 strong, with 90 guns, deployed on a frontage of four miles on a low ridge behind the shallow River Nebel. The position appeared to be so defensible that Tallard fully expected Marlborough to retreat. Thus the coalition troops succeeded in surprising the Franco-Bavarians by appearing on the battlefield (after a nine-mile approach march) at 8.00am on 13 August. Marlborough had spotted one major enemy weakness. The French and Bavarian armies were deployed side by side, with infantry in the center of each army and cavalry on the wings. Thus, the overall enemy center (the "hinge" between the French and Bavarians) was held only by cavalry. This proved a major error.

The French artillery opened fire, but by 10.00am, Marlborough was deployed along the left and center of the position. Eugene's force marched to take up position on the right, and was not in place until after midday. At 12.30 the allied attack began. Lord Cutts was dispatched against Blenheim village, with his infantry marching in four lines, and the cavalry in two. This was the most heavily defended section of the enemy line, and therefore, Marlborough reasoned, the place where Tallard would least expect to be attacked. The objective was to force Tallard to reinforce this point and thus weaken other parts of the line. This plan worked. Two assaults were thrown back by the French, but as a result the garrison was swollen from nine battalions to 27.

Marlborough hoped to achieve a

similar result at the village of Oberglau. He called off the attacks on Blenheim at 2.30pm and ordered a force ten battalions strong against Oberglau, held by nine battalions under the Maquis de Blainville. The Prince of Holstein-Beck, commanding the allied force, was defeated and pushed back, leaving a dangerous gap in Marlborough's center. Marlborough realized the danger and reacted swiftly. He asked Eugene for the support of Fugger's cavalry brigade, which duly arrived and checked a large body of French horse Marsin had sent to exploit the opportunity. This episode reflects well on both men, for Eugene was in need of the cavalry himself. The struggle in the center resulted in the advantage passing to Marlborough. Holstein-Beck's men advanced once again and this time succeeded in their task. With the result that de Blainville's garrison was now bottled up in Oberglau. With large numbers of enemy herded into the two villages, the time had arrived for Marlborough's main attack against the enemy center.

The center cannot hold

On the right, the Bavarians had fought bravely, absorbing Eugene's attacks without giving any indication of an imminent collapse. However, by 4.30pm Eugene was beginning to make progress towards Lutzingen, thus preventing reinforcement of the Franco-Bavarian center merely by continuing the battle. Half an hour earlier Marlborough had sent the 23 battalions and 90 cavalry squadrons of his center against the French positions between Blenheim and Oberglau. The initial attacks were unsuccessful as Tallard brought up his reserve (nine battalions), but at about 5.00pm Marlborough ordered a general assault on the French. The French center began to cave in under the weight of a massive attack. The French cavalry was routed, and as Eugene advanced on the right, the enemy position became hopeless. By nightfall, Tallard and the garrison of Blenheim

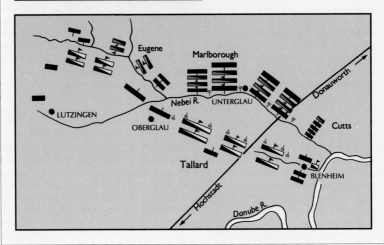

had surrendered and the Franco-Bavarian army had been decisively smashed. Tallard and the Elector had lost 38,000 men, including 14,000 prisoners. The price that Marlborough and Eugene had to pay was heavy – 12,000 casualties – but Vienna was saved and Bavaria was open to the allies.

Blenheim was Marlborough's finest battle. Again, he demonstrated a degree of courage in attempting to assault the powerful enemy position, for defeat deep in central Europe would have been a political, as well as a military, disaster. His army, a polyglot collection of national contingents was far less homogenous than was the Franco-Bavarian force, and yet Marlborough had led it to one of the greatest victories of modern times.

His initial plan is worthy of admiration: by seizing the initiative and forcing Tallard to dance to his tune, he succeeded in negating his numerical advantage. The strong support given by Eugene was evidence of the trust that existed between the two men, and played a significant part in making the ultimate victory possible. One could go on to number the praiseworthy aspects of Marlborough's genius as a tactician, but perhaps one more prosaic aspect of generalship may be highlighted. It was Marlborough's meticulous attention to administrative detail that ensured that his army was able to march across Europe to Bavaria and arrive in a condition fit to fight. Marlborough was far more than an excellent battlefield commander: he was a master of all facets of warfare.

DECEMBER 1757

LEUTHEN:
Frederick the Great's masterpiece
The Seven Years' War

The battle of Leuthen is the supreme demonstration of Frederick of Prussia's mastery of tactics. In it, Frederick and his Prussian army (35,000 men and 167 guns) decisively defeated Prince Charles of Lorraine and the Austrian army (65,000 men and 210 guns).

The year 1757 tested Prussia to its limits, but, as a result of Leuthen, it ended in triumph. Frederick was faced with invasion from all sides, but, at Leuthen he was able to overcome the handicap of inferior numbers and inflict a crushing defeat on the Austrians at a time when it appeared that Prussia must succumb to the sheer weight of the enemy coalition. By defeating his enemies in detail, Frederick was able to stave off defeat.

The story of the Leuthen campaign starts in early November 1757. On 5 November, Frederick clashed with a combined French and Imperial army under Prince Sachsen-Hildenburghausen and the Prince of Soubise at Rossbach in Saxony. Despite having only 22,000 men at his disposal, Frederick defeated the 41,000-strong enemy force. This timely victory freed him to turn against the Austrians, who were threatening Silesia with some success. On 22 November, a Prussian army had been defeated at Breslau and its commander taken prisoner.

Marching against the Austrians

Frederick now marched an army of 13,000 effectives into Silesia. Covering 170 miles in the staggeringly short time of 12 days, he arrived at Liegnitz to rendezvous with the scattered Prussian forces that had survived the Breslau debacle. Reinforced to 35,000 men, with 167 guns, Frederick marched on the Silesian capital. Barring his progress was an Austrian force under the command of von Daun and Prince Charles of Lorraine, with 65,000 men and 210 guns.

The Austrian infantry was deployed on a front some five miles long, running north to south from the village of Nippern, through Leuthen in the center to Sagschutz. Behind them was the Schweidnitz stream. Their cavalry was massed on either side of the Breslau road, which ran through the right center of the Austrian dispositions. It was a strong, although not unassailable, position, For their part, the Prussian aim was to feint towards the Austrian right to buy time to deploy against the Austrian left, and then to mount an oblique attack to turn the Austrian left flank.

At 5am on 5 December 1757 the Prussians advanced from Neumarkt. Their advance guard of 10 infantry battalions and 60 squadrons of cavalry ran into their opposite numbers at Borne. Here, Frederick's light cavalry fought a brief action with Austrian outpost cavalry, taking 600 prisoners, including the Austrian commander, General Nositz. The remainder of the Austrians were pushed back.

Using the dead ground

Near Borne was the Schon-Berg, a small mound from which Frederick, who had ridden in the forefront of his army, was able to gain a clear view of the Austrian positions; however, the lie of the land meant that he could conceal his force in dead ground. The consequences of this were dramatic. When Frederick sent his advance guard forward against the enemy right, the Austrians took this as the Prussian main thrust, rather than recognizing it as a diversion. Consequently, Daun's cavalry and nine infantry battalions were rushed north to throw back the Prussians. Though they were successful in this, what this meant in the long term was that a substantial part of the Austrian reserve had been committed in the north, just as Frederick was preparing to launch a major attack in the south, five miles away.

So far, Frederick's plan had worked well. One major advantage that he enjoyed over the Austrians was a detailed knowledge of the terrain over which the battle was to be fought. Silesia was home ground for the Prussians, who had fought many mock battles over this particular plain. However, it needed the genius of a Frederick to convert a potential advantage into an actual one. He ordered his army to wheel to the right and head south, the nature of the ground making it possible for his men to march across the Austrian front in two columns – both concealed from the Austrians by wooded hills. Perhaps surprisingly, in view of their previous experiences of Frederick, Charles and Daun concluded that he had decided to withdraw, but what he was in fact doing was pivoting his forces around the village of Lobetinz to attack the extreme Austrian left. Before the attack began, Frederick became caught up in an exchange of artillery fire while reconnoitering the enemy line from an exposed position. Having survived this, he personally supervised the deployment of his forces for the assault.

The oblique attack

At about mid-day the Prussians emerged from cover. They were heading for the extreme Austrian left in "oblique order," with their

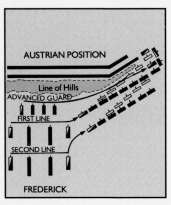

FREDERICKIAN VICTORY
Leuthen marked the triumph of the Prussian military machine. Though heavily outnumbered, Frederick (left) cleverly used dead ground to conceal his troop movements, which enabled him to launch a concentrated oblique thrust against the surprised Austrians (below).

AUSTRIAN POSITION

Line of Hills

ADVANCED GUARD

FIRST LINE

SECOND LINE

FREDERICK

erick's left-wing launched a perfectly timed stroke to hit Lucchessi, the Austrian cavalry commander, on three sides. The Austrian horse having been routed, the Prussians then attacked the enemy infantry, who, after a final show of resistance, broke and fled the field. By nightfall, Frederick was assured of a great victory.

A Frederickian victory

The battle had cost the Austrians perhaps one-third of their army. Their losses amounted to 22,000 men, including 12,000 prisoners, 131 guns, and 46 colors. The Prussians suffered 6,400 casualties. Following up his victory, Frederick moved against Breslau, which fell to the Prussians on 19 December at a cost to the Austrians of a further 17,000 men and 81 guns.

Leuthen was Frederick's finest victory. During the course of the battle, he demonstrated his command of almost every element of generalship. Strategically, the campaign is almost a text book example of how a large force can be defeated by a smaller one through bold offensive action and clever use of interior lines of communication. Tactically, his plan was both simple and bold, for conventional wisdom had it that an attempt to march across the enemy front would invite counterattack in flank and defeat. However, by accepting the odds of such a gamble, Frederick was able to compensate for the inferior size of his force by ensuring that it was concentrated at the decisive point.

Frederick was also well served by his subordinate commanders and his men – a reflection on the army that he had molded. The diversionary force in the north played its part to perfection; Dreisen's counterstroke in the south dashed the last Austrian hopes of salvaging anything from the battle. *Napoleon*'s oft-quoted verdict on Leuthen was simple. He called it "a masterpiece of movements, maneuvers and resolution". Alone, it is sufficient to immortalize Frederick as one of the great commanders of all time.

battalions echeloned to the left. Frederick had managed to achieve a massive local superiority over his opponents. The lead units, three battalions of Wedel's advance guard, came into contact with the Austrian line after 1.00pm. The Prussians, supported by artillery, assaulted Sagschutz and then began to roll up the Austrians towards Leuthen. The staggered formation allowed Frederick to feed more and more battalions into the fighting and thus keep up the pressure on the disintegrating Austrian line. In an attempt to stem the Prussian advance, Nadasti, the Austrian commander in this sector, threw in his cavalry. They had some initial success, but Ziethen countercharged and repulsed the Austrians.

Charles initially reacted to the crisis on his extreme southern flank by piecemeal reinforcement and by ordering Lucchessi on the northern flank to send back the cavalry he had been given to counter the initial Prussian diversion. Later he attempted to reface his entire line to present a solid front with its flanks

resting on Leuthen and Rathen. In response, Frederick ordered an attack on Leuthen itself at 3.30pm. By this time, the Austrians were packed into the village in dense formations, which suffered heavily from Prussian artillery. However, their spirited resistance forced Frederick to throw in his reserves before a Captain Mollendorff, at the head of a battalion of the élite Prussian Garde eventually fought his way into Leuthen.

The Austrians, however, reformed behind the village, and brought heavy artillery fire to bear on the Prussians. Worse, 70 squadrons of cavalry began to move towards the Prussian left flank. To meet this threat, Frederick deployed a battery which included 10 siege guns on the Butterberg, to support his infantry, which, after an initial failure, began to force the Austrian infantry into retreat. The advance of the Austrian right-wing cavalry, which would have endangered Frederick's position if it had been left unchecked, was checked by von Driesen, the commander of Fred-

OCTOBER 1805

TRAFALGAR:
Nelson's greatest victory

Trafalgar was the last battle in a struggle for maritime supremacy between Britain and France that had lasted since the late 17th century. Nelson's inspired choice of tactics and leadership, combined with the courage and seamanship of the British fleet, not only ended the immediate threat of invasion by Napoleon, but marked the beginning of more than a century of domination of the world's oceans by the Royal Navy. As befits a battle with such mighty results, it was one of the most decisive sea battles of the age of sail; it was also the last to be fought on the high seas.

The build-up to battle
The Trafalgar campaign can be said to have started when Napoleon began to assemble an Army of England along the coast of northern France. The First Consul understood little of the complexity of naval operations and his plan of operations reflected this ignorance. The combined Franco-Spanish fleets, were to break through the British blockade of their harbors and rendezvous in the West Indies, hopefully forcing the Royal Navy to pursue them. The combined fleets would then double back to the English Channel, arriving at Boulogne in mid-summer to escort Napoleon's invasion fleet of flat-bottomed barges across the Channel.

In the event, only Admiral Villeneuve in Toulon succeeded in breaking out of port, in March 1805. He eventually arrived at Cadiz, having sailed to the West Indies and back again. Nelson arrived from England on 28 September to take command of the British fleet. He realized to the full the gravity of the situation facing Britain and laid his plans accordingly.

Not just victory, destruction
The commander of the British fleet was well aware of the importance of the "Nelson touch" – the charisma and streak of unorthodoxy that gave him the ability to inspire confidence, admiration and love. He thus made a typically theatrical gesture at 11.45am on the morning of the battle, by signaling to the fleet "England expects that every man will do his duty." More importantly, before the battle Nelson entertained his captains on board his flagship, Victory, to ensure that each of them knew exactly what part they were to play in the battle that lay ahead. Nelson clearly and candidly explained his objectives and tactics to the men who would actually have to carry them out. Nelson's captains were enthusiastic, the admiral himself likening their reaction to "an electric shock." His plan was to attack the center and rear of the line of the combined fleets, to break through and engage in what Nelson called "a pell-mell battle." The Franco-Spanish van would thus be excluded from the combat until it was too late. In emphasizing close action, Nelson stressed that "no Captain can do very wrong if he places his ship alongside that of an enemy." It was a plan that contained some risk, but Nelson had every confidence in his fleet and was well aware that the enemy were no match for the British in skill. Nelson was not merely looking for a victory, but for destruction.

On 19 October Villeneuve put to sea, harried by his imperial master, but, by early on 21 October, he realized that Nelson was sailing to intercept him. He ordered a return to port; but this time, however, he was unable to escape. As the British fleet closed on Villeneuve, the French admiral ordered the combined fleets to form line of a battle, which they did with some difficulty.

In contrast to the inexperienced French and Spaniards, who had never before operated as a fleet, the 27 British ships-of-the-line smoothly formed into two columns and sailed menacingly towards the enemy. Nelson had decided to lead from the front instead of taking position in the center, the usual place for the fleet commander. He thus had Victory placed at the head of one column, while his second-in-command Collingwood led the other in Royal Sovereign.

Pell-mell battle
Collingwood's leeward column was in action first at noon. Royal Sovereign closed on the enemy rear and cut through their line between the Spanish Santa Anna and the French Fougueux. Then Royal Sovereign's gunners began to wreak revenge on Santa Anna for the heavy fire that the Spanish vessel had brought to bear on the British during Collingwood's advance. Royal Sovereign had pulled away from the remainder of the column and was heavily engaged by the French ships Neptune and Fougueux while she was engaged in her two-and-a-half hour struggle with Santa Anna, but at length Belleisle and Mars came up to break the enemy line. As Nelson had anticipated, the Franco-Spanish rear broke up into a "pell-mell battle."

Victory came under long-range fire at 12.15pm. By then, Nelson had seen Collingwood move into action and had signaled his frigate captains to use their initiative in deciding how best to bring their vessels to bear on the enemy. This decision is a tribute to the enormous confidence that Nelson had in his fleet, and is indicative of his command methods, which were at variance with the conventions of the early 18th century, where frigates were not employed in major set piece battles. *Victory* surged ahead of the windward column, first veering towards the enemy van to confuse Villeneuve further and then switching back to crash into the enemy line between *Redoubtable*, commanded by Jean Lucas, and *Bucentaure*, which was flying Villeneuve's flag. Nelson was granted his wish to be in the thick of the fighting. *Victory* was pummeled by gunfire as she approached, causing heavy casualties and her wheel to be smashed. A total of 159 men were killed on Nelson's flagship that day. Many of them died because of the heroic efforts of Lucas. He steered *Redoubtable* alongside *Victory* and grappled it. Gun fire raked the *Victory*, bringing down her mizen topmast. This was "pell-mell" with a vengeance, and Nelson ordered a party of marines, conspicuous in their red uniforms, to take cover. This decision sealed Nelson's fate. In the absence of the marine's covering fire, French marksmen were able to pick their targets. At about 1.15pm Nelson, in full uniform and wearing all his orders and decorations, was hit by a musket ball fired from 15 yards above his head.

Nelson had died at 4.30pm. By then it was clear that he had achieved a remarkable victory. In all, Villeneuve had lost 18 out of 33 ships and 14,000 men. 1,500 Britons were casualties, but not a single British vessel had been lost.

Nelson's death was a blow to the British, but he had ensured that Napoleon would be unable to mount another serious challenge at sea. In addition, British control of the seas made it possible for *Wellington* to conduct his operations in the Peninsula, which were to be instrumental in helping to ensure Napoleon's downfall.

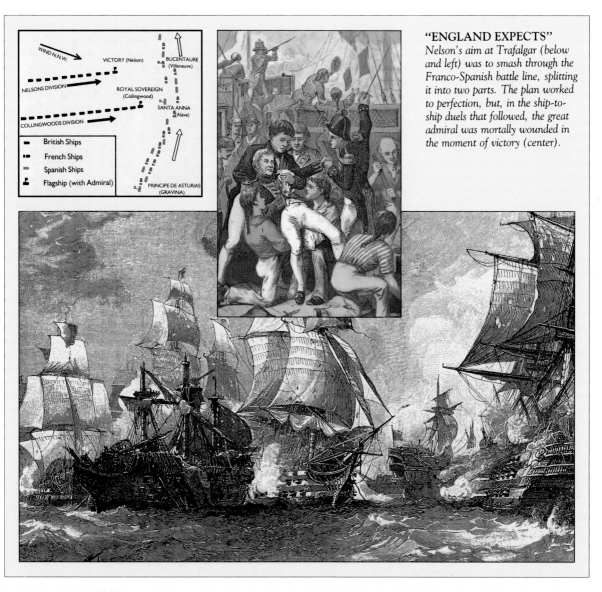

WIND N.N.W.

NELSONS DIVISION

COLLINGWOODS DIVISION

VICTORY (Nelson)

BUCENTAURE (Villeneuve)

ROYAL SOVEREIGN (Collingwood)

SANTA ANNA (Alava)

PRINCIPE DE ASTURIAS (GRAVINA)

- British Ships
- French Ships
- Spanish Ships
- Flagship (with Admiral)

"ENGLAND EXPECTS"
Nelson's aim at Trafalgar (below and left) was to smash through the Franco-Spanish battle line, splitting it into two parts. The plan worked to perfection, but, in the ship-to-ship duels that followed, the great admiral was mortally wounded in the moment of victory (center).

DECEMBER 1805

AUSTERLITZ:
Napoleon's classic victory

Exactly twelve months after crowning himself Emperor of France at Notre Dame, Napoleon inflicted a crushing defeat on an Austro-Russian army deep in Moravia. Technically, it is commonly regarded as his greatest victory.

Losing the advantage
The Austrians threw away one of the allies' greatest advantages over the French – their potential superiority in numbers – by prematurely advancing into Bavaria on 2 September before *Kutusov* and his Russians arrived to support them. The Austrian commander, Mack, apparently assumed that Napoleon would advance through the Black Forest and positioned himself accordingly, in the process dispersing his force of 43,000 men in a haphazard and near suicidal manner. Napoleon struck like a cobra and, on 20 October, Mack surrendered at Ulm.

Defeat into victory
Although the main Austrian force had been defeated, Kutusov's Russians remained in the field. He retreated back through Bohemia and Moravia, and Napoleon pursued him. It was a dangerous gamble; the French supply system was breaking down, and while Napoleon was moving away from his base, Kutusov was falling back on his and growing progressively stronger as a result. The Russian rearguard, under Bagration and Miloradovitch, fended off attempts to bring their main force to battle. By late November, the campaign had ground to a halt, with both armies confronting at each other in eastern Moravia. Napoleon desperately needed a battle but was too weak to initiate one. Instead, he tempted the allies to attack by making a show of his weakness, encouraging them to believe that they would be able to regain Vienna. Kutusov, indeed, was opposed to an attack, but was overruled by Tsar Alexander I.

The allied plan, devised by the Austrian general, Weyrother, underestimated the French army and overrated the ability of the allies to carry out a relatively complex maneuver. In effect, the main attack was to be made against the extreme French right, across the Goldbach stream. Once this flank was turned, the line was to be rolled up to the north. The main defect of the plan was that Weyrother paid little attention to the possibility of a French counterblow, and it was precisely such a stroke that Napoleon was planning. He had given orders for Bernadotte's I Corps, and Davout's III Corps to join the main army in a classic example of his ability to concentrate force at the decisive point. Broadly, he intended a wide sweep across the plain at the north of the battlefield, into the enemy rear. Soult's corps were to storm and capture the commanding Pratzen Heights in the center of the Allied position, which Napoleon judged would be empty as the allies concentrated on his right, which he kept deliberately weak as bait. This flank was to be defended along the line of the Goldbach.

Dawn at Austerlitz
Napoleon deployed 73,000 men and 139 guns: the Allies (of which the Russians were in a majority) 85,500 and 278 guns. At about 7.00am on 2 December, the unwieldy Allied columns under the Russian, Buxhowden, were coming into action against the villages of Tellnitz and Sokolnitz on the extreme French right. The outnumbered French fought back fiercely and the arrival of Davout's corps, after an exhausting approach march, ensured that the allies were unable to break through. Thus the major plank in the allied plan collapsed almost immediately.

At 8.30am, Kollowrath's column, which was to form the remainder of the force to envelop the French right, were ordered to move off of the Pratzen Heights. Napoleon at 9.00am, ordered Soult to attack the Pratzen Heights, which were apparently empty of allied soldiers. However, a column of allied soldiers was still crossing the plateau, en route to the battle in the south. Thus Soult found himself fighting an unexpected battle and his position became critical when a number of allied counterattacks were launched. About 10.30am two Russian Grenadier regiments, which had been moving south, came up against Soult's right flank (St Hilaire's Division), the Russians having simply been ordered to about turn and attack the French on the Pratzen Heights. Having survived this, the other assaulting division (Vandamme's) found its eastern flank under attack from two Austrian brigades. Only the timely arrival of six 12-pounder guns – IV Corps Reserve Artillery – enabled the French to fight off this challenge.

Decision on the Pratzen
One more allied effort on the Pratzen was still to come. At 1.00am Grand Duke Constantine led the Russian Imperial Guard, the only allied reserves in that part of the battlefield, up on to the Pratzen. With artillery in close support, the Guard destroyed a French battalion

and captured an eagle standard. Soult's battle line started to crumble, but Bessieres committed the cavalry of the French Imperial Guard to his support, while, on Napoleon's instructions, Drouet's Division of Bernadotte's corps were thrown into action. The Russian Guard recoiled. With the two most important points on the Pratzen Heights, the Pratzenburg and the Stare Vinohrady, safely in French hands, Napoleon was in a position to make his next move.

On the northern flank, Lannes's V Corps, supported by Bernadotte's I Corps, crashed into Bagration's Russians, backed up by Liechtenstein's cavalry. A large cavalry melée developed, with the French pushing back the Russians. The Santon Hill, the key to the French left flank, was threatened by Bagration in midmorning, but by midday, Lannes was pushing the Russians back. Bagration narrowly escaped being cut off from the rest of the allies to the south, but nevertheless had fought well enough to frustrate Napoleon's planned advance across the northern plain. Napoleon was thus forced to improvise a response to this check to his original plan, and the manner in which he did so demonstrated his true greatness. He made the Pratzen the pivot of his army and switched his forces south against the allied columns still stuck fast on the Goldbach. With the divisions of Vandamme and St Hilaire in the lead, and the Imperial Guard in reserve, the French attacked the flank and rear of the main allied columns. At the same time, fortuitously, the French defenders along the Goldbach launched a frontal attack. The allied armies began to crumble. Some troops, notably Keinmeyer's Austrians, broke out of the trap, but most fell back in disorder, were surrounded and surrendered. According to legend, thousands were drowned in the lakes at the southern end of the battlefield, but, in truth, probably only two men were drowned in what were actually shallow fishponds.

AUSTERLITZ *Having tempted the Austro-Russians to strip their center, Napoleon launched a telling counter-stroke to capture the key central heights. Their possession enabled him to envelop the enemy left wing (above and below).*

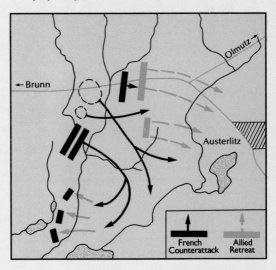

By 4.30pm, the battle was over. The Austro-Russian casualties amounted to some 27,000; those of the French, to about 8,300. On 5 December an armistice came into effect; and by the Peace of Pressburg (26 December 1805) the war between Austria and France was ended, on terms that effectively cost Austria its influence.

JUNE 1815
WATERLOO
Napoleon crushed

Napoleon and *Wellington* faced each other across a battlefield only once – at Waterloo in June 1815. Napoleon's bloodless reconquest of France that spring had compelled Wellington to resume his military career and take command of the Anglo-Dutch forces in the Netherlands. This was a force far inferior to his Peninsular army. At Waterloo, Wellington's army was to consist of 67,000 men – of which only 23,000 were British, and few of these were veterans. The rest were untried Hanoverians, Dutch-Belgians, Nassauers and Brunswickers, some of whom were of doubtful loyalty. Wellington was supported by an 89,000-strong Prussian army under *Blücher*. Together, they outnumbered Napoleon's Armée du Nord. However, from the beginning of the campaign Napoleon's strategy had aimed to divide the two allied armies and destroy them in detail. He desperately needed to achieve a quick victory to break up the enemy coalition and achieve a compromise peace.

A fight to the finish
The battle of Waterloo began at 11.00am when the French artillery opened fire on Wellington's positions. This had little effect on most of Wellington's carefully-positioned infantry, but Bylandt's Dutch-Belgian brigade, which was not behind cover, suffered heavy casualties. 30 minutes later Napoleon's brother Jerome launched a diversionary attack on Hougomont château. Although Jerome was ultimately to pour more than two divisions into the struggle, Wellington soon had the measure of the situation, and ordered a mere four light companies of the Guards to reinforce the garrison. The château, although bat-tered, held out throughout the day against the French assaults. The struggle absorbed troops that would have been of greater use elsewhere.

At approximately 1.00pm the first Prussians were sighted and Napoleon at last gave Grouchy direct orders to abandon his dilatory pursuit of *Blücher*'s army, defeated at Ligny the previous day, and to join him on the battlefield. These arrived too late to have any effect. At noon Grouchy, 15 miles away, had heard the sound of gunfire, but chose to follow his orders rigidly and continue to shadow 3rd Prussian Corps to Wavre, rather than march towards the sound of the guns. But at 1.30pm it seemed as if the battle would be won without him. The massed columns of D'Erlon's four infantry divisions advanced against Wellington's center. Bylandt's bri-gade broke and fled; the farm house of La Haye Sainte was swamped, its King's German Legion garrison remaining as an island of resistance. The British general Sir Thomas Pic-ton led his division forward and brought the French to a halt. Picton was killed during the counterattack and the battle was still in the balance when Wellington sent for-ward two brigades of heavy cavalry, the Household and Union brigades. They smashed into D'Erlon's dense columns and drove them back. The center had been stabilized, but the British cavalry then got out of con-trol and rode towards the French lines. They were counterattacked with devastating effect by French lancers, and the duke was left with-out an effective heavy cavalry force for the remainder of the battle.

By 3.00pm, Napoleon and Ney were aware that Grouchy would not be able to get into action that day. Ney mistook a tactical retirement ordered by Wellington for a full-scale retreat and sent forward cavalry unsupported by artillery or infantry. While this was an under-standable error, Ney's insistence on making massed cavalry charges against unbroken squares for an hour and half after he had dis-covered the truth was not. In con-trast to Ney, who seems to have totally lost his head, Wellington coolly rode up and down the ridge, encouraging his men, giving orders, always managing to be in the thick

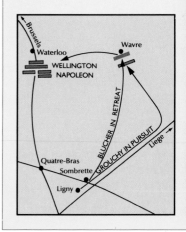

"A CLOSE-RUN THING"
Wellington's objective at Waterloo was to keep Napoleon at bay until Blücher's Prussians could come to his aid. Napoleon's plan was to smash straight through the allied center and drive on Brussels, but troops were diverted to support a secondary action and the main central thrusts failed (below). Both sides showed great courage – a key moment was the celebrated charge of the Scots Greys against the French 1st Corps (right).

of the action. In this battle of attrition, both sides suffered heavily, but it was the Duke's forces that prevailed; to one of his staff officers, it seemed that "while he was there, nothing could go wrong." At 5.30pm the allies beat off a combined infantry/cavalry attack, while Napoleon had been forced to commit units of his Imperial Guard to push Bulow's Prussian IV Corps out of Placenoit on his right.

The crisis of Waterloo

At 6.30pm it suddenly seemed if the road to Brussels was all but open. Ney succeeded in taking La Haye Sainte, by using an all-arms combined attack, which served to show what a similar effort might have achieved if launched earlier. Wellington's center was extremely weak, and was now exposed to close

range artillery fire. Wellington improvised a defence, personally rallying wavering Brunswick and Nassau troops and ordered troops from his left flank to move towards the center. As always, the mere prsence of the duke, apparently impervious to fear, proved to be of incalculable value in maintaining morale. But it is very probable that if Napoleon had launched a major attack at this point, it would have succeeded. Despite Ney's request, the emperor refused to release his remaining reserves – the Imperial Guard – and the opportunity passed. At 7.00pm, half an hour too late, Napoleon did authorize an attack by the Guard on Wellington's center right. Ney had had five horses shot from under him that day. He led the Guard, deployed into two columns up onto the ridge. With the Prus-

sians arriving in large numbers, it was Napoleon's last throw.

A personal victory

The Imperial Guard suffered from British fire, but still pushed some allied troops back. Then they came up against Maitland's British Guards Brigade. Wellington himself gave the order – "Now, Maitland, now's your time!" The 2nd and 3rd battalions of 1st Guards rose from their concealed position, poured fire into the French columns and followed up with a bayonet charge. For the first time in history, the Imperial Guard broke and ran. Their rout was completed by a well timed flank attack by the 52nd Light Infantry. Standing in his stirrups, Wellington waved his hat three times. The message was clear – the whole line was to advance to final victory.

BLÜCHER
Gebhard Leberecht (1742-1819)
PRUSSIAN FIELD-MARSHAL
Napoleonic Wars

It is one of the ironies of history that the greatest Prussian commander of the Napoleonic Wars began his military career fighting against the Prussian army. The future Field-Marshal Gebhard Leberecht von Blücher, Prince of Wahlstadt, was born in Mecklenburg and joined a Swedish cavalry regiment at the age of 14. Three years later, in 1760, he was captured by the Prussians and persuaded to take a commission in their 8th Hussars, with whom he saw more service in the last years of the Seven Years War. In 1773, Blücher resigned his commission after he had been passed over for promotion: Frederick the Great replied to his request bluntly: "Captain Blücher has leave to resign and may go to the devil as soon as he pleases."

Life as a farmer soon palled, but Blücher's reputation for drinking, womanizing and gambling proved an insuperable barrier to reinstatement as long as Frederick remained alive. His successor, Frederick William II, proved more amenable and appointed Blücher as a major in his old regiment, now called the Black Hussars, with eight years backdated seniority. Blücher served with his regiment against the fledgling French republic in 1793-5. Although the Prussians were militarily unsuccessful, Blücher won a hard-fought action at the head of his regiment at Landau in May 1794. He was rewarded with promotion to major-general.

Prussia took no part in the wars against the French from 1795 until 1806. In the latter, Blücher commanded a cavalry force at the disastrous Battle of Auerstadt (14 October). In the subsequent retreat, he commanded a force that was forced to surrender at Lübeck in November. However, his efficient handling of the retreat ensured that he was one of the few Prussian command to emerge from the 1806 debâcle with his reputation enhanced. With Napoleon dominating Prussia, Blücher was too out-spokenly anti-French to be given an active military command. It was not until 1813, and Prussia's defection from the French alliance in the wake of Napoleon's disaster in Russia, that Blücher again took the field.

Victory at Waterloo

As the principal Prussian commander, Blücher took a prominent role in the campaigns in Germany in 1813 and in France in the following year. Although he was on the losing side at Lützen and Bautzen (2 and 20 May 1813), he defeated Macdonald at the Katzbach (26 August 1813), and commanded the Prussian contingent at Leipzig (16-18 October). There, Napoleon was decisively beaten, and Blücher was promoted to the rank of general field marshal. In the 1814 campaign Blücher was bested on several occasions by Napoleon, but never conceded defeat. His reward was to occupy Paris in April and thus

BLÜCHER THE BRAVE *"Papa" Blücher has Napoleon gripped firmly by the neck in this 1814 cartoon.*

end Napoleon's first period as emperor. His role in the *Waterloo* campaign of 1815 was crucial and is discussed elsewhere (*see Wellington*). Suffice it to say that he recovered from the defeat at Ligny on 16 June to deliver the *coup de grâce* to Napoleon at Mont St. Jean on 18 June.

Blücher's strengths as a commander were his courage and determination, rather than his brains. Indeed, he suffered from bouts of insanity, at one stage believing he was pregnant, and carrying an elephant! Blücher relied on his chiefs of staff, first von Scharnhorst and later von Gneisenau, to supply the army intellectual power. Nevertheless, it was Blücher's aggression (which earned him the nickname "Marshal Vorwärts," or "Forward") and his loyalty to his British allies which proved the decisive factor at Waterloo, rather than von Gneisenau's cool appreciation of the situation. He over-ruled von Gneisenau's hesitations, insisting on marching to Wellington's aid, and thus ensured Napoleon's final defeat. After the Hundred Days campaign, Blücher retired from active service. He lived life to the full, gambling and hunting, until he died in 1819, mourned by all as the "Father of the Fatherland."

CAMPBELL
Sir Colin, Baron Clyde of Clydesdale (1792-1863)
BRITISH FIELD MARSHAL
Crimean War and Indian Mutiny

Colin Campbell was one of the longest serving and most successful of 19th-century British generals. Starting his military career as a subaltern in the Peninsular War, Campbell overcame his lowly social origins – a positive bar to advancement in the aristocratic British army of the day – and eventually emerged as a national hero.

Colin Campbell was born in Glasgow on 20 October 1792. His father, John Macliver, was a carpenter, but Colin's paternal grandfather had been the Laird of Ardnave, who had lost his lands as a result of the unsuccessful Stuart rebellion of 1745. Colin àdopted his mother's maiden name when his maternal uncle Colonel John Campbell bought him a commission in the 9th Foot (later the Norfolk Regiment).

Dour, cautious and courageous

Colin Campbell was almost a caricature of a dour, cautious but courageous Scottish soldier. In 1808 he was sent to Portugal and saw much action. He took part in *Wellington*'s first Peninsular War victories at Rolica and Vimero, and fought in *Moore*'s Corunna campaign in 1809. Later that year he was sent to the Low Countries, where he caught the notorious "Walchern Fever" and was invalided home. On his return to the Peninsular theater, he fought at Barossa (1810), with the Spanish at Tarifa, and at Wellington's crushing victory at Vittoria (1813). However, his luck turned against him at the siege of San Sebastian in 1813, where he was wounded three times. Campbell was then returned home to recuperate, with a substantial pension.

Campbell could not be kept out of action for long, however. In 1814 he served against the USA, and three decades of largely unrecognized military service followed. During this period, he lived the life of a typical colonial soldier of the time, spending long years abroad on garrison duty interspersed with bouts of active service overseas. Thus Campbell served in British Guiana in 1823, putting down the Demerera uprising. In 1835 he at last gained command of a regiment (the 9th Foot). Two years later he exchanged into the 98th. It was the Opium, or First China War (1841-43) that finally brought Campbell public recognition. He distinguished himself at the head of the 98th and was mentioned in dispatches and created a Companion of the Bath. Already, the hallmarks of his

style of generalship were discernable; a slow, methodical, and cautious approach that reflected his determination to economize on his soldier's lives.

Campbell's campaigning in India commenced with the Second Sikh War (1848-9). He had been commanding a brigade in China, but was promoted and commanded a division in that campaign. This was followed by three difficult, but successful, years of campaigning on the northwest frontier. He spent 1853 in semi-retirement in England, but, as Britain prepared to send an army to fight Russia in the Crimea, Campbell was recalled to the colors. In the subsequent war, he commanded the Highland Brigade with great distinction.

The "Thin Red Line"

At the Alma (20 September 1854) Campbell led his brigade forward and took a full part in clearing the heights of the enemy. At Balaclava (25 October 1854) Campbell's handling of his Highlanders passed into legend. Facing a charge by a massive body of Russian cavalry, he ordered the 93rd Highlanders to deploy to face them, warning "There is no retreat from here, men! You must die where you stand!" His nerve and caution were a valuable counter to the impetuosity of the Highlanders. As the Russians drew closer, he had to restrain the 93rd's urge to charge with an angry "Damn all that eagerness!" and the cavalry were driven off by musketry. The stand of the "Thin Red Line" made Campbell a national hero. Campbell was promoted to command the 1st Division, and was involved in the siege and storming of Sebastapol.

Campbell returned to India in 1857 as a lieutenant general and commander-in-chief in succession to Sir Patrick Grant. The Indian Mutiny had broken out in May, and Campbell's task was to restore order. He chose to do this in a typically slow and methodical way, much to the frustration of many observers who saw his caution as out of place in the desperate times of 1857. He relieved Lucknow in November (*see Outram*), taking the garrison back to Cawnpore. Outside the latter town Campbell smashed a rebel force on 6 December and then brought the surrounding areas to heel, using methods which seem brutal in retrospect but were considered normal in the emotionally charged climate of the time; the infamous massacre of the British garrison at Cawnpore had occurred only months before. Campbell returned to Lucknow in March 1858 and took the city. More operations lay ahead, but by the time of his promotion to the rank of full general in May, he had reasserted British control of northern India.

Ennobled as Lord Clyde, Campbell returned to Britain in 1860 to a hero's welcome and a field marshal's baton. The campaign to crush the Mutiny had been achieved with the minimum of British casualties, an achievement for which Campbell's careful planning and execution was largely responsible. Although this earned Campbell the unkind nickname of 'Sir Crawling Camel', the men under his command appreciated his Fabian strategy. His death in 1863 robbed the British army of one of its safest and most reliable commanders.

CHARLES
Archduke (1771-1847)
AUSTRIAN FIELD-MARSHAL
Napoleonic Wars

The Archduke Charles was the leading Austrian general of his generation, winning a reputation as a fine field commander, an important military reformer and an influential military analyst.

ARCHDUKE *Charles, imperial Austria's best general.*

The brother of the Emperor Francis I, Charles was a sickly and solitary child, who was instructed in military matters by a former adjutant of *Frederick the Great*. At the age of only 21, he was serving as a major-general against Revolutionary France, seeing action at Jemappes (6 November 1792). In 1793, as governor-general of the Austrian Netherlands, he defeated the French invaders at Neerwinden (18 March 1793), but was defeated himself by Jourdan at Fleurus (26 June 1793).

A thinking soldier

Charles spent the next two years in research, examining the reasons for Austria's defeat. He was particularly critical of the low standard of Austrian generalship, a problem that bedeviled the army throughout the period. In 1796, Charles was appointed to command the Army of the Rhine as a field marshal. Despite the handicap of having to submit plans to a council of war, on which powerful rivals were represented, his campaign was successful. Charles won impressive victories at Rastadt, Amberg and Würzburg over the French generals Moreau and Jourdan. Transferred to the Italian theater, Charles pursued a cautious strategy rather than seeking a decisive battle.

In the so-called War of the Second Coalition, Charles once again opposed Jourdan, whom he defeated at Stockach (25 March 1799). His attempt to campaign in combination with a Russian force under the obstinate Suvorov was not a success, however, and Charles was relieved of his command in February 1800. In December he was reinstated after the disastrous defeat at Hohenlinden (3 December 1800) but so complete was the French victory that peace was signed the following February.

Emerging from the war with his reputation intact, Charles held a series of important posts over the next few years, including the governorship of Bohemia and the war ministry. In the latter role, he forced through some important reforms in the Austrian command structure and created a regular corps of *Jäger* (light infantry). His influence waned when he opposed the drift towards a Russian alliance and the renewal of the war with France,

which he foresaw would be disastrous for Austria. The campaigns of Ulm and *Austerlitz* proved him correct, but by winning the battle of Caldiero in the secondary Italian theatre (29-31 October 1805) he enhanced his reputation. With the return of peace, Charles spent the years from 1806 to 1809 engaged in further army reforms.

The renewal of war in 1809 led to the first direct confrontation between *Napoleon* and Charles. The latter was defeated at Abensberg-Eggmuhl (20-22 April 1809), but at Aspern-Essling (21-22 May 1809) Charles inflicted the first outright defeat in the field that Napoleon had ever suffered. At one point Charles personally steadied his men by appearing in the front line bearing a standard. At Wagram (5-6 July 1809), however, Napoleon gained his revenge, and Charles was defeated, although not before inflicting heavy casualties.

Charles never held high command or high office again after Wagram. In many ways, he was an unlucky commander. He suffered from epilepsy, and his subordinates were – in comparison with their French counterparts – grossly inferior. While his personal courage was not in doubt, he lacked the ruthlessness of a Napoleon in that he often seemed hesitant to force a decisive battle. However Charles' work as a reformer and his writings on military matters deserve recognition. *Wellington* – like Charles, a masterly tactician – rated him as Napoleon's finest continental opponent.

CHARLES XII
(1682-1718)
SWEDISH KING
Great Northern War

The short reign of Charles XII was dominated by the Great Northern War of 1700-21. In it, Charles acquired an impressive military reputation as a result of his campaigns; yet, as a result, Sweden was eliminated as a first-class power.

RASHNESS *Charles XII over-taxed Sweden's resources.*

Charles was born on 17 June 1682, succeeding to the Swedish throne in 1697 and ruling, like his father Charles XI, as an absolute monarch. Charles had had a grueling apprenticeship, deliberately warping his personality to be remote and aloof, spending much time developing military skills. In the first years of his reign, he devoted considerable time to studying his father's written guidance on the problems of kingship. It was not the problems of peace, however, that occupied most of his attention – it was those of war.

Threatened by a coalition

In 1700 Sweden was threatened by a coalition of Russia, Denmark, and Poland-Saxony. In a series of campaigns in 1700-2, Charles' experienced generals broke up the coalition, with the king himself playing a relatively minor role, although his confidence and responsibility increased with the passage of time. By 1702 Charles had become the *de facto* as well as *de jure* Swedish commander. Denmark had been beaten, and Russia defeated at Narva (20 November 1700). Charles then concentrated on Augustus of Poland-Saxony with a singleminded determination that amounted almost to monomania – although this gave the Russians under Peter the Great time to recover and reoccupy their Baltic provinces.

Charles' victory at Poltosk (April 1703) and that of his general Rehnskjold at Fronstadt (1706) pushed the Swedes into effective control of Poland. He then turned his attention to the Russians, for whom he had much contempt – once saying "There is nothing in winning victories over the Muscovites; they can be beaten at any time." In 1707 the Swedes attacked Russia from their Polish bases. The Russians had spent the years since 1701 retraining their army and were now a more formidable force than at the time of Narva. Charles won a battle at Holowczyn (4 July 1708) but the Russians retreated, conducting a scorched earth policy, much as *Kutuzov* was to do just over a century later.

Charles attempted to link up with the Cossacks under Mazeppa to the south, but Peter defeated the Cossacks in October. Worse still, from Charles' point of view, a Russian force destroyed the Swedish supply train at Lesnaya (9-10 October 1708). Again, Charles' monomania surfaced, and he could only think of gaining revenge on Peter. He retreated through the winter to the Ukraine, losing 20,000 men in the process. In 1709 he advanced, to be defeated at Poltava (28 June). Shortly before the battle, he was wounded. His army surrendered, and he fled south to Turkish territory.

Decline and fall

Charles remained at his camp in Bender (in Moldavia) until 1714, attempting both to rule distant Sweden and to persuade the Turks to attack Russia. In 1713, he was besieged by his unwilling hosts, and at last, in 1714, Charles arrived back in Swedish Pomerania, after an epic journey. Charles set about defending Sweden from its Baltic enemies, but in 1718 he was killed in an invasion of Danish Norway. Rumor had it that he was shot by one of his own men.

Charles was undoubtedly an above-average soldier and an extremely efficient military administrator, who greatly influenced the Swedish army in such matters as inter-arm co-operation. However, some historians have detected a strand of lunacy in his mental make-up. His obsession with defeating first Augustus of Poland-Saxony and then Peter the Great led him to over-stretch Sweden's military resources, and by the time of his death Swedish resources were exhausted. The Russia of Peter the Great had replaced Sweden as the dominant Baltic power.

CONDÉ
Louis de Bourbon (1621-86)
FRENCH GENERAL
Thirty Years' War, Wars of Louis XIV

Louis II de Bourbon, Prince de Condé, epitomizes the ideal of the warrior prince – a chivalrous leader self-confident to the point of arrogance and brave to the point of recklessness. However, there was more to Condé than this. His sure tactical understanding, his ability to recognize and seize the decisive moment on the battlefield and his sheer tenacity of purpose won him a string of brilliant victories that amply proved his military ability. Put at its simplest, his aim was always to deliberately seek battle and then win it.

The young Condé achieved early prominence as Governor of Burgundy in 1638, where he led his first campaign at the age of 19. Just three years later, he was entrusted with the command of the French army opposing an invading Spanish force, operating from the Spanish Netherlands. The situation did not seem a promising one as far as the French were concerned, since Louis XIII was on his death bed and the country was in crisis as a result. Another man might have adopted a cautious policy of containment – but not Condé. Instead, he advanced to Rocroi, where he sought battle with the opposing army of Francisco de Melo. Condé's victory on 19 May 1643 saved France; at the same time, he destroyed what had been the most respected infantry in Europe.

Victory at Rocroi

Rocroi shows Condé at his best and the tactics he employed there were to be his hallmark for the rest of his career. The French infantry were used to enmesh the Spanish foot. Meanwhile, Condé, placing himself at the head of his right-wing cavalry, beat Albuquerque's opposing force. Keeping his troops well in hand, he turned the Spanish flank and then launched his cavalry on the flank and rear of the enemy, his infantry simultaneously renewing their pressure from the front.

Turenne, France's other great general of the time, might have been content with forcing the Spanish to withdraw, but this was not Condé's way. He kept up the pressure until de Melo's force was completely destroyed. Spanish losses were 20,000 to Condé's 2,000 – a stunning victory for the French.

Battling the Bavarians

After Rocroi, Condé was sent to take command of the Alsace front, which Turenne was reorganizing. Here, he faced the Bavarians under Mercy. Again, Condé carried the war to the enemy and in three bloody battles at Freiburg (3 August, 5 August and 9 August 1643) drove Mercy across the Rhine. In the first two battles – as at Rocroi – Condé sought to outflank his enemy. Finally, the French maneuvered themselves into a position from which they could attack the Bavarian rear.

The Bavarian threat had not been eliminated, however. A year later, Condé was ordered back to the aid of Turenne, whose forces had been badly mauled by those of Mercy. Arriving with reinforcements, Condé took control, while Mercy fell back to Nordlingen, where he entrenched his forces. Unable to turn a flank. Condé launched a three-pronged frontal attack against the Bavarian center. The Bavarians rallied, but, with the battle in balance, Mercy was killed.

Noticing the consequent slackening of the enemy attack, Condé charged again. Meanwhile, Turenne had beaten back the enemy right wing. Leaving the center, Condé led the French reserves to support his fellow general and so clinch victory – though its cost meant that it was a Pyrrhic one as far as the French were concerned.

Having suffered heavy casualties at Nordlingen, Condé was more cautious the next time he came up against an enemy in a similarly strong defensive position. This was at Lens on 20 August 1648, where he faced an entrenched Spanish force. Determined to lure the Spanish out of their position, Condé feigned a retreat. Putting himself at the head of the elite body known as the *gens d'armes*, Condé foiled an attack by the heavy Lorrainer cavalry serving in the Spanish ranks. Then, having succeeded in luring the Spanish forward, Condé turned, took their left wing in front and flank and then swung his cavalry round to attack their rear and routed them.

Out of favor

Condé was now at the height of his powers, but, unfortunately for him, he became involved in the French internal struggles known as the *Frondes*, opposing Louis XIV. After this, though he was restored to command, he was out of favor. His last great action was at Seneffe on 14 August 1674, where he routed William of Orange.

In a period when absolute monarchy was curtailing princely power, Condé was a political anachronism, as his unfortunate involvement in the *Frondes* showed. As a battlefield commander, however, he was supreme. Unlike many of his contemporaries, he understood that the true objective of battle was the destruction of the enemy, and it was on the battlefield that he surpassed the generals of his era in both conception and execution.

CROMWELL
Oliver (1599-1658)
ENGLISH ROUNDHEAD GENERAL
English Civil War

Politician, statesman, and also a formidable soldier, it is remarkable that Oliver Cromwell was recognized as none of these until well into his forties. Previously, he had lived the life of an East Anglian country gentleman, serving as MP for his birthplace, Huntingdon, and then for Cambridge, where he had been educated. Although associated with the Parliamentarians in their opposition to

ORIGINAL IRONSIDE *Cromwell's military reforms enabled the Roundheads to beat Charles I in the English Civil War.*

Charles I, Cromwell had made no great mark on his time before the outbreak of civil war.

When civil war broke out in 1642, Cromwell seized Cambridge Castle. Although he had no previous military experience, he raised a troop of cavalry from East Anglia and fought in the Parliamentarian army at Edgehill (23 October 1642). Ironically, it was probably Prince Rupert's cavalier horse that gave Cromwell a rapid and telling military education – the theory that Cromwell served as a mercenary in Europe in his youth is almost certainly unfounded. Cromwell saw the devastating effect of a powerful cavalry charge, but also saw the need for a disciplined marshaling of this force. One of the trademarks of Cromwell's cavalry was their charge at a fast trot, rather than a headlong gallop, and the fact that they did not lose the initiative gained by their charge by undisciplined pursuit of their enemy.

The manner in which he recruited and trained his "Ironsides" reflected the personality of Cromwell himself. His troopers were godly men of good character, for the most part yeomen, well equipped and self disciplined. Cromwell felt only this type of man had the belief and commitment to withstand the king's more experienced cavalry. Like Prince *Rupert*, he adopted the charge, rather than the use of fire arms, as the basic cavalry tactic. In sharp contrast to his Royalist rival, the discipline of Cromwell's regiment, and later that of the cavalry of the New Model Army ensured that he was always able to rely on them to obey orders.

Cromwell cut his teeth in a series of battles in eastern

England in 1643, as colonel of a regiment of well trained and disciplined horse. His regiment featured prominently at Gainsborough (28 July) and Winceby (11 October). The following year, Cromwell himself was appointed by the leading Parliamentarian general, Sir Thomas Fairfax, to command the cavalry of the army of the Eastern Association. At Marston Moor (2 July 1644) the discipline of his cavalry was decisive in winning the Parliamentarians the victory. Cromwell, though wounded, returned to the battle to break a determined stand by a Royalist infantry regiment, Newcastles' Whitecoates.

Cromwell's highly developed sense of order and discipline was offended by the presence of well-connected, but militarily inept, men, such as the Earls of Manchester and Essex, at the head of the rebel armies, and he and likeminded allies succeeded in forcing all MPs to resign their commissions under the "Self Denying Ordinance". Cromwell's outstanding talents earned him a "temporary" commission to allow him to serve in the field.

The New Model Army
Cromwell was now appointed to command the cavalry of Fairfax's New Model Army, the first truly professional army that England had seen. At Naseby on 14 June 1645, the cavalry played a prominent role in defeating the Royalist army, and by the end of the First Civil War Cromwell's reputation as a soldier was firmly established. His military career was far from over. When Royalist sympathizers renewed the fighting in 1648, Cromwell marched north and crushed his Scots opponents in a victory of annihilation at Preston (16 August 1648). Apart from being one of his first major victories as an independent battlefield commander, this battle demonstrated that his talents were not merely confined to commanding cavalry, for Preston was in large part an infantry battle.

In 1649, after the execution of Charles I, Cromwell was despatched to the English colony of Ireland in his first totally independent command. He won notoriety by putting the garrison of Drogheda to the sword, demonstrating the same streak of ruthlessness that had been revealed in his similar treatment of the garrison of Basing House in 1645. His action, although shocking to modern opinion (and even some contemporaries), was in accordance with the strict letter of the rules of war and served as an example to other Irish rebels. The final spasm of the Civil War came in 1650-1. In the role of captain-general of the Parliamentarian forces, Cromwell smashed the supporters of Charles II at Dunbar (3 September 1650), and exactly 12 months later broke a Scots invasion at Worcester. Both these actions bore the Cromwellian hallmarks of efficiency, discipline and flexibility, and made Cromwell master of England and Scotland. After various constitutional expedients had been attempted, he became Lord Protector – military dictator – in 1653.

Cromwell ruled England with as firm a hand as he had commanded his Ironsides, and brought to the country a much needed period of stability. Although his reputation has suffered a decline in recent years, he should be remembered as one of the better rulers of 17th century England. In military terms, he began the process of re-establishing England's military reputation in Europe, which was to come to full flowering under *Marlborough*. His forces waged a successful war against Spain, seizing Jamaica in 1655; attempted to break the commercial stranglehold of the Dutch in the First Dutch War of 1652; and fought alongside the French (who were beginning to emerge as the dominant power of the period) in the Low Countries. As a commander, Cromwell's greatness rested on his dedication and his absolute belief in his Divinely-appointed destiny, although his reputation as a psalm singing, Puritanical killjoy has been exaggerated. How Cromwell would have fared fighting against an army commanded by one of his great continental contemporaries, such as *Condé*, is, of course, impossible to say. His achievements in his brief military career, begun late in life, would suggest that he would not have been totally out of his depth.

EUGÈNE
Prince of Savoie-Carignon (1663-1736)
FRENCH SOLDIER IN IMPERIAL SERVICE
War of the Spanish Succession

Field Marshal François Eugène de Savoie-Carignon, *Marlborough*'s loyal ally at *Blenheim* and Oudenarde, was a brilliant soldier in his own right. Born in Paris, he had an unhappy and dangerous childhood, his father having been forced to flee from the city as a result of his involvement in a plot against Louis XIV. This legacy had a major consequence, since Eugène entered the army of the Holy Roman Emperor Leopold I

THE ALLY *Eugene's support was vital to Marlborough in the war against France.*

in 1683, Louis having refused to allow him to join the French army. He came to prominence during the war Austria waged to liberate Hungary from the Turks (1684-88) and, by 1693, at the age of only 30, he was a field marshal. Eugène served as commander-in-chief of the imperial forces in Italy during the War of the Grand Alliance (1688-97). In the latter year, while commanding on the Turkish front, he won an outstanding victory at Zenta (11 September 1697), which put an end to Ottoman hopes of reconquering Hungary.

The War of the Spanish Succession, which began in 1701, was to win Eugène further glory. In that year, he defeated the French generals Catinat and Villeroi, although he was himself beaten by Vendôme at Luzzara the following August. In 1704 he served alongside Marlborough for the first time, playing a major part in the Allied victory over the Franco-Bavarian forces at Blenheim (13 August). Recalled to the Italian theater, Eugène demonstrated his command of mobile operations in 1706 by outmaneuvering the French force besieging Turin and then proceeding to drive the French out of Italy – no mean feat in an age dominated by sieges and a determination to avoid pitched battles whenever possible.

Renewing his partnership with Marlborough in Flanders, Eugène fought in the battles of Oudenarde (11 July 1708) and Malplaquet (11 September 1709). Eugène customarily led from the front – he was wounded twice at Malplaquet, but stayed with his men on the field of battle. Eugène continued to serve his emperor well after the conclusion of the war in 1713, once again fighting the Turks. In his last campaign as a field commander in 1716, he captured Belgrade against heavy odds. He lived on until 1736, acting as a trusted military advisor to the crown.

Eugène was a cultured man, whose interests ranged far beyond the purely military sphere. He had a thorough grasp of his profession in all its aspects, undertaking some significant reforms, particularly in the field of cavalry, of which he was a brilliant commander. He was also an unselfish and a loyal ally, who was capable of inspiring great loyalty from his men. Perhaps the greatest tribute to Eugène as a soldier came from *Napoleon*, who listed him among the seven great commanders of history.

FREDERICK THE GREAT
(1713-86)
KING OF PRUSSIA
Seven Years' War

Frederick II of Prussia is one of the handful of monarchs to have earned the soubriquet of "the Great". He was the outstanding soldier of the era between the death of *Marlborough* and the emergence of *Napoleon*, and made Prussia into a great military power. In most of his campaigns he was outnumbered, but he compensated with bold offensive action, based on the discipline and maneuverability of his troops. His greatest single achievement was to survive overwhelming odds of 20 to 1 to emerge victorious from the Seven Years' War.

Born in 1712, the son of Frederick William, the first King of Prussia, Frederick had a harsh upbringing. His father was a brutal near-psychopath, who used his eccentricities as a cover for building a powerful army of 80,000 men without exciting the envy of the Hapsburgs. This, along with a full treasury and a well organized and compliant kingdom, were to be his most important legacies. Frederick himself had to endure humiliations at his father's hands, including attempts to crush his artistic temperament. (On one occasion Frederick was forced to watch the execution of his closest friend, who had helped

him in an attempt to flee the country.)

This upbringing may explain Frederick's career: the tension between his love of the arts, including playing the flute and a lengthy correspondence with Voltaire, and his remorseless, aggressive militarism. When Frederick succeeded to the throne in 1740, he almost immediately went to war. His objective was to seize Silesia, then a province of the Austrian Empire. He demanded the province as a *quid pro quo* for supporting Maria Theresa's claim to inherit the Hapsburg lands of her father, Charles VI. The acquisition would nearly double the population of Prussia to 3,750,000. When Maria Theresa refused to cede the province, Frederick demonstrated for the first time the streak of aggression in his character, and went to war.

On the offensive against the odds

The first Silesian war was typical of Frederick's style of warfare – a swift offensive designed to shatter his enemies before they could attack him. Moving against Silesia in December 1740, he was successful at first, but an Austrian counteroffensive brought Frederick to the verge of defeat at Mollwitz (10 April 1741). The Prussian infantry, trained by "the old Dessauer" (Leopold of Anhalt-Dessau), under the command of the aged Field-Marshal von Schwerin, succeeded in snatching a victory only after the Prussian cavalry had fled and Frederick had taken Schwerin's advice to follow them. Not surprisingly, reform of the mounted troops became a high priority for Frederick thereafter. The battle of Chotusitz (17 May 1742) was a Prussian victory and brought the First Silesian War to a conclusion. By the treaty of Breslau later that year Silesia was ceded to Prussia.

In 1744 Frederick began a second Silesian war, in anticipation of Austria's attempt to retake its lost province. His army had been expanded and retrained in the intervening years of peace, so he was able to lead 80,000 men into Bohemia on the outbreak of war, capturing Prague on 2 September 1744. He was forced to withdraw, as he found that his army was overstretched, but was able to save Prussia from defeat when he won a brilliant victory at Hohenfriedburg (4 June 1745), on Silesian soil, over the invading Austrians, under Prince Charles of Lorraine. True to his principle of taking offensive action at all times, he followed up by launching a second invasion of Bohemia, but again was forced to retire. He brushed aside an Austrian force attempting to block his line of retreat at Sohr (30 September 1745), inflicting 8,000 casualties. He was then faced with an Austro-Saxon assault on his homeland, which he defeated by taking advantage of his interior lines of communication to make rapid thrusts against the invading columns. The battles of Hennersdorf, (23 November) and Kesselsdorf (15 December) resulted in the treaty of Dresden in December 1745. Frederick was confirmed in his possession of Silesia: it remained Prussian and then German for exactly 200 years.

The Seven Years' War

In August 1756 Frederick signaled the beginning of the

PRUSSIAN GENIUS *Frederick the Great made unscrupulous use of his superb army to expand his country's borders.*

Seven Years' War by invading Saxony, at a time when the "Diplomatic Revolution" had aligned France with Prussia's enemy, Austria. All too aware of the weakness of Prussia's strategic position, Frederick hoped to strangle this potentially hostile coalition in its cradle, while all his life Frederick nursed a deep-seated hatred for Saxony, which some have traced to a sexual disease contracted by him while on a visit to the Saxon court as a youth. This precipitate occupation of its territory provoked the construction of the coalition against Prussia that Frederick had feared. Despite a victory over the Austrians at Lobositz in October 1756, and again against Prince Charles at Prague (6 May 1757), Frederick rapidly found himself in trouble. He lost the battle of Kolin (18 June 1757) and then had to react to threats from all sides. He again exploited the advantage of being able to move on interior lines of communication, moving first against the French army advancing from the west. Having failed to force a decisive action here, he then turned to face the Austrians advancing from Bohemia and the Russians slowly crossing into East Prussia. In addition, a 100,000-strong French army had invaded Hanover, the territory of Frederick's ally, George of England, en route to Prussia, while a small force of Swedes threatened Frederick from Pomerania. At Rossbach (5 November 1757), after yet another rapid change of front, a joint Franco-Austrian army was defeated by a much smaller Prussian army with the loss of 8,000 men.

Victory at Leuthen

Only one month later, on 6 December 1757, Frederick achieved perhaps the greatest of all his victories – this time over the Austrians at *Leuthen*. Here, his brilliant feint attack, rapid wheeling marches and use of the terrain enabled him to overcome odds of over two to one. The Russians were his next victims at Zorndorf (25 August 1758), and despite a defeat at the hands of the Austrians at Hochkirchen (14 October 1758), the strategic situation at the end of the year was more favorable than Frederick could have reasonably have hoped. He had thrown back the invasion attempts made by his adversaries and had survived their onslaught intact. However, the price that Prussia paid for this respite was high. The finely tuned army that Frederick had led into Silesia in 1756 was no more.

In the years of peace, Frederick had made many reforms. The cavalry was transformed into a formidable force, which, under the command of Seydlitz, performed magnificently in the Seven Years' War. In addition, light infantry and horse-drawn, mobile artillery were introduced. These reforms, allied to the celebrated discipline and endurance of the Prussian infantry, had allowed Frederick to win his great victories, but the quality of the army was no longer as high as early years. In a war of attrition, Prussia could not hope to compete with the vast reserves of manpower that France, Russia and Austria possessed. Already fighting with greatly inferior numbers (37,000 to 90,000 at Hochkirchen, for example), the declining quality of Frederick's army was to lead to defeats in the last phase of the war.

A man of iron

In the years 1759-63, Prussia survived by a combination of luck and skill. Frederick's unparalleled ability as a tactician and his iron will kept the Prussian ship of state afloat, even after such defeats as Kunersdorf (12 August 1759), when he lost 20,000 men against the Russians, and the occupation of his capital, Berlin, by the enemy.

Frederick's conduct of this war for national survival is perhaps one of his greatest achievements. At Liegnitz (15 August 1760) and Torgau (3 November 1760), he bought time with hard-fought victories, which allowed him to take advantage of the death of Tsarina Elizabeth of Russia, and her replacement by the Prussophile Peter III, who made peace. With one enemy removed, shortly to be followed by another, Sweden, Frederick was free to look south and west. At Burkersdorf and Freiberg (21 July and 29 October 1762) Frederick won further victories. Finally the war came to an end with an armistice that November.

Frederick reigned for another 23 years, and his death in 1786 brought an era to a close. His place in German history was assured; his reign saw significant movement in the historical process by which the center of political gravity in Germany shifted from Vienna to Berlin.

Frederick's claim to be one of the greaterst commanders of history is founded on his extraordinary tactical and strategic ability, and above all his refusal to admit defeat, even when in an apparently hopeless military situation. He was not the creator of his army; rather he took over an existing force and turned it into the finest in

Europe. His desperate fight for survival in many ways foreshadowed the type of war fought between 1792 and 1815, as he adapted or ignored the conventions of 18th-century warfare as he saw fit and risked battle for the sake of decisive victories. Frederick exerted almost as great an influence over the Prussian army after his death as he did when alive. It remained a rigid copy of that of Frederick's day and failed to move with the times out of excessive reverence for "old Fritz". Ironically, it was destroyed in 1806 by the army of his true heir, *Napoleon*.

GUSTAVUS ADOLPHUS
(1594-1632)
KING OF SWEDEN
Thirty Years' War

Gustavus Adolphus of Sweden has been described as the "Father of Modern Warfare". His prowess as a commander enabled him not only to rekindle the Protestant cause during the Thirty Years' War (1618-48) but his military reforms and tactics influenced succeeding military commanders throughout Europe.

Gustavus was born in 1594 in Stockholm, his grandfather being Gustavus I, the founder of the Vasa dynasty. His father became king (as Charles IX) in 1599 after a civil war against Sigismund of Poland; hostilities between Sweden and Poland simmered until the late 1620s. Charles wisely chose to give his son the fullest training in statecraft and military affairs. Thus in 1611, at the age of

MILITARY REVOLUTIONARY *Gustavus Adolphus launched a military revolution that was to transform the way in which war was fought across Europe.*

only 16, Gustavus commanded the Swedish forces in East Gotland and fought a number of battles against the Danish invaders.

In October 1611 Charles IX died, and, although legally under age, Gustavus became king with full executive powers. The wisdom of the decision of the *Rigsdag* (the Swedish parliament) to waive the normal rules was demonstrated by the king's first political act. His appointment of Axel Oxenstierna as Chancellor began a long and fruitful partnership between the two men. Faced with war against Denmark, Poland and Russia, Gustavus struck first at Christian IV of Denmark. He carried the war to the enemy by invading Denmark, even though a Danish army was on Swedish soil. The daring plan failed. The Danish war was brought to an end in 1613, on unfavorable terms to Sweden, but Gustavus had found time to deal with the Russians. The ensuing campaigns of 1614-17 ended the war with the Muscovites, this time on Swedish terms.

Military revolutionary
In these early campaigns, key elements of Gustavus' style of command were already apparent. His boldness has already been mentioned; one facet of this willingness to take risks was his predilection for seeking decisive battles, which was unusual in an age dominated by sieges. As a youth he had studied the campaigns and reforms of Maurice of Nassau and now set out to emulate and improve on them. The creation of a firm administrative base, the introduction of his system of discipline into his conscript army, and the adoption of radical new tactics and formations, helped produce the most formidable land fighting force in Europe.

In 1617, Gustavus began his long series of wars with Poland. After the capture of the ports of Polish Livonia, a two year truce intervened. In 1621, the Swedes returned to Livonia, and in a series of campaigns gained control of large swathes of the southern Baltic coast. At length, in 1629 the exhausted Poles agreed to a six-year truce. Although less well known than his German campaigns, the Polish wars can be seen as one of Gustavus' finest achievements. He had weakened the Poles by expanding Swedish territory at their expense and by gaining control of the ports through which they exported their grain. This sophisticated strategy succeeded in making Sweden the dominant Baltic power, a position the Swedes were to retain for a century. The Polish wars also gave Gustavus and the Swedish army much practical battle experience.

The Thirty Years' War
In 1630 Gustavus landed in northern Germany, not only to take up the sword on behalf of the Protestant cause, but also to defend his dominions. As he wrote, "All the wars that are on foot in Europe have been fused together," and *Wallenstein*'s armies were threatening his Baltic possessions. The first year of campaigning was spent consolidating his base area. Gustavus occupied the port of Stettin, and then spread out into the rest of Pomerania. In 1631 he took the offensive. After his brilliant victory at Breiten-

feld in September 1631, the road to Vienna and a swift peace appeared open. However, Gustavus chose to pursue a more cautious and subtle strategy by striking at some of the richest imperial territories on the Rhine. At the battle of the River Lech (16 April 1632) he crossed the river under the cover of a smoke-screen, and heavily defeated the imperial forces. The great *Tilly* was mortally wounded during the battle.

The return of Wallenstein as imperial commander-in-chief led to a decline in Gustavus' fortunes. Wallenstein seized the strategic initiative and forced the Swedes to respond. At Alte Veste (3 September 1632) Gustavus was repulsed when he attacked a strongly fortified position. Not only were Swedish losses heavy but, worse, Gustavus' reputation was dented. At Lützen, near Leipzig (16 November 1632) the Swedes attacked Wallenstein's entrenched army. It was a Swedish victory, but Gustavus paid a dire price for his method of command – leading from the front. He was shot dead when, isolated from his main forces in a fog with an escort only three strong, he was attacked by enemy cuirassiers.

Gustavus' record on the battlefield, although perhaps of less historical importance than his military reforms, was nonetheless impressive. He had, by force of arms, established Sweden as a great power and intervened decisively on the Protestant side in the struggle in Germany. His care for his men, as well as his military prowess, earned him popularity among his troops; and his fondness for decisive action led *Napoleon* to count him among the great captains of history.

HOWE
Richard, Earl of (1726-99)
BRITISH ADMIRAL
Wars against France

"Black Dick" Howe, as he was nicknamed by his men, was one of the greatest admirals to serve in the Royal Navy during the age of sail. He developed a revolutionary signaling system, and, based on this, broke away from the rigid "line of battle" tactics that had previously dictated British naval warfare.

Howe was one of three distinguished brothers; General William Howe (1729-1814) fought in the American War of Independence, while Brigadier Viscount (George) Howe (1724-58) had been killed in America during the Seven Years' War. Richard Howe's career began in 1740 when he served with Anson's fleet in HMS *Severn*; six years later, he was wounded fighting the French in the War of the Austrian Succession. Howe rapidly established himself as a man destined for high rank, becoming a captain when he was only 20 years old.

Howe spent the first part of the Seven Years' War (1757-63) serving in home waters. Much of his duties consisted of the blockade of French ports, but in 1759 he saw action at Quiberon Bay, when a French fleet under de

"BLACK DICK" *Admiral Howe's greatest achievement – the defeat of the French fleet on 1 June 1790 – was achieved after his recall from retirement from the Royal Navy.*

Conflans was destroyed by Sir Edward Hawke. Howe's ship HMS *Magnanime*, led the British van and captured the French vessel *Héros*. Typically, Howe took *Magnanime* as close as he possibly could to *Héros* before opening fire, ensuring that the combat would be conducted on terms favorable to the British. Howe's next appointment perfectly suited his aggressive temperament. As a commodore, he was responsible for mounting raids against the French coast, flying his flag in *Magnanime*.

The next phase of Howe's career took him into an administrative post on the Board of Admiralty, and then treasurer of the navy. Howe was once more back on active service during the American War of Independence, this time as a rear-admiral. During this phase he co-operated with his brother William, leading to the British victory at Brandywine, but resigned over a political dispute with the government in London in 1778.

In 1782, however, Howe was given command of the Channel Fleet. His most urgent task was the relief of Gibraltar. The Rock had been under siege by the Spanish for two years, and two attempts to relieve the garrison (under Sir George Elliot) had failed; the third, organized by Howe in 1782, succeeded. The following year, Howe became First Lord of the Admiralty for five years, and then retired, his career apparently over, in 1788.

However, the newly ennobled Earl Howe had two great services to render the nation. The first was the naval victory of "The Glorious First of June". In 1790, Howe had emerged from retirement to take command of the Channel Fleet again, as war with Revolutionary France threatened. Four years later, aged 66, he trapped the French fleet, commanded by Villaret-Joyeuse, which was escorting a convoy of vessels transporting grain from the New World to relieve famine in France.

Employing his favorite tactic of close action, Howe abandoned the conventional line of battle and ordered his ships to cut the enemy line and engage in a close quarters melée. Howe inflicted a heavy tactical defeat on the French, who lost seven ships, but the escape of the all-important grain convoy was of greater long-term significance, since it reached its home port.

Almost the last act of Howe's career came in 1797, when he was appointed to negotiate with mutineers at Spithead. Howe was trusted by the fleet, and his concern for the welfare of the ordinary sailor was well known. He played a crucial part in ending the mutiny, later receiving a well-earned Order of the Garter.

How was in many ways the archetypal British sailor of the 18th century – aggressive, disciplined and dedicated. He was a shy man with a brusque manner, who rarely showed his emotions, but was far from being merely a simple seadog. He was a thinking sailor; his system of signals was introduced in 1782 and used well into the next century. Tactically, his innovative break from the line of battle was the inspiration for *Nelson* at *Trafalgar*.

KUTUSOV
Mikhail (1745-1813)
RUSSIAN GENERAL
Napoleonic Wars

The Prussian military theorist Karl von Clausewitz wrote that "the prudent and wily Kutusov was . . . (Napoleon's) most dangerous adversary". As the commander-in-chief of the Russian armies during the 1812 campaign, Kutusov ended a long and distinguished career by presiding over the destruction of Napoleon's Grande Armée.

Mikhail Ilarionovich Kutusov was born in St Petersburg in 1745, the son of a military engineer. His army career began when he entered the artillery and engineering school at the age of 12. He first made his name as an officer of the newly raised *Jäger* (or light infantry) Corps. After service in Poland (1764-9), he fought with the *Jägers* against the Turks from 1770-4 and 1788-91. In these campaigns he served under two men who greatly influenced his style of generalship – Alexander Suvorov and Count Peter Rumyantsev.

Kutusov survived two serious head wounds (including the loss of an eye) and emerged from the Turkish campaigns as a major-general with a reputation for consummate courage. From 1793-8 he was employed away from the battlefield, as ambassador to Constantinople and governor of Finland. His next active command was in the 1805 campaign in Bavaria and Austria. True to Rumyantsev's principles, Kutusov retreated before Napoleon's advance, forcing the French into a dangerously overextended position and giving time for the other Russian army, under Buxhavden, to join him. However, Kutusov's advice was ignored by the Tsar, and against Kutusov's will, the Austro-Russian forces attacked at Austerlitz on 2 December, where they were decisively defeated (*see Austerlitz*).

After a spell in semi-disgrace, Kutusov once again assumed command against the Turks in 1811. He won a considerable victory at Rushchuck in December, and by May 1812 the Turks had been knocked out of the war – thus releasing Russian troops to oppose the imminent French invasion. Kutusov was still distrusted by Tsar Alexander, however, and until August served in the lowly capacity of commander of the St Petersburg militia.

Borodino and "General Winter"

The advance of Napoleon's armies deep into Russia led to public clamor for Kutusov to be given command in the west, and eventually Alexander gave way. On 29 August 1812 the 67-year-old Kutusov arrived at his new command. He continued with the unpopular policy of retreat begun by his predecessor, Barclay de Tolly, but on 7 September he halted 60 miles west of Moscow to give his army the battle it desired so dearly. The battle of Borodino was a Pyrrhic victory for Napoleon. He inflicted losses of 40,000 on Kutusov, but, in turn, sustained 30,000 casualties, weakening further his already depleted army. Kutusov withdrew in reasonable order, abandoning Moscow to the French, who entered it on September 14.

To Napoleon's surprise, Alexander did not sue for peace and on 19 October the French began to evacuate the fire-gutted city. Kutusov checked the French at Maloyaroslavets on 24 October, and thereafter followed Napoleon, choosing to harry the retreating French, rather than seek another major action. Kutusov was much criticized for this, but the Russian army was in little better shape than Napoleon's, and he preferred to allow the Russian climate to deliver the *coup de grâce*. The remnants of the once mighty French army had recrossed the Russian frontier by mid-December. Napoleon had lost 300,000 men; Kutusov only 50,000 less.

Although Kutusov was created Prince of Smolensk for his part in the 1812 campaign, his advice to exercise caution in 1813 was ignored by the Tsar. Kutusov died, worn out by the rigors of active service, on campaign in Germany in April 1813. His claims to greatness has sometimes been challenged. At Borodino, he sunk into lethargy and his liking of luxurious living on campaign was notorious. However, he succeeded in winning the affection and respect of his men (following the example of Suvorov) and in both 1805 and 1812 pursued shrewd strategies based on lengthening his opponent's lines of communications, while falling back on his own.

MARLBOROUGH
John Churchill (1650-1722)
BRITISH GENERAL
War of the Spanish Succession

Marlborough was one of the finest soldiers that Britain has ever produced. As the leader of a polyglot coalition of English, Dutch and Austrians, he took on and defeated the armies of the most powerful state in Europe in a series of campaigns that marked the transition of Britain from an insignificant off-shore island into a great power. However, in the best tradition of the hero of a Jacobean tragedy, Marlborough fell from power as a result of political intrigue when he was at the height of his success. Although later restored to royal favor, he never fought another battle.

The life of Marlborough

John Churchill was born in Devon in 1650, the son of a Royalist squire. Throughout his life he was an opportunist. He came to the Stuart court as a young man through the influence of his sister Arabella, the mistress of the Duke of York, later James II, and then became the lover of Lady Castlemaine, the mistress of Charles II. However, he saw service on the battlefield as well as in the bedroom, fighting in Tangier in 1668, at the naval battle of Sole Bay in 1672, and in the service of Louis XIV of France. In 1674 he married Sarah Jennings, a lady-in-waiting and close friend of the future queen, Anne.

In 1685 Churchill led James II's army against the Duke of Monmouth, the Protestant pretender to the throne, but three years later deserted his patron, the Roman Catholic James, to join William of Orange, the Dutch Protestant who had married Anne and now had landed in England at the invitation of the leading Protestant nobles to overthrow James. As a reward, Churchill was created Earl of Marlborough in 1689. It was the death of William III in 1702, which left Anne alone on the throne, that gave Marlborough real power. As Captain-General of the Anglo-Dutch forces and the power behind the throne, Marlborough began his campaigns against another old patron – Louis XIV of France.

Heading a coalition

The Anglo-Dutch forces were fighting to prevent Philip, the grandson of Louis, from succeeding to the throne of Spain. Marlborough's role in what became known as the War of the Spanish Succession began with his invasion of the Spanish Netherlands (modern Belgium) in June 1702. By seizing the French fortresses on the River Meuse, he opened up the river to Dutch trade and was rewarded by elevation to a dukedom. His next stroke was the most daring of his career. He marched his army 250 miles, deep into Germany, aiming to knock France's ally Bavaria out of the war. This campaign culminated in the victory of *Blenheim* (12 August 1704), fought with his Austrian ally *Eugène* of Savoy. Marlborough's reward

from Austria was to be made a Prince of the Holy Roman Empire. Anne granted him £100,000 and ordered a palatial residence, Blenheim Palace, to be built for her favorite.

Marlborough's next victory was at Ramillies, in Flanders, where he defeated a French army under Villeroi on 23 May 1706. After a tentative probe against the French left, Marlborough smashed through Villeroi's center, and the French army fled. Marlborough capitalized on his triumph by capturing several important towns in Flanders, including Antwerp and Dunkirk. Two years later, however, he was to be faced by a more formidable enemy – Marshal Vendôme. The latter took the offensive, seeking to defeat the allied armies in detail, and was successful in bringing Marlborough to battle before he could be reinforced by Eugène's army (although Eugène himself arrived to command Marlborough's right wing). The resulting battle was fought at Oudenarde on 11 July 1708. Here, the French were presented with a golden opportunity to win victory by attacking the weak Allied right, but confusion among the French commanders frustrated this plan. Instead, Marlborough enveloped the French army and inflicted 18,000 casualties on it, while suffering losses of only 7,000. Oudenarde showed that Marlborough's talents were not confined to a setpiece battle; it proved that he was capable of improvizing a plan and carrying it out to devastating effect. He was thwarted in his next endeavor, (a joint invasion of France by his own and Eugène's army), by the pusillanimity of his Dutch allies, so had to be content with the capture of Lille on 11 December 1708.

A frustrating period followed, as the allies negotiated with France and squabbled among themselves. As a result, most of Marlborough's energy was spent on political, not on military, affairs. On 11 September 1709, however, while laying siege to Mons, Marlborough accepted the battle offered by Marshal Villars at Malplaquet. This was the British commander's hardest fought victory. Both Eugene and Villars were wounded, with Boufflers taking command of the French army. Marlborough launched a massive blow against the French center, which caused their line to stagger, but the timely commitment of reserves stabilized the situation. However, he had one last card to play; the last remaining reserves were thrown into action. With their reserves already committed, the French center gave way, but, in sharp contrast to his earlier victories, Marlborough was in no position to pursue his enemy. The allies had suffered 21,000 casualties as against the French 12,000. Mons duly fell, but Marlborough was destined never to fight another pitched battle.

Fall from favor

Anne's relations with Marlborough's wife had deteriorated sharply by 1711, and that year the Tories came to power in Britain. They stood for a "blue water" strategy, based on naval power, and were opposed to the commitment of an army to fight on the European continent. Thus, Marlborough was regarded by his home govern-

THE FIRST CHURCHILL *John Churchill, Duke of Marlborough, combined military genius with political skill in his conduct of his long campaign against Louis XIV's France.*

ment as a political enemy, despite his attempts to remain above party strife. He was relieved of his command and went into exile, accused of misappropriating public funds. By the time George I came to the throne in 1714 and rehabilitated him, the war was over.

An old folk song, "Lord Marlborough", has the Duke saying

"I was beloved by all my men
And Kings and Princes likewise".

Indeed there rarely has been a general as popular with his men as was Marlborough. This was based on his concern for their welfare, which was in turn the product of his meticulous attention for detail. Unlike many of his contemporaries, he ensured that his men were always well fed and clothed, for instance. The news of his recall to England led to genuine displays of sorrow from his army's rank and file.

Marlborough's ability to co-operate with his fellow commanders and his tact when dealing with political figures was also of great importance. He held together a coalition of quarrelsome and sometimes reluctant allies largely by the force of his personality, for his responsibilities were not confined to the battlefield alone. He was director of the coalition's grand strategy – in effect, the supreme commander – but without the ability to insist on the unquestioning obedience that such a position

deserves. In addition, Marlborough was one of the most powerful politicians in England.

As a man, Marlborough had his faults – he could be mean with money, and was highly ambitious – but, as a general, he stands firmly among the great captains of history. His depth of political vision puts him on a par with *Napoleon*, while, in an era of many sieges, much maneuvering, but few pitched battles, he was a rare attacking general, who was constantly seeking to force his enemies to fight. Above all, "Monsieur Malbrook" was the first English military leader to strike fear into the hearts of the French since Henry V, 300 years earlier.

MOORE
John (1761-1809)
BRITISH GENERAL
Napoleonic Wars

"We'd not have won, I think, without him." Thus did the Duke of *Wellington* sum up the contribution of Sir John Moore to the Peninsular War. Moore was born in Scotland, the son of a doctor, and was commissioned into the 51st Foot in 1776. He saw service in the American Revolutionary War from 1779 to 1783, and, after a spell serving in other regiments, was appointed to command the 51st in 1790. Two years later Britain became involved in the wars against the fledgling French Republic. In 1794-5 Moore fought in Corsica, which led to him being given temporary command of a brigade. He then served in the West Indies and in the Irish Rebellion of 1798. In the two latter campaigns he made effective use of troops with which his name is still associated. These were the light infantry – men who fought in loose skirmish order, ahead of the close formations of "line" infantry.

Moore was wounded in the battle of Alkmaar during the Anglo-Russian invasion of Holland in 1799, and again at Alexandria in 1800, where he commanded a division in the British force sent to Egypt under Sir Ralph Abercromby. In 1803 he was back in England. As one of the most promising young commanders in the army, Moore was a natural choice to command a brigade on the Channel coast, where forces were being concentrated to meet the threat of French invasion.

At Shorncliffe camp in Kent, Moore set about training his men in skirmishing tactics – marksmanship, the use of cover, and individual initiative. He based his disciplinary system on example and encouragement, rather than relying on the harsh discipline of the lash. Although he was far from being the first British commander to recognize the need for light troops, his brilliance as a trainer of men has led to the general recognition of the justice of his claim to be the "patron saint" of the Royal Green Jackets and light infantry regiments in the modern British army.

Retreat to Corunna

In 1808 Moore survived a mission to support the Swedes,

during which his attempt to carry out hopelessly unrealistic instructions meant that he only narrowly avoided imprisonment by the mad Swedish king. After the Convention of Cintra (*see Wellington*) Moore received his first independent command – that of the British expeditionary forces in the Iberian peninsula.

In October 1808 Moore advanced into northern Spain to co-operate with the Spanish forces there, but soon discovered that the latter had been defeated, while the logistical support he had been promised was sadly lacking. However, he saw an opportunity to inflict a damaging defeat on the French by moving his 27,000 men against Soult, who was about 100 miles from Madrid and unaware of Moore's presence. On 22 December, however, Moore learned that Soult and *Napoleon* himself were advancing on him. This unwelcome news forced him to abandon his daring plan and instead embark on a nightmare retreat over the mountains of north-western Spain to the coast. He skilfully used his light troops to cover his retreat, conserving his ragged, exhausted army. In spite of his army being in poor shape, Moore then turned on Soult outside the port of Corunna on 16 January 1809 and defeated him in a defensive battle. At the moment of victory, however, Moore was killed.

Although his army was evacuated successfully by the Royal Navy, Moore's reputation suffered as a result of the campaign. Moore's character – efficient, upright, brave and a little priggish – had made him enemies. While he undoubtedly committed some errors, notably in not turning to fight defensive actions before reaching Corunna, the bold stroke he launched there suggests that he had a shrewd grasp of strategy. In addition, by diverting Napoleon from menacing southern Spain for several months, and by keeping the flame of resistance to the French burning in Spain during the darkest period of the Peninsular War, Moore's efforts paid ample dividends, as Wellington, his successor, recognized. The tribute he paid to Moore might refer to this – it might equally well refer to Moore's ability as a trainer of men, for Wellington made good use of the so-called "Shorncliffe boys" in his campaigns from 1808 to 1815.

NAPOLEON
(1769-1821)
FRENCH EMPEROR
Napoleonic Wars

In 11 years, the military genius of Napoleon Bonaparte enabled him to rise from obscurity to become Emperor of the French. At the peak of his career, he ruled either directly or indirectly most of continental Europe and had won renown as the greatest soldier since *Alexander the Great* and as a dynamic and reforming administrator. Yet, Napoleon possessed a fatal flaw; he was a gambler on the grandest of scales, with the fate of Europe as the prize. Eventually, in attempting to defeat Russia, he over-

reached himself. Within three years his empire had collapsed and he was exiled, to spend his last years on a remote Atlantic island, a prisoner of his bitterest enemy, Britain.

Napoleone Buonaparte (as he was christened) was born on 15 August 1769 in Corsica into a family of the petty nobility. He was educated at military schools in France, and in 1785 was commissioned as an artillery officer. With the eruption of the French Revolution in 1789, Napoleon became a Jacobin, a political radical. His family were forced to flee from Corsica, and he abandoned his early Corsican nationalism to concentrate on building a career in France.

A "whiff of grapeshot"
Napoleon's rise to prominence as a soldier began with his skillful command of the French artillery against the British at the siege of Toulon in 1793. His reward was promotion to general of brigade and commander of the artillery of the Army of Italy, with whom he campaigned in 1794.

After a spell during which he was out of favor for politi-

THE "LITTLE CORPORAL" *In the eyes of many commentators, Napoleon was the world's greatest soldier since Alexander the Great, his flaw being his propensity to gamble.*

cal reasons, Napoleon re-established himself in 1795 by dispersing a royalist mob in Paris by artillery fire, the notorious "whiff of grapeshot". This episode brought Napoleon – who now chose to render his surname in the French form as "Bonaparte" – command of the Army of Italy. He fired his poorly-equipped and dispirited men with his own enthusiasm and led them to a series of victories over the Piedmontese and Austrians, most notably at Lodi (10 May 1796) and Rivoli (14 January 1797). Then, taking a major gamble, he marched into Austria, advanced to within striking distance of Vienna, and so forced the Austrians to make peace.

The master of Europe

Now a popular hero, Napoleon displayed the extent of his strategic vision by deciding to strike a blow at Britain by attacking her eastern trade. Narrowly avoiding interception by Nelson's fleet, he landed in Egypt in July 1798, smashing a Mameluk force at the Battle of the Pyramids on 21 July. However, *Nelson* destroyed the French fleet in harbor at Alexandria, thus stranding the French in the Levant. The campaign suffered a further setback when the invasion of Syria was brought to an abrupt halt by Napoleon's failure to take Acre. Deserting his army, he made his way to France and became involved in the coup of 18 Brumaire (9 November 1799) against the ruling Directory, from which he emerged as the *de facto* ruler of France, as the first of three consuls of the Consulate.

Earlier that year, the military situation in Europe had appeared dire, but it had greatly improved by the time Napoleon returned to France. Nonetheless, he again took the field against the Austrians and narrowly defeated them at Marengo (14 June 1800). With the conclusion of a general peace in 1802, Napoleon was able to tighten his grip on France, crowning himself and his wife Josephine as Emperor and Empress in 2 December 1804. This was one of the reasons for the peace not lasting for long. Napoleon's aggressive foreign policy quickly stirred up another coalition against France. He prepared to invade England, but even before his fleet was shattered by Nelson at *Trafalgar* he had already been forced to march east. In perhaps his most brilliant campaign, Napoleon won great victories at Ulm (17 October 1805) over the Austrians and at *Austerlitz* over an Austro-Russian force (2 December 1805). Napoleon then crushed Prussia at the battles of Jena-Auerstadt (14 October 1806) and then marched into Poland to take on a Russian army. After a nightmarish winter campaign and a murderous, drawn battle at Eylau (2 February 1807), he at last won a victory at Friedland (14 June 1807).

The resulting Treaty of Tilsit with Tsar Alexander II marked the zenith of Napoleon's career. Europe was remodeled to suit the two emperors, and Alexander agreed to participate in the so-called Continental System, Napoleon's attempt to ruin Britain's trade by closing Europe's ports to British shipping. However, Napoleon was now faced with the problem of policing the whole of Europe, and his ambition was not yet sated. Attempts in 1807-8 to coerce Britain's ally Portugal and to put his brother Joseph on the Spanish throne misfired, resulting in the damaging six-year-long Peninsular war. In 1809 Napoleon once again had to fight the resurgent Austrians, receiving a serious check at Aspern – Essling (21-22 May), but winning an attritional blood-bath at Wagram (5-6 July 1809).

Divorcing Josephine, who was childless, Napoleon now married Marie-Louise, the Austrian emperor's daughter, who provided him with a male heir. However, just as relations with Austria appeared to have stabilized, those with Russia deteriorated. In order to force Alexander back into the Continental System, Napoleon invaded Russia in June 1812. For the first time, a Napoleonic gamble failed. A pyrrhic victory at *Borodino* (7 September) was followed by the retreat from Moscow and the destruction of the Grand Armée. Suddenly, all of Europe rose up against Napoleon. In August 1813, Russia and Prussia were joined by Austria and at Leipzig (16-19 October 1813) Napoleon was decisively beaten.

With *Wellington*'s British army advancing over the Pyrenees, having won a series of victories in Spain, in 1814 Napoleon fought a number of brilliant, but ultimately futile, actions in eastern France against the Russian, Prussian and Austrian invaders. On 11 April, 1814, the inevitable happened; Napoleon was forced to abdicate, his armies defeated and his capital occupied. After a few months in exile on the island of Elba, in March 1815 Napoleon once again returned to disturb the peace of Europe. He raised an army of veterans, but was finally and irrevocably defeated by Wellington and *Blücher* at *Waterloo* on 18 June 1815. He died in exile on St Helena in 1821.

The greatest since Alexander

As a propagandist, Napoleon was without peer, but much of the legend he fostered is firmly based on truth. He was a clear-sighted, vigorous and resilient man of action and the master of the calculated gamble, although in his later campaigns he lacked the drive of his early years. Napoleon was not a military innovator. His genius lay in taking existing elements and adapting them for his own purposes. Thus his tactical system, of infantry columns covered by skirmishers and backed by massed artillery was developed in the late 18th century. On a strategic level, his use of the "battalion carée", by which army corps – balanced all-arms formations – could be maneuvered so as to be ready to face the enemy from any direction, brought him victory after victory. Not the least of Napoleon's talents was his ability to inspire men, so that the young conscripts of 1814 – the "Marie Louises" – fought with the same fervor as the men of 1805.

Napoleon was a rare example of a man whose talents equalled his ambition, which bordered on the megalomaniac. His reign witnessed the apogee of French military power, while his political and social reforms molded Europe for a century. Napoleon's shadow was to hang over succeeding generations of soldiers, to the extent that it could almost be said that he was more influential dead than alive. He is simply one of the greatest soldier/statesmen of history.

NAVAL GENIUS *Nelson and his "band of brothers" laid the foundations for a century of British naval supremacy.*

NELSON
Horatio (1758-1805)
BRITISH ADMIRAL
Napoleonic Wars

Horatio Nelson has been acclaimed as the finest naval commander in history. His qualifications as a hero were impeccable; after a glittering string of victories, he was killed in the battle that laid the foundations for a century of British naval dominance.

Nelson was born in 1758 in Norfolk, the son of a parson. Through the influence of his uncle, Maurice Suckling, who had been comptroller of the navy, he embarked upon a naval career in 1770. With the exception of an expedition to the Arctic in 1773, most of his early service was spent in the West Indies. Nelson took part in the American War of Independence, and was promoted to post captain in 1779, before his 21st birthday.

Already Nelson was showing signs of promise. He took his profession seriously, and single-mindedly set about mastering the skills of seamanship. He also exhibited the traits that were to characterize his later career – aggression, a propensity for leading attacks on land, ruthlessness and the willingness to act on his own initiative. After the loss of the American colonies, for instance, Nelson rigorously enforced the generally laxly observed laws against trading with the newly-born USA, despite incurring his commander-in-chief's wrath.

Nelson married Mrs. Nesbit, a widow, in 1787. Until 1793, he was on half pay, but, with the coming of war with revolutionary France, he was given command of HMS *Agamemnon*. The next year he lost the sight of his right eye while conducting amphibious operations in Corsica. In the next three years he gained much experience of sea warfare, commanding an independent squadron as a commodore. It was in this period that he formed his low opinion of French naval seamanship.

First major action

Nelson's first major fleet action was fought under the command of Admiral Sir John Jervis off Cape St Vincent (14 February 1797). Here, Nelson distinguished himself by attacking the mighty 130-gun Spanish *Santissima Trinidad* with his own 74-gun *Captain*, thus delaying the Spanish fleet at a vital moment; he then boarded and captured *San Nicolas* (80 guns) and the three-decker *San Josef*. For his part in Jervis' victory, Nelson was promoted to rear-admiral and created a knight of the bath.

In July 1797 Nelson lost his right arm in an unsuccessful attempt to capture Santa Cruz, Tenerife, but in 1798 he was back in the Mediterranean, pursuing Napoleon to Egypt. Having narrowly missed the French fleet at sea, Nelson caught up with it at Aboukir Bay on 1 August 1798 and destroyed it. He sent his 13 ships into the bay, running the gauntlet of shore batteries, and succeeded in getting between the 13 enemy men-of-war and the shore. All but two of the French ships were destroyed or captured. The battle stranded Napoleon in the Middle East and doomed his Egyptian expedition to ultimate failure.

Created Baron Nelson of the Nile, Nelson's next task was to defend Naples. Nelson was created Duke of Brontë by the king of Naples and began his much publicized affair with Emma, the wife of the British minister, Sir William Hamilton. On returning to England in 1800, he separated from his wife and recovered from a painful head wound he had received at the Nile battle. Nelson feared that his career was over, but in 1801 he was promoted to vice-admiral and sent to attack the Danish fleet, which, as part of the Baltic league of armed neutrality, was thought to pose a threat to Britain. One of his actions during the battle of Copenhagen (1 April 1801) has passed into immortality. He placed his telescope against his blind eye, remarking "I have only one eye – I have a right to be blind sometimes". Thus he ignored the signal from his superior, Admiral Hyde Parker, to break off the action, and went on to win the battle. The battle contributed to the disruption of the league, and earned Nelson a viscountcy as a reward for his disobedience.

Build-up to Trafalgar

After a temporary cessation of the war with France, Nelson was appointed in 1803 to command the Mediterranean fleet. Two years of blockade duty followed, while Napoleon stood poised to invade England, if he could only gain – however briefly – naval superiority. After a campaign that took him to the West Indies and back to Europe, on 21 October 1805 Nelson fought his last battle, off Cape Trafalgar. It was a crushing victory, but Nelson paid with his life. His corpse was preserved in a cask of brandy and brought back to England, where in January 1806 it was interred in St Paul's cathedral.

As a commander, Nelson scorned inconclusive actions and always sought to destroy his enemies in a decisive battle. He was a daring, resourceful leader who, like Napoleon, was always prepared to use unorthodox methods and to take calculated risks; his tactics at Trafalgar and the Nile provide good illustrations of this. He never left things to chance, however; his apparently easy expertise was acquired the hard way. One of his greatest gifts lay in knowing when to diverge from pre-arranged plans or to ignore orders and to act on his own initiative. This is the mark of the truly great commander.

Nelson was more than a great naval tactician and strategist; he was a charismatic leader with the gift of inspiring love and devotion. He was careful to ensure that his captains – his "Band of Brothers" – were aware of his plans and methods, and that they felt part of an overall team. Likewise, he was popular among his men. However, Nelson could be extraordinarily vain, one incident in particular is revealing of the way that he manipulated his charm. In 1805 he met Sir Arthur Wellesley (later the Duke of *Wellington*). At first Nelson talked, as Wellesley later said, " . . . all about himself . . . in really, a style so vain and so silly as to surprise and almost disgust me." On learning of Wellesley's identity, his manner changed; "a more sudden and complete metamorphosis I never saw . . . I don't know that I ever had a conversation that interested me more." From the first part of the conversation, Wellesley "should have had the same impression of a light and trivial character that other people have had, but luckily I saw enough to be satisfied that he was really a very superior man . . . " or, as the Garter King of Arms said in his enlogy at Nelson's funeral, "the Hero who in the moment of Victory fell, covered with Immortal glory".

GALLANT MARSHAL *Ney's courage and dash in action won him the accolade of being the "bravest of the brave".*

NEY
Michel (1769-1815)
FRENCH MARSHAL
Napoleonic Wars

There have been generals of greater ability than Michel Ney, but few have matched his courage and power to inspire fighting men. He was born in Saarlouis in 1769, the son of a cooper, and enlisted in the 5th Hussars in 1787. Ney benefitted from the opportunities offered by the collapse of the French monarchy, rising swiftly through the ranks of the Revolutionary army. He came to prominence as a cavalry commander on the Rhine; by August 1796, he had been wounded in action (the first of his many wounds) and had been promoted to the rank of general of brigade. He played a significant role in Moreau's victory at Hohenlinden in 1800, having been promoted to general of division the previous year. Command of the French army that invaded Switzerland in

1802 further enhanced the reputation of "la rougeaud" (the redhead), as Ney was nicknamed, as a brave and skilful general. In 1804, he was among the 18 generals promoted by *Napoleon* to the position of Marshal of the Empire.

Brave, but impetuous

Ney was at his best serving as a corps commander under Napoleon, although the two men did not campaign together until 1805. At Elchingen on 14 October, Ney's VI Corps attacked 9,000 Austrians threatening to escape from Napoleon's encirclement at Ulm (*see Austerlitz*). After a furious argument with his superior, Murat, Ney personally led a French force to capture the key bridge, and then assaulted the town itself. The enemy retreated and thus left Ulm completely surrounded. The Austrian commander, Mack, surrendered on 20 October with 32,000 men.

Ney's conduct here reveals many facets of his personality: his courage and his methods of leading from the front, but also his inability to co-operate with other marshals unless under the direct supervision of Napoleon. His career over the next few years was chequered. Exactly twelve months after Elchingen, Napoleon destroyed the Prussians at Jena, but Ney's impetuous and unsupported advance almost led to a disaster for French arms; in the Polish campaign of 1807 Ney's impetuosity succeeded in provoking a confrontation with the Russians before Napoleon would have wished it.

Ney's conduct at the battles of Eylau and Friedland redeemed his reputation, and in June 1808 he was created Duke of Elchingen. Serving under Marshal Massena in Portugal in 1810, however, he was little short of insubordinate and was relieved of his command.

Last to leave Russia

Recalled for the 1812 campaign in Russia, Ney performed prodigies of valor. He was wounded at Smolensk and commanded the rearguard on the retreat from Moscow (see Kutusov). At Kovono Bridge, 13 December 1812, he fought in the front line, firing a musket like a common soldier, and he claimed to be the last French soldier to leave Russian soil. He was created Prince of the Moscowa in 1813.

Ney was wounded twice in the 1813 campaign in Germany, and in 1814 proved that he had moral, as well as physical, courage by acting as spokesman for the other marshals in insisting that Napoleon abdicate. He retained his titles under the Bourbons, and when Napoleon escaped from Elba rashly promised to bring him back to Paris in an iron cage. Despite this pledge, he rejoined Napoleon and was his operational commander at Waterloo (see Waterloo).

Ney – nicknamed "the bravest of the brave" by Napoleon – was adored by his men. It is as a fighting general that he is best remembered; he was too argumentative and impulsive and lacked the intellectual skills to be a truly great captain. It is noticeable that his generalship suffered after his chief of staff, the Swiss theorist Jomini, defected to the allies in 1813. Ney's end was ignoble. He was tried for treason by the Bourbons in 1815, and executed by firing squad on 6 December.

OUTRAM
Sir James (1803-63)
BRITISH GENERAL
Indian Mutiny

Sir James Outram was one of the finest British soldiers and political officers to serve in India during the middle years of the 19th century. He was remarkable as much for his political sensitivity as for his military competence. Outram was born in Derbyshire on 29 January 1803. His father was a naval surgeon, and James was educated at Marischal college in Aberdeen. In 1819, at the age of 16 he joined the Bombay army as a cadet and quickly showed promise. He established his reputation when he raised a unit from among the Bhil tribesmen, an episode that required him to show tact and understanding of Indian

ways and customs. This experience was to be invaluable in his later career as a political officer.

Outram's first taste of campaigning came in the ill-conceived and mismanaged First Afghan War of 1839-42. He rendered valuable service in that campaign as a soldier, but it was as a political officer that he made his greatest contribution. He was appointed to Sind, on the north-west frontier, and through his diplomatic

MUTINY HERO *Outram helped put down the Indian Mutiny.*

handling of the various tribes and factions was able to keep that unruly province quiet during the Afghanistan campaign. Unfortunately, much of his good work was undone by the high-handed and clumsy actions of Sir Charles Napier, who was appointed to administer Sind in 1843 and imposed a harsh treaty on the Mirs, or chieftains. Outram was dismissed by Napier, but was still able to persuade the Mirs to accept the unpalatable terms.

After briefly campaigning in Bombay in 1844, Outram resumed his career as a political agent. He was dismissed from one post for uncovering and publicising corruption, but in 1847 was appointed Resident in Lucknow. In this post, Outram was responsible for the initial decision to annex the state of Oudh. This was a major cause of the Indian Mutiny, for it underlined the Indian potentates' fear that the British had designs on their territories. The Oudh annexation eventually took place in 1856; one year later, the Mutiny began, threatening the British hold on the Indian sub-continent.

Relief of Lucknow

Early in 1857 Outram, by now a major-general, was commanding an expeditionary force in Persia. There he achieved some success, winning the battle of Khushab, but, when the Mutiny erupted in May, he was hastily recalled, appointed Chief Commissioner of Oudh and also given command of the Dinapore and Cawnpore divisions. He arrived at Cawnpore in September.

Outram had been appointed to succeed Sir Henry Havelock, who was advancing to relieve Lucknow, but chivalrously agreed to let Havelock continue in command as a mark of respect for the latter's achievements. This divided command was not altogether a success, but the joint force reinforced the garrison of Lucknow on 25 September. Outram then assumed command, and successfully defended the city until Campbell relieved him on 17 November. The British were extracted from the city, and Campbell marched on to Cawnpore. Outram was left with a force exceeding 4,000 men to keep watch on the city of Lucknow (now rebel held) from the Alambagh, a defensible position outside the city. In March 1858, Campbell returned and he and Outram invested the city.

On 9 March, Outram began preliminary attacks, which were marked by atrocities committed by British troops as reprisals for the acts of savagery perpetrated by the mutineers. By 22 March, Lucknow had fallen after heavy fighting. Outram was rewarded with a baronetcy, promotion to lieutenant-general and appointment to the governor's council as military representative. Typically, almost his last act in India was to act as a restraining influence on Lord Canning, the viceroy, and so was able to win over the great native landowners.

Outram was admired for his upright and generous character. At the end of the Sind affair, he gave away 30,000 rupees of prize money to charity because of his disgust at British policy. He was friendly and approachable to his subordinates, and his popularity was not limited to the army. After his death in France in 1863, partly caused by his exertions during the Mutiny, he was given a hero's funeral and buried in Westminster. Had his attitudes towards the native population been more widely emulated by other British soldiers and administrators in India, the Mutiny might never have broken out.

RUPERT
Prince (1619-82)
GERMAN SOLDIER IN ROYALIST SERVICE
English Civil War

"Rupert of the Rhine", as Prince Rupert was commonly known, was perhaps the finest Royalist cavalry commander and strategist of the English Civil Wars. He was the son of the Protestant Elector Palatine, who was forced to flee from the kingdom of Bohemia when Rupert was only two. Rupert made an impressive military debut in Dutch service in 1637-8, gaining a thorough grounding in the art of war, but was captured in 1638 and imprisoned for three years by the imperialists. After his release he joined the forces of his uncle, Charles I of England, who was preparing to fight the rebellious Parliamentarians. Rupert was appointed to command Charles' cavalry, and took part in the first major action of the civil war at Edgehill (23 October 1642). Rupert drew up a sensible plan for the battle, but although his men routed the Parliamentary cavalry, they then got out of control and recklessly pursued the broken enemy. Rupert was unable to rally them. This was an all too frequent occurrence. Though Rupert trained his men in the "Swedish" tactics used by *Gustavus Adolphus*, relying on shock action rather than firepower, all too often the indiscipline of the Royalist horse when it came to exploiting success nullified his undoubted qualities as a cavalry commander.

Rupert's sound grasp of strategy is illustrated by the fact that he advised his uncle to follow up the victory at Edgehill with a direct advance on London. If Charles had pursued this aggressive strategy, the Great Rebellion might have been crushed before the end of 1642. Instead, the king prevaricated. In the long war that followed, Rupert was given plenty of opportunity to display his virtuosity as a vigorous and dashing general. In 1643 he won the Battle of Chalgrove Field (18 June) and took Bristol; the following year, he raised the Parliamentary siege of York by forcing the enemy to face him at Marston Moor (2 July 1644). This was typical of Rupert's bold approach, but was a costly move for the Royalist cause. Rupert met his match as a cavalry commander in *Cromwell*, when his cavalry was defeated by Cromwell's Ironsides. The Royalist army as a whole suffered a similar defeat, and the north of England was lost to the Royalist cause.

History, if not battles, undecided

After his escape to the south from Marston Moor with 6,000 men, Rupert was appointed to command all of the Royalist forces, but his authority was undermined by factionalism in the king's circle. Against his will, he gave battle at Naseby (14 June 1645) against Fairfax's New Model Army. Rupert's plan was sound, but, as at Edgehill, he lost control of the impulsive Royalist cavalry and the Parliamentarians won a significant victory. Rupert's enemies, led by Lord Digby, seized on Naseby as an opportunity to further weaken his position. After he was forced to surrender Bristol in September 1645, Rupert was dismissed by Charles. Convinced that the Royalists were in an impossible situation, Rupert left England in 1646.

In exile Rupert commenced upon the second phase of his active service – as an admiral. From 1649-53 he commanded a Royalist fleet, which preyed on the shipping of the fledgling English Republic. After the restoration of Charles II to the English throne in 1660, Rupert com-

ROMANTIC CAVALIER *Prince Rupert was an able cavalry commander, but too impetuous to be totally successful.*

manded the English fleet with some success in the Second and Third Dutch Wars (1665-67 and 1672-74).

Rupert was not merely a man of war. He was a cultured and intelligent man, a member of the Royal Society, an artist and a scientist. However it is as the archetypal dashing cavalryman, that he has been remembered, courageously leading charges with much drive and élan. Rupert cannot be entirely absolved of the blame for the impetuosity of his cavalry, a failing which his Parliamentarian rival Cromwell managed to overcome. He was, without doubt, unlucky in having some of his soundest advice ignored and in having to jostle for the king's ear with a crowd of jealous and less talented rivals. If he had been serving in one of the contemporary armies on the continent, rather than in the amateurish forces of Charles I, he would probably have enjoyed more success as a commander than he did in the Civil War.

DE RUYTER
Michiel Adrienszoon (1607-1676)
DUTCH ADMIRAL
Anglo-Dutch Wars

De Ruyter was perhaps the greatest of all Dutch seamen at the time when the Netherlands were challenging Britain for naval supremacy. He was born at Flushing in 1607, and first went to sea at the age of nine in a merchant vessel. The first half of de Ruyter's life was spent in merchantmen, but the Dutch seaborne empire of the early 17th century offered much scope for men to gain experience of naval warfare as well as trade. In 1641 de Ruyter commanded a fleet of 15 ships as a rear admiral in support of Portugal, at that time in rebellion against the United Province's enemy, Spain.

His next taste of action was in the First Anglo-Dutch War of 1652-54, in which de Ruyter began to demonstrate the characteristics that were to be his trademark — aggression, audacity and courage. Early in the war, de Ruyter was escorting a convoy when he was attacked by enemy ships near the Channel Islands, but he succeeded in escaping. On 28 September 1652 he was present in the fleet of Witte Corneliszoon de With at the battle of Kentish Knock. De With was defeated by an English fleet under Blake but de With's replacement as Dutch commander, Tromp, gained revenge off Dungeness (29 November 1652). De Ruyter served with great courage and skill in this battle and also in "The Three Days Battle" off Portland in February 1653. In July Tromp led the Dutch fleet out to try to break the English blockade, but was heavily defeated off the Texel. De Ruyter, as ever, emerged from the battle with his reputation enhanced and, on this occasion, with his ship, Lam, reduced to little more than a wreck. He was now regarded as one of the foremost Dutch admirals.

The years separating the end of the first from the beginning of the Second Dutch Wars were not, for de Ruyter, years of peace. He commanded a fleet sent to aid Denmark in the Baltic (1659), and was involved in attempts to curb piracy in the Mediterranean. Even before the Second Dutch War began in 1665, he had clashed with English ships off the coast of West Africa. With the formal declaration of war, de Ruyter attacked Barbados and then made for home, where he was appointed lieutenant-admiral In June 1666 he was engaged in the running "Four Days Battle" in the Channel. The outnumbered English fleet, under Monck and Prince Rupert lost about 20 ships and de Ruyter only seven. However, the next few months went badly for the Dutch. De Ruyter was defeated by Monck on 25 July, losing 20 ships to only one English vessel and then was pinned to his own coastline.

Sailing up the Medway
In June 1667, de Ruyter took spectacular revenge and in doing so inflicted the most humiliating defeat on the Royal Navy in British naval history. Taking advantage of the fact that the bulk of the fleet was laid up in Chatham (partly through lack of funds and partly because peace negotiations were underway at Breda), de Ruyter boldly sailed up the Medway. For two days de Ruyter maintained his challenge to English national pride, and then he withdrew, having destroyed much of the fleet and captured the English flagship, Royal Charles. The English hurriedly made peace. Samuel Pepys wrote in his diary that "in all things, in wisdom, courage, force, knowledge of our own streams, and success, the Dutch have the best of us and do end the war with victory on their side."

The final clash
The final clash between England and the Netherlands for maritime and commercial supremacy began in 1672. This time England was in alliance with Louis XIV of France, who invaded the Netherlands by land. De Ruyter launched a pre-emptive attack against an Anglo-French invasion fleet at Sole Bay, and succeeded in wreaking havoc before he was forced to withdraw. In the Third Dutch War de Ruyter was on the strategic defensive, but took the tactical offensive whenever possible. Thus in 1673 he attempted to sink blockships in the Thames estuary, and harried the Anglo-French fleet by conducting a kind of maritime guerrilla campaign. In the two battles of the Schonveldt (7 and 14 June 1673) de Ruyter emerged from harbor to inflict sharp defeats on the allies. His last, and possibly most important, victory against his old English adversaries was at the Texel (11 August 1673), in which he managed to shield an important convoy on its trip home, thus breaking the English blockade.

Although England made peace in 1674, Louis XIV fought on; de Ruyter died fighting the French in the Mediterranean off Messina in 1676. With his death, the Dutch attempt to gain naval supremacy began to falter. In an age of many great fighting sailors, de Ruyter was one of the greatest. His exploits won him the devotion of his friends and the admiration of his enemies; he was probably the greatest figure in Dutch naval history and one of England's most skillful enemies.

SAXE
Hermann-Maurice (1696-1750)
MARSHAL-GENERAL OF FRANCE
War of the Austrian Succession

Marshal de Saxe, the victor of Fontenoy, was a distinguished field commander who also had great influence as a theorist of war. Hermann-Maurice was born at Goslar on 28 October 1696, the bastard son of Elector Frederick August I of Saxony, who later became King of Poland, and Maria Aurora von Konigsmarck. In 1711 his father gave him the title of Count of Saxony (in French, Comte de Saxe). It is possible that the desire to overcome the stigma of his illegitimacy explains both his ambition, and his strivings to attain a throne for himself. He came close to achieving the latter, when in 1726, he became involved with Ann Ivanova, Duchess of Courland and the future Tsarina of Russia. The elective throne of Courland became vacant, and with Anna's support, de Saxe became the duchy's ruler. However, in 1722 he was expelled by the Russians to prevent him marrying Anna. With his hopes of marriage thwarted, he returned to Paris, now destined to achieve fame as a general in the service of France rather than spend his life as a minor Baltic princeling.

Learning from great contemporaries
Military influences loomed large in the young Hermann-Maurice's life. He much admired Marshal Count von der Schulenberg, a leading soldier of fortune of the day. At the age of 13, de Saxe first saw action at close quarters, serving in the army of *Eugène of Savoy* in Flanders. He entered French service in 1719 as the colonel of a German regiment, purchased for him by his father, having already had spells in Russian and imperial service.

De Saxe now began a serious study of the art of war, soon gaining a reputation as an efficient soldier, a good regimental officer and a talented trainer of men. He also earned an entirely deserved reputation for hard living and womanizing. This did not prevent him from becoming a major-general in 1720, however. In the War of the Polish Succession (1734-38), he served under Marshal Berwick and his particular patron, the Duc de Noailles. De Saxe won laurels at the siege of Phillipsburg in 1736, and emerged from the war as a lieutenant general. Ironically, de Saxe was fighting to unseat his brother, who had been elected King of Poland, and the command of the Saxon army had in fact been offered to de Saxe.

War of the Austrian Succession
At the outbreak of the War of the Austrian Succession in 1740 de Saxe served with the French forces in Bohemia. In November 1741 he assaulted Prague and captured it by sending a force to scale the walls. In April 1742 he defeated an Austrian force at Egra. Although the French were forced out of Bohemia the same year, de Saxe's reputation had been enhanced by the campaign. After the defeat at Dettingen (1743), de Saxe was appointed to assist de Noailles, the *de facto* French commander-in-chief, and he played an important role in whipping – on occasions, literally – the French army back into shape. After a period of campaigning on the Rhine, in January 1744 de Saxe took command of an army at Dunkirk. It was intended that de Saxe would land in Britain to support the "Young Pretender", the Stuart Prince Charles Edward ("Bonnie Prince Charlie"), but a storm destroyed the French fleet in March and de Saxe was added to the long list of would-be invaders of England.

Marshal of France
In March 1744 Saxe became a marshal of France, and the period of his greatest successes began. In May 1745 he besieged Tournai, in Flanders, and when the so-called Pragmatic army, under the Duke of Cumberland, advanced to relieve the city, de Saxe gave battle at Fontenoy (11 May 1745). His army absorbed the allied attack, although at one point the situation was so grave that de Saxe, sick with dropsy, had to personally intervene to rally his men. The French then counterattacked to win de Saxe's greatest victory. A series of the most important towns in Flanders fell into his hands as a result, including Brussels and Antwerp, which were taken in February 1746. At Raucoux on 11 October 1746 de Saxe added the oft-beaten Prince Charles of Lorraine to his list of victims (*see Frederick the Great*).

The final phase of de Saxe's career was spent campaigning in the Netherlands. He was appointed Marshal-General of France in 1747. Only two other men had ever received this title, and its bestowal was confirmation that de Saxe had become one of the most powerful men in France. His last battle was at Lauffeld, near Maastricht, on 2 July 1747 where he overcame the handicap of an army of indifferent quality to defeat Cumberland again.

In 1732 de Saxe had written *Mes Reveries* (My Thoughts), which were a distillation of his research and ideas on the practice of war. These contained a number of forward-looking ideas, including the establishment of all-arms combat groups, and the use of light infantry. He attacked the immobility of 18th-century warfare, and put forward sound ideas on training and discipline and morale. The book was published posthumously. Though de Saxe has tended to be overshadowed by Frederick the Great, he was much admired by *Napoleon*.

SCHWARZENBERG
Karl Philipp von (1771-1820)
AUSTRIAN GENERAL
Napoleonic Wars

Schwarzenberg has sometimes been likened as a commander to *Eisenhower*. Both men served as the supreme commander of a heterogeneous group of national armies, the former against *Napoleon* and the latter against Hitler.

C-IN-C *Schwarzenberg, the Eisenhower of his day.*

Both have been scorned as mere co-ordinators, rather than true fighting generals. Both, however, crowned their careers with an undeniable achievement – leading their respective coalitions to victory.

Prince Karl Philipp von Schwarzenberg was born in Vienna in 1771. He rose quickly in the army of the Hapsburg empire, seeing his first active service at the age of 17 against the Turks. By 1800, he was a major-general, and distinguished himself by covering the retreat of the beaten Austrian army after the battle of Hohenlinden that December. At Ulm, five years later, he again plucked personal glory out of an Austrian defeat, by fighting his way out of Napoleon's encirclement of Mack's army with a force of cavalry.

The diplomatic soldier

Apart from service in the 1809 campaign, Schwarzenberg spent the next few years carving out a reputation in the diplomatic sphere. He was intimately involved in the negotiations leading to Napoleon's marriage to Marie-Louise, the daughter of the Austrian Emperor, sealing an alliance between the old adversaries. In the role of diplomat, he won Napoleon's trust and admiration. Thus Schwarzenberg was a natural choice for the commander of the contingent that Austria was forced to contribute to the Grand Armée for the invasion of Russia in 1812.

The Austrians advanced as far as Pinsk but fought as little as possible, and quietly withdrew into Austrian territory when the news of Napoleon's disastrous retreat from Moscow reached them. Schwarzenberg then commanded the so-called army of observation in Bohemia in 1813, while the Prusso/Russian forces fought Napoleon in Germany. Following an unsuccessful attempt at mediation, Austria entered the war against Napoleon that August and Schwarzenberg was appointed supreme commander of the allied forces. He had 500,000 men under his control, including 230,000 of the army of Bohemia, which he continued to command.

War of attrition

From the very first, Schwarzenberg chose to pursue a strategy of attrition. The Trachenberg plan of August 1813 aimed, as Radetzky, Schwarzenberg's chief of staff wrote, "to avoid any unequal struggle and so to exhaust the enemy, fall upon his weakened part with superior strength and to defeat him in detail". When faced by Napoleon in person, the allied forces would retreat, but others would advance against his subordinates and defeat them. This frank recognition of Napoleon's superiority, and the formulation of a strategy to take account of it, was a mark of Schwarzenberg's flexibility of mind.

Schwarzenberg's tenure of the supreme command was by no means an easy one. The allied monarchs constantly interfered in the decision-making process, while the ultimate aims of the coalition partners were far from identical. In contrast to the Prussian lust for revenge, the Austrians were not entirely convinced that a decisive defeat of Napoleon was in their interests. However, Schwarzenberg's tact and diplomacy were instrumental in holding the alliance together. He defeated Napoleon at Leipzig in October 1813, and then led the armies of the coalition into France in 1814.

Schwarzenberg was paralysed in 1817 and died in 1820. His military epitaph perhaps should be the truthful, but tactless, toast once proposed by Blücher to "the commander-in-chief who had three monarchs at his headquarters and still managed to beat the enemy".

SHAKA
(c.1787-1828)
ZULU KING
Zulu Wars

The Zulu chieftain Shaka was perhaps the finest soldier that Africa has ever produced. An innovative tactician and strategist, he was the architect of a formidable army that built a powerful empire – an army that, 50 years after Shaka's death, was to defeat British regulars in open battle in the Zulu War.

Shaka was born in extremely humble circumstances, probably in 1787. His mother, an eLangeni woman called Nandi, became pregnant by the Zulu chief Senzangakona, the head of what was then a small and uninfluential clan, who, however, considered themselves to be of higher status than the eLangeni. Indeed, Shaka's name originated in an insult, for iShaka was an intestinal beetle, believed to cause menstrual irregularities, which, the Zulu elders claimed, was the true cause of Nandi's "pregnancy". This cruel name reflects the misery of Shaka's childhood as an outcast among the Zulus and later among the eLangeni; his experiences then undoubtedly played a major part in forming his adult personality, which was marked by ambition, ruthlessness and a total disregard for human life.

When Shaka was about 16, he came under the protection of Dingiswayo, king of the Mthethwa. The latter had succeeded in forming the various tribal clans into a confederation under his leadership, partly by organizing his army into disciplined regiments and recruiting defeated enemies into his forces (Shaka absorbed these lessons, later applying them when king of the Zulus). He served in Dingiswayo's army and obtained a formidable reputation as a warrior. Legend has it that a victory in single combat led to Shaka being appointed to command the iziCwe regiment. He then began to develop the methods that he would later apply to the entire Zulu army. He equipped his men with a stabbing assegai, in place of a lighter version, which was used as a missile weapon. He developed a tactic (demonstrated in his famous single combat) of using a heavy hide shield as a weapon with which to expose the side of an enemy to an assegai thrust. The usual oxhide sandals were dispensed with, in order to increase speed; and his Mthethwa men were hardened to be able to cover as much as 50 miles at a trot. Adolescent boys, (the uDibi), were allocated to supporting regiments to carry weapons and other equipment.

The "buffalo" formation

Shaka's strategic innovations consisted of the introduction of the famous "buffalo" formation. Units were formed into four sections – two "horns", the "chest" and the "loins". The "horns" were trained to outflank an enemy force and eventually encircle it, while the "chest" engaged the enemy frontally. The men in the "loins" formed a reserve, often sitting facing away from the action so as not to get overexcited. Shaka would direct the battle by the means of runners. Further, Shaka was prepared to use methods previously unknown to his culture – such as a scorched-earth policy when Zululand was invaded by the Ndwandwe in 1819.

Shaka took control of the Zulus in 1816 and raised regiments on the Mthethwa pattern. Although the Zulus had previously been unimportant, and he had only a few warriors, he began to bring neighboring clans under his control and, after the death of Dingiswayo, started to fashion an empire of his own. In 1819 he crushed the Ndwandwe, after surviving perhaps the hardest-fought battle of his career at Gqokli Hill the year before. By the time of his death, Shaka had brought 250,000 people under his sway.

The name of Shaka was synonymous with bloodshed. He was merciless to his enemies, and enforced his will by the instillation of terror, founded on a reputation for casual murder of any who displeased him: he was responsible, in one way or another, for about 2 million deaths during his reign. In 1828 Shaka himself was murdered by two half-brothers. Already, cracks were beginning to appear in the edifice he had created. War-weariness, and disillusionment with Shaka's very individual style of leadership – which included the enforcing of chastity on most of his warriors – undermined the morale of the army. Nevertheless, Shaka's achievements cannot be denied.

TAYLOR
Zachary (1784-1850)
US GENERAL AND PRESIDENT
Mexican-American War

Zachary Taylor was a regular soldier with much frontier experience who earned popular renown as a result of his victories in the Mexican-American War of 1846-47.

Taylor was born in Virginia on 24 November 1784. His father had a military background, having fought in the

THE FRONTIERSMAN *Zachary Taylor won notable victories in the Mexican War and went on to become US president.*

recently concluded American War of Independence as an officer, and Taylor became a regular officer in the 7th US Infantry in 1808. He was to see much service against the Indians on the frontier. In 1812, as a captain, he successfully defended Fort Harrison, Indiana, against a large warband and was promoted to the rank of major as a result.

Soldiering on the frontier

The years following the end of the War of 1812 against the British in 1815 were lean ones for the US army, and Taylor was fortunate to be retained in the service – to ensure this, he reverted to the rank of captain. Two decades of arduous frontier soldiering and eventual promotion followed. In 1832, as commander of the 1st Infantry, Taylor – now a colonel – fought in the Black Hawk war. Five years later he campaigned in the swamps of Florida as the effective commander of the US field army.

In 1835, Seminole Indians had massacred 107 men of the 4th Infantry under Captain Dade, and an exhausting guerrilla war started. It was to last for six years. The US army was ill-prepared for this type of irregular warfare and a series of US officers tried – and failed – to defeat the Seminoles. In July 1837 Taylor was ordered to take command and on 25 December managed to force them to fight a conventional action near Lake Okeechobee. The result was a convincing victory. Promoted to brevet brigadier-general, Taylor then developed an intelligent long term strategy to defeat the Indian guerrilla campaign, based on building forts every 20 miles or so, and then mounting frequent sweeps through the surrounding district to flush out hostile Indians. When Washington complained about the slowness of progress, Taylor asked to be given a fresh command and returned to the frontier, with his headquarters at Fort Smith, Arkansas.

In early 1846 Taylor was sent from Corpus Christi, Texas, to the Rio Grande. Texas had won its independence from Mexico in 1836 and, on appealing to Washington, had later been absorbed into the USA. Taylor's march brought him into territory claimed by Mexico and provoked war. Taylor's 3,800 men were opposed by 5,700 Mexicans, whom Taylor defeated on 8 May at Palo Alto. The following day Taylor attacked at Resaca de la Palma and pushed the Mexicans back over the Rio Grande. By skillful generalship, Taylor had succeeded in ensuring that US losses were light. He invaded Mexico proper on 18 May, five days after the official declaration of war.

"Old Rough and Ready"

Democratic President James Knox Polk disliked Taylor and had serious reservations about his professional competence, even saying that "He is brave but does not seem to have resources or grasp of mind enough to conduct a campaign". Taylor clashed with Polk over the government policy of sending untrained volunteers to serve with his forces. Taylor was a blunt man, not given to diplomatic language. Polk, who had a cold and reserved character, was greatly offended by Taylor's intemperance. To make matters worse, Polk rightly suspected both Taylor and Winfield Scott (see below), who were both Whigs, of harboring presidential ambitions.

Polk had no wish to see either man ride to power on the back of a victory. He thus opposed Taylor's plan to strike into Mexico in August. Taylor, however, ignored Polk and captured Monterrey after stiff fighting; his 6,000 men were opposed by 10,000 Mexicans under de Ampudia (20-24 September). After an armistice, disowned by Polk, Taylor took Saltillo (16 November). Polk sought to deny Taylor the glory of an advance to Mexico City, and reluctantly appointed Scott to command an expedition to be sent by sea to Mexico. Taylor was stripped of many troops and ordered on to the defensive. However, in February 1847 a Mexican army under President Santa Anna moved against the northern forces under Taylor, hoping to exploit the division of the US force. At the battle of Buena Vista, Taylor won his last victory (22 February 1847).

Buena Vista effectively brought Taylor's part in the war to an end. In 1848 Polk's fears were confirmed when Taylor defeated the Democratic candidate and was elected President. He died in 1850 before he could complete his term of office.

Taylor was far from the incompetent portrayed by Polk. Although he had little formal education, he proved to have a sound grasp of the various arts of war. At Palo Alto, for instance, he won a pitched battle of the traditional sort; he took Monterrey by street fighting; and his strategy in the Seminole War foreshadowed some of the techniques of modern counter-insurgency. His nickname of "Old Rough and Ready" neatly summarizes his approach to warfare.

TILLY
Johann Tserclaes (1559-1632)
FLEMISH MERCENARY IN BAVARIAN SERVICE
Thirty Years' War

Tilly, commander of the forces of the Catholic League for much of the Thirty Years' War, was an able, but conventional, general. Though successful for a number of years, he proved unable to match the new tactics and dynamism of *Gustavus Adolphus*. Born in Brabant, at the family seat of Tilly, his childhood, however, was spent in exile in Germany, where he was educated by the Jesuits. His father, who had been forced into exile

THE MERCENARY *Tilly, one of the key Catholic commanders of the Thirty Years' War.*

in 1568 was reconciled with the rulers of the Spanish Netherlands in 1574 and the young Tilly joined a Walloon regiment. He cut his military teeth at the siege of Antwerp, serving under the great *Parma*. The latter, whom Tilly greatly admired, died in 1592; in 1594, Tilly joined the army of Emperor Rudolph II, with whom he fought against the Turks.

Tilly's move into the service of the Holy Roman Emperor was to shape the pattern of the rest of his life. He incurred the displeasure of Rudolph's successor, Matthias, and offered his sword to Duke Maximillian of Bavaria in 1610. The conflict that was to rage across Germany for three decades broke out eight years later, and in 1620 Tilly led the army of the Catholic League into action against the Protestants of Bohemia. The League had been created in 1610. Its forces amounted to some 25,000 men, including the Bavarian army, which Tilly had turned into an extremely effective fighting force. In concert with an imperial army commanded by de Bucquoi, Tilly crushed the rebel Protestant forces of the Elector Palantine at the battle of the White Mountain (8 November 1620). Prague fell and was sacked; a similar fate was to befall central European towns and cities.

Until Gustavus, victorious

Tilly then turned his attention to eradicating Protestant support in Germany, winning victories at Wimpfen (6 May 1622), investing and storming Heidelberg in September of the same year, and inflicting devastating losses on the army of Christian of Brunswick at Stadtlohn (6 August 1623). Christian of Denmark entered the war in 1625 in an attempt to arrest the apparently irresistable onward march of the Catholic forces. Once again, Tilly's shrewd generalship and his mastery of the "Spanish" tactics of the *tercio* combined with the efficiency of his soldiers to overwhelm a Protestant opponent and the Danes were destroyed at the battle of Lutter (24-27 August 1626). At this time Tilly was co-operating uneasily with the Bohemian mercenary *Wallenstein*, who had been hired by Emperor Ferdinand II to command an imperial army with the intention of lessening his dependence on the Catholic League forces. Between them, Wallenstein and Tilly extended Catholic control over most of northern Germany and continental Denmark, but in 1630 the former fell victim to the jealousies of members of the League and was dismissed from his command. Tilly took up the unwelcome burden of command of both armies. He was now forced to serve two masters – Maximillian and Ferdinand II – who were frequently at odds with each other.

In 1631 Tilley campaigned against Gustavus Adolphus of Sweden. He besieged and took Magdeburg in May, which was then sacked and pillaged, 25,000 civilians being killed. At Breitenfeld on 17 September 1631 Tilly once again used the tried and tested tactical methods that had won him so many battles, but was badly beaten by Gustavus, who employed radically new tactics. Tilly, however, succeeded in returning to the fray by the end of the year. In 1632 he prepared to counter a Swedish invasion of Bavaria, only to be defeated again by Gustavus at the battle of the River Lech (15-16 April 1632) – an action in which Tilly was severely wounded. He died on 30 April 1632 at Ingolstadt.

Tilly was a consummate professional soldier who, within the limits of the tactical conventions of the day, was the equal of any other general. When, as an old man, he was faced with a totally new type of warfare, he found himself out of his depth. His death is symbolic of the end of an era and the passing of the style of warfare of which he was an undisputed master. His personal conduct, in particular his allegiance to first Rudolph and them Maximillian, stands in sharp contrast to the machinations of his self-centered rival, Wallenstein.

TURENNE
Henri de la Tour d'Auvergene (1611-75)
FRENCH GENERAL
Thirty Years' War, Wars of Louis XIV

Though Turenne surpassed other contemporary generals in his achievements, he remained a man of his time. Exceptionally gifted tactically – especially in the tactics of maneuver – on the battlefield itself he was conventional and sometimes even cautious.

Turenne's family had a military background, so he was literally born to the profession of arms. He gained experience serving with the Dutch and the Swedes and soon showed his command talents. By 1643 he was recognized as one of Europe's most able generals and so was sent to take command of the remnants of a Franco-German army that had recently been beaten by Mercy's Bavarians. Always a great husbander and manager of his men, Turenne was soon on the offensive.

Turenne and Condé
Reinforced by *Condé*, the French beat Mercy at Freiburg (3 August to 9 August 1644), Turenne leading the key flanking movements that turned the tide of battle in favor of the French forces. The following year, Turenne advanced into Germany, but his over-extended army was surprised by Mercy at Mergenthein and defeated through the rashness of one of Turenne's subordinates. The arrival of Condé with reinforcements stabilized the situation; Mercy was defeated and killed at Nordlingen.

These campaigns highlight the essential differences between Turenne and Condé. The latter was the master of the aggressive attack and the destruction of the enemy on the field, no matter what the cost. Turenne, on the other hand, preferred to out-maneuver his opponents and destroy their effectiveness by forcing them to retreat. In combination, the two men were extremely successful.

The willingness to co-operate was one of Turenne's major strengths. In 1648 he combined with the Swedish general Wrangel to surprise the opposing imperialist forces at Zumarhausen on 17 May. At the battle of the Dunes in Flanders on 14 June 1658, Turenne, now in command of a combined Anglo-French army, routed the opposing Spanish. His English troops, under Morgan, seized a key dune on the Spanish right, while French cavalry outflanked them on the left. Faced with these twin threats, the Spanish collapsed.

A four-front war
Two subsequent campaigns in Flanders – in 1667 and 1672 – ushered in a new style of European warfare. Large armies now operated in combination on several fronts. There were no major battles, though several towns were captured; the presence of Louis XIV inhibited Turenne's freedom of action. What became clear was that French aggression had stirred up a hornet's nest, with the formation of a coalition of the Dutch, Spanish, German and imperialists. Louvois, Louis' minister of war, now had to mobilize men and materials for a war on four fronts.

Turenne was despatched to Alsace to hold off the imperialists. At Sintzheim (16 June 1764), he surprised and defeated Caprara, the imperialist commander, but his army was not strong enough to exploit this success and he was forced to recross the Rhine. Early the following month, he returned to the right bank, where his men devastated the Palatinate (the area between the Rhine and the Neckar) be-

MARSHAL OF FRANCE
Turenne, the master of maneuver on the battlefield.

fore withdrawing once again. In the meantime, the imperialists themselves marched northwards, eventually crossing the Rhine at Strasbourg. Anxious to attack them before they could be reinforced by a powerful Prussian force, Turenne forced battle at Entzheim on 4 October 1674. There, though he failed to win a decisive victory, he established a clear moral ascendency over an enemy army of nearly twice his strength.

The arrival of the Prussians brought the strength of the imperialist army up to 57,000 men, at which point Turenne fell back. It was now very late in the campaigning season and the winter weather in the Vosges Mountains and the Black Forest was severe. Thinking that the French had gone into winter quarters, the imperialists settled down to spend the winter on French soil. They had reckoned without Turenne, however. At the start of the 1674 campaigning season, he had vowed that he would not let the imperialist army winter undisturbed in France and he was now to be as good as his word. Deciding on a shock winter campaign, he broke quarters in December and, screened by the Vosges, marched his men in separate columns south to Belfort. On 31 December Turenne's 28,000-strong army debouched from the Belfort Gap on to the plain of the Rhine. The imperialists; scattered in quarters and cantonments all over the region, were taken completely by surprise by the arrival of the French. Desperately they tried to concentrate their forces between Colmar and the little town of Turckenheim. There, the two armies clashed on 5 January 1675, the imperialists being taken in flank and forced back over the Rhine. During the next campaigning season, Turenne sought to capitalize on his advantage, but he was killed by a cannon shot at Nieder Sasback before he could set the seal on his greatest campaign.

The master of planning and maneuver, Turenne always measured the risks of any action against its possible rewards. His final campaign amply demonstrated his ability to conceive and execute a grand tactical concept, even though his death meant that it could not be fulfilled.

WALLENSTEIN
Albrecht Eusebius Wenzel von (1583-1634)
BOHEMIAN MERCENARY IN IMPERIAL SERVICE
Thirty Years' War

Twice commander-in-chief of the armies of the Holy Roman Empire, Wallenstein's ability as a general was matched by his naked greed. His career, in sharp contrast to that of his contemporary *Tilly*, was dominated by his worship of the twin gods of wealth and power. Wallenstein was born into the minor nobility of Bohemia on 24 September 1583. In 1606 he converted from the Protestantism of his birth to Catholicism, which opened the possibility of a career in the service of the Holy Roman

Empire. This piece of opportunism brought Wallenstein a swift reward, for his spiritual counsellor, a Jesuit, arranged his marriage to an extremely wealthy widow, who died in 1614 after only five years of marriage, leaving Wallenstein a substantial landowner. His inherited wealth allowed him to further ingratiate himself with the emperor. He paid for a mercenary cavalry regiment to fight in the Venetian war of 1618.

ENIGMA *Wallenstein, though a fine commander, alienated his masters.*

In the same year, Wallenstein's Protestant compatriots in Bohemia revolted against the empire, but he remained loyal. His calculated risk paid off handsomely. After serving with a cavalry regiment that he raised, Wallenstein was rewarded for his distinguished service and loyalty by the restoration of his lands (confiscated by the rebels) and appointed Governor of Bohemia. Given permission to mint debased coinage, he acquired vast estates off rebel nobles for prices far below their actual value. In 1625 Wallenstein was granted the title of Duke of Friedland to accompany his private kingdom in north-east Bohemia. By that date he was one of the richest and most powerful men in the empire, but still his ambitions were not satisfied.

Personal power, not integrity
The Emperor Ferdinand II was eager to assert his independence from his powerful ally, Maximillian of Bavaria, whose Catholic League army was the only effective fighting force that the empire could call upon for aid. On the entry of Christian of Denmark into the Thirty Years' War on the Protestant side in 1625, Wallenstein offered to recruit and pay for a 24,000-strong army. Wallenstein's "expenses" would be extracted from conquered Protestant areas in the form of loot or taxes. Wallenstein ensured that his regimental commanders gave their loyalty to him – and not to Ferdinand – by lending them money to recruit troops, who were lavishly equipped from factories on his lands.

On 25 April 1626, Wallenstein's new army won its first victory, at Dessau over Mansfeldt. This further strengthened Wallenstein's hand, and the emperor was forced to allow him greater independence and to recruit up to 70,000 men in order to retain his services. As if to demonstrate his indispensability , he forced the Hungarian rebels to accept peace in December 1626 and, with Tilly, inflicted defeats on the Danes and extended Catholic control over much of northern Germany.

In 1628 Wallenstein's attempt to take Stralsund was thwarted. This brought about the collapse of his ambitious plan to create an imperial trading company to challenge the commercial domination of the English and

Dutch. In addition, he began to forge links with Protestant north German states, such as the Hanseatic towns, and to press for conciliatory terms to be offered to the Protestants. This, indeed, was a strange move for the supreme commander of the army of the Catholic emperor and was symptomatic of his increasingly independent stance. As a reward for his services, Wallenstein became hereditary ruler of the duchy of Mecklenburg, but his rapid advance to power had earned the jealousy and fear of the German princes. An imperial army was a dangerous and unwelcome novelty, and rulers from both sides of the religious divide had reason to fear for their independence. In 1630 they forced the emperor to dismiss Wallenstein.

The embittered Wallenstein began to negotiate with *Gustavus Adolphus* of Sweden to form an alliance to attack the emperor. At Breitenfeld in September 1631 Tilly's army of the Catholic League was destroyed by the Swedes, and Ferdinand reinstated Wallenstein. The mercenary demanded and received stiff terms for returning to imperial service. After a successful campaign, in which he drove the Swedes from southern Germany, he repulsed Gustavus at Alte Veste in August 1632 but was defeated at Lützen (16 November 1632). However, with the death of Gustavus in the latter battle, the main threat to the Catholic cause was removed, and Wallenstein suddenly became vulnerable as a result. This time, he overreached himself; by refusing imperial orders and, intriguing with France, Saxony, Sweden and Brandenburg while at the same time protesting his loyalty to the emperor, he was left in a position where his word was deemed worthless by all. In 1634 his subordinates mounted a coup against him, and he was murdered by a group of English and Scots officers.

Wallenstein was a complex man, who combined an intense belief in astrology – which may have contributed to his misguided belief in the loyalty of his officers – with hardheaded calculation. He showed great ability as a military administrator; the preparations for war of his imperial army were, for the time, very thorough. To arrive at a verdict on Wallenstein's caliber as a general is more difficult. While his victories were impressive, they were achieved against inferior opponents. When faced by the genius and new tactics of Gustavus he was, like Tilly, unsuccessful.

WASHINGTON
George (1732-99)
AMERICAN GENERAL
American War of Independence

At the end of the American War of Independence, Washington described his army as "composed of Men sometimes half starved; always in Rags, without pay and experiencing, at times, every species of distress which human nature is capable of undergoing." His success in defeating a disciplined, efficient regular opposition with such raw material guarantees his place in any listing of the great commanders of history.

Washington was born in Virginia in 1732, the descendent of immigrants from Northamptonshire. His father was a tobacco planter, owning several plantations, so Washington had a comfortable upbringing. One of the formative experiences of his life occurred between the ages of 16 and 19, when he surveyed the largely unexplored Shenandoah Valley. Later, Washington served as an officer in the Virginia militia. As a lieutenant colonel, he accompanied them on an expedition to the Ohio River against the French in 1754. The following year he served as an ADC to General Braddock, and escaped with his life from "Braddock's Massacre" that July.

His political career began in earnest in 1758, when he became a member of the Virginian House of Burgesses. Washington became opposed to British rule as the government sought to recoup the expense of protecting the colonies by taxing the colonists themselves. Thus he opposed the Stamp Act of 1765. As a respected and wealthy man, he was a prominent member of the two Continental Congresses that set themselves up as an alternative government to the colonial administration. Despite his limited experience as a soldier, in June 1775 he was appointed commander of the rebel forces.

A struggle for survival

The first years of the war were a constant battle for survival; to have nursed the revolutionary cause through this phase was not the least of Washington's achievements. Although he forced the British to abandon Boston in March 1776, he was beaten at the battle of Long Island on 27 August and forced to retreat, being defeated time after time as he retired through the state of New York, although the British never won a decisive victory. For his part, Washington had occasional successes; he brought off a spectacular surprise success at Trenton on 26 December 1776, and then inflicted a defeat on a column of British reinforcements at Princeton. By this time, he had realized the futility of attempting to defeat the British by fighting conventional campaigns. Instead, as he himself wrote, the American strategy should be "on all Occasions [to] avoid a general Action." Instead, what he termed "a War of Posts" would be fought. This was an attritional strategy. By forcing the British to hunt him down, Washington hoped to overstretch their resources and exhaust them, and this strategy was eventually to bear fruit, earning *Frederick the Great*'s admiration. However, the Continental Army was not, as might have been expected from such a declaration, a guerrilla force; it was modeled on contemporary European lines.

The immediate result of this strategy were meager. Washington was defeated at Brandywine in September 1777 and forced to withdraw to Valley Forge, where his army endured a terrible winter of privation, but received some excellent training from a former Prussian staff officer, Baron von Steuben. Washington gave the Prussian his full support, and von Steuben displayed remarkable respect for the differences in attitude between

FATHER OF HIS COUNTRY *George Washington kept the Continental Army together to win American independence.*

European soldiery and the products of a frontier society in producing a reasonably disciplined army. Washington was thus able to face 1778 with greater optimism.

In 1778 France entered the war against the British, French naval power acting as an effective counterweight to the Royal Navy, which have given the British a great advantage in earlier years. Washington fought an indecisive battle at Monmouth, which, however, forced the British to withdraw; the performance of the Continental Army here was particularly encouraging. He then remained watching the British in New York while the main battles of the next three years were fought in the south. In September 1781, however, with the aid of French regulars and seapower, he forced a British army under Cornwallis to surrender at Yorktown. Although the war dragged on for another two years, Yorktown ensured that the British could never again pose a serious threat to the independence of their former colonies. Washington was acclaimed as a popular hero, becoming the first president of the USA in 1789.

Overcoming handicaps

Washington overcame considerable difficulties to achieve his eventual success. He was overwhelmed by pressure of work, lacking an effective staff; the quality of his forces at no time matched that of his enemy; he accepted no pay and took no leave; and he had to cope with political pres-

sures to fight a more aggressive war – a policy that Washington knew all too well would lead to disaster if adopted. While not a great battlefield commander, he showed a shrewd appreciation of strategic realities in his handling of the war and great tenacity and willpower.

WELLINGTON
Arthur Wellesley, 1st Duke of (1769-1852)
BRITISH
Napoleonic Wars

Britain's finest military leader since *Marlborough* and the vanquisher of *Napoleon*, Arthur Wellesley was the fifth son of an impoverished Anglo-Irish peer. He was educated at Eton and a French military school at Angers, where he was not regarded as an outstanding pupil. For the want of a better career, Wellesly was commissioned into the 73rd Foot in 1787. Thanks to the system of purchasing promotion and some judicious exchange of regiments, he was a lieutenant-colonel by 1794 commanding the 33rd Foot (now part of the Duke of Wellington's Regiment) at the age of 25. He fought in the ill-fated Walcheren campaign of that year against Revolutionary France, at one stage being put in temporary command of a brigade. He was later to say that this campaign taught him at least "what one ought not to do, and that is always something."

Sent to India with the 33rd Foot in 1796, Wellesley began to apply himself seriously to his profession, and started to cultivate the self-discipline that was later to earn him the soubriquet of the "Iron Duke". He abstained from gambling and heavy drinking, for instance – these were among the usual diversions of the average British officer of the day. The arrival of his elder brother, Lord Mornington, as Governor-General of Bengal gave his career a fillip. Wellesley defeated Tippoo Sahib, a native ruler allied to the French, at Seringapatam in 1799. Later, in his first major independent command, Wellesley (promoted to major-general in 1802) gained an impressive, but costly, victory over the Mahrattas at Assaye in 1803. This Indian apprenticeship brought him a knighthood the following year, but, more importantly, much practical experience of campaigning and the political problems of exercising command.

The Peninsular War

Wellesley spent the next few years pursuing a political career in England. In 1807 he commanded a brigade in an expedition against Copenhagen, the Danish capital, and was the victor at Kioge that August; the following year, he was dispatched to Portugal to support the Portuguese, who had recently risen against Napoleon. He won the victories of Roliça and Vimiero (17 August and 21 August 1808), but was then superceded by two more senior generals, who signed the Convention of Cintra. This

THE IRON DUKE *Wellington's ability to strike from the defensive served him well in the Peninsular War in Spain.*

allowed the beaten French to be transported home in British ships. Following the death of *Moore* in 1809, Wellesley returned to command the British forces in Portugal, and his long and successful campaign in the peninsula began in earnest.

Striking first at Soult at Oporto, Wellesley defeated the French commander on 12 May 1809, following up his victory with an invasion of Spain in co-operation with Spanish forces. Despite victory at Talavera (27-28 July), however, he was forced to fall back on his base in Portugal, disillusioned by the incompetence of the Spanish leadership and the poor quality of the Spanish armies. In future, Viscount Wellington (as he became after Talavera) would rely on his own army. This included large numbers of Portuguese, trained by a British general, Beresford, who were to become, in Wellington's words, the "fighting cocks" of the army.

In 1810, Marshals Massena and *Ney* led another French army into Portugal. At Bussaco (26 September 1810) they were defeated in a classic Wellingtonian defensive victory. The Anglo-Portuguese, in line on top of a steep ridge, drove back the advancing French columns. Wellington then fell back to Lisbon, which was protected by a powerful system of fortifications – the celebrated Lines of Torres Vedras. While Wellington was kept supplied by the Royal Navy, the French starved in a countryside swept bare by his "scorched earth" policy, until they were forced into retreat the following April. Wellington pursued them to defeat Massena at Fuentes d'Onoro in May.

This was one of the British general's hardest fought battles, and one of the relatively few in which the French attempted to out-maneuver him.

1811 saw the elimination of the French threat to Portugal. The following year, Wellington took the offensive. He besieged and captured the frontier fortresses of Civdad Rodrigo and Badajoz, the so-called "keys of Spain", and then decisively defeated Marmont in an opportunistic offensive victory at Salamanca on 22 July. After occupying Madrid, and being created a marquis, Wellington once again retired on Portugal. Although this was a disappointing end to the campaign, the French had been forced to abandon much of southern Spain to the Spanish guerrillas in order to concentrate on the British.

The following year, Wellington ignored Madrid and headed to the north-east; by outflanking the French, he forced them into a wholesale retreat, and at Vittoria on 21 June he won a decisive victory, which sealed the fate of Napoleon's Iberian adventure. It also won Wellington a field-marshal's baton. From September to December, Wellington and Soult fought a bitter series of actions in the Pyrenees, before the British invaded France in early 1814. Wellington's campaign, which had begun in Oporto five years before, ended with the battle of Toulouse on 10 April 1814, after which he heard that Napoleon had been forced to abdicate by the advance of *Schwarzenberg*'s forces from the east.

The "conqueror of Europe"

Wellington's reputation had by now reached dizzy heights. Beethoven composed a battle symphony to celebrate Vittoria; and wherever he went, Wellington was fêted as a conquering hero, the "conqueror of the conqueror of Europe". When in March 1815 the news of Napoleon's escape from Elba reached the Congress of Vienna, where Wellington was representing Britain, Tsar Alexander I of Russia expressed the general feeling when he told the newly created duke: "It is for you to save the world again".

Wellington's final victory at *Waterloo* broke Napoleon's power for ever. Wellington then resumed his political career, becoming Prime Minister from 1828 to 1830. He was unpopular as a politician, while his conservative influence tended to stifle attempts at army reform, but at the end of his life he regained his earlier popularity. The popular image of the 'Iron Duke' was bolstered by his pithy, patrician comments (such as referring to the soldiers he commanded as the "scum of the earth"), but he was not hard-hearted and possessed a good deal of personal charisma. He was admired by his soldiers as a fine fighting general, who ensured that they were well-fed, and was sparing of their lives, if only because he was well aware that his army could not be replaced if it was destroyed. He was courageous under fire, and a consummate professional in an army of amateurs; the blunders he had seen on the Dutch campaign were never forgotten.

Wellington had a brilliant eye for terrain, which maximized the defensive power of his sturdy infantry, which he deployed in a two-deep line, thus allowing volly musket fire. Wellington used a thick cloud of skirmishers to drive away the French *voltigeurs*, and then completed the damage caused by the fire-fight with a bayonet charge. As the battles of Salamanca and Vittoria proved, among others, Wellington had an equal flair for the attacking battle. He also possessed wide strategic vision; in Spain, he used his army as a mobile élite force to strike rapid and devastating blows against the French, who were overstretched in trying to hold down large tracts of the countryside against the of the Spanish guerrillas.

Wellington was perhaps the finest soldier Britain has ever produced. Like Marlborough, his only equal, he made the British army a force to be feared.

WOLFE
James (1727-59)
BRITISH GENERAL
Seven Years' War

"Mad is he? Then I hope he will bite some of my other generals!" George II's trenchant comment aptly sums up the character of James Wolfe, one of the greatest British military heroes of the 18th century. Wolfe was unpredictable, arrogant and emotional – a man whose brilliance, some believed, balanced on the edge of insanity. He was killed in action at the age of only 32, but, at least according to his admirers, even his brief military career showed promise of true greatness.

Wolfe was born into a military family in Westerham, Kent, in 1727. As was the custom of the time, he exchanged between regiments in order to gain promotion. While serving as the 16-year-old acting adjutant of the 12th Foot, Wolfe fought at Dettingen in 1743. His promise was noted at an early stage, and in 1745 he acted as an aide-de-camp to General Hawley at Culloden, the battle in which the last hopes of the Jacobite Pretender to

the British throne were finally extinguished. At the end of the War of the Austrian Succession (1740-48) Wolfe was a major with much experience of campaigning behind him. He was still only 21 years old.

Promoted to lieutenant colonel in 1750, he commanded the 20th Foot (later the Lancashire Fusiliers) and won a reputation as a brilliant trainer of men and as an efficient and keen, if somewhat eccentric, regimental officer. His dynamic and feverish activity may be explained by his poor health. He suffered from consumption and from bouts of depression, and, perhaps in compensation, was throughout his life driven by an inner demon, which lead to his reputation for madness among some of his less well-motivated peers.

Wolf's chance to prove himself came in 1757. The Seven Years' War (1757-63) again ranged Britain against France, and Wolfe was the only man to emerge with an enhanced reputation from a disastrous expedition to Rochefort, on the French Atlantic coast. As a result, he was appointed a brigade commander in an expedition against the fortress of Louisberg in Canada. Under the overall command of Amhurst, Wolfe distinguished himself in a series of daring operations, beginning with an amphibious assault that he led in person (9 June 1758). News of his activities reached the elder Pitt, the mastermind behind the British war effort, and on his return to England Wolfe was appointed to command the force to be sent against Quebec, but promoted to the rank of major-general for the purposes of the expedition.

The British arrived outside Quebec in June 1759, after a dangerous journey up the St Lawrence river. Wolfe's force of about 5,000 effectives was not strong enough to assault the formidable fortress system protecting the city, which Montcalm, the French commander, defended skillfully. The latter showed little indication of being obliging enough to come out to fight, having a numerically strong, but unreliable, army. Wolfe was faced with dissension among his senior commanders, and was extremely sick, so he decided on a risky strategem.

Storming the Heights of Abraham
On 12 September 1759, Wolfe's troops took to the river and landed at the foot of the Heights of Abraham. They scrambled up the steep slopes to deploy on the plain beyond. Perhaps imagining that this was only an advanced guard, Montcalm marched out to meet Wolfe, but was defeated, both men perishing in the course of the battle. Wolfe's victory led to the capture of Quebec; a year later the whole of Canada was British.

The capture of Quebec and the manner of his death turned Wolfe into an instant hero. As a result some extravagant claims have been made about what he might have achieved had he lived – and had he survived his persistant ill-health. Historical evidence, however, casts a shadow over such claims. While the final act was unquestionably brilliant, the earlier stages of the siege of Quebec were a failure, and it might also be doubted whether the individualism and temperament that Wolfe displayed during the campaign fitted him for high command.

STRANGE GENIUS *When told that Wolfe was "mad", George II wished that he "would bite some of my other generals."*

The Nineteenth Century

Following the defeat of Napoleon in 1815, Europe was at peace for four decades. The next war of major importance in which European armies were involved was fought in the Crimean region of southern Russia. Then a series of nationalist uprisings resulting from the ferment of the revolutionary year of 1848, led to a series of wars from 1859 to 1870 whose outcome changed the political structure of Europe. In 1859 Austria fought a Franco-Italian coalition, a bloody conflict that led to the formation of an independent united Italy. Then, in the wars of German unity, Austria was again defeated – this time by Prussia. The last link in this nationalist chain was the Franco-Prussian war, fought between Prussia, its German allies and France to decide which of the two would be the dominant military power on the European continent. This was followed, once again, by a 40-year period of peace.

US expansionism

Within those years of European conflict – 1859 to 1870 – a great civil war had also been fought out in the USA between the Confederate states of the south and the Federal states of the north. Out of the bitterness of that war – and out of a need to find new horizons – the USA expanded into the largely unexplored areas of the west, but continental America was not the only region in which the USA developed. The decades following the civil war saw the USA engaged in creating a Pacific empire, of which the Philippines was the most important acquisition. The reasons for this were simple. The USA, which had been a largely rural economy before the civil war, became within a very short time a leading industrial power and was suddenly aware of its own importance on the American continent. Bearing in mind the dictates of the Monroe Doctrine, it was now clear that Spanish imperialism in Cuba could not be tolerated and the US set about destroying the influence of Spain as surely as the US had formerly used the threat of armed intervention to crush that of Napoleon III's France in Mexico. If the USA could not create a benevolent Anglo-Saxon sphere of influence, the US could at least ensure that its Central and Latin American neighbors did not represent a threat to its sovereignty.

Into Africa

The struggle by European powers to occupy Africa, the last remaining unexplored continent, resulted in wars that were only of local importance. Even those fought by the Boer farmers of South Africa against the British were not wars in the accepted sense of the word – they were more partisan or guerrilla engagements. It was in the Far East that the next major conflicts erupted, the outcome of the decadence of Manchu China and the rising power of Japan. As a result, large areas of former Chinese territory, notably Korea, were left without a strong ruler. Russia entered that vacuum and consequently was soon involved in hostilities with the Japanese, who also laid claim to them. The resultant war cost Russia its fleet and the defeat on land of the Tsarist forces by the Japanese army.

One major power, however, was left out of the imperialist scramble.

Germany, which had become one nation only after the other great powers had already divided the world into respective spheres of influence, resented its lack of colonies and assuaged its hurt feelings by saber-rattling and the adoption of an aggressive foreign policy. Germany was now not a state with an army, but an army controlling a

state. It was no empty boast that "The German army is the German people under arms."

In the first decade of the 20th century, the other powers of Europe, confronted by a dynamic nation of 80 million industrious, highly literate and disciplined people, reacted in one of two ways. Some nations were determined to crush Germany by force of arms if need be. The others feared the Reich and wished to ally themselves to it out of that fear. The alliances and pacts that were concluded turned the continent into two armed camps. In the one were the Central Powers – Germany, Austria-Hungary and Italy. Aligned against that group were the Entente powers – France and Russia. There were some nations of Europe whose alliances did not bring them automatically into war. The British, for example, though they abandoned their traditional policy of "splendid isolation" to form the *Entente Cordiale* with France, were not duty bound to go to war if France was attacked. It was only when Germany violated Belgian neutrality that Britain became involved.

The armaments race

Britain had long been aware of Germany's intention to rival the Royal Navy through the construction of a modern fleet. The German navy was large, modern and aggressive. The

"SOMEONE HAD BLUNDERED"
The survivors of the Light Brigade after Balaclava. Their charge was "magnificent, but not war."

army was known to be a finely tuned instrument and the whole nation had been mentally prepared to welcome war when it came. For her part, France longed for revenge for the humiliation of 1870 and so was likewise keen to fight. The whole of Europe was expecting war and it needed very little to create the conditions which brought it about. The spark that destroyed the old European order was the assassination of Franz Ferdinand, heir to the throne of Austria-Hungary, by a Serbian nationalist in the summer of 1914. Within four weeks, a minor Balkan war between Serbia and Austria had escalated to become a major conflict in which most of the nations of Europe were soon involved.

The armies which embarked on

the First World War were the beneficiaries of the industrial advances that had occurred throughout the 19th century. The railway age had begun only 20 years after the battle of Waterloo in 1815; yet, within a single generation, western Europe was covered with complex and widespread railway networks. The same development had occurred in the eastern areas of the USA and it was in that country that the railway first showed what a major part it had to play in military operations. The US Civil War was, therefore, the first war in which railway junctions became strategic objectives. A railway system meant that no longer did armies march on foot as had been the case since the beginning of warfare. Now they could be conveyed to battle far faster and would arrive on the battlefield less fatigued.

The telegraph was another invention to be first used widely in the US Civil War. As a result of its invention, it was no longer necessary for despatch riders to gallop between the commander-in-chief and his subordinates. The telegraph transmitted messages more speedily and more reliably than could the horsed aide de camp. Thus, together, the railway and the telegraph revolutionized warfare. The speed with which an army could be mobilized was an important factor in a nation's preparation for war, as was that of how quickly the mobilized forces could be deployed for battle. The army that could achieve both the quickest had a great advantage over its opponents.

Germany was the one nation in Europe which had refined those two skills to the ultimate degree. The Germans accomplished this through the Prussian military staff system, which had been working to make warfare scientific since the reforms of Scharnhorst after Prussia's defeat by Napoleon. The refinement was finally accomplished by von *Moltke*, chief-of-staff of the Prussian army in the wars fought against Denmark, Austria and finally France. The Prussian system of military conscription was adopted throughout Germany, so that there was always one

VICTORIA'S "LITTLE WARS"
Colonial campaigns were poor preparation for modern European warfare, as the British were to find.

part of the male population undergoing training. Behind that trained body was a vast reserve of men who had completed their national service, but were liable for recall in the event of war. Prussian mobilization techniques and deployment plans were so thorough that a unit's mobilization order contained a railway timetable. Each unit knew by which train it had to travel to reach its concentration area.

A school for war
A simple telegraph message to all units set the whole mobilization machinery into operation. Another telegraph message moved the mobilized armies from their concentration areas to their sector of the battlefield where the chief of staff's plan, which had been agreed in advance and whose precise details were familiar to each senior commander, was put into action. Thus, the Prussian system was a masterly example of military organization and efficiency. To ensure that the plan ran smoothly, there were general staff officers in all major formations from supreme command down to divisional level. Those men acted in the name of the chief of staff and their advice was usually heeded, since they brought the same train of logical military thought that the

chief of staff himself employed to any problem that arose. To those dedicated and well-trained professionals, the lure of war was not the emotive joy of commanding men in battle, although they were also competent in that. Rather, war was a whole series of theoretical problems for each of which there was a logical solution. It was a school for war whose structure was finally smashed, not by external enemies, but by Adolf Hitler, Führer of the Third Reich.

Battle plans and actualities
The mobilization of the other European armies was slower than that of Germany. Many Russian conscripts spent days walking to their regimental depots and then footmarched for many more days in order to reach their concentration area. It was upon the slowness of her enemies to mobilize that Germany's war plan of 1914 – the *Schlieffen* Plan – was predicated. Swift mobilization and deployment would mean that a line of armies would be in position along the western frontier shortly before the outbreak of war. When hostilities began the right-wing armies would strike quickly through Belgium and extend across Flanders. When those armies were in line, they would advance southwards to battle.

The French Plan XVII was based upon vengeance for 1870 and proposed an advance into Alsace-Lorraine. Nothing would have suited the German purpose better. When the crack French armies struck eastwards, they would leave their backs only weakly guarded – and into that all but defenceless rear the German right wing armies would strike to crush the French between the frontier defences and the armies guarding them.

It was estimated that it would take some six weeks to accomplish the defeat of France through the Schlieffen Plan. Then, the German railway system would rush the armies in the west to the Eastern Front. In the meantime, any Russian advance, which, owing to the slowness of Russia's mobilization, could not be with the bulk of its forces, would have to be held by the Austro-Hungarian army, with minimal German support. Austria, after all, would have to carry the burden in the east for only six weeks – the time it would take for the Schlieffen Plan to succeed in the west. Then the German armies fresh from the campaign in France would arrive, the Central Powers would smash the Russian hosts and the war would be won.

To ensure the maximum deployment of the Austro–German field armies, certain other nations would also carry a small burden. Italy's support would mean that Austria did not need to keep troops needed in the east guarding the Austro-Italian frontier. Romania, with whom Austria had had a secret treaty since 1881, would put her army into the field to protect the Austrian right wing on the Eastern Front. Neither of those two nations carried out their obligations, but this was not to influence the development of the German battle plan. Schlieffen's plan rolled – and failed.

New technology

Advances in other areas of industry produced the internal combustion engine, which powered motor vehicles as well as the first aircraft. In armaments, too, there had been improvements in propellants as well as in weapons; it was on the battlefields of the US Civil War that the

THE HELIOGRAPH *Inventions like the heliograph were pressed into service to solve the age-old problem of communication on the battlefield.* [1]

prototypes of the machine gun had been employed, for instance. The development of breech-loading rifles increased the infantry's rate of fire from two or three rounds per minute to 15 rounds of aimed and accurate fire per minute. With such a curtain of bullets being fired into such clearly visible targets as long lines of brightly dressed soldiers, it was self evident that formal attacks in the old fashioned, Napoleonic sense of frontal assault were suicidal.

What is surprising is that the military took so long to realize the potency of the new weapons and the need to rethink infantry tactics. In the US Civil War, both sides launched their infantry into frontal assaults against a resolute enemy in prepared positions. The lessons of the futility of such tactics had still not been learned by either side in the Franco-Prussian war, although von Moltke had begun to consider the problem, but, in the opening campaigns of the Russo-Japanese war, 40 years after the US Civil War, columns of infantry of both sides were still being launched in a series of frontal assaults until the terrible losses forced the combatants into trench warfare. Armies went below ground and by removing their infantry from the surface produced the situation of the "empty" battle-

field. Here, the British, who had learned how destructive modern weapons could be from the Boers, produced a professional army, skilled in musketry and at digging trenches and emplacements. They adopted a neutral color for their uniforms and, as a result of the Boer War and campaigning on the northwest frontier of India, had come to terms with the concept of the "empty battlefield" before other European powers. The Austro-Hungarian army had also adopted the new battlefield techniques of camouflage and trenches, but the French infantry attacked in the scarlet and blue uniforms of the Second Empire, using the tactics of that period. French officers thought it chic to die wearing white gloves. In the opening campaigns of 1914, the German infantry also attacked shoulder to shoulder in human waves, until British musketry and French artillery fire forced a change in tactics. The Russians, however, used the human wave tactic in both world wars.

By 1914, armies, or at least some of them, were conveyed by train to a concentration area, then embussed and brought up to the front as far forward as it was possible to drive. In the sky aircraft flew on reconnaissance, trench strafing or on bombing missions. On the ground the degeneration within months from a war of maneuver into one of trench warfare was not to be broken until the marriage of the internal combustion engine to an armored shell produced the tank.

War had come a long way – from long lines of splendidly uniformed soldiers, obvious and visible and intended to be so, into a muddy trench in which a dun uniformed warrior was afforded scant protection from the lethal devices of the enemy. Did the romance of war die with the empty battlefield? Had it died when a gunpowder weapon fired by a peasant could kill a nobleman? Has it died at all, for there is still majesty in warships, virility in armored fighting vehicles and beauty in aircraft? Romance has not died on the battlefield; it has merely changed.

Technology and war:
The railway and the telegraph

Although it had been developed for commercial use, the military potential of the railway was soon perceived. In the middle years of the 19th century it stimulated what was literally a revolution in the way in which war was waged. As early as the 1820s, Prussian industrialists had mixed self-interest with patriotism and sought to persuade the government of the railway's potential usefulness. In 1835 a commission of enquiry into the use of the railway was set up. Fortunately for the Prussians, its pessimistic conclusions did not retard the development of military railways.

At first, thought on the use of railways was essentially defensive, as was demonstrated in the revolutions of 1848. Beleaguered governments were able to concentrate troops rapidly against outbreaks of revolutionary violence. The steam locomotive also offered defence against foreign, as well as internal, enemies. For example, Prussia's strategic position was weak, situated as she was in the center of Europe and surrounded by potential enemies. A Prussian economist, Friedrich List, argued that an extensive rail network would allow the army to exploit "interior lines of communication" – that is, to be concentrated centrally and quickly moved to the appropriate frontier. In a similar fashion, Britain built railways in order to be able to mass its army at Aldershot in Surrey, instead of maintaining coastal garrisons.

Offensive potential

It was not long before the offensive potential of the railway was recognized, however. The Franco-Austrian war of 1859 saw their first large-scale offensive use, when Napoleon III's army was moved by rail to the theater of operations in northern Italy in 11 days. It would have taken his uncle, the first Napoleon, nearer 60 days to march a similar distance.

The French strategic rail system transported over 600,000 men and nearly 130,000 horses during the course of the war. Roughly half the men were taken directly to Italy. The performance of the railway was rather more impressive than that of the adversaries, but the lessons of the campaign were closely studied by the Prussians. When war came with the Austrians in 1866, the combination of a relatively efficient rail system with an excellent well-organized army produced a convincing Prussian victory.

The success of the Prussians in overcoming the teething problems of railways should not be overestimated. The 1866 campaign was beset by problems as was that against France in 1870. Although rail eliminated much of the sweat involved in actually reaching the area of operations, the movement of supplies still presented great difficulties. It was relatively easy to move large amounts of supplies from depot to railhead, but less easy to distribute food, clothing, and ammunition to the troops in the field. In 1866, thousands of tons of supplies were stranded at the railheads because of congestion on the tracks. A further problem was the difficulty often experienced in persuading civilian rail officials and soldiers to cooperate harmoniously. This problem was highlighted by the chaos that resulted when the French army mobilized in 1870. One unfortunate general was reduced to telegraphing to Paris: "Have arrived at Belfort. Not found my brigade . . . What should I do? Don't know where my regiments are".

The US Civil War

The US Civil War was dominated by the railway – indeed, it can be argued that the Confederacy's lack of railway track predestined it to defeat, for railways

IN COMBAT *Union troops set up a telegraph line under enemy fire. Speeding up communication improved command.*

represented economic power. Of the 30,000 miles of track existing in 1860, about 20,000 lay in the north. This allowed the Union to move the munitions from the factories to its armies, and to move the armies themselves. In a vast country with few major roads, railways were, if anything, of even greater importance than in Europe.

Another new invention, the electric telegraph, also proved its worth in the war. The USA had some 50,000 miles of telegraph wire prior to the outbreak of the war; by 1865 there were 65,000 miles. The telegraph allowed commanders to maintain contact with separated formations and with their superiors. At a time when the expansion of the battlefield had rendered personal command – such as that exercised by Wellington and Napoleon only 50 years earlier – impossible, the electric telegraph represented a breakthrough of immense importance. The major drawback of the telegraph was that it was easy to cut or tap the land lines. The introduction of Marconi's "wireless" technology was another major advance, but the ability to transmit and receive the human voice was still some years distant.

Trends confirmed

The last quarter of the 19th century saw the trends of the previous 25 years confirmed. By the outbreak of the First World War, France and Germany both had massive strategic railway systems, while Russia was building one apace. The railway also entered the diplomatic sphere; in 1896 and 1898 the Italians and the Germans signed railway conventions and Russia received large loans from France – as did Turkey from Germany – specifically to build strategic railways. The Russians attempted to counter the threat that they correctly perceived the German strategic railways system posed in two ways. In order to hinder a German invasion, they constructed their track with a broader gauge than the standard European one and deliberately left communications in Poland underdeveloped.

The inflexibility of the telegraph was matched by that of the railway. The very usefulness of the railway forced strategy into a straightjacket. When moving through underdeveloped territory, armies could often advance only at the speed at which it was possible to lay track, and large numbers of troops were needed to protect these arteries. Only just over 20 per cent of the British forces in South Africa in March 1901 were deployed as fighting troops, for instance, the rest being tied down protecting lines of communication, or forming garrisons.

By the time of the First World War, so dependent were the armies of Europe on the use of railways, that it has been argued that the need to keep to railway timetables was a major contributory factor in inflaming the August 1914 crisis into war. When the Kaiser, on the eve of war, wanted to ignore France and turn the German armies on Russia alone, his chief of staff, von Moltke, was forced to dampen the "All-Highest's" enthusiasm. "I answered His Majesty," wrote Moltke, "that this was not possible. The deployment of an army a million strong was not a thing to be improvised . . . If His Majesty were to insist on directing the whole army to the east, he would not have an army prepared for the attack but a barren heap of armed men disorganized and without supplies." The railway was now a vital part of the fabric of war.

ON THE RAILS *Armored trains were a major feature of the US Civil War.*

MAY 1863
CHANCELLORSVILLE:
Lee's tactical masterpiece

Chancellorsville was fought between the Army of Northern Virginia, under Robert E. *Lee*, and the Army of the Potomac, commanded by General Joseph *Hooker*. Lee's subordinate commanders were "Stonewall" *Jackson*, "Jeb" *Stuart* and Jubal Early, while General Sedgwick was in command of the two corps which made up Hooker's left flank. In total, the Confederates had 60,000 men in the field as opposed to "Fighting Joe's" 134,000; however, inspired flank attacks by Lee won him a decisive victory. His conduct of the battle demonstrated to the full his gifts of command, courage and tactical skill.

A general who finds himself outnumbered and in danger of having both his flanks turned by the enemy might well be prudently advised to avoid battle, or, if forced to fight, to stay on the defensive. However, at Chancellorsville – outnumbered and outflanked though he was – the brilliant Confederate commander Robert E. Lee rejected both these options. Instead, he went over to the offensive, striking against the Federal troops on both his flanks and defeating them in turn.

Build up to battle

Previously, the Federals had launched a number of unsuccessful offensives in an attempt to capture Richmond, the Confederate capital, the last, in November 1862, having been repulsed with heavy loss. As a consequence of that defeat, President Lincoln dismissed Burnside and replaced him with Hooker, who reorganized the dispirited Union soldiers. With reinforcements, his army of the Potomac numbered 134,000 men; Lee had only 60,000 Confederates under command.

The principal town in the area was Fredericksburg, through which ran a railway line which was used to carry reinforcements and supplies to the Federal Army. The town itself was on the western bank of the Rappahanock river. By holding the area, the Federal army could block any advance by the Confederates towards Washington.

Lee's army was positioned south of the Rappahanock, which had two main fords, both located to the west of Fredericksburg. A lateral road ran westwards to Chancellorsville about 10 miles distant. That small town, standing at a cross roads, was thus the most strategically important point on the battlefield.

The Federal plan

Hooker had seven corps at his disposal, each between two and three divisions strong. He intended to take three corps (some 70,000 men) and march westwards until he was well past Lee's left flank. He would then detach a cavalry force, which would ride south and position itself so as to cut off the Confederate retreat. Hooker himself would then swing his force across the river, with his own right flank protected by a tributary of the Rappahanock. Once across, he would change direction again and move eastwards towards Fredericksburg, aiming to roll up Lee's left flank. As the Federal advance moved east, it would also gain the other river ford, across which Hooker could march his remaining corps to reinforce the advance. In order to keep Lee occupied, two further corps (some 40,000 men) would make a demonstration at Fredericksburg under the command of General Sedgwick.

Hooker's plan was sound in theory, but in practice, Lee enjoyed

a key advantage – he deduced Hooker's intentions in advance. "Jeb" Stuart, the Confederate cavalry commander, was the finest leader of reconnaissance and scouting operations in either army and his reports were always informative and accurate. On 29 April, Lee acted on the intelligence Stuart had brought him and deployed for battle accordingly. It was clear that the forces led by Hooker would launch the main Federal assault, while Sedgwick's two corps formed the secondary thrust. Lee therefore sent one division against Hooker and then reinforced it with another two. Facing Sedgwick, he left Jubal Early, with one division of 10,000 men.

Crossing the Rappahanock

By 1 May Hooker's army had crossed the Rappahanock, captured the strategic road junction at Chancellorsville and was attacking eastwards up the lateral road to Fredericksburg. When Lee arrived on the battlefield, he ordered an immediate counter-attack – a move whose audacity so confounded Hooker that he halted his own assault, despite the objections of his subordinate commanders. Thus, by the end of the first day of battle, the military initiative was firmly in the hands of the outnumbered Confederate forces.

That night, Lee and "Stonewall" Jackson devised an even more audacious plan. Their forces facing Hooker would be divided. While Lee, with 17,000 men, held Hooker's superior force at bay, Jackson, with 26,000 men, would ride out and envelop the Federal right flank. The successful conclusion of the Confederate plan obviously depended upon Hooker remaining dominated by Lee's determined grip on the conduct of the battle.

A battle of wills

Hooker did remain dominated and, if not inactive, then certainly non-aggressive. "Stonewall" Jackson moved his men into position undetected and, shortly after 5.00pm on 2 May, they thrust unexpectedly out of the tangled undergrowth and stunted trees of an area known as the Wilderness. Hooker had hoped that this almost impenetrable terrain would protect his right flank, but, when faced with this strong surprise attack, his units were flung back in disorder which only nightfall prevented from degenerating into rout. Now tragedy intervened. Jackson's intention was to cut Hooker off from his supply lines across the Rappahanock fords. As he returned from a reconnaissance patrol, a nervous Confederate sentry opened fire and mortally wounded Lee's most indispensable subordinate.

This tragedy, however, did not alter the course of the battle. On 3 May, Sedgwick opened his demonstration. Although Hooker's demands for reinforcements had stripped him of most of his men, he nevertheless attacked. The fury of his assaults drove Jubal Early's division from its defensive position on Marye's heights and down the lateral road towards Chancellorsville. To meet this thrust, Lee halted his operations against Hooker and, leaving only a holding group in position, turned his forces and marched them up the lateral road to come to the aid of the hard-pressed Early. The following day, he struck at Sedgwick and forced him to retreat. He then turned his forces once again and marched them back against Hooker, only to find that his beaten opponent's army was streaming back northwards in defeat back across the Rappahanock.

The battle of Chancellorsville was over, opening the way for Lee's second invasion of the North and the battle of Gettysburg two months later. A potential defeat for the Army of Northern Virginia had been converted into a victory over

CHANCELLORSVILLE *Union artillery repulses Confederate troops (above), but the battle as a whole was a tactical triumph for Robert E. Lee (below).*

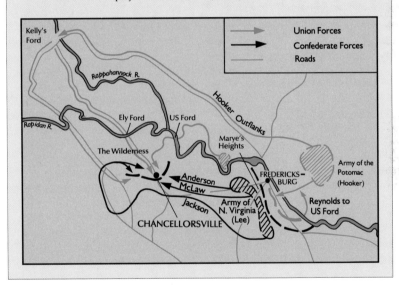

the Army of the Potomac, a force superior in both numbers and equipment. Lee was helped by the fact that he had the advantage of interior lines, which enabled him to deploy units rapidly from one threatened flank to the other, while Confederate reconnaissance and scouting were unquestionably superior. The morale of the Southern soldiers was high. They also possessed a commander of genius in Robert E. Lee, whose boldness in action and speed in executing his plans dominated Hooker.

In the battle, the Confederates lost 12,754 men killed, wounded and captured, as against the Federal 16,792. Chief among the Confederate casualties, however, was the one man whom Lee could not afford to lose. "Stonewall" Jackson died of his wounds. Chancellorsville, in fact, was the last great Confederate victory won by Lee. If, as in the eyes of many authorities, it was his finest battle, then it also was the high point of Confederate military skill.

MAY 1864-AUGUST 1864

THE ATLANTA CAMPAIGN:
Sherman's "March to the Sea"

From very early on in the Civil War, the city of Atlanta was of vital economic importance to the Confederacy, housing vital armaments works and a main supply depot. It was also a key rail center on the line from Chatanooga to the east coast. For these reasons, its capture was a vital first stage in the strategic plan devised by Ulysses S. Grant, the Federal commander-in-chief, in his bid to finish the war. The Atlanta campaign, which lasted from May to August 1864, saw General Johnston, the Confederate commander, and his 60,000 men valiantly resisting the offensive thrusts of Sherman's army group – the Armies of the Cumberland, of the Tennessee and of the Ohio – which numbered around 100,000 men in total.

The Federal masterplan
For summer 1864, Grant had planned a wide-ranging strategy. Federal control of the Mississippi had already led to the isolation of the Confederate heartland of Virginia from the deep south. Now, while Grant himself kept Lee's army occupied in the eastern theater of operations, Sherman, in the western theater, was to drive down the Decatur railway line to capture Atlanta, advancing from there to Savannah and then to the sea. At that point, he would be at Lee's back and the Army of Northern Virginia would be crushed between his and Grant's forces.

Sherman's drive into the South started with his capture of Chatanooga in November 1863. There, he rested his armies and, with the exception of minor skirmishes, no events of military significance took place until late the following spring. On 5 May 1864 the Federal army group marched out of Chatanooga to seek out Johnston and destroy him in the field.

A fighting retreat
Johnston, although heavily outnumbered, conducted a brilliant fighting retreat, delaying the advance of the Federal forces by using his cavalry to harry their lines of communication and by attacking isolated Federal garrisons. His chief aim was to make Sherman's advance too costly to continue by fighting set-piece battles in good defensive positions, while Sherman, with equal skill, maneuvered so as to pass around Johnston's flank.

The first Confederate delaying action was at Dalton, an important rail junction, followed by further battles at Resaca and Cassville, another railroad center. In a bold strike, Sherman then bypassed the Confederate forces holding prepared positions at Allatoona and raced to reach the high ground at Marietta before Johnston could establish a position there. Sherman's gamble failed; as a result, he found himself committed to frontal attacks against Kenesaw Mountain, only 25 miles from Atlanta and the key to its capture.

After a few minor skirmishes, Sherman launched his forces at Kenesaw against good troops in prepared positions. The result was a Federal disaster, Sherman losing 3,000 men and Johnston only 800. The Federal commander then tried a vast outflanking movement around the mountain to bypass the Confederate left flank; to avoid encirclement, Johnston retreated again – this time taking up position in the strong defences of the Chatahoochie river, six miles from Atlanta. Once more, Sherman outflanked his enemy, who was thus forced to retire from the river line to positions along the Peachtree Creek, just short of the city.

Johnston had carried out a brilliant fighting retreat at very little cost. Now, however, as he prepared to march out to meet the enemy, he was relieved of his command. This humiliation showed how little the civilian government understood of what he had achieved. In a series of delaying actions, he had slowed the advance of Sherman's vastly superior forces to a rate of around a mile a day, but his dogged defence lacked the glamour the south had come to expect of its generals. His replacement, the impetuous Hood, was confidently expected to provide the dash it was thought his predecessor had lacked.

Battle for Atlanta
Instead of conserving his effectives, Hood, though he based some of his thinking on the battle plan that Johnston had devised, was determined to take the counter-offensive. Facing him was General Thomas's Army of the Cumberland, which formed the right wing of the Federal army group. Hood intended to attack Thomas as soon as the latter's army had crossed Peachtree Creek, since it would then be out of contact with the other Federal armies and so could not count on them for support. In the event, the Confederate attack was repulsed and Hood was forced to retreat into Atlanta itself, having lost 4,000 much-needed men. The three Federal armies then concentrated to the north and the east of the city. Hood countered with an attack upon the left wing of the Army of the Tennessee, but, although this achieved complete surprise in its initial stages, Sherman soon rallied his

men and quickly held the Confederate offensive.

For days the battle continued on two sides of the city. Then Sherman, aware that his forces were not strong enough for a siege and that time was against him because of the vital role he had been given in Grant's overall strategy, sought to force a result by sending raiding parties to cut the railroad lines through which Atlanta was supplied. These raids were unsuccessful, however, while Sherman's attempts to storm the Confederate defences failed because of the sheer strength of the positions.

From Atlanta to the sea
Determined to force the issue, Sherman now decided to march his entire army group to the south of the city. This was a bold plan, since the gigantic wheeling movement was fraught with danger. Had the Confederates struck out of Atlanta against the Federal flank as the wheel was being made, they might have rolled up Sherman's battle line. In the event, however, the audacious Federal move succeeded. Leaving just a single corps to guard his lines of communication, Sherman drove down the railroad, defeating the forces that Hood had sent out to intercept him.

Hood, in Atlanta, was now cut off. Destroying those military stores he could not take with him, he evacuated the city and it was entered by units of the triumphant Federal army on 2 September. All civilians were promptly ordered to leave Atlanta. It was to become a military camp that would nourish Sherman's advance.

Though Atlanta itself might have fallen, Hood's army was still active and Sherman realized that he had no time to seek to pin down the Confederate commander. Such an effort would have compromised Grant's strategy. Instead, he sent the Army of the Cumberland back to Nashville and Chatanooga with orders to pursue the southern troops, while, he, with only 68,000 men under command, set out on the next phase of the campaign.

The Atlanta campaign was one of the most decisive in the whole of the Civil War. What it demonstrated was Confederate skill in fighting delaying actions, Sherman's genius in his decision to take the risk of marching his army down Hood's flank and the importance of the railroads in determining the movements of both sides. It ended with a major Federal force situated in the heart of the Confederacy. Sherman's continued advance tore out that heart, as he cut a destructive swathe through Georgia on his march to the sea.

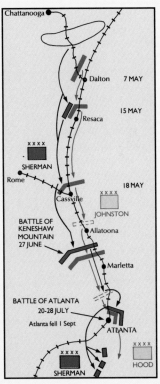

ATLANTA *Confederate troops stand their ground at Resaca (above left) in their fighting retreat through the mountains of Georgia. Despite their spirited resistance, Sherman eventually took Atlanta (above right).*

SEPTEMBER 1870

SEDAN:
Prussia's Cannae-style victory

The war fought between France and a coalition of German states led by Prussia had as its climactic the battle of Sedan, fought on 1 September 1870. If the Franco-Prussian War was Bismarck's war, then the battle of Sedan was *von Moltke*'s battle.

The speed with which Prussia could mobilize and put troops into the field had been demonstrated against Austria in 1866, but had seemingly gone unremarked by the French. By the end of July, 380,000 German soldiers were concentrated into three huge armies west of the Rhine between Trier and Gemersheim. The remainder were held facing Austria until it became clear that the Austrians would not intervene in the war.

Facing that great host lined up along the Franco-German frontier, Napoleon III had 224,000 men in eight separate corps forming a line extending from Thionville to Strasbourg and then echeloned back to the complex of fortresses – Metz, Nancy and Belfort. The first engagement took place on 2 August, whereupon the emperor, aware of the nearness of the Prussians, prepared for battle by grouping his eight corps into two armies – the Army of Lorraine (five Corps) under the command of Marshal *Bazaine* and the Army of Alsace (three Corps) under Marshal *MacMahon*.

The road to Sedan
A series of battles, fought between 4 and 18 August, struck both the French armies and separated them. The French regrouped – MacMahon at Châlons and Bazaine at Metz into whose fortress complex he withdrew. Under orders from the government, McMahon left Châlons and marched north intending, by an indirect route, to link up with

Bazaine in Metz. The time that it took to make this unnecessary maneuver allowed the Prussian commander, von Moltke, to group his armies. He used First and part of Second Army to besiege Metz. The remainder of Second Army, now know as the Army of the Maas, moved west to support Third Army, which had moved to block McMahon's advance.

On 29 August, the Army of Alsace attempted to cross the Maas, but was flung back and forced northwards in the direction of Sedan. Clashes during that day and on the following two days pushed back the French into the bend of the river around the city. By 31 August, Third Army and that of the Maas had begun to encircle the French. McMahon's troops were to be eventually compressed into the bend of the Maas, where they were overlooked by the Prussians who held the high ground around the town. By nightfall on 31 August, Moltke was moving his artillery and infantry up, but, as yet, his forces were still too weak to do more than form a broken cordon of infantry, the gaps between the Prussian columns being covered by a cavalry screen of Uhlaus.

On the river's right bank, the Army of the Maas moved towards Bazeilles to block the southern approaches to Sedan and two corps of Third Army reached Donchery to the north-west of the town. During the night an attempt to reinforce the Army of the Maas, by putting a Bavarian corps across the river, was contested by French marines. The sound of firing alerted the troops in and around Sedan. The battle had opened and German units began marching towards the gunfire. The Army of the Maas moved before

0500, the Saxons starting to advance towards Daigny while the Prussian Guards, on the Saxon right, moved along the road between Villers and Arnay.

Trapped at Sedan
Because of the thick morning mist it was not until 0600 that the Prussian guns came into action and the first of their barrages wounded MacMahon. Command of the army then passed to General Ducrot, who quickly realized that he would soon be completely encircled but that the Prussian ring was still too weak to resist a firm blow. He then decided to move the army westwards towards Mezieres, where a French corps was holding the road open.

A dramatic intervention then occurred. General Wimpffen, who had joined MacMahon's army only the previous day, produced a secret order empowering him to take command should MacMahon be killed or wounded. At 0900 he countermanded Ducrot's orders, instead directing the army to march eastwards towards Metz. This conflict led to confusion within the trapped force and the troops to the north of Bazeilles began to move eastward along a fordable small river, the Fond de Givonne.

At Daigny to the right of the Fond de Givonne, Saxon 12 Corps captured the dominant ridge to the south of the Sedan-Givenchy road, but, between Daigny and the village of Givonne, a minor crisis threatened the Germans. In that sector the Prussian Guard and its artillery had still not deployed for battle when a column of some 6,000 troops came into sight. This was part of the French infantry force marching as a result of Wimpffen's orders, which promptly charged for

TRIUMPH AT SEDAN
Superb staffwork and the fighting qualities of the German troops, including the Uhlans (left), forced the main French armies into encirclement and surrender at Sedan (below) in the Franco-Prussian War. Swift action at Sedan might have saved the French from disaster, but General Ducrot, who succeeded the wounded McMahon, was himself replaced by Wimpffen, who ordered the army eastwards, rather than westwards. After a day of bitter fighting, Napoleon III himself negotiated the final French surrender.

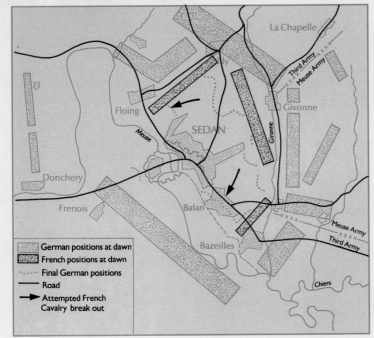

- German positions at dawn
- French positions at dawn
- Final German positions
- Road
- Attempted French Cavalry break out

near Fleigneuax. The French fell back to their main position on the ridge to the south of the road between Floing and Illy. German artillery was brought forward to bombard them, but seemed to be unsupported. Against this exposed target, General Gallifet launched his brigade of Chasseurs d'Afrique, a crack cavalry regiment, but the charge, unsupported by the French artillery, was smashed.

At 1100 the French infantry was put into the assault to force back the weak enemy forces on its front. It advanced with élan, gaining ground until Prussian reinforcements came forward and drove the attack back, first into and then out of the village of Floing. By noon French cohesion was breaking as orders were countermanded and then changed again. To smash a way through at Floing and thus escape the encirclement, an entire French cavalry division was ordered to attack. Its commander was killed as he made a reconnaissance and his successor, Gallifet, led a succession of gallant, but fruitless, charges.

Late in the afternoon Moltke considered that he now had sufficient troops available to order a general advance and his men in the east and north of the battlefield moved forward. In the south, however, Wimpffen was still making desperate, but unsuccessful, attacks against the Bavarian corps which had captured Bazeilles. He was still determined to batter a way through, but Napoleon III, who had been with MacMahon's army throughout the day, was not prepared to see more of his soldiers killed and decided to surrender. The day had been a disaster for French arms. More than 100,000 soldiers were taken prisoner together with 558 guns. Those killed and wounded numbered 17,000.

For years, the Prussian staff had taken the battle of Cannae as the model for their military operations. At Sedan the armies moving separately but grouping around the enemy had destroyed him totally, achieving another Cannae.

the guns, protected only by a thin screen of infantry. With all speed, the artillery was brought into action and a barrage of shells cut the attacking French column in two. The rear units, which had been most heavily shelled, scattered but the leading battalions, numbering some 2,000 men, pressed on. The Guard infantry jog-trotted into battle and formed line. Under the combined fire of musketry and artillery, the French attack was destroyed. The Prussian Guard then prepared to attack the Bois de la Garenne and sent out patrols to reach the Belgian frontier.

Meanwhile Third Army, which had begun to march as early as 0230, had crossed the Maas at Donchery and established contact with the right wing of the Prussian Guard

MAY 1905
TSUSHIMA:
Annihilation in the Pacific

The naval battle of Tsushima was fought on 27 May 1905 between the Russian Baltic fleet, which had sailed around the world to give battle and a Japanese fleet close to its home bases. The battle was a watershed action. For nearly a century after *Trafalgar*, battles at sea had been minor affairs but Tsushima was an action as decisive as had been Trafalgar – both in respect of the number of ships involved and in the effect it had upon ship construction. It was also the first major battle in which wireless telegraphy was used to any great extent.

The two fleets
The rivalry that had grown up between Japan and Russia at the turn of the century for the control of Manchuria and Korea led to a situation in which Japan needed to destroy the Russian Far Eastern Fleet and capture the naval base at Port Arthur if her own troop convoys were to reach the future battle areas safely. Naval battles, fought on 10 and 14 August, 1904, had destroyed the Russian Far Eastern Fleet, leaving the Japanese navy in command of the sea. To restore the Russian position in the Far East, Tsar Nicholas II then ordered the Baltic Fleet, renamed the 2nd Pacific Squadron, to sail from the Baltic on an epic 18,000-mile voyage half-way around the world to meet, engage and defeat the Imperial Japanese Navy.

In charge of the fleet was Admiral Rozhestvensky, a man who had held no previous sea-going command. His armada was made up of 39 vessels, whose speed was restricted to about nine knots – that of the slowest ship. Five of the 12 warships were new. Of the others, some were more than 40 years old, their main armament consisting of muzzle-loading

cannon. The Japanese fleet numbered about 93 ships, of which four were modern battleships and eight armored cruisers. All the Japanese vessels were capable of speeds in excess of 18 knots. Their guns were modern and the shells they fired were filled with a newly invented high explosive of tremendous power, detonated by highly sophisticated, instantaneous fuses.

Voyage to catastrophe
Rozhestvensky's voyage was dogged with misfortune. It lasted for almost seven months before the Russians were in a position to prepare for the final dash to Vladivostok. In the Straits of Korea, persistent thick mist blanketed the Russian armada, filling Rozhestvensky with confidence that he might slip through the Tsushima Straits without detection and reach his destination safely. He was to be disappointed. The Japanese commander, Admiral *Togo*, was very well aware how close to him the Russians were and was ready for battle in every respect. On the morning of 27 May 1905, the mist cleared sufficiently for the Russian ships to be sighted advancing in two parallel columns; shortly after mid-day they entered the Straits of Tsushima. Togo now put to sea.

While still seven miles distant from the Russian columns, and therefore out of range, Togo steamed across their front – in effect, crossing the Russian "T" – his intention begin to engage the enemy's left hand column, which he had been advised was the weaker one. To counter that maneuver, the Russians turned north-eastward and then due east, hoping to escape the Japanese. Togo then executed a maneuver, which, against a more

aggressive enemy, could only have resulted in disaster. He ordered his whole fleet to reverse its course while under Russian fire.

Rozhestvensky's intention was to outrun the Japanese, but this was a vain one. With their superior speed, the Japanese ships quickly overhauled him and the two fleets engaged each other broadside for broadside at a distance of about 7,000 yards. Now was seen how efficient and thorough had been the Japanese training. Their gunfire was fast, accurate and destructive. Their new, powerful shells struck the Russians hard and first the flag ship, *Suvorov* and then an older battleship were hit and destroyed. Rozhestvensky was wounded and transferred to a destroyer. The Russian return fire was unco-ordinated and inaccurate. Within two hours the battle had been decided. Four of the Russian battleships – the *Suvorov, Alexander III, Borodino* and *Oslyabya* – had been sunk and seven other vessels had struck their colors.

Togo continued the bombardment until 1900. Then he released into the gathering darkness his light forces, which hunted the fleeing Russians throughout the night. Only one cruiser and two destroyers of the 39 ships of the Russian armada ever reached Vladivostock.

Immediately after Tsushima, the Royal Navy's First Sea Lord, Admiral Sir John Fisher, was jubilant. The policy he had long advocated of a fast, all-big gun ship had been vindicated and he declared that traditional battleships were "as obsolete as the Ark". Tsushima therefore set in train Fisher's cherished Dreadnought construction program, in which all the major navies of the world eventually competed. It sparked off a naval revolution.

ANNIHILATION AT TSUSHIMA *Having steamed half-way around the world from its home ports (right), the Russian Baltic Fleet was annihilated by the Japanese at Tsushima in one of the most decisive sea battles in history (above). Admiral Togo, the Japanese commander, ordered his ships to make a daring U-turn while within range of the Russian guns to bring his fleet on to a parallel course, when superior Japanese gunnery could take its toll.*

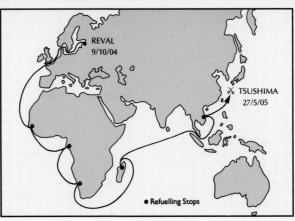

REVAL
9/10/04

TSUSHIMA
27/5/05

● Refuelling Stops

BAZAINE
Achille F (1811-1888)
MARSHAL OF FRANCE
Franco-Prussian War

Achille Bazaine, a future Marshal of France, started his army career in 1834 as a private soldier. However, his career is not a classic instance of a low-born warrior rising through the ranks to the pinnacle of high command. In reality, Bazaine had failed to pass the entrance examination to military college and enlisted to gain through bravery in action the commission that his intellectual qualities had denied him.

Born in Versailles in February 1811, Bazaine served in the army in Algeria, where bravery in action won him the lieutenant's commission his intellectual skills had not achieved. Once commissioned, he rose quickly through the courage he displayed on various battlefields. He campaigned in both Spain and in Mexico, having served as a brigadier in the Crimea and in the 1859 campaign against Austria at the battle of Solferino.

Disaster against Prussia

Bazaine was undoubtedly courageous, but courage alone is not enough to win battles against a superbly led and well equipped foe, as the events of the Franco-Prussian War were to show. After the war's first skirmish at Saarbrucken, Napoleon III divided his forces into the Army of Lorraine, made up of five corps and commanded by Bazaine and the Army of Alsace, three corps under McMahon. Bazaine, in an effort to protect as much territory as possible, positioned his corps so far apart that they could not provide each other with mutual support. Occupying three sectors of Lorraine, they now faced the Prussian 1st and 2nd Armies.

Bazaine's II Corps, holding the high ground at Spichern, was speedily attacked by superior Prussian forces. Though the French held throughout 6 August, they withdrew when it was clear that encirclement was imminent. Surprisingly, Bazaine made no attempt to reinforce this isolated corps, which was holding a strategically important feature barring the way into France through the Vosges Gap. His whole army then began to retreat, closely pursued by von Moltke's 1st and 2nd. The speed of the Prussian pursuit not only gave the French no time to prepare a defence; it also cut across Bazaine's lines of communication. Even more seriously, Moltke had separated the Army of Lorraine from the Army of Alsace. His plan was obvious – to destroy each army separately. A French reorganization led to the formation of the optimistically-named Army of the Rhine, again commanded by Bazaine. He promptly fell back upon the fortified city of Metz, closely pursued by the Prussian 1st Army.

A battle and a siege

Determined to reach Verdun to join forces with McMahon, Bazaine marched out of Metz, but, on being inter-

cepted by the Prussian 2nd Army, deployed the Army of the Rhine between the Orne and Moselle rivers. The Prussians attacked on 16 August and there followed a series of small, but bitter, battles at Mars la Tour, Vionville and Rezonville. In these the French cavalry, inspired by Bazaine, carried out a number of furious charges to smash a breach for the rest of the army and the Prussians responded with their own cavalry charges to check the furious French assaults. On 17 August, unable to break through, Bazaine fell back on Metz and took up a new defensive position facing westwards to where the Prussian armies stood – between him and Paris.

During the battle of Gravelot-St Privat, fought the following day, Bazaine seems to have been overwhelmed by events. He allowed his VI Corps to be attacked all day by an overwhelming Prussian force without sending it reinforcements. The result was that the Army of the Rhine now found itself besieged in Metz and its timid efforts to break out and advance to support McMahon were repulsed. On 27 October, with the war all but ended, the Metz garrison surrendered. Bazaine was subsequently court-martialled and sentenced to be shot by firing squad, but this was later commuted to 20 years imprisonment. He did not remain a captive for long. With the help of his devoted wife, he escaped and reached Spain, where he died in exile in 1888.

A gallant and thrusting soldier who was adored by the men he commanded, Bazaine seems to have lost his confidence when facing the Prussians. His emperor Napoleon III went into exile; the commander of the Army of Alsace, McMahon, became President of the Third Republic. Bazaine alone was made the scapegoat for France's humiliating defeat in the summer of 1870.

BENEDEK
Ludwig August von (1804-1881)
AUSTRIAN GENERAL
Austro-Prussian War

Ludwig August von Benedek was one of the most tragic figures in the history of the Austrian imperial army. Not only did he take the blame for the Austrian defeat at Koeniggraetz in 1866, but he was officially forbidden to make any subsequent attempt to clear his name.

Benedek, the son of a doctor, was born at Sopron in Hungary on 14 July 1804. He entered the Maria Theresa military academy in 1822, from which he was gazetted into the 27th Infantry Regiment. In 1833, he was transferred to the general staff. He first came to the notice of his superiors during 1846, when he played a conspicuous part in putting down a revolt in western Galicia, and won renewed attention in the 1848 Italian campaign, where, as Radetzky's chief of staff, he planned the victory over the Piedmontese at Curtatorne. He was also responsible for the Austrian success at Mortara in the following year and as an acknowledgment of repeated acts of bravery received Austria's highest award, the Maria Theresa Order. Archduke Albrecht was so impressed with Benedek's ability that he presented to him the sword which had been worn by the Archduke *Charles*.

Benedek showed his ability in defeat as well in the 1859 war against Napoleon III's Franco-Italian coalition. The disastrous defeat inflicted on the Austrians at Solferino was saved from becoming a rout by his 8th Corps, which formed the Austrian right wing. Benedek's troops held fast when the center corps broke and, in a skilfully conducted operation, covered the retreat of the main body. This brilliant act of generalship added to Benedek's growing reputation; he became the idol of the army.

A man of action

Benedeck was a man of action, impatient with paper work and the bureaucracy that surrounds a senior commander. His pressing need to be kept busy was met by burdening him with offices. It seemed, indeed, that any military task could be given to him. In January 1860, he was chief of the general staff; in April the same year, he took over as Governor of Hungary; a year later, he was commander-in-chief of the Austrian forces in Venetia and the Alpine provinces. He was promoted out of turn to the rank of major-general, while the noble status given him through the award of the Maria Theresa Order allowed him a seat in the House of Peers. It seemed that the triumphs of his past had assured for him a secure future, but all this was to change with the Austro-Prussian War of 1866.

Beaten by the Prussians

By making an alliance with Italy, Prussia forced the Austrian army to fight a two-front war. The command of the army facing Prussia was almost forced upon Benedek. His protest that he knew "every tree in Italy, but not one in Bohemia" was seen as an expression of modesty and not the acknowledgment of a soldier aware of his own shortcomings. His objections were ignored and he took the field against *von Moltke*.

The speed of Prussia's mobilization gave Moltke the military initiative and he struck before Austria and its Bavarian, Hanovarian and Saxon allies were ready. The Prussian commander attacked in the west first, one of his three armies destroying those of Hanover and Hesse. His other two armies then struck in the east to defeat the Saxons. Two Prussian armies now invaded Bohemia and moved down upon the Austrian army.

Benedek, aware that he was facing superior forces armed with better weapons, planned to group his forces round Olmutz and to meet the Prussians upon ground of his choosing. Though he was ordered to advance and take the initiative, aware of his force's weakness and lacking confidence in himself, his staff and his army, he suggested to the Emperor Franz Joseph that peace should be made, citing Prussian successes against Hanover, Saxony and in a number of minor battles in Bohemia. However, his proposal was rejected on the grounds that no decisive battle had yet been fought.

Benedek accordingly obeyed the orders to fight and his army, seven corps strong, occupied the high ground at Koeniggraetz. Had he been more aggressive he might have defeated the two Prussian armies advancing towards him by attacking each in turn before they could join forces, but he did not. Even at the opening of the battle at Koeniggraetz, he might still have won the day, since, when the battle started, only the two Prussian armies were on the battlefield. This meant that the Austrians would enjoy numerical superiority until the forces of the Crown Prince entered the battle and he was miles away. Benedek decided to let the Prussians exhaust themselves in attacks against his well-chosen positions before he sent his two reserve infantry corps and his cavalry divisions into a massive counter stroke.

Deceived by von Moltke

Moltke's frontal assaults against the Austrian center were intended as a deception to hold Benedek's attention, while the other Prussian armies outflanked him and cut his line of retreat. However, the fulfilment of the Prussian plan depended upon the Crown Prince who, late in the morning, had still not reached the field. Until he did, the Prussian central divisions bore the burden of battle. Their attacks were smashed by the Austrian artillery and at midday, Benedek, chain-smoking on the heights of Lipa, was convinced that the time for his counter-attack was fast approaching. The signs were favorable. The Prussian center was tiring, the army on the one flank seemed to be making no determined assault and the Crown Prince was still absent. Benedek, unaware that the Army of the Elbe had begun to outflank him, was confident that victory was only a matter of time.

Within 30 minutes, however, this confidence had been shattered. To confront the Crown Prince's army, which had at last begun to arrive in force, Benedek could deploy only his two reserve corps – the very troops he had reserved for the counter blow. Determined to keep his reserves intact, the Austrian units fighting in the Swiep woods were ordered to form a defensive front against the Crown Prince, but then were struck by a Prussian asault before they could take up their defensive positions. To meet the situation, Benedek was forced to commit unit after unit from his reserve; in the words of a Prussian officer-poet, "The whole day long with rifle and pack, there flooded forward in repeated attack a snow-white sea – the enemy's marvellous Army." The attacks of the white-coated Austrian infantry withered in the fire of the Prussian infantry's needle guns, which could be loaded and discharged four times faster than the Austrian muzzle-loading muskets. It was the victory of technology over bravery.

The Austrian cavalry, at last, entered the battle – not to crown a victory, but to cover the retreat, which had become inevitable. Benedek pulled back the remnants of his defeated army across the Elbe to Olmutz and the positions which he had intended originally to occupy.

Blame had to be apportioned for the lost battle. Benedek – once hailed as a hero – became a scapegoat and only the direct intervention of the Emperor prevented his court martial. He was allowed to retire and to retain his military privileges on the undertaking that he would make no attempt to clear his name. The Austrian semi-official publication *Oesterreichs Kaempfe* wrote of him: "A career filled with achievement, distinction and fame deserved a less tragic end. Dispassionate judgement will not forget the successes he achieved in earlier decades in the Emperor's service and these will ensure, despite the recent tragic blow, that he is remembered with honor." Unable to speak in defence of his conduct, he died an embittered man in Graz on 27 April, 1881.

DEWEY
George (1837-1917)
US ADMIRAL
Spanish-American War

George Dewey became a national hero as a result of the crushing naval victory he won over the Spanish fleet in Manila Bay during the Spanish-American War. In recognition of his services, Congress authorized the creation of the special rank of Admiral of the Navy for him.

Dewey was born in Montpelier, Vermont, on 26 December 1837, the son of a doctor. He graduated from the US Naval Academy at Annapolis in 1858 and served in the Union fleet during the US Civil War, taking part in several battles, including New Orleans and Port Hudson. His post-war service was varied and promotion was steady. By 1898, he hadbeen made a Commodore and was commanding the US Asiatic squadron.

"Remember the Maine!"
On 15 February 1898, the existing tension between Spain and the USA sharpened, when the USS *Maine* blew up in Havana harbor in mysterious circumstances. Spain was accused of sinking the ship and the USA prepared for war. The Assistant Secretary of the US Navy, Theodore Roosevelt, accordingly telegraphed Dewey, ordering him to sail his Asiatic squadron, consisting of five cruisers and two gunboats, to Hong Kong, there to prepare for action against the Spanish colony of the Philippines.

On 25th April, four days after the USA had declared war on Spain, Dewey received orders to sail from Hong Kong and to destroy or capture the Spanish Pacific fleet. The first problem he had to solve was that of coal. Since there were no US Navy coaling stations en route, he spent his time negotiating with British companies to furnish him with colliers while his ships prepared for sea. On 27 April, with his fueling problems solved, Dewey sailed for Manila Bay, where the Spanish fleet lay protected by a minefield. Among the civilians who accompanied Dewey's squadron, was the US Consul at Manila, who had brought with him the first detailed report on the Philippines that the US Navy had been able to obtain for over 20 years!

On the night of 30 April, the Asiatic squadron was in Philippine waters. Some time around midnight, Dewey led his ships into Manila Bay, sailing across the Spanish minefield without loss. Inside the bay was a squadron of Spanish warships – four cruisers and three gunboats. Though the Spanish fire-power was inferior, they were supported by shore batteries mounted around the harbor. Dewey calmly positioned his ships. There was no hostile reaction. Then at 5.40 am, he turned to Gridley, the captain of the flagship, and gave him the instruction, "You may fire when you are ready."

The US squadron steamed backwards and forwards along the moored line of Spanish ships positioned off the fortified naval base of Cavite Island. The US gunnery was fast, accurate and destructive, the range between ships seldom rising above 2,000 yards. At 7.35 am, Dewey withdrew to rest and regroup. Behind him in Manila Bay, the Spanish squadron had ceased to exist. Dewey had carried out his orders. At the cost of eight wounded, he had sunk Spain's sole Pacific squadron and had set in train the destruction of Spanish power in the Far East. That process was hastened by the Filippino leader Aguinaldo whom Dewey had landed in the Philippines to raise a guerrilla army against the Spanish garrison.

Although the Cavite naval base surrendered at midday, as the result of a renewed bombardment, Dewey's force did not have sufficient military muscle to occupy Manila itself. While waiting for the arrival of US troops, Dewey instituted a naval blockade, which provoked a further crisis. Germany was sympathetic to Spain and a force of German ships arrived outside Manila, intending to land supplies. Dewey informed the German squadron commander that he was prepared to fight if necessary and the intruders promptly withdrew. The blockade was maintained until the end of June when the awaited convoy of troop transports arrived. Backed by a bombardment from Dewey's squadron, an attack was launched on Manila, but it surrendered after only token resistance.

The determination and speed of action with which Dewey faced the problem of sailing into a mined and well-defended harbor, as well as the firmness with which he confronted the German squadron, are evidence of the quiet authority which he had shown throughout his service life. After Manila, for which victory he was granted the title of Admiral of the Navy, he served on several naval advisory boards until his death in 1917.

FARRAGUT
David (1801-1870)
US ADMIRAL
US Civil War

David Farragut has gone down in naval history as the man who issued one of its most celebrated orders – "Damn the torpedoes. Full steam ahead." His years of devoted service to the US Navy culminated in his command of the Federal fleet in the Civil War.

Farragut was born at Stoney Point, Tennessee, on 5 July 1801. He was given a midshipman's warrant at the unusually early age of eight through the intervention of a relative who had adopted David upon the death of his mother and had influence in the navy. In the war of 1812, between the USA and Britain, the twelve-year-old Farragut served in the frigate *Essex* in a campaign against the British whaling fleet in the Pacific Ocean. So many British prizes were captured that the young Farragut was made prize master of one whaler. By the age of 24, he was commanding the schooner *Ferret*, but reductions in the size of the US navy lessened his chances of promotion and the prospects of sea-going command. It was not until 1855 that he reached the rank of captain; however Farragut had demonstrated his seamanship to such effect over the years that in 1859 he was given command of the steam sloop *Brooklyn*.

Blockading the Confederacy

When the Civil War broke out, Farragut, who had been living in the south, moved north to serve with the Union navy and was given command of a blockading squadron, operating in the Gulf of Mexico. In early spring 1862, however, he was ordered to sail his fleet up the river Mississipi to meet a second Union naval group sailing down the river from New Madrid. The meeting of the two fleets would not only halt river traffic; more importantly, it would also cut the Confederacy in two. The fleet Farragut assembled for the operation consisted of eight steam ships, nine gunboats, and 20 mortar-carrying vessels, together with a great number of miscellaneous craft. He was given a large military force to support him.

On 24 April 1862, Farragut make the first move in the campaign by attacking New Orleans, the largest port at the mouth of the Mississipi. A Confederate squadron of 11 vessels trying to intercept the Federal group was engaged and in a short sea-fight nine Confederate ships were destroyed. New Orleans was abandoned by its garrison and the town surrendered. Farragut then converted it into a Federal naval base, from which he could resume his attack up the Mississippi and take Vicksburg. Though his first attempt to capture this strongly defended and well-fortified port did not succeed, he regrouped his ships, bringing his mortar boats close in to provide covering fire as the squadron ran the gauntlet of Vicksburg's batteries.

Once past the Confederate guns, Farragut steamed upriver to link up with the other Union fleet as planned. His ships ran the Vicksburg gauntlet again in order to attack the *Arkansas*, which had fought its way through the Union ships to reach the safety of that port.

In recognition of his services, Farragut was now promoted rear-admiral and, in March 1863, set out to attack Vicksburg again. This time, the Union efforts were ultimately successful, although it took a siege to bring about its fall. The blockade swept Confederate shipping from the river and the Confederacy was divided, Virginia now being isolated from the trans-Mississipi states. This was of major significance.

Though the Union navy had established a strong and secure blockade on the inland rivers, the situation at sea was less satisfactory. Many Southern ports, the most important being Mobile, were havens for blockade runners. Farragut was determined to put an end to this.

Mobile was situated within a bay whose narrow entrance was guarded by Fort Morgan. Farragut concentrated his squadron of four ironclad monitors and 14 wooden ships and in August 1864, set out to give battle. Running the gauntlet of Fort Morgan's cannon, Farragut brought his ships into Mobile Bay and deployed them in battle formation. He could see that his chief surface opposition would come from the Confederate ironclad *Tennessee*. What he could not detect was the field of sea-mines, known in those days as "torpedoes", the Confederates had laid to the approaches to the inner harbor.

The Federal squadron's advance soon ran into difficulty. *Tecumseh*, the leading monitor in the first line, struck a mine and sank within minutes, while desperate maneuvers by the other leading ships to avoid both the mines and collisions with the vessels following them put the whole operation in jeopardy. It was then that Farragut turned his flagship directly into the minefield, ordered that he be tied to the rigging and issued his famous order "Damn the torpedoes. Full steam ahead."

Farragut gambled that many of the mines would have become ineffective through their long immersion in the water. Fortunately for him, his judgement was proved correct; in the ensuing battle, the *Tennessee* surrendered, as did two small forts protecting the harbor. It was the high point in Farragut's career; the victory won him promotion to the rank of admiral.

Following his retirement from the navy, Farragut dedicated himself to the task of reconciliation between the states. He is remembered not so much for the order he gave at Mobile, as for the successful blockade of the lower Mississippi and the decades of devoted service he gave the US navy.

GRANT
Ulysses S (1822-1885)
US GENERAL
US Civil War

Ulysses S Grant was to the Union what Robert E *Lee* was to the Confederacy – its best strategist and its most renowned general. There can be no doubt that, had Grant been in command of the Union forces at the outbreak of the US Civil War, it would have ended far more quickly with a Federal victory.

Grant was born in Mount Pleasant, Ohio, on 27 April 1822. He showed no academic ability at school or at West Point – indeed, as a West Point cadet, he lacked any sort of military inclination. However, he was finally gazetted into the 4th Infantry Regiment. He fought in the Mexican War, his bravery under fire leading to a field promotion to first lieutenant after the battle of Molino del Rey, while his courage at Chapultepec won him further promotion to captain, though he considered that the war had been fought to extend the hated system of slavery. Perhaps this was one of the reasons for his decision to resign his commission in 1854 – another was his lack of interest in a military career.

A new life as a result of war

Grant, however, got little satisfaction out of farming, real estate, or the other civilian professions he tried. He sunk into a profound melancholia, which was only saved from becoming a mania by the outbreak of war. Grant promptly volunteered to serve in the Union forces.

What Grant had hoped for was an immediate combat assignment, but, at first, he was confined to administrative positions. Nor was he, to begin with, granted a commission in the US Army, but was issued with one by the state government of Illinois, for whom he raised and trained an infantry regiment. It was not until April 1861 that Lincoln gave him a field command in the Union ranks with the rank of brigadier.

Grant was one of the first Union commanders to realize that the war could be decided in the western theater, rather than the eastern one, where its earliest battles were fought in Virginia, as both sides concentrated their forces to defend Washington and Richmond, their respective capitals. During January 1862, Grant made his first move in the west, leading a fleet of gunboats and soldiers from Cairo, Illinois, to move against the chain of Confederate forts guarding the Tennessee and Cumberland rivers. Fort Henry was taken on 6 February, from which Grant advanced to take Fort Donelson. The Confederate forces in the area were now faced by three Union armies – Pope on the right, Grant in the center and Buell on the left.

In an attempt to break Grant's hold on the Cumberland and Tennessee rivers and thus to stave off the Federal encirclement, the Confederates launched an attack, which Grant beat off, following this up by counterattacks, which drove the Confederates back into Fort Donelson. When the fort's commander asked for surrender terms, Grant replied: "No terms, except an unconditional and immediate surrender." The combined Union forces of Grant and Buell then went on to capture Nashville, so opening up the Tennessee river.

Aggression and initiative

Grant was now promoted major-general, although there had been widespread criticism of the heavy losses he had incurred during the campaign – particularly at Shiloh, where he lost 13,000 out of the 63,000 men in his army. As commander of the Army of the Tennessee, a post he assumed during July 1862, Grant found that his forces were widely spread out and in a tactically unsound situation. The Confederates had realized this as well, but their resulting offensive was met by an immediate counterattack. Grant's policy was to keep the initiative; this, he was convinced, could best gained by aggressive action.

In the first week of October 1862, following the battle of Corinth – though his success here was incomplete –

DEFIANT GIANT *Grant's determination was instrumental in turning the tide of civil war in favor of the Union.*

Grant, with Memphis and Corinth in his hands, moved against Vicksburg. From January to March 1863, he waited patiently for the water level of the Mississippi to fall, so that he could move his army across it and deploy to attack the city. The following campaign lasted just over two weeks, during which Grant's forces crossed from the west to the east bank and marched to take up position between Vicksburg garrison and a second Confederate force at Jackson. Grant's first blows drove the Jackson force back, after which he turned against the Vicksburg garrison, defeating it at Champion's Hill on 16 May. Grant had gained the initiative. Pemberton, the Confederate commander, and 30,000 of his men, were trapped in the city.

The latter stages of what became known as the "big black river" campaign is a clear demonstration of the full measure of Grant's abilities. He had fought and defeated numerically superior forces in five separate engagements and had trapped a large enemy force inside Vicksburg. As a result of its surrender on 4 July, the Union gained control of the Mississippi, so splitting the Confederacy in two.

On 17 October Grant was given overall command of the western theater of operations and promptly relieved Chatanooga, which had been under siege. By the first week of December, his forces had cleared Confederate troops out of Tennessee and the way was open for *Sherman* to march through Georgia in a strategy designed to encircle the south. When Lincoln appointed Grant to be General-in-Chief of the Union forces on 9 March 1864, the new commander at last was able to implement his long-desired plan for a concerted campaign by the various Federal armies now in position on the separate war fronts. Though Robert E Lee's brilliant defensive strategy staved off defeat, the end of the war came in spring 1865, with Grant's army facing Richmond and others advancing through the Shenandoah Valley and Georgia. The last surviving Confederate army was trapped and Lee surrendered at Appomatox Courthouse.

Fluctuating fortunes

In the post-war years, Grant's fortunes fluctuated dramatically. He was hailed as a military hero, becoming head of the war department in one administration and eventually being elected President for two terms. Yet, there were times when he was so poor that he had to sell his wartime sword and he was eventually declared bankrupt. In an effort to ensure his family's financial security, he began to write his war memoirs, even though he was dying of cancer. His iron will kept him writing until his book was completed. Published posthumously, it was an enormous success and the royalties saved his family from destitution.

Grant was accused of being a drunkard, of butchering his men and of fraud. The fraud charges arose because of the trust he placed in unreliable subordinates, whom he then supported through thick and thin with the astonishing loyalty for which he was renowned. There is no evidence to show that he was uncaring about his men's lives, but the fact that he smoked to excess and was profane cannot be doubted. Lincoln's comment on being told that Grant drank was to ask for the name of his whisky – in order to send some to his other field commanders. Lincoln's words: "I need that man; he can fight" were the finest recommendation of Grant's generalship.

HANCOCK
Winfield Scott (1824-1886)
US MAJOR-GENERAL
US Civil War

Winfield Scott Hancock made a name for himself in the war with Mexico, as a diligent and conscientious organizer. It was the US Civil War that gave him the opportunity to demonstrate his qualities as a fighting man, particularly in the handling of his brigade during the 1862 campaign in the Peninsula during a series of attacks against Marye's Heights. At the battle of Antietam, he commanded a division and went on to lead II Corps in the Army of the Potomac.

Foresight at Gettysburg

At Gettysburg it was Hancock who appreciated the key importance of Cemetery Ridge, which he promptly and expertly prepared for defence. It was as well that he was so thorough in that work and in the training of his men, for

TURNING POINT *Winfield Scott Hancock's greatest moment came at Gettysburg, when he broke Pickett's charge.*

it was against his corps that the last full-scale Confederate attack – Pickett's charge – was launched in the afternoon of 3 July 1863. During the battle, which Robert E *Lee* had hoped would decide the course of the Civil War in favor of the Confederacy, Hancock was so severely wounded that he was out of action for six months.

Hancock recovered sufficiently to resume command of II Corps and during August 1864, led a combined infantry/artillery force to cut the railway line at Ream's station, south of Petersburg, which was being besieged by Federal troops. The fury of the counter-attacks the Confederates launched to keep open this important railroad link shook the Union troops, but Hancock rallied them and flung back the southern assault before going on to complete the destruction of the railroad.

Opposing the "carpetbaggers"

The strain of campaigning re-opened Hancock's wound, however, and he saw no more active service during the war. However, he remained in the army and fought in several campaigns against the Indians before being appointed to command the military district of Louisiana and Texas. In this post his outspoken comments on the evil of the "carpetbaggers" – the derisory nickname given to Republican civil administrators and grasping northern businessmen in the conquered south – and his refusal to employ his troops on duties he considered denied southern civilians their constitutional rights, made him so many political enemies that he asked to be relieved of command in order to stand as Democratic candidate in the 1880 Presidential election. To do this, he had to resign his commission, but returned to the army when he was defeated by Garfield.

Hancock, a brave and competent soldier who refused to pervert the course of natural justice in the interests of a prejudiced minority, was never given the chance to demonstrate his undoubted tactical abilities to the full. He is remembered chiefly as the commander who broke Pickett's charge at Gettysburg.

HOOKER
Joseph (1814-1879)
US GENERAL
US Civil War

There are some commanders who would be flattered and honored if the epithet "fighting" was to be attached to their name. Joseph Hooker, for all the fact that he was said to have been a braggart, took the opposite view and the newspaper accolade – "Fighting Joe" – was one he rejected and despised. It was given him because he took part in every major battle in the eastern theater of operations during 1862, the first year of the US Civil War.

Hooker was born in November 1814 in Massachussets and, after graduation from West Point, was gazetted into the artillery. Although promotion came regularly – he was a lieutenant-colonel during the Mexican War – he resigned his commission in 1853 to farm in California. On the outbreak of war, however, he returned to the north and was appointed brigadier of volunteers.

"Fighting Joe" in action

Hooker's aggressive instincts demonstrated themselves from the opening weeks of the war. He was one of the group of Union commanders who unsuccessfully tried to convince *McClellan* to advance and to seize Richmond in June 1862. In the bitter fighting at Antietam on 17 September, his 1st Corps opened the Union assault, but what should have been a co-ordinated blow struck by all three Union corps, degenerated into individual assaults, each of which was beaten back by the Confederates with heavy loss. Hooker himself was wounded during the fighting.

Not long after he returned to active service, Hooker was appointed to the command of the Army of the Potomac. He took up the appointment at the end of January 1863 and, having carried out a thorough reorganization of the army, launched it against *Lee* near Chancellorsville.

Hooker's battle plan was for one part of the Army of the Potomac to launch a demonstration at Fredericksburg, so as to attract Confederate attention, while he, with the main body, carried out an encircling march through an area known as the Wilderness. A third group, cavalry and guns, would make an ever wider westward sweep, so as to cut Lee off from his base in the Confederate capital at Richmond. However, the Union plan, though bold, failed. The Fredericksburg demonstration was dealt with by one part of Lee's army, while his main body marched westwards to confront Hooker. Although the Union force was numerically superior, it promptly went onto the defensive. While Hooker was thus static, Lee slipped "Stonewall" *Jackson* around his flank; following a long march, Jackson was positioned at Hooker's back.

The Army of the Potomac was trapped between the two Confederate groups and Hooker's units fell back in disorder. Meanwhile, Lee, leaving only a skeleton force to face Hooker, marched his army back to Fredericksburg, crushed the enemy there and then returned to complete the destruction of the main Union army.

Lee then invaded Pennsylvania. Hooker responded by moving his army parallel to the Confederate line of march, but his new-found caution caused him to lose several opportunities to strike at Lee as the Confederates marched northward. In an argument over what battle plan should be adopted to defeat the Confederates, Hooker tendered his resignation. He had often threatened this before, but this time it was accepted.

No longer at the head of the Army of the Potomac, but still a prominent Union general, Hooker, together with 2nd Corps, was transported from the eastern theater on a 1100-mile-long rail journey to strengthen the forces gathering to raise the siege of Chatanooga in the western theater of operations. When the offensive opened, his corps led the Federal advance through a breach that had been forced in the Confederate line near Look Out Mountain and relieved the town. The Federal forces under *Grant*, now superior in number to the Confederates, now moved against the new Confederate positions. Hooker's corps, forming Grant's right flank, stormed the Look Out Mountain positions and captured them. The capture of that important feature opened the way for the invasion of Georgia. However, when the post of commander of the Army of the Tennessee became vacant, Hooker was passed over in favor of *Sherman*. He promptly resigned his commission and retired.

Hooker was unfortunate. In his first battles, he was not a good field commander and, by the time he had gained proficiency, other, more able, generals had been found. He was probably at his best at corps commander level; as events showed, it was clear that control of the Army of the Potomac was beyond his capabilities. He was a competent professional soldier, but not beyond a certain level.

JACKSON
Thomas J "Stonewall" (1824-1863)
CONFEDERATE GENERAL
US Civil War

"Look, there is Jackson standing like a stone wall. Let us resolve to stand here . . . " This battle cry steadied the Confederate troops as the Union divisions marched forward into a new attack at the first battle of Bull Run. The nick-name "Stonewall" stuck, though it was not in any way descriptive of an outstanding tactician, who was renowned for his mobile, fast hitting raids.

Jackson was born in Clarksburg, Virginia, on 21 January 1824, into a family so poor that he saw the army as his only chance of escape from a life of unending poverty. Such was his diligence at West Point that he graduated 17th in his class and was gazetted into the artillery. Like many of those who rose to command positions in the Confederate and Union armies, Jackson fought in the Mexican War, where he took part in the battles of Cerro Gordo and Chapultepec. He was twice promoted for con-

Jackson then returned to the Shenandoah Valley and, his movements concealed by a mountain range, marched through the only pass in the Blue Ridge mountains to attack and drive back a Federal force at Front Royal. He was now in a position to menace Banks' rear. Swinging westward again, Jackson drove Banks back northward, overhauling and bringing him to battle at Winchester. Banks and his army were flung back across the Potomac, Jackson capturing a great quantity of arms and supplies, plus a substantial number of prisoners.

Alarmed at Jackson's mobility and the threat he posed to the Federal capital, Lincoln now ordered the army based around Fredericksburg to co-operate with the other Federal forces in surrounding Jackson at Harpers Ferry. On Jackson's left lay Fremont, in front of him was Banks and Shields, leading a contingent from the Fredericksburg force, now appeared on his right. The wily Jackson was not to be trapped, however. He sent his cavalry to delay the hesitant Fremont, while he himself trekked southwards with his captured arms and supplies. He escaped one Federal encirclement, but knew that Fremont and Shields were keeping pace on either side of his line of retreat, intending to cut him off at Port Republic. His cavalry was sent, once again, to hold off Fremont, while he defeated Shields at Port Republic to make good his escape. Jackson had converted the intended demonstration into a major campaign that had ended with him foiling a Union force four times his number. More than that, he had saved Richmond for the Confederacy.

The irreplaceable commander

Aware that Lincoln was concentrating his armies to destroy him, Lee needed accurate knowledge of Union movements and so now sent Jackson to observe Pope's army. His corps was attacked at Cedar Mountain on 9 August, however, only Jackson's personal rallying of his troops preventing a Union victory.

Determining to attack Pope, Lee now ordered Jackson to march quickly to position himself in the rear of the Union army. He and *Longstreet* would then join him and destroy Pope's army in a concerted assault. Jackson covered 54 miles in two days to take up position and, having located the main Union supply depots, burned them. Flaunting his presence to conceal the advance of the other Confederate units, he lured Pope into attacking him on 30 August 1862. The unwary Union commander was then taken in the flank by Longstreet's corps and flung back across the Bull Run river.

The Confederate forces then invaded the north. Jackson captured Harpers Ferry, 4,000 prisoners and a mass of stores before joining the main southern force at Antietam Creek, where the Union commander, *McClellan*, had intended to trap Lee's army. On 17 September, the bloodiest single-day battle in the whole US Civil War was fought. McClellan's plan to launch a concerted attack against Lee degenerated into a series of unco-ordinated assaults against Jackson's corps.

Jackson again demonstrated his mobility at Chancellorsville in May 1863, when Lee, caught between two

THE SOUTH'S "STONEWALL" *Jackson was one of the best commanders the south produced during the US Civil War.*

spicuous gallantry and, by the end of the war, had reached the rank of brevet-major. While subsequently serving in Florida, however, he had a fierce argument with his commanding officer and resigned his commission in 1851.

Back in Virginia, Jackson was one of the witnesses at the execution of John Brown in 1859. On the outbreak of the US Civil War, he was appointed as a colonel in the Confederate army and ordered to hold the strategically important town of Harpers Ferry, positioned at the confluence of the Potomac and Shenandoah rivers and also a major railway junction. He held it.

A threat to Washington

In the late spring of 1862, Jackson, by now a major-general, embarked on the campaign that was to make him a household name throughout the Confederacy – and the north as well. Union forces were threatening Richmond, the Confederate capital, and Robert E *Lee*, in a counter-move, decided to panic the Union government by menacing Washington. Jackson, with 18,000 men, was to make a demonstration in the Shenandoah Valley, with the aim of drawing the Union forces away from the Confederate capital towards him. Two Union armies swallowed the bait – one, under Fremont, striking from the west and a second, under Banks, moving down from the north. Aware that, of the two men, Banks was the less able general, he confronted him with a screen of only 8,000 men. He then advanced westward against Fremont, who promptly halted his advance in the face of the threat from Jackson.

Union armies, detached Jackson's corps on a wide enveloping sweep, which then rolled up *Hooker*'s right flank. Jackson determined to make the victory even more complete by cutting Hooker off from the Rappahannock river ford. He rode out at night to conduct a reconnaissance and returning to his own lines was shot and mortally wounded by a nervous sentry. "Stonewall" Jackson, a deeply religious man, had often expressed the wish to die on a Sunday. On Sunday 10 May, 1863 he succumbed to his wounds.

Jackson was undoubtedly Lee's finest lieutenant and many historians have wondered whether the Confederacy would have lost the war had he lived. The evidence provided by his brilliant field operations suggests that the south, with such commanders as Lee and Jackson, might well have fought the US Civil War to a stalemate.

KITCHENER
Herbert Horatio (1850-1916)
BRITISH FIELD MARSHAL
19th-century Colonial Wars,
First World War

Herbert Horatio Kitchener was a Victorian household name. His imperial victories, notably against the fanatical hordes of the Khalifa at Omdurman, firmly established him as one of Britain's leading soldiers; such was his prestige that, on the outbreak of the First World War in 1914, he was the only natural choice as Secretary for War.

Kitchener was born in Listowel, County Kerry, on 24 June, 1850. He was privately educated and then entered the Royal Military Academy, Woolwich, from where, in January 1871, he was gazetted into the Royal Engineers. Prior to his passing-out from the academy, he had served as a volunteer with the French army in the Franco-Prussian War, during which he frequently demonstrated his skilled horsemanship and bravery by carrying despatches across country.

Kitchener's early career in the British army was spent on survey work in Palestine; in 1883, he was posted to Cairo as second in command of an Egyptian cavalry regiment. It was in the Sudan, during the Nile expedition of 1884-85, that he first distinguished himself by outstanding acts of courage and it was to be in the Sudan, 11 years later, that he fought the battle that brought him public renown. The campaign in which Kitchener destroyed the dervish armies of the Khalifa also revenged the murder of General Gordon by the Mahdi, the Khalifa's predecessor. Kitchener's victory was thus the fulfilment of the 1884-5 campaign – the reconquest of the Sudan.

Action at Omdurman
Lord Salisbury, the British prime mininster, chose Kitchener to command the expedition because of the reputation he had earlier gained as a first-rate soldier, as well as for the administrative qualities he had shown as Governor of Zanzibar, of Suakin and as Adjutant General in Cairo. Kitchener was also the *Sirdar*, or commander-in-chief of the Egyptian army, units of which were also to take part in the forthcoming campaign.

Kitchener considered the daunting task he had been given. He was to take a punitive expedition hundreds of miles into a desert region, there to find and to destroy a numerically superior enemy, who, moreover might be concentrated anywhere in that wilderness. His first priority was to establish a supply route to bring in stores and to evacuate the sick. The only natural route was the River Nile, but the Nile was navigable only as far as the first cataract at Wadi Halfa. At that place the river swings westward to form a great bend before it comes back to take up its original direction at Atbara. Kitchener, with his engineering training, saw that the way to overcome the obstacle was to build a railway line from Wadi Halfa to Atbara, across the neck of the river's westward bulge. He dismissed the objections of those who doubted that the work could be carried out and by a combination of brilliant organization and ruthless dedication pushed the line forward at the rate of 1½ miles per day.

By the end of 1897 the railway had been completed and was in operation. Kitchener then began to build up his army for battle. Outfitted with the supplies and strengthened by the reinforcements he had requested, he proposed to advance towards Khartoum, the capital of the Sudan and the center of the Khalifa's power. He had also set up a blockade of the Nile with a flotilla of gunboats, which patrolled the river between Atbara and Khartoum. Kitchener intended to use them as mobile artillery during the battle. Meanwhile, the Khalifa had concentrated his forces. He sent one group to launch guerrilla attacks against the advancing British, while he himself stayed with the main body grouped at Omdurman, outside the Sudanese capital. A clash between the two forces was only a matter of time.

Defeat of the Mahdi
Through native spies, Kitchener received information of an imminent dervish attack on 2 September. This intelligence was confirmed by cavalry reconnaissance, which reported 50,000 of the enemy only five miles from the British positions. Before first light that morning, the British army, positioned on the Plain of Kererri, near Omdurman, was ordered to "stand to". Kitchener deployed his force in a semi-circle behind a *zaraba*, or fence, of camel thorn, erected along the front of the perimeter. Some 20 minutes later, the dervishes launched their first attack from the south-west, masses of men charging on foot, horseback and on camel along an eight mile front. Kitchener held back his artillery fire and watched, as the enemy masses swung in towards the British/Egyptian perimeter. When the dense crowd of dervishes was only 2,000 yards away, the artillery began its bombardment with the Maxim machine guns, positioned between the British and Egyptian brigades, following it into action. Despite the losses this caused, the der-

vishes pressed home their attack; at 200 yards from the *zaraba*, Kitchener's infantry was given the order to open volley fire. The bullets that were fired were dum-dum rounds, which inflicted frightful wounds. They were outlawed by international agreement two years later.

The dervishes in the south-west launched other attacks, but these, too, were smashed. Then from the north-east, out of the Kererri hills, came a series of charges by the main dervish body. These were repulsed as well. By 8.30am, the assaults from both directions seemed to have lost their fury and Kitchener, confident that the battle had been won, sent out a cavalry regiment to cut the dervishes off before they could retreat into Khartoum. The 21st Lancers trotted forward to clear what they supposed to be a group of skirmishers and were surprised to find immediately to their front a natural ditch crammed with the enemy. The lancers charged, reformed and attacked again.

That error on Kitchener's part might have had serious consequences for the 21st Lancers, but he was to make another and more potentially disastrous mistake that

morning. Still convinced that the dervish army had been beaten, he ordered a general advance. The move forwrd broke the British line and exposed Kitchener's left flank. The Khalifa, realizing that his enemy had made a tactical blunder, ordered his army into another attack. The charge that resulted was directed at Hector McDonald's 2nd Sudanese Brigade, which formed the British rearguard. This brigade was still positioned in line facing southwestwards, where it had stood all morning facing the dervish attacks. It opened fire and broke the charge with accurate musketry. Then from the north-east the Khalifa ordered in a second attack against the isolated Sudanese. Coolly, McDonald took his soldiers through the complicated drill movements of changing front. His troops, marching as if on parade, formed a new line to face the assault of some 20,000 dervishes. With a battalion of the Lincolnshire Regiment, which had moved up in support, they smashed what proved to be the final enemy attack as effectively as they had dealt with the previous ones. The battle was now won and, for a loss of 500 men, Kitchener had reconquered the Sudan. The dervishes lost 11,000 killed.

Battling the Boers

Following his victory Kitchener was sent to South Africa, where the British army was meeting with little success in its struggle with the Boer guerrilla commandoes. He became chief-of-staff to Lord Roberts and eventually succeeded him in overall command. Once again, he gained a victory – this time by grasping the basic tactics of successful anti-guerrilla operations. Deprive the enemy of food supplies and of the population which supports him and he is isolated and can be destroyed. Kitchener carried out a "scorched earth" policy and set up camps into which the Boer women and children were concentrated. Those ruthless methods broke Boer resistance in the field.

From India to the War Office

Kitchener's next post was that of commander-in-chief in India where, despite criticism from influential quarters, he carried through the amalgamation of the three separate presidency armies. Out of that former, cumbersome, tripartite system evolved the splendid Indian Army. The need to modernize other imperial and colonial military forces then took Kitchener on a two-year tour of inspection from 1909 to 1910. The reforms which he proposed were carried out and resulted in greater efficiency. In 1911 he returned to Egypt to take up his former post as Agent, or Governor.

When the First World War broke out in 1914, Kitchener was on leave in Britain and accepted, reluctantly, the post of Secretary of State for War. It was not one in which he was happy. He had not been give the chance to reorganize the British forces; in his opinion, the regular army was too small to have any impact in a major war, while the territorial army was inefficient. He was one of a small minority of men in power who believed that the war would last for years and so insisted that the army must be expanded. His call for volunteers, backed by a drawing of

PILLAR OF EMPIRE *Kitchener's imperial triumphs included the defeat of the Mahdi at Omdurman in the Sudan.*

the heavily-moustached Kitchener pointing a finger above the slogan "Your King and Country need you", had an electric effect. Within a short time, the million men for whom he had asked had come forward in a unique patriotic response.

Conflicts of opinion with other military leaders and with politicians on the direction of war strategy led to decisions being made without reference to him. He was faced by a coalition of men who, like Haig, had influence at court or who, like Lloyd George, had opposed the war in South Africa and Kitchener's methods of winning it. He was powerless against that circle of enemies and his influence declined. In the end, however, Kitchener perished heroically. In June 1916, while leading a liaison mission to the Russian Front, he was drowned when *HMS Hampshire*, the cruiser on which he was sailing, struck a mine and sank.

LEE
Robert E (1807-1870)
CONFEDERATE GENERAL
US Civil War

Without doubt, Robert E Lee was the most able soldier ever produced on the North American continent, exhibiting a skill in maneuver and a strategic brilliance that have never been surpassed. In personal habits he was courteous, handsome in appearance, brave in battle and cool in judgement. In a rough and violent age, his impeccable manners and speech were a byword. He was teetotal, did not smoke or swear and was deeply religious.

Born on 19 January 1807 in Virginia, Lee entered West Point in 1825, and graduated fourth in his class. Commissioned into the Corps of Engineers, he saw service in the Mexican War as chief-of-staff to Winfield Scott who wrote of him, "he (Lee) was the very best soldier I ever saw in the field."

A cruel dilemma

After serving as Superintendent at West Point, Lee went on to command the crack 2nd US Cavalry. The outbreak of the Civil War called for his most difficult decision. He had served in the US Army for decades and in fact had been offered command of the Union army by Lincoln. He rejected slavery, was opposed to secession and was also aware that the south was economically backward in comparison with the north. Yet, the ties of honor, blood, race and custom were too strong for him to resist. He resigned his commission and accepted a generalship in the Confederate forces. He was not, at first, given a field command; instead, he was made military adviser to Jefferson Davis, the Confederate president. His first thought was to consider the tactical and strategic situation in which the south was placed.

The theater of war extended from Virginia, whose Atlantic seaboard was dominated by the Union navy, along

THE GREATEST CONFEDERATE *Robert E Lee, commander of the Army of Virginia, was a master of battlefield strategy.*

the Mississippi and as far as Texas. That 3,000 mile-long battle front was only loosely connected – if at all – so making an overall military strategy extremely difficult to conceive and execute. Both sides' main armies were concentrated into a relatively small area of territory in the north-eastern states, within which lay their two capitals – Washington and Richmond. The Potomac river formed the frontier between the Union and the Confederacy.

Virginia, in which the principal battles were fought, was naturally divided by mountain ranges into an eastern and a western theater of operations. Lateral communication between these two theaters was limited, so railways therefore were of key importance. In the deep south, the Mississipi was another worry for Lee, for it was the natural route to the western theater. If Union forces won control of the waterway, then the Confederate states south of the Mississipi would be separated from Virginia, leaving the Virginians isolated.

Lee was also aware that two further factors adversely affected Confederate hopes of success. From a white population of 4½ million, only a small army could be recruited, while such heavy industry as the Confederacy possessed was located around Richmond, only 100 miles from Washington. Under such circumstances, Lee considered the south's accepted strategy – to remain on the defensive to conserve its few resources – to be incorrect. Instead, he argued that the Confederacy must attack and carry the war to the enemy. His belief was that the invasion of northern territory would force the Union to concentrate its armies to meet the attackers. A decisive battle would result and the casualties the Confederates would inflict on the Union forces, would compel the north to make peace. Lee was confident that the high standard of military skill in the Confederate armies would bring victory in the single decisive battle he proposed.

Thrusting into the north

On 1 June 1862, Lee was given command of the Army of Northern Virginia, and ordered to resolve the crisis arising from a Federal invasion, which was threatening Richmond. While he fortified the city with field defences and prepared it to withstand a siege, Lee ordered a cavalry force under "Stonewall" *Jackson* to thrust along the Shenandoah Valley and to threaten Washington. As Lee had anticipated, Lincoln, concerned for the safety of his capital, reinforced his troops along the Shenandoah at the expense of those facing Richmond. With a Federal force now firmly committed to holding the valley, Lee could bring Jackson's corps by train to reinforce his own command. The Confederates now fought and won the battle of Manassas Junction. Fearful for his exposed army, Lincoln withdrew it from before Richmond, thus giving Lee the freedom to attack General Pope, whom he defeated in the second battle of Bull Run.

Lee was now confident he could gain the strategic victory he had planned. Intent upon a decisive battle, he led the Army of Northern Virginia into the Cumberland Valley during September 1862. However, his scheme was frustrated. The Union commander, George *McLellan*, moved his army faster than Lee had anticipated and trapped part of the Confederate force at Antietam Creek in Maryland, where, on 17 September, the bloodiest single-day battle of the US Civil War was fought. The Confederacy lost 12,000 men and the Union 17,000 but, even more significantly, Lee had failed to fight the decisive battle. He withdrew to Fredericksburg in Virginia, where he defeated one Union army, under Burnside, during December 1862 and another, commanded by *Hooker*, in May 1863.

Decision at Gettysburg

Lee's army, now 75,000 strong, now invaded the north once again, still in search of the decisive battle. The Confederates advanced up the Cumberland Valley and then turned eastwards, intending to strike at Washington from the north. The Union army that had confronted Lee at Fredericksburg now abandoned its siege and maneuvered to keep itself between Lee and the Federal capital. Patrols of both sides clashed at Gettysburg on 1 July 1863 and battle was joined on the following day, with Lee attacking and Meade (who had replaced Hooker), standing on a defensive line built on high ground.

Gettysburg was the high tide of Confederate hopes, but, when the fighting died away on 4 July, Lee knew that he had not gained the victory for which he had striven.

He withdrew back into Virginia. Gettysburg had cost him one-third of his troops; Lee realized that his army no longer had the strength to fight and win the war in a single, set-piece battle.

Lee versus Grant

The scale of operations in the eastern theater of war now diminished. The new Union commander, Ulysses S *Grant*, realized that a military decision would be easier to obtain through a war of maneuver in the west. His actions quickly won the strategic initiative there.

To stop Lee reinforcing his western armies, Grant acted aggressively against Richmond, so forcing the Confederate commander to retain his troops around the southern capital. In that campaign, Lee, although outnumbered and outgunned, demonstrated his strategic brilliance by anticipating every move that Grant made. His economy of effort in countering the Federal operations was masterly and his application of the military sciences unsurpassed in the history of war on the North American continent.

However, Lee did not have the strength to defeat Grant – nor to halt *Sherman*, whose outflanking march took him through Georgia to the sea. Lee, who assumed command of all the southern armies in February 1865, did manage to win the Confederacy a little time in the hope that political moves might still bring victory, but his hopes faded when one of his armies operating in the Shenandoah Valley was eventually trapped and defeated, while even the delaying actions fought by Johnston against Sherman only postponed the inevitable. Sherman's army swept northward, thrusting at Lee's back, but, before he could bring the Confederate commander to battle, Grant had broken through at Richmond. Lee surrendered on 9 April and Johnston later that month. The military strength of the Confederacy had been broken and the US Civil War was at an end.

Robert E Lee, a superb strategist and military engineer, whose field fortifications anticipated the trench warfare of later conflicts, did not long survive the end of the Civil War. A heart condition, which had affected him for years, was aggravated by the strain of command and he died on 12 October 1870.

LONGSTREET
James (1821-1904)
CONFEDERATE GENERAL
US Civil War

James Longstreet has long been an enigma to military historians. If he was as dilatory as some assert, the question is why did *Lee* think so highly of him? If he was not, why did he not act more promptly at Gettysburg?

Longstreet was born in January 1821, at Edgfield, South Carolina. He graduated from West Point in 1842 and saw service in the war with Mexico, during which he demonstrated such outstanding courage that he was twice promoted in the field – once from lieutenant to captain and then from captain to major. Supporting the Confederacy in the US Civil War, he commanded a brigade at the first battle of Bull Run, leading it with such ability that he was promoted major-general. Indeed, such was Lee's confidence in Longstreet that he now placed half of the Army of Northern Virginia under his direct com-

SCAPEGOAT? *Longstreet, blamed for Gettysburg.*

mand. During the second battle of Bull Run and at Antietam, Longstreet showed once more the panache in attack and the tactical flair that had distinguished him in earlier battles. Given command of 1st Confederate Corps, he demonstrated at Fredericksburg that he was as skilled in fighting a defensive battle as he was in leading an attacking one.

The puzzle of Gettysburg

Much of the post-war criticism of Longstreet stems from his actions – or lack of them – at the battle of Gettysburg. Following the first clashes on 30 June, the battle lines had been drawn up by 1 July. At a battlefield conference late that night, Longstreet, whose corps had not yet arrived on the battlefield, argued that the Confederate force should maneuver round the Union left flank and threaten Washington. Lee, however, knew it was essential for him to capture the high ground south and east of the town upon which the Union army was deployed. He rejected Longstreet's plan and issued orders for a combined attack by his three corps the following morning. However, it was not until the afternoon, that Longstreet, whose corps Lee had ordered to open the general assault, went into action.

The fury of Longstreet's attack drove back the Union left flank based around Little Round Top, one of a pair of low hills. For hours, Longstreet's men fought their way across the cultivated valley south and west of Gettysburg and up the hills and ridges and, time after time, their assaults were driven back. The breakthrough for which they were striving eluded them. Lee had planned for the whole Confederate line to go into action, but it was not until the last of Longstreet's attacks ebbed away that first Ewell's and then Hill's corps moved forward. Though their assaults were many and well-directed, they failed to seize the vital high ground from the determined Union defenders as well.

Lee decided that he would now assault the Union line on Cemetery Ridge frontally, using ten brigades of infantry. Longstreet opposed this plan, pointing out that the tired Confederate troops would be attacking the strongest sector of the enemy line. Lee insisted that the

attacks went ahead. Longstreet refused to move in support, for he would not order his men into what he considered to be a suicide operation. The great assault – Pickett's famous charge – failed and its survivors flooded back in retreat.

The Confederate forces had failed to win the battle of Gettysburg and much of the blame was laid at Longstreet's door for his slowness in getting into action on 2 July. As if in answer to his critics, Longstreet demonstrated how speedily he could move at Chickamauga that September, when he exploited a crucial mistake made by Rosencrans, the Union commander. While deploying his divisions after the fighting of the previous day, Rosencrans left a gap in his line. Longstreet, seizing the opportunity, flung his men forward to smash through the Union left and center and drive the Federals from the field.

Longstreet was wounded during the battle of the Wilderness in May 1864 and consequently was out of action until October. He then played a leading part in defeating the Union attempt to cut the last remaining Confederate railway link into besieged Petersburg. It was Longstreet's final major action in the US Civil War.

In post-war analyses of the Civil War campaigns, Longstreet was blamed for delays and slowness and was practically accused of having lost Gettysburg for the Confederacy and consequently the war. He died in January 1904 an embittered man. More recent and less subjective studies suggest that, although his actions were undoubtedly deliberate, he was steadfast and reliable.

McCLELLAN
George B (1826-1885)
US GENERAL
US Civil War

George B McClellan is a classic case of a commander promoted beyond his abilities by an amateur. Though he was an effective organizer and administrator, he was not a skilled leader in battle.

McClellan was born in Philadelphia in December 1826 and graduated from West Point in 1846, after which he was gazetted into the Corps of Engineers. After service in the Mexican war, McClellan was selected to be one of a board of officers that was sent to study European military systems; the board visited Sevastapol during the Crimean War. Upon returning home, however, McClellan resigned to work as a senior railroad administrator.

Organizer and administrator

In the first months of the US Civil War McClellan served as a major-general of volunteers in Ohio; subsequently, he was appointed to command all the military forces Ohio had raised, with a regular army commission. He showed his willingness to take the military initiative at Philippi on 3 June 1861 and at Rich Mountain in July, successfully clearing western Virginia of Confederate troops.

McClellan's skill in organizing and administering large bodies of men was brought to Lincoln's attention and, after the first battle of Bull Run, he was put in command of all the various unorganized military bodies grouped around Washington. McClellan quickly formed these into proper detachments – this was the foundation of what eventually became the Army of the Potomac. Following this, Lincoln, who was dissatisfied with the field strategy proposed by Winfield Scott, the ageing commander-in-chief, replaced him with McClellan, expecting that he would demonstrate the same skill in the conduct of large-scale military operations as he had shown in administration.

Lincoln, however, was quickly disillusioned. The new commander-in-chief was hesitant and timid. Faced with the problems of administering an army, of planning operations across a wide-flung battle front and also fighting battles in the field, McClellan developed a neurosis. He refused to move against the Confederate forces, because he believed that they outnumbered him. Lincoln had appointed him because he had ability, but he lacked the crucial trait that wins wars. He lacked the lust for combat – the *sine qua non* of a fighting commander.

Disaster in the field

In an effort to lighten his burden, Lincoln relieved McClellan of his post as commander-in-chief, on 11 March 1862, leaving him free to concentrate on the Army of the Potomac. This was then marched, via the Peninsula, towards Richmond, but *en route* McClellan was once again plagued by doubts, when he learned that *Lee* was moving against him. Fearing himself to be confronting a Confederate Army superior in number to his own, McClellan hesitated – once at Yorktown, which he invested in April and May; and again at the end of June when the battle of Gaine's Hill might have led to the capture of Richmond. Lincoln, now concerned for the safety of Washington, order him to pull back into northern Virginia, assuring the fearful McClellan that he would be reinforced by Pope's army. Before the two forces could link up, however, Lee struck and on 29 August the second battle of Bull Run was fought. Pope was saved from total defeat by the intervention of McClellan's forces, who arrived piecemeal on the field and were committed immediately to battle. In that two-day fight, Pope's army was all but destroyed and it was McClellan, using all his skills in training and in organization, who reformed it.

Now, an order from Lee, detailing the Confederate moves and dispositions, fell into McClellan's hands. But although he knew the Confederate forces to be strung out and, therefore, in a tactically unsound position, McClellan made no immediate move against them. When he did, at Antietam Creek, his unco-ordinated attacks incurred casualty figures that were simply too large for Lincoln to accept. McClellan was replaced and his military career was effectively at an end. He sought to make a name for himself in politics, fighting the presidential election of 1864 as a Democrat, but was beaten.

McClellan was an excellent administrator and successful organiser, but he was no fighting commander. Indeed, from his actions and attitudes, he was clearly unsuited to the stresses of high command. It was his tragedy that men of the calibre of *Grant* or *Sherman* were not to hand when Lincoln needed a dynamic fighting man.

McMAHON
Marie Maurice (1808-1893)
MARSHAL OF FRANCE

Marie Maurice McMahon led Napoleon III's forces to their disastrous defeat at Sedan in the Franco-Prussian War of 1870. The Prussian victory here confirmed the emergence of a new military force and marked the end of France's role as the premier martial nation of Europe.

McMahon's military career began early. At the age of 19, he was already on active service in Algeria, fighting against the Emir of Mascara, Abd el Kader. During the campaign, the young McMahon won a reputation for repeated acts of bravery in the fighting for the city of Constantine. By the time of the Crimean War he was a divisional commander and, during the war, added to his firmly established reputation for courage the cachet of being a first-class leader of men in battle. In September 1855, the French and British armies stormed Sevastapol, the principal French objective being the Malakov strongpoint. In this battle, McMahon's division played a vital part and was instrumental in bringing about the capture of Sevastapol on 9 September.

McMahon was now one of Napoleon III's favorite commanders. In the war against Austria in 1859 – particularly at Magenta – McMahon's actions were considered by Napoleon III to have been of decisive importance. In recognition of his efforts, the emperor created him Duke of Magenta. A Marshal of France at the age of 51, McMahon then spent a number of years as Governor-General of Algeria, where he had served as a young officer.

Debacle at Sedan

When Napoleon III declared war on Prussia on 15 July 1870, the French army was ill prepared for action. After the first frontier clashes, the emperor divided the field force to create two armies, of Alsace and Lorraine. The Army of Alsace, with three corps, was placed under McMahon. On 6 August, his I Corps flung back a Prussian reconnaissance group, but was then outflanked by the Prussian Crown Prince. McMahon's withdrawal to avoid encirclement opened the road to Paris.

The shaken Army of Alsace fell back before its Prussian pushers, but, having regrouped, McMahon marched to relieve Marshal *Bazaine*, now invested in Metz. However his line of march was not eastwards, as might have been expected, but northwards to Belgium and then southeastwards towards Bazaine. The delay this indirect route caused gave *Moltke* time to deploy the Prussian armies to their best advantage with the result that McMahon found himself trapped in the bend of the Meuse at *Sedan*. In the battle that followed, McMahon took little active part, for he had been wounded on 31 August and had delegated command to General Ducrot. As a sign of the confusion into which the French had fallen, Ducrot was immediately superseded by Wimpffen, who claimed that the French war minister had given him the authority to take over should McMahon be incapacitated. The battle itself was a brutal and bloody affair that was only brought to an end when Napoleon personally rode forward to surrender his forces to the Prussian king.

Sedan was not McMahon's last battle, but his defeat of the Communards in 1871 was a campaign fought against fellow Frenchmen. Within a few years of the war's end, McMahon, whose simplicity and dignity inspired confidence, was elected president of the Third Republic. As president, he suffered greatly from abuse and accusations of disloyalty from left-wing politicians; it was, therefore, with relief that he laid down the office and retired. The courageous, yet modest, McMahon devoted the remaining years of his life to working for veterans' associations and speaking at ex-service rallies.

VON MOLTKE
Helmuth (1800-1891)
GERMAN FIELD MARSHAL
Franco-Prussian War

Helmuth von Moltke was the creator of the Prussian army that forcibly unified Germany by defeating Austria and then went on to establish Germany's military hegemony in Europe through his defeat of France in the Franco-Prussian War. A thinking soldier as well as an active combatant, he also created the modern general staff system, which was the model for all other major powers.

Moltke was born at Parchim in October 1800 into a family of minor Prussian aristocrats. The Moltke family moved to Holstein while Helmuth was still a child and, as a Danish citizen, he was chosen to serve as a page at court and then in the Danish army. He returned to Prussia at the age of 21, where he was gazetted into the 8th Infantry Regiment. Evan as a subaltern, his tactical skills as displayed on maneuvers and his grasp of military doctrines marked him out as an exceptional officer. His drawback was his need for a second source of income, which he found in authorship. Showing remarkable diligence, he completed the German translation of nine of the volumes of Gibbon's "Decline and Fall of the Roman Empire" within 18 months of starting the task. Though he never received the full fee for the translation, he was later to declare that the knowledge he gained from it more than compensated for the paltry sum he was paid.

During his time at the Prussian war academy, Moltke was given leave to serve with the forces of Sultan Mahmoud in the Russo-Turkish War of 1828/29, when he demonstrated the calmness he was to exhibit in battle throughout his life. At Nazib in June 1829, his artillery held back the victorious infantry of Mehmet Ali and was the last unit to leave the field. Returning to Germany, he published an account of his experiences, which sold well and gave him financial security. From then on, he rose steadily through the ranks of the Prussian general staff, becoming its chief during 1857. In that post, he set about re-organizing the Prussian army, which was no longer the efficient force that had been created in the immediate post-Napoleonic period.

Reforming the Prussian army
The first product of Moltke's re-organization was a staff system in which the chief of staff of any major formation was a graduate of the Prussian war academy. This meant that such officers were members of an elite group of skilled professionals, who spoke with the authority of the chief of the general staff and dealt only with the execution of military operations. Transportation, supplies and other non-combat functions were handled by officers trained in those branches of service. Each chief of staff produced battle plans for his superior and gave advice that was usually heeded, since it contained all the information required for a decision to be reached.

Moltke then turned to the problem of mobilization and the speedy deployment of the army. He had long studied the use of railways and the telegraph in military operations and their employment in the US Civil War. The increase in rates of fire and accuracy of musketry, together with the greater destructive power of modern artillery also all demanded new battlefield tactics and training.

Unifying Germany by "blood and iron"
Prussia's large conscript army was backed by civilian reservists, an industrial base capable of equipping these forces and, finally, by an expanding, efficient railway network. Moltke utilized all the resources for the first of the wars of German unification against Denmark in 1864. One far-reaching result of the Prussian success was that Kaiser Wilhelm I, impressed by Moltke's handling of the army in action against the Danes, was prepared to leave battlefield control to his chief of staff.

Following the short campaign against Denmark, Moltke re-organized the Prussian artillery and reconsidered the battlefield tactics that had been employed. He had seen that old-fashioned, frontal assaults by massed infantry and cavalry were obsolete and wasteful in manpower. He would win his future victories through flanking attacks and by indirect approach. What this meant was that his armies would march separately towards the enemy but would concentrate to fight him. While one of them held the enemy front fast, the others would maneuver round the flanks. The enemy, now surrounded, would be forced to launch costly mass assaults to try to break through the Prussian ring; when he was sufficiently weakened, he would be destroyed by a simultaneous attack launched by the encircling armies.

The first war in which these new concepts were

PRUSSIAN PLANNER *As chief of the general staff, von Moltke built up the formidable Prussian war machine.*

employed was the 1866 campaign against Austria and her mainly Catholic allies in the German states. Moltke was aided by Bismarck's political activities, which kept France and Russia neutral and enlisted Italy as Prussia's ally. Thus the Austrian army was forced to fight on two fronts, grouping the bulk of the imperial forces – the army of the North – to face the Prussians as they moved into Bohemia, having defeated Austria's German allies.

As a result of Moltke's mobilization, Prussia fielded three armies, totalling 250,000 men – 20,000 more than Austria had available to meet the attack. Wilhelm I delegated full command to Moltke and the Prussian commander ordered his three armies to march separately towards the chosen concentration point.

On 2 July 1866, the rival forces were grouped near the key road and rail junction of Koeniggraetz in Bohemia. Battle was joined during the following day, with Prussian victory as the result – even though Moltke's plan to surround the Austrian army did not succeed completely.

Birth of an empire

Once again, there were lessons to be learned and new tactics to be developed. These were put into practice in Moltke's final war against France, fought in order to determine whether Germany or France would be the principal European power. Moltke equipped the Prussian artillery with steel, breech-loading cannon, while refinements to the doctrine of encirclement and destruction were introduced and mobilization plans overhauled. At the end of the reorganization Moltke was able to deploy an army of 500,000, superbly equipped Prussian soldiers in less than three weeks and could triple the number, if

required, within six months. Moltke had such confidence in the force he had developed, that in reply to Bismarck's question on the odds of a Prussian victory, he said that these were 80 per cent in its favor.

By the first week of August 1870, Moltke had assembled three armies along the frontier and engaged the French before they were deployed for battle. A series of minor engagements dispersed Napoleon III's forces, which the French command then sought to concentrate. At *Sedan*, the mass of Napoleon's army was trapped; in the battle of encirclement that followed, Moltke's tactics forced a mass surrender, by 104,000 French troops – and Napoleon himself – being taken prisoner.

After the war, convinced of the dependence of what was now the imperial German army upon railways, Moltke continued to refine his mobilization plans. Each unit was given an allotted place in the overall plan, the individual commanders knowing the trains on which their men would be transported, for each set of operational orders had included a railway time-table. The whole mighty apparatus could be set in motion with one single, telegraphed message. It was a remarkable planning achievement and a fitting memorial to Moltke's abilities.

Because of his calm, quiet nature, Moltke was known as the "Great Silent One." The most vivid pictorial memorial of him was a painting of the crisis point of the battle of Koeniggraetz in 1866. In this painting, the tall, gray-faced von Moltke and his staff are depicted watching the struggle. Wilhelm and Bismarck are showing concern at the prospect of an Austrian breakthrough, but the quiet, calm bulk of the "Great Silent One" reassures them. Copies of this painting were once to be found in every Prussian schoolroom – an eloquent testimony to the commander, who more than any other, was responsible for the military muscle that helped to create a unified Germany under Prussia's hegemony.

NOGI
Maresoke (1849-1912)
JAPANESE GENERAL
Russo-Japanese War

At the turn of the century, Japanese colonial expansion in the Far East resulted inevitably in a confrontation with Russia. The resulting conflict – the first modern, major one between an eastern and a western power – produced many outstanding Japanese commanders. Of these, Maresoke Nogi was as prominent on land as Admiral *Togo* was at sea.

SAMURAI *Nogi, leader of the attack on Port Arthur.*

Nogi was born on 11 November 1849 at Yamaguchi, into an old Samurai family. Graduating from military school in 1871, he rose steadily and in the war with China during 1894/1895, led the dawn attack upon the fortifications of Port Arthur, going on to capture the town.

Shortly after promotion to the rank of lieutenant-general and the command of a division, Nogi retired, but, within four years, was recalled to duty for the imminent war with Russia. In May 1904, he was appointed to command Japanese 3rd Army with the task of investing Port Arthur, while 2nd Army moved northwards to confront a Russian offensive. The defence of Port Arthur was in the hands of the incompetent General Stoessel, who, in fact, had little to fear. The port was surrounded by rings of defences and fortified hills. Its garrison of 40,000 men was supported by more than 500 guns and was adequately supplied to withstand a siege. Reinforcements increased the strength of 3rd Army to twice that of the Russians, but the Japanese had less artillery. The 3rd Army was not yet powerful enough to take the town.

The siege of Port Arthur
During the first week of July, Nogi, who had been surprised by a swift Russian sortie, carried out a detailed reconnaissance of the Russian defences. From this, there then developed, later in July, strong, localized attacks mounted to test the strength, speed of reaction and combat efficiency of the Russian garrison.

Nogi's first main attack was launched on 7 August against the eastern hills, which were captured on the following day. His second offensive opened on 19 August, when the Japanese regiments, set out in mass formation, attacked Hill 174 on the north-western sector and fortified positions in the north-eastern area of the defensive perimeter. In superb demonstrations of military valor, Nogi's close-packed columns stormed forward into the rapid fire of the Russian machine guns. In the frequent night attacks, the defenders illuminated the battlefield with searchlights and flares and continued to slaughter Nogi's troops. The five-day battle ended with the Japanese having gained Hill 174 and some forts at the cost of 15,000 men. Until the heavy artillery Nogi had requested arrived, extensive mining work was undertaken and sap heads pushed out from the Japanese trenches, which now completely surrounded the port.

At the end of the second week of September Nogi, although still lacking his siege artillery, decided to undertake a third attack – this time against the north and north-western sectors. The tactic of close-packed columns of infantry advancing against machine-gun fire was repeated throughout the remaining days of September and the result was the same – small gains for the loss of thousands of dead. By 20 September, the north and north-western objectives had been gained, but the tactically important Hill 203, the key to the entire defence, was still in Russian hands. The arrival of the heavy guns in October, the destructive power of their bombardment and the completion of the mining and sapping operations around Hill 203, were a prelude to the next infantry

assaults, which lasted for three days, from 30 October to 1 November. These were wasteful and gained nothing.

A determined Japanese infantry assault was then planned to finally capture Hill 203. The assault started at 9.00 am with a simultaneous, two-pronged attack against the eastern and northern forts. For ten days, waves of Japanese fought their way uphill and into the fortifications that ringed the position. Their ferocious attacks, carried out across a hillside covered with dead, were met with equally ferocious Russian counter-attacks. On 4 December the last defenders were destroyed and Japanese guns on the hill crest opened fire upon the Russian fleet trapped in the harbor. The siege did not end completely until 1 January 1905, when the last fort fell.

Nogi then marched his army to join the main Japanese forces in the battle for Mukden. In that operation, 3rd Army played a decisive part, driving back the enemy right wing and thereby forcing the Russians into retreat.

At the end of the war, Nogi returned to Japan, where he served as a member of the emperor's supreme war council. When the Mikado died, Nogi, as a demonstration of Samurai loyalty, committed hari-kari (ritual suicide). It was all part of the tradition of fearlessness in the face of death in which he and his soldiers had fought – one which enabled him to commit Japanese troops to repeated and unflinching frontal attacks against the destructive fire-power of modern weapons.

SHERIDAN
Philip (1831-1888)
US GENERAL
US Civil War

The fiery-tempered Philip Sheridan, one of the most distinguished Federal commanders of the US Civil War, almost had no army career at all. He was very lucky to have passed out from West Point as he took five years to graduate – the result of being suspended for a long period as punishment for striking a cadet sergeant.

When the US Civil War broke out, Sheridan was recalled from his post as quartermaster in south-west Missouri to take up a fighting command with the 2nd Michigan Volunteer Corps as their brigadier. His skilful handling of his corps in the summer 1862 fighting brought him promotion to the command of an infantry division. However, the full extent of his military skills were first demonstrated when he was made commander of the Army of the Potomac's cavalry in April 1864.

Cavalry genius
By this time, cavalry no longer possessed the power as a shock weapon it had enjoyed in former days; cavalry units were more usually employed in reconnaissance, or in raids to create unrest in the enemy rear. It was in this type of operation that Sheridan excelled himself, gaining the sort of reputation which had once been enjoyed only by

Confederate cavalry commanders as a result of the four raids he launched during this period. In one of these, during Grant's southward strike that May, Sheridan's 10,000 troopers were moving against the defences of Richmond, when they were confronted by "Jeb" *Stuart* with 4,500 horsemen. In the resulting clash the Confederates were driven from the field and Stuart was mortally wounded.

In an attempt to split the Southern forces, *Grant* ordered Sheridan to launch a further raid during June 1864, its purpose being to divert Confederate attention. However, *Lee* would not be drawn, countering Grant by detaching two Confederate cavalry divisions, which intercepted Sheridan and brought him to battle at Trevilian station. After two days of confused, but bitter, fighting, Sheridan was forced to withdraw. The thwarted Grant now determined to block off the Shenandoah Valley, through which the Confederacy could threaten Washington. He gave Sheridan command of the Army of the Shenandoah, with orders to devastate Virginia and to destroy the Confederate forces in the valley.

Sheridan's offensive opened slowly, but then gained in momentum. At Opequon Creek, in a brilliant display of battlefield command, Sheridan turned the Confederate left flank and then struck the center. The Confederates pulled back, but were savaged again only three days later at Fisher's Hill, where Sheridan, using the same tactics as at Opequon, forced the enemy troops back with heavy casualties. As Sheridan moved down the Shenandoah Valley, he destroyed everything that might have been of use to the south.

The final campaign
Sheridan rested his army, while he waited for orders from Grant as how it was next to be employed. While he was attending a conference in Washington, however, Jubal Early launched a surprise attack on the Army of the Shenandoah and all but scattered it. Just as defeat seemed certain, Sheridan, who had ridden at top speed for over 20 miles, arrived on the battlefield. Exhibiting masterly powers of leadership, he rallied his shaken army and led it into a counter-attack, which drove the Confederates from the field. He joined Grant on 26 March 1865 for the final campaign. His cavalry sought to encircle Lee's flank, but the Confederate commander marched two divisions to encircle the encirclers and attack Sheridan's left flank. By reinforcing the battle line, Sheridan eventually drove back the enemy. At Five Forks, he smashed the Confederate front and flank and by forcing these back uncovered the enemy right wing. This gave Grant the opportunity to order a general assault.

Sheridan flung his cavalry into action as the southern forces began to collapse, Lee's attempt at an orderly withdrawal from Petersburg being harassed by Sheridan's raids along the Confederate flanks. At Saylor's Creek, Sheridan took the initiative when two southern corps sought to delay Grant's pursuit, moving quickly to position himself behind the southern troops along the creek while a Union infantry corps attacked frontally. The Confederate force

surrendered. Sheridan then anticipated that Lee would move towards Lynchburg and intercepted him at Appamatox Courthouse where, after a short battle, Lee finally surrendered.

In post-war years, Sheridan served in Mexico but his harshness raised criticisms and he was relieved of his command in 1867. He then travelled to Europe to observe the Franco-Prussian War. In 1888, the year in which he was promoted full general, Sheridan died. Throughout his life, Sheridan displayed a pugnacity, which, when utilized in military sense, brought him fame. He had a magnetic force of personality, which won him the fiercest loyalty from his men. Without question, he was a superb cavalry commander.

SHERMAN
William T (1820-1891)
US GENERAL
US Civil War

William Tecumsah Sherman was an uncomplicated man of action, respected by the men he commanded despite being a strict disciplinarian. A fighting soldier to his finger-tips, he found daily routine boring and frustrating.

Born on 8 February 1820 in Lancaster, Ohio, Sherman graduated from West Point in 1840, sixth in a class of 42. He was commissioned into the 3rd Artillery Regiment, but,

REALIST *Sherman thought "war is hell".*

after 14 years of regimental duty, conscious of the poor prospects of promotion, he resigned. Subesquently, he experimented with several civilian careers, before securing the superintendency of a military academy.

Learning from experience
Sherman's path back into the service was not straightforward. Shortly after the outbreak of the US Civil War, Sherman wrote to Lincoln to offer him advice on the Louisiana situation. Lincoln ignored it. Sherman, indignant at this rebuff, at first resolved not to fight for either side, but was soon persuaded to accept a colonelcy in the Federal forces. However, his opinion of Lincoln remained low. He was contemptuous of the president's control of the war, seeing his actions as amateurish and not meeting the need of the moment. In particular, he ridiculed Lincoln's appeal for short-term volunteers as Sherman was convinced that the war would be a long and bitter one. However, Sherman's grasp of command in the field was rusty, as his poor handling of his troops during

the first Battle of Bull Run demonstrated. His own uncertainties – and the sudden attacks of depression from which he suffered as a result – led to him raising so many false alarms about Confederate attacks that there were doubts as to his mental balance.

It was as a subordinate to Ulysses S *Grant* that Sherman regained his confidence. He now showed the ability to plan operations down to the minutest detail, a characteristic that marked his subsequent career. Guided by Grant, he fought and won the battle of Shiloh in April 1862; in May, by this time a major-general, he was ordered with 40,000 men to capture the strategically-important city of Vicksburg. His planning for this amphibious operation was excellent, but he was abruptly superseded by the incompetent McClernand.

Sherman was not finished with the Mississippi, however. In April 1863, he launched a demonstration along the Yazoo river to attract Confederate attention while Grant prepared for the battle of Champion's Hill and then went on to destroy Confederate supplies at Jackson and to blockade a Southern force in Johnson. His aggressive action soon cleared the Mississippi. When Grant was promoted and the post of overall commander of the Army of the Tennessee consequently became vacant, Sherman's abilities and Grant's recommendation ensured that he filled the post.

The "march to the sea"
Sherman now prepared to undertake the operations with which his name is forever associated. His army marched for a month in order to link up with Grant's forces and then fought a series of small, but important, battles which cleared Tennessee of Confederate troops. The way was now clear for Sherman to march into Georgia. During May 1864, he led 100,000 men from Chatanooga towards Atlanta, the advance being contested by a Confederate army under Johnston. The tactical skills of those two able commanders was demonstrated at Dalton, Resaca and Cassville, but on 27 June Sherman fought an uncharacteristic battle, for which he has been criticized by historians. Making no attempt to maneuver at all, he launched a frontal assault against Kenesaw Mountain, the key to Johnston's position before Atlanta. His attacks, though pressed home with great gallantry, were completely unsuccessful and cost him 3,000 casualties.

This proved to be only a minor check. Aided by a change in the Confederate command, the cautious Johnston being replaced by the more aggressive Hood, Sherman broke through and on 1 September his troops entered Atlanta (the Confederate forces had evacuated the city the previous evening). During November 1864, after only a short pause for regrouping, his army marched forward to the sea some 300 miles away, rolling up the Confederate positions and defeating the forces which were put into the field against him. Sherman was determined to destroy the Confederate will to fight, so his troops cut a deliberate swath of destruction on their march. Savannah was captured and offered to Lincoln as a Christmas present;

during February, Sherman occupied Columbia, which was then burnt to the ground. Sherman had reached Goldsboro before he decided to pause to allow his troops to rest, before moving forward again to Petersburg, where Grant's forces were positioned. However, before the roads had dried sufficiently to allow the advance to Petersburg to be resumed, the last battles of the war had been fought. Grant, with Sheridan's cavalry blocking Lee's attempt to link with Johnston, trapped the Confederate commander-in-chief at Appamatox. The US Civil War was over.

Sherman's campaign had been a brilliant military success, but the way in which it was accomplished has been harshly criticized. His decision to let his army live off the land as it swept through the south and the wholesale killing of cattle and confiscation of foodstuffs that resulted meant that it could be truly said "famine follows Sherman". His soldiers' brutality towards the civilian population was attacked; it was widely believed that the repressive measures he instituted might almost have been deliberate terror tactics.

Post-war promotions raised Sherman to the rank of lieutenant-general by 1866 and full general in 1869. In the same year, he became general-in-chief of the army, holding that post for 14 years. Unlike Grant, he lacked political ambitions. When he was asked to run for the presidency, he declined with the famous refusal "I will not accept if I am nominated and will not serve if elected." He died on 14 February 1891 in New York.

STUART
James E B ("Jeb") (1833-1864)
CONFEDERATE GENERAL
US Civil War

There is no doubt that the most able commander of light cavalry on either side in the US Civil War, was the flamboyant and daring "Jeb" Stuart.

Stuart was born on 6 February 1833, in Virginia, graduating from West Point in 1854, as a cavalry lieutenant. He served with the US cavalry for five years. At the outbreak of the Civil War, however, he resigned his commission and enlisted in the Confederate forces, with the

DASH *"Jeb" Stuart, brilliant cavalryman, was the Confederacy's darling.*

rank of lieutenant-colonel. Although he was technically commissioned into the Confederate infantry, Stuart served exclusively with the cavalry.

It was during the first battle of Bull Run, fought on 21

July 1861, that Stuart first showed his extraordinary ability as a cavalry commander. McDowell, in command of the Union forces, had planned to turn Beauregard's flank force, but was himself outflanked. Stuart's regiment played a distinguished part in the battle and in the pursuit of the scattered northern troops, an achievement that was recognized by his promotion to brigadier-general.

Flair and imagination

Stuart possessed the twin qualities of flair and imagination and was able to communicate his enthusiasm to the men he commanded. Throughout the winter of 1861/62, in between scouting duties, he trained his troops, leading them on swift "in and out" raids, to which the Union commanders had no answer. Their own attempts at similar operations were foiled by Stuart's extensive and well led outpost patrols.

In June 1862 Stuart carried out the most famous of his many scouting operations – perhaps the most celebrated of the entire Civil War. That spring, the Union army, under *McClellan*, had begun an advance towards Richmond, the Confederate capital. In order to counter the move Robert E *Lee*, the Confederate commander, needed to know the strength of the Union forces and the areas which they had reached. Stuart rode out on 12 June and did not return for three days. In that time, he had taken his force of 1,200 men round the entire Union army and, not content merely with reconnaissance, had also burned a great deal of enemy stores. The campaign that followed was based upon the intelligence which Stuart had supplied; and although the inexperience of his other subordinates denied Lee victory, McClellan was forced to retreat. Lee went on to invade the north in September and Stuart, whose troopers had already created panic by raiding Union headquarters at Catlett's Station, screened the Confederate advance through the Shenandoah Valley. He used his artillery to great effect to repel the 14 infantry assaults the Union forces launched during the battle for Fredericksburg on 13 December.

Chancellorsville and after

Stuart, now a major-general, next played a major part in the Chancellorsville campaign of April 1863. The Union plan called for a demonstration to be made at Fredericksburg, while the rest of the Federal army, under *Hooker*, struck southwards across the river west of the town to attack Lee's left flank. The Union commanders had reckoned without Stuart.

Made aware by Stuart's excellent scouting that the Fredericksburg movement was only a feint, Lee marched against Hooker, who promptly halted his advance and went over to the defensive. "Stonewall" *Jackson* was then ordered to make a wide outflanking march to attack Hooker's right wing, with Stuart's cavalry in support. Their job was to protect the flanks of the advance and to reconnoiter and secure the ground ahead of it. The move ended with a successful attack, which flung back Hooker's flank in disorder.

When "Stonewall" Jackson himself was wounded, Stuart assumed overall command. By his aggressive actions, he so dominated Hooker that the latter failed to react when Lee hurried his troops back to Fredericksburg to smash the Union forces there. Hooker's army then was forced to retreat back across the Rapahannock river.

In order to keep the strategic initiative, Lee then prepared to invade the north for the second time, again ordering Stuart to protect the flank of the advance. Stuart was preparing to carry out those orders when, on 9 June, he was taken by surprise in his encampment at Brandy Station by a Union cavalry raid. The excellence of the training he had given his troops then proved itself. The Confederates rallied and there followed the largest mounted cavalry action of the war. Of the 12,000 Union soldiers who were engaged, 900 were killed or wounded. Stuart lost 500 of his 10,000 strong force, but held the Federal attacks.

Blunder at Gettysburg

However, despite this success, things were about to go badly wrong for the Confederacy. Lee's custom of giving his subordinates discretionary orders – that is, orders they could choose not to follow at their discretion – led to unfortunate consequences as the Confederate advance got under way. Taking advantage of this loophole, Stuart gave up the task of guarding the flank, undertaking instead a raid that took him round the Union army in central Maryland. Lee, deprived of his principal source of intelligence, was consequently unaware of how close to him the main Federal army was. A skirmish between patrols in the little town of Gettysburg quickly developed into one of the key battles of the war. In this, Stuart took no part. When he finally reached Gettysburg on the second day of battle, it was too late – and his cavalry were too tired – to have any effect upon its outcome. Together with Lee, he fell back in retreat.

The campaigns of 1863 reduced the numbers under Stuart's command, while some Union cavalry commanders were now starting to exhibit the same flair. Indeed, it was a cavalry raid that was to cause Stuart's death. During the Federal campaign on May 1864, a cavalry corps, under General *Sheridan*, struck southwards in a raid on Richmond. On 11 May, outside the city's suburbs, Sheridan's 10,000-strong corps clashed with Stuart's 4,500 veterans. Overwhelmed by the weight of numbers, the Confederates were driven from the field. Stuart, who had been mortally wounded during the fighting, died in Richmond the following day.

The Confederacy was fortunate enough to be well endowed with good cavalrymen. None of them, however, was as gifted in the special type of military operation – scouting and reconnaissance – in which Stuart excelled. Though he may have been neither a strategist nor a good tactician, he did not need to be. His brilliance lay in his reconnaissances, which were thorough, and in his reporting, which was both informative and accurate. Robert E Lee's description of him as "the eyes of the army" expressed in five words the true worth to the Confederacy of "Jeb" Stuart.

TOGO
Heimachiro (1848-1934)
JAPANESE ADMIRAL
Russo-Japanese War

One of the bitterest memories of Heimachiro Togo's childhood was the sight of Commodore Perry's US naval squadron violating, as Togo thought of it, the sacred isolation of Japan by sailing into Tokyo harbor. It was a humiliation which ruled Togo's life and his determination to avenge it became an obsession.

Born on 27 January 1848, Togo entered a provincial naval school at the age of 18 and became a cadet in the imperial Japanese navy during 1870. Selected to train with the Royal Navy in England, he spent eight years studying gunnery, naval engineering and mathematics. He was promoted to command the cruiser *Naniwa*, and, by 1903, he had risen to the rank of vice-admiral. As commander of the Japanese fleet, Togo had the reputation of being a hard disciplinarian, whose training methods were thorough to the point of brutality. This harshness, however, produced a super-efficient fighting force.

War against Russia
On 10 August 1904, Togo's ships and those of the Russian Admiral Vitgift clashed in the Yellow Sea. Japanese naval gunfire sank a cruiser; the other ships of the Russian Far Eastern fleet fled into neutral ports and were interned. Only a few reached the safety of Vladivostock. Though the Japanese vessels had also been damaged, Togo had time to repair this, analyze the battle and to take steps to improve the already high standard of seamanship of his sailors. The Russians could pose no threat during this period of re-training, for Togo's victory had destroyed their naval power in the Far East.

Humiliated by the defeat, Tsar Nicholas II ordered his Baltic Fleet to sail around the world to the Pacific and annihilate the Japanese. After a long and tiring voyage, lasting nearly seven months, the miscellaneous collection of Russian ships met Togo's fleet, crewed by fresh, well-trained seamen, in the *Tsushima* straits. Before the battle Togo, whose respect for *Nelson*'s seamanship amounted almost to idolatary, sent his men a signal similar to the one that Nelson had ordered to be hoisted before going into action at Trafalgar – "England expects that every man this day should do his duty."

Annihilation at Tsushima
While he was still out of range of the Russian fleet, Togo crossed their "T", intending to attack the weaker of the two enemy columns. The Russians promptly changed course, endeavoring to turn in a smaller radius and then to outrun the Japanese. To counter this maneuver, Togo now had to swing his fleet round so as to bring it on a parallel course. The maneuver left his fleet open to Russian fire – but none came, save for a few salvoes. A shell struck Togo's flagship and wounded him seriously in the thigh. In samurai fashion, his impassive face showed no sign of the pain he must have been suffering and he would not leave the bridge even to have his wound dressed by his ship's surgeons.

Battered by the superior Japanese gunfire, several Russian ships struck their colors, a number were sunk and others foundered. It was a naval disaster. As night fell, Togo ordered his cruisers, destroyers and torpedo boats to keep up the pursuit. In a single day, the Baltic Fleet had been almost completely annihilated. Only three of its ships reached Vladivostock.

Togo's success brought him promotion; in 1913, he was created admiral of the fleet and ennobled, following a successful four-year period as chief of naval staff. He was also a permanent member of the emperor's military council until his death in 1934. He brought to the navy the characteristic samurai traits of selfless devotion to the Mikado and singleness of purpose in pursuit of an objective.

Completely impassive and stoical, he was as unsparing of himself as he was of those whom he commanded. His tactical skills were of the highest order and he was lucky enough to be able to support these personal abilities with first-class ships and highly trained men. By defeating the Russians in 1904 and in 1905, the samurai Togo, had not only avenged the humiliations of his childhood but had created for Japan a world-class fighting navy.

VICTOR OF TSUSHIMA *Togo, creator of imperial Japan's great navy, was an old-school samurai who was not afraid to learn from the West many of his fellows despised.*

WOLSELEY
Garnet (1833-1913)
BRITISH FIELD-MARSHAL
19th century Colonial Wars

There are very few military commanders whose names have passed into vernacular usage. "To Rommel" was a verb used in Germany during the Second World War to imply fast and decisive action. In Victorian and Edwardian times, the term "all Sir Garnet" – meaning that everything was in excellent order – commemorated Garnet Wolseley, the archetypal "model of a modern major-general," as Gilbert and Sullivan satirized him in *The Pirates of Penzance*.

"ALL SIR GARNET"
Garnet Wolseley, Victorian Britain's "model of a modern major-general".

Born in Ireland in June 1833, Wolseley saw his first action in Burma, where he received the first of the several wounds he was to suffer in his country's service. The most serious of these was in the Crimean War; a shell splinter struck him in the face, costing Wolseley the sight of an eye. His most successful operation was his penultimate campaign – the defeat of the forces of Arabi Pasha. The operation stands as an excellent example of his methods. In common with good commanders, he was skilled in picking right men for the job, ensuring that his subordinates were completely in the picture at all times. Not only did he plan each operation with meticulous care; he also possessed a flexibility of mind, which allowed him to grasp tactical opportunities on the battlefield.

The Wolseley school

It was during the expedition he led to suppress the Riel rebellion in Canada during 1870 that Wolseley began to put the methods described above into practice. He handpicked his subordinates carefully, looking for officers with the gifts of leadership and tactical ability. He planned each detail of the campaign carefully in advance, playing special attention to logistics, and even selected the season of the year in which his force would set out. The success of the expedition showed that such attention to detail paid dividends – Wolseley set out, fought and returned without losing a man. Even more importantly, as far as the British government was concerned, was the fact that he did not overspend the money set aside to fund the campaign.

The attention to detail that Wolseley had shown against Riel made him the obvious choice to command the 1873 expedition against the Ashanti slave traders in West Africa. Aware of the evil reputation of the Gold Coast as the "white man's grave", Wolseley chose to campaign in the dry season, when there would be little rain to breed fever. Before the main expedition sailed from England, he himself led a small advance party to reconnoiter the line of advance and plan every phase of the campaign. Wolseley intended his soldiers to spend as little time as possible in acclimatization after disembarkation. His plan was for a quick advance into the interior, where he would meet the Ashanti in battle, destroy the slavers and then re-embark. In the event, the whole operation was not only successful, but once again, was kept within budget.

War within budget

Wolseley was now the Victorian imperial general *par excellence*. Nine years after the Ashanti War, he fought what was probably his greatest campaign, when he took command of the force Britain sent to defeat a nationalist uprising in Egypt. For this expedition, Wolseley had one cavalry and two infantry divisions under command.

Clever deception work completely hoodwinked the Egyptian commander, Arabi Pasha, as to the direction of the eventual British thrust. Aggressive demonstrations by a diversion force at Alexandria convinced Arabi Pasha that the British attack on Cairo would come from the north, but, in fact, the main British force eventually landed in Ismailia.

Wolseley planned for the main battle of the campaign to be fought around the fortress of Tel-el-Kebir, but, before he could attack, he needed a forward base from which to operate. The small town of Quassassin was chosen. It had the advantages of being on the railway line and close to the Suez Canal. Wolseley, however, feared that his advance was beginning to outstrip its supplies and so ordered a halt. Luckily, his cavalry reconnaissance patrols soon captured an Egyptian provision train only 10 miles from the town. An abortive Egyptian attack was then beaten off, but inferior numbers meant that the British did not pursue the fleeing enemy.

Wolseley knew that he must defeat Arabi Pasha quickly in a set-piece battle; he must also not allow him to fall back upon Cairo. When all his preparations had been made, he night-marched his army to attack the Egyptians at first light. The battle was soon over, Arabi Pasha and his troops being totally routed.

Unfortunately, his return to Egypt in 1884 to relieve the besieged Gordon in the Sudanese city of Khartoum was not as successful. Political dilatoriness and rivalries in London so delayed the progress of the relief column that Khartoum had fallen to the Mahdi and Gordon had been murdered long before the expedition could raise the siege.

Wolseley became commander-in-chief of the army in 1895; he died in 1913. A highly-skilled staff, meticulous planning, decisive action, an ability to deceive the enemy and a flexibility of mind were his classic hallmarks. However, his decided views and his patronage of officers who agreed with them – such officers were referred to as members of Wolseley's "ring" – made many enemies.

The First World War

When the First World War broke out in 1914, the participating nations were mentally prepared for only a short conflict. "Home by Christmas", was the common belief. The German war plan, the *Schlieffen Plan*, was based upon a six-week war in the west, and a slightly longer campaign in the east, while the French Plan XVII similarly was predicated upon a speedy victory. It was also quite widely believed that no nation could sustain the financial burden of a long war, so, by definition, it must be a short one.

The weapons with which the armies were equipped reflected the fact that contemporary wars tended to be of short duration, for those arms were usually updated versions of weapons which had been in standard service for years. In one respect only was there a difference between the 1914 armies and those which had preceded them. A new invention, the aircraft, now formed part of the military establishment of the major armies.

War in the air

Though it was only just over a decade since the first flight of a heavier-than-air machine, in those few years there had been swift developments. Aircraft had been used by Italy to bomb the Libyans during the 1912 war and in September 1914, it was airplane and not cavalry reconnaissance that first alerted *Joffre*, the French commander-in-chief, to the change of direction by von Kluck's army and so opened the way for his crucial counter-offensive on the Marne. Throughout the war, there was a continuing and rapid development in aircraft design, speed and armament as both sides fought to gain air superiority. Aircraft progressed from the stage of being solely reconnaissance vehicles, through that of being fighter machines intended to gain command of the air and into bombing aircraft. Quite early in the war, there were airmen who realized the terrifying potential of the air arm. Bombers could be used to destroy strategic objectives located a long way behind enemy lines, such as railway marshalling yards and Zeppelin sheds. And if military targets could be attacked, then why not the arms factories supplying the armies in the field? By 1918, plans for a strategic bombing offensive had been drawn up and the first stages began, but the war ended before the full power of the bomber could be deployed.

Trench warfare

The war of maneuver that had opened the land war was soon halted and after a race for the Channel ports, the armies on the Western Front were forced into trench warfare. The rest of the war in the west is the story of how the generals, all of whom had been trained for a war of movement, tried to break the resulting deadlock. For the greatest part of the war, the belief prevailed that, by bombarding the enemy trenches, sending in infantry to create a breach and using cavalry to exploit it, mobility would be restored. These tactics failed repeatedly, as did the use of poison gas to overwhelm the enemy or of liquid fire to burn him out.

Then, in the fall of 1916, the British introduced tanks on to the battlefield – armored fighting vehicles intended to destroy the enemy's barbed wire defences, cross his trenches and create the breach ready for cavalry exploitation. Tanks were rushed into service prematurely. The first were underpowered and were not used in sufficient numbers to be effective. By 1918, however, enough tanks were available to spearhead successful offensives, though, once again, the war ended before the full potential of the tank could be realized.

The Germans, for their part, did not believe tanks were the answer. To break the stalemate, they relied upon gunfire and sophisticated infantry tactics. The same sophistication produced the concept of "elastic" defence in the middle years of the war – a front line thinly held by riflemen, but with a greater density of machine guns at their disposal. Behind that first line stood reserve groups ready to absorb the enemy blow and behind them again, storm troop detachments to launch counter-attacks. Such tactics were eventually adopted by most armies.

In offence General Hutier also devised special tactics for German use that were the opposite of the conventional practice. In Hutier attacks, any strong center of enemy resistance was not assaulted – instead it was by-passed and left to the troops following up the advance. According to Hutier the speed of the advance was the all-important factor – the enemy must not be given the time to reform his ruptured front. These tactics, originally devised for infantry warfare, were to form the basis of German armored operations in the Second World War.

Naval war

On the allied side, both Russia and France started the war with mass armies. Britain only had a small professional land force, but, at sea, the Royal Navy reigned supreme. In Scapa Flow and its other Scottish bases, the Grand Fleet watched and waited for the German High Seas Fleet to steam out to battle. The

Germans did indeed make several forays into the North Sea, one of which led to the battle of *Jutland*, though this inconclusive affair was not the decisive "great smash" that had been anticipated. One reason why *Jellicoe*, the British commander-in-chief, did not gain a total victory was because he would not pursue the retreating enemy for fear of submarines. As he explained, "It is suicidal to forego an advantageous position in big ships by risking them in waters infested with submarines. The result might seriously jeopardise the future of the country by giving over the command of the seas to the Germans." The Royal Navy had superiority in big ships and he intended to retain it.

Jellicoe was acutely aware that he might, in Churchill's words, "lose the war in an afternoon". In his view he might also lose it to submarines, described by one senior British sailor as that "damned un-English weapon". Germany had great faith in its U-boats and the losses they inflicted upon merchant shipping brought Britain close to

WAR OF MOVEMENT *"Whippet" tanks in action in 1918. The tank broke the stalemate of trench warfare.*

starvation in the fall of 1917. The introduction of the convoy system helped to resolve the crisis. Meanwhile, the big ships of both navies waited in harbor – the Royal Navy aware of the fragility of its supremacy and the Germans not daring to make another attempt to challenge it.

The Russian revoluton

Though Russian losses on the Eastern Front were catastrophic, it was not military defeat that forced Russia out of the war, but revolution. The first revolution, which overthrew the Tsar in February 1917, did not immediately lead to a collapse, the new Kerensky regime being prepared to stay in the war and to mount offensives. To drive Russia completely out of the war and to release the mass of German troops in the east for the great offensive in the west planned for 1918, the German high command transported Com-

munist leaders across Germany to foment a second revolution. Lenin's Bolshevik revolution took Russia out of the war and enabled the German armies to enter upon their cherished offensive.

The allied counterattacks in the west which drove back the Germans and brought the war to an end were fought by armies which now included contingents of soldiers from the USA. The Western powers had lost one great ally through the defection of Tsarist Russia, but had gained another, and stronger one in the USA. The war, which had begun as a Balkan quarrel between Austria and Serbia, had escalated into campaigns fought in Europe, in Africa and in Asia. It destroyed four empires – Austria-Hungary, Germany, Russia and Turkey.

A war that France had entered determined to revenge the humiliation of 1870 ended with a Germany dreaming of revenge for the humiliation of 1918. The armistice of 1918 was just that – a pause between conflicts. The next one was only 20 years away.

AUGUST-SEPTEMBER 1914

ADVANCE INTO FRANCE:
The Schlieffen Plan in action

In 1914, the German army planned to win its victories as von *Moltke* had won his in the wars of 1864, 1866 and 1870. What the German general staff was seeking was a classic battle, patterned on Cannae, which would result in the envelopment and complete destruction of the enemy. This belief was in line with the rest of contemporary European military thought, the notion being that, in the event of war, a series of minor engagements would lead inexorably to the decisive battle. Little notice was taken of the way in which the US Civil War had been fought and few conclusions were drawn from it as the first modern-style conflict. This lack of foresight meant that, throughout Europe, armies were organized, armed and trained for short wars and led by generals who were convinced that a war could be won quickly by an all-out assault.

As far as Germany itself was concerned, however, there was a second reason why the Germans needed a swift Moltke-style victory. The Germans and their allies faced an enemy coalition which was of superior numbers. Of their two principal enemies, France, which could mobilize quickly, was considered to be a more serious threat than Russia, whose mobilization and deployment would be slow. The German General Staff based its war plan, therefore, on fighting a short, victorious campaign in the west, after which its excellent internal lines of communication would enable the troops in the west to be rushed to the Eastern Front, where they would meet and destroy the incompletely mobilized Russiana.

The battle plan for the campaign in the west was named after the German commander who had formu-lated it – Count Alfred von Schlief-fen. In this plan, seven German armies were to be deployed. Those on the right wing would make their approach march through Belgium and northern France, flanking the French defences and carrying out a right hook encirclement. The central and left wing German armies would hold their ground. Schlief-fen's main concern was to make the right wing strong enough to overlap the armies of the allied left wing. However, Schlieffen's successor, Colonel-General von Moltke, anti-cipating a French thrust for Metz, redeployed his forces to meet the anticipated thrust, so weakening the right wing in favour of a stronger center. This redeployment des-troyed the Schlieffen concept – though when the war in the west opened in August 1914, this weak-ness did not show. By 17 August, the German armies were lined up ready to open the southerly drive on the following day.

Meeting the plan
The Franco-British forces on the left wing of the allied armies marched northwards into Belgium, where they were struck by German 1st and 2nd Armies as these swung south-wards aiming to envelop the allied wing. The commanders of those days were tied to the concept of linear defence, in which any breach in the battle line, which could not be closed by immediate counter attack, resulted in a withdrawal by the units on either flank in order to keep the line intact and solid. Forced to conform to that policy of an unbroken front, the Franco-British forces retreated towards the river Marne, while the Belgian army withdrew into the fortress systems of Antwerp and Maubeuge. Three

German corps were detached from the right wing to invest them; then, on 25 August, German supreme command detached two more right-wing corps and sent them to bolster the front in East Prussia. The German right wing, weakened even be-fore the outbreak of war by von Moltke's adjustment to Schlieffen's plan, had been further reduced in strength to a critical level.

The "miracle of the Marne"
In the first days of September, the five armies of the German right wing and center were advancing, extended on a broad front between Flanders and Verdun, while 6th and 7th Armies, on the left wing were moving slowly westwards towards Nancy. Yet, the situation on the extreme right gave Moltke cause for concern. Because it had been weak-ened by the loss of five corps, it could not by-pass Paris to the west as had been intended; 1st Army, in fact, was forced to contract its front to pass to the east of the French capital. Moltke's fear was that, if the German advance continued south-eastwards, it might be trapped be-tween the French forces massed around Verdun and the newly-formed 6th Army grouped round Paris. He could no longer expect to encircle the French armies from the west and drive them onto the guns of 5th and 6th Armies. Rather, Moltke had to guard his own extreme right flank against the 6th Army round Paris. Accordingly, he halted his 1st and 2nd Armies, ordering them to form a front facing the city, leaving only three corps from 3rd Army to maintain the southward drive towards Troyes. He directed 4th and 5th Armies to carry out operations to permit 6th and 7th Army to advance to the line of the

THE MAN BEHIND THE PLAN *Count von Schlieffen (left), chief of the German general staff, died before he could see his celebrated plan in action (below). He developed it to deal with the problem of a two-front war, in which Germany had to defeat France in the west before the cumbersome Russian army could be fully mobilized. With typical Prussian ruthlessness, Schlieffen was prepared to violate Belgian neutrality in order to facilitate the German right-wing's sweep towards Paris – he wanted the last man on the right to "brush the Channel with his sleeve". His last words were "only make the right wing strong", but his successor, von Moltke, tinkered with the plan, with fatal results.*

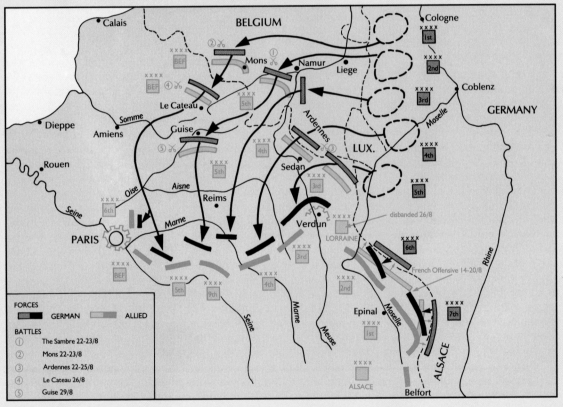

FORCES
GERMAN   ALLIED

BATTLES
① The Sambre 22-23/8
② Mons 22-23/8
③ Ardennes 22-25/8
④ Le Cateau 26/8
⑤ Guise 29/8

Mosel, while, to strengthen 6th Army in its attacks against the Nancy fortress system, he committed six fresh divisions, his last remaining reserves.

An allied counter-attack, initiated by French 6th Army thrust out of Paris. To counter that move, von Klück, commanding 1st German Army, detached some units that were still moving southwards and swung them to face north-east. The movement opened a gap between the inner wings of 1st and 2nd Armies and the commander of 2nd Army, without advising von Klück of his intention, gave the order to retreat. Von Klück was forced to conform. Within a day, the three other armies of the German right wing had pulled back. The Schlieffen Plan had failed to produce a quick victory as its original architect intended.

JUNE 1916
THE BRUSILOV OFFENSIVE:
Russia's greatest triumph

Not until the last months of the First World War did the allies have a generalissimo, with the appointment of Foch to the post. There had, of course, been attempts to co-ordinate allied military policy, particularly, at the Chantilly conference of December 1915. The Russian operation of 1916, known as the *Brusilov* offensive, came about as a result of that conference, plus demands from the French for Russian help in the face of the Germand onslaught at *Verdun*.

Russian dispositions

In 1916, the Russian armies were deployed in three huge groupings – North Front, facing the Baltic countries, West Front, to the north of the Pripet marshes, and South-West Front to the south of them. At a *Stavka* (high command) conference on 14 April, the chief of staff, General Alexeivitch, told his subordinates that an offensive had been ordered and directed West Front to carry out the principal attack and capture Vilna. Success, he assured his listeners, was almost guaranteed, for the Germans, only about 62,000 men strong, were confronted by a Russian host of 1,220,000. Although South-West Front had a less important role in Alexeivitch's plan, the battle on its sector might be harder, because its 512,000-strong force faced an Austro-Hungarian Army Group of 441,000 men. North Front would mount diversionary attacks to draw German strength away from West Front's main effort.

However, neither the commander of North or West Front was optimistic about the prospect of such an offensive. It was left to Brusilov, commander of South-West Front, to rekindle confidence.

In a flamboyant gesture, he said he was prepared to take sole responsibility for the offensive, even going as far as to declare that he had no need of other troops than those already under his command. His confidence infected the other commanders and an offensive was planned which, if successful, would restore the morale of the Russian army.

Brusilov in action

Facing Brusilov stood Boehm-Ermolli's Austrian Army Group in an extensive system of field fortifications between Pinsk and Czernovitz. Safe behind its barbed wire entanglements and sheltering in deep, underground dug-outs, the Austrians had developed a dangerously complacent, defensively-minded attitude, ignoring not only the Russian bombardments, which steadily destroyed their barbed wire, but also all other indications that an offensive was imminent. Their counter-preparations were minimal. As the main weight of the Russian operation was to be borne by West Front, Brusilov, whose South-West Front had a subordinate role, was not given any strategic objectives and his own battle orders were limited to directives to capture the enemy defence lines.

Brusilov's Front opened its assault on 3 June 1916, with a six-hour bombardment of the Austrian positions. Then the Russian infantry, specially trained for this operation, charged from the sap exits, some of which were only just short of the Austrian forward positions, and overran the first trench lines. By 10 June, Brusilov had driven a deep, wide breach into the Austrian front, the result being a crisis at high command level. Neither Germany nor

Austria had sufficient reserves available on the Eastern Front to meet the situation and both were forced to rush reinforcements from France and Italy respectively.

Brusilov's failure to name a strategic objective was one factor that slowed his attack. Much of his cavalry, which could have been used to thrust into Austrian rear areas, was assigned to hold captured trenches. The salient which South-West Front had created was subjected to heavy attacks. Despite those counter-blows, the advance continued, while Brusilov's success encouraged Alexeivitch to reinforce South-West Front to whom he at last allotted strategic objectives, including Kovel, and important communications center. On West Front, a halt was made to regroup.

The advance was resumed in July. Under the double pressure of the two Russian Fronts, the Austrian and German units opposing them gave ground, but withdrew into an extensive trench system which the tiring Russian troops were unable to penetrate. The most competently planned and efficiently conducted Russian military operation of the First World War had failed in its ultimate objectives.

Although it had not achieved a breakthrough, the Brusilov offensive had achieved a long-term strategic success. The Central Powers were alarmed at the élan with which the Russians had opened the battle and the excellent planning that had characterized the operation. They decided that, rather than expose their troops on the Eastern Front to the possibilty of another massive Russian assault, they would retain in the east the forces that had been rushed there from other theaters of war. This was to effect the conduct of operations in France and the Tyrol on the Italian Front.

In human terms, Brusilov's offensive had cost Boehm-Ermolli's Army Group 475,000 soldiers, a loss that dangerously weakened the Austro-Hugarian Army in the field.

Another advantage to the allies was that Romania, which had hitherto remained neutral, was emboldened by the apparent strength of the Russian army to declare war on the Central Powers. On the negative side, the high hopes which the Russians had entertained of this major operation were dashed. Discontent in the homeland and at the front resulting from the failure of the offensive was to set in motion a chain of events which led to the overthrow of Tsar Nicholas II.

OFFENSIVE IN THE EAST *Alexei Brusilov (above left) mastermined Russia's most successful offensive of the war (above right) in 1916. He struck against the Austrians in Galicia; their front was saved from collapse only by substantial German reinforcement.*

JUNE 1916
JUTLAND:
The "great smash" in the North Sea

"There seems to be something wrong with our bloody ships today." Admiral *Beatty's* terse comment on seeing two British battle-cruisers sunk within half an hour of each other has passed into history as a crucial summing up of British tactical fortunes in the battle of Jutland (known to Germans as Skagerrak), fought between the British Grand Fleet, commanded by Admiral Sir John *Jellicoe*, and the German High Seas Fleet under Admiral Reinhard Scheer in 1916. The battle took place in the North Sea, from approximately the estuary of the Elbe river to the southern end of western Norway.

The naval rivalry between Britain and Germany had resulted in a massive building program, the British producing 28 giant Dreadnoughts, carrying either 12-inch or 15-inch guns. The faster, but lightly armored, battle-cruisers were armed with 11-inch or 13-inch guns. The German fleet consisted of 16 modern battleships, six pre-Dreadnought battleships and five battle-cruisers. The heaviest gun the German ships carried was 12 inches. The total number of ships in either fleet was 151 British to 99 German.

British naval strategy was based on the blockade of the North Sea bottling the German fleet inside its home waters. The Admiralty, through a network of secret agents could be certain of receiving warning of the German fleet putting to sea, while inefficient German naval signaling also betrayed details of sailings and operations. Nor did the Germans know that the Royal Navy had got possession of their code. The strategy common to both sides was to lure the opposing fleet away from its bases, coal and ammunition supplies and destroy it in detail.

To provoke the Royal Navy, the Germans had made several sorties into the North Sea. They had, on occasions, bombarded British coast towns, while an inconclusive naval encounter between Beatty and von Hipper was fought at the Dogger Bank in January 1915. At a naval conference in February 1916, however, Scheer won the Kaiser's permission to employ the German fleet more aggressively. Scheer's battle plan was to bombard East Anglian towns with Hipper's battle-cruisers. When the British battle-cruisers sailed to intercept, they would be attacked by the rest of the High Seas Fleet and destroyed before the Grand Fleet proper could intervene.

Scheer intended to use submarines and Zeppelins for reconnaissance, but, late on the morning of 30 May, he was advised that the Zeppelins could not be used because of adverse winds, while most of the U-boats had returned to port. The alternative plan was for the fleet to keep close to the German side of the North Sea, advertising its presence by intercepting neutral shipping off the coast of Norway.

The Germans sail
Scheer's Signal 31 Gg 2490, put the new German plan into effect. In another attempt to lure the British away from their Scapa Flow base, the German High Seas Fleet put to sea. It was divided into von Hipper's screening group of 40 vessels, including five battle-cruisers, and the main body, under Scheer. The Germans headed for the Skagerrak; early in the afternoon of 31 May, the screening force, ahead of Scheer's, was nearing the south-western exit.

By noon on 30 May, Jellicoe knew that the German navy was preparing for action and at 1740 he

was ordered by the Admiralty to "concentrate eastward of the Long Forties ready for eventualities." Accordingly, Jellicoe's main force sailed out of Scapa Flow and Cromarty, while Beatty's battle-cruisers left Rosyth to screen and to reconnoiter ahead of the Grand Fleet. Beatty's force of 52 ships including six battle-cruisers and a squadron of four Dreadnoughts, was some 70 miles ahead of Jellicoe.

The High Seas Fleet sighted
At 1420 on 31 May, the cruiser, HMS *Galatea* sighted some German vessels checking on a neutral ship. Fire was opened almost simultaneously. The battle of Jutland had begun. On receipt of *Galatea's* news Beatty, with his forces sailing eastward in two line-ahead columns, altered course to the south-east. A sea-plane flown off by HMS *Engandine* – the first use of aircraft in a naval battle – signaled back the position of the light forces in Hipper's group and at about 1530 visual contact was made between the two screening forces.

Hipper was sailing due south. Beatty's two columns turned on a parallel course and opened fire. Hipper responded and the excellent training of the German gunners soon became evident. HMS *Lion*, Beatty's flagship, was hit several times and two of his battle-cruisers were sunk. The aggressive Beatty at first ordered his ships to engage the enemy more closely, but, sighting Scheer's main battle group, he then swung his ships on a northward course, confident that Hipper and Scheer would pursue him and that they would be caught by the Grand Fleet proper.

At 1800, Jellicoe came in sight, his force advancing in six parallel

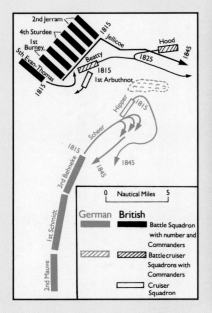

columns. Beatty promptly swung his double columns eastwards, so as to be ahead of the main British body. That easterly course also took him across the front of the German fleet and its bases. (In this maneuver the ships making it are able to concentrate all their armament on the enemy ships forming the "up stroke" of the T, while the enemy vessels can only use their forward guns).

A general action

Within half an hour, both fleets were engaged in general combat with British fire concentrated on the leading German battle-cruisers of Hipper's squadron. In the fast and furious fight, Hipper's flagship SMS *Lutzow*, was put out of action, but the Royal Navy lost HMS *Invincible, Defence* and *Warrior*. In between the lines of heavy ships, the light forces – destroyers and torpedo boats – wheeled and charged, carrying out daring torpedo attacks upon the major units.

By 1845, the Grand Fleet formed a half circle around the head of the German squadrons. Scheer made smoke and, covered by the attack of his destroyers, changed his course by 180 degrees to take his ships out of range. Jellicoe, aware that he lay between the Germans and their bases, made no attempt to follow, but maintained his course. Scheer then realized that, by turning northward, he could escape the Grand Fleet. He reverted to his original course. Ahead of him, he thought he would find only the last ships of the British line, but was shocked to discover the main body of the Grand Fleet once again blocking his path. He had had his "T" crossed for a second time. Battle was rejoined and once again the High Seas Fleet turned away, leaving Hipper's four surviving battle-cruisers to steam in a "battle charge" straight towards the British to cover Scheer's withdrawal. They were accompanied on that death ride by flotillas of destroyers, whose attacks caused Jellicoe to turn away.

Contact lost

Contact between the two main groups was lost and in the oncoming darkness Scheer turned firstly northwards and then swung south-east, cutting through the rear ships of Jellicoe's fleet. In the night-time encounters, the High Seas Fleet and Scheer escaped.

The battle of Jutland, although it was not realized at the time, marked the end of naval warfare, as it had been traditionally fought by fleets within sight of each other. The result was a strategic victory for the British and tactical one for the Germans. The threat the Royal Navy posed stopped the High Seas Fleet from making another major sortie and thus, strategically, Britain had gained the victory. The casualties he inflicted gave Scheer the tactical victory. The Royal Navy had lost three battle-cruisers, three cruisers and eight destroyers. The German fleet lost one pre-Dreadnought battleship, one battle-cruiser, four light cruisers and five destroyers.

FEBRUARY-DECEMBER 1916

VERDUN:
Carnage in the mud

There are many commanders in the history of warfare who have ordered attacks or offensives aware that these will result in bloody losses. Only one commander in recent military history based a whole battle on a calculation of the losses he would inflict on the enemy. That commander was von *Falkenhayn*. The enemy he intended to bleed white was France and the area in which he proposed to conduct this operation was Verdun.

In a cold analysis, which, when converted into action, would result in the deaths of hundreds of thousands of German and French troops, the German chief of staff was planning the final great, decisive battle, which, with a successful "bleeding white" of the French army, would lead to a break-through and reintroduce mobility to warfare on the Western Front. The Verdun operation would also be the first major German offensive action in the west since the failure of the *Schlieffen Plan* in 1914, which had resulted in the creation of a French salient projecting into the front of the Crown Prince's Army Group at Verdun.

As far as the French high command was concerned, the Verdun position, which was centered on the massive fortress complex protecting the city and standing on the banks of the Maas river, was a quiet one. Consequently, a great number of its guns had been transferred to other sectors of the front, as had much of its garrison. In mid-February 1916, the front line trenches and chain of supporting permanent defences were held by only five divisions, although that number had been increased to eight with a further three in reserve by 21 February, the starting date for the opening German attack.

Bleeding France white

Falkenhayn's offensive started with a massive nine-hour barrage fired by 1,400 guns – the biggest concentration of artillery seen on the Western Front to that date. This was followed at 1700 hours by an infantry attack launched by three corps of German 5th Army on an eight-mile front. The first assault broke through the French front line defences and, by 24 February, the second line had been taken. Shaken by the fury of the attack and the heavy losses his troops had suffered, General Herr, the local French commander, proposed to withdraw his forces from the eastern bank of the Maas – where they were being slowly destroyed – to the western bank. The response from *Joffre*, the French commander-in-chief, was both immediate and dramatic. He rushed whole corps of infantry and artillery to support the collapsing front and he threatened any commander who ordered a withdrawal with immediate court martial. The reinforcements were then grouped into 2nd Army and placed under the command of General *Petain*. Joffre had fallen into Falkenhayn's trap. He was sending his men into a battle of attrition, just as his German opposite number had arranged when planning the attack.

Before the reinforcements had reached the front, however, the situation had become even more critical for the defenders. On 25 February Fort Douaumont fell, but not to the storming rush of assault troops fighting down a staunch defence in hand to hand combat. A German patrol from the 24th Infantry Regiment entered the fort, drove out the few defenders that were found there and occupied it. On the same day and under terrible pressure, the French units on the river's eastern bank were driven back still further.

These successes marked almost the limit of German gains, however, for thereafter, they made little appreciable progress. Strong French reserves were thrown in, regardless of losses, and they stemmed the advance. French artillery reinforced the defence, pouring enfilade fire from the western bank of the river and forcing the Germans to extend the area of the front to include that sector, too. Falkenhayn's original plan for a limited assault on a narrow front had suddenly degenerated into an offensive on a wider front.

A battle of attrition

The battle of attrition that followed the failure of the initial German assaults quickly assumed proportions never before witnessed in the history of warfare. The landscape became almost lunar through bombardment. All vegetation was destroyed and the thick clay of the Verdun region degenerated into clinging, knee deep mud after only short rainy periods. There could be no talk of trench positions under such conditions, so the infantry of both sides usually lived in shell holes, on ground upon which lay thousands of unburied dead. The living waited to attack or to be attacked, their life expectancy certain to be brief.

Petain was very much a soldier's soldier and his understanding of the dreadful battle conditions led him to do his best to ensure his units were relieved at frequent intervals. He kept up their morale by ensuring that supplies reached them regularly through the organization of truck convoys along the only link between the front line and the rear areas. The 40-mile-long secondary road to Bar le Duc – the so-called *Voie Sacré* (Sacred Way) – carried fleets of trucks at 14-second intervals, day and night. To prevent delays or traffic jams due to shelling, maintenance units filled in every shell crater within minutes.

A third German offensive on 9 April, against both sides of the salient failed and had died away by 29 May. The mainpoint of the German assault swung to the east against Fort Vaux, which finally surrendered on 9 June. During June, the main effort was made in the west and, in the face of a new secret weapon – phosgene gas bombardment – the French line wavered. Petain, indeed, recommended that the west bank positions be abandoned, but he was overruled by Joffre. On 11 July, Falkenhayn ordered the Crown Prince to temporarily assumed a defensive posture.

France had suffered more than 500,000 casualties, but Germany had lost more than 434,000 troops. Shocked by the terrible toll of the battle and by von Falkenhayn's failure, the Kaiser intervened to replace him on 27 August by von *Hindenburg*, with *Ludendorff* as his Chief of Staff. The new commanders, who had never been enthusiastic about the Verdun plan, ordered a completely defensive posture to be assumed. No more attacks would be undertaken. French counter-attacks, led by Mangin, were launched with élan and by October 24, Fort Douamont had been recaptured. Fort Vaux was regained on 2 November. After a lull of several weeks, Mangin reopened his attacks and by mid-December he had almost reached the position from which the French had been driven in February. The campaign had ended.

The personality of the rival commanders makes an interesting contrast. On the French side there was Joffre, who looked and acted like a peasant, and Petain, the soldier's soldier, who commanded at Verdun until he was succeeded by the flamboyant *Nivelle*. This ambitious and

CARNAGE IN THE MUD *French troops come under artillery fire as they pick their way up to the Verdun front line (above). The battle (right) was deliberately planned by the German high command as a cold-blooded experiment in attrition to "bleed France white".*

French Line Feb. 1916
Furthest German advance July 1916
Forts

1 Marre   4 Noulainville
2 Belleville   5 Tavannes
3 St. Michel   6 Vaux
            7 Douaumont

confident general was to lead the French army down the road to mutiny in 1917. The last of the Verdun commanders was Mangin, who succeeded Nivelle. Swarthy, dour and reliable – he was a rock of man. One of the Verdun trio coined the famous French rallying cry, "They shall not pass."

On the German side, there was von Falkenhayn, the confident, smiling chief of the general staff whose brilliant strategic brain encompassed the "bleeding white" of the French Army. His immediate subordinate, the German Crown Prince, did not agree with Falkenhayn's logic and believed that the whole campaign had been mounted to gain the city and fortress of Verdun. His feelings may well be imagined when, firstly, von Falkenhayn ordered a defensive posture to be adopted and, secondly, when the prizes which his army had gained fell so quickly back into French hands.

ALLENBY
Edmond H (1861-1936)
BRITISH FIELD-MARSHAL
First World War

Allenby's nickname – the "Bull" – was no misnomer, for his huge frame shook with anger whenever he was upset, which was frequently. However, he must have possessed a mordant sense of humor since the title he chose when he was raised to the peerage was Megiddo. This is the site on which the Bible tells us the final battle between good and evil will be fought.

Allenby was born in Southwell, Nottinghamshire, on 23 April 1861. From public school he entered Sandhurst, graduating into the cavalry in 1882 and joining the Inskilling Dragoons. His first service postings were in Africa – in Bechuanaland in 1884 and Zululand in 1888. He returned to the continent to fight in the Boer War in which he gained the reputation of an excellent cavalry commander. Rising steadily through the military establishment he became a major-general by 1909; he was then appointed Inspector of Cavalry, a post he held until the outbreak of war in 1914.

"Take Jerusalem before Christmas"
Allenby was commander of the British Expeditionary Force's cavalry in France and Flanders until it became clear that mounted troops had no role to play in trench warfare. He was then given a field command and led 3rd Army on the Somme and at Arras. His great opportunity came in the summer of 1917, when he was sent to take command of the expeditionary force in Egypt and Palestine, with the simple order to "take Jerusalem before Christmas." Determined to succeed in this mission, his first move was to transfer the British headquarters from the comforts of Cairo to the front line. Like all great commanders, Allenby identified with the ordinary soldiers he led and he was prepared to share many of their privations.

His insistence that no victory could be expected without reinforcements brought him the divisions he needed; to supplement the standard cavalry force, he also raised camel detachments, combining the two to create the Desert Mounted Corps. A master of deception, he then took the Turks by surprise by a swift switch of forces to move against Bersheba, whose wells were vital to any subsequent advance. The Australian Cavalry Brigade captured these at last light on 31 October 1917.

Still moving swiftly, Allenby struck at and divided the Turkish 7th and 8th Armies, which fell back to avoid being trapped. The arrival of General *von Falkenhayn* to assist the Turkish command slowed down but could not halt the advance; Jerusalem fell on 9 December.

Forward to victory
There was only little activity in Palestine during the early part of 1918, as Allenby's force was reduced in strength as divisions were transferred to the Western Front, where

"THE BULL" *Allenby's successes against the Turks confirmed his reputation as a cavalry commander.*

Ludendorff's great offensive was in full swing. Consequently, pressure could only be maintained on the Turks through Lawrence and his Arab guerrillas. To aid Arab recruitment, Allenby's name was corrupted by British propagandists to *El Nebi*, (a promised one of God). When he was again reinforced, Allenby once again went into the offensive to live up to this. Using dummy stocks of stores and other classic deception tactics to foil the enemy commander – now Liman von Sanders who had replaced von Falkenhayn – he thrust up the coast, releasing his Desert Mounted Corps to exploit the breach his infantry had created. The crucial battle opened on the morning of 19 September, and quickly developed according to plan as the Turkish armies began to disintegrate under the blows of the allied divisions.

By 22 September the battle of Megiddo had turned into one of pursuit; in quick succession the chief cities of Lebanon and Syria fell to Allenby's assaults. By the end of October, Turkey had sued for an armistice. In a well planned and skilfully led offensive, Allenby's forces had fought their way forward over 360 miles of desert in 38 days, defeating three Turkish armies in the process. It was an excellent example of all-arms co-operation carrying out a well-planned operation based on use of firepower and exploiting the opportunities presented to Allenby's forces by a war of movement.

For a man who was feared for the ferocity of his temper, Allenby was a simple, sincere, even humble man. He refused to enter Jerusalem in a staff car, making his official entry into the city on foot. His life-long hobbies were ornithology and botany and he pursued these actively until his death in 1936. As a general, he was one of the finest cavalry commanders in the history of the British army, being adept at the use of cavalry not just in isolation as a shock weapon, but as an integral part of a combined modern military force.

BEATTY
David (1871-1936)
BRITISH ADMIRAL
First World War

One of the less happy results of the battle of Jutland, fought in 1916, was a newspaper campaign which credited Beatty and his battle-cruiser squadrons with bearing the burden of the battle, while condemning *Jellicoe*, the overall commander of the British Grand Fleet, for holding his ships back. Although the newspaper stories were wrong, it was not an unbelievable account, for Jellicoe looked like a country curate while the dashing Beatty had the air of a reincarnation of an Elizabethan sea dog.

Born at Stapely, Cheshire, on 17 January 1871, Beatty entered the Royal Navy as a midshipman at the age of 13. When he was only 25 he was already commanding a squadron of Nile gunboats, supporting *Kitchener*'s expedition to the Sudan. During the Boxer Rebellion, his service was recognized by promotion to captain; when he was in 1910 promoted rear-admiral he was, at 39, the youngest man to hold that rank for over a century. From sea-going commands, he was posted to the Admiralty to become flag secretary to the First Lord, Winston Churchill, before going back to sea and the command of a battle-cruiser squadron.

Photographs of Beatty always show him with his cap set at a jaunty angle, his hands firm set in the side pockets of his jacket and his jaw thrust aggressively forward. This stance mirrored his pugnacious philosophy – an all-out policy of aggression towards the enemy with which Churchill heartily concurred. Within a month of the outbreak of war, Beatty had fought and won the battle of the Heligoland Bight, sinking four enemy ships. In January 1915, his battle-cruisers intercepted von Hipper's battle-cruiser squadron at the Dogger Bank. The *Blücher*, a heavy cruiser, was sunk, but a misunderstood signal from *Lion*, Beatty's flagship which had been crippled in the action, enabled the other German ships to escape the British and regain port without further loss.

The "great smash"
In common with all his countrymen, what Beatty was waiting for was a decisive clash between the British Grand Fleet and the Imperial High Seas Fleet, but, due to the German Kaiser's protective attitude to his ships, the first major fleet action of the war did not take place until *Jutland*, fought at the end of May 1916. Beatty's battle-cruisers, in the van of the fleet, clashed with Hipper's squadron, which was scouting ahead of the main German force and two British battle-cruisers were quickly lost. Beatty ordered his ships to engage the enemy more closely, then turning away to lure the High Seas Fleet on to the Grand Fleet's guns. Beatty led the line of British ships that crossed the German "T" twice in one battle. The result was a tactical victory for the Germans, but a strategic one for the British. The Royal Navy lost more ships, but the Germans thereafter made no serious attempt to challenge British naval supremacy.

Succeeding Jellicoe
Jellicoe's wireless silence after the battle led to wild rumors of defeat in Britain and, to satisfy their readers, the newspapers made Beatty, who had always had a good press, the hero of Jutland. He himself did not directly contradict those stories; indeed, at the official enquiry into the conduct of the battle, he implied that Jellicoe had not pressed home his attacks as hard as he ought to have done. Eventually, he succeeded Jellicoe as commander-in-chief, when he was instrumental in introducing the convoy system to protect British merchant shipping against the U-boat menace. He accepted the surrender of the German fleet in November 1918, and then became First Sea Lord.

As his country's leading sailor, Beatty fought hard to maintain the strength of the Royal Navy in the face of the drift towards disarmament that followed the war. His powerful arguments were understood by the public to whom he had always been a charismatic figure cast in the mould of Drake and the other naval heroes of the Elizabethan period.

BRUSILOV
Alexei Alexeivitch (1854-1926)
RUSSIAN GENERAL
First World War

The optimistic commander whose Front, or Army Group, launched the most successful Russian offensive of the First World War in 1916, served three regimes – that of the Tsar, Kerensky's short-lived republic and the Soviet dictatorship.

Alexei Brusilov was born into a military family in Tiflis in Georgia. He was commissioned in 1872 and served in the Russo-Turkish war of 1877/78. His rise through the Russian army hierarchy was unremarkable, for he gave no indication that he possessed the qualities of military greatness. What he did have was the gift of gaining his soldiers' loyalty and confidence and he was at his happiest when among them.

From command of the cavalry school, at which he had been a student, Brusilov rose to take over the Warsaw military district and then that of Kiev. In 1914 he commanded Russian 8th Army of the South-West Front in the advance against the Austrians through Galicia towards Lemberg and the fortresses at Przemysl. That November, when the Russian right wing came under pressure from the counter-offensive spearheaded by *Mackensen's* 9th Army, it was Brusilov's tactical skill that prevented a German break through.

The Brusilov offensive
During the early part of 1915, there was a regrouping and a re-organization of the South-West Front. Brusilov took over as its commander; though he held this post until 1917, it is for the 1916 offensive to which he gave his name that he is chiefly remembered. The background to this is as follows.

From the opening days of the war, the Tsar's armies had suffered terrible losses in a series of bloody battles. In the spring of 1916, the French government – confronted with the German attack at Verdun – appealed, as it had done in 1914, to the Russians to launch an offensive to draw off German forces from the west. Accordingly, the Russian army was ordered to prepare for a new assault, even though at a *Stavka* (supreme command) conference the Tsar's senior generals openly doubted whether such an offensive could be successful. Only Brusilov displayed optimism, declaring himself ready to go into action even without support. His enthusiasm won his fellow commanders over and a general attack by all three Fronts was then agreed.

The offensive opened in June 1916 and continued until the end of August, with Brusilov's South-West Front making the most spectacular advances. Although local strategic objectives had been allotted to all three Fronts, the offensive's overriding purpose was to relieve the strain on the French – and, in that respect, Brusilov succeeded brilliantly. His storming advance panicked the German high command, who hastily rushed divisions eastwards to bolster up the Austrians. However, a later attempt to extend the scope of the offensive failed and the Russian troops, whose morale was now beginning to falter, settled down grimly in their trenches for another bitter winter.

The revolution and after
In the army re-organization that followed the February revolution, Brusilov was made commander-in-chief. That summer, Kerensky, Russia's new leader, again under French pressure, asked Brusilov to launch a second offensive. But, though Brusilov was personally popular with the rank and file and could talk to his troops as one soldier to another, this was no substitute for the discipline that had hitherto held the army together and the revolution had destroyed. The 1917 offensive failed, the front collapsed and the October revolution brought the Bolsheviks to power. Brusilov was wounded so severely in the fighting that accompanied the October revolution that he was inactive for several years.

In common with many other Tsarist officers, Brusilov's prime loyalty was to his country – rather than restricted to the support of a particular system of government. Thus, when the Soviets attacked Poland in 1920, he helped to plan the Soviet offensives and at the end of the campaign was appointed inspector of cavalry. He held this post until 1924, when he retired. He died in Moscow two years later.

The 1916 Brusilov offensive was the most competent Russian military operation of the First World War. It was well-planned, the troops were rehearsed in the parts they were to play and the offensive was well executed. Brusilov's planning ability, his enthusiasm and his gift of inspiring his men mark him out as one of the most successful Russian commanders of the First World War.

CADORNA
Luigi (1850-1928)
MARSHAL OF ITALY
First World War

Luigi Cadorna, chief of staff of the Italian army during much of the First World War, presided over Italy's greatest defeat at Caporetto. It was his tragedy that he was forced to shoulder the total blame for this catastrophy and so fell from power before the war was brought to a triumphant conclusion.

Cadorna was born in Pellanza in Piedmont on 4 September 1850. He entered military academy in 1865 and was gazetted in 1868. He rose swiftly. By the age of 30, he was already a brigadier; by 1905, he was a divisional commander. In 1910, he became commander of 4th Corps, with the rank of lieutenant-general; in 1914, he was appointed chief of staff of the Italian army.

When war broke out in 1914, the Italians, though bound by treaty to the Central Powers, remained neutral. Then, on 23 May 1915, they declared war on one of their treaty partners – Austria-Hungary. Cadorna had already completed his preparations for war against his former ally, having secretly mobilized the Italian army in order to gain the strategic initiative as soon as war was declared.

Italy at war
Cadorna's battle plan was for a fan of armies to move against Austria, his ambitious aim being to reach Vienna via the Lubliana Gap. The 1st Army, facing the South Tyrol salient, initially would adopt a defensive posture, while 4th Army drove northwards towards Toblach. On 4th Army's right flank was the Carniac Group, with two tasks – firstly, to advance north-eastwards towards Austria's southern provinces and secondly to cover the left wing of 2nd and 3rd Armies in their eastward advance towards Slovenia.

However, the advance of Cadorna's forces was not the storming assault that the Austrians had feared. By contrast, it was slow and hesitant. Had the Italians been more aggressive, they might well have won a decisive victory, since, until the Austrians rushed divisions back from the Eastern Front, the only forces available to meet the Italian offensive were amateur rifle clubs.

Stalemate set in on the Isonzo river. In the first four battles of the Isonzo, Cadorna's armies failed to break through the Austrian Alpine defences. Three years of warfare in the mountains followed, neither side being strong enough to drive the other back to reach lower ground. By 1917, both sides were fighting the 12th battle of the Isonzo. What followed next was a breakthrough – but by a combined Austro-German army at Caporetto. This military disaster led to Cadorna's fall, though he represented Italy on the inter-allied military council set up at Versailles. He retired from the army on 2 September 1918.

For the rest of his life, Cadorna's ambition was to clear his name as the man responsible for the disaster at Caporetto, which he tried to achieve through the publication of his memoirs. In 1924, he was made a Marshal of Italy and died on 21 December 1928 at Bordighera. Irrespective of where the blame for Caporetto lay, it is clear that the task Cadorna set himself when the war with Austria opened would have had little chance of success, even had he handled initial operations more aggressively. He had sought to gain a decision as the result of attacks in a terrain that naturally favored the defence, not the offence. Though it was a measure of the confidence Cadorna reposed in his soldiers that he had been so ambitious, it was a confidence that was misplaced. However, his failure was not a reflection upon his leadership, nor upon the courage of the men he commanded. It was the terrain, more than the enemy, that defeated him and his soldiers.

CHILLING STRATEGY *Erich von Falkenhayn masterminded the strategy of attempting to bleed the French army to death in a vast battle of attrition at Verdun.*

FALKENHAYN
Erich von (1861-1921)
GERMAN GENERAL
First World War

Erich von Falkenhayn was one of the finest strategists produced by the German army during the First World War, though his abilities were overshadowed by the achievements of *Hindenburg* and *Ludendorff*. He was a brilliant example of German staff training.

Falkenhayn was born in Prussia on 11 September 1861, and was gazetted in 1880. After a period of regimental service, he was selected for general staff training and, alternating between regimental and staff posts, rose steadily through the military hierarchy. By 1913 he had become Minister of War for Prussia; following the failure of the *Schlieffen Plan* in 1914, he succeeded von Moltke as chief of the general staff.

A new strategy

The situation Falkenhayn inherited was as follows. The great mass of the German army was positioned in an area extending from the north-east of Paris to the Franco-German frontier and down to Switzerland, the right flank, in Flanders, being only lightly held. Operations had ceased to be ones of maneuver, being replaced by the stalemate of trench warfare. It was Falkenhayn's task to devize a strategy that would revitalize the front and produce the victory that had eluded his predecessor.

It was the right flank that concerned Falkenhayn the most, for he feared that the British might attempt to land a force in the Channel ports to out-flank him. His move to prevent this, by extending the battle line westwards, led to the so-called "race to the sea" by the contending armies. The BEF and Belgians prevented the Germans from capturing the vital ports, but the only other result was that positional warfare became the order of the day along the entire battle line.

Falkenhayn nevertheless saw the west as the principal theater of operations. France had to be defeated. Then Germany's chief foe, Britain, would be unable to fight a major land campaign on the continent. Though Russia was too powerful to defeat, given the demands of two war fronts, operations in the east had shown that the Russians could be held in check by a numerically smaller German force. The strategy, he felt, must therefore be to remain on the defensive in the east until victory was won in the west. Russia could then be crushed.

This decision was opposed by the German and Austrian commanders fighting on the Eastern Front – particularly by *Hindenburg* and *Ludendorff*, who had become national figures as a result of their victory at Tannenberg. They told the Kaiser that total victory in the east was possible and won his support for a further series of offensives. Falkenhayn, for his part, deliberately reduced the scale of Western Front operations in order to build up a strong reserve, which he intended to deploy as the situation demanded. Then, Italy's entry into the war and the consequent need for Austria to reinforce its southern front necessitated an increase of German strength in the east to counterbalance the lost Austrian units. This need could be met only by drawing upon the reserves Falkenhayn had so carefully husbanded.

Attack in the west

The offensive on the Eastern Front in the first months of 1915, satisfied Falkenhayn that his theory had been correct. His reasoning now satisfied the volatile Kaiser, who agreed to von Falkenhayn's plan to mount an offensive of his own – in the west. Its intention was literally to bleed France white and Verdun was chosen as the best possible killing ground.

The campaign opened during February 1916. In a 10-month battle, France lost more than 500,000 men, as against the German 400,000, but Falkenhayn had been prepared for this. He had calculated that his reserves of manpower were greater than those of his enemy. His losses, he believed, could be made good. Those of the French could not.

The fall of von Falkenhayn

However, the scale of German casualties was too high for the Kaiser to accept. He replaced Falkenhayn, who then went to command operations against Romania, which had entered the war on the allied side during August 1916. Falkenhayn now showed his detractors how brilliant he could be in the field, defeating the Romanian army in the battle of the Arges river during the first week of December. He was then employed in Palestine where the Turkish 7th and 8th Armies had been badly hit by *Allenby*'s offensive.

Falkenhayn arrived in Palestine on 13 November 1917 and, with his usual energy and decision, had soon established a firm line running from the sea to Jerusalem. He fought a successful defensive battle against Allenby, but was then replaced by Liman von Sanders. His final command was 10th Army in Russia in 1918. Three years later, he died in retirement at Lindstedt near Potsdam.

Falkenhayn's grasp of strategy made him aware of more than the confines of continental warfare, a view that limited most of his contemporaries in the German army. He realized that Britain was Germany's chief enemy and that her defeat alone would bring victory. For that reason, he supported the policy of unrestricted U-boat warfare aimed at destroying the British merchant shipping fleet and so starving Britain into surrender. His pragmatic approach to the problems of war allowed him to propose in 1914, that a separate peace be made with Russia in order to allow Germany to concentrate upon a one-front war. His dispassionate advocacy of a campaign of attrition, as against the French at Verdun, stemmed from the logical viewpoint that a victory – even a Pyrrhic one – is still a victory.

FOCH
Ferdinand (1851-1929)
MARSHAL OF FRANCE
First World War

Ferdinand Foch, the generalissimo who led the allied armies to victory in the First World War, was an aggressive leader whose character had impressed itself upon the French people in the first weeks of the conflict. Asked at that time what the situation was on his front, he replied tersely: "My right wing is in retreat. My left wing is withdrawing. My center is disintegrating. Situation is excellent. I am attacking."

Foch was born in Tarbes on 2 October 1851, and fought as an infantryman in the Franco-Prussian War; in 1871 he entered the Nancy military academy and was gazetted from there into the artillery. He soon showed that he had a gift for words, especially when combined with military thought in his various treatises on the conduct of warfare. Believing that the French had lost the Franco-Prussian war by being too defensive, his writings constantly stressed the war-winning importance of attack. "War is positive in nature and admits only of a positive solution," he wrote. "Offensive is the law of war. The great captain is one who can transmit this idea to his men."

The apostle of attack

Foch's belief in the offensive fitted well with French military thought, particularly after the appointment of *Joffre* as commander-in-chief. It was to find its ultimate expression in the battles of 1914-18 on the Western Front, where the offensive philosophy was explored to its extreme limit. However, unlike many of his disciples, Foch was not an unthinking general as far as the possibilities of the offensive were concerned. As a lecturer in the Ecole Supériere de la Guerre, he stressed that élan in attack had to be supported by fire power and that both officers and men had to be aware of how to fully exploit the capabilities of the weapons they used. As an example, he demonstrated that the poor performance of the French mitrailleuses at Sedan in 1870 was due not to their inadequacy as a weapon, but to the fact that very few of Napoleon III's commanders knew how to deploy them to best advantage. He also proved by other examples that any attack made by a half-trained infantry mass against a well-armed enemy was sure to fail.

Élan, Foch argued, was not sufficient on its own. Attacks had to be planned, use had to be made of ground and the activities of infantry, cavalry and artillery had to be impeccably co-ordinated.

Foch at war

At the outbreak of war in 1914, Foch was commanding 20 Corps of the French 2nd Army, which, though initially spearheading the French attack into Lorraine, soon found itself driven back by two German armies. Foch's handling of his men during this battle was the instrumental factor ing them in detail. Given the pressure of Ludendorff's repeated attacks, it seemed as if the German plan might well succeed, especially since the pessimistic Petain was more concerned with the defence of Paris than in supporting his British allies. *Haig*, the British commander-in-chief, appealed to London for the appointment of a supreme allied commander to resolve the situation and Foch, on 3 April 1918, was made the man of the hour.

The victory offensive

Ferocious fighting continued, as the Germans continued to seek a decisive breakthrough and the allies made moves to halt them. The climax of the German assaults came in with the second battle of the Marne, after which the allied armies were able to move into the counteroffensive that Foch had been planning. This was to be a double assault – one blow striking from Verdun and the second in the Lens area of northern France.

Foch's aim was not to destroy the German armies in the field, but to capture the key railway junctions on which they depended for their supplies. By smashing the German logistical system on the Western Front, their front-line troops would be forced into inexorable retreat. To support these main thrusts, other attacks would be made in Flanders and on various sectors along the allied battle line. The offensive opened late in September and by the beginning of November the Germans had been forced to the armistice table.

The war was over and the part played by Foch in it had been a decisive one. It was not one without personal loss, for his son had been killed in action. His characteristic response was to remark that now he had even more reason to want to defeat the enemy.

GENERALISSIMO *Ferdinand Foch, the apostle of the offensive, became allied supreme commander in 1918.*

in preventing the German capture of the city of Nancy. In recognition of the ability he showed, he was speedily transferred to the command of the newly-raised 9th Army, a formation the French high command positioned in support of 4th and 5th Armies to give weight to the counterattack which Joffre proposed to launch against the German right wing. That offensive, driving northwards, met the German armies head on as they moved southwards and culminated in the victory of the Marne.

With the initial crisis mastered, a new one developed in the Channel coast area, where both sides "raced to the sea". In the First Battle of Ypres the British Expeditionary Force, faced by a major German assault, was aided by French troops under Foch's command. His army was kept in support of the British; in time, it grew in size to become the Army Group of the North, part of which was involved in the Somme battle in 1916.

That year saw a temporary downturn in Foch's fortunes. Very much Joffre's protege, he was eclipsed when the latter was replaced by *Nivelle* and then by *Petain*, the hero of Verdun. Foch was, however, soon to receive not only a Marshal's baton, but also the post of allied Generalissimo. His appointment came about as the result of the success of the German offensive of March 1918. This had been launched at the junction of the Franco/British armies with the intention of separating them and destroy-

FRENCH
John D (1852-1925)
BRITISH FIELD-MARSHAL
First World War

The little cavalryman who led the British army into first war in western Europe for nearly a century was the victim of a military intrigue, which caused him to be removed from his command and posted, at the end of 1915, to a non-combatant post in charge of Home Forces in the United Kingdom.

John Pinkstone French was born in September 1852 in Kent and was commissioned into the cavalry in 1874. He demonstrated his command capabilities and skill in handling cavalry during the war in South Africa. The campaign there had not been going well until Lord Roberts arrived and took over command from Buller. Roberts realized that the British army could not defeat the Boers by conventional means – by slow and methodical assaults – but would need to be as mobile as the enemy.

The formation of mounted infantry units was the first step in that new direction and French was promoted to command two such brigades. His opponents were the skilful Boer leaders de Wet and de la Rey, but French, in a number of swift and daring assaults, defeated them both. On 15 February 1900, he raised the four-month-long Boer siege of Kimberley, finishing the battle with a cavalry charge which drove the enemy from the field. When the Boers retreated under the pressure of Robert's advance, they were cut off at the Modder river by French's cavalry, whom he had force-marched from Kimberley.

As a result of his successes in the Boer War, during which he was promoted first major-general and subsequently lieutenant-general, French was made inspector general and then chief of the imperial general staff, rising to the rank of field marshal. Though he was forced to resign as a result of the so-called Curragh Mutiny in March 1914, he was recalled to lead the British Expeditionary Force to France on the outbreak of war only five months later.

French in France
French's four divisions marched into Belgium and took up position on the left of 5th French Army. There, outside the town of Mons, part of the BEF was struck by 1st German Army. The rifle fire of the British regulars decimated the enemy units sent in against them, but French was forced to conform to the withdrawal that the 5th Army commander had begun, without advising his British allies. During the retreat, one of French's corps was heavily engaged at the battle of Le Câteau, the biggest battle that the British army had fought since Waterloo, in which it was opposed by the whole of the German 1st Army. Concerned at the losses his force was suffering and the seeming indifference of his allies, French was determined to preserve what remained of his army by refusing to obey *Joffre*'s orders and to act on his own initiative instead. However, he was overruled by *Kitchener*, the Secretary of State for War, who ordered him to conform to French plans.

In the confused military situation at the beginning of September 1914, German 1st Army was pulled back across the Marne to avoid being outflanked. The change in direction that resulted from this move opened a gap between German 1st and 2nd Armies into which the BEF marched, conforming with Joffre's general advance. The German armies withdrew from the Marne. The French held the German attacks during the first battle of Ypres, where the old British army was destroyed, but failed to smash the enemy line at Neuve Chapelle in March 1915. He was reluctant to involve the BEF in Joffre's ambitious offensive to recapture the industrial region of northern France and, when his own attacks failed in the battle of Loos, French was blamed for their failure.

He had long been the victim of a scurrilous campaign by *Haig* and General Wilson, a francophile who, together with another francophile, Kitchener, considered the field marshal unsuitable for his command because of his acknowledged problems in dealing with with Joffre and his subordinates. Accordingly, French was replaced in December 1915 and posted back to the United Kingdom.

There is no doubt that French was a difficult person, who found it hard to communicate with or trust foreigners. He had been in the Sudan at the time of the Fashoda incicent when a French military force had tried to claim British territory. He had also witnessed the pro-Boer sentiments of the French with distaste. He was, thus, an unwilling ally, but once he was totally involved he was absolutely loyal and dependable. He was prickly, being quick to take offence, and was stubborn in defence of his principles. A brave and skilful soldier, he showed himself to be as able to organize and command an expanding British army in France and Flanders as he had been in South Africa. He was given no chance, given the conditions of trench warfare, to use the British cavalry in the way which he would have liked. Had he had that opportunity, then he might have scored as complete a victory over the Germans in 1914 as he had over the Boers more than a decade earlier.

HAIG
Douglas (1861-1928)
BRITISH FIELD-MARSHAL
First World War

Douglas Haig, the handsome cavalryman who rose to become commander-in-chief of the British Army in France and Flanders during the First World War, is still a figure of controversy even today. Was he, in the cynical, dismissive words of British Prime Minister David Lloyd George, "brilliant to the top of his riding boots", or, as some military historians argue, was he a military commander of too great stature for the limited mind of a party politician to grasp?

Haig was born into a prosperous family of whisky distillers on 19 June 1861. He graduated from the Royal Military Academy in 1895 with first-class honors, choosing the 7th Hussars as his regiment. Then, because of his excellent staff college results, he was selected to serve under *Kitchener* in the reconquest of the Sudan and fought with the Egyptian cavalry at the battle of Omdurman in 1898. A year later he became chief of staff to General Sir John *French* in South Africa where, in addition to this staff posting, he also was given field commands, particularly in the final stages of the war, when he led mounted columns in sweep and search operations against the Boer commandos.

Before 1914
Haig had shown in the Boer War promise of military distinction. This led to his being selected to work on the reorganization of the British army, which was initiated by Haldane, the war minister in the Liberal government of 1906. Through this, Haig became familiar with the intricate structure and organization of the army; it was due to the Haldane Committee's reforming efforts that the expeditionary force Britain was able to field in 1914 was the

best eqiuipped that had ever been sent to fight overseas.

One of the weaknesses of the British system was that the staff college courses prepared their entrants to be no more than corps commanders. Unlike the German system, there was no long and formal schooling to train officers to command an army, or an army group. As far as the British were concerned, there had been no need for this in the past – nor would there be in the future. No one had anticipated a war of the scale of the First World War; so when in 1914, the existing British corps expanded to become armies, they were led by men whose training had not prepared them for the level of command involved. Haig, though regarded by his contemporaries as an educated soldier, was in some ways a victim of this lack of military foresight.

Taking French's place

Haig went overseas in command of 1st Corps in 1914 and led it through the great opening battles of the war, plus overseeing its expansion into 1st Army. Becoming increasingly concerned with what he saw as the incompetence of *French* to lead what was becoming a mass army, Haig wrote to George V, a personal friend of long standing, with his complaints. His was not the only criticism of the British commander in the field, the result being that French was replaced by Haig in December 1915.

The first major military operation in which Haig was involved as commander-in-chief of the British army on the Western Front was the Somme offensive. Haig, however, had no confidence in the operation because he could see no strategic sense in it. Furthermore, the proposed French participation in the offensive was reduced to a minimal level as a result of the demands of Verdun, so the battle became a primarily British affair. On the first day of the offensive alone, the British army lost 20,000 killed, with double that number being wounded or taken prisoner. Though the offensive relieved the German pressure upon the French, this was the Somme's sole benefit. By the time the battle ended the British had advanced little more than 8 miles and lost 420,000 troops.

Haig was not deterred by these losses, however, and the following year planned the battle that brought about even greater condemnation of his strategy than had the Somme. This was Third Ypres. It had been Haig's intention in 1916 to capture the Passchendale ridge to the north of Ypres as a prelude to an advance towards Ostend and Zebrugge, but the Somme offensive had taken its place. Now, he argued fervently again for his plan; even enlisting Admiralty support. In the face of the U-boat offensives, he argued the Germans had to be denied the use of their Belgian bases. The alternative, so Haig and his allies claimed, was the possibility of Britain being starved into surrender. Despite their misgivings, Lloyd George and his colleagues gave Haig the authority to proceed.

The only factor Haig could not influence was the weather – and this proved to be his worst enemy. What he required above everything else was a long dry period. He did not get it. Rain started to fall on the first day of the

BLUNDERER? *Haig's strategy was bitterly criticized, not least by Britain's premier, David Lloyd George.*

offensive, its effects being made worse as a consequence of the long preliminary bombardment, which had destroyed the drainage ditches. Consequently, the rain was not carried away and the ground was churned into deep mud. Despite the terrible conditions, Haig nonetheless kept up his attacks until the second week of November, for he had convinced himself that the German armies were cracking. When the fighting stopped, the battle had cost Haig around 300,000 casualties.

"With our backs to the wall"

The failure at Third Ypres led to a complete collapse of confidence in London. Lloyd George could not replace Haig; what he could do – and did – was to refuse to reinforce Haig's armies. This led to dire consequences when the British came under attack during *Ludendorff*'s offensives in the spring of 1918. The German intention was to drive a wedge between the British and French armies and then to destroy them in detail. Haig and his armies stubbornly resisted the German pressure, but, at the same time, the British commander began to fear that *Petain*, his French opposite number, was more concerned with defending Paris than with fighting a unified battle. Accordingly he appealed to Lloyd George for the appointment of an allied generalissimo. In a rare display of agreement, both agreed that Foch was the man.

Foch's appointment did not immediately end the danger, however. Having been rebuffed at the junction of the allied armies, Ludendorff tried again against the British armies in Flanders. The situation was desperate and Haig issued a powerful rallying call in his celebrated "backs to the wall" order of the day. The tenacity of his troops and Haig's skilful defence frustrated the German drive. By August 1918, the allies had contained and held the fury of the German offensives and were ready to mount their own counterstroke. This was initiated by Haig; on 8 August, his success was such that Ludendorff decided that the war must be ended.

A controversial commander

Haig fought the final battles of the war with the flair and ability of a truly great commander. However, considerable hostility pursued him even after the war and he found himself reviled by many who had never grasped the realities of the military situation. This feeling, however, was not shared by the thousands of soldiers he had commanded and for whose benefit he helped to found the Royal British Legion and the Poppy Day appeal – a fund that bears his name. He died in London in January 1928.

Haig was an inarticulate man – the product of an social system that was suspicious of people who were glib with words. Whether he was an intriguer, going behind French's back to complain to George V about the latter's inadequacy, or whether he was concerned for the future of the army, is a matter of conjecture. Whether he was wrong to have persisted with his attacks on the Somme and at Third Ypres is also a matter of opinion. But the fact that he did an excellent job in shouldering his responsibilities – unprepared though he was for them – is unquestioned. Few, if any, of his contemporaries could have done better in the face of a situation for which they had never been trained and so were forced to learn by crude experiment.

HAMILTON
Ian (1853-1947)
BRITISH GENERAL
First World War

Ian Hamilton was considered by his contemporaries to be one of the most talented commanders of his day but, to posterity, he is the man responsible for the disastrous campaign in Gallipoli in the First World War. His career came to an end there when he was relieved of his command in October 1915, a humiliation that brought to an end four decades of military service, during which Hamilton gained the reputation of having seen more fighting than any other British senior officer.

Hamilton, the son of an army officer, was born on 16 January 1853, in Corfu and was gazetted into the Gordon Highlanders, with whom he served in the Second Afghan War. He took part in the expedition that was sent to relieve Gordon in Khartoum and then returned to the east, where he fought in the Burma wars as well as on the north-west frontier of India. In 1902, after fighting in the Boer War, he was knighted and promoted lieutenant-general. In 1904 he was sent by the War Office as an official observer of the Russo-Japanese War, which gave him considerable insight into the problems both sides faced in modern land warfare.

Genesis of disaster

The background to the Dardanelles disaster is a complex one, but it is worthy of study since it showed that Hamilton was by no means solely to blame. When Turkey entered the war against the allies, forcing the Dardanelles to open up a Black Sea supply route to Russia became a priority. A purely naval task force having failed, an expeditionary force was hurriedly assembled to seize the Gallipoli peninsula and Hamilton was given command. However, administrative blunders at home caused the initial landings to be postponed, thus giving the Turks time to strengthen their defences. In addition, further naval bombardments, intended to destroy the Dardanelles forts, had served only to warn the enemy that an attack was imminent.

Finally, two landings were made on 25 April 1915 – one at Cape Helles and the other at Ari Burnu – but neither attack gained the dominant high ground, which was the chief objective. Turkish counter-attacks at Ari Burnu drove back the Anzacs (the troops from Australia and New Zealand) – Hamilton ordering them to hold their narrow beach head at all costs – while other counter attacks pinned down the British at Cape Helles. Soon, both landing areas were ringed by trenches and positional warfare followed. A third landing, made at Suvla Bay in August, was intended to outflank the Turks investing the Anzac positions at Ari Burnu, but Hamilton's plans for a co-ordinated assault from all the beachheads came to nought in the face of determined Turkish resistance.

Had the War Office in London sent Hamilton the reinforcements for which he had asked, had he been given the staff officers he needed to control the three, widely-separated combat areas and had he driven his subordinate commanders harder, then a victory might well have been gained. But Hamilton, like Robert E *Lee*, did not so much issue orders as suggest a course of action to be followed. Nor did he possess the ruthless driving force that was needed to win success. He tried always to see the best in men, even in those whose unsuitability for command was clearly evident. Consequently, his orders at Gallipoli were not forced home with the vigor that was needed, as opposed to the speed of reaction of his adversaries, Liman von Sanders and Kemal Attaturk.

Ultimately, the defeat of Serbia confounded the strategic plan to drive Turkey out of the war and the Gallipoli campaign no longer had a purpose as a result. At the end of December 1915, the Suvla Bay and Ari Burnu beachheads were evacuated, with Cape Helles following in January 1916. Hamilton, however, had already been relieved of command, the scapegoat for an operation that had failed because, so rumor said, it was never intended to succeed. There were many among the allied leaders at the most senior levels who were convinced that the main war effort had to be made on the Western Front and that allied resources should not be frittered away in side shows. Gallipoli had been a side show.

Hamilton, now faced the prospect of long years of retirement with equanimity. His loyalty was such that he never sought to clear his name.

HINDENBURG
Paul Beneckendorff von (1847-1934)
GERMAN FIELD MARSHAL
First World War

Field Marshal Paul von Hindenburg became Germany's military father figure during the First World War and subsequently last president of the Weimar Republic. However, though an imposing leader physically, he was more of a figurehead than a true leader.

Hindenburg was born on 2 October 1847 at Posen. The son of a military family, he entered the Prussian army via cadet and military academies and was gazetted into the 3rd Guards Regiment during 1866. As a young officer, he fought first in the Austro-Prussian and then in the Franco-Prussian wars. Graduating from the Prussian war academy, he joined the general staff; his subsequent career alternated between staff and regimental duties. In the latter capacity, he commanded the 91st Regiment and then, for eight years, 4th Corps in Magdeburg. At the age of 64 he retired from the army, after a routine career.

Recalled to the colors
Hindenburg's recall to duty in 1914 came about as a result of the advance of the Russian 1st and 2nd armies through East Prussia and the failure of von Prittwitz, the commander of 8th Army, to master the resulting crisis. He was teamed with a new chief of staff, Erich *Ludendorff*, whom he met for the first time on Hanover railway station. On their journey east, the two men studied the situation and Hindenburg reviewed the plan of action which Ludendorff had already prepared. His approval of the forthcoming offensive marked the birth of a partnership that was to bring Germany close to total victory – always provided the offensive plan was successful.

At Marienburg, the headquarters of 8th Army, Hindenburg was briefed by Hoffmann, chief of the army's operations staff and he found that the latter's plan to beat the Russians was essentially the same as the one he had worked out with Ludendorff. From Russian signals, which were being sent uncoded, the Germans were able not only to identify and locate every major enemy unit, but also to learn the intentions of the Russian commanders. It was learned that *Rennenkampf*'s 1st Army, in the north, was plagued by supply difficulties and so had had to halt its advance until rations and ammunition columns had been

FATHERLAND'S HERO *Though more of a figurehead than a great military thinker, Hindenburg was hailed as the man who had saved the fatherland at Tannenberg.*

brought forward. *Samsonov* and his 2nd Army, in the south, was still advancing northwards; although its progress was slow, this army represented the greater menace.

Triumph at Tannenberg
Armed with this intelligence, Hindenburg withdrew the corps to ring his left flank facing Russian 1st Army, leaving a single cavalry division in position to screen him from the enemy. The infantry were then rushed by train or marched on foot southwards, where they began to encircle the Russian 2nd Army. As a native of East Prussia, Hindenburg had a detailed knowledge of the terrain and so was aware how difficult it would be for a major force to advance as a cohesive body through the swampy, heavily forested areas of his Prussian homeland. He also knew where he could best concentrate his own troops and site his artillery batteries.

On 24 August, units of 2nd Army, moving blindly forward, ran into German 20th Corps, which pulled back, drawing the Russians into a trap. Samsonov was convinced that his forces were pursuing a beaten enemy, but he was soon to be disillusioned. Other German corps then encircled and destroyed 2nd Army, then turning north to inflict a similarly stunning defeat on 1st Army. For a loss of only about 40,000 men, Hindenburg had gained a victory that overshadowed the failure of the *Schlieffen Plan* in the west; he had also inflicted over 250,000 casualties on the two Russian armies.

Hindenburg did not rest on these laurels. During the last two weeks of September, he came to the aid of his Austro-Hungarian ally, which had borne the brunt of the fighting in Galicia. He moved four corps to Cracow in Poland, grouping these into 9th German Army under his own command. The offensive he launched pre-empted a Russian assault, thwarting the Russian plan to invade the industrial area of Silesia. On 1 November 1914, he was appointed commander-in-chief of the Austro/German forces on the Eastern Front; shortly thereafter, his clever maneuvers drove a wedge between Rennenkampf's 1st Army and the reconstituted 2nd Army.

This successful offensive not only destroyed Russia's last chance to invade German territory, but also stabilized the Eastern Front until February 1915, when Hindenburg opened a double offensive – one thrust to the north of Warsaw and the other in Galicia. The offensive, with pauses for reorganization and to deal with enemy counter-attacks, lasted until June and brought about a virtual collapse of the Russian armies. Only the onset of fall rains saved them from total disaster.

Transfer to the west

In the summer of 1916, however, Hindenburg, by this time a national idol, was posted to the Western Front. German military planning in 1914 had called for the major effort to be made in the west. In 1915, the emphasis was to gain a decision in the east, but now, it was thought that victory on the Eastern Front was impossible and the military emphasis changed to the west once again.

Hindenburg and the inseparable Ludendorff quickly realized that the German armies in the west were over-stretched and were in no position to undertake major operations, following the losses incurred at Verdun and on the Somme. Indeed, in Hindenburg's opinion, it was essential to shorten the German line so as to release sufficient troops to create a strong reserve. Accordingly, during March 1917, a withdrawal to a strong defence system – known to the allies as the Hindenburg Line – was carried out.

At the same time, it became increasingly clear that the burden of command was taking its toll on the 71-year-old Hindenburg's health and that it was Ludendorff who now made the military and the political decisions. This was kept from the German people, who still considered Hindenburg to be the national savior. In November 1918, however, it fell to Hindenburg to advise the Kaiser that he should abdicate. Ludendorff had already been forced to resign, because the allies would not sign an armistice while he retained his authority. Hindenburg, however, was seen as the man who could hold both army and nation together at this critical moment.

Hindenburg retained his personal charisma even in the post-war years; in 1925, it won him the presidency of the Weimar Republic. By now senile, Hindenburg's one aim was to preserve national unity and governmental authority in the face of economic depression and rising political violence; on 30 January, 1933, he overcame the constitutional crisis by appointing Hitler chancellor, believing that the traditional conservatives in the government could control the radical Nazis. Hindenburg did not live to see the results of his appointment, for he died in the fall of 1934, still seen as the epitome of the Prussian spirit of self-sacrifice in the national interest.

VON HOETZENDORFF
Conrad (1852-1925)
AUSTRIAN FIELD MARSHAL
First World War

In the years following the First World War, many military historians credited Conrad von Hoetzendorff with having had the finest strategic mind of any of the period's commanders. Like most great military leaders, Conrad also had the gift of anticipating tactical trends and of developing them – a gift he showed in his creation of the Austro-Hungarian mountain troop forces.

Born at Penzing, a suburb of Vienna, on 11 November 1852 into a military family, Conrad was gazetted into Feldjaeger Battalion No. 11, with which he saw active service in the Bosnian campaign of 1878 and that in south Dalmatia in 1882. As a brigadier in Trieste in 1899, Conrad demonstrated on maneuvers a flair for original thinking and for training his men along unconventional lines. Knowledge of his ideas spread through the army via his writings, for he was a gifted author. In view of the aggressive attitude of Italy, as commander of 8th Division in the Tyrol, he busied himself in the creation of what was to prove the finest force of mountain troops in the world. Passionately believing that thorough training, however arduous, saves blood on the battlefield, he tested his soldiers to their limits, despite being rebuked by Archduke Franz Ferdinand, inspector-general of the army. Aware that the Austrian artillery was badly organized, he laid plans to improve it, but, though he put them into effect when he rose to high rank, they had not been completely carried through by the outbreak of war in 1914.

A man who wanted war

Through Franz Ferdinand's influence, Conrad, now promoted to the rank of general and ennobled, became chief of staff of the armed forces. In that premier position, he was brought into the political arena, where his well-known demands for military action against his country's enemies were condemned by the liberal and anti-militaristic factions of Austro-Hungarian society. Conrad saw the empire as threatened by Italy to the south and by Serbia to the south-east. Convinced that the aggressive policies of those countries could only be countered by pre-emptive action, Conrad produced a succession of war plans, which brought him into conflict with the Emperor Franz Josef and the foreign minister. Franz Josef saw Conrad's demands for war as infringing upon his own prerogative to determine foreign policy and relieved him of his post. Conrad was demoted to inspector-general of the army, but the Balkan Wars and the resulting close alliance of Serbia with Russia, showed the correctness of his thinking. Reinstated as chief of staff, he promptly proposed a pre-emptive strike against Italy, which at that time was fighting a colonial war in Libya. Conrad considered that no reliance could be placed upon Italian loyalty to the triple alliance of Austria, Germany and Italy. He, therefore, strengthened the fortifications of the Alpine region and built up his heavy artillery.

War plans and war

During the last years of peace in Europe, Conrad produced two war plans. One was for use in the event of action against Serbia alone (Plan B – Balkans), while the second provided for dual operations against Serbia and Russia (Plan R). German/Austrian military strategy called for Germany to make its main effort in the west, using the *Schlieffen Plan* to attack and destroy France in six weeks. While that campaign was in operation, the Austrian and Romanian armies would hold the front in the east, virtually without German support. After the French had been destroyed, the combined Austro-German-Romanian forces would smash Russia.

Such, at least, was the plan, but, in 1914, muddle took the place of planning. Advised that Austria contemplated hostilities only against Serbia, Conrad first activated Plan B. Then he found himself at war with both Russia and Serbia. To further complicate the situation, Austria's ally, Romania, declared its neutrality, so the armies that should have formed the Austrian right wing were non-existent. Conrad's intricately-planned timetable was thrown into temporary confusion while he regrouped his forces. The Austro-Hungarian army then took up the burden of the war in the east, but with singular lack of success. It took German aid to destroy Serbia and Montenegro, as well as to drive Romania out of the war. Russia, too, won its greatest successes against the Austrians – a fact that the German high command was not slow to point out. Conrad might strive and plan for a decisive victory, but, without German support, he lacked the means to achieve it.

During December 1916, the new Emperor, Karl, took over command of the army. Conrad who had been passed over for the post of commander-in-chief of the Austro/German armies on the Eastern Front, suffered a further humiliation in being dismissed as chief of staff. The emperor gave him field command on the Italian front and, in June 1918, Conrad's Army Group participated in a final offensive. It failed to gain its objectives and he retired. He died at Mertgentheim on 25 August 1925.

Conrad's great tragedy was that the army with whose command he had been entrusted was flawed. He himself was aware of this, but he was not given the time to create a fighting machine capable of carrying out his strategy. The Austro-Hungarian army, through no fault of its own, was unequal to the demands made upon it by its brilliant commander, Conrad von Hoetzendorff.

JELLICOE
John Rushworth (1859-1935)
BRITISH ADMIRAL
First World War

John Jellicoe, a small, mild man with a prominent nose, commanded the British Grand Fleet on the outbreak of the First World War. He was described by Winston Churchill as "the only man who could lose the war in a single battle in one afternoon." The responsibility he bore was therefore awesome.

John Rushworth Jellicoe was born on 5 December 1859, and entered the Royal Navy during 1872. As soon as he could, he concentrated on a subject that had always fascinated him – that of naval gunnery – and had soon gained a reputation as an expert in the field. This brought him to the attention of the influential Admiral John Fisher, who was seeking to modernize the navy's ships and improve its tactics. With Fisher's patronage, Jellicoe was soon made director of naval ordnance and then rear-admiral of the Atlantic fleet. In 1908, he became third sea lord, and then commanded in succession the Atlantic and the Home Fleets before taking over leadership of the Grand Fleet – Britain's premier battle fleet – in 1914.

AWESOME RESPONSIBILITY *John Jellicoe could have "lost the war in an afternoon", according to Churchill.*

Leading the Grand Fleet

British naval strategy's long-term aim was either to annihilate the German fleet if it put out to sea, or to keep it bottled up within its home ports. Both sides believed that there must be, at some time, a decisive clash and the two fleets accordingly made sweeps of the North Sea, hoping to lure the opposing navy into a forced engagement under unfavorable terms. Jellicoe, fully aware of his awesome responsibility, left such aggressive sweeps to his subordinates, keeping the main battle fleet at Scapa Flow awaiting the time when he could strike the decisive blow. It was, therefore, his commanders who won publicity for their feats, rather than the shy commander-in-chief who had planned them.

Jellicoe had another powerful ally. British naval intelligence had broken the German naval code and so were able to help him in planning battle-cruiser sweeps. They were also able to warn him when the German navy was about to make a sortie, so that he could deploy his ships to meet it accordingly.

The fleets clash at Jutland

Though there were several clashes between units of the opposing fleets during 1914 and 1915, the only full-scale battle between the Grand Fleet and Imperial High Seas Fleet took place at Jutland at the end of May 1916. Jellicoe, warned that a German fleet had left harbor, took the Grand Fleet to sea, with *Beatty*, the battle-cruiser commander, in the van. However, Jellicoe was also advised that Admiral Scheer's flagship had not sailed – an incorrect piece of intelligence – and so anticipated that only a portion of the enemy navy – probably its battle-cruisers – was in the Skagerrak. He did not know that the whole High Seas Fleet had steamed into the North Sea.

The first clash between Beatty's screening squadrons and von Hipper's battle-cruisers cost Beatty two of his ships; he turned towards Jellicoe, confident that he would draw the Germans after him and so on to the guns of the battleships of the Grand Fleet. The Germans pursued – then, in the words of one German senior officer, "The whole horizon became a mass of flame as the British heavy guns opened fire upon us." What that officer was witnessing was the crossing of the German "T" by the Grand Fleet, the German ships being enclosed within a shallow arc of British vessels.

Jellicoe, now aware of the enemy's true strength and therefore that this was the major clash that had been so long anticipated, steamed at top speed to place his fleet between Scheer, the German commander-in-chief, and his home bases. As the long line of British ships crossed the enemy "T", they concentrated their fire upon the leading German squadrons. Under this savage gunfire Scheer retreated, but Jellicoe did not pursue. Enemy destroyers, making repeated torpedo attacks upon his capital ships, caused him to turn away so as not to hazard them.

When, after a quarter of an hour, the German admiral realized that he was not being pursued, he turned back onto his original course, only to have Jellicoe cross his "T" again. It was now twilight and again the German fleet turned away – this time making good its escape in the gathering darkness. Jellicoe had no intention of fighting a night action. He knew that German gunnery was as accurate by night as it was by day and that that of the Royal Navy was not. Enemy gunnery techniques, which he had studied, made him acutely aware that his was the inferior position. He maintained a course that should have resulted in a continuation of the action during the following morning. He was disappointed. The High Seas Fleet had escaped him in the night and had returned to its home ports. Maintaining wireless silence to avoid the risk of alerting U-boats, Jellicoe headed for his bases. Scheer, on arriving in Germany, claimed a victory which the British Admiralty was in no position to refute because of Jellicoe's silence. Technically, the Germans were correct. They had sunk three battle-cruisers, three cruisers and eight destroyers for a loss of one second-line battleship, one battle-cruiser, four light cruisers and five destroyers. Strategically, however, the British had had the best of it, for the High Seas Fleet was never to fight another action.

What the British public had expected, however, was a *Nelson*-style victory, not an inconclusive battle. Ships of the Grand Fleet were greeted with boos, while the newspapers, to whom Beatty was a hero through his battle-cruiser exploits, accused Jellicoe of bungling the battle. At the subsequent Court of Enquiry, Beatty's statements seemed to substantiate this.

Jellicoe became First Sea Lord, but retired from the navy shortly afterwards. The achievements of that introspective man, with his gold-rimmed spectacles perched on the end of his nose, were not understood or appreciated until the end of the war. Then, on a gray November morning, the massed squadrons of the once-proud German navy steamed into Scapa Flow to anchor under the guns of the Grand Fleet in surrender. It was Jellicoe's patient long-term strategy that had brought about this end; the surrender of the German fleet was his victory.

JOFFRE
Joseph (1852-1931)
MARSHAL OF FRANCE
First World War

Joseph Joffre was an archetypal French peasant – albeit a uniformed peasant who rose to the rank of Marshal of France. Moustached, gaitered and deliberate, he was slow to act, but firm in action. The outward calm and unruffled attitude of this stocky old man served to reassure his subordinates – and the French people – in times of crisis, as events in the First World War were to show.

Born at Rivesaltes in the Pyrenees in January 1852, the young Joffre saw action for the first time in 1870, when, after passing out from the Polytechnique the previous year, he manned a cannon in the defence of Paris against its Prussian besiegers. He then served with distinction on

ranteed Belgian neutrality in perpetuity and were hopeful of British aid. Michel was therefore relieved of his command, to be replaced by Joffre.

Encouraged by the so-called "young Turks" of the high command, Joffre now produced his Plan XVII – the plan with which France went to war in 1914. This called for an all-out offensive to be launched eastwards into Alsace-Lorraine by the bulk of the French army, but allowed for two armies to be detached to oppose the Germans, should they attack through Belgium. The unfortunate facts were firstly that the Germans were defensively well-prepared for such an offensive and secondly that Joffre expected any attack via Belgium to be a feint.

The "miracle of the Marne"

When the war came in 1914, Joffre started out by following Plan XVII to the letter, using his 4th and 5th armies to oppose what he took to be the German feint, while ordering the others to launch the long-planned offensive. Luckily, he quickly realized that the thrust through Belgium was in fact the main German effort in the west and was calm enough to keep his head and act accordingly. He promptly called off the eastward advance of his own frontier armies – this had been held by the German defences in any case – and then, with remarkable flexibility of mind and action, devised a new plan from the debacle. This was for a counter-attack against the advancing Germans, for which two new armies, composed of fresh troops, were created to reinforce the troops who, together with the British Expeditionary Force under General Sir John *French*, had been in action on the allied left wing since the opening days of the war.

Before the operation could be launched, however, Joffre was advised that the German thrust had changed direction, to pass to the east of Paris, not to the west. This meant that a gap had opened up between the German 1st and 2nd armies, which the allies could now exploit. Recognizing his opportunity, Joffre grouped 6th army – one of the newly-organized formations – around the French capital and on 4 September launched it against the open German flank.

Out of this counter-offensive, there developed the battle of the Marne, one of the most important battles of the First World War. Joffre fought it with great skill; although no clear-cut allied victory resulted, it halted the German offensive – the Germans were forced to retreat to the line of the River Aisne – and consequently stopped Germany from winning the war in the west.

Stalemate in the west

Following the Marne, the allies and the Germans fought a further succession of battles as both attempted to side-step and out-flank each other in a stately "race" to the sea. When the Channel coast was reached, both sides entrenched and a military stalemate resulted. In a series of attempts to re-open a war of movement, Joffre launched various offensives that winter and in the spring of 1915, but gains were minimal and costly, while none of them achieved the strategic breakthrough he sought.

many colonial expeditions in the Far East, the Sudan and to Timbuktoo. Even as a junior commander, his skill in planning operations and the speed with which he executed them marked him out as a soldier destined for advancement. He rose steadily through various staff posts, making a special study of fortification – a factor which was to be of help to him when he came to conduct the defence of *Verdun*. By 1911, he had become chief of the French general staff.

The birth of Plan XVII

At the time when Joffre took up this post, French plans to deal with a German attack in the event of war were undergoing substantial revision. Previously, the aim had been to remain on the defensive, but now, as a result of staff discussions with the Russian general staff, it was mutually agreed that both nations would take the offensive if attacked. The French had to adjust their existing war plans accordingly.

Plan XVI, drawn up by General Michel, the commander-in-chief, called for a pre-emptive French invasion of Belgium, so as to forestall the Germans, who, in Michel's opinion, would be launching their main offensive across the Franco-Belgian frontier. However, such an act was impossible to contemplate politically – the French were conscious that, like Britain, they had gua-

After failing to capture Vimy Ridge, he reduced the scale of his operations to rest his exhausted troops, only to resume them later in the year with the same lack of success.

Verdun and the Somme

Joffre now believed that planned co-operation between the allies would bring about military success. Accordingly, at a conference in Chantilly, he proposed that the 1916 battle plans of the allied armies should be co-ordinated. This was agreed in broad outline, though the delegates did not go into more detailed planning. This was left to Joffre and General Sir Douglas *Haig*, the new commander-in-chief of the British armies in France – both of whom believed that 1916 would see the decisive "big push" to end the war. Joffre's intention was to launch a major offensive on the Somme to bring this about and the aim, once again, was to break the trench deadlock.

The Germans, however, were to strike first. Throughout 1915, Germany's main efforts had been made on the Eastern Front against the Russians, with the intention of driving them out of the war. Despite substantial territorial gains, the Germans failed to destroy the Tsarist armies and so turned westward again to seek a decision on the Western Front. Their aim was to deliberately seek an objective for which the French would be forced to fight, regardless of loss; the place they chose for this experiment in "bleeding France white" was the centuries-old fortress city of Verdun.

The battle for Verdun was the most serious crisis that Joffre had had to face since the Marne, but he mastered it by skilful deployment of his reserves and by finding men of the right caliber to conduct operations in the field. Nevertheless, as more and more of Joffre's troops were drawn into the fighting, the promised French support for the Somme offensive dwindled and, in the event, little more than a token force took part.

Paradoxically, in successfully delegating command at Verdun, Joffre was sowing the seeds of his own downfall. *Petain*, the senior field commander for the key stages of the battle, became a national hero, though, when fierce German attacks in July almost broke through the French front, it was Joffre who steadied Petain's nerve, turning down his request for a tactical withdrawal. Then, the Somme offensive – a fruit of the Chantilly conference – forced the Germans to withdraw 15 divisions from the Verdun sector, while more troops had to be transferred to the Eastern Front to meet the summer Russian offensive.

Decline and fall

After the fighting at Verdun, on the Somme and in the east, the armies of both sides needed a period of rest and no major operations were undertaken until the late fall of 1916. Joffre's armies then went over to a counter-offensive, but this petered out, just as political confidence in Joffre's ability had also begun to wane. As stories about the initial unpreparedness of the French at Verdun began to circulate, the French decided that Robert *Nivelle*, another Verdun hero, had the secret of victory; accordingly he replaced Joffre that December.

Joffre's fall from prominence was total, though at *Foch's* insistence, he rode alongside him in the victory parade of 1919. Returning to retirement, he died on 3 January 1931. Attacked at the time for lack of imagination and complacency, posterity has been kinder to Joffre than were his contemporaries. Backed by an army which he had infused with his own qualities, he had destroyed the German war plan of 1914, emerged victorious from the 1916 Verdun offensive and thereby had laid the foundations for eventual allied victory.

KRAUSS
Alfred (1862-1938)
AUSTRIAN GENERAL
First World War

In political history, Alfred Krauss is known as the Austrian officer who welcomed the German annexation of his country in March 1938. In military history, the same man is remembered for the reputation he gained as the finest corps commander in the armies of the Central Powers during the First World War.

Krauss was born at Zara in 1862, entered the Austro-Hungarian army via cadet school and military academy and was gazetted as a lieutenant. After a short period of regimental duty, he entered staff college and, at the outbreak of war in 1914, was commanding 29th Infantry Divison as part of Potiorek's army group, fighting in Serbia. The Austrian advance was halted and driven back by the Serbs, who then concentrated their forces to meet Potiorek's counter-attack in the triangle between the Save and Drina rivers. Krauss saw a weakness in the enemy dispositions and flung his units against the crack Timok Division, the leading Serbian formation. With the enemy army thrown into confusion by Krauss's prompt and decisive action, Potiorek was able to launch his forces into a successful advance.

Krauss at Caporetto

By 1916, Krauss had become chief of staff to the Archduke Eugene, the Austro-Hungarian army group commander on the Italian Front and planned an offensive which would strike through the Alps to reach the north Italian plain. Although the operation, the fifth battle of the Isonzo, did not achieve the anticipated breakthrough, it did gain jumping-off ground for future offensives, when, in 1917, the German high command released six divisions for operations on the Italian Front. These were grouped as 14th German Army, Krauss' 1st Austrian Corps. being included in its order of battle. The plan was to launch a counter blow in response to the Italian offensive on the Isonzo – the 11th battle along that river line. The attack's main weight was to come in 14th Army's sector between Flitsch and Tolmein – and specifically, in Austrian 1st Corps area. It was a desperate undertaking. The Austro-German armies, fighting in Alpine regions, were to

UNDERRATED AUSTRIAN *Alfred Krauss was a brilliant leader in both the offensive and the defensive.*

launch an offensive perilously late in the year in the hope that it would be concluded before the onset of winter.

On 24 October, Krauss's corps took its first objectives at the end of 40 hours of non-stop battle. His success on the right wing of 14th Army initiated equally successful operations by other corps, which forced Italian 2nd and 3rd Armies to retreat to the Tagliamento river. By 5th November Krauss had crossed this obstacle and was leading the general advance towards the Livenza river, which he crossed on 7 November. Only three days later, the Austro-German armies, with 1st Austrian Corps in the van, were approaching the Piave.

Ahead of Krauss lay Monte Grappa, a massive feature forming the cornerstone of the Piave defences. It had to be taken before the advance could continue. It was a key objective – one that would have been difficult even for fresh troops to take, but Krauss' men, although exhausted by the previous fighting, went into the attack with a determination to succeed. Their assaults had soon gained the whole northern side of the feature, except for the highest peak, which remained in Italian hands until the end of the war. This was the Caporetto offensive's last blow. The onset of winter, one of the most bitter in living memory, forced the supreme command to break off the offensive, with its final objectives unachieved.

Krauss, by 1918 a full general, was transferred to command the eastern army in the Ukraine, but saw no further major action. With the armistice and the collapse of the Austro-Hungarian forces, as the minority nationalities began to desert in droves, Krauss performed his last ser-

vice to the defunct empire by leading his army back into the heartland of German Austria. In post-war years Krauss, a strong Pan German, worked for the union of Austria with Germany, but his efforts were not realized until 1938, when the *Anschluss* took place. Krauss was greeted effusively by Hitler for the efforts he had made to bring the union about, but he did not live to see the results of incorporation within the Third Reich had upon Austria, for he died late in 1938.

Krauss was the product of a staff system based upon excellence, not upon social position or money. To his years of study in the higher war college, he added an original mind and tactical brilliance. His military skills were of the highest order, whether used in the defensive or in the offensive.

LETTOW-VORBECK
Paul von (1870-1964)
GERMAN GENERAL
First World War

During the First World War, there was only one German commander who fought almost continuously against enemy forces many times superior to his own in size and remained undefeated when the armistice was signed. That man was Paul von Lettow-Vorbeck and the troops he led were the *Schutztruppen* – German East African native contingents, commanded by white officers.

Lettow-Vorbeck, the son of a Prussian general, was born in Sarlouis on 20 September 1870. As a young soldier, he took part in the expedition that was sent to crush the Boxer Rising in China; he had also fought against the Herero and Hottentot uprisings in German South-West Africa before returning to the fatherland to join the general staff in Berlin. There, his specialist subject was colonial warfare, at that time an unusual topic in the general staff curriculum, for Germany had entered the scramble for empire late. The Germans established themselves in their largest colony – East Africa – only during 1884; however, when war broke out in 1914, the *Schutztruppen* were a small but very efficient military body, with a reputation for first-class musketry.

Isolated in Africa
When war broke out, German East Africa was surrounded by enemy colonies and Lettow-Vorbeck had only 11,400 Askaris and 2,700 white officers under command – a force inferior in numbers and equipment to its adversaries. Nevertheless, he decided upon attack to seize the military initiative. While small detachments of *Schutztruppen* kept an eye on the Belgians in the west, the bulk of the German forces moved northwards into Kenya, capturing the small border town of Taveta. The panic-stricken Kenyan civilians promptly demanded the despatch of an adequate British force to protect them, but, in fact, the Germans were too few in number to exploit the incursion

they had made. Lettow-Vorbeck therefore had to be content with the launching of sporadic raids to blow up the Uganda railway line.

British/Indian reinforcements soon landed in Africa and mounted an operation at the end of October, with the aim of capturing Moshi, believed to be the main German military base. The pincer operation that was mounted was a disastrous failure. Two brigades disembarked in the German port of Tanga, the first of which marched into the jungle heading northwards towards Moshi. Its leading battalions were ambushed by a *Schutztruppe* company, who pursued the Indian recruits back to the beaches. Lettow-Vorbeck rushed some Askari companies down from the north to reinforce his Tanga garrison and reconnoitered the town by bicycle. Having disposed his men, he was able to greet the second British brigade with well-aimed fire. The British rallied and the *Schutztruppen* were in danger of being overwhelmed until two more companies arrived by train and entered the battle. The result was rout. The British fled and re-embarked with such haste that they left behind their ammunition, machine guns and wounded. Following their victory at Moshi, the Germans then repulsed the attack of the brigade forming the northern pincer. With its defeat Lettow-Vorbeck raided deeper.

Africa's "Scarlet Pimpernel"

During 1915, more British reinforcements arrived and there were soon two divisions hunting the elusive German commander and his *Schutztruppen*. Lettow-Vorbeck now had to face General Smuts, who decided that maneuver, rather than confrontation, was the way to defeat the Germans. However, his attack upon Taveta, which opened on 8 March, failed to capture the *Schutztruppen* main defences.

Lettow-Vorbeck then broke off the action and rushed his forces to defend Moshi against the South African cavalry. Smuts' infantry pursued the Germans, but a new attack on 20 March, was only a repetition of the earlier engagement – a thinly held outpost line, a strongly defended main line and a slipping away into the jungle before the British encirclement had been completed.

Nevertheless, Smuts' force, now three divisions strong, eventually overran much of German East Africa, putting Lettow-Vorbeck on the defensive. He lost the important town of Kondor Irangi and his attempts to recapture it by conventional infantry assault failed with heavy loss. Bad weather and sickness then halted the British advance and gave Lettow-Vorbeck an opportunity to regroup and re-organize. An attempt in June 1916 to trap the Germans along the line of the Lukigura river succeeded only in destroying the *Schutztruppen* rearguard, which fought to the last man. The sacrifice meant that Lettow-Vorbeck had escaped to fight again. On the German East African coast, however, the British captured Tanga and Dar-es-Salaam, while, in the west, the Belgians also attacked.

Things looked black for Lettow-Vorbeck, but, from his native sources, he learned that the Belgians were not planning a further advance. This enabled him to withdraw the *Schutztruppen* garrisons from that now quiet sector to reinforce the exhausted companies of his main force, which was in action against the British in the south-eastern corner of the colony. Smuts then planned to starve out Lettow-Vorbeck's men by seizing their supply centers. Kibata was captured, but then retaken by the *Schutztruppen* at the point of the bayonet.

The British summer offensive was mounted to capture Lindi, the only port remaining in German hands. Fighting there lasted until October; and in one of the last actions, 18 *Schutztruppen* companies and six artillery pieces smashed nearly two British divisions. But, though the Germans had won a tactical victory in that set-piece battle, they had suffered a strategic defeat. Their heavy losses could not be made good, while those of the British could and were. The strength of the *Schutztruppen* had sunk to 267 white officers and 1,700 Askaris, 30 heavy and seven light machine guns and a couple of mountain guns and there was now little territory left in German hands. Despite this, Lettow-Vorbeck would not surrender and prepared for an all-out guerrilla war, deciding to base his surviving *Schutztruppen* units in Portuguese East Africa, which he promptly invaded.

A guerrilla campaign

The South African commander, Deventer, in charge of the field force, watched the German/Portuguese frontier with 30,000 troops, while columns totaling 80,000 men scoured the Portuguese territory for Lettow-Vorbeck and the small group of *Schutztruppen* accompanying him. At one point, it seemed that the German force was trapped but on 28 September 1918, Lettow-Vorbeck escaped from the threatening encirclement and re-entered German East Africa. Then, in the first week of November, his forces invaded northern Rhodesia; by 12 November, the *Schutztruppen* were 150 miles inside the colony. The next day, Lettow-Vorbeck captured a British despatch rider and learned that the war was over; on 25 November his force of 155 officers and 1168 Askaris surrendered – "the capitulation of an army that had not lost to an army that had not won."

LUDENDORFF
Erich (1865-1937)
GERMAN COLONEL-GENERAL
First World War

Two men dominated the German military machine for the greater part of the First World War. The first was Paul von *Hindenburg* and the second was Erich Ludendorff, Hindenburg's chief of staff on the Eastern Front and later his deputy in the west.

Ludendorff was born at Kruszvenia near Posen on 9 April 1865. By 1908, he was leading the section of the general staff responsible for planning the army's concen-

MASTER PLANNER *In partnership with Hindenburg, Erich Ludendorff came close to winning the war for Germany.*

tration and movement. At Liège, in the opening days of the First World War he demonstrated his personal courage under fire. During the fighting for the key fortresses in eastern Belgium, the German assaults lost their impetus in the face of heavy enemy artillery fire. Ludendorff, who was serving on the staff of one of the assault corps, walked calmly up the road leading to the fortresses through the thick of the Belgian fire. Inspired by his example, the shaken soldiers resumed their advance to capture their objectives. The German advance then resumed.

The partnership with Hindenburg

Meanwhile a crisis had developed on the Eastern Front. Von Prittwitz, the commander of the German 8th Army defending East Prussia, proposed to evacuate the province in the face of invasion by two Russian armies. He was replaced by Hindenburg, to whom Ludendorff was appointed as chief of staff. The latter's plan of action was simple. He proposed that the corps on 8th Army's left wing be withdrawn and marched southwards to surround and attack Russian 2nd Army. After 2nd Army had been destroyed, the German forces would be rushed back northwards to crush 1st Army.

The two-part operation was brilliantly successful; it was followed by a series of Austro-German offensives in 1914 and 1915, which drove the Tsarist armies back until they could no longer threaten German territory. The victories which the armies of the Central Powers won on the Eastern Front between 1914 and 1916 were due to the collaboration between Ludendorff and his overall commander and the skill with which they operated as a team.

From east to west

In August 1916, with the situation in the east stabilized, the successful duo were posted to the Western Front, where Ludendorff was appointed Hindenburg's deputy. His first advice was to halt the German offensive at Verdun; he them moved swiftly to prioritize the needs of the front as against those of the homeland. His view was that a program of priorities would have to be resolved and a national war effort planned if the war was to be won. That planning, in Ludendorff's opinion, had to be the responsibility of the military.

Ludendorff saw the war in terms of a global conflict, not simply as a war restricted to the European mainland. Among the problems which his active mind considered was that of German settlement in the occupied areas of Russia. His influence, which by now had extended into the political arena, was instrumental in engineering the downfall of the German Chancellor, Bethmann-Hollweg, who opposed his plans for unrestricted submarine warfare. In Ludendorff's opinion, U-boats could blockade the Entente powers and starve them into surrender by the unrestricted sinking of their merchant shipping. He realized, too, that Germany's manpower resources were running low. For that reason he proposed to maintain a defensive posture on the two main fronts, throughout 1917, so as to concentrate upon driving Italy out of the war. To maintain the confusion of revolution in the east and to ensure that the Russian army did not act offensively, he made a strange, tacit alliance with the Bolshevik leaders, transporting them across Germany in a sealed train to take advantage of the February revolution.

As Bethmann-Hollweg had forecast, unrestricted U-boat warfare resulted in the USA entering the war on the allied side. Ludendorff, who had accepted this as a calculated risk, believed that the U-boats could sink enough US troopships to halt their sailings. Meanwhile, the German troops in the east, having nothing to fear from a Russia in turmoil, would be transferred to France and Flanders, where Ludendorff was planning to open a war-winning offensive in early 1918. Although nominally still Hindenburg's deputy, it was clear that Ludendorff had become the directing brain and driving force of the German war machine.

"The Kaiser's battle"

The 1918 offensive was intended to separate the French and British forces and to destroy them in detail. On 21 March 1918, 67 divisions, backed by 3,000 guns, attacked the 26 divisions holding the British line; these were supported by fewer than 1,000 pieces of artillery. Despite impressive initial gains, the offensive failed to achieve a breakthrough. Ludendorff then swung the point of maximum effort towards Flanders, but was again thwarted. Changing the direction of his assault once more, he flung 40 divisions south-westwards from the Aisne at Paris. As in 1914, the French army halted the Germans on the Marne and then slowly forced them back.

Although Ludendorff had won a tactical victory – he had gained, in a matter of weeks, ten times more ground than the allies had won in all their 1917 operations – he had failed in his strategic intentions. More significantly, the loss of nearly a million men had so reduced German strength that it no longer had the power to hold out against allied counter-attack. Ludendorff, as a realist, accepted that bitter fact and demanded that an armistice be secured. In October 1918, Prince Max of Baden, the new German Chancellor, asked for terms, but, because the allies refused to negotiate while Ludendorff retained power, also demanded his general's resignation.

Flirtation with Hitler

In the immediate post-war years Ludendorff lived in Sweden, where he involved himself in a nationalist political movement demanding "German Freedom." Upon his return to Germany, he was attracted to Hitler's nationalist policy and marched in the front rank of the Nazis during the abortive Munich putsch in November 1923. A year later, he was serving as a deputy in the Reichstag, holding a seat until 1928. During that time, he stood, unsuccessfully, for the presidency, advocating strongly nationalist policies. In his latter years, however, he disagreed with the policies of the Nazi government, taking up religion and becoming almost a recluse.

Ludendorff, a believer in the Clausewitzian theory of total war, died at Tutzing on 20 December 1937. He had realized, as had few other German professional soldiers, that military operations cannot be conducted in isolation, but form part of a whole, made up of political, economic, industrial and civilian factors.

MACKENSEN
August von (1849-1945)
GERMAN FIELD MARSHAL
First World War

August von Mackensen epitomized the popular ideal of the Hussar officer. He was a handsome, dashing, moustachioed soldier and a superb horseman, who gained a reputation for bravery in battle and swiftness of action.

Born at Leipnitz, near Wittenberg, on 6 December 1849, the son of a minor landowner, Mackensen entered the army against his father's wishes, serving as a one year volunteer in the 2nd Lifeguard Hussar Regiment. He saw service with his regiment during the Franco-Prussian War, then leaving the army to study agriculture, but later returning to it. He did not enter the war academy, which was the usual route of advancement, but was posted directly to the general staff in 1880. Following this, spells of regimental duty were succeeded by periods of service on the staff.

In 1891, after a period as Chief of Staff of 4th Division,

Mackensen served for two years as adjutant to the great von Schlieffen; he was then selected as an *aide de camp* to Kaiser Wilhelm II. He held that post for five years before going on to command the Lifeguard Hussar Brigade in 1903 and XVII Corps by 1908. This was the formation he led at the outbreak of the First World War.

Victory over the Russians

Mackensen came to prominence on the Eastern Front in November 1914. Then, Russian operations had led to the danger that 9th Army might be outflanked by the Russian 1st Army, which could then roll up the whole Austro-German battle-line. Von Mackensen was given command of the threatened army and reacted with his usual energetic leadership. In a counter-offensive against the northern flank of the advancing Russians, he forced a breach between their 1st and 2nd Armies. This not only halted a Russian drive, which, had it succeeded, would have resulted in the invasion of Upper Silesia; it also forced the Russians back on to the defensive, thereby stabilizing the battle line before the onset of winter.

In the spring of the following year, the Austrian and German high commands planned a pre-emptive offensive at Gorlice-Tarnov, with the aim of destroying any Russian threat to the Carpathians. Mackensen commanded the newly formed 11th Army, which contained formations from both partners; he was positioned between the Austro-Hungarian 4th Army in the north and the Austro-Hungarian 3rd Army in the south. Mackensen's force was to be the spearhead of the attack. The offensive was such a brilliant success that, to capitalize on it, a further thrust was launched on 12 June 1915 to recapture Lemberg. With the fall of Lemberg, von Mackensen was promoted to field marshal and given command of an Army Group charged with the task of capturing the fortress of Brest-Litovsk, which fell on 25 August 1915.

At the conclusion of that campaign, he was posted to the south-eastern front to command an Army Group for the campaign against Serbia. The operations he mounted not only destroyed the Serbian army but, more importantly, opened a land link with Turkey, the other main ally of the Central Powers. During the final months of 1916, Romania, which had entered the war on the side of the Entente, was attacked and Mackensen's troops drove through the Dobruja, crossed the Danube and entered Bucharest on 6 December. He then took up the post of supreme commander in Romania. At the war's end, he was still serving on the Eastern Front, and was interned in Romania until December 1919.

Von Mackensen's service to Germany extended from the Franco-Prussian War and across two world wars. In the early years of the Third Reich, the elderly field marshal, in full dress uniform, was a familiar sight at most military parades, where the Nazis sought to demonstrate their links with the old imperial army by parading one of its most popular commanders. He died during November 1945, near Celle, the last of the senior German Army commanders of the First World War and, undoubtedly, the most famous Prussian hussar since Ziethen.

MONASH
John (1865-1931)
AUSTRALIAN GENERAL
First World War

During the First World War, only a few Dominion officers rose by virtue of outstanding ability to high command. The Australian John Monash was one of the few; his leadership of the Anzac Corps made him one of the most distinguished corps commanders of the war.

Monash was born in Melbourne on 27 June 1865, and, after university, became an engineer. He had joined the University of Melbourne officer cadet training unit in 1884, and was commissioned into the garrison artillery in 1908. He went overseas with the Australian Expeditionary Force and, during the Gallipoli campaign, commanded 4th Australian Infantry Brigade. Elements of the Australian forces then moved to the Western Front, where Monash helped to raise and to train 3rd Australian Division. During the battle for the Messines Ridge in 1917 his division played a leading part.

Monash's finest hour came in the spring of 1918, when *Ludendorff* mounted a series of attacks which would, he hoped, bring him final victory in the west. The first of these struck at the junction of the French and British armies and an early blow fell upon 3rd Australian Division holding the line east of Amiens. Monash fought an excellent defensive battle and his skill, together with the staunchness of his soldiers, helped to check the assaults. For his part in halting the German drive upon Amiens, he was promoted to command the Anzac Corps, part of Rawlinson's 4th Army, in succession to General Birdwood. As the Anzac commander, he played a leading part in the counter-offensives launched on the Somme in July 1918 to recapture the ground that had been lost in the first weeks of the German spring attacks.

Monash and the Anzacs
The battle for which Monash is best known was the capture of Villers Brettoneux ridge on the Somme during July 1918. His plan was a model one, in which infantry and armor were supported in their attacks by waves of low-flying aircraft "strafing" the enemy. To ensure absolute secrecy, no telephone conversations were permitted to mention the operation and written orders were kept down to a minimum. The date chosen for the attack was a deliberate compliment to the US troops attached to the Anzac Corps, who would be making their first assault on Independence Day.

Only one feature of Monash's plan did not need to be used. He had ordered a smoke screen to cover the advance of the infantry and tanks across the rolling, open countryside. None was needed. Moving forward across the dry chalk soil, the tanks raised so much dust that the attackers were completely hidden and so excellent was the co-operation between all arms that the operation succeeded with very low casualties.

On 8 August, supported by waves of tanks, the Anzac Corps attacked without the preliminary artillery barrage that had so often in the past only alerted the enemy. The Germans, neither anticipating an attack on that sector nor alerted by artillery preparation, were caught off guard and Monash's divisions attacking in thick fog gained an outstanding victory. The attacks that day, carried out on either side of the Hamm-Amiens road, made such progress and captured so many prisoners that Ludendorff referred to it as "the black day of the German army." From participation in that victorious battle, Monash went on to plan and to execute the capture of Mont St Quentin, which fell to his corps on 31 August. That victory helped to reduce the German salient at Amiens.

The next major task was for the British army to smash through the Hindenburg Line, one of a series of German defensive positions. It was at a military conference at which *Haig* and *Foch* were present that Monash energetically rejected the supreme commander's plan for a frontal assault by Anzac Corps. He suggested a number of places where a flank attack would have a better chance of success and won Haig over to his plan. Together, they persuaded Foch to accept it.

Anzac Corps' participation in the Hindenburg Line offensive was successfully completed by 1 October. Monash's advance had prepared the way for the succeeding stages of the operation, which were successfully concluded by 5 October. The British main thrust then moved away from the Somme area to Flanders and the role played by Monash's corps in the final battles leading up to the armistice was less spectacular than those of July, August and September.

Monash was not a long-term professional soldier and did not have years of staff training behind him. He lacked, as a consequence, the flair that the most outstanding commanders possess. What he did have, as a compensating factor, was the engineer's approach to a problem, seeing it in three-dimensional detail. His campaigns, particularly those fought after he took up divisional and then corps command, carry the marks of meticulous planning and thorough execution. He was deeply aware of the efforts which his troops made to carry out his plans and his deep affection for the men he commanded was reciprocated.

NIVELLE
Robert (1856-1924)
FRENCH GENERAL
First World War

In 1917 the handsome, dashing Robert Nivelle led the French army down the road to mutiny when the offensive bearing his name ended in disaster with fearful loss of life. His meteoric rise was paralleled only by the speed of his fall; after the failure of the Champagne offensive he launched that April, he never held high command again.

Nivelle was born in Tulle on 15 October 1856, graduating from the Ecole Polytechnique in 1878 as an artillery officer. There followed the usual round of colonial campaigns and duties of a professional French soldier of the day, first in Indo-China and then in North Africa. In August 1914, by which time he had reached the rank of colonel, Nivelle was commanding an artillery regiment; by October he had become a brigadier. In 1915, his rise continued. Early that year he was leading a division and by its end 3rd Corps. He was becoming noted as a successful and lucky commander.

In March 1916, during the Verdun offensive, it was Nivelle's corps that halted the German assault, so he was the natural choice as commander of 2nd Army, when *Petain* was promoted to take change of an army group. Nivelle's carefully planned counter-offensive, in which key use was made of a creeping barrage behind which the infantry advanced, recaptured nearly all the gains that it had taken the Germans six months to achieve within a week. Nivelle was hailed as the man of the hour and was the obvious choice to succeed *Joffre*.

The Nivelle offensive

Nivelle now began to plan an offensive which he claimed would win the war outright. One vast, stupendous blow would achieve in a single operation what Joffre's constant nibblings at the German defences had not brought about – a strategic breakthrough. In previous operations, the enemy could seal off any small penetration that had been created and bring forward reserves to counterattack, but a great offensive all along the line would put the Germans under such pressure that they would not be able to deal with the situation. The resulting breakthrough, followed by exploitation of the main breaches, would inevitably restore mobility and bring victory. So, at least, ran the optimistic Nivelle's argument.

Above all, Nivelle promised that violence, brutality and rapidity were to be the keynotes of his campaign. There would be no wasteful attrition – the enemy front would be captured within hours. This optimism infected the whole French army. Now, at last, a commander had emerged who had a clear cut scheme to break the deadlock of trench warfare. The end of the war would surely be the result.

Indeed, Nivelle managed to secure something that Joffre had never enjoyed fully. To ensure the full coordination of the allied blows, Lloyd George, impressed by the English-speaking Nivelle's charm and intelligence, agreed that the British army should be placed under his direct command, but the arrogance of the French commander upset the British generals and led to cooled relations. A compromise gave *Haig*, the British commander-in-chief, the right to appeal against any order he received from Nivelle which he thought might prejudice the safety of his army.

During the period that Nivelle was preparing his offensive, the Germans themselves took a hand. They pulled back from their positions around Arras, as a result shortening their lines and releasing a number of divisions

THE OPTIMIST *Nivelle's belief in his "formula" to break through the German line led to disaster.*

for use on other sectors of the front. This meant that the enemy now had more troops available to meet the offensive and should have served as a warning to Nivelle. It did not. Nor did he appear concerned that breaches of security – to say nothing of his own bombastic public statements – had compromised his plan.

Build-up to disaster

In essence, this plan was for five French armies in total – three in the first line and two in the second – to attack either side of Reims and scale a succession of ridges leading up to the Chemin des Dames. The area was heavily wooded and the Germans, forewarned of the attack, had strengthened their defences throughout the entire area. As the time for the offensive to open approached, doubts began to be raised about the plan's viability, both Petain and Michelar, the commander of the army group involved, thinking it too ambitious.

The British played their part first, landing a series of attacks between 9 and 15 April, which were carried out by 1st and 3rd Armies at Arras. During the battle, Canadian troops stormed and captured Vimy Ridge, but the British advance then slowed. Three days later, however, Nivelle opened his own war-winning offensive, with Micheler's army group attacking along a 40-mile front between Reims and Soissons.

The French operation opened badly. The German air

force had gained air superiority and dominated the battle-field area. On the ground, Nivelle's famous creeping barrage outpaced the infantry, who were slowed down by the wooded ridges they had to scale. The tanks that should have supported the infantry were mostly destroyed by German artillery fire before they could get into action. Pushing forward with great heroism, Nivelle's gallant infantrymen were only able to reach the German first line. They advanced no further. In five days the French officially lost 120,000 men, but many believe that the actual figures were much higher.

It was clear that Nivelle's offensive had failed – but he still went on attacking. The results of the offensive were even more catastrophic than the casualty figures implied, for its failure led to the collapse of morale throughout the French army. A few initial acts of insubordination soon swelled into a rash of mutinies. Troops were prepared to hold and to defend their trench lines, but would not attack. The calming influence of Petain solved the immediate crisis, but it was a long time before the French fully recovered. Meanwhile, the disgraced Nivelle was sent off to command a corps in distant Algeria.

The fact that Nivelle's claim that he had a plan that would bring movement back into the war was accepted so easily demonstrates how deep was the national longing for a strong man to save France. No other reason can explain not only why his plan was adopted but why he was allowed to put it into effect. He had been told in confidence before the battle opened that his was "the last Army of France". French reserves of manpower had been bled white by Verdun and apart from the men made available for his offensive there were no more. Such a warning should have made any general aware of the gravity of his responsibility, but in Nivelle's case this appears to have gone unheeded.

Nivelle's confidence in his own ability was undoubted. His fluency, his charm and his logical arguments convinced many that this was the master of the battlefield whom they were seeking. They were terribly wrong as the cemeteries of Champagne show.

PERSHING
John J (1860-1948)
US GENERAL
First World War

Popular history has it that the first words Pershing uttered on setting foot on French soil were "Lafayette, we are here!" This seems unlikely, since the grim-faced figure of "Black Jack" Pershing was an unlikely character to have expressed so emotional a sentiment.

Pershing was born into a poor family in a rural community outside Washington on 13 September 1860. In his early teenage years he was a schoolteacher until he passed the entrance examination for the US military academy. He graduated from there in 1886; although he had not

shone academically, he was already exhibiting those powers of command and leadership he was later to demonstrate in full measure. He achieved the highest cadet rank and was president of his class.

Upon graduation, Pershing was gazetted into the cavalry and saw active service fighting the Indian tribes. His academic gifts improved, as witnessed by his success in a Bachelor of Law examination in 1893. In the Spanish-American war, he was decorated for bravery, going on to fight in the Philippines, where he established his reputation as a first-rate fighting soldier in the battles on Mindanao. He also attracted the attention of Theodore Roosevelt, who had him promoted in one step from subaltern to brigadier general. This move made Pershing very unpopular, however, since he had been promoted over the heads of a great many other officers.

From Mexico to France

In March 1916, Pershing led a punitive expedition into Mexico in pursuit of Pancho Villa's bandits, who had attacked a US cavalry post. Although inconclusive in its results, the campaign demonstrated Pershing's tenacity and ability. He fought a 10-month campaign in poor terrain, against a hostile population with great skill; although Villa himself was never captured his band was dispersed.

Pershing returned to the USA during April 1917 and was then sent to France as commander-in-chief of the US expeditionary force. The presidential directive he received was that the US forces were a separate and distinct component, whose identity had to be preserved, and, as far as Pershing was concerned, he was prepared to uphold this in the face of the severest pressure from the USA's political and military allies. Indeed, his determination to do this amounted in its single mindedness almost to fanaticism. He insisted on choosing the region in which his army would fight, selecting Lorraine, which had direct lines of communication to ports on the coast. Nor had he any intention of wasting his highly-trained soldiers in the futility of trench warfare; he believed that the million men he expected to have under command by the spring of 1918 should be a powerful attack force.

From the small circle of men who had constituted the officer corps of the USA's regular army, Pershing selected those on whom he could rely. He was a harsh taskmaster, realizing that sweat in training saves blood on the battlefield. What the American Expeditionary Force (AEF) was training for was a series of operations that Pershing had planned against a German salient around St Mihiel on the Lorraine front. However, the appointment of *Foch* as allied generalissimo to deal with the crisis resulting from the great German offensives of the spring of 1918 caused Pershing's position to be reviewed. In view of the gravity of the situation, he offered troops from the AEF to reinforce the French line, although as soon as it was practicable to demand their return he did so. Then the St Mihiel operation was threatened with cancellation, when Foch demanded that US forces be committed as he, rather than Pershing, directed. Pershing refused to accept this dictate, though he did agree to participate in the general allied offensive once his own St Mihiel plan had been executed. Both operations succeeded, the AEF advance eventually reaching the outskirts of Sedan. The armistice halted all further military operations.

By the time of the armistice, Pershing had fought only one offensive of short duration with only a limited number of divisions. It was his ill luck not to have commanded more troops in major operations, but his place among the great commanders is nevertheless secure. His major achievement was the creation of a two million strong army in under two years. The victories he won with only part of that force demonstrated the worth of the hard training he had given his men.

Pershing was a hard man. To his severe natural disposition was added a bitterness that arose out of personal tragedy. While assembling his forces for the 1916 operation in Mexico, Pershing heard that his wife and daughters had been burned to death in a fire at their home. To overcome his grief, he submerged himself in his duties, shunning unnecessary social contact and working with single-minded concentration upon his many tasks. What emerged from that period of seclusion was a grim-faced, aloof and ruthless figure, who shouted down the European politicians who sought to alter his attitude to the employment of US troops with the firm statement "I will not be coerced." Perhaps this was an expression of his personal philosophy, for "Black Jack" Pershing was as unyielding as granite.

PETAIN
Phillipe (1856-1951)
MARSHAL OF FRANCE
First World War

Phillipe Petain's life ended in tragedy. Hailed as the savior of France for his fine generalship in the First World War, he was condemned as a traitor for his collaboration with the enemy in the period from 1940 to 1945.

Petain was born on 24 April 1856, in Cauchy à la Tour, in the Pas de Calais, the son of a wealthy peasant. In 1878, he was gazetted from St Cyr into the 24th Battalion of Chasseurs. Eventually his ability won him the professorship of tactics at the Ecole de Guerre, where he rejected the view of most of his contemporaries that attack under any circumstances was France's best policy in the event of war with Germany. Instead, he stressed the advantage that modern weapons gave the defence. His criticisms of current military dogma perhaps explains why, though he was given command of a brigade at the ourbreak of war, he was not given the rank that was customary with such an appointment.

Petain's career was also unusual in the fact that, when the First World War broke out, he had seen no active service in his 36 years in the army. However, he quickly showed that he possessed superb field skills. From briga-dier, he rose to command a division and then, during the Artois battle of 1915, the 33rd Corps. His skilful leadership there brought him command of 2nd Army positioned around Verdun in the face of *von Falkenhayn's* all-out attack. There, he inspired the French defenders with the famous battle-cry, "They shall not pass." He was capable of more than words, however, and it was his military skill and tenacity that ensured that the Germans did not make him eat his words. Only once did his iron resolve waver, when, during July 1916, the fierceness of the German attacks threatened a break-through. *Joffre* rushed reserves to him and Verdun held out.

From that successful defence, Petain was called to master an even more serious military crisis. The *Nivelle* offensive of 1917, which had promised the ordinary French soldier so much, had been a disastrous failure. The terrible casualties the offensive caused demoralized the rank-and-file of the fighting divisions, while news of the revolution in Russia inflamed anti-war feelings. The result was mass mutiny when the troops were ordered to undertake a new attack. They simply refused to leave their trenches. Ordered to take over from the disgraced Nivelle, Petain, who had become a national hero through the defence of Verdun, set about the task of restoring his army's morale.

Petain's finest hour

Petain had the common touch – the gift of understanding the moods of the troops and of communicating with them. He gained the confidence of the *poilus* and won for them better pay, improved rations and furlough. He was able to commute most of the death sentences that had been handed down by court martial, arguing that the French army had suffered enough. Having gained the soldiers' trust, he then organized a chain of carefully-planned offensives with limited and realizable objectives. The first of these was in the Verdun area against German 5th Army. On 20 July 1917, after an eight-day barrage, two French Corps went over the top and drove a three mile wide salient into the German defences. The success was a heartening one, since the enemy had not just been driven from prepared positions, but had also suffered heavy losses in the attack.

Three months later, on 25 October 1917, an attack upon the Laffaux salient not only eliminated it, but led to a consequent German withdrawal from along the Chemin des Dames. Through such limited operations, the French army regained its former fighting spirit, which it demonstrated once again during the German offensive of March and April 19018. Petain and *Haig*, the British commander-in-chief, were inspired by *Foch* to create a common defensive strategy to prevent the Germans driving a wedge between the allied armies. The success of that policy slowed down and then halted the German offensive – *Ludendorff's* final throw in the west.

With Petain as commander-in-chief of the French armies, the Americans in the line under *Pershing*, Haig in command of the British and Foch as overall generalissimo, the Germans were pushed back along the entire

WAR WINNER *Petain's dogged defence of Verdun in 1916 was a key step in his rise to the supreme command.*

Western Front until an armistice was signed at the beginning of November 1918. As a reward for his outstanding services, which had contributed so much to the allied victory, Petain was promoted Marshal of France on 21 November 1918. In the inter-war years he held a succession of high military and diplomatic posts, including that of war minister.

From Verdun to Vichy
The collapse of the allied front in the face of the German blitzkrieg in the west in May 1940 brought Petain out of semi-retirement to become deputy premier in Reynaud's cabinet. By this time, however, Petain was approaching senility and his natural caution had turned to complete pessimism in the face of the German onslaught. He emerged as the figurehead leader of the peace party that practically forced Reynaud's resignation; the armistice quickly followed.

There now opened the most tragic stage of Petain's career. As leader of unoccupied (Vichy) France, he sought to lead the French people into collaboration with Germany. He did this because of his belief in a Christian Europe, united against Bolshevism, as well as part of his efforts to reduce the demands of the German occupiers. In the confusion that followed D-Day, Petain was arrested by the Germans on 20 August 1944, and taken to the castle of Sigmaringen, where he was captured by French security agents towards the end of the war. A treason trial followed, but the sentence of death, passed on 15

August 1945, was commuted by General de Gaulle to life imprisonment on the island of Yeu, where Petain died on 23 July 1951.

Petain's greatest gift was the ability to inspire his soldiers, a gift only marginally greater than those of outstanding tactical skill, diplomacy and intellectual power. Never afraid to argue against accepted theories, whether these were military, social or political, Phillipe Petain went to his grave in the firm belief that he had never compromised his honor.

PLUMER
Herbert C (1857-1932)
BRITISH FIELD-MARSHAL
First World War

It has been said that Herbert Plumer's physical appearance was the inspiration for Low's famous cartoon character, Colonel Blimp. Though Plumer's choleric face and sweeping white moustaches were a gift to any cartoonist, he was greatly admired by his troops and was, in fact, one of the best British commanders of the First World War.

Plumer was born in 1857 and gazetted in 1878 into the Yorkshire and Lancashire Regiment. His service was the usual round of imperial garrison duties until the Anglo-Boer War of 1899-1902, where he first distinguished himself. The Boer commanders were mounted riflemen, whose guerrilla tactics could not be countered by conventional military methods. The way to beat the Boers was for the British to form their own mounted infantry detachments, so as to "out-Boer the Boers." One of the leaders of those newly formed British detachments was the 43-year-old Colonel Plumer and, when the war in South Africa ended, he was considered to have made a significant contribution to the victory.

Plumer at Ypres
During December 1914, Plumer was given command of 2nd Corps, which was expanded in May 1915 to become 2nd Army. Plumer's army held the Ypres salient for the whole of the First World War – Plumer himself became the British expert on the region. His main concern was the salient that had been created around Ypres in the autumn of 1914, when, by holding the town, the British stopped the German onrush towards the Channel ports. What resulted was a bulge nearly 12 miles wide projecting deep into the German lines. Most British army units on the Western Front fought in the battles of the salient at some time or other.

The Germans held the high ground around the salient, which ran in a semi-circle from Passchendale Ridge in the north to Mount Kemmel in the south, while the British were on the marshy, low ground. Many attempts were made to destroy the salient, principally the huge assaults of 1914 and 1915, but the British, too, carried out their own offensives, with the army capturing high ground.

Messines and Third Ypres

Such was the situation up to 1917, the year in which the main British effort on the Western Front swung back to Ypres from the Somme region, where the 1916 offensive had failed. *Haig*, had long set his heart on a war-winning offensive in Flanders and, as a preliminary to it, directed Plumer to capture the Messines Ridge.

Aware, from previous failed assaults, of the difficulty of the task, Plumer decided that he would literally flatten the ridge, using a chain of 19 massive mines, which had been excavated deep under the German positions. After a ferocious artillery bombardment, the mines were finally detonated on 7 June 1917. Though two misfired, the results were exactly as Plumer had hoped. Plumer's infantry moved forward and battled for what remained of the Messines Ridge with a demoralized enemy. The position was taken for the loss of 17,000 men – an exceptionally low figure by First World War standards. The Germans lost 7,500 men taken prisoners and 18,000 dead.

The Messines Ridge operation had several purposes. Firstly, its success would give the British a piece of the high ground; secondly it would straighten out the southern wall of the salient; thirdly, a demonstration in that area would distract German attention from the salient's northern wall, where Haig intended to launch his now imminent major offensive to capture Passchendale. This offensive failed in its intended purpose. The main burden of the fighting fell upon *Gough's* 5th Army, but German tenacity and the persistent bad weather, which turned the ground into a morass, frustrated his effort. In an attempt to revive the failing offensive, Haig asked Plumer to extend the area held by 2nd Army – in effect, to take over a vital sector from Goughs. With Plumer's step-by-step approach, the Passchendale ridge was captured.

Plumer was then rushed to Italy, where an Austro-German attack had all but destroyed the Italian army at Caporetto, but in the spring of 1918, at Haig's insistent demand, he was brought back to Flanders, where *Ludendorff's* offensives were threatening to smash the salient. Plumer's return strengthened the resolve of his veteran 2nd Army and ended the chance of a breakthrough.

Plumer was not a flamboyant commander, but one whose hard work and concentration upon details always produced results. Quite early in his career in the Ypres salient, he realized that the only way to achieve results was by a succession of small gains. It was this cautious and methodical approach that led to his army only being allotted a secondary role in the Third Ypres operation, until it became clear that Gough's more adventurous plan could not succeed. Whereupon, Plumer was given the task and brought it off.

Plumer was a gentle, courteous and considerate man. His deep concern for his men was a byword; for their part they appreciated that their commander would not risk their lives in risky adventures. His calm, and studious approach to the problems of battle did not win him the accolade of a military genius – but Plumer achieved results with minimal losses, which is the true measure of a great commander.

RENNENKAMPF
Paul Karlovitch (1854-1918)
RUSSIAN GENERAL
First World War

Paul Rennenkampf was one of the two Russian field commanders who led the ill-fated offensive into East Prussia at the start of the First World War. For this, he has gone down in history as a talentless commander, yet it was his military skills that led to his rapid preferment in the Tsarist army of the day.

Rennenkampf was born on April 1854 in Estonia, graduating from the Helsingfors Infantry Junker School in 1873. His academic gifts and considerable ability marked him out for early promotion; he entered the general staff academy, from which he graduated during 1882. He was given his first field command in the Boxer Rebellion of 1900, where he led a cavalry brigade; during the Russo-Japanese War of 1904/5, he commanded a Transbaikal Cossack division. Later in 1905, he was placed in command of an expedition sent to suppress a revolt in Eastern Siberia and then spent two years in the east. His next important post was as commander of the Vilnius Military District, an appointment he took up during 1913.

The road to disaster

When the First World War broke out in August 1914, Rennenkampf was in command of 1st (Nieman) Army and was ordered, together with 2nd (Narev) Army, to thrust towards East Prussia. The intention was to panic the German supreme command into switching troops from the west to the Eastern Front, so relieving the hard-pressed French armies. Accordingly, on 17 August, Rennenkampf's army began its advance, aiming for Koenigsberg.

Ahead of the main body of the army, he deployed a mass of Cossack cavalry with considerable skill, the light, mobile horsemen moving fast across the difficult East Prussian terrain. His right-wing corps also made good progress, but the formations in the center and on the left found it more difficult to get through the swamps and heavily forested areas of the province. Rennenkampf accordingly halted the advance of his right wing to allow the other corps to come forward. The inaction enabled *Hindenburg* and *Ludendorff* to redeploy the bulk of German 8th Army to the south to attack 2nd Army, leaving only a thin cavalry screen facing Rennenkampf.

Samsonov's 2nd Army was soon in disarray, but here personal feelings came into play. Rennenkampf and Samsonov hated each other – they had actually come to blows on Mukden railway station during the Russo-Japanese War, an incident that had been witnessed by Colonel Hoffman, now in charge of German 8th Army's planning staff – and so failed to come to his assistance. The victorious Germans swung against Rennenkampf's 1st Army and smashed it in its turn. Surprisingly, Rennenkampf was not relieved of his command, but similar inactivity during the 1916 *Brusilov* offensive, finally cost him his job. During the civil war, in which he took no active part, he was captured at Taganrog by Soviet troops and was executed by them during March 1918.

SAMSONOV
Alexander Vassilievitch (1859-1914)
RUSSIAN GENERAL
First World War

Alexander Samsonov will go down in military history as the general who led his army to total disaster at Tannenberg in 1914. He was born on 2 November 1859, graduating from the St Nicholas Cavalry School in 1877 with the rank of lieutenant. In the same year, he demonstrated both his bravery under fire and tactical skill in the Russo-Turkish War, after which he entered the general staff academy. He graduated from there in 1884.

A swift rise
As early as 1902, Samsonov was a major-general at the age of only 43; during the Russo-Japanese war, he commanded, firstly, the Ussuri cavalry brigade and then a Siberian Cossack division. His rise continued, despite the Russian defeat; in 1906 he was appointed chief of staff of the prestigious Warsaw military district.

The next year Samsonov won a signal honor. He was elected by the leaders of the Don Cossacks to be their Altman – an uncrowned king of the Cossack peoples. In 1909 he was appointed Governor of Turkestan and head of the Turkestan military district, posts that he held until shortly before the outbreak of the First World War in 1914. This found him in command of 2nd Army.

Disaster at Tannenburg
The sensible course of action for the Russians to take on the outbreak of war would have been to delay any offensive until their mobilization was completed – indeed, this was what the Germans had counted on in devising their war plan, which called for the bulk of their forces to be concentrated in the west to knock France out of the war before turning to deal with the slow-moving Russians. The swift pace of the German advance in the west led to a plea for help from the French, however; in response Tsar Nicholas II ordered his armies to advance westwards towards East Prussia without waiting to complete their mobilization. The intention was honorable, the result was disastrous.

Samsonov's 2nd Army was one of the two armies spearheading the assault; the other – 1st Army – was led by *Rennenkampf*. Their task was to create such panic and confusion in the German defence that the German supreme command would be forced to transfer forces from the west to bolster up the Eastern Front. At the start, the opening phases of the offensive were so successful that von Prittwitz, commanding German 8th Army, decided

SUICIDE AT TANNENBURG *Russian defeat led Alexander Samsonov to kill himself on the battlefield.*

to retreat behind the line of the Vistula river and abandon East Prussia to the enemy. Unfortunately for the Russians, he was promptly replaced by von *Hindenburg* and *Ludendorff*, who quickly reassessed the situation.

The initial Russian advance had been carried out reasonably quickly, but then its pace had slowed due to the lack of roads and railways in the difficult country. The Germans, on the other hand, were now highly organized and were operating on interior lines. They were able to leave only a thin screen of defenders to face Rennenkampf and switch the mass of their troops to attack Samsonov. The two Russian armies were so widely separated that they could not support each other – even had their commanders been agreed on the best course of action to adopt. Rennenkampf and Samsonov were bitter enemies, having once even come to blows on Mukden station during the Russo-Japanese war. Thus, when German 8th Army opened its assault upon Samsonov, there was no aid coming from Rennenkampf.

Von Hindenburg, exploiting his personal knowledge of the area, was able to isolate Samsonov's army and to destroy it in detail in a battle that continued throughout the last two weeks of August 1914. The Germans then attacked and smashed 1st Army. But Samsonov was not to witness this second defeat. In despair at the disaster, he had committed suicide in an East Prussian forest.

The Second World War

The opening campaign of the Second World War against Poland was a final testing ground for the tactics that all main armies were to adopt until 1945. Though some aspects of the campaign might be described as conventional – the collaboration of artillery and infantry, for instance – what became clear was that the tank and tactical bombing had totally transformed the pace of war. Indeed, the German high command used the Polish campaign to see whether the combination of panzers and aircraft could create the conditions of blitzkrieg – a lightning war.

New tactics, new weapons

In May 1940, however, when Germany launched its attack in the west, one new and revolutionary tactic was introduced – that of "vertical envelopment". In this, highly-trained paratroops parachuted, or were landed by glider, to attack strategic targets. By taking advantage of the element of surprise and through the superb training of the men taking part in them, most paratroop operations were very successful. At Fort Eben Emael in Belgium, less than 100 paratroopers attacked and seized this key fortress, with a 2,000-strong garrison, while other airborne units captured the crucial road and railway bridges across which the German army headed westwards to win total victory within 60 days of the campaign's opening blows.

This was one way in which air power was transforming the face of war. Another was the notion of air superiority and its effect on ground and sea operations. After the fall of France, for instance, the Luftwaffe had to beat the RAF in order for Hitler's sea-borne invasion of Britain to succeed. Here, the RAF

had an inestimable advantage in its possession of one of the key secret weapons of the war – radar. Through its use, German aircraft could be detected flying towards the British coast at distances in excess of 100 miles.

This meant that RAF fighter squadrons could keep out of battle until the last moment, so gaining

more combat time in the air than their German adversaries.

Radar thus helped to negate the Luftwaffe's numerical superiority. Later, used at sea, it allowed ships to engage targets hidden in fog or darkness, while bombers could use it to strike at targets through the thickest of cloud cover.

Radar was only one of a number of

items of electronic equipment which were developed and used during the war. The proximity fuse gave anti-aircraft shells a hitherto undreamed of accuracy. In the sea war in the Pacific, naval artillery using proximity fuses shot down Kamikaze pilots who were determined to sink a US ship at the cost of their own lives. In Germany the SS had developed, against army opposition, an infra-red tank gun sight. The device put an end to the days when nightfall ended a battle, or fog and smoke could protect a target from attack. Nothing was now undetectable.

The rocket, although not a new invention, made its debut on the modern battlefield. In the Second World War, rockets were scaled down in size by the Germans and the Americans to be used as close range, anti-tank weapons. One projector, the German, single-shot panzerfaust became, according to Goebbel's propaganda, the favorite weapon of women and girls, because it was portable and easy to use.

The Soviets, on the other hand, resurrected the idea of Congreve's 19th-century rocket batteries with their Katushyas. The Germans retaliated with the Nebelwerfer, a six-barreled rocket mortar. The shell filling was variable – one variety used liquid oxygen, whose destructive power was enormous.

The perfection of the Blitzkrieg
Land warfare progressed from Poland, where the techniques of Blitzkrieg were tried out, through the campaigns in the west where they were further developed and into the war with the USSR where they were perfected. However, this was not the work of the Germans, but rather of their Soviet adversaries. Having used geography as a defence in depth to help them bring the Wehrmacht to a halt, the Soviet army turned the blitzkrieg against the Germans.

AIR POWER *Rocket-firing Typhoons in action at Falaise. Air superiority was now a battlefield prerequisite.*

Naval and air factors

At sea the major units of the navies no longer fought fleet versus fleet gun battles, although there were ship versus ship engagements, of which the sinking of the *Hood* and *Bismarck* are perhaps the most famous. There were improvements in submarine equipment – snorkels to allow a U-boat to remain submerged for longer and improved engines, but nothing else of significance. What became clear was that aircraft carriers were now the key element in fleet operations, but also the most vulnerable one. The most significant factor in naval warfare was that the submarine, the dive bomber and the torpedo bomber had made the battleship obsolete. Air power was now the dominant factor.

Nowhere was this more clearly seen than in the battle of Midway in the central Pacific in June 1942. The fleets involved never came within sight of each other; what counted were the strikes launched from the US and Japanese carriers. In one of the decisive battles of the war, the sinking of the Japanese carrier force gave the strategic initiative back to the USA.

Air developments, however, followed a predictable path until the development of the jet engine took aircraft out of the internal-combustion era and into a new age. The fighter and bomber aircraft of the Second World War fulfilled the same role as they had in the First World War, only on a bigger scale. RAF Bomber Command, building upon the knowledge of strategic bombing the RAF had gained during the First World War, applied this with great determination between 1939 and 1945. Initially, at least, this was a policy which had its opponents, notably the 1939 Air Minister himself. It was suggested at the outbreak of war that the Black Forest made an excellent target. Sir Kingsley Wood is said to have retorted, "Do you not realize that this is private property? You will be asking me to bomb Essen next."

This was the age of total war, however, and the bombers of the RAF and US air forces went on to

FROM BLITZKRIEG TO BLITZ *A Heinkel III medium bomber approaches the center of London as the Luftwaffe unleashes the blitz in the fall of 1940. Goering's air force, however, had been designed for tactical battlefield support and was ill-equipped for strategic bombing.*

KEY TO THE BATTLE *Radar and efficient direction of the RAF's fighter squadrons were two of the keys to British success in 1940.*

FIRST JETS *Germany led the way in jet propulsion, but this Heinkel "people's fighter" was developed too late to see much active service.*

devastate Germany. The USAAF raided by day, the RAF by night. This was war of a type that had not been envisaged by those who had engineered its opening.

In the last years of the war, the Germans produced their "reprisal" (Vergeltung, or V) weapons. There was a whole series planned but only two entered service. The VI – a pilotless, ram-jet flying bomb, was more destructive than the V2 rocket, but it could be intercepted and destroyed. The V2 could not be stopped. The V2 bombardment produced one half of a terrible partnership which was formed shortly after the end of the war and has since that time dominated the world. The other partner in that fearful combination was the atomic bomb. The first of those was dropped over Hiroshima, the second over Nagasaki with a very high loss of life. More people had been killed in conventional air raids, but over a longer period. In an atomic explosion, thousands perished in a matter of

OLD AND NEW *The success of Japanese torpedo bombers at Pearl Harbor in 1941 demonstrated that the days of the battleship were numbered.*

seconds. It was that scale of destruction in so short a time which many critics of nuclear warfare found appalling. The other side of the picture was that the destruction of two Japanese cities probably saved the life of millions of allied servicemen.

Special development

One interesting development – not a new tactic, but an improvement upon an old one – was the proliferation of small specialist units throughout the war. The British SAS and Commandoes paralleled the German Brandenburg units. At sea, explosive motorboats and frogmen, both pioneered by the Italians, were widely used by all major navies. In the air, only the Germans and the Japanese had squadrons of fliers dedicated to self destruction as a result of crashing

their aircraft into the enemy. The Japanese *Kamikaze* sought to destroy allied ships, while in Germany young men in old machines dived their aircraft into the "boxes" of American bombers. However, the major German effort, made on 7 April 1945, had so little effect upon the US fliers that they ascribed the mid-air collisions between Flying Fortresses and Messerschmitts to bad piloting by the Luftwaffe's last reserve of airmen. This was the Luftwaffe's last throw of the war.

At the end of the war, the weapons and tactics of future conflicts were already evident – rocket projectors and electronic devices, small expert bodies of men trained to fight in every type of terrain in fast, hard-hitting missions, in advance of or in conjuction with conventional forces. All these would be employed in a conventional, non-nuclear war. In the worst possible scenario – an all-out nuclear war – they, like the rest of mankind, would be redundant.

Air Power

It is significant that a long war has a telescoping effect upon the length of time usually taken to develop new weapons. Who can believe that aircraft would be as highly developed as they are today if there had been no wars to inspire research? The Wright brothers first flew in 1903. Within 15 years aircraft had evolved sufficiently to be capable of flying relatively long distances carrying heavy bomb loads. In the inter-war years there was, of course, some development, but it was slow. The Second World War speeded up research and improved engine and aircraft design. Within a period of six years between the outbreak and the end of the Second World War, air forces had passed out of an age of propellor-driven monoplanes into one of jet engines and, eventually, supersonic speeds.

Birth of air combat

Less important than the design or performance of the flying machine is its military application. The first aircraft – low-powered and unarmed – were seen as reconnaissance vehicles; indeed, it was a pilot's report in 1914 that von Klück's army had changed direction that led to the allied counter-thrust in the first battle of the Marne. Reconnaissance pilots soon armed themselves with pistols or shotguns to drive off enemy aircraft and, out of such encounters, there evolved the two-seater reconnaissance machine, fitted with a machine gun mounted onto a traversing ring on the rear cockpit.

Aerial combats between reconnaissance machines then evolved into a form of warfare of its own as the fighter aircraft was developed to intercept and destroy those of the enemy. The single-seat fighter or "scout" fulfilled not only standard reconnaissance duties, but set out to gain mastery of the air space over the battle area. In addition, they escorted the specialist bombing machines which had by then been designed, built and taken into service.

Air power – a war-winner?

Even before the armistice brought the First World War to a close, visionaries such as Trenchard, Douhet and Mitchell had appreciated that air power gave war a new dimension, and that the bomber was a potent weapon, which, if used correctly, had a major strategic role to play in future conflicts.

The thinking of those first advocates of air power can be reduced to a simple thesis: the vital components of the enemy's war machine are determined and then destroyed, using bombers which will always get through. Their contention was that strategic bombing would act faster than conventional blockade, was more devastating and was cheaper. The one extra prerequisite they had was that an air force must be a

FIGHTING "SCOUTS" *The Dutch aircraft designer Anthony Fokker designed several warplanes for imperial Germany, including the Fokker triplane fighter (below).*

BOMBER KILLERS *Though the belief in the 1930s was that "the bomber will always get through", this proved not to be the case. The monoplane fighter proved an extremely efficient bomber killer, as the Hawker Hurricane (below) and the Focke-Wulf 190 (left) both proved.*

separate service. It could not be controlled by soldiers, who would not grasp its potential and employ the strategic air weapon tactically.

Hitler's Luftwaffe, for instance, was designed as a tactical, not a strategic, air arm. Although it was a separate service with its own supreme commander, it was subordinate to the Combined Service Supreme Command (the Oberkommando der Wermacht, or OKW), whose leaders were soldiers. German military thinking had always concentrated on continental land warfare. Strategy, so far as the German Army High Command (the Oberkommando des Heeres, or OKH) understood it, related to movements by armies in Europe. The concept of global strategy, while existing, was irrelevant. Germany was a central European state, whose army would win its victories in continental warfare. The Luftwaffe was shackled to that narrow concept and could not develop beyond it.

There had been men in Germany who saw aerial warfare in the same way as Mitchell, Douhet and the others. General Wever, the Luftwaffe's first chief-of-staff, was one of them, but a fatal air crash in 1936 brought the ex-fighter pilot, Goering, into full authority. He filled the senior echelons of the Luftwaffe with his war-time fighter comrades and the opportunity

to build a strategic air arm was lost. However, there were also economic and political reasons for this. In Germany, there was a shortage of aluminium, while, at the same time Hitler was demanding a bigger and bigger air force. For the equivalent amounts of aluminium, Goering could produce five twin-engined short-range aircraft, or three four-engined long-range machines. The Führer ". . . does not ask how powerful are the bombers, but just how many we have . . .", was Goering's comment.

As a consequence, the Luftwaffe went to war equipped with short-range machines, which could carry only a small bomb load. Hitler's bomber arm can be considered, therefore, as little more than long-range artillery, suitable for the short, fast campaigns that OKW envisaged.

The RAF viewpoint

The other air forces of the European land powers – France, Italy and the USSR – were also dominated by the army, as was that of the USA until the 1930s. Britain's alone was not.

Detached from the European mainland, Britain was faced by a Germany whose industrial might lay not only in the Saar and Ruhr, but also in the Saxon and

Silesian provinces. What the British needed, therefore, was a bomber capable of flying deep into the Reich, dropping a sizeable bomb load and then returning to its home base. The plan was for such raids to be made in daylight, but fighter opposition made this unacceptable. Night bombing was the only solution. The bombers were to fly in a stream, which would have the bonus of extending the length of the raid and consequently of lowering enemy morale further.

Finding the target

Air force theorists had long accepted that, for a pilot to fly by night and to pin-point a specific target without causing civilian damage was to demand the impossible. It was clear that civilians would become casualties as a consequence of bombing inaccuracy, and, out of that acceptance, there evolved the rationalization that civilian casualties would shatter morale and would thus shorten the war. Such a strategem was a logical extension of Douhet's principles. From 1942 onwards, this was the philosophy of RAF Bomber Command as it bombed Germany's cities to destruction.

The US tactic

By this stage of the war, the US air forces – chiefly the 8th, located in eastern England – had begun operations. In contrast to the RAF, the USAAF squadrons flew by day and not as a stream, but in huge "boxes" of bombers, flying in layers one above the other. In theory, the "boxes" were self-protecting, given the defensive armament of the B17 Flying Fortress with which most of the squadrons were

DAY AND NIGHT *US Boeing B17 "Flying Fortresses",
heavily armed and flying in defensive "box" formations, took the
air war to the Reich by day (above), while RAF Lancasters carpet-
bombed its crumbling cities by night (below).*

equipped. A "box" of 300 bombers could utilize 3,900 machine guns forming interlocking defence zones, which, in theory, made the "box" impregnable. The penalty was reduced bomb weight.

New technology

Offence and defence rivaled one another in technological innovation. British efforts to locate and destroy targets more accurately led to radar sets being fitted in the RAF's bombers. German night fighters also used radar to locate their targets. The Luftwaffe pioneered the development of the jet fighter – but, thanks to Hitler, who demanded it be redesigned as a bomber, this came too late to influence the course of the air war. The jet engine revolutionized air warfare by raising speeds to supersonic level; today, a pilot

controls not the aircraft, but the computers which fly it, which, in turn, control the aircraft's armament. It is all a far cry from the wood and fabric aeroplanes of the First World War.

Two inventions late in the Second World War – the rocket and the atomic bomb – were combined in the post-war years to create an inter-continental weapon carrier with a warhead of terrible destructive power. In view of this monstrous marriage, it would seem that the aircraft, at least in strategic terms, has become obsolete within eight decades.

Air force leaders, however, are as unwilling to accept that their service is now as out-of-date as were the horsed reconnaissance detachments the aircraft replaced. They point to the use of aircraft in recent conflicts as evidence that they are still needed – but there is no gainsaying the fact that the aircraft has diminished in importance to become solely a tactical weapon. *Harris*, who fought desperately to ensure that his squadrons were not diverted from their strategic task to become a tactical army support force in the battle for Normandy, Mitchell, who demonstrated that naval power had been superseded by air power, Douhet whose principle that the bomber would always get through was accepted as an unassailable truth in the 1930s – all would be dismayed that the power they advocated so strenuously and the techniques they pioneered have passed away in so short a time, despite attempts to revive them.

TOO LITTLE, TOO LATE *Hitler's "intuition" held up the introduction of the Messerschmitt Me262 jet fighter (above left) until it was too late, while the V2 (below) never justified the resources devoted to its development.*

Tank Warfare

It is a matter of opinion as to who first realized the possibility of a tracked, man-carrying armored machine. A Colonel Burstyn of the Austro-Hungarian army is said to have designed such a vehicle in 1912, only to have it rejected on grounds of cost. Germany seems not to have even recognized the politics of such a machine, seeking instead to break the trench deadlock with new artillery and infantry tactics. Only when it was realized how successful were these mobile pill-boxes did the Germans build their own machines. France and Britain seem to have developed ideas along parallel lines, but both worked in such secrecy that no concepts or techniques were shared.

As far as Britain was concerned, two men were chiefly responsible for tank development – Colonel Swinton, who proposed the idea to the government, and Winston Churchill, who rescued Swinton's plan when it was rejected. After a series of tests in December 1915, the first machines were produced and sent to the Western Front. They first went into action during the latter stages of the 1916 Somme battle, but over unsuitable ground and in too few a number to break through the German lines.

Tank design

It must be appreciated that the internal combustion engines of the period were very low-powered; the Mark I tank's 110hp engine had to propel a large steel box carrying two 6pdr guns and four machine-guns as well as a crew of nine men. The maximum speed that could be obtained under optimum conditions was only slightly more than walking pace.

The principle purpose for which the tank had been designed – to smash a gap through the enemy's barbed wire and cross his trenches – made the first models an infantry close-support weapon, with a radius of action of just over 20 miles. By the end of the First World War, however, advances in design had produced a smaller, turreted vehicle which, because of a reduction in weight and an increase in engine power, had gained in speed and range. The function of these so-called "whippet" tanks was that of armored cavalry, though the war ended before they could demonstrate their full battlefield capabilities.

Fighting philosophies

In the post-war period, professional soldiers were divided about the future of the armored fighting vehicle and its use in war. Mechanical unreliability and the inability of tracked vehicles to climb the sort of steep slope that a horse could negotiate led to the retention of cavalry by most armies. The value of the tank as a shock weapon, as the cavalry had once been, was undisputed. The question was did armor have any greater purpose than fighting in support of the infantry?

In the German army, discussions on the recent, lost war produced several theories to explain defeat. The consensus was that military operations had lacked battlefield mobility. What was required, when maximum pressure applied at a given point achieved a break-through, were mobile forces in armored vehicles, supported by self-propelled (SP) guns, to exploit the situation. Logistical problems could be overcome by making supply and ammunition columns part of the armored break-through battle group. Such warfare would be a triumph of all-arms collaboration – armored cavalry, armored infantry, armored artillery and an

AN ERA OF EXPERIMENT *In the First World War, many ingenious ideas were tried out in an attempt to produce an effective trench-crossing vehicle before the design of the first tank was ultimately developed.*

THE FIRE-BREATHER *Many special adaptations were made to tanks in the Second World War. This Churchill VII, nicknamed the "crocodile", carried a flame-thrower.*

armored supply system all ranging unchecked to strike at the enemy's heart.

In England and France, the tank was still considered to be, at official level, the hand-maid of the infantry. However, there were other voices, outside and inside both armies, who saw armor not as a close-support weapon – nor, in the German fashion, as a task force with quasi-strategic aims – but as a wholly strategic weapon, capable of winning the most wide-ranging victories.

What those theorists were proposing was nothing less than the overthrow of conventional military beliefs. Military thought concentrated upon linear warfare and concern for the flanks. In the new armored warfare

there would be no need to worry about flanks, because the speed of armor, used en masse, would give the enemy no time to build up a force to threaten them. That advance would be headed by a spearpoint of battle tanks. Behind that narrow, penetrating spearpoint, the expanding spearblade would cut a wider swathe through the enemy. The shaft of the spear would be the supply echelons. Infantry would need to be conveyed in armored carriers in order to carry out tasks for which armor was unsuitable. A high level of liaison with the air force would provide air support, either to carry out reconnaissance, or to act as "flying artillery" to bomb and destroy any pockets of resistance ahead of the armored spearhead.

Birth of the blitzkrieg

Thus, in the minds of theorists and some far-sighted serving soldiers the concept of a fast war, a lightning

179

war, a blitzkrieg had been born and was developing. The theories were discussed in most major armies, but found greatest response among German junior commanders, who were able to test them in practice in the USSR. In the late 1920s, the Soviets not only provided German industrialists with factories in which they could produce arms in defiance of the Versailles treaty, but allowed the German army to carry out clandestine maneuvers in the USSR. When Hitler's accession to power put an end to this, maneuvers were conducted in Germany, using motor cars covered with plywood to represent tanks. The German army in the 1930s was the only one in which field commanders were capable of handling tanks en masse.

The tank in action

The early stages of the Second World War in Europe ran very much as the German high command had predicted, with blitzkrieg operations practiced in Poland, developed in France and perfected in the first two summer campaigns in Russia. However, once the Soviet army leaders developed their own blitzkrieg techniques, it was they who bested the Germans. The armies of the western allies had no real opportunity to carry out such operations except on a very minor scale after the Falaise Gap operation in August 1944 and Patton's thrust through a collapsing Germany towards the Czechoslovak border in April 1945.

Certain limitations influenced tank tactics for much of the Second World War. In all armies the lack of

compensators meant that a vehicle had to halt to fire its main armament if it hoped to achieve accuracy. Then, too, tank battles usually ended at last light for lack of a night sight. Towards the end of the war, compensators, which enabled a gun to be fired accurately while the vehicle was on the move, and infra-red sights, which allowed tank battles to be continued after dark, or in fog, were introduced. Armored operations also produced the need for a great number of non-fighting armored machines and those needs were met by conversion of standard chassis. Chief among these machines were command tanks. It was usual for commanders of armored formations to

THE TANK EVOLVES *One of the first tank prototypes (below) is put through its paces for the benefit of the watching infantry, while (above) a 1920s experimental model shows how design gradually evolved. Experts of the day were divided as to whether the tank's future was as infantry support, or as an independent fighting weapon.*

direct the battle, if not from the front, then certainly from a well forward position. Communication was, thus, a vital element in battlefield control, German wireless sets being excellent in that respect. In Russian formations at regimental and lower levels, only the commanders had a transmitter/receiver. The subordinate vehicles had only receivers.

There were armored recovery vehicles, bridge layers and ammunition carriers. In the British Army, the 79th Armored Division consisted almost exclusively of what were nicknamed "funnies" – machines that threshed the ground to detonate land mines, that carried bombard-type guns to destroy concrete emplacements, flame-throwing tanks and swimming tanks. Every likely battlefield eventuality could be catered for by 79th Armored Division.

Tank design today is still a compromise between the three governing factors and, although some excellent machines have been produced, there has been little development from the 1945-pattern mold. The question as to whether there is a future for armored fighting vehicles depends upon the way in which warfare itself develops. In conventional warfare, even with the present-day sophistication in anti-tank weapons, the tank has a role. However, it may well be that, in any future war, helicopters will usurp the role of armor.

"ACHTUNG PANZER!" *A panzer commander poses in the turret of his PzKw IV during the blitzkrieg against France in 1940. Inspired by commanders such as Guderian, Germany led the way in the new school of tank warfare.*

MAY 1940-JUNE 1940

BLITZKRIEG IN THE WEST:
The battle for France

In May 1940, the German army, having concluded successful campaigns in Poland and Scandinavia, began an operation which within 60 days had smashed France, driven the British Expeditionary Force from the continent and had defeated both Belgium and Holland. When that campaign ended, Hitler was the master of Europe and controlled a seaboard which, extending from northern Norway to the Spanish frontier, outflanked the British isles. Yet the plan for this campaign – generally regarded as one of the most brilliant in military history – was in fact a second thought and not the German High Command's original intention. This was for a broad repeat of the *Schlieffen Plan* of the First World War.

Bad weather and vacillation within the German High Command led to repeated postponements of the offensive in the fall of 1939; it was put off indefinitely when a light aircraft, with key drafts of the plans on board, strayed off course and crashed in Belgium. It was then that *von Manstein*, chief of staff to *von Rundstedt*, commanding Army Group A, laid before his superior a revolutionary alternative plan. It called for the main German thrust to be made not in Holland and north Belgium, but in southern Belgium, driving out of the heavily forested, hilly, Ardennes region. The plan had several advantages. Firstly, the main thrust would come from a direction that would take the allies totally by surprise. The lack of adequate roads in the area had convinced the conventionally-minded allied commanders that no major enemy attack could be made through the Ardennes, which they regarded as impassable for tanks.

The second advantage followed on from the first. Convinced that the German main effort would be made in the north, the allies would send their best troops to meet what in fact would be a diversionary attack. When the German effort was made, it would fall on second-line troops, who would offer little resistance. The swift westward advance across France that would follow would cut off the allied armies in the north from those south of the Somme, so trapping the former between *von Bock*'s Army Group B and von Rundstedt's Army Group A.

Hitler's gamble

So radical a plan would hardly have stood much chance of acceptance had not Hitler, by a strange coincidence, also thought of the Ardennes as the logical springboard for the attack upon France. He adopted Manstein's plan enthusiastically. The keyword of the operation was to be speed. The German divisions striking from the Ardennes to the coast had to move quickly before the allied divisions in the north could pull back out of Belgium and escape the encirclement that was planned for them. In the opening stages of the operation, too, a new weapon would be employed – airborne troops. These would be dropped or air-landed to knock out the key Belgian fortress of Eben Emael, which guarded the Albert Canal, plus several bridges on the line of advance and also The Hague, the seat of the Dutch government. The whole campaign in the west depended upon the airborne units gaining their objectives; in fact, the operational plan was geared to open five minutes after the airborne assault had been launched.

The contesting armies were approximately equal in number. The Allies put a total of 144 divisions into battle and the Germans 138. However, the Germans had several factors working in their favor. Firstly, they had more armored units – 10 panzer and four motorized – at their disposal, as opposed to the seven (including armored brigades) of the allies. In addition, the German armor was concentrated in what was termed the *schwerpunkt* (thrust point), while the Allied armor was spread out in general support of the infantry, as had been the practice in the First World War. As far as the other vital element in blitzkrieg warfare – air support – was concerned, the Luftwaffe had 1,100 fighters, 325 dive bombers and 1,000 conventional medium bombers at its disposal. Against this, the allies fielded 1,000 fighters and 400 bombers. The Germans also employed the Luftwaffe to support the army in a tactical role, but the allies had no such detailed plans. Many of their fighter squadrons were allocated to home air defence, while the bombers had been trained for strategic, rather than tactical, operations.

The first stage of the campaign in the west went as OKW had planned. The airborne landings in The Hague, Moerdijk and Dortrecht paralyzed Dutch resistance and were instrumental in smashing the Dutch army within days. The French and British armies, reacting to what they saw as the main German offensive in the north, advanced into Belgium to meet it, according to the so-called Dyle plan, prepared by General Gamelin, the allied commander-in-chief. But behind them and to the east, the great mass of von Rundstedt's Army

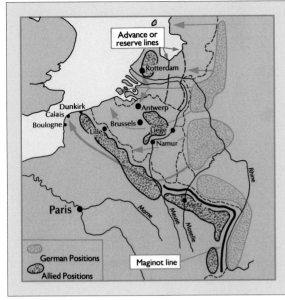

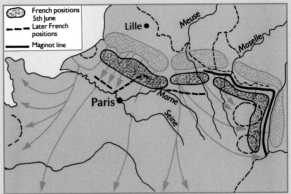

BLITZKRIEG IN ACTION *The German invasion plan worked almost to perfection. The armored thrust from the Ardennes (left) swept through to the Channel as planned, encircling the allied northern armies and leaving the French to fight unaided (above).*

Group A burst out of the Ardennes. The great guns of the fortress of Eben Emael did not oppose the advance; the whole complex had been put out of action within hours and surrendered within a day.

Total surprise, total victory

The first major obstacle was the Meuse river and it was not until 12 May (D-Day plus 2) that the leading elements of the German panzer divisions had struggled through the Ardennes and had reached better tank country. Opposing the crack panzers were the French 9th and 2nd Armies – neither of which contained first-line units. The French formations were swept aside or over-rolled by blitzkrieg tactics. By 14 May, the pattern of German operations was fully developed. A mighty mailed fist was striking across the rear of the allied armies in northern Belgium, too strong to be resisted. In the north Hoepner's 16th Panzer Corps, (Army Group B) was striking southwestwards between the Sambre river and the city of Mons. Below it *Hoth's* 15th Panzer Corps, (Army Group A), was heading for Cambrai and Arras. A long way to the south, Reinhardt's 41st Panzer Corps was heading due west to pass between Albert and Arras and *Guderian's* 19th Panzer Corps, three divisions strong, with its left flank resting on

the Somme river, was making for the Channel ports.

The swift and unrelenting drive westwards separated the allied armies in northern Belgium from those south of the Somme just as the Germans had intended. Powerful though the allied northern group was, it now lay trapped between two more powerful German ones. It was cut off from its bases and could not be reinforced, while the allied commanders found their reserves insufficient to launch sufficiently powerful counter-attacks from the south. The only hope of escape lay in the Channel ports and it thus became vital that these be held for as long as possible to allow the armies to be evacuated. This had been accomplished by 4 June.

When the last troops left the Dunkirk beaches, the German armies in Flanders had achieved a spectacular, though hard-fought, victory. On several occasions their panzer advances had been upset – once by de Gaulle's counter-attack against Guderian's 10th Panzer during 17/18 May and then by the British attack on *Rommel's* 7th Panzer Division to the south of Arras – but these were local successes.

France falls

After a short pause for regrouping, the German forces were ready to open the second and final phase of

the battle for France. On 5 June, three panzer corps spearheaded the attack across the Somme and four days later the remaining two panzer corps struck across the Aisne. There was very little French armor to resist those assaults; it had been lost in ill-conceived defensive battles or consumed in counter-attacks at Peronne and Abbeville. The German southward march was bitterly contested, but Paris was entered on 14 June. The German advance then drove south and west to outflank the Maginot Line.

French resistance crumbled in the face of the German advances and Marshal *Petain*, the hero of Verdun, asked for terms. On 25 June 1940, the battle for France ended. Both sides' losses – 40,000 German and 100,000 French – were bitter, but the Germans had gained a complete victory in a shorter time and at less cost than a comparable single battle of the First World War.

Hitler, the political revolutionary, had used revolutionary military methods to defeat Germany's enemy, France. The theory of blitzkrieg – armor and aircraft working in close collaboration – and assaults from two new directions, out of the Ardennes and from the air, had been sufficient to first unbalance and then to destroy the allied armies in the west in a decisive campaign in less than two months.

AUGUST-OCTOBER 1941
KIEV:
A battle of encirclement

In any battle they fought, German commanders were guided by the classic Cannae principle, seeking to surround and totally destroy the opposing army. The great von *Moltke* had achieved this at Sedan in 1870; in 1941, it seemed as if this objective had been achieved in a number of encirclement battles on the Eastern Front, of which Kiev was the greatest.

The German supreme command's intention was to defeat the Soviet army west of the Dnieper river. The task was the responsibility of Gerd von *Rundstedt*'s Army Group South, one of the three that Hitler flung against the USSR. Rundstedt intended to thrust for Kiev, to pass along the valley of the Dnieper and then to strike for the Black Sea. This left hook would pass behind the armies of Marshal Budyenny's South West Front, a massive force of 69 divisions. It was Rundstedt's aim to move his 50 divisions so quickly that the Soviets simply would not have time to retreat. Once the strike for the Black Sea had been completed and Rundstedt stood at Budyenny's back, the Soviet armies, forced to fight on a reversed front, would be crushed.

From planning to reality
The situation did not develop quite as von Rundstedt had planned. The infantry armies on his left wing were having difficulties in crossing the huge Pripet Marsh, as were those of the right wing of Army Group Center. By contrast, the forces on the outer wings of both army groups were making good progress, the result being the creation of a salient north and south of Kiev.

In a move to speed the advance of the inner flank armies, Hitler at first ordered one of the panzer groups of Army Group Center to support Army Group South, but he then realized that it was better to allow the salient to develop, so that it could then be encircled by panzers and then destroyed, together with the mass of Soviet units within it. *Guderian*'s panzer group would form the northern pincer, while von Kleist's panzer group would form the southern one. To prevent the Soviets in the salient from realizing that they were being outflanked, the 6th Army would demonstrate to threaten Kiev.

The German objectives
The lack of communications in western Russia in those days made railway and road junctions and crossings strategic objectives. In the Kiev operation, the most important communications feature was the Moscow-Kiev railway line. The capture of the junction at Konotop would cut the rail link through which Budyenny's armies were supplied. Konotop was thus a prime objective for Guderian's panzer group, but to reach it he had to drive south-eastwards for more than 120 miles through the Soviet armies defending the Desna river line.

Nevertheless Konotop was specified as the eastward point of the advance for Guderian's panzers. They would then swing in a giant southerly wheel to reach Romny, where they would join up with von Kleist's panzer group, which would have struck northwards across the Dnieper river at Kremechug. Once the junction of both panzer groups had been achieved, the Soviet forces within the salient would be trapped. For its part, the supporting infantry would march along both encircling arms, striking north or south, as opportunity dictated, so as to cut the salient into small sections, which could be more easily mopped up and destroyed.

Battle begins
The Kiev encirclement proper began on 21 August 1941, although there had been preliminary battles as Guderian's forces fought their way through a mass of Soviet armies towards and then across the Desna river. In a *coup de main* on 25 August, the Moscow-Kiev railway line at Shostka was cut, a feat that made the capture of Konotop redundant. Now Guderian's panzer group could begin its giant wheel southwards, fighting all the time not only against a determined enemy, but also the vagaries of the terrain and weather and supply problems.

Alarmed that Guderian's drive had all but separated the Ukraine from central Russia, the Soviet high command took action to defeat him. On 28 August, massive armored counter-attacks were launched at Shostka, but the line held. Budyenny, too, aware of the danger of total encirclement, asked Stalin's permission to evacuate the salient, but the Soviet dictator not only refused his request, but actually reinforced the pocket. Along the whole length of the salient's northward wall there was bitter fighting, as the trapped Soviet forces struggled to break through the German infantry. The units in the south attempting to cross the Dnieper and reach safety were forced back.

At the eastern end of the salient, Guderian's armor was battling against Soviet attacks from east, west and south. On 29 August, Geyr von Schweppenburg, commander of the 24 Panzer Corps, positioned 3rd and 4th Panzer side by side and launched them in a massive south-

THE GREAT ENCIRCLEMENT *In the battle for Kiev, twin thrusts by the cream of the Reich's panzers (left) ended with the encirclement of 69 Soviet divisions (below). More than 650,000 Russian prisoners were taken, but the battle was only a tactical, rather than a strategic, victory, since, to fight it, the Germans had halted their drive on Moscow.*

wards punch. Two days later, von Kleist's panzer group crossed the Dnieper and established a bridgehead near the city of Kremechug, which fell on 8 September. The northward advance towards Romny then began. Within two days, faced with Guderian's pressure from the north and von Kleist's from the south, Budyenny lost control of his armies within the salient. Fighting without central direction, they made frantic efforts to hold apart the closing panzer jaws, but their uncoordinated efforts failed.

The trap springs shut

At 6.00pm on 15 September, Guderian's Panzer Group 2 and von Kleist's Panzer Group 1 met near the little town of Lubny, to the south of Romny. The encirclement was complete, but that was not the end of the battle. The trapped Russians fought heroically to escape and the fighting did not end until the first days of October.

When it did, what was rightly described as the mightiest action of the war to date was concluded. A million Soviet troops had fought in the salient, of which more than 665,000 were captured. Budyenny was not one of them, since Stalin had ordered his rescue by air. Yet, despite appearances, the Soviet army had not been destroyed. Germany had underestimated the numbers that Russia could put into the field. The succession of encircle-

ment battles in 1941 had weakened the Soviet army, but had not destroyed it.

When Kiev was all over, it was seen that a Cannae-style victory had been achieved, but it was a tactical, not a strategic, triumph. To win it, Hitler had halted an offensive that would in all probability have captured Moscow and perhaps won the war in five months, as he had planned. Even as the prisoners taken in the Kiev operation were being counted, a German supreme command memorandum was issued which admitted that the army could not win the war in 1941. A winter campaign by an army not equipped to cope with its rigors was the consequence of the victory.

JULY 1943
KURSK:
Tank armies clash

In western eyes the battle of Kursk, fought in central Russia during the late summer of 1943, refers to the failed German *Citadel* operation. The Soviets, however, consider the battle as a two-part operation – the first to counter *Citadel* and the second the mounting of their own offensives, *Kutuzov* and *Rumyanstsev*. Again, it is more usual for westerners to view *Citadel* as a local defeat for the German army on the Eastern Front and not to see it, as the Soviets do, as the decisive battle of the Great Patriotic War. Soviet literature claims that the true consequence of the Kursk operation was the wresting of strategic military initiative from German hands. This was the measure of the Soviet Army's victory.

The Russians prepare
As a consequence of the Soviet 1942/43 winter campaign, a blunt salient had been driven into the German front in the east. Two Russian Fronts held the salient, with others in reserve.

The great Soviet commander *Zhukov* was well aware of the danger this salient posed. He outlined to Stalin the strategic advantages the Germans would gain were an attack to pinch out the salient to succeed. He forecast the direction the German thrusts would take and warned that an enemy success would outflank Moscow from the south-east. Zhukov detailed the Soviet options as either to undertake a pre-emptive blow, or else to fight a defensive battle. He recommended the latter option, intending to bleed the Germans to death in a war of attrition as they fought their way through the Soviet defences. When they were weakened sufficiently, a Soviet counter-stroke would destroy them.

The Stavka, conscious of the need for flexibility in the face of the new German offensive, discarded the former piecemeal method of reinforcement and created a huge reserve force – the Steppe Front – under *Koniev*'s command. It is an axiom of war that God is on the side of the big battalions – and, for this battle, Stavka ensured that God would be on the Soviet side. They achieved a fourfold numerical superiority in men and a twofold superiority in artillery and armored forces. Into the salient battles, they put 1.3 million troops, 20,000 cannon, 3,500 tanks and self-propelled guns, plus 26,650 aircraft. In the reserve Steppe Front there were an additional 580,000 men, 9,000 guns and 1,639 tanks. The Kursk salient held no less than 40 per cent of the Soviet army's infantry and armored strength. And the Soviets had one further advantage that outweighed all others. Their intelligence had obtained most of the details of the German plan.

Citadel is launched
On 4 July, Stavka warned Vatutin, the Voronezh Front commander, and *Rokossovsky*, commanding Central Front, that the German offensive was imminent. It was time to initiate the tactical counter-measures Zhukov had prepared. The most important of those was an artillery barrage to be fired over the German positions immediately preceding their attack. It was anticipated the bombardment would cause the enemy severe casualties, but more importantly it would damage German morale before the battle opened. Rokossovsky attached such importance to this opening barage that during it he used up over half his allocated stock of artillery

ammunition. At 0220 the guns of his Central Front opened up, so blanketing the German artillery that counter-battery fire did not begin until 0430.

Shortly after 0530, 4th Panzer Army attacked towards Oboyan, but was held by 6th Guards Army until *Hoth*, concentrating his panzer force, smashed through 67th Guards Division and continued the advance. On the right of 4th Panzer Army, Army Detachment Kempf forced crossings of the Donets against the fierce opposition of 7th Guards Army and established a bridgehead on the river's eastern bank. In the south, therefore, the advance towards Kursk seemed to be rolling well. In the north, the downward thrust by *Model*'s 9th Army did not have a flank guard, as Hoth had in Kempf's Army Detachment. Thus Model was obliged to detach units as he advanced, so weakening his main effort. Despite this disadvantage, his army smashed through the front of 13th Red Army and it took massive Soviet air strikes against the panzer spearheads to hold them and so allow the Soviets time to reform their front. However, the furthest advance made by 9th Army on the first day of battle was less than five miles.

Throughout the following days, German infantry and armor struggled to capture the high ground and to clear the way forward for the panzer break-out, but without success. Their attacks were flung back by heavy and repeated counter-attacks and their panzer thrusts were smothered in an almost unceasing barrage of shells. Hoth, however, concluded that Stavka had already committed its armor and that he had defeated it. The breakthrough, he decided, was imminent. He regrouped his panzers and strengthened the attack towards Oboyan. On the Russian side, Vatutin was ordered to hold the German drive until reinforcements could be sent to him from Steppe Front.

Crisis in the south

With his assault upon Oboyan stalled, Hoth changed the direction of his thrust towards the Byelgorod-Kursk road, but made little ground on that sector. He changed direction yet again and swung north-eastwards towards Prokharovka seeking to force a break-through there.

On that sector stood the fresh formations of 5th Guards Tank Army and 5th Guards Infantry Army. Zhukov knew that the crisis of the battle in the south was at hand and that, if *Rotmistrov's* 5th Guards Tank Army could smash Hoth's panzer thrust, then *Citadel* would have failed. The Russian commander ordered the two guards formations into action, with the result that, as the tank army drove down from Prokharovka towards Yakovlevo, the 48th Panzer Corps of Hoth's army was striking upwards. Two armored armadas were about to collide.

Back on the northern sector the drive by Model's 9th Army was weakening. His armored thrusts were making little progress through the lines of Soviet defences and to force a breakthrough he committed his infantry supported by tanks. Both suffered crippling losses in their attempts to storm the Soviet positions. By 9 July, Model's advance had been halted and he was forced onto the defensive. His units had penetrated only the first part of the Soviet defence systems and had been bled white.

By the evening of 12 July, Hoth realized that he could not continue with a frontal assault and decided on a flanking maneuver. Zhukov returned from the Briansk front where he had been directing *Kutuzov* and co-ordinated the operations of the two Red Army fronts within the salient. He realized from Hoth's flank assault that he was too weak to

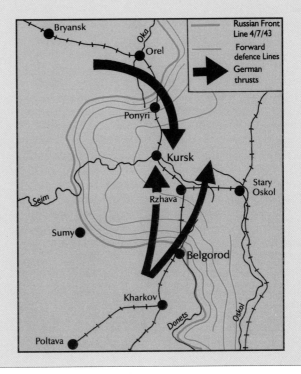

TANKS IN CONFLICT *Kursk (below) was the biggest tank battle of the war and ended in German defeat (above). The intention had been to cut off the Soviet troops in the Kursk salient, but the tank drive failed in the face of fierce Soviet resistance.*

force a decision and that, therefore, the battle of Kursk had turned in favor of the Soviet army. Hitler realized this too, but his order to break off the battle was challenged by both Manstein and Hoth, who were convinced that a breakthrough was not only impossible but imminent. Hitler insisted and in Manstein's bitter phrase: "Operational control on the Eastern Front was given away to the Russians."

JANUARY-MAY 1944
CASSINO:
Breaking the Gustav Line

The battles of Cassino in 1944 will go down in history as among the most ferocious of the Second World War. The four offensives had a common aim – to allow the allied armies in Italy to penetrate the gap between the mountains around Cassino and the Tyrrhenian Sea in order to capture Rome. They were fought between German 10th Army and 15th Army Group.

The allies had landed in Italy during September 1943, and by the end of the year were approaching the Gustav Line, a chain of carefully prepared defences whose focal point was the town of Cassino. The town lies at the entrance to the Liri valley, a narrow strip of land between the mountains and the sea. No direct advance upon Rome was possible without passing through the valley; in order to enter it, Cassino, behind which rose Monte Cassino and the other peaks extending eastwards across nearly the whole width of Italy, had to be taken. It was the allied attacks to force a way into, and then through, the Liri valley and the German attempts to hold them which forms the story of the battles for Cassino – four bloody offensives lasting nearly six months.

Battles on the Rapido
The only way to reach Cassino town was across the Rapido river, which itself was the first of the Gustav Line's three lines of defences. The second was built in the mountains and the third ran through the town. The task of capturing those objectives was given to US 5th Army, while, on its left, a British corps was to cross the Garigliano river to advance and occupy the ground between the Tyrrhenian Sea and the US forces and enter the Liri valley.

The British thrust on 17 January

1944 opened the first battle of Cassino. The weight of that drive alarmed General von *Senger und Eterlin*, commander of German 14th Panzer Corps, which was holding the right wing of German 10th Army. He appealed for reinforcements to meet the British assault and *Kesselring* released the last two divisions of his strategic reserve. In the Cassino town area, troops of 36th (Texas) Division were ordered to cross the Rapido. They were launched in unsuitable craft across a fast-flowing, icy river and then into ill-prepared assaults across unreconnoitered ground. The operation was a complete disaster, the 36th losing 2,066 men without gaining a single one of its objectives. To balance that defeat, the crossing by 34th Division, which had been made higher up the Rapido, was successful and a bridgehead was gained.

In an attempt to split the German forces in the Cassino sector, the allied high command then launched an amphibious assault at Anzio, between Cassino and Rome. An attempt to break out of the beach-head failed due to the speed of Kesselring's reaction, and the Anzio forces were boxed in within their beach-head perimeter.

Stalemate at Cassino
During 24 January French colonial troops advanced so far through the mountains on the US right that a movement to out-flank Cassino seemed possible. However, the possibility was not developed. In the town sector, 36th Division was still launching fruitless attacks, while 34th Division had been hauled into a frontal assault against Monte Cassino. An attempt to get tanks across the Rapido failed. The vehicles were bogged down in mud and were

destroyed by German shell fire.

To aid the US assaults in the mountains, 4th Indian and 2nd New Zealand Divisions were now formed into 2nd New Zealand Corps. The British 78th Division was also taken out of reserve and all three formations were moved to the Cassino sector. Their task was to capture the town, to seize the hill on which the monastery stood, to enter the Liri valley and to cut the main road to Rome. Meanwhile in the mountains, US troops had captured Point 593 (Monte Calvario), which dominated the town but were thrown off it by German counter-attack, recaptured it and were flung back for a second time. The 36th Division was ordered to make a frontal assault to capture the feature. With its total failure, the first battle of Cassino was at an end.

On 12 February, the newly formed 2nd New Zealand Corps began to arrive from the Adriatic sector and within a few days had taken over the US positions. *Freyberg*, the New Zealand commander, was convinced that the Germans had observation posts in the abbey and demanded that the building be bombed to destruction. The abbey buildings crumbled but were not destroyed because of the thickness of the walls; in the ruins, the Germans now set up observation points from which they could direct artillery fire upon allied units moving across the plain towards Cassino. During that same night – 18 February 1944 – the first detachments of German paratroops entered the Cassino area. The whole area was now defended by some of the finest formations of the German army – the 1st Airborne, 15th Panzer Grenadier, 5th Gebirgsjaeger (Mountain) and 44th Hoch und

Deutschmeister Divisions.

Freyberg's new attack was planned for 24 February. This was to be a massive effort on a narrow front, but the continuing bad weather cancelled the opening of the offensive and in the relative lull a mass bombing of Cassino was undertaken on 15 March, followed by a massive artillery bombardment, in which 195,696 shells were fired into the town. Nevertheless, the advancing infantry were repulsed by the surviving paratroops and the intention to trap the German troops in the Cassino area between the Indian and New Zealand Divisions was not realized. Although tanks were brought into action during 19 March, they could make little progress through the rubble and, on 22 March, the final New Zealand attack failed to gain its objectives.

Breakthrough at last

The Allied commanders now sought to starve out the Cassino garrison by attacking its supply routes. They also decided to launch British 8th and US 5th Armies in one huge operation to bludgeon a way through the defences. A total of 17 allied divisions were in the line, giving them a slight numerical superiority over the Germans.

Plans were also laid to deceive the Germans into believing that a new landing would be made north of Rome and that no new operations were intended on the Cassino front. So successful were these deception operations that several German commanders were on leave when the final offensive was launched on 11 May with 1,600 guns opening up along an 18-mile front. It was a truly allied offensive – Frenchmen, Tunisians, Algerians, Poles, Americans, British, Indians, New Zealanders and Italian units fighting in one battle line. Two days later, Kesselring was forced to commit his last reserves to create rearguards behind which the troops in the Cassino area could retreat. By 17 May the French had forced a way through the mountains and were in a position behind Cassino. The Germans,

conscious that the French would cut them off if they did not withdraw, began to pull back. At 9.45am on 18 May, the Poles entered the abbey; within minutes, the historic "Cracow" trumpet signal sounded the victory and the Polish flag flying above the ruins showed that the battle for the monastery had ended.

The four battles of Cassino had cost the allied forces approximately 350,000 men killed, wounded and missing. The objective of the fighting, the city of Rome, fell on 5 June. There have been many criticisms of the operation, General Fuller, for instance expressing these with the words "tactically the most absurd and strategically the most senseless campaign of the whole war."

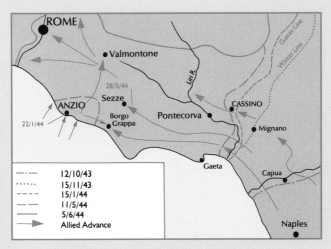

BATTLE AT CASSINO *The battle for Cassino (above) degenerated into a First World War-style battle of attrition, even massive allied artillery bombardments (below) and blanket bombing raids failing to dislodge Cassino's fanatical defenders.*

JUNE-AUGUST 1944
D-DAY:
The battle for Normandy

At the beginning of June 1940, the British Expeditionary Force was driven from the continent. Immediately preparations began for a re-entry into Europe, the planning, preparation and construction of the invasion force taking four years. On 6 June 1944, allied armies disembarked upon the coast of Normandy and in an 11-month campaign liberated occupied Europe and destroyed the German armies fighting against them. The account here deals with the period from D-day to the crossing of the Seine.

Planning Overlord
The original battle plan for the invasion had provided for the landing of five assault divisions but this was felt by both *Eisenhower*, the allied supreme commander, and *Montgomery*, who was to lead the ground forces in the field, to be too few for success and and two further sea-borne and an airborne division were added to the invading force. The assault would land on a chain of beaches extending along an area of over 35 miles in the Baie de Seine to the east of Cherbourg. Even after years of all-out production by two great industrial nations, there were still equipment shortages – notably of the vital assault landing craft. Eisenhower, in fact, actually postponed the original D-day date in order to obtain an extra month's landing-craft production for the allied armada.

Once the five divisions had made the initial assault, there was to be a rapid build-up and break-out from the beachhead. The British were eventually to field 14 divisions, the USA 20, the Canadians three, and the French and Polish one each. The allied air force, 11,000 aircraft strong, included 5,000 fighters; this

was to gain and hold air superiority before D-day. To transport and to protect the allied convoys, there were 6,000 vessels. Against this, the German forces on the western coast of Europe, between Holland and Spain, numbered 38 infantry divisions, with a further four in reserve at Calais and another three in Normandy. In the immediate area of the D-day beaches – an area held by *Rommel*'s Army Group B (7th and 15th Armies) – there were four coastal defence divisions – not first-line formations – with two infantry and three panzer divisions in reserve, together with garrison troops in Cherbourg. More German divisions were to be brought in as the fighting developed, though these arrived piecemeal, rather than as part of a logical overall plan.

The allied plan was for landings on five main beaches. *Bradley*'s 1st Army would land on *Utah* and advance up the Cotentin peninsula to capture Cherbourg. Other units of 1st Army would land on *Omaha* the gap between the two beaches being covered by two airborne divisions dropped some way inland. British 2nd Army, plus a Canadian division, would land to the east of *Omaha* on *Juno, Sword* and *Gold*. To protect the British eastern flank, an airborne division would be landed in the area of the Orne river.

It was the task of 2nd Army to attract the bulk of the German panzer forces to its front. This would leave the US command free to build up 1st Army to a point where its forces could break out of the beachhead and make a vast wheel to reach open country. At that point the 3rd Army under George *Patton*, would be landed to advance through the gap 1st Army had created to begin a battle of pursuit.

D-day and after
The allied invasion fleet carrying 176,000 troops, preceded by airborne drops and an extensive bombing campaign, sailed for Normandy and landed the five assault divisions on 6 June 1944. By nightfall, all the troops were ashore and had dug in. There had been some anxiety on *Omaha*, where US commanders had rejected specially-designed British armored fighting vehicles, which would have blown gaps in the sea wall through which the infantry had to pass in order to move inland. So serious was the crisis that Bradley considered evacuation, but by mid-morning the situation had been resolved.

German plans to meet the invasion were not clear cut and decisive. Rommel had intended to meet and defeat the allies on the beaches, where they were at their weakest. He improved the local defences, setting up anti-barge obstacles topped with anti-tank mines. However, his strategy was in direct contrast to that of von *Rundstedt*, the Supreme Commander West, who wanted the allied landing force to be destroyed in a mobile battle, fought away from the landing areas. Hitler further complicated the situation through his obsessive belief that the main invasion effort would be made in the Pas de Calais area and held 15th Army in position there to meet it. As head of OKW, he also ordered that no reserve panzer divisions could be put into action without his express order. When the allied forces landed, the Führer was asleep and no one at his headquarters dared to wake him. Thus the panzer divisions that might have been used to defeat the allies on the beaches were not released until D + 1 – too late to be effective in Rommel's

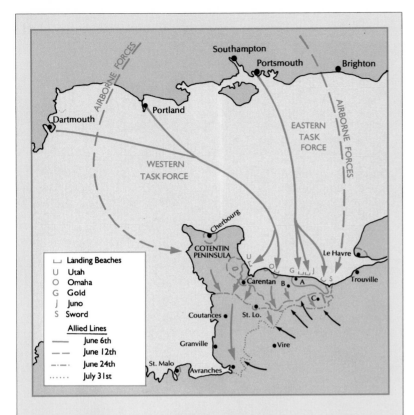

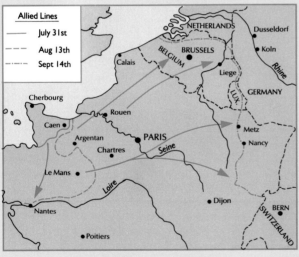

D-DAY AND AFTER *The Germans were taken by surprise by the allied landings in Normandy (above) and failed to win the battle of the beaches. Eventually, the allies broke out and, in a vast wheel, encircled the German defenders in the Falaise pocket.*

27 June and Bradley was building up for the breakout. This occurred on 25 July, with Collins making the principal effort; two days later, his divisions had reached Avranches, smashing a gap in the German line. Patton's 3rd Army exploited the gap and swung in a vast sweeping movement towards Le Mans.

Hitler, who had finally accepted that Normandy was the actual invasion area and not a feint, now ordered a counter-attack. What he wanted was a panzer thrust from Mortain towards Avranches to halt the US drive, throw back their forces and destroy the allied armies in Normandy. The operation had no chance of success and indeed gave the allies an advantage. The Germans had created a salient and this very soon became a pocket within which the greatest parts of 7th Army and 5th Panzer Army were trapped.

The British and Canadian drive south from Caen towards Falaise and Patton's swift-moving armored forces could not prevent the escape of part of the trapped German troops, however. Furious German counter-attacks to hold back the advancing allied armies, the efforts of the ordinary soldiers, and the skill of their commanders all combined to ensure that the retreat to the Seine never became a rout. Paris was liberated on 25 August, and with its liberation the campaign in Normandy was at an end.

During the campaign, 50 German divisions had been committed to Normandy and, at the end of the battle, only ten could be considered to be effective fighting units. In three months, the German army had suffered twice the number of casualties that it had sustained during Stalingrad. *Guderian* condemned the supreme command for the debacle. "While our panzer units still existed, our leaders had chosen to fight a static battle in Normandy. When our motorized forces were squandered and destroyed, they were compelled to fight the mobile battle they had hitherto refused to face."

plan.

The pattern of the fighting over the weeks following the landing saw a build up of allied strength and assaults by both sides – the allies to enlarge the perimeter and the Germans to contain it. Montgomery's attempts to capture Caen, which would act as a pivot when the breakout came, was frustrated for weeks by a strong German defence backed by SS panzer divisions. Moving out from *Utah*, however, Collin's 7th Corps had captured Cherbourg by

191

AUCHINLECK
Claude (1884-1981)
BRITISH FIELD MARSHAL
Second World War

The tall, imposing Claude Auchinleck had all the attributes of a natural leader of men. Yet his skills as a commander, though recognized by the men serving under him at the time, were not generally recognized until the history of the Second World War came to be written.

Auchinleck was born into a British military family on 21 June 1884, and passed out from Sandhurst into an Indian infantry regiment in 1904. He served in the Middle East in the First World War; in post-war years, he was closely associated with the policy of the "Indianization" – that is, of giving command opportunities to Indian officers – of the Indian army. From an appointment at the Quetta staff college, he went on to command several of the campaigns fought on the north-west frontier. In 1938, he was general officer commanding the Meerut military district and it looked as if his uninterrupted rise through the Indian army military hierarchy would take him to the post of commander-in-chief. However, the outbreak of the Second World War interrupted temporarily the smooth flow of his career.

Recalled from India
In 1940 Auchinleck was given command of the allied forces which briefly held the Norwegian town of Narvik

THE "AUK" *Auchinleck's defensive victory at the first battle of El Alamein stopped Rommel, but did not stop Churchill replacing him as British commander-in-chief.*

in the late spring and early summer of 1940. Following the British evacuation from Dunkirk, Auchinleck took over Southern Command and set up the first anti-invasion defences. In December 1940, he returned once more to India to take up at last the post of commander-in-chief, but his tenure was short-lived. In July 1941 he was ordered to replace *Wavell* as commander-in-chief in the Middle East. Auchinleck had no desert experience – and he came from the Indian army, rather than being a British army regular. This distinction – though subtle, or, indeed, meaningless to the untutored – led to some difficulties for Auchinleck in his new post, for some senior British commanders resented his appointment. However, Auchinleck's personality soon won over these who had initially opposed him.

Command in the desert
Unlike *Rommel*, Auchinleck did not lead his men in the field, delegating this responsibility to field commanders. On two occasions, however, he intervened directly to save 8th Army from disaster. The first time he did this was during the winter offensive of 1941, when Cunningham's plan to trap and destroy Rommel's forces went wrong. The intention had been to launch a drive along the northern, coastal area, linking up with the garrison of besieged Tobruk, while a second thrust swept up out of the desert south of Tobruk. Rommel would be caught be-

tween the pincers. However, the British tank assaults deep in the desert were repulsed, while the slowness of the northern pincer gave Rommel the chance to seize the initiative and thrust towards Egypt.

The 8th Army field commander, General Cunningham, believed himself trapped and decided to retreat, but Auchinleck kept his nerve and ordered the army to stand fast. He realized that Rommel had overreached himself and that it was the Germans who would have to withdraw. Under unrelenting British pressure, Rommel retreated to his original positions.

However, Rommel was not Auchinleck's only adversary. Wavell had been dismissed for lack of aggression and now Churchill began to lose faith in his successor as Auchinleck steadfastly refused to mount offensives for no clear strategic purpose. Rommel, however, had a strategic prize – the Suez canal – and, to gain it, undertook a series of attacks during January 1942, which drove 8th Army, now commanded by Ritchie – Cunningham's replacement – back to a strongly fortified and heavily mined defensive line at Gazala. On 28 May 1942, the Axis armies attacked in a brilliantly executed operation, which turned the southern flank of the British line. Just when it seemed that Rommel was trapped, he concentrated his armor and broke out, overrunning 8th Army's rear areas. Ritchie ordered a withdrawal on 13 June, which soon threatened to become a disorderly rout.

Auchinleck moved from his headquarters in Cairo to the forward area and took over direct control of the battle. He then fought successful delaying actions at Mersah Matruh and at Alam Halfa – each action weakening the enemy. By the end of June, Auchinleck had brought the battered 8th Army back to a defence line at El Alamein, which he had begun to build shortly after taking up his Middle East appointment. Here he regrouped and prepared for the next Axis thrust. This was not long in coming, but the weakening effect of Auchinleck's earlier defensive battles meant that the Germans no longer had the strength to break through.

It was from that line at El Alamein that the Axis forces were finally driven back in October 1942. By that time Auchinleck was no longer in the Middle East. He and Ritchie were both relieved of their commands in August 1942. Montgomery took over from Ritchie and Alexander replaced Auchinleck,

Return to India

Restored to the post of commander-in-chief India, Auchinleck was now faced with Japanese attempts to invade the sub-continent. He set about strengthening the Indian army and deploying it to meet the enemy threat. His organizational skills supplied the men and arms that were needed to win eventual victory in Burma. In 1947 he left the land which he had served for decades and settled in Morrocco, where he died in 1981.

Auchinleck was a big man – both in stature and in character. He exuded confidence and is remembered by those who served under him as a soldier's soldier, refusing to allow himself privileges his men could not enjoy.

BOCK
Fedor von (1880-1945)
GERMAN FIELD MARSHAL
Second World War

Fedor von Bock was one of the most senior and experienced German military commanders during the early years of the Second World War. Yet, after he had been retired in 1941, Hitler refused to offer him any other military appointment.

Von Bock was born in Kustrin on 3 December 1880, into a military family. He entered the army as an ensign and was gazetted into the 5th Guards Regiment during 1898. As early as 1913, he showed promise of future ability and was posted to the staff of the Prussian Guards Corps. For much of the First World War, he served on the staff of von *Mackensen*'s army in Galicia and, by 1929, had risen to the rank of major-general. In 1935, he was commanding a corps. Three years later, as commander of 8th Army, he led the march into Austria and then went on to command 1st Army Group, with the rank of colonel general.

A professional leader

During the war with Poland in 1939, von Bock led the northern army group – this played the most prominent part in the campaign – and in 1940 commanded Army Group B for the war in the west. On 19 July 1940 came his promotion to Field Marshal. For the war with Russia the next year, von Bock was given command of Army Group Center, with the responsibility of breaking through the Soviet armies and of driving on to Moscow. Under his command was a force of 49 division, 11 of which were panzer. The left flank of his Army Group was made up of Panzergruppe 3, with the 9th and 4th Armies in the center and Panzergruppe 2 forming the right wing. Opposing him were the armies of the Soviet West Front, comprising the 3rd, 4th and 10th Armies – a seemingly imposing force of 23 infantry divisions, six cavalry divisions and nine tank brigades.

Despite the successes achieved by von Bock in the opening stages of the campaign, Hitler now decided that Moscow was not the principal objective and so halted the attack on 21 August 1941. Army Group Center was then used as a holding force, from which units were taken to reinforce the offensives being mounted by the other Army Groups in the north and south. This move was condemned by von Bock for it gave, as he saw it, time for the retreating Soviet forces to regroup, to reinforce and to prepare their defences in front of the Soviet capital.

Operation Typhoon

The order to resume the attack upon Moscow was not given until 6 September; the actual offensive, Operation *Typhoon*, was launched four weeks later. For the operation, von Bock's Army Group was reinforced to give it a strength of 70 divisions – more than 1,000,000 men – and the time-table drawn up by OKW expected that the 200-mile advance to reach and capture the city would be completed by the end of October. Von Bock planned a pincer operation, with the left (northern) arm being the more powerful of the two.

Typhoon opened in fine fall weather, but this soon deteriorated into heavy, persistent rain. The rain, as Bock complained in a diary entry, delayed his troops far more than did the Soviet army. Conditions worsened, forcing the operation to be broken off for a time – it was not resumed until the second week of November. This further delay was to cost the Germans dear.

It soon became clear to von Bock that he would not be able to gain the objectives he had been set, even though his northern wing was still advancing and Moscow itself was now only 20 miles away. He feared the weather would turn against him again, while he also suspected that the Soviets had taken advantage of the delay to build up their forces defending their capital. Nevertheless, he opened what was planned to be the crucial final assault, but found himself up against an enemy whose strength increased daily and winter conditions, for which the German armies were neither prepared nor equipped. His troops, having fought almost without a break since June, were also nearing exhaustion.

Bock realized the hopelessness of the situation, expressing his bitterness in his diary entry for 1 December. The OKW daily communique had reported: "In the Moscow area, German infantry and Panzer units are maintaining their advance towards the Russian capital." Von Bock dismissed this entry as "a pipe dream". His signals to OKH were even more direct; in a memorandum, he declared that ". . . a continuation of the attack is without point or purpose, because our forces are at the end of their strength. . . ."

Here, politics intervened – and the wish of the Führer. Von Bock demanded that the offensive be terminated, but the reaction of his immediate military superiors was cowardly. They were not prepared to issue such an order, but left it up to him. This meant that the responsibility – and Hitler's consequent fury – would fall upon von Bock alone. Von Bock acted. Two days later, on 3 December, he ordered the attack of his left wing to be halted and pulled back his right-wing units. Moscow had been saved and the way had been opened for the launch of the Soviet winter counter-offensive, in which fresh Siberian troops drove the Nazi armies back along the line.

Even though it could be argued that von Bock would indeed have taken Moscow had it not been for Hitler's earlier delay, the Führer's revenge was swift. He allowed his most experienced military commander to retire on medical grounds. On 18 December von Bock's career ended; a superb strategist, whose gifts had contributed to victories in two key campaigns, was not employed again. Von Bock died in an allied air attack in the last weeks of the war. According to reports he was killed firing his pistol at aircraft "strafing" the street in which he lived. It was a fitting ending for a dedicated Prussian commander of the old school.

BRADLEY
Omar N (1893-1981)
US GENERAL
Second World War

The mild mannered Omar Bradley, Eisenhower's right hand in Europe, was right on many occasions, but wrong on one major one. He advised Eisenhower against the capture of Berlin. Bradley believed that it would cost 100,000 troops to take the city in exchange for a mass of ruins, hungry civilians to house and feed and a tenancy that would be measured in months, as it had already been agreed that Berlin would form part of the Soviet zone of occupation. The cost was too heavy for what Bradley saw only as a prestige objective. What he failed to realize was the political advantage Berlin's capture would bring.

Bradley was born on 12 February 1893, in Clark, Missouri. He graduated from West Point in 1915, and served in the 14th Infantry Regiment during the First World War. In the immediate post-war years Bradley lectured in mathematics at West Point, attended the general staff school in 1929 and the war college in 1934. In 1941, with the rank of brigadier, he was commandant of the infantry school at Fort Benning, and went on to lead the 82nd and then the 28th Infantry Divisions.

Involvement in Overlord
During the North African campaign, Bradley took over the 2nd Corps from *Patton*, leading it in the final stages of the campaign and into Sicily. He was then transferred to Britain in fall 1943 to be chief of US ground forces and general officer commanding 1st Army.

Bradley's first task came on D-Day, when his army landed as planned on two of the D-Day beaches – coded *Utah* and *Omaha* – which were more than 10 miles apart. Reports soon indicated that, while the *Utah* landings had been successful and the troops there were advancing inland, there was chaos on *Omaha*. The local commanders had rejected the offer of specially-converted tanks to negotiate the beach; the lack of supporting armor meant that US infantry could not advance. The confusion was compounded as the landing craft carrying fresh waves of infantry to the beaches lost direction and literally began dumping troops wherever they could. So bad was the confusion that Bradley seriously considered re-embarking his units, but slowly order was restored and the infantry moved inland.

The next step was the breakout from the beachheads and this was led by 1st Army. Throughout the latter weeks of June and the first weeks of July, it had been making gains. Bradley's 7th Corps, under *Collins*, had swung up the Cotentin peninsula to capture Cherbourg, while his other divisions advanced towards St Lo, which was taken on 18 July. It was at St Lo that Bradley's breakout began, with, once again, Collins leading the assault. Combined with the British pressure at Caen, this was to lead to the collapse of the German front.

THE QUIET AMERICAN *Bradley rose to become Eisenhower's right-hand man during the drive through France.*

The advance into Germany

With the arrival in Normandy of Patton's 3rd Army, the planned organization of 12th US Army Group was accomplished. Bradley now held equal status with *Montgomery*, who had previously been in command of all allied field forces on the continent. Patton's troops poured through the gap that 1st Army had created and then in a great right wheel began to trap the German forces that had been containing the allied bridgehead.

Soon Bradley's army group was in full pursuit of those remnants of German 7th Army and 5th Panzer Army that had managed to escape from the allied encirclement at Falaise. Bradley crossed the Seine and liberated Paris on 25 August, but his advance then faltered, due to a shortage of fuel. Although the US drive was now slower paced than formerly, Patton reached the Maas river and 1st Army, led by Hodges, took Mons. By the end of September 1944, Bradley's 12th Army Group was closing on the German frontier.

Bradley and Montgomery now submitted separate plans to Eisenhower for operations inside Germany. Montgomery's, which depended on success in the airborne drop to capture the Rhine bridges at Arnhem, failed, and Bradley's forces, reinforced by 9th Army, together with Dever's 6th Army Group, moved to destroy the German armies west of the Rhine in preparation for the assault across the river. The German counter-offensive in the Ardennes halted the advance, but, after Hitler's armies had been contained and flung back, it soon resumed.

During February 1945, the allied armies completed the clearing of the west bank of the Rhine: on 7 March, Bradley crossed the river via the undamaged bridge at Remagen. With Bradley and then Montgomery both firmly established east of the river, Germany's defeat could only be a matter of a few months at the most, but Bradley's encirclement and seizure of the Ruhr reduced this to a matter of weeks. His armies streamed eastwards into the heart of the Reich. Patton reached Pilsen in Czechoslovakia and would have gone on to capture Prague, had he not been halted, while *Simpson* and his 9th Army was across the Elbe and preparing to burst out of the bridgeheads there to drive onto Berlin when Bradley halted him. By this time, with the addition of 15th Army to his establishment, Bradley was leading over 1,250,000 men in the field.

Bradley was a quiet spoken, well-mannered man, who, having given an order, expected it to be carried out thoroughly and swiftly without his interference. Nor did he welcome interference from his superiors. Once he had been given a job, he would carry it out. He needed no supervision. Because of his reluctance to interfere with a subordinate's operations, he at times seemed not to exercise sufficient control over Patton – but that was Bradley's way. His aim was to teach by example, a reflection of the early days when he had lectured at West Point. Quiet, dependable, an excellent administrator and a sound tactician – this was Omar Bradley.

CHUIKOV
Vassili I (1900-82)
SOVIET GENERAL
Second World War

One of the most influential of the group of middle level commanders with whom *Zhukov* surrounded himself and whom he used to staff important command posts was Vassili Chuikov, the hero of Stalingrad. Chuikov's leadership of 62nd Army was decisive in halting the German offensive and in launching the Soviet counter thrusts.

The son of a peasant, Chuikov was born on 31 January 1900, in a village just outside Moscow and joined the Soviet Army as a raw recruit in April 1919. There is no doubt that his membership of the Communist Party aided his promotion; during the Civil War, he rose to the command of a regiment within two years from his enlistment. In 1925 Chuikov graduated from the Frunze Military Academy and then specialized in the study of Far Eastern affairs. As a result he was posted as a military advisor to Chiang Kai Shek and remained in China from 1926 to 1937. In the last year of his secondment he began to study the techniques of mechanized warfare and, by 1939, he was in command of one of the armies that fought against Finland before returning to China as military attaché. When the USSR was attacked by Nazi Germany in June 1941, Chuikov was recalled to serve in defence of his

SIEGE OF STALINGRAD *Chuikov's defence of Stalingrad was the turning point of the war on the Eastern Front.*

homeland. He commanded a succession of armies – 64th, 62nd and 8th Guards – the last-named from April 1943 until the end of the war.

Defending Stalingrad

Chuikov's most successful battle was the defence of Stalingrad in command of 62nd Army. He was only 42 when, together with Shumilov's 64th Army, he halted the massive Nazi assaults.

Chuikov's arrival on the Stalingrad front was less than auspicious. The German offensive of the summer of 1942 had driven the Soviet forces back towards the Volga river and, during 25 July, while Chuikov was en route to the front, panzer units struck at the junction between 62nd and 64th armies and began to roll them up. It was no time for half-measures. As he drove to the front-line, Chuikov found himself confronted with a great mass of soldiers who had broken under German air and tank assault and were in full retreat. This was not the time for gentle handling or soft talk. By brute force he literally forced back the stream of panicking troops, formed them into units and set up a battle line. However, despite the brutal methods he used to restore the situation in this instance, Chuikov was not a commander who expected his soldiers to bear hardships that he did not share. His headquarters were an ancient burial mound near the banks of the Volga, a vantage point that the Germans made every effort to capture. He was thus often in the forefront of the battle.

Meanwhile in the industrial sprawl of Stalingrad itself, Chuikov inspired his men to fight a tenacious defence – not just battling from house to house but from room to room. Here, he had an advantage denied to the German commander, von Paulus. Behind Chuikov lay the Volga, across which he could ferry supplies and reinforcements while wounded and exhausted troops could be evacuated eastwards to safety. The Germans had no such reliable supply line, their communications being over-extended and subject to partisan attack. The way in which German wounded were evacuated was inefficient, while it was seldom possible for the German command to rotate battle-worn units, given the intensity of the fighting. Aware from personal experience of the power of the dive bomber – his headquarters had been attacked several times – Chuikov realized that close-quarter fighting would eliminate the threat, since it meant that the Luftwaffe could not bomb for fear of hitting German troops.

Stalingrad relieved

While Chuikov and his army fought their desperate and bitter battles within the factory complexes and rubble that had once been the city of Stalingrad, other Soviet forces had begun to strike at the enemy lines to the north and south of the city. A breakthrough was made in the sectors held by the troops of Germany's satellites – Italy and Romania – and the Soviet forces stormed through those breaches. Even had von Paulus wanted to withdraw in the face of this counter offensive and even had Hitler been prepared to agree, it would have been impossible for 6th Army to do so, since Chuikov's grasp on it was so strong that the German units would have found it impossible to disengage and retire.

Cut off, encircled and starving, the remnants of what had been one of Hitler's crack armies fought on until the beginning of 1943, when the last pocket of German resistance surrendered. Chuikov's ruthless determination had played a major part in the destruction of an entire German army. One even greater honor was to fall to him. After fighting his way across western Russia, Poland, the Oder river and into Berlin, it was Chuikov that a German delegation from Hitler's bunker approached on May Day to ask his terms for a truce; on 2 May General Weidling, the commandant of Berlin, formally surrendered the city to the Soviet commander.

This was a proud moment for Chuikov. In post-war years he held a number of command positions, including the supreme command of Soviet troops in Germany; in 1972, he was senior Inspector General in the Ministry of Defence. He died in 1982.

Chuikov possessed a number of soldierly qualities. He was tough and had unbreakable nerve, as he demonstrated in the early days of battle in Stalingrad. However, although he showed great tactical skill and ability – his troops established the first bridgeheads across the Oder in January 1945, for instance – circumstances denied him the opportunity to demonstrate any strategic gifts he may have possessed. He was a loyal subordinate, rather than a command initiator.

CLARK
Mark W (1896-1984)
US GENERAL
Second World War

Mark Clark was undoubtedly a brave man; he was also capable of showing great skill in the planning of military operations. Yet, as a commander, his judgement was often suspect; he was so hated by many of the troops serving under him that a group of them sought to persuade the US Congress to launch an investigation into his handling of the Rapido river crossing during the 1944 Italian campaign. It was also widely believed that his personal vanity led him to order 5th Army to capture Rome, rather than concentrate on trapping the enemy north of Monte Cassino, and that this decision led to the prolongation of the entire campaign.

Clark was born on 1 May 1896 in a New York barracks, where his father was a serving officer. On graduation from West Point, he was posted to an infantry regiment; within a year, the young Clark was wounded while serving with the US expeditionary force in France. He fulfilled various army assignments during the inter-war years, but promotion was slow. By 1939 he had risen only to the rank of major. The expansion of the US Army after the outbreak of war brought with it more speedy advancement, however, and by 1942 he had reached the rank of major general and was chief of staff of Army Ground Forces. That July, he was serving in Britain, commanding the US ground forces in Europe, when he was selected by Eisenhower to assist in planning Operation *Torch*, the forthcoming allied invasion of French North Africa. In order to establish how the French garrison would react to the allied assault, Clark was landed by submarine to meet Vichy French commanders at a secret conference outside Algiers, where he displayed considerable gifts of diplomacy and clarity of expression. During the campaign that followed, Clark served as Eisenhower's deputy.

The invasion of Italy
Following the North African campaign, Clark was selected to lead 5th Army, the Anglo-American force that launched the allied invasion of Italy by landing at Salerno in September 1943. His advance up the Italian peninsula was bitterly contested at every river crossing and mountain pass by an enemy intent on holding the allies south of Rome. At Cassino, for instance, the Germans halted the allied advance for over four months; here, Clark's leadership during the Rapido river crossing in January 1944 brought condemnation from 36th Division, which suffered bitter losses in the battle.

In an attempt to outflank the German Cassino defences, a further Allied landing was made at Anzio, behind the enemy lines, in January 1944. The assault took the enemy by surprise, but Lucas, the ground-forces commander, did not press forward – even though his advanced scouts reached the suburbs of Rome – but

waited for his tanks and heavy artillery to arrive. Clark, who was in Lucas's headquarter supported him in this mistaken decision. While the allies waited, the Germans acted. So successful were *Kesselring*'s counter measures that the allies came close to being driven into the sea.

The breakout from the beachhead and the breakthrough at Cassino finally occurred almost simultaneously in the latter half of May 1944. The Anzio force advanced eastwards through the Alban Hills, but Clark then deflected it northwards to take Rome. This meant that the German 10th Army, which might otherwise have been trapped, in fact escaped.

Clark continued in command in Italy. By April 1945 he was a full general in rank and commanding 15th Army Group. His final offensive opened on 9 April; its success led to the unconditional surrender of Axis forces in Italy, the first of the capitulations that ended the war. He went on to serve as US high commissioner in Austria until 1947, a period in which he needed all his diplomatic skills when conducting negotiations with the USSR; he was called up to use these again in 1952/53 as commander of the UN forces in Korea, when he took part in the negotiations that brought the Korean War to a close.

Mark Clark was a competent professional soldier, but lacked flair. His diplomatic ability was, however, remarkable, as he repeatedly demonstrated.

COLLINS
Joseph L (1896-)
US GENERAL
Second World War

Described by Omar *Bradley*, his superior officer, as "one of the outstanding field commanders in Europe", Joseph Collins demonstrated in north-west Europe the same qualities of leadership and battle spirit he had previously shown in the Pacific in the Second World War.

Collins was born in New Orleans on 1 May 1896, and graduated from West Point in 1917. His peace-time duties involved him in the normal round of overseas and home postings; late in December 1941, he was sent to work on the defences of Hawaii and he remained in the Pacific for the next three years. His 25th Infantry Division played a significant part in the short, but hard-fought, New Georgia battles of July-August 1943, which formed part of *MacArthur*'s double thrust through the Solomons and along the northern coast of New Guinea. It was at that time that Collins received his nick-name "Lightning Joe" from the wireless code name for his division.

Into action in Normandy
In February 1944, Collins was promoted and sent to Europe to lead 7 Corps in the coming D-Day invasion. Under his aggressive handling, his corps forced its way across the base of the Cotentin Peninsula and, on 18 June, 12 days after the landings on *Utah* beach, swung

northwards and struck out for Cherbourg, which fell on 27 June, after days of bitter struggle. The capture of a major port early in the campaign had been one of the main objectives of the D-Day planners and, although Cherbourg's harbour installations had been wrecked, the unloading of supplies across the beach commenced immediately. It was a tribute to the reputation that Collins had earned that his corps had been chosen to capture this prime objective.

The next stage of the campaign was the break-out from the Normandy bridgehead. The first move was made at St Lo on 25 July, Collins' corps leading the massive assault, which reached Avranches only six days later. Through the gap 7 Corps had created, Patton's newly-arrived 3rd Army now struck in a vast right wheel, seeking to outflank the German armies in Normandy. Hitler, observing what he thought was Patton's isolated thrust, decided on a large-scale counter-attack. He ordered an all-out panzer effort to strike across the base of the Cotentin Peninsula; by swinging northwards, the panzers would smash 3rd Army, so bringing about the collapse of the whole American front in Normandy.

However, the air support provided by rocket-firing RAF Typhoons, together with firm resistance on the ground, in which 7 Corps played a distinctive part, stemmed the enemy attack, leaving the German 7th Army and 5th Panzer Army in a vulnerable salient. A pincer operation, carried out by US, Canadian and British troops, turned this salient into a pocket, within which the enemy forces were trapped. Collins' corps helped to close the ring around them and in the pursuit to the Seine that followed the Falaise battle and the subsequent thrust to the German border, 7 Corps was usually in the van of the allied advance.

Advance into Germany
Soldiers of 7 Corps were the first US troops to reach German soil and Aachen, which fell to Collins on 21 October, was the first German city to be captured by the allies. When Hitler's Ardennes offensive led to the fear of a breakthrough, *Montgomery* asked for Collins to take a key post in the counter-offensive since he considered him to be one of the most aggressive corps commanders in the allied forces. Continuing his drive into Germany, Collins captured Cologne on 6 March 1945 and was active in the Remagen bridgehead on the Rhine. From there, his corps moved on to participate in the great battle of encirclement around the Ruhr; when the German forces there surrendered on 17 April, it raced for the Elbe, reaching the river on 25 April. The German surrender came only five weeks later. Collins, promoted lieutenant-general on 16 April 1945, spent little time in the army of occupation. He returned to the USA to become involved in planning the allied invasion of Japan. He was engaged in this task when the war ended.

The militarily aggressive Joseph Collins was also a man of great charm and friendliness, optimistic and enthusiastic. There is no doubt that he was the finest corps commander in the US forces in Europe.

DIETRICH
Josef (1892-1966)
GERMAN SS OBERSTGRUPPEN-FUEHRER (COLONEL-GENERAL)
Second World War

Though the SS is popularly associated with concentration camp brutality and other atrocities, it was also one of the most respected fighting forces of the Second World War. The Waffen (Armed) SS, as the fighting branch was known, possessed a unique aggressive spirit, which brought victory on many battlefields. The man, more than any other, who was responsible for this SS battle ethos was Josef "Sepp" Dietrich.

The son of working-class parents, Dietrich was born in Bavaria on 28 May 1892. He enlisted in the 1st Uhlan regiment in 1911, transferring to the 42nd Infantry regiment at the outbreak of war and then into 5th Storm battalion and finally the 13th Bavarian Tank Detachment. By the end of the war Dietrich had been promoted sergeant-major. In post-war Germany, he soon became involved with right-wing nationalist extremists. He joined the Oberland Freikorps in 1919, fighting the Polish annexation of Silesia, and took part in the Munich Putsch of November 1923, when Hitler tried to overthrow the Bavarian government, though he did not formally join the Nazi party until 1928. Accepted into the SS, he soon became one of Hitler's bodyguards. He showed his flair for organization when the SS units in southern Bavaria were regrouped. He became a Reichstag member in 1930 and in the following year became the commander of Hitler's bodyguard – the SS Leibstandarte.

One state, two armies
The creation of a Party army – the Waffen SS – was opposed by the Wehrmacht generals, the traditional defenders of the state, but Hitler eventually had his way. In the first military operations the Waffen SS fought, its soldiers were kept firmly under army control, but, as the Waffen SS expanded during the Russian campaign, it achieved independence. Dietrich, commander of the Leibstandarte regiment in 1939, saw his force grow from division to corps strength. A fighting general, he often led his men in person on the battlefield.

Dietrich commanded 6th Panzer Army in the battle of the Bulge in December 1944, but even SS élan could not win Hitler victory in his last offensive in the west – nor indeed could it achieve miracles in the final German offensive of the war on the Eastern Front, which was launched in Hungary in the spring of 1945. During the subsequent fighting for Vienna, Dietrich commented bitterly, "We are called the 6th Panzer Army because we still have six panzers on strength."

Dietrich was tried as a war criminal and sentenced to imprisonment for life. He was paroled in 1955, only to be re-arrested by the West German government and sentenced to 18 months imprisonment for the part he had played in murders committed by the Nazi party.

Leaving aside moral and legal issues, it is clear that the comradeship that Dietrich fostered between SS officers and their men was of a kind unknown to any contemporary army. Any SS soldier, for instance, had the right of direct appeal to the most senior of his commanders, a fact that helped to form a bond of trust between officers and men unrivaled in both the Wehrmacht and the allies' fighting formations. This bond was strengthened in the many campaigns in which SS officers, following Dietrich's example, led infantry attacks in person. The result was a unique fighting spirit, which made the Waffen SS the best fighting formation of the war.

Dietrich's working-class background was reflected in his speech, habits and manners. Despite his crudeness, he possessed a charisma that inspired deep loyalty. Above all, he was a fighter. That was the measure of his achievement for Germany in the Second World War.

DOENITZ
Karl (1891-1980)
GERMAN ADMIRAL
Second World War

The admirals of the Third Reich's navy understood the principles of global conflict better than did the commanders of the German army, whose concepts were limited to continental warfare. The navy's first supreme commander, Admiral *Raeder*, saw commerce raiding as his fleet's most important practical priority, this to be carried out chiefly by surface vessels. His successor, Karl Doenitz, however, was convinced, that submarines were the key weapon – it is not hard to understand Doenitz's point of view, since he had served in the U-boat arm during the First World War and was fully aware of the submarine's potential. Effective deployment of U-boats, he believed, could this time bring Britain to its knees.

Doenitz was born on 16 September 1891, in Gruenau -Berlin. On his graduation from naval academy, he volunteered for the U-boat branch of the service, but was captured by the Royal Navy during October 1918, while attacking an allied convoy off Sicily. He was held prisoner until 1919. In the post-war navy, Doenitz commanded the cruiser *Emden*.

When, as a consequence of the 1935 Anglo-German Naval Agreement, the German navy embarked on an ambitious expansion programme, Doenitz was given the task of re-creating the U-boat fleet. In 1936, he was appointed commander-in-chief submarines and started to train his future U-boat crews intensively. He also planned the submarine tactics that would be used in the coming war, of which the "Wolf Pack" was to be the most successful. He also endeavored to increase the numbers of U-boats in service, also seeking ways of improving their range, speed and armament.

Divided priorities
Doenitz believed that Britain was Germany's main enemy and also realized how dependent the British were on seaborne trade. If his U-boats could sink sufficient ships, Britain would be starved into surrender. However the demands Doenitz made both before and during the war for a larger share of Germany's steel production so that more U-boats could be built were opposed by the army, who wanted to establish tank and vehicle manufacture as industry's main priority. As a result, Doenitz was never supplied with the number of U-boats he demanded in order to defeat Britian, although several U-boat offensives came close to achieving this result. Those were collectively termed the battle of the Atlantic.

The battle of the Atlantic
Belatedly, Doenitz convinced Hitler that U-boats could be a war-winning weapon and the Führer authorized an expanded construction programme. The number of U-boats that could be deployed on operations correspondingly increased; between January and March 1943, merchant ship sinkings rose so dramatically that Britain's food reserves were reduced to a dangerously low level. By May, however, the situation had changed, with new counter-measures including radar and effective air patrols. One convoy fighting a running battle with 51 U-boats, sank five of the seven destroyed. Total U-boat losses for the month were 38 – 12 more than the German shipyards could build. Doenitz withdrew his U-boats from the unequal battle; between May and September 1943, not a single allied ship was lost in the North Atlantic sea-lanes through submarine attack.

On 30 January 1943, Doenitz had succeeded Raeder as overall supreme commander, but, although he now had the whole navy to administer, the U-boat arm remained his chief interest. Faced with his Atlantic defeat, he sought constantly to improve the technology available to his crews. To increase his U-boats' endurance, he introduced supply submarines, called "milch cows". He also improved underwater speed and endurance, fitting his U-boats with Snorkel breathing tubes and improved engines. As Germany was forced into unusual measures to fight the sea war, Doenitz introduced new types of naval craft – explosive torpedo boats, human torpedoes and one-man submarines. A new U-boat offensive opened at the end of 1944, to be resumed in early 1945. The U-boat arm fought until the eleventh hour; at the end of the war 398 submarines were still on active service, compared with the 98 with which Germany had entered the war. The U-boat war had cost Doenitz 781 submarines and a total of 32,000 sailors.

The last Führer
In the will he dictated before killing himself in his Berlin bunker, Hitler named Doenitz as his successor as Führer. Doenitz took over power on 1 May 1945 and immediately opened talks to end the war, though he naively supposed that, even though the Reich was collapsing around him, he could conclude a separate peace with the western

allies. This attempt at partial capitulation was rejected, but Doenitz determined to try to spin out the surrender negotiations. In Germany's eastern provinces, millions of refugees were still being evacuated by sea to safety in the west. Until the Germans signed the instrument of unconditional surrender, Doenitz's ships could sail to evacuate the refugees. The German delegates, therefore, played for time and it was not until 9 May 1945 that the war finally ended with signature of the surrender terms.

For the next few weeks, Doenitz's administration of a small enclave of German territory was tolerated, since the allies needed its help on controlling the immediate postwar refugee problem. On 23 May, however, Doenitz was arrested. Subsequently, he was tried at Nuremberg as a war criminal and sentenced to 10 years imprisonment.

Although Doenitz possessed considerable strategic gifts, some of the views he held were dangerously flawed. His belief that his U-boats could sink allied ships faster than they could be built ignored completely the known ship-building resources of Britain and the USA. His political naivety in believing that the western allies would consider signing a separate peace demonstrated an unbelievable degree of insular arrogance. However, he was a brilliant operational tactician – not the least of his assets being his ability to divorce himself mentally from the knowledge that he was sending men out to almost certain death. His cold and dispassionate nature is clearly revealed in photographs; he was a leader to be respected, rather than a commander to be loved.

DOWDING
Hugh (1882-1970)
BRITISH AIR CHIEF MARSHAL
Second World War

Solitary and introspective, Hugh Dowding on the face of it was an unlikely choice as the commander of the flamboyant young men of RAF Fighter Command in its first major battle of the Second World War in the summer of 1940. It was his insistence that stopped the British War Cabinet squandering the RAF's last modern fighters in a futile attempt to bolster up the French army; it was his persistence that won the battle of Britain and so put an end to the threat of German invasion. Yet he was removed from command after the battle, since it was claimed he had been too operationally cautious.

Born at Moffat in Dumfries on 24 April 1882; Dowding graduated from the Royal Military Academy, Woolwich, in 1900 and joined the Royal Artillery. As early as 1913, he was showing an interest in aviation; he qualified as a pilot at the Uphaven Central Flying School the same year. At the outbreak of war in 1914, Dowding was posted to a squadron, but after a month's active service, was transferred from flying duties to the staff. Another short period in command of a squadron on active service was followed by a posting back to Britain to set up the wireless

school of the Royal Flying Corps and then command of 9th (HQ) Fighter Wing during the battle of the Somme. When the Royal Flying Corps became the Royal Air Force in 1918, Dowding was promoted to the rank of brigadier and attached to RAF headquarters in the Middle East.

Promotion and advancement
The two decades between the armistice and the outbreak of the Second World War were times of promotion and advancement for Dowding. In 1929, he became Air Officer Commanding Fighter Command Air Defence of Great Britain. In those days when Fighter Command numbered fewer than 200 single-seater aircraft, the pilots all knew their commander personally and he knew each of them individually. His punctuality and efficiency were well known, his insistence upon compliance with regulations winning him the nickname of "Stuffy". He also believed in the element of surprise; frequently, a signal announcing an inspection would be received as his aircraft came in to land.

Between 1930 and 1936, Dowding served on the Air Council for Research and Development. Recognizing the threat of Hitler's Germany – and the menace of the new Luftwaffe – he insisted that the RAF be equipped with a fast, monoplane fighter aircraft, armed with eight machine guns. He also demanded bullet-proof windshields and championed the introduction of radar. In 1939, he returned to Fighter Command as Air Officer Commanding-in-Chief, with the rank of Air Vice Marshal and introduced the new battle tactics which had been developed as a result of aircraft improvements. His grasp of technical detail was phenomenal – and it needed to be, for under his aegis were not only the squadrons of Fighter Command and Anti-Aircraft Command's guns and searchlights, but also the Royal Observer Corps and the all-important chain of radar stations.

The battle of Britain
In June 1940, Dowding's strategic foresight probably saved Britain from defeat even before the Luftwaffe ventured across the Channel. He realized that France was defeated and hence resisted Churchill's demand to send still more of the RAF's precious fighter squadrons to aid the French. How right he had been was proved in the later summer. That July, the Luftwaffe began an air offensive to gain the necessary air superiority to cover a seaborne invasion and the only force which stood between the Germans and the realization of their plan was Fighter Command. Though the RAF was heavily outnumbered – both in terms of pilots and machines – Dowding did have a key advantage. Contemporary fighters had only a limited combat radius; the Germans – even though they were now flying from French airfields – could remain in battle for only a matter of minutes before having to return to their bases to refuel. This meant that the main thrust of the Luftwaffe's assault would inevitably be launched against the south-east. This key sector was the responsibility of 11 Group, commanded by Keith Park.

Dowding's strategy, therefore, was to refuse to engage the enemy over France or out to sea; the Luftwaffe was forced to come to the RAF over England. Nor did he need to maintain massive standing patrols, for his radar stations, plus the indomitable men and women of the Royal Observer Corps, could provide the RAF with an accurate picture of enemy activity in time for his pilots to get themselves airborne and into an attacking position.

At his headquarters in Bentley Priory, Dowding watched the plotting tables as the Luftwaffe sought to destroy Fighter Command. German intelligence had forecast that this would take only four days, but at the end of ten days victory had still not been achieved. German strategy, which had been aimed at luring the RAF into unequal battle, had clearly failed. Therefore, in an effort to force the British to accept combat, the Luftwaffe's high command now switched the thrust of their offensive from air-to-air engagements to attacks upon Fighter Command bases, which the RAF would have to defend. This change of plan brought them close to success, as the pilots and machines of Fighter Command were gradually worn down, pilot loss being the critical factor.

Crisis overcome

At this moment of crisis, however, the Germans suddenly switched their strategy again – a move that was to cost them the battle. In response to a bomber attack upon London, the RAF bombed Berlin and the outraged Führer ordered immediate reprisal. In the three week lull that followed while the Luftwaffe prepared its all-out blow, Fighter Command's damaged airfields were repaired and new aircraft and pilots brought in to reinforce the depleted ranks. Preparations were put in hand to meet a new German fighter onslaught, but none came, at least not in the form of a sustained major attack. Hitler, realizing that the pre-conditions for a successful invasion had not been met, canceled.

Dowding's Fighter Command, although outnumbered by more than two to one, had defeated the German offensive. It was not just the tactical reverse which the Germans considered it to be – it was a major strategic defeat that changed the course of the war. As a result of the Luftwaffe's failure, Hitler turned eastwards into the USSR, where he was to be beaten as decisively on the ground as he had been in the skies above Britain.

EISENHOWER
Dwight D (1890-1969)
US GENERAL
Second World War

Modesty, it is said, is its own reward; however, particularly in military matters, it is the flamboyant character that makes the headlines. Thus the keen military skills of the modest, quiet Eisenhower were overshadowed by the more vivid natures of several of his subordinate commanders. Eisenhower, the supreme commander of allied forces in north-west Europe from 1944 until the end of the war, has often been considered mistakenly to have been simply the chairman of a committee of military leaders. To view him only in that light ignores the fact that he was a skilled strategist, who, before D-Day, had already planned and executed the invasions of Sicily and Italy.

Dwight Eisenhower was born in Denison, Texas, on 14 October 1890, the third of seven sons of a working-class family. When he was a year old, the family returned to its original home in Kansas to rejoin a strict German Protestant sect and the young Eisenhower grew up in simple, pious and modest surroundings. He entered West Point in 1911, eventually graduating third in his class. During the First World War, the key point of his service was his involvement with tanks – first at one of the early training schools and then as commander of a training center. His post-war career saw the conventional mixture of overseas and domestic postings, but there were incidents in it to mark him out as a potential senior commander. In 1926, for instance, he passed out top of a class of nearly 300 students from the command and general staff school. Two years later, he graduated from the war college, after which he served in several staff appointments, including a spell with *MacArthur* in the Philippines during 1935.

Towards supreme command

Eisenhower's great opportunity came during the 1941 US maneuvers in Louisiana when his work as chief of staff of 3rd Army attracted the attention of General *Marshall*; given Marshall's good opinion and that of MacArthur, Eisenhower was marked out for a high field command. This came late in 1942, when he led the allied forces during the Anglo-American invasion of North Africa, both *Montgomery* and *Alexander* subsequently coming under his command. After the campaign had been successfully concluded in May 1943, Eisenhower then planned and carried out the conquest of the island of Sicily, when he found that he needed not only to control the fighting, but also the incipient rivalry between Montgomery and *Patton*. In September 1943, Eisenhower's armies invaded mainland Italy; it was shortly after the initial landings at Salerno that Eisenhower first came up against Montgomery's stubbornness in the face of his orders when 8th Army's advance was not pressed forward as quickly as Eisenhower had requested.

D-day and after

Eisenhower did not remain in Italy for long; soon, he had returned to Britain with the task of leading the allied invasion of north-west Europe. Determined to establish a good working relationship with his allies – he told his staff that anyone unable to work with the British would be shipped home in disgrace – he set up an effective supreme command, making Montgomery ground forces commander in the field. However, it was Eisenhower's decision to launch the invasion of France on 6 June 1944, which took considerable courage in the face of adverse weather conditions.

THE COMMANDER *Eisenhower's ability to work closely with his allies made him the ideal choice for supreme command.*

The broad strategy of the *Overlord* campaign had been worked out early on in the planning stages. Basically, the British and Canadian armies were given the task of drawing the bulk of the panzer divisions to their sectors, while the US forces built up their strength in preparation for a breakout. This would lead to an advance that would not only capture the port of Cherbourg – a prime allied objective – but would free Patton's army to launch a massive right hook to outflank and encircle the German 7th Army. The campaign, however, seemed to hang fire and, for a time, there were considerable recriminations between the various commanders involved; at one stage Eisenhower was urged to take over personal command of the forces in the field.

During August, the breakout finally occurred, but, as the allied armies raced across France, Eisenhower was faced once again with the conflicting demands of Patton and Montgomery, both of whom proposed a single massive thrust to the German frontier by the armies under their respective commands. Eisenhower, however, was more cautious, favoring a slower, but surer, advance on a broad front by all his armies, including the forces that by this time had been landed in southern France.

Eisenhower's plan depended on adequate supplies reaching his armies, and it was the failure of the supply system to achieve this that led to a slowing down of the advance and consequent heavy criticism of his leadership. Here, he was ill-served by Montgomery, who failed to capture Antwerp and the Scheldt estuary quickly. For lack of a major port, apart from Cherbourg, the great allied advance eventually was slowed to a crawl in the late fall of 1944.

From the Ardennes to the Alps

The gradual strangulation of the allied advance – and the formidable defensive abilities of his soldiers – gave Hitler the opportunity to turn the tables on Eisenhower, or so he thought. In the utmost secrecy, he prepared a counter-offensive in the Ardennes, which in December 1944 struck a weak sector of the US front, taking Eisenhower by surprise. However, he did not panic. He reacted swiftly to deploy his forces to seal off the enemy penetrations and then to drive the Germans back in rout. Once across the Rhine, his armies quickly moved to surround the Ruhr, the heart of German industry, and captured it in a hard-hitting campaign. The end of the war was now in sight.

It was now that Eisenhower made two surprising decisions that were to have a major impact on the post-war situation. With his armies driving eastwards, it seemed clear that *Simpson's* 9th Army, which was only 60 miles away from the German capital, was poised to capture Berlin. Instead of receiving the expected order to advance, however, Simpson was ordered to halt on the Elbe. With the backing of Marshall, Eisenhower had decided that the city was of no military significance. Instead, he turned southwards in order to seize the so-called Alpine Redoubt, a defensive complex in the mountains which his intelligence had informed him would be the scene of the last Nazi stand. The redoubt was a myth; Berlin, as the Russians realized, was the political reality. Though a fine field commander, Eisenhower had shown his political naivety.

The first five-star general in the US army since *Pershing* from December 1944, Eisenhower went on to command the armies of occupation; he then became chief of staff of the army and subsequently first commander of NATO. Entering politics, he served two terms as President of the USA. He died in March 1969.

Some great commanders project a magnetic force of personality and are adored by their men. Eisenhower was not such a general. His deeply religious background emphasized the importance of modesty and lack of outward show. For what he lacked in showmanship, however, he compensated with warmth, friendliness and optimism, though this second quality was exploited by some, who perhaps saw it as a weakness. He disliked the isolation of supreme command, for he was by nature a gregarious man, a loyal friend and a faithful ally. If his strategy was conservative, then it reflected the conservatism of his nature, which was based on clear-cut traditional values. These brought him happiness and honor.

FREYBERG
Bernard (1889-1963)
NEW ZEALAND GENERAL
Second World War

Bernard Freyberg, the commander who bore the stigma of having insisted upon the destruction of the abbey at Monte Cassino during the Italian campaign of 1944, showed by this that he cared more for the lives of his men than for the fate of a building, however ancient and venerable. He was acutely conscious that the men of the New Zealand division he commanded represented a very high proportion of the country's male population and that the death of each and every one was a terrible loss. His philosophy was that a building could always be rebuilt.

Freyberg was born in Surrey, England, on 21 March 1889, but, when he was still a young child, his family emigrated to New Zealand. He joined the New Zealand army in 1909, but returned to Britain in 1914 to serve with the Royal Naval Division during the First World War, notably in Gallipoli. It was in that campaign that he was decorated for bravery for swimming a great number of times by night to carry out reconnaissance of enemy-held beaches. When the division returned to the Western Front, Freyberg's continued bravery resulted in the award of the Victoria Cross. Before the end of the war he had risen to the rank of brigadier – at the age of 29, he was the youngest brigadier in the army. He then went on to command 29th Infantry Division.

Leading the New Zealanders

At the outbreak of the Second World War, Freyberg was given command of the New Zealand expeditionary force, which he led in the early desert campaigns. He then was put in command of the survivors of the ill-fated expedition to Greece, who were now forming the garrison of Crete. Soon after his arrival in spring 1941 – and before a proper defence could be organized – he was warned of imminent German attack, which promptly followed in May. The Germans, urged on by *Student*, had selected Crete for airborne assault.

Although Freyberg's troops outnumbered Student's paratroops, the Germans had command of the air and their dive bombers smashed the few gun positions that had been established. Protected by a Luftwaffe umbrella, the paratroops had soon established themselves and Freyburg found it impossible to expel them from the footholds they had gained. Their bridgehead around Maleme airfield was expanded and reinforced – firstly with other airborne units and then with the crack Gebirgsjaeger (Alpine) Division. By 31 May, Freyberg had been forced to evacuate the island. Of the garrison of 30,000, about half reached safety in Egypt.

From the desert to Cassino

Back again in the desert, Freyberg commanded 2nd New Zealand division with distinction; during the fighting at Mersah Matruh, where his division was cut off, he managed an able withdrawal, but during the break-out, he was badly wounded – one of the nine wounds he suffered during his career. He returned to lead his division into the battle of El Alamein, where it held a vital sector of the battle line. *Montgomery* chose Freyberg to command the final assault which broke through Rommel's last line of defence and the skill and fury of the attacks he planned forced Axis withdrawal. That retreat did not end until May 1943, when the surviving Axis forces in Africa surrendered, the crack 90th (Light) Division insisting upon surrendering to Freyberg's division.

Freyberg soon found himself in Italy, where the allied advance up the peninsula was halted by the Germans at every natural obstacle. South of Rome, the enemy high command built the so-called Gustav Line, based on two rivers – the Garigliano and the Rapido – the pivot point being the town of Cassino, lying at the foot of the mountain of that name. At Cassino the mountains run nearly into the sea, so an army holding the narrow gap between them and the coast can halt any advance.

The first of the offensives to break through the gap was mounted by the US 5th Army. Fighting lasted from 17 January to 11 February 1944, but each of the series of US attacks was bloodily repulsed. For the second battle, Freyberg's 2nd New Zealand Corps (2nd New Zealand Division and 4th Indian Division) was brought into the line. High on the topmost peak of Monte Cassino stood a Benedictine abbey, which overlooked the whole of the plain in front of the town. Convinced that the Germans were using the building as an observation post – they were not – Freyberg demanded that it be destroyed and, on 15 February, 142 B 17s dropped 253 tons of bombs on it, followed up by a second wave of 82 aircraft. The abbey was badly damaged, but not destroyed. Since the allies had been the first to violate the venerable building, the Germans now moved into the ruins.

It is easy to be wise after the event. The bombing of the abbey and town of Cassino neither denied observation positions to the Germans, nor did it destroy the defenders. Neither did the other raids which carpeted the town with bombs or the ground offensives launched under Freyberg's direction throughout the following weeks. In fact, the air raids had an opposite effect to the one intended, for they provided the German paratroops holding the position with a vast desert of rubble favoring the defence and impassable to allied tanks. The Germans held out in the ruins until May 1944 when the final offensive smashed its way into the gap and both the town and the abbey were captured.

There was a peculiarity in Freyberg's position, which was found in other Dominion forces. He was directly responsible to his own government for the New Zealand forces – not to the British government nor to the British army. Aware of the responsibility he carried for the lives of his men, Freyberg was determined to see that they were not wasted in useless attacks. He insisted that his soldiers be well fed and equipped, a demand that no British commander at his level could make. Freyberg's men respected him for the care he showed for their welfare. Personally brave, he led a division of men whose bravery was legendary – they were all trying to "out-Freyberg Freyberg". At his level of command, he had no opportunity to show any latent gifts of strategy he may have possessed, but he was an accomplished tactician.

GRAZIANI
Rodolfo (1882-1955)
MARSHAL OF ITALY
Second World War

Rodolfo Graziani, a future Marshal of Italy and one of the leading Italian commanders of the Second World War, was born on 11 August 1882 in Filettino and entered the army in 1908. He served throughout the First World War in front-line units; it was widely understood in Italy that his abrasive manner and the ruthlessness he displayed was directly attributable to his experience as a combat soldier.

After a period spent in staff duties and on home service, Graziani was posted to Africa, where he took command of the Somali corps in 1935. The following year, he was created Viceroy and commander-in-chief in Ethiopia, leading the Italian expeditionary force in its conquest of the kingdom; by October 1939, he had become chief of the army general staff. As such, he was well aware of Italy's unpreparedness for war and therefore opposed Mussolini's decision to declare war in June 1940. Nevertheless, Mussolini appointed him commander-in-chief in Africa and governor of Libya.

The Libyan fiasco
Mussolini had convinced himself that, with the fall of France, Britain would soon capitulate and that all he needed to secure booty for Italy at the eventual peace conference was "a few thousand dead" to show that Italy had fought. Accordingly, convinced that the campaign would be an easy one, he ordered Graziani to advance and conquer Egypt. Graziani, however, did not share his Duce's belief in Britain's weakness; instead, he proposed that his army should be built up and that such an offensive should be undertaken no earlier than the spring of 1941. Though he delayed for as long as he could, Mussolini eventually issued a formal edict – advance or resign. Graziani's 10th Army, a force of some 300,000 men, was to attack during September.

The Italian advance guard accordingly left the frontier post of Fort Capuzzo on 13 September, with the main body following. The Italians captured the small town of Sidi Barrani the following day, but at the end of seven days, they had advanced only 60 miles into Egypt. Graziani then halted the advance and his engineers constructed a fan of seven fortified camps in which the Italians took up position. There they remained inactive for a further three months. During that time, emboldened by the absence of British response, Graziani believed that

he could go on and conquer Egypt without German assistance. The 3rd Panzer Division, which had been selected for African service, was stood down, but the period of Italian euphoria was brief.

Delighted by this Italian inaction, the British commander-in-chief, Archibald *Wavell*, prepared a counterblow. Against the 10th Army, he could pit only two divisions – the 7th Armored and 4th Indian – totaling 30,000 men with General O'Connor in field command. Despite this numerical inferiority, the British struck at Graziani's army on 9 December 1940.

Very soon an offensive that had been planned as a limited five-day operation to drive the Italians back to the frontier wire had generated such momentum that the Italian 10th Army had virtually disintegrated, with thousands of its soldiers taken prisoner. Wavell's force had all but destroyed the Fascist position in North Africa. Only the prompt despatch of a German relief force – the Afrika Korps – and Churchill's decision to divert troops to Greece saved the Italians from total defeat.

Defending Mussolini
The Italian humiliation caused Mussolini to relieve Graziani of his command; he was replaced by General Gariboldi. The disgraced Graziani was flown back to Italy, where a court of enquiry found him guilty of dereliction of duty. He remained unemployed until the Allied invasion of Italy in the fall of 1943 and the rescue of the fallen Mussolini by the Germans. Graziani accompanied the Duce when he later fled northwards to found a Fascist republic, saying that he had sworn an oath of loyalty to Mussolini and to the alliance with Germany. In recognition of that loyalty, he was appointed Minister of Defence in Mussolini's rump government. In August 1944, after the allied invasion of southern France, Graziani was given command of the Ligurian Army and defended the Franco-Italian frontier against the French.

In the last weeks of the war, Mussolini sought to escape from Italy and Graziani escorted his leader as far as Lake Como. Assuming that the Duce would cross without delay into Switzerland, Graziani returned to the soldiers of his Ligurian Army and on 29 April surrendered.

A civil tribunal found Graziani guilty of crimes against the people and sentenced him to 19 years imprisonment. However, he served only three months of his sentence before being released on medical grounds. He died on 11 January 1955.

GUDERIAN
Heinz (1888-1954)
GERMAN COLONEL-GENERAL
Second World War

Heinz Guderian is renowned as the founding father of panzer warfare. During the 1930s, notably in his book *Achtung Panzer*, he developed the revolutionary tactics of the blitzkrieg, which Hitler's armies were to put into practice with stunning effect in the opening campaigns of the Second World War. In those campaigns Guderian played a key part.

Guderian, born on 17 June 1888, the son of a Pomeranian infantry officer, was commissioned during 1907. In 1915, while serving on the staff, he became interested in battlefield mobility; in the post-war Reichswehr, he became a fervent advocate of the potential of the tank. Chief among the small group of German officers who advocated the employment of armor in mass, rather as an adjunct to infantry operations, Guderian put forward the theory of an armored battle technique that formed the basis of the blitzkrieg. Work in the Reichswehr Ministry as Inspector of Lorried Troops allowed Guderian to develop his ideas and, by 1936, he was commanding 2nd Panzer Division. Within two years he was not only a corps commander but had also been named as Commander of Mobile Troops. The Polish campaign of 1939 and the war in France during 1940, allowed him to demonstrate in a practical way, that his theories were sound. The war with Russia, in which Guderian commanded Panzergruppe 2, the equivalent of a Field Army, gave him the chance to prove the correctness of the blitzkrieg principle at a strategic level. This he ably demonstrated in the battle for *Kiev*, in which the German panzers successfully encircled a mass of Soviet armies. Of the million Soviet soldiers who fought in the battle, more than 665,000 were captured. Nearly 1,000 tanks had been destroyed and over 3,000 guns taken.

The Kiev encirclement showed that certain of Guderian's theories of lightning war worked. It was essential to direct the battle from the front, not from a headquarters far removed from the action. The use of sophisticated communications techniques, allowing for great flexibility in command was another Guderian innovation. Liaison between his panzers and the air force was tight and effective. But, though blitzkrieg could work, it could do so only if the pre-requisite of aerial superiority had been accomplished. In the Kiev operation, Guderian took risks, particularly in allowing his armor to outrun its supplies, and these would have been disastrous against a more flexibly-minded enemy, or one which enjoyed command of the air.

Guderian's well-known bluntness and short temper led Hitler to relieve him of his command on more than one occasion. He was first dismissed in December 1941, but was recalled in 1943 to become inspector general of panzers. In 1944, he was made chief of the army general staff, but, the following March, a final quarrel with the Führer led to him being sent on indefinite sick leave. At the end of the war, he surrendered to the US forces.

"HURRYING HEINZ"
Guderian was the true pioneer of panzer warfare.

HARRIS
Arthur T (1892-1984)
BRITISH AIR CHIEF MARSHAL
Second World War

Arthur Harris is probably one of the most controversial commanders of the Second World War; indeed, controversy about his role and achievements started almost as soon as the war had ended. With victory, all the most senior British military and naval commanders were ennobled, but Harris, the commander-in-chief of Bomber Command for the key period of the war, received only a knighthood. The reasons for this apparent snub have never been fully revealed, but it may well have been that influential people in Britain considered his policy of all-out bombing to have been immoral – once the war had been won. For his part, Harris passionately believed that wars could be won quickly by shattering the morale of the enemy's home-front and that air power was the most effective way of achieving this.

Harris was born in Cheltenham in 1892, emigrating to Rhodesia as a young man to work as a tobacco planter. On the outbreak of the First World War, he joined the 1st Southern Rhodesian regiment and took part in the campaign in German South-West Africa. When the fighting there was over, he returned to Britain, where he joined the Royal Flying Corps, becoming a pilot in 1916. His obvious powers of leadership brought him command of bomber squadrons, as well as of night-fighter units operating against the Zeppelin airships bombing London.

Taking over Bomber Command

Post-war service in the empire followed, during which Harris developed the policy of what became known as "air control" – using RAF bombers against rebel tribesmen in Iraq. He rose to the rank of Air Vice Marshal and to the command of 5 Bomber Group. As deputy chief of the air staff, he headed a purchasing mission to the USA; in 1942, he finally took over the leadership of Bomber Command from Sir Richard Pearse.

At this time, Bomber Command was a confused, badly led force. There was no clear philosophy of what it should do or achieve – it was far from being the war-winning weapon it had been predicted that it would be in pre-war days. This Harris was determined to change. His first task was to infuse his command with his own single-minded determination to bomb Germany into submission. He believed that his men should not be asked to risk their lives on pointless raids and all the missions they flew must have the firm purpose of destroying the enemy. He also believed – and in this would accept no counter-argument – that Bomber Command must be in control of its own operations. The cabinet might suggest a target – but he and his staff would decide whether or not it should be attacked. Nor would he allow his bombers to be subordinated to the other services. Airmen alone, he argued, knew their capabilities and those of their aircraft.

Within three months of taking up his post, Harris captured the headlines with the launch of the first-ever 1,000-bomber raid on Cologne, for which even his training squadrons were pressed into service. The campaign to smash German industry now got underway, a list of priority targets being raided by "boxes" of US bombers by day and RAF bomber "streams" at night. As a result of his own night-flying missions and his command of bomber squadrons during the First World War, Harris had long been aware of the problems a heavy bomber faced at night locating a small target. Accordingly, he pressed for the fitting of advanced navigational aids, including radar, into his bombers, arguing that this was imperative if a strategic bombing offensive was to be launched successfully. Such measures improved the accuracy of his aircrews. Tactically, he developed the art of timing the arrival of the main bomber stream effectively to achieve the greatest possible concentration of aircraft over the target to overwhelm the enemy defences.

Harris was a great believer in training and it was his excellent training methods that produced the first-rate young commanders that were needed to lead the new Bomber Command he had created. In pursuit of greater accuracy, he formed crack "Pathfinder" squadrons to locate and mark the targets for the main bombing stream. Aware, also, of the need for pin-point bombing, Harris formed 617 Squadron from a group of Bomber Command's most experienced crews; their missions included the successful destruction of the Ruhr dams, the Bielefeld viaduct, and the U-boat pens on the French coast. The same squadron also sank the *Tirpitz*, Hitler's last battleship, at anchor.

Bomber or butcher?

By 1943, Bomber Command had become a formidable destructive machine; now, Harris believed, entire cities could be destroyed, so leading to the collapse of the German war effort and of civilian morale. That summer, he ordered the saturation bombing of Hamburg to see whether a man-made "fire-storm" could be created. The results proved that the theory was practical. Incendiary bombs, dropped en masse, created a ring of fire, which expanded inwards to create a hurricane-force wind as oxygen was sucked in to feed the flames. Harris went on to use the same technique against other German cities. His intention was to "bomb Germany so persistently and so severely that her power to make war will be crippled. We will bomb her for all the world – especially Italy and Japan – to see and to ponder."

However, opposition to Harris' blind faith in bombing was growing – on practical, as well as on ethical, grounds. German civilian morale did not collapse; indeed, with the relocation of vital war industry and the determination of the work force, German war production, as was shown after the war, was increasing, not diminishing. Rather than being the finely-tuned weapon of Harris' dreams, Bomber Command was a bludgeon, rather than a rapier, suited to the mass bombing of cities, but to little else. Losses to the German defence were also increasing.

CONTROVERSIAL COMMANDER *Harris caused considerable controversy with his all-out blanket bombing strategy.*

Harris stubbornly refused to change his tactics. In 1944, he launched his biggest campaign yet – against Berlin. For the cost of 600 to 700 aircraft (and given US assistance), he would "wreck the city from end to end" and "win the war." But the Reich's capital proved too tough a nut for Harris and his bombers to crack and he was forced to abandon the offensive. Another source of criticism was his refusal to attack what he termed "panacea targets," such as the oil industry. He also resisted the switching of his bombers to a tactical role as part of the preparations for D-Day; though he was overruled, he resumed the strategic offensive as soon as he could.

It was Harris' bombing of Dresden on 14/15 February 1945, however, that produced the greatest controversy – it is thought by many not only to have cost him his peerage, but his aircrews a campaign medal. The fire storms his bombers raised destroyed practically the whole city and led to 100,000 civilian casualties. Harris, who believed that no German city was "worth the bones of a single British grenadier", simply stated that Dresden was a justified military target – indeed, the Soviet army had asked for it to be bombed to slow the flow of German units through it.

Whether Harris was a great commander or not will always be a matter of controversy. He had no such doubts. The ethical question did not concern him; he was content to be judged by results. Subsequent historical analysis suggests that his single-mindedness was wrongly directed, but equally it can be argued that he was the man for the job as it was conceived at the time.

HEINRICI
Gotthard (1886-1971)
GERMAN GENERAL
Second World War

Gotthard Heinrici was one of the German army's most distinguished panzer leaders and certainly its finest exponent of defensive warfare. The tall, blunt East Prussian was also the commander who decided that Berlin was indefensible in 1945 and consequently was dismissed for "sabotage of the Führer's orders."

Heinrici was born in Gumbinnen on Christmas Day 1886, and was gazetted in August 1906 as a cavalry lieutenant. During the First World War, he alternated between front line service and staff postings; by 1933, he had reached the rank of colonel. Hitler's reintroduction of conscription and the consequent expansion of the Wehrmacht gave added impetus to Heinrici's career and by September 1941 he was commanding 43rd Corps. In January 1943, having reached the rank of Colonel General, he was leading 4th Army. His appointment as commander of 1st Panzer Army was announced on 15 August 1944; towards the end of the war, in March 1945, he was placed in charge of Army Group Vistula.

Master of the defensive

Heinrici thus spent most of the war on the Eastern Front. Although he demonstrated skill in attack – particularly in the advance on Moscow – he soon became recognized as the Wehrmacht's leading specialist in defence, starting with that first winter in Russia. He dealt with crisis after crisis throughout the war, but faced his greatest challenge during the final Soviet offensives.

At the end of March 1945, *Zhukov's* 1st Bylo-russian and *Koniev's* 1st Ukrainian fronts were positioned along the line of the River Oder – the last great natural obstacle to the east of Berlin. The Soviets had come to the end of a long, hard-fought offensive, which had started from central Poland, and both commanders hoped that they might be able to rest and regroup their forces before launching the final battle for Berlin. Their men were tired, their vehicles needed servicing and they had outrun their supplies. However, they were given scant time to rest, since Stalin was determined that his armies should be first into the Nazi capital. Accordingly, Zhukov, who was nearer the city, was ordered to attack it directly, while Koniev was ordered to swing around it to the south.

The battle for Berlin

During the early hours of 16 April, more than 22,000 guns on Zhukov's front fired the opening barrage and the Soviet infantry then launched their mass attacks. Heinrici, who had been in command of Army Group Vistula for just a matter of weeks, had only 30 divisions under command – and many of these were divisions in name only – but he had already made defensive preparations to minimize the effect of the Soviet blows. He realized, however, that he had no hope of defeating so heavy an assault. The best that he and his understrength formations could do was to slow down the Soviet advance.

The heaviest concentration of shell-fire fired on that first day of battle fell on the divisions of 9th Army blocking the direct route to Berlin. Here, Heinrici took advantage of the Soviet command's rigid insistence upon following time tables and working to routine. A Soviet deserter had revealed when the Soviet artillery barrage would start and had also said that it would be concentrated against the dominant Seelow Heights. Heinrici accordingly put into action a tactic that had served him well in the USSR; he ordered the forward trenches to be evacuated, so that the barrage fell into thin air. When the barrage lifted, the German grenadiers hastily re-occupied their positions, ready to give an unpleasant surprise to the advancing infantry, who expected to meet only minimal resistance from the pulverized defenders.

The spirited German defence of the Seelow heights halted the Soviet advance totally, for, until the high ground had been captured, no general forward movement was possible. Even when Zhukov's forces, after suicidal frontal assaults, finally managed to seize the heights on 17 April, he came up against further German units, which Heinrici had placed on the Berlin road to bar the way forward. Furious at Zhukov's delay, Stalin accordingly ordered Koniev to swing his armies into action to attack Berlin from the south.

So far, Heinrici had done better than anyone had the reasonable right to expect – but he was now up against another enemy. This was his own Führer. Totally out of touch with reality, Hitler was feverishly planning a counteroffensive to save his capital. The 9th Army to the south, 12th Army to the west and Army Group Steiner to the north were to disengage themselves and strike simultaneously to annihilate the thrusting Soviet columns.

Heinrici realized that the orders he accordingly received from OKW were impossible to execute. The 12th Army, locked in fighting US forces on the Elbe, was expected to disengage itself to change front and advance towards Berlin. The 9th Army, battling with its back to Berlin, was similarly expected to swing around to move westwards to link with 12th Army. Steiner's army group, taking its name from SS general Steiner, existed in name only and had no hope of cutting off the armored pincer of *Rokossovsky*'s armies in north Germany.

Berlin, therefore, could not be saved by the forces deployed around it. The sensible course of action, as Heinrici saw it, was for him to form a front in Mecklenburg and to conduct a fighting retreat so as to stop the meeting of the British and Russian armies in the Baltic area for as long as possible. He, of course, was aware that the Kriegsmarine was making an all-out effort to evacuate cut-off civilians and troops from eastern Germany to safety in the west. The longer he could keep the allies out of the harbors along the western Baltic and in Schleswig-Holstein, the more Germans could be evacuated to safety. He, therefore, ignored his wireless orders to attack.

"A traitor to the Reich"

On 28 April, however, while the fighting in Berlin was at its height, Keitel, head of Hitler's OKW, managed to make his way to Heinrici's headquarters, hoping to revive the flagging assaults which Hitler had ordered to relieve the besieged capital. On learning that Heinrici was pulling back, Keitel threatened to charge him with sabotage. His threats were reinforced by Colonel General Jodl in a telephone conversation that evening, who bluntly told Heinrici either to obey the Führer's orders or take the consequences, which would include reprisals against his family. Heinrici refused point blank to carry out the suicidal frontal operation and the Reich's last great soldier was immediately relieved of his command.

Although Hitler had destroyed much of the old Prussian staff systems, he could not eradicate the long-established tradition that a commander has the duty to question orders that run contrary to the military situation as he judges it. Heinrici was one of the few who dared to challenge the Führer's orders. He was an honest, upright man, who, even with his family under threat, could not be deflected from what he saw as his primary duty – to rescue as many of his fellow countrymen as possible from the wreckage of the Reich.

HOTH
Hermann (1885-1971)
GERMAN COLONEL-GENERAL
Second World War

Hermann Hoth emerged as one of Germany's leading tank commanders in the east during the Second World War largely through the leadership of the 4th Panzer Army. From the time that Hoth took command during April 1942, until he relinquished the post during Novem-

ber 1943, he and his troops fought in the most important battles on the Eastern Front.

Hoth was born in 1885 in Neuruppin, the son of a prosperous businessman. He entered the army as a cadet in 1904, and was gazetted into the 72nd Infantry regiment a year later. He was soon posted to the supreme command, where he worked for Colonel Nicolai, head of the imperial military secret service. He then served in various staff appointments during the First World War.

In November 1938, Hoth became commander of 15th Corps, which he led during the Polish campaign and in France. For Operation *Barbarossa*, he was given command of Panzergruppe 3, which formed part of Army Group Centre. His skilful strategic thinking and clever tactical handling of a potentially dangerous situation enabled 4th Panzer Army – at that time commanded by von Kluge – to cross the Duna river and advance towards Moscow, the Soviet capital.

When the thrust towards Moscow was halted – temporarily by Hitler's order and them by inclement weather – Hoth was sent first to command the 17th Army in Army Group South; he then took over the 4th Panzer Army at the end of the Soviet winter offensive. His new army was to act as the spearhead of Army Group South during the 1942 German summer offensive.

Drive towards Stalingrad

Hoth's first move was to pincer out the Issyum-Kharkov pocket. When the offensive proper was launched, Voronezh quickly fell to his 48th Panzer Corps on 6 July and a subsequent thrust down the Don towards Rososh put Hoth into a position from which he could threaten the Russian rear areas. By 21 July, with the mass of his Panzer army now south of the Don, Hoth turned north-eastwards and struck towards Stalingrad. By 2 September, his units – a panzer corps, an infantry corps and Romanian formations – had reached the western outskirts of the city. The speed of Hoth's advance forced Stavka (the Soviet high command) to transfer troops from the sector on which the 6th German Army, under von Paulus, was fighting, thus relieving the pressure on that formation.

Stalingrad's importance in the battle plans of both the German and Soviet armies lay not so much in its economic or strategic value than in its morale value. Hitler was determined to take the city because it bore Stalin's name; Stalin was equally determined not to lose prestige by allowing it to be captured.

The battle for Stalin's city

Hoth studied his intelligence reports and conferred with his panzer commanders. It was clear that the cornerstone of the Soviet defensive ring was the high ground at Tundotovo. The well-prepared Soviet positions there could not be taken by frontal assault, since this would result in unacceptably heavy infantry losses. Nor was it a suitable objective for Hoth's armor. An alternative plan had to be found in order to keep up the pressure.

Hoth regrouped his units, withdrawing his panzer and motorized divisions from the front line and replacing them with infantry formations. He then concentrated his armor to attack as a single force, striking northwards into the flank of the Soviet 64th Army. Hoth's intention was to outflank the Soviet positions on the lower heights of Beketovka and Krasnolsarmeisk and then swing his attack to take the high ground to the south of Stalingrad.

On 30 August, Hoth's panzer and motorized formations broke through the Soviet defensive system at Gavrilovka. By the close of the following day, the 24th Division had penetrated deep into the Russian defences and had cut the rail link between Stalingrad and Karpovka. Thus one pincer arm around the Soviet forces to the south and west of the city was on the point of creation. An advance southwards by Paulus' 6th Army would create the second pincer arm, with the result that the Soviet formations outside the city would be crushed between its two jaws. An advance into the heart of Stalingrad would follow. However, von Paulus lacked Hoth's flexibility; by not moving quickly enough, he allowed the Russian forces to escape from the trap.

Nevertheless, an advance towards and into Stalingrad began; by 14 September, Hoth's troops had captured the city's southern sector. The battle then was intensified, as Stalin committed more and more troops to Stalingrad's defence and, on 19 November, the Soviets moved into the counter-offensive. Hoth's 4th Corps, which had been holding his army's northern flank, was cut off and pushed back towards the city. Hoth ordered the 29th Motorized Infantry Division into action and stemmed the advance of Soviet 57th Army, which had broken through to the south, but now the sector of the front held by 6th Romanian Corps was pierced by the Soviet 51st Army. Hoth's immediate response was to plan a strike at the Russian flank, but Army Group South ordered him instead to set up a defensive front in order to protect 6th Army's flank.

Failure at Stalingrad

On 24 November, Hitler intervened. He ordered the encircled troops to hold out at all costs, promising that they would be supplied from the air until they could be relieved. Paulus and his army prepared for a siege. For its part, Hoth's force, which had suffered heavily in the first Stalingrad battles, was now reconstructed, so that it could undertake the vital mission of breaking the Soviet ring and relieving 6th Army. The two German armies were only 60 miles apart and, by 19 December, seven days after he had opened his attack, Hoth's spearheads had covered 20 of them. To succeed in its mission, his army needed support, but Hitler stubbornly refused to allow 6th Army to break out towards Hoth – nor would he transfer troops from the Caucasus to support Hoth's offensive. The 4th Panzer Army would have to force a break in to raise the siege unaided.

At this point, a further disaster struck the crumbling German front, when a new Soviet offensive broke through the Italian 8th Army in the middle of December. To launch a counter-strike against the attacking Soviet divisions, 26th Panzer was hastily transferred from Hoth's command – a decision that put an end to any chance of

rescuing von Paulus's army. Hoth was forced to pull back 57th Panzer Corps, which had spearheaded his advance, in order to hold back the Soviet armies now striking westwards. By skilful tactical handling, he thwarted Stavka's attempts to outflank Army Group South and also prevented the destruction of the German armies on the Upper Don.

In March 1943, when the Russian winter offensive came to an end, the Germans prepared a counter-blow. This was Operation *Citadel*, launched at Kursk in July 1943. Hoth's 4th Panzer Army bore the brunt of the ambitious pincer operation Hitler had planned, becoming involved in the greatest tank battle in history. His forces, battering their way slowly northwards through the Soviet defences, met Rotmistrov's 5th Guards Tank Army in a head-on clash of armor. More than 1,000 armored vehicles took part in the resulting battle and casualties were heavy on both sides. Despite the losses which he had suffered – losses that could not be made good – Hoth was still prepared to continue, but Hitler now canceled the operation. The Germans had finally lost the strategic initiative in the east, which remained in Soviet hands for the remainder of the war.

Kursk was Hoth's last major battle. He retired from active service during November 1943, though he was briefly recalled during April 1945 to command the Hartz Mountain defence area.

JEREMENKO
Andrei I (1892-1970)
SOVIET GENERAL
Second World War

The time-table for Operation *Barbarossa* – the code name given to the Nazi invasion of the USSR – depended for its success upon the German armed forces beating the Soviet army in the field before the rainy season put an end to military operations. That the Germans failed to keep to their time-table was due, in the opinion of a great number of soldiers and historians, to one particular Soviet commander, Andrei Jeremenko. The skilled defensive battles he fought around Smolensk in the first weeks of the German invasion, critically delayed the German advance upon Moscow, allowing time for reinforcements to be brought up and defences prepared.

Jeremenko was born in October 1892, in a village near Kharkov, the son of a Ukrainian peasant. Conscripted into the army during the First World War, he was promoted to the rank of corporal for bravery. During the civil war he successively led a partisan unit and a Soviet cavalry reconnaissance unit before becoming chief of staff in a cavalry regiment and, finally, a regiment's second-incommand. He fought successfully against the White Russians under Denikin and Wrangel and then served in the invasion the USSR launched against Poland, which was defeated outside Warsaw.

Stemming the German advance

By 1939 Jeremenko was a corps commander; in 1940, he was in command of an army in the Far East. Immediately after the German attack on 22 June 1941, Stalin ordered him to fly back to Moscow and a week later he was given command of West Front. The situation Jeremenko found when he arrived at his battle headquarters was disastrous. The force and weight of the German invasions had fragmented the front and the Soviet units now under his command were fighting without central direction from main headquarters. Serious though he had assumed the situation to be, Jeremenko was shocked to learn just how little control he could exert over his front-line forces. The first discussion he held with his staff showed that West Front was on the brink of collapse.

Jeremenko decided that, if he could not direct his front-line units adequately, he would bring forward crack troops from the rear to form a strong second line. Until these arrived, the embattled Soviet forces must make the most strenuous efforts to form a cohesive front. Using draconian threats, Jeremenko forced the Soviet air force in his sector to put every available machine into the air to attack the advancing columns of *Guderian's* and *Hoth's* panzer armies. Then, while the German columns were recovering from the air assaults, he thrust forward an élite tank group, equipped with T 34s and KVs. The appearance of these new types of tank on the battlefield threw the Germans into disarray, as they found that their anti-tank guns could not penetrate the tanks' armor.

A victim of success

Jeremenko had successfully carried out the orders of his superior, Marshal *Timoshenko*, to halt the Germans, but his reward was to be superseded by him. He became Timoshenko's deputy. Shortly afterwards, a panic spread through the Soviet army, as the German advance still continued to roll forward. Waves of courts martial and summary execution marked Stalin's efforts to force his forces to stem the German tide. Despite his success in re-forming the shattered front and delaying the German thrusts in his sector, Jeremenko was nevertheless under suspicion, because he had not totally succeeded.

By October, it was clear that the Germans had finally decided to strike for Moscow and Jeremenko was given the task of holding the Briansk sector of the front against them. During the mid-October battles there, he was badly wounded in an enemy air attack and spent two months in hospital. On his return to active service, he took part in the bitter fighting at the western approaches to Moscow, leading the 4th Assault Army. A year later, as part of *Zhukov's* key team of generals, he was fighting at Stalingrad and then in the Russian summer campaign of 1943. In May 1945, his troops liberated Prague.

The tall and powerfully-built Jeremenko, like the other senior officers whom Zhukov grouped around him, was overshadowed by the latter's abilities. Thus, Jeremenko had little opportunity to display his strategic gifts; however, at Smolensk, Moscow and Stalingrad, he was able to show his outstanding tactical skills.

KEMPF
Werner (1886-1964)
GERMAN GENERAL
Second World War

The name of Werner Kempf, one of the most successful panzer commanders of the Second World War, is not as familiar as those of *Rommel, Hoth* or von Kleist. However, his ability as a great commander is unquestioned.

Born in 1886 in East Prussia, Kempf first joined the 149th Infantry Regiment but was then transferred to the marines, with whom he served in Flanders before being given a staff appointment. In the post-war Reichswehr, he was posted to No 1 Motorized battalion and then to the staff of the Inspectorate of Mobile Troops. There he studied and developed theories of armored warfare, particularly the concept that the tank was not an infantry auxiliary, but a weapon in its own right.

For the war against Poland, Kempf, now a major-general, was given command of an ad hoc division. He led this with such success that he was promoted to 48th Panzer Corps, which he directed throughout the opening stages of Operation *Barbarossa*. Concentrating his corps into a single powerful fist, he smashed through the Stalin Line and then launched his panzer formations in a series of lightning strikes that soon flung a pincer to the north of Uman and then on to Novo Archangelsk. Three Soviet armies were trapped inside the Uman pocket, but this was by no means the greatest victory of fall 1941 in which 48th Corps played a major part.

The Kiev encirclement

The largest of those encirclements was that of *Kiev*; here the part Kempf played was vital to the success of von Kleist's Panzergruppe 1, which formed the southern arm of the pincer. By 10 September Kempf's corps had reached Kremechug on the Dnieper river. Immediately he put all his engineer units to work and within a day the Dnieper had been bridged.

Kempf himself led the break out from the Kremechug bridgehead, driving northwards to the Sula river. The bridge across the Sula, vital to the Panzergruppe's advance, was captured intact and the drive carried on to Lubny. On 14 September, units of Kempf's corps met the spearheads of *Guderian's* Panzergruppe, which had been striking southwards. In the operation, the three panzer divisions of Kempf's 48th Corps captured more than 109,000 of the 650,000 Soviet troops taken prisoner.

Fall from favor

On 15 February 1943, Kempf formed Army Detachment Kempf – another ad hoc panzer grouping – his task being to deal with the dangerous situation that had developed around Kharkov, which was threatened by the last Soviet attacks of their winter offensive. Then, with that clearing-up operation successfully completed, Kempf was positioned on the right flank of 4th Panzer Army in preparation for the summer offensive, the German intention being to pinch out the huge salient centered on Kursk the Soviet army had carved out in its winter battles. The role of 4th Panzer Army was to drive northwards towards Kursk, where it would meet *Model*'s 9th Army striking southwards, so completing the encirclement. Kempf crossed the Donets river against the opposition of 7th Guards Army and established bridgeheads on the eastern bank. He then ordered his 2nd Panzer Corps to fan out and swing northwards, a move intended to reduce Soviet pressure on 4th Panzer Army's right flank. The offensive, however did not succeed and when Hitler broke it off, the military initiative passed to the Soviets.

During August 1943, Kempf's Army Detachment, now renamed 8th Army, was ordered into action to halt the advance of Vatutin's Voronezh Front towards Kharkov. Kempf, however, decided to withdraw from the city and save his army – a decision that Hitler condemned as disloyal and cowardly. The outraged Führer relieved Kempf of his command and he remained on the sidelines for the rest of the war.

KESSELRING
Albert (1885-1960)
GERMAN FIELD MARSHAL
Second World War

"Smiling Albert", as Kesselring was nicknamed by his troops, was one of Nazi Germany's leading commanders. He was the only senior German soldier to start and finish the Second World War in a top command position; he was also unique in starting the war as a Luftwaffe commander and ending it in charge of a major part of the Reich's ground forces.

Kesselring, the son of a professor, was born in Lower Franconia on 20 November 1885. He was gazetted into the 2nd Bavarian Foot Artillery Regiment as a *fahrenjunker* (volunteer officer cadet) in 1904 and became a lieutenant of artillery in 1906. He swiftly showed promise; by 1913, he had become regimental adjutant to the 1st Bavarian Foot Artillery. During the First World War, he proved himself a first-rate staff artillery officer and, in 1918, was seconded to the general staff. He stayed in the Reichswehr after the war, becoming a major in 1925.

Architect of the Luftwaffe
Kesselring was the protegé of Hans von Seeckt, chief of the *Truppenamt* (the post-war command organization), who gave him a series of wide-ranging responsibilities. He encouraged Kesselring's interest in the potential of air power and, as a consequence, Kesselring played a leading part in the training and organization of the clandestine air arm that was to emerge as the Luftwaffe in 1935. Kesselring then transferred to the air force as chief of administration and state secretary in the Air Ministry; the following year, he became the Luftwaffe's chief of staff.

Becoming involved in the controversy between the advocates of a strategic or a tactical air arm, he chose the tactical side; the quarrels this led to in Luftwaffe supreme command led to his posting away from Berlin to the command of Luftkreis III (this became Luftflotte I in 1939).

Poland, France and Britain
During the 1939 Polish campaign, Kesselring's Luftflotte I saw action for the first time, Kesselring himself flying with his forces. This was a habit he maintained – he was shot shot down five times during his career. In 1940, he took command of Luftflotte II for the attack in the west. Here, Kesselring's early career as a soldier was reflected in his tactics. The Luftwaffe's role, as he saw it, was not to fight its own independent battle; he used his aircraft tactically to give support to the ground troops.

In the Battle of Britain, however, Kesselring made a tactical blunder that, in the opinion of many experts, cost the Luftwaffe the campaign. He agreed with Hitler and Goering's decision to change target priorities from RAF airfields to the bombing of London. Kesselring believed that daylight attacks on London would force the RAF into a fight to the finish, but, in fact, his previous tactics were inflicting far more damage on Fighter Command. Transferred to the east with his Luftflotte for the Russian campaign, he again proved his tactical mastery in the opening stages of Operation *Barbarossa*, with well-

"SMILING ALBERT" *Kesselring was recognized universally as one of the most gifted German commanders of the war.*

planned sorties against the Soviet air force – much of which was destroyed on the ground – and close support of German ground operations.

Command in the Mediterranean

In the winter of 1941, however, Kesselring was posted to Italy to provide much-needed support for the flagging Italian war effort in the Mediterranean. The idea had been for Kesselring to combine command of Luftflotte II with that of the entire southern theater of war, but, in practice, he found himself restricted by the jealousies of the Italians and Rommel's determination to preserve his independence of action. It took all Kesselring's considerable diplomatic skills to establish a modus vivendi between the conflicting views and priorities of the Italian and Rommel – not to mention the demands made by Hitler from Berlin.

In October 1942, however, with the collapse of the Axis forces in the Western Desert, Kesselring was finally given the chance to effectively exercise his powers as commander-in-chief south. Now the only German commander to control units of all three fighting services, he was soon to show his mastery of the defensive battle.

Back to soldiering

In the face of allied invasion in 1943, Kesselring convinced Hitler that it was essential to defend Italy south of Rome. This decision condemned the allied armies to a slow, bitter battle up the length of the Italian peninsula, which Kesselring made harder by turning every river and mountain range into a major barrier. His brilliant defensive tactics at Cassino delayed the allied advance for nearly six months, while his ability to react to a crisis enabled him to hold the allied landings at Anzio in check, even though these had taken him completely by surprise. The allied troops soon recognized Kesselring's worth; however, allied politicians gave him little credit for his determined defence. They attributed the slow advance of their armies to the failings of their own commanders, rather than his tactical determination.

Kesselring in defeat

Towards the end of 1944, Kesselring initiated secret negotiations with Allan Dulles, head of the US OSS in Switzerland and the Archbishop of Milan, seeking to end the war in Italy. Kesselring, however, was not prepared for peace at any price; he remained loyal to Hitler and had not supported the July 1944 bomb plot against the Führer. He realized the war was lost and wanted to end it while Germany was in as strong a position as possible. He certainly did not stop fighting. Transferred to the west to take supreme command of the faltering German forces there in April 1945, he fought on until the Reich's capitulation. He then surrendered to the US Army.

Events in the Italian campaign – notably an SS massacre of civilian hostages as reprisal for a partisan bomb attack in spring 1944 – led to Kesselring's trial on war crimes charges in 1947. He took complete responsibility for the actions of his subordinates and was condemned to

death by a military court. Subsequent protests led to this sentence being commuted to one of life imprisonment. By now suffering from a heart condition, he was paroled in 1952 and died in 1960.

Few commanders in history have been as respected by their adversaries as was Kesselring. "Smiling Albert" was recognized by all soldiers – German and allied alike – as a first-rate tactician, a skilled diplomat, a general who was loyal to his subordinates and an honorable foe.

KLUGE
Hans von (1882-1944)
GERMAN FIELD MARSHAL
Second World War

Hans von Kluge, who succeeded von *Rundstedt* on 2 July 1944 as supreme commander in the west, arrived in France convinced of Hitler's strategic genius. Within weeks, now aware of the true situation in Normandy, and in despair at being implicated in the July bomb plot to kill Hitler, he committed suicide. Known throughout the German army as "clever Hans", he had fought and lost his last great battle.

Von Kluge was born at Posen on 30 October 1882 and was gazetted into the 46th Field Artillery Regiment in 1901. During the First World War, he served at the front and on the staff, rising after it to the command of the 2nd Artillery Regiment in 1930. Three years later, he was Inspector General of Signals Troops, commander of the 6th Infantry Division in 1934 and finally 6th Corps the following year. In 1938, he was retired together with, many other senior officers whom Hitler considered might oppose his plans. Like many of them, however, von Kluge was recalled to duty in 1939, when he was given command of 4th Army for the Polish campaign. Here, he showed his true metal. His army's rapid advance on either side of the Vistula river was a major contributory factor to the encirclement of the Poles at Kutno and the swift conclusion of the campaign. He continued in command of 4th Army in the blitzkrieg in France in May 1940, crossing the Meuse and then, with his left flank resting on the Somme, moving northwards to help trap the allied armies around Dunkirk. In the second phase of the campaign, Kluge's army, forming the right of the German line, struck through Normandy to capture Cherbourg.

Hitler's favorite

So far, Kluge had shown that he was possessed of more than the normal amount of military competence, but he still had to impress Hitler to take the necessary step forward to become one of the Führer's most trusted generals. His actions in December 1941, when he brought about the degradation and expulsion from the army of General Hoepner, opened the way to this advancement. In the bitter conditions of that first winter on the Eastern Front, Hoepner asked von Kluge for authority to pull back one of his corps, which was in danger of being surrounded and destroyed. When von Kluge ordered him to stand firm, Hoepner disobeyed the order. The furious von Kluge reported what had happened to Hitler, who promptly ordered Hoepner's dismissal. Shortly afterwards, von Kluge was promoted to command Army Group Center.

For nearly two years, von Kluge held his sector of the front, skilfully deploying his forces to meet every Russian assault. Hitler put him in overall command of the great summer offensive of 1943 against the Kursk salient, but the Führer's prevarication and a fourfold Russian superiority destroyed von Kluge's hopes. Nevertheless, he kept his army group intact throughout the severe Russian attacks that fall and winter before hastily being ordered to Normandy.

Faith in the Führer

Even at this late stage of the war, von Kluge had not lost faith in his Führer. En route to Normandy, he was ordered to Hitler's headquarters and briefed on what was expected of him in France. Hitler's glowing confidence inspired von Kluge, who believed the Führer's boasts that the Reich's secret weapons were bringing Britain to its knees and that consequently a decisive victory in Normandy was within von Kluge's grasp.

Once in France, however, von Kluge quickly realized the German armies in France were facing a desperate situation, but despite this he dutifully prepared to obey Hitler's orders and launch an offensive at Mortain. The hope was that the Germans could cut off the Cotentin Peninsula and so trap *Patton*'s forces, which by this time were starting their main thrust. Von Kluge knew the attack was doomed to fail, given allied superiority – particularly in the air – but when it did Hitler's comment was simply "Success only failed to come because Kluge did not want to be successful . . . ". The Führer's judgement was influenced by a letter von Kluge had sent him on 21 July, in which he advised Hitler that the Normandy front must inevitably break and that the German armies there would be destroyed unless they were allowed to retreat.

The sole consequence of Hitler's Mortain offensive was the creation of a salient. This rapidly became a pocket, within which von Kluge's armies were soon all but encircled, but he could not convince the Führer of that fact. Hitler's opinion was that "every meter of Norman soil is worth 10kms of soil in any other part of France" and he ordered the offensive to be resumed without delay. The demand was insane – and von Kluge knew it, but even "clever Hlans" could not convince his Führer.

There now occurred a mysterious incident, which contributed greatly to von Kluge's disgrace. He mysteriously absented himself from his headquarters for most of 14/15 August. Officially, he was en route to the headquarters of 5th Panzer Army, but some historians believe that he was in fact trying to meet with a group of US officers at Avranches to arrange the surrender of the armies under his command. Eventually, he did arrive at 5th Panzer Army late at night, explaining that traffic congestion had delayed him.

Whether a surrender had been discussed or not soon proved immaterial, for on 17 August von Kluge was relieved by *Model*, who was totally loyal to Hitler. Von Kluge was ordered to return to Germany forthwith; he was not only under suspicion for having been out of contact on 15 August, but he was also suspected of being a party to the July bomb plot. On his way back to Germany, von Kluge took poison near Verdun, where he had served as a young officer in the First World War. In his suicide note, he assured Hitler that he had been loyal, but urged him to end the war.

Von Kluge's suicide removed one of the most able German generals of the Second World War. Though he was not a thrusting, vigorous commander, he was a loyal, dependable and efficient one, determined to try his best even in the face of insuperable odds. His character can be summed up in his reply to critics of the Mortain operation – "It is the Führer's order". Illogical though the orders he received might be, von Kluge would do his best to carry them out. His was not to reason why.

KONIEV
Ivan S (1897-1973)
MARSHAL OF THE SOVIET UNION
Second World War

Stocky and bald-headed, Ivan Koniev was one of the core of first-class generals whom *Zhukov* brought together to fight the key battles of the Eastern Front against the Germans in the Second World War. Yet, he was more of a party official than a Soviet commander of the classic military mold.

Koniev was born on 16 December 1897 in Lodenyo in northern Russia, the son of a farmer. Conscripted into the Tsarist army at the outbreak of the First World War, he served in an artillery regiment on the Galician front, where he was promoted to the rank of corporal for his bravery under fire. With the outbreak of the Bolshevik revolution of 1917, he joined the Communist party and enlisted into the Soviet army the following year. Koniev's political zeal won him an appointment as commissar of the Nikollsk region; during the civil war, he commanded firstly an armored train and then became the commissar of a rifle brigade. Sent to the Far East, he fought there against Kolchak's White Russian armies; after this, he played a leading part in the brutal and bloody repression of the naval mutiny at Kronstadt.

From commissar to general

Political influence and growing military expertise combined to win Koniev a place at the Frunze military academy and then the war school. Between 1931 and 1938, he commanded an infantry division in the Far East, surviving the period of Stalin's massive purges of the Soviet officer corps, in which thousands perished. Indeed, he benefitted from them, being promoted to com-

COMRADES *A party official who became a first-rate general, Koniev won the trust of the Russian dictator Stalin.*

into conference. There he made it clear that it would be the Soviet armies that would capture the Reich's capital; the question was which of them was better placed to do so. Both commanders expressed confidence that they would succeed, but, as Koniev's troops were further away, Zhukov was given the job. Koniev was ordered by Stalin to support Zhukov's left wing, at the same time moving to reach the Elbe as quickly as possible so as to block any further American advance.

All the Soviet commanders involved believed that the battle for Berlin would be hard and bitter. Aware of the need for speed, Koniev for his part, demanded a supporting artillery density of 250 guns per kilometer of front to open the way for his advance. Koniev's troops met with patchy German resistance – the city of Breslau, however, held out tenaciously – while Zhukov's troops were held up by the stubborn *Heinrici*. Accordingly, Koniev was ordered to swing part of his Front into Berlin; with his troops' arrival, the battle was swiftly concluded. The war in Europe was over.

Koniev was not a born military leader, but primarily a party official who developed into a competent defensive commander and then a first-rate attacking leader. He displayed a ruthlessness towards officers and men who failed to achieve their objectives that was quite out of keeping with the friendly smiling front he presented publicly. Like all his contemporaries, he was overshadowed by Zhukov, but in fact was being groomed by the suspicious Stalin to take over that great commander's duties. Such was the confidence of the Soviet leader in his party comrade, Ivan Koniev.

mand a corps. He was then put in command of the 2nd Far Eastern Army and finally the Baikal Military District.

Koniev saw his first action in the Second World War in the fall of 1941, when he was transferred from 19th Army to the Smolensk sector of the front, where he tried to halt the advance by *von Bock's* Army Group Center upon Moscow. As part of *Zhukov's* reorganization of the capital's defences, Koniev was given command of the West and then of the Kalinin Fronts and played a key role in Moscow's successful resistance.

The drive to the Oder
Koniev's subsequent career saw him involved in almost every major Soviet campaign. During Operation *Citadel* – the German codename for their 1943 summer offensive against Kursk – he created the huge mass of reserve armies grouped together as the Steppe Front; he then led them in the field to advance on and capture Kharkov.

Promoted to the command of the 1st Ukrainian Front, Koniev's troops drove swiftly through southern Poland in the fall of 1944 and reached the Oder river – the final natural barrier before Berlin – on 23 January 1945. Here the Soviet armies halted to regroup for the final thrust at the German capital. Now Stalin intervened. Learning that Simpson's 9th US Army was only 60 miles (100km) from Berlin and that it might drive forward to capture the city; the Soviet leader called both Koniev and Zhukov

MACARTHUR
Douglas (1880-1964)
US GENERAL
Second World War

Each of the combatants in the Second World War produced commanders of great ability – some of whom turned apparent defeat into victory and disaster into success. But out of the entire gallery, one figure stands out as the greatest strategist of all. He was Douglas MacArthur, the most brilliant US general of the war. Perhaps he was fortunate, since his great strategic mind was free to range across the vastness of the entire Pacific theater of war, rather than being confined to small battle areas, or to single countries.

MacArthur was born on 26 January 1880, at Little Rock, Arkansas into a military family. Even as a cadet, he was already demonstrating his tremendous intellectual gifts and leadership potential, graduating top of his class and becoming senior cadet in the West Point corps. Early in his army career, he served in the Philippines and Korea; his first really active service came on the US expedition to Vera Cruz in April 1914, when US troops occupied the town in a punitive action.

MacArthur in France

When the American Expeditionary Force went to France in the First World War, MacArthur commanded its 42nd (Rainbow) Division, leading his men into the second battle of the Marne with outstanding success. In the immediate post-war years, he commanded the US occupying forces in the Rhineland before returning home to become commandant of West Point and chief of staff of the army from 1930 to 1935. He officially retired from the US army on 31 December 1937, but continued to serve in the Philippine army as a field marshal – a title that had been bestowed upon him in 1936, when he went to the islands as military adviser to prepare the Philippines for eventual independence.

Pearl Harbor and its aftermath

Mounting tension in the Pacific region as Japan came closer to war with the USA led to MacArthur's recall to active service; on 26 July 1941, he was nominated as commander of the US and Philippine forces in the islands. He had little time in which to plan and prepare. The Japanese attack upon Pearl Harbor on 7 December was followed the next day by a heavy air raid on the island of Luzon, which preceded its invasion, followed by that of

"I SHALL RETURN" *The charismatic MacArthur (right) was probably the greatest US commander of the war.*

the other islands of the Philippines group.

Under the pressure of the Japanese thrusts, the main body of MacArthur's forces was pushed southwards; a second invasion then threatened to trap it in a pincer movement. MacArthur's response was to conduct a fighting retreat to Bataan, which so slowed down the pace of the Japanese advance that their operational time-table, which depended upon speed for its success, was thrown out of gear. MacArthur's success was all the more remarkable, since, out of his 130,000-strong army, only 22,400 were trained soldiers. His Filipino recruits, however, learned so quickly that it was not until May 1942 that their last resistance was overcome, after which they turned to guerrilla warfare.

"I shall return"

Two months before the capitulation, MacArthur was ordered by President Roosevelt to leave the islands and, after a hazardous journey by sea and air, he arrived in Australia on 17 March 1942. There he made his famous promise to the Filipinos – "I shall return" – and set to work without delay on plans for the defeat of the Japanese and the reconquest of the islands he had been forced to abandon. To conduct the war in the Pacific, which was principally a US area of operations, Washington divided the theater into the south-west Pacific region, under MacArthur, and put Admiral *Nimitz* in command the remainder. MacArthur's area of direct responsibility included Australia, New Guinea, the Dutch East Indies and the Philippines.

In view of the allied commitment to make the defeat of Germany their priority, the first operations MacArthur was able to launch were limited, but, though his offensives may have been small in scope, they were nevertheless important to the course of future operations. He himself bitterly resented the priority which had been given to Europe and made no secret of his feelings. This was by no means the only controversy in which the strong-minded MacArthur became involved. During June 1942, after the US victory at Midway, MacArthur and Admiral King, the local naval commander, differed over the best choice of strategy. Though they were both agreed that the next offensive should be launched in the New Guinea area to deal with Japan's chief air and naval base in the south-west Pacific, which was located at Rabaul on the northern coast of New Britain, they differed as how best to implement the New Guinea undertaking. King proposed a series of operations to capture the islands between the Solomons and New Britain – in other words a navy-orientated plan. MacArthur demanded an army controlled direct thrust to Rabaul. A compromise was reached, with King placing Halsey's 3rd Fleet under MacArthur's command. The final plan was for a double thrust to isolate Rabaul. The fleet would advance up the chain of islands from Guadalcanal to the St Matthias islands, while the troops of 6th Army jumped up the northern New Guinea coast in a series of landings. They would then land in New Britain and advance towards the common objective.

A staged reconquest was very much part and parcel of MacArthur's strategy. In the last week of February 1944, he personally led the invasion of Los Negros island and established an airbase there. He then bypassed Japanese 18th Army, which was grouped between Madang and Weiwak to hold western New Guinea, and struck at Aitape, which the Japanese had thought to be so secure that it was defended by a minimal garrison. In a brilliant operation, which opened on 1 April and was concluded 26 days later, MacArthur cut off the enemy army, whose units then disintegrated and vanished into the jungle where they stayed until the war's end.

The war's last stages

Late in 1944, the army and navy chiefs again disagreed as to the direction of Pacific strategy. The navy demanded an assault upon Formosa or China to precede the attack upon Japan; MacArthur argued for the attack to be made through the Philippines. Despite the formidable defences that the Japanese had set up, he saw the liberation of the islands as a debt of honor. His plan was accepted.

In the last year of the war, MacArthur and his subordinates showed amazing flexibility in their direction and control of operations. The skilful use of US paratroopers in the reconquest of Manila and the assault landings and the attacks against fanatical Japanese resistance – all showed the US commanders at their best. The Luzon campaign cost the Americans 8,000 killed, but the Japanese lost 192,000. In that operation MacArthur fulfilled his promise to the people of the Philippines, striding through the surf towards the Philippine shore, head high, his face marked by emotion.

From June to August 1945, MacArthur and his staff worked on plans to invade the Japanese home islands in a two-stage operation. It was expected that the first stage would be launched in November 1945 and the second in March 1946. How long the fighting would last and what it would cost in human lives – both American and Japanese – could only be hinted. The most optimistic estimate was that the fighting would take two years and there would be about three million dead, one million of whom would be American. However the dropping of two atomic bombs at Hiroshima and Nagasaki brought the war to a swift end and on 2 September 1945, MacArthur, a newly-created General of the Army, received the Japanese surrender on board the USS *Missouri* in Tokyo Bay.

There are some men to whom fate is generous. Born into a famous military family, Douglas MacArthur grew up to be a handsome and distinguished man. Brilliantly gifted in military matters, he also showed rare diplomatic skills in the five years he then spent in charge of the US occupation of Japan. When ordered to Korea to take charge of the UN forces fighting to protect the South from the Communist north, he showed he had lost none of his strategic and tactical skills. Nor, unfortunately for him, had he lost his ability to create controversy. When he called for atomic bombs to be dropped on China, President Truman promptly relieved him of command. Though he defended his policies in brilliantly composed and eloquently delivered speeches to both houses of Congress, his military career was over. His valedictory address to the cadets of West Point was a masterpiece of classical oratory – dignified, but moving. He died in April 1964.

MANSTEIN
Erich von (1887-1973)
GERMAN FIELD MARSHAL
Second World War

It is generally accepted in military circles that Erich von Manstein was the finest Axis strategist of the Second World War. In 1940, when the campaign in the west was being discussed, the supreme command was faced with the problem of how the operation should open. The first proposal for a re-run of the 1914 Schlieffen plan was unacceptable to Hitler. He adopted von Manstein's unconventional plan for a thrust through the "impassable"

Ardennes, with the result that the battle ended with complete victory over the western allies within six weeks.

Von Manstein was born into a military family in 1887 and was gazetted into the 3rd Guards Regiment in 1906. He was wounded in the fighting around Ypres in November 1914, and thereafter served on staff duties on the Eastern, Western and Balkan Fronts. In the post-War German army, he served as chief of staff to two of Germany's most distinguished soldiers – Beck and *von Rundstedt*. In the 1940 campaign, he led 38th Corps which spearheaded the battle for France and was the first German unit to cross the Seine. The gratified Hitler chose him for a field command in the forces which were to invade Britain in Operation *Sea Lion*.

Master of the offensive

In the opening offensives of the German invasion of the USSR in 1941, von Manstein's 56th Panzer Corps advanced 200 miles in a four-day drive to reach the Dvina river. By mid-July, his troops were driving on to Leningrad, the USSR's second city. Von Manstein was then posted to Army Group South and again demonstrated his abilities as a brilliant tactician and clear-thinking strategist with his invasion of the Crimea and capture of Sevastapol. However, his greatest test came in the winter of 1942/43 in the face of the Soviet army's massive offensive, which had destroyed 6th Army at Stalingrad and was now driving on towards Kharkov. The swift pace of the Soviet advance threatened to trap the German forces in the Caucasus, but Manstein managed to hold the Don crossings, so allowing an orderly withdrawal.

The lure of Kharkov

Von Manstein's proposed strategy – to let the Red Army exhaust itself and then to cut it to pieces – required a bait to draw the Soviets forward. Kharkov was that lure: here, von Manstein clashed with Hitler. His plan required the Germans to withdraw from the city, but Hitler ordered that the city be held to the last man. A stormy meeting between the two men followed, but the Führer was finally convinced by von Manstein's plan. To the south of the salient the Soviet advance was creating, three panzer corps would breach the Soviet South West and Voronezh Fronts and attack each in turn. With both Soviet fronts in disarray, 2nd Panzer Army would thrust southwards from Briansk to meet Manstein's northwards-thrusting pincer and so trap the Soviet forces.

Von Manstein's reading of Soviet intentions was faultless. He knew that the Soviet commanders would simply drive westwards until ordered to halt, despite the fact that their troops had almost outrun their supplies. The intelligence for which he had been waiting finally arrived. The Soviet armor had run out of fuel and had ground to a halt. Von Manstein promptly launched his massive counterattack. The first assault he launched struck South West Front, cutting off the tank and infantry corps of its spearhead forces.

Manstein turned next against the Voronezh Front, destroying the 3rd Tank Army. The first spring thaw then set in and mud slowed the pace of Manstein's drive. In one last effort to gain complete victory before the thaw halted operations, he struck across the Mush river and crushed the remaining Soviet forces facing him. Kharkov was recaptured, while in the final phase of Manstein's series of counter-blows, the Grossdeutschland Division recaptured Byelgorod.

Though the Soviet winter campaign had now been smashed, this was the German army's swan song in the east, as well as Manstein's last victory. Thereafter, despite its efforts at Kursk that summer, the Wehrmacht gained no further strategic successes against the Soviets. Hitler, for his part, did not forgive Manstein for his opposition and in March 1944, dismissed him. In the last days of the war Admiral Doenitz sought unsuccessfully to contact von Manstein in order to offer him the leadership of OKW. It would have been a post without authority, for the Third Reich both men had served was dead.

Von.Manstein's brilliance lay in his ability to foresee, as if clairvoyantly, the various stages of a battle from both sides. He realized that the "impassable" terrain of the Ardennes would be guarded by a second rate army and that the western armies would play into his hands by advancing into Belgium. Thus, when the Germans thrust out of the Ardennes, they would find the space to maneuver. The Crimean operation, the Don crossings, the Kharkov strategy were all evidence of the skills of an exceptional, gifted commander; it was the allies' good fortune that Hitler was incapable of appreciating them.

MARSHALL
George C (1880-1959)
US GENERAL
Second World War

George Marshall's career disproves the theory that the victories of peace are less renowned than those of war, for his name is remembered less for his military gifts than for the economic plan he initiated to aid war-shattered Europe in the late 1940s. In recognition of that plan, he is the only professional soldier ever to have been awarded the Nobel Peace Prize.

Marshall was born on 31 December 1880 in Unionstown, Pennsylvania, graduating from the Virginia Military Institute in 1902 with the rank of lieutenant of infantry. His regimental service was limited, for he quickly went on to study for the staff. He went with the American Expeditionary Force to France in the First World War, when he served as chief of operations with 1st Division; by the time the war came to an end, he was chief of operations for 1st Army.

Marshall made his post-war career in executive posts; from 1927 to 1932, he was principal instructor at the infantry school at Fort Benning. Rising steadily through the command structure of the US army he became deputy chief of staff in 1938 and chief of staff on 1 September

1939. In that post, Marshall recognized that his top priorities were to expand the army and then to prepare it to meet the challenge should the USA enter the war. Statistics ably demonstrate how successful he was in the first of these tasks; from a peace-time strength of 200,000 in 1939, the US army had 8,500,000 men serving in it by the end of the war.

Chief of staff

As Roosevelt's senior military advisor, Marshall attended all the main war-time conferences and directed US military policy throughout the war. His influence on allied strategy was substantial. He opposed, for instance, Churchill's wish for an indirect approach through the "soft underbelly of the Axis" in Italy and the Balkans, advocating instead a direct cross-Channel assault into France. Marshall was of the opinion that such an operation could be mounted in 1942, even though the tragic failure of the Dieppe raid had shown the formidable nature of the German defences. He advocated it again in 1943, although it was clear that the allies were at that date incapable of carrying out a successful landing and fighting the subsequent campaign. Indeed, Marshall had hoped to be supreme Allied commander when the invasion came, but, because he was considered indispensable in Washington, the job went to *Eisenhower*, who had already demonstrated his military skills during the invasions of North Africa, Sicily and southern Italy.

Achilles heel

Marshall's suspicion of Britain's intentions and his dislike of many British commanders led him to influence Eisenhower, not always wisely, in the conduct of operations.

IN THE PENTAGON *As chief of staff, Marshall masterminded the war effort and ably supported his field commanders.*

Though, as a commander, he should have tried to consider military operations dispassionately, Marshall in fact was incapable of overcoming a narrow, nationalistic approach whenever US troops came under British field command, as in the post D-day period. For this reason, though thousands of miles away from the battlefield and concerned also with events in other theaters of war, he insisted that the armies in Europe advance towards the Rhine in concert, rejecting *Montgomery's* concept of a single thrust across the north German plain, and his determination that the armies he had raised should play a decisive part on the field led Eisenhower first to take charge of land operations and then to decide not to make the final thrust into Berlin. Neither Marshall nor Eisenhower appreciated the political significance of the capture of the German capital; instead, they decided to concentrate on capturing the mythical Alpine Redoubt, in southern Germany. An objective assessment of the available intelligence data would have shown that the so-called redoubt did not exist.

From soldier to statesman

In the immediate post-war period, Marshall attempted to mediate between the Chinese Nationalist Chiang Kai Shek and the Communist Mao Tse Tung in September 1945. Two years later Marshall, now Secretary of State, proposed his celebrated plan of economic aid to enable Europe to rebuild the damage of the Second World War and, at the same time, resist the spread of Communism. In 1950, a special act of Congress was passed to allow him to become Secretary of Defence since as a serving officer he was ineligible to hold the office. Through his efforts the Korean War was contained. Awarded the Nobel Peace Prize in December 1953; he died in October 1959.

Any judgement of the achievements of George Marshall must first recognize his considerable gifts of organization. His expansion, reorganization and administration of the US Army were incredible achievements. However, his strategic horizons were limited. He seemed unable to grasp that successful military operations are dependent upon complete and thorough preparation, while, though understandable, his narrow nationalistic approach to the command of US forces could have caused considerable problems in the field, had it not been for the charm and tact of the man he had chosen to serve as allied supreme commander – Dwight D. Eisenhower.

MODEL
Walther (1891-1945)
GERMAN FIELD MARSHAL
Second World War

When allied airborne troops were parachuted around Arnhem on 17 September, 1944, Walther Model, the commander of Army Group B, whose headquarters were in the town, was convinced that the whole allied operation had been mounted to capture him. The high opinion Model had of himself was not entirely unjustified, for the "Führer's fireman", as he was known, was one of the most outstanding, as well as flamboyant, commanders in the German army.

Model was born at Genthin, near Magdeburg, on 24 January 1891, the son of a Prussian director of music. He was gazetted a lieutenant in 52nd Infantry Regiment and served as a front-line soldier throughout the First World War, being wounded many times and receiving several awards for gallantry. During the Polish campaign of 1939, Model, now a major-general, served on the staff of 4th Corps and then 16th Army. He commanded 3rd Panzer Division in the opening offensives of the war with the USSR, when his dynamic leadership during the battle of encirclement around *Kiev* in September 1941, brought him to Hitler's attention. Model's 3rd Panzer, which formed part of *Guderian*'s Panzer Group smashed 13th Red Army and spearheaded the German advance across the heavily defended Desna river line and for more than 150 miles to link up with von Kleist's Panzer Group in the greatest encirclement in military history up to that time.

Model was promoted to the command of 41st Corps and was then given command of 9th Army, which he led during Operation *Citadel*, the 1943 summer offensive, which Hitler planned to regain the strategic initiative for his forces after the Stalingrad debacle. Model's task was to drive south towards Kursk to meet *Hoth*'s 4th Panzer Army striking north. The aim of the plan was to eliminate a dangerous Russian salient and destroy the massed Soviet armies within it, but, despite initial tactical successes, the operation was a disaster. Neither German force gained its objectives; then a Soviet counter-offensive struck Model's army. *Citadel* was terminated.

During the following year, Model commanded Army Group North and then Army Group North Ukraine. In both posts he made a point of rushing to the key sector when the Soviets attacked and restoring the situation. This special ability won him his nick-name. He demonstrated his talent yet again during the summer, when a Soviet offensive broke through Army Group Center and struck towards Warsaw. Model swiftly re-established a battle line, which held the advancing Soviet forces to the east of the Polish capital.

The Führer's fireman

With the situation in the east stabilized, in August 1944, Model was ordered to the Western Front. Again, the front gradually stabilized after the German retreat – though this was to do more with shortage of supplies on the allied side than German defensive capabilities. The Arnhem operation was an attempt to break through to the Rhine and end the war in 1944. To meet the situation, Model mustered every man – even convalescents – and threw 9th SS Panzer Division, which was refitting in the area, into action. His decisive action led to the total defeat of the allied operation.

Model now had to face disaster in his turn in the so-called "battle of the bulge". It was not until 3 November 1944 that Model and the other senior commanders in north-East Europe learned of the Führer's proposed masterstroke in the Ardennes, which Hitler had scheduled should be launched on 25 November. Model argued that the preparations for such an offensive could not be completed in time and that the strategic aims of the operation – the thrust to Antwerp – was unrealistic. At a Führer conference in Berlin on 2 December – the original date for operations was indeed postponed – he and the other field commanders sought to convince Hitler that the offensive was over-ambitious; Model himself told Hitler bluntly that the operation, as planned, could not possibly succeed. This was not the first time that Model had spoken so openly to the Führer. Once, when Hitler commented that the spirit of the soldiers of 1943 was not as good as in 1941, and asked where that spirit had gone, the enraged Model told him that the men of 1941 were dead and buried in Soviet soil.

Disaster and defeat

Hitler insisted that his original plan be followed to the letter, but the results were as Model had forecast. The offensive failed. By March 1945, the allies had crossed the Rhine and by April the whole of Army Group B was encircled in the Ruhr. Model's request to withdraw his troops was rejected by Hitler and counter-attacks by the encircled troops to smash the US ring of steel surrounding them were beaten back. On 15 April, aware that even he could not save the situation, Model ordered discharge papers to be issued to his soldiers.

Like many good commanders, Model was a soldier's soldier and his men knew that he would not sacrifice them in a hopeless cause. Monocle in eye and peaked cap set at a jaunty angle he was a familiar figure in the most forward positions and he did not hesitate to take part in battle himself. However, his honor as a German field marshal would not allow him to surrender. On 21 April 1945, he shot himself. For years, his body lay in an unmarked grave near Ratingen but was then disinterred and reburied in a German military cemetery in the Ruhr.

MONTGOMERY
Bernard Law (1887-1976)
BRITISH FIELD MARSHAL
Second World War

Montgomery was a modern equivalent of one of Cromwell's Puritan Ironsides. His father was an Anglican bishop and Montgomery's self-confidence owed much to his faith. He never doubted his own abilities, particularly after making his name. He was convinced that he was guided and protected by God and that therefore his plans and ideas had to be correct.

Montgomery began his army career at Sandhurst, but his time as a cadet was a troubled one – he was suspected of bullying his fellow cadet-officers. Gazetted into the

Royal Warwickshire Regiment, he fought on the Western Front at the start of the First World War, being so severely wounded at the battle of Mons that he was given up for dead. For the rest of the war, he served on the staff, where he developed an expertise in organization that he was to demonstrate in the campaigns of the Second World War.

Between the wars, Montgomery's career followed a conventional enough pattern. He lectured in the staff colleges in Britain and India; by 1937, he had risen to the rank of brigadier. At the time, he was serving in Palestine, where he organized swift raids on Arab areas to help reduce the number and weight of Arab attacks on the Jewish settlements.

From Europe to the desert

At the outbreak of the Second World War, Montgomery commanded 3rd Division of the British Expeditionary Force in France. He emerged from the fighting in Belgium in May 1940 with his reputation for efficiency and bravery enhanced and, in the post-Dunkirk period, commanded 12th Corps, followed by 5th Corps, before taking over South-Eastern Command. A physical fitness fetishist, Montgomery ordered his men to take part in cross-country runs and rigorous PE routines. His own spartan habits – he was a teetotaler, a militant non-smoker and

retired to bed every night no later than 9.30pm – plus the demands he made on his men had their detractors, but he was fortunate enough to enjoy the support of the chief of the imperial general staff and the war minister.

Nevertheless, Montgomery appeared a strange choice to take over command of 8th Army in the Western Desert in August 1942. Indeed, he was not the first choice, but the substitute for General Gott, who had been killed in an air crash in the desert. The situation Montgomery faced was simple. His new command had been driven back to El Alamein and was faced by a confident foe, poised for a final thrust to bring victory.

"Hitting Rommel for six"

As if by instinct, Montgomery grasped the needs of 8th Army. He knew that he could always replace his officers if they let him down, but that he needed to gain the confidence of the rank-and-file. He achieved this, not just by his breezy confidence, or by insisting on putting all ranks "in the picture", but by fighting and winning the defensive battle of Alam el Halfa. This led to triumph at El Alamein, which was followed by total allied victory over Rommel and his Italian allies in North Africa within six months. As Churchill said, if inaccurately: "Before Alamein, we never had a victory. After Alamein, we never had a defeat".

THE DESERT RAT *Though difficult to work with, Montgomery proved his ability as a hard-hitting desert general. In Normandy, however, his strategy came under considerable attack, notably from his US allies.*

Leading Overlord

Montgomery went on to lead 8th Army in Sicily and Italy before returning to Britain to prepare for his role as field commander of the allied ground forces in the D-Day landings. Here, he had the first of his major disagreements with Eisenhower, who, Montgomery believed, failed to recognize his strategic intentions, which were to draw the bulk of the German panzers away from the US forces and on to his own front. This would pave the way for a US break-out. The plan, however, took longer to accomplish than Montgomery had predicted and, consequently, Eisenhower took over supreme command in the field himself, making *Bradley* co-equal with Montgomery as an army group commander.

"A bridge too far"

Even as the allies raced in pursuit of the retreating Germans, Montgomery was at loggerheads with Eisenhower as to the future conduct of the campaign. Montgomery believed a single thrust, with the whole weight of the allied war machine behind it, would win the war; Eisenhower preferred a general advance on a broad front. Perhaps this dispute led Montgomery to abandon his usual caution and launch Operation *Market Garden* – a series of airborne landings designed to lay a paratroop "carpet" to seize the key bridges in northern Holland and so open the way to an armored thrust across the Rhine and into the Ruhr. The over-ambitious operation failed and there was further criticism when Montgomery's forces were slow in capturing Antwerp

The end of the war

Montgomery, however, bounded back to favor through his success in containing Hitler's Ardennes offensive, though his buoyant manner – and subsequent breezy comments – deeply offended many Americans. Montgomery's contempt for Eisenhower was now well-known and the supreme commander acted by relegating Montgomery's armies to a secondary role in the final offensives of the war. Nevertheless, it was at Montgomery's tactical headquarters that the instrument of German unconditional surrender was signed.

After the war, Montgomery served as chief of the imperial general staff and then at NATO before finally retiring. Even in his last years, he was no stranger to controversy, as the publication of his memoirs showed.

NIMITZ
Chester W (1885-1966)
US ADMIRAL
Second World War

The courtesy, tact and calm nature of Chester Nimitz were a by-word in the US navy; he also possessed highly developed strategic and tactical skills, which he demonstrated to the full as commander-in-chief in the Pacific.

Born in Texas on 24 February 1885, Nimitz graduated from the US Naval Academy at Annapolis in 1905. In the years before the First World War, he commanded both surface and submarine vessels, becoming an expert on underwater warfare as well as a naval engineering specialist. During the war, he served on the staff of the commander of the Atlantic Fleet (Submarines) and in the post-war period he rose steadily, eventually becoming commander of a battleship squadron in 1938.

After Pearl Harbor

Nimitz's unruffled calm and firm grasp of the situation in the days following the Japanese attack on Pearl Harbor in December 1941 impressed the Secretary of the Navy, Knox, deeply. He accordingly appointed Nimitz to the command of the US Pacific Fleet, promoting him to the rank of Admiral; subsequently the area of Nimitz's responsibilities were extended to cover the entire Pacific area, outside *MacArthur*'s command.

Nimitz was determined to assume the offensive, sending his aircraft carriers on strikes against Japanese-held islands. His tactical skills were clearly shown during the battle of Midway in June 1942, when the Japanese lost four carriers to US air strikes. As a consequence, the previous enemy naval superiority in the Pacific theater was reduced almost to parity, which, in turn, allowed greater naval support to be given to land operations in the Solomons and New Guinea areas.

In September 1943, with allied strength increasing, Nimitz was able to initiate operations across a vast area; the following year he was also able to support MacArthur in his reconquest of the Philippines. This expansion of activity let to the key naval battles – that of the Philippine Sea and Leyte Gulf – whose successful outcome finally broke Japanese naval power. Japan's decline was such that its fleet could not prevent Nimitz's forces from invading Iwo Jima and Okinawa, from which islands his aircraft raided the Japanese homeland. His key role in the eventual allied victory was formally recognized on 2 September 1945, when Nimitz signed the instrument of Japanese surrender as the representative of the US navy.

Command methods

Like Nelson before him, Nimitz relied heavily on his subordinates, calling a conference of his captains before battle and listening to their views. He, however, took the decisions. Once these had been made and his orders issued, he did not interfere in the way his subordinates executed them. Indeed, he did not accompany the fleet into battle for fear that by being present he might inhibit his commanders. He relied upon those whom he had chosen and was never disappointed.

Nimitz, without doubt, was one of the great strategists of the Second World War. His strategic and tactical brilliance produced a chain of victories in wide-ranging operations throughout the south Pacific. This was not the least of his gifts, for the sheer size of the theater of operations demanded strategy on a grand scale, capable of being produced only by a gifted commander.

PATTON
George S (1885-1945)
US GENERAL
Second World War

The most striking personality among the military commanders of the Second World War was undoubtedly George S Patton. Other leaders may have had an individual trait to distinguish them, but only Patton was flamboyant enough to wear a pair of Colt 45 pistols, one on each hip. He was also the most inspired leader of armor the US army has ever produced.

Patton was born in California in 1885. Graduating from West Point in 1909, he was gazetted into the cavalry, the branch of the service with which he identified for the rest of his life. His first active service was as an *aide de camp* to General *Pershing* during the punitive expedition against Mexico in March 1916. Following the USA's entry into the First World War, Pershing was put in command of the expeditionary force that was sent to France, Patton accompanying the US commander-in-chief as chief of the headquarters defence troops.

From horses to tanks
When the first US tank units were formed, Patton was selected for tank training; he went on to organize and then lead the 1st US Tank Brigade in the St Mihiel offensive of September 1918, when the US 1st Army, in conjunction with the French, eliminated a salient that had been held by the enemy for four years. Patton's brigade also took an active part in the allied offensives that brought the war to a close; in the US attack in the Meuse-Argonne sector, he was wounded and was also awarded two medals for bravery.

In the inter-war years, Patton served as both a regimental and a staff officer, graduating from staff colleges and lecturing on the principles and tactics of armored warfare. He had already established a reputation for being a strict disciplinarian, filled with a love of armored troops – his men showed him a reciprocal degree of loyalty. He sought to give his soldiers a unit identity through their dress. He himself wore, for a short time, a gilded helmet topping an immaculate uniform, while his troops were issued with neck scarves in order to distinguish tankmen from the rest of the army.

Blunder in Sicily
In the allied landings in French North Africa in November 1942, Patton commanded the western task force. Light initial resistance from the Vichy French forces was quickly overcome; Patton's duties were then chiefly ceremonial until March 1943, when he was given command of 2nd US Corps, which had been badly mauled by the Afrika Korps in the Kasserine Pass. Patton took firm control of the battered units, so infusing its men with his own aggressive spirit that the corps played a very prominent part in the final battles in Tunisia.

"BLOOD AND GUTS" *Controversial yet brilliant, Patton's drive made him the leading US tank commander of the war.*

The next year of Patton's life was one during which his reputation was tarnished. His anti-British feelings – particularly his dislike of *Montgomery* – came to the surface during the allied invasion of Italy, but it was his attitude to one of his own men that nearly led to his recall in disgrace. Visiting a hospital, Paton slapped a shell-shocked soldier in the face. Hastily transferred to Britain, where the plan was for him to play an active part in the invasion of north-west Europe, Patton's indiscreet political statements became so notorious that he was reprimanded by *Eisenhower*, the allied supreme commander, and sidetracked to command the dummy diversionary forces.

A reputation redeemed
Patton could not be kept out of the Normandy campaign for long, however. When the US breakout at Avranches in August 1944 was accomplished, it was Patton and his 3rd Army that stormed across France to the Meuse before fuel shortage forced a halt. His organizational skills and his tactical flexibility were further demonstrated during December 1944 when his troops moved at breathtaking speed to relieve the pressure on *Bradley*'s troops during the German Ardennes offensive – the "battle of the Bulge". In hours rather than days, Patton's army, which had been facing eastwards when the German attack opened, was swung around northwards to contain the enemy salient and then reduce it.

Having played a major role in the defeat of Hitler's last offensive in the west, Patton turned east again in a series of attacks that brought him to the Rhine and then across the river. The crossing, a surprise operation, cost Patton 34 men killed or wounded. Four days later, his armored spearheads were more than 100 miles further east into Germany. Eventually, he was to thrust down the Danube valley into Austria and western Czechoslovakia by the time the war ended.

Patton's action in this last period of the war – and in the immediate post-war period – again made him the subject of adverse comment. In his drive, his policy of destroying any village or town offering even token resistance to his forces by artillery and bombing was bitterly criticised. He was also savagely attacked when he ordered an armored column to relieve a prisoner-of-war camp, in which one of his relatives was held captive, and the column was almost totally destroyed.

Patton also distrusted the Soviet – more than once, he suggested that the allies should exploit Russian military weakness by attacking their armies in eastern Europe. This added to his unpopularity. Then, always a pragmatist, he retained Nazi officials in the posts they had held under Hitler in his military administration of the southern zone of occupied Germany. Eventually, Eisenhower transferred him from 3rd Army to 15th Army, which was little more than a name and a collection of military historians analyzing the campaign in north-west Europe. He was killed in a car crash in late 1945.

Patton remains a controversial figure. His detractors see him as having been a profane, arrogant bully, taking a childish delight in wearing medals and other items of outward display, and as an over-emotional figure, who ordered his army chaplains to pray for good weather in order that military operations might continue. His supporters see him as a brilliant commander of armored forces, flexible, dynamic and thrustful, with a high standard that he expected others to attain. What cannot be doubted is the efficiency and *esprit de corps* he created in the armies he commanded. Though his troops might nick-name him "old blood and guts" – "our blood, his guts" – they would fight for him in a way that few other commanders could equal.

RAEDER
Erich (1876-1960)
GERMAN ADMIRAL
Second World War

The tragedy of a commander who sees his battle plans brought to nought by enemy action can only be surpassed by that of one whose political master cannot appreciate the policies which he proposes. It was the fate of Grossadmiral Erich Raeder, the architect of the navy of the Third Reich, that Hitler could not grasp the fundamentals of basic naval strategy.

Raeder was born at Wandsbeck near Hamburg on 24 April 1876, and entered the imperial navy in 1894. In the First World War, he served under von Hipper in the battle of the Dogger Bank, in command of a cruiser; after the war, he stayed in the navy, rising to become chief of naval staff. During 1935, he was appointed supreme commander. In German naval circles, Raeder was known as a "big ship" man, and he launched an intensive construction program, a key element of which was a force of "pocket" battleships, which combined high speed, long range and powerful armament to make them perfect commerce raiders. The Anglo-German Naval Treaty of the same year gave Raeder the green light to plan a truly modern fleet, which would contain traditional battleships and an expanded submarine wing. Building continued, but his Plan Z, produced during 1939, warned that naval parity with Britain could only be achieved by 1945 and if war did not intervene.

The realities of war
When war came, Raeder realized that a direct, major confrontation between the surface ships of the Royal Navy and the Kriegsmarine would result in a defeat for the German service. His strategy was based, therefore, on blockade, relying upon commerce raiders and submarines to halt the flow of supplies to Britain. The conquest of Norway in spring 1940 gave the German navy bases between the Baltic and the Arctic which its commerce raiders could utilize, while the conclusion of the war with France meant the Kriegsmarine now had bases extending along the French Atlantic coast to the north of Spain. The British, were, therefore, outflanked to the north and to the south. The Norwegian effort, however, cost Raeder dear, for his surface losses meant he was in no position to provide even minimal naval support for the invasion of Britain in the summer of 1940.

Raeder's strategy of commerce raiders and U-boats was successful. The *Admiral Scheer* broke out into the Atlantic late in October 1940 and returned in March 1941, after a successful mission. Nearly a year later, however, Raeder moved three of his major surface units, the battle-cruisers *Scharnhorst* and *Gneisenau* and the heavy cruiser *Prinz Eugen* from Brest to Norway. The Grand Admiral had changed his strategy. The re-grouping would tie down a major part of the British Home Fleet to watch them, especially with the *Tirpitz*, Germany's sole surviving battleship, already in Norwegian waters. The German threat was twofold. The heavy units might break out into the Atlantic to attack the convoys crossing between Britain and the USA. Secondly, they might, in conjunction with the Luftwaffe, attack the British convoys sailing with supplies to Soviet Russia. Those threats would prevent the full deployment of the Royal Navy against the U-boat menace.

One of the major successes gained by Raeder's strategy was the destruction of convoy PQ 17 in July 1942 but, against that, in December 1942, a German naval force broke off battle against an inferior British one. Hitler was infuriated, even though his own orders had been that capital ships were not to be hazarded. He accused Raeder's navy of cowardice and declared that surface ships had no purpose, that he would have them scrapped and their guns mounted in fixed fortifications. Raeder was unable to convince Hitler that the Kriegsmarine's strategy had succeeded; nor would he accept the destruction of the fleet he had for so long labored to create. He resigned his post as the navy's supreme commander in 1943 and thereafter played no further part in the conduct of the war. In 1945 he was arrested, tried as a major war criminal at Nuremburg and sentenced to life imprisonment. For medical reasons he was released on 26 September 1955. He died on 6 November 1960.

ROKOSSOVSKY
Konstantin K (1896-1965)
MARSHAL OF THE SOVIET UNION
Second World War

Konstantin Rokossovsky's most distinctive physical feature was his set of stainless steel teeth, which replaced the natural ones that had been knocked out of his mouth by NKVD (now KGB) agents. In common with a great many Soviet officers, Rokossovsky had been arrested during the purges of 1936-37, when he was charged with spying for Japan and Poland. Unlike many of his contemporaries Rokossovsky was fortunate, since he could prove that the evidence presented by the prosecution was false. The NKVD claim to have on record recent personal testimony from the man who had denounced Rokossovsky had to be a lie, for the man concerned had been dead for nearly 20 years. Though he escaped the firing squad, however, such was Stalin's paranoia that Rokossovsky was nevertheless imprisoned.

Konstantin Rokossovsky, the son of a railway engineer, was born on 9 December 1896, in Veliki Luki. He was called up into the army upon the outbreak of the First World War and was both decorated and promoted for bravery. Soon after the October revolution, he volunteered for the Red Guard and then the Soviet army, serving as a cavalryman in the civil war and rising to the command of a regiment by 1920. At the end of the civil war, Rokossovsky was selected for staff training at the Frunze Academy, the next major step in his career being the command of a Kuban Cossack Corps in Manchuria. It was while in command of that formation that he was arrested, tried and imprisoned.

Like many officers who had been victims of Stalin's purges, Rokossovsky was released from a concentration camp during 1940. He was restored to his former command and then went on to raise and to lead 9th Mechanized Corps. Nevertheless, the German attack in 1941 found the USSR with only a few commanders of similar stature. Luckily Zhukov was not only an able commander, but was also a good judge of men. Rokossovsky was one of a group of four he selected – the others were Vatutin,

Chuikov and Yeremenko – all of whom quickly demonstrated their suitability for high command positions.

Rokossovsky rehabilitated

Rokossovsky was selected for advancement by Zhukov as a result of his handling of 9th Mechanized Corps in the opening days of the war, when it counter-attacked Kempff's Panzer corps successfully on 26 June to temporarily halt the German advance. The next month, Rokossovsky was accordingly transferred to command 16th Army and from there to command, in succession, the Briansk, Don, Central, Byelorussian and then 2nd Byelorussian Fronts (he was commanding the last at the end of the war). As a Front commander, he played a leading part in all the major battles of what in Soviet history is termed the Great Patriotic War.

The successful defensive battle that Rokossovsky fought at the gates of Moscow in 1941 was followed at the end of 1942 by his first major offensive, in which his Don Front smashed through German 6th Army at Stalingrad and initiated its encirclement and destruction. As a member of Zhukov's successful command team, Rokossovsky played an important part in the Russian battle plan at Kursk the following year. As the commander of the Central Front, it was his task to meet and contain the massive, southward thrust by Model's 9th Army and then to drive the Germans back in a general counter-attack.

Model had hoped that, by concentrating his forces on a relatively narrow front, he would pierce the successive lines of Russian defences, but Rokossovsky's five armies – the 65th, 70th, 13th, 2nd Tank and 65th Army (in reserve) – were skilfully deployed to slow down the German thrust. This they achieved in a matter of days and then halted it completely. A little later the Soviet counter-attack opened, flinging Model back into retreat.

This marked the end of the last major German strategic initiative in the east.

In the 1944 summer offensive, Rokossovsky headed the Sovet drive into central Poland, but was held to the east of Warsaw by Model. The Soviet commander was then moved to the northern sector of the Russian battle line where, during February 1945, he helped to trap the German armies between Stettin and Koenigsberg against the Baltic. With this major German force encircled and therefore neutralized, the final battle for Berlin could open. In that offensive Rokossovsky's 2nd Bylorussian Front had the task of protecting the right wing of Zhukov's forces as they drove towards the German capital and of defeating *Heinrici*'s opposing Army of the Vistula. It was a mark of his success that he was selected to command the victory parade in Moscow on 24 June 1945. At the request of the Polish government, he was then appointed Poland's Minister of National Defence, being given the title of Marshal of Poland to add to his Soviet one.

Like all those who had lived in the USSR under Stalin, Rokossovsky had been hardened by the experience, but he had learned to be pragmatic. To be brought from a concentration camp and restored to the command of a major military grouping demands a very flexible approach to problems, policies and people. Like most of the Soviet military leaders who rose to high command during the war, Rokossovsky was overshadowed by Zhukov, behind whom stood Stalin – a dictator who tolerated neither mistakes nor disobedience. Of Rokossovsky's ability as a tactician on the battlefield, there can be no doubt, as the attack by his inexperienced tank crews against Kempff's veterans showed. His personal courage could not be questioned, for he had a record of bravery going back as far as the First World War.

ROMMEL
Erwin (1891-1944)
GERMAN FIELD MARSHAL
Second World War

Erwin Rommel's military skills won him a place as one of the truly great commanders of the Second World War – particularly, though not exclusively, because of his ability to handle armor en masse. It was his masterly tank tactics, plus other aggressive battlefield skills, that won him the nickname of the "Desert Fox" in North Africa. Later, when German fortunes were in decline, he showed equal defensive capabilities.

Rommel was born in November 1891 at Heidenheim and entered the army in July 1910, being gazetted as a lieutenant in the 124th Infantry Regiment. During the 1917 campaign in Italy, his conspicuous bravery was rewarded by the award of imperial Germany's highest decoration – the *Pour le Merite*. By 1937 he had reached the rank of colonel and the following October was selected to command the Führer Escort Battalion. After that came a post

DESERT FOX *Rommel's Afrika Korps successes made him Hitler's favorite general, but by the time of D-Day Rommel had become disillusioned with his Führer.*

as instructor in the war academy at Wiener Neustadt and on 1 August 1939, with Hitler's keen support, he was promoted to the rank of major-general.

From France to the North African desert

On the outbreak of war, Rommel was in command of the military detachments at Führer Headquarters; in recognition of the abilities he showed in that post, he was rewarded with command of 7th Panzer Division, which he led into the French campaign in 1940. Here, Rommel showed such drive that his formation won the nickname of the "ghost division".

In early 1941, Rommel – now a lieutenant-general – was put in charge of a totally new formation – the Deutsches Afrika Korps – which Hitler had decided to send to the aid of his Italian allies. Over the years, the command was enlarged and became firstly Panzer Group

Africa and subsequently Panzer Army Africa. Rommel himself became a colonel-general in January 1942 and a full field marshal that June, after a brilliantly executed offensive had all but destroyed the British 8th Army. Rommel's offensive, fought in the heat of summer, brought the Axis forces to within 60 miles of Alexandria, but this was to prove the high water mark of their advance. Rommel's thrust was checked by Auchinleck at the first battle of El Alamein and his subsequent attempts to break through the British defence were defeated at Alam Halfa.

The Axis forces were over-stretched and short of supplies; in contrast, *Montgomery*, 8th Army's new commander, was receiving plentiful reinforcement. Rommel, now a sick man, flew back to Germany on leave, but, while he was absent from his post, 8th Army opened its decisive counteroffensive at the El Alamein position. Rommel promptly flew back to Africa, where, having made his customary quick assessment of the situation, he launched a series of counterattacks, but to no avail. Firstly, Rommel was short of tanks – and the supplies to fuel them – but, more importantly, Montgomery did not waste his armor in "cavalry-style" charges, as had his predecessors. Rommel lost the resulting slogging match and was forced to withdraw from Libya, pursued by Montgomery. Though he managed to delay the British advance on a succession of natural defence lines, he fell further back into Tunisia, where during February 1943, he took up command of Army Group Tunis.

"The longest day"

Flown home from Tunis by the Führer's direct order, Rommel advised on the plans for the defence of Italy, but his next active command was of Army Group B, in France, where he was subordinate to the Supreme Commander West, Field Marshal von *Rundstedt*.

Rommel soon came into conflict with von Rundstedt as to how the allied invasion was to be met and defeated. In contrast to von Rundstedt, who intended to keep the key panzer divisions in reserve away from the coast, Rommel insisted that they be stationed as far forward as possible. This was the only way, he argued, in which the German armor could smash the landings at the point where they would be most vulnerable – on the beaches. He was also keenly aware of allied air superiority. The argument went up to Hitler, who characteristically decided to reserve for himself the decision as to how, where and when the panzers would ultimately be employed. Rommel and von Rundstedt thus had the worst of both worlds. In his dual capacity as Inspector General of Coastal Defences, however, Rommel was able to ensure his directives were obeyed, particularly the siting of fixed defensive positions and the thickening of the beach defence belts by the erection of under-water obstacles and the planting of thousands of land mines. All depended on where the allies would attack Hitler's vaunted Atlantic Wall.

Neither Rommel nor von Rundstedt anticipated the eventual invasion site, so the allied landings in Normandy took both men by surprise. Rommel energetically strove to contain the perimeter of the allied bridgehead; he achieved an outstanding success by repulsing Operation *Goodwood*, the offensive the British mounted in July. Here, it was Montgomery's bad luck that he chose to launch his thrust in an area east of the Orne river that Rommel had personally reconnoitered and along which he had located a series of defence lines. Rommel had read the British commander's mind, anticipating correctly that Montgomery would attack on that sector because he had failed to achieve a breakthrough on any other.

Rommel stationed his units one behind the other to a depth of ten miles – far deeper than the British had expected. In the front line were placed the three infantry Divisions of 86th Corps, behind which was 21st Panzer, reinforced by a battalion of Tiger tanks. Behind lay a defensive line, the strongpoints of which were fortified villages. The German artillery belt, placed on the northern side of the Bourgebus ridge, formed the fourth line. Dug in on the ridge itself were the SS Panzergrenadiers and behind them, again, an SS armored battle group of tanks, plus more grenadiers.

Rommel's last success

Rommel knew that he was in a strong position. Montgomery's tanks would not be able to deploy until they had crossed the three Orne bridges in single file, while his artillery would be in no position to cover the armor until the guns, too, had been brought across the river. German observers on the Bourgebus ridge would soon determine the direction of the British thrust.

Rommel was also aware of the standard allied procedure for overcoming such tactical disadvantages and laid his plans to defeat the anticipated aerial bombardment. He simply pulled back his forward units, so that the bomb loads of more than 4,000 aircraft fell into thin air. Once the bombardment had been completed, Rommel's men re-occupied their bomb-cratered positions in time to meet the Anglo-Canadian armored assault.

What the allies were confronted with was a strong German defence, made up of first-class soldiers holding first-class positions and well supplied with ammunition. By evening, many British and Canadian tanks were ablaze and the objectives had not been gained. All that was achieved was a small increase in the area of the British perimeter at a cost of 200 tanks and 1500 casualties.

Death of a hero

Rommel, however, was unaware of the success of what was to be his last battle. His staff car had crashed while under air attack and he had been badly injured. Before he had recovered sufficiently from his wounds to return to active service, he was under suspicion of having been involved in the bomb plot to kill Hitler. The Führer gave Rommel a choice. He could take poison, in which case it would be announced that he had died as a result of his wounds and his family would not be threatened. The alternative was arrest, a state trial and public disgrace. Hitler's one-time favorite commander chose suicide.

ROTMISTROV
Pavel A (1901-   )
CHIEF MARSHAL OF THE SOVIET ARMED FORCES
Second World War

Pavel Rotmistrov was a passionate believer in the power of armor used en masse; as a lecturer at the Stalin Academy of Mechanization and Motorization before the war, he advocated the strategic use of tanks as a war-winning weapon. At Kursk in 1943, he was to demonstrate his mastery of his subject in a battle that led to the destruction of the cream of the Nazi panzer force.

Rotmistrov was born on 23 June 1901, in the village of Kovorova in north Russia; he joined the Soviet army in 1919 and the Communist Party in the same year. As a dedicated Communist, he fought in the Russian Civil War and took part in the bloody and savage repression of the 1921 mutiny at Kronstadt. His party membership, together with his natural skill in soldiering, ensured him entry into the Frunze Military Academy in 1931.

From theory to practice

Through a study of foreign works on the theory of amored warfare and from evaluating the evidence of the German campaigns in Poland and in France, Rotmistrov was firmly convinced that the potential of armored vehicles fighting en masse and in pursuit of strategic objectives was almost limitless, provided that certain conditions obtained. Only en masse, he believed, could tank forces be truly effective. He was therefore dismayed when the Soviet tank armies were split into brigade-sized infantry support units – exactly the role the defeated French had given their armor in 1940. Shortly before the German invasion of the USSR, however, this destructive policy was reversed and an attempt was made to reamalgamate the tank brigades into major formations. It was too late for this policy to be put into effect completely by the time of the Nazi attack and, as Rotmistrov had feared, the scattered Russian armored forces were unable to halt the panzer onslaught.

After several appointments, Rotmistrov was given command of 7th Tank Corps, which he led during the Stalingrad battles. On 14 December it was his corps that spearheaded the assault that 5th Shock Army launched to smash the German bridgeheads on the Don; as a reward for its part in the operation, his command was later regraded and numbered as 3rd Guards Corps. His skilful handling of the corps contributed greatly to the successful outcome of operations against 1st Panzer Army during January 1943 in the Soviet attack to recapture Rostov.

Tank versus tank

During the initial battles that marked the launching of the German summer offensive of 1943, 5th Guards Tank Army, which Rotmistrov now commanded, was under Stavka (Soviet High Command) control as part of the strategic reserve. Known as Steppe Front and commanded by *Koniev*, the Stavka intended to use this not only to open the Soviet counterattack, but also to lead the advance that would follow with Kharkov as its objective. The German aim was to smash the huge Soviet salient that was bulging into the Nazi lines, with German armies driving from north and south to meet around Kursk. Although the Soviets had been long

TANK COMMANDER
Rotmistrov, the USSR's leading exponent of tank warfare.

aware of the German plan and though they outnumbered the enemy, the German pressure forced Stavka to release formations from Koniev's reserves quite early in the battle. One of these was Rotmistrov's Guards Tank Army. He was ordered to take up a position between Oboyan and Prokharovka and then, together with 5th Guards Infantry Army, to drive south towards Bykovka. The Soviet aim was to outflank the panzer force striking northwards towards Kursk.

In the event the weight of the German attack meant a reduction in the scale of the proposed counter-thrust; Rotmistrov's army was left to bear the brunt of the battle largely unsupported, though he had the backing of 10 artillery regiments *Zhukov* was able to allocate him. Nevertheless, his tank formations deployed and began their drive to battle against *Hoth*'s 4th Panzer Army. On a battlefield not more than 3 miles long by 4 miles wide was to occur the mightiest clash of armor ever seen in military history up to the present date. German pressure came from two sides, the main attack of some 600 vehicles coming from the west and a smaller force of some 300 machines driving up from the south.

Leaving part of his force to fight a defensive battle against the Germans in the west, Rotmistrov made his main effort in the south. He had a slight numerical advantage, while his troops were equipped principally with the battle-tested T34 tank. On the other hand, the Pkwf V and VI, with which the Germans were equipped, still showed signs of having been rushed into service too quickly before the many technical defects in their design had been solved.

The decisive tank battle was fought out on 12 July 1943, with Rotmistrov watching seated on a hillside near Prokhorovka. At the end of the day literally hundreds of tanks lay destroyed and burning on the battlefield. Though the Germans had won a tactical success, the strategic victory belonged to Rotmistrov since he could replace his tank losses while the Germans could not. Moreover, on that one day, he had destroyed the myth of German superiority in panzer operations.

Rotmistrov went on to lead his army in the battles of autumn 1944 on the north/central front, which led to the

Soviet breakthrough into East Prussia and Lithuania. From then until the end of the war, he was deputy commander of the armored and mechanized troops of the Soviet army; he then held a senior military post in the Far East before becoming the senior inspector general in the Soviet Ministry of Defence.

Rotmistrov was at his most able when it came to the tactics of armored warfare, although he also showed an excellent grasp of strategy. This tactical skill was evident at Kursk, when he realized that his T34s were outgunned by the 88mm armament of their German adversaries, but that this advantage would be nullified at close range. He accordingly ordered his armored regiments to engage the enemy at close quarters; despite their heavy losses, this order was instrumental in smashing the German attacks. No-one played a more telling part in winning that victory than the heavily moustached and bespectacled figure of Pavel Rotmistrov.

VON RUNDSTEDT
Gerd (1875-1953)
GERMAN FIELD MARSHAL
Second World War

To the plaintive question "what shall we do now?", asked by Field Marshal Keitel, chief of Hitler's OKW, after the allied invasion of Normandy in June 1944, the curt retort of Gerd von Rundstedt – "make peace, you idiot" – is a clear indication of the forthright nature of the Reich's senior field marshal. It also shows that German general staff officers of the old school did not regard themselves as "rubber stamps", but as experts, who expected their criticisms, objections and suggestions to be listened to and acted upon by their superiors. Gerd von Rundstedt was a soldier of the pre-First World War general staff, some of whose oldest members had served under the great von *Moltke*. He thus absorbed the influences and attitudes of those men and was certainly not afraid to speak his mind.

Von Rundstedt, himself the son of a general, was born on 12 December 1875, at Aschersleben; following service in a cadet academy at Potsdam, he was gazetted as an infantry officer in 1892. After a short period of regimental duty, he joined the general staff in 1907, part of his job being to help to re-organize the Turkish high command. He served as a staff officer throughout the First World War, and during the post-war Weimar period he was involved in the clandestine rearmament effort.

First clash with the Führer
In those inter-war years, Rundstedt rose through the Wehrmacht command structure; by 1938, he was commanding 1st Army Corps in Berlin. That year, Hitler, having dismissed his War Minister, von Blomberg, and the commander-in-chief of the army, von Fritsch, nominated his own favorite general, Walter von Reichenau, to take over the latter post. This was unacceptable to the

army's senior commanders. Acting as their spokesman, von Rundstedt told Hitler that he had made the wrong decision and maintained his opposition until a compromise was reached with the appointment of von Brauchitsch. Given this opposition, it was probably with relief that Hitler accepted Rundstedt's retirement on the grounds of age in the same year.

Back into service
Shortly before the outbreak of war in 1939, however, Hitler recalled von Rundstedt from retirement to command Army Group South in the Polish campaign. Rundstedt speedily demonstrated his ability to conduct fast and mobile warfare; his units swiftly advanced to a position between the Poles' western armies and their capital, Warsaw. There, in the bend of the Bzura river, Rundstedt destroyed the bulk of the Polish effectives. He was to win even more distinction in the attack on France – again being prepared to speak his mind.

Early in 1940, during the planning stages of the campaign, von Rundstedt was convinced that *Manstein's* audacious advocacy of a thrust out of the Ardennes was the plan that should be adopted, even though this conflicted with orthodox opinion. Here, he was fortunate that Hitler, for once, shared his belief.

For the campaign in the west, Rundstedt commanded Army Group A, which consisted of four infantry armies and a panzer group. The massive concentration of armor he commanded smashed through the French and in two separate drives – the first through Sedan and to the Channel and the second against the remaining French forces south of the Somme – gained total victory within six weeks. A grateful Führer promoted von Rundstedt to the rank of field marshal and named him as supreme commander in the west, a command that extended from Norway almost to the Mediterranean.

When it was decided to turn on the USSR, von Rundstedt was given command of Army Group South, his task being to destroy the Soviet army west of the Dnieper river. In a succession of brilliant operations, his forces completed the greatest encirclement in the history of warfare by killing or capturing more than a million Soviet soldiers. Now, however, von Rundstedt had his first setback. By October 1941 Army Group South had reached the Don river, but its drive was now so strongly contested that he ordered a withdrawal – the first strategic retreat that the German Army had been forced to make during the war. He defended his decision against all the criticisms of OKW, but the strain brought on a heart attack and he asked to be relieved of his command – pre-empting Hitler's intention to replace him.

Back to the west
Von Rundstedt remained inactive until March 1942, when he was reappointed supreme commander in the west. He was again relieved of command after his failure to defeat the D-Day invasion, but was recalled once more when the German front in north Belgium was ruptured in September 1944. Von Rundstedt restored the military

situation and went on to launch the last major German offensive in the west – the "battle of the Bulge" – in December 1944, though he made no secret of his view that it was an ill-timed operation. After its failure, he organized the subsequent retreat to the Rhine. In March 1945 he was relieved of command and, at the end of the war, was captured at the spa of Bad Toelz. He was held by the British as a war criminal, but was released in May 1949 on grounds of ill health. He died on 24 February 1953.

In the campaigns von Rundstedt fought in Poland, France and southern Russia, he showed a masterly command of the skills of mobile warfare. In the years of Germany's military decline, he also demonstrated his skill on the defensive. All his campaigns, whether in attack or defence, were excellent examples of thoroughness in planning and speed of execution. Although Hitler – particularly in the last years of the war – had nothing but contempt and hatred for his military commanders, he did show "the old gentleman," as he called von Rundstedt, a degree of respect which he gave to no other leader of his armed forces. The Führer may have not accepted the field marshal's advice, but, in a crisis, it was to von Rundstedt the Führer turned to overcome it.

SENGER UND ETTERLIN
Fridolin (1891-1963)
GERMAN GENERAL
Second World War

Fridolin von Senger und Etterlin's claim to fame as a commander lies in his stubborn defence of Monte Cassino, which held up the allied advance in Italy for many crucial months. Yet, paradoxocally, his greatest military success was his greatest personal tragedy. A deeply religious Catholic and a lay member of the Benedictine Order, he saw the Benedictine mother church at Cassino totally destroyed by war.

Fridolin von Senger und Etterlin was born at Waldshut on 4 Spetember 1891. He entered the army during the First World War, serving in an artillery regiment. In 1921, he was selected as a candidate for general staff service, but, though he passed the qualifying examination, he was returned to regimental duty for being over the age limit. After 1935, with the massive expansion of the army, more staff officers needed to be trained and Major von Senger was accordingly detached from his regiment and posted to the general staff. In 1939, he served as commander of a regiment of motorized cavalry and then led a brigade in the 1940 campaign in France, where his brigade raced *Rommel*'s 7th Panzer Division to capture Cherbourg. Late in 1942, he commanded a panzer division spearheading an attempt to relieve the encircled 6th Army at Stalingrad. Although this failed, von Senger gained other successes in southern Russia, for which he was promoted to the rank of lieutenant-general and given command of a corps in Italy.

The Italian campaign
In the summer of 1943, Mussolini was deposed and the Italians were seeking to extricate themselves from the war. The resulting confusion led to fighting between the German units garrisoning the islands in the Tyrrhenian sea and the Italians. Hitler ordered von Senger to shoot all the Italian officers who had been taken prisoner in the fighting, but he refused to obey the Führer. However, his success in carrying out the evacuation of German forces from Corsica without loss, despite allied air and naval supremacy, brought him congratulation from Hitler, rather than a reprimand or dismissal.

Having accomplished the tricky task of evacuating the German garrisons, von Senger took up command of 14th Panzer Corps, part of German 10th Army. When he took up his command, his corps was conducting a fighting retreat from the Volturno river towards the Gustav Line, a chain of brilliantly sited mountain defences that had been constructed behind two swift flowing rivers with the small town of Cassino as its focal point. At Cassino, the mountains ran to within a few miles of the sea, leaving only a narrow gap – the Liri Valley – through which ran the main road and rail route between the south and Rome. The allies could only advance towards the Italian capital through the valley; to enter the valley, they first had to capture Cassino.

Battle at Cassino
It is with the battles of Cassino that the name of Fridolin von Senger und Etterlin is most closely associated. Allied strategy was to launch a frontal assault to take the town, followed by a landing behind the Gustav Line at Anzio to take the German forces in the rear. The plan was confounded by the German supreme commander, *Kesselring*, who, though taken by surprise at Anzio, promptly formed the 14th Army to pin the allies on the beaches, so leaving the forces in Cassino free to deal with the frontal assaults of US 5th Army.

The US 5th Army launched a series of unsuccessful attacks – the first battle of Cassino – from the middle of January to 12 February 1944. The British 8th Army, leaving only skeleton forces on the Adriatic sector, was then moved across the peninsula and 2nd New Zealand Corps was put into the fight. It was during this second battle – from 15 to 18 February 1944 – that the New Zealand commander, Bernard *Freyberg*, demanded the bombing of Cassino's venerable monastery, which he claimed was being used by the Germans as an observation point. Von Senger evacuated the monks but, more importantly, requisitioned army lorries to take the abbey's moveable treasures to safety. Despite the bombing, the New Zealanders failed in their turn, as did a third attempt to take Cassino in March.

The order now went out that Cassino had to be taken at all cost. The allies regrouped to strike again during May in a fourth battle. In this, they finally forced their way into the Liri Valley, the resulting pressure aiding the break-out from Anzio. Under pressure, German 10th Army withdrew northwards.

Allied success at Cassino seemed likely to trap 10th Army in the hills, while the Anzio break-out had all but destroyed 14th Army. A strong thrust by the Anzio forces eastwards would have trapped the Germans, but, at that critical moment they were saved by Mark *Clark*, commander of US 5th Army, who decided to divert his forces to the capture of Rome. The reprieve allowed Kesselring to rebuild his shattered front. On his right flank, there were only isolated units fighting desperate defensive battles. Kesselring decided that he would fill the gap with von Senger's corps.

Because of the pressure under which he was fighting, von Senger could not simply take his corps out of the line and switch it across to its new position. Instead, he would have to side-step his units, dropping off a formation in one position or absorbing another in the westward side slip. His task was to take his corps of five front-line divisions across the front of the allied armies, at the same time conducting a fighting withdrawal. The operation lasted two weeks; at the end of it von Senger's 14th Panzer Corps, the only effective unit of 14th Army, was positioned ready to block 5th Army's drive northwards to Florence.

Von Senger's defence of Cassino and the westward movement of his corps described above demonstrates very clearly that, although he had not had the same long and arduous training for high command as other German generals, he possessed a natural battle ability that made him their equal. Despite his lack of formal training, von Senger's planning, admistrative and organizational skills were in the best tradition of the general staff. Himself an anti-Nazi and an Anglophile, Fridolin von Senger und Etterlin demonstrated his modesty in his description of the Cassino battle. In it he did not praise his planning skills or tactical ability; he praised his subordinates – in particular, the junior officers – and the men they commanded. He knew that, without the fighting ability of ordinary soldiers, even the best-laid plans do not succeed.

SIMPSON
William H (1888-   )
US GENERAL
Second World War

During part of the campaign in north-west Europe in 1944/45, the order of battle of *Montgomery*'s 21st Army Group included US 9th Army, led by the bald-headed William H Simpson. Montgomery had no more loyal US supporter than "Big Simp", as he was known throughout the US army.

William Simpson was born in Texas in 1888, the son of a Confederate veteran. He served in France during the First World War, becoming chief of staff of the 33rd Division after the armistice. In the years preceding the Second World War, he commanded the 30th and then the 35th Divisions before being given command of 12

Corps. His leadership of all these formations was impeccable; by September 1943, he had been promoted to the rank of lieutenant-general and given command firstly of the 4th Army and then of the 8th Army (subsequently renumbered 9th Army).

Serving with Montgomery
Simpson's command formed part of Omar *Bradley*'s 12th Army Group as it approached the Siegfried Line on the German border in October 1944; in December, however, it was transferred to Montgomery during the Battle of the Bulge. The German Ardennes offensive had taken the allies by surprise and, in a regrouping to contain the assault, *Eisenhower*, the supreme allied commander, placed all US forces on the north of the salient the German thrust had created under British field control. After the offensive had been crushed, Simpson and 9th Army stayed with the British, forming the right wing of Montgomery's Army Group as it advanced eastwards into Germany towards the Rhine.

During this period, Simpson and his army played a leading part in the Roer Valley offensive – they had been involved in fighting there even before the Ardennes offensive had opened. In February 1945, 9th Army was given the task of crossing the Roer river as part of the general plan of advance. Despite being baulked by floods when the Germans opened the Roer dam sluices, Simpson pressed home his attacks and by 10 March, his forces, together with the other allied armies, were positioned on the west bank of the Rhine.

The lost prize
During the first week of April 1945, Simpson and 9th Army came under Bradley's command again, as Eisenhower had decided that 12th US Army Group would make the final thrust into the heartland of the dying Reich. Simpson believed that, as his army had the least distance to cover, it would soon receive orders to advance and take Berlin, but he was to be disappointed. On 15 April, Bradley flew to 9th Army headquarters and told Simpson that he was not to advance from the positions they were holding along the Elbe. The thinking at SHAEF headquarters was that the city was now simply a political objective and that the last remaining center of Nazi resistance was in the south – the so-called Alpine, Redoubt. "The only thing that stood between us and Berlin", commented one 9th Army officer, "was Eisenhower." Obeying his orders, Simpson stayed in position while the Soviet army fought for and captured Berlin.

Because the alert, intelligent Simpson spent only a short time in Europe, he had little opportunity to demonstrate his undoubted ability as a field commander. The limited number of operations he did conduct demonstrated the thoroughness with which he planned, his insistance on excellent reconnaissance and his keen military judgement. He was a true military professional, competent and able without being flashy. In the words of Eisenhower: "Simpson was the type of leader that the American soldiers deserved."

SLIM
William (1891-1970)
BRITISH FIELD-MARSHAL
Second World War

In 1915, the young "Bill" Slim's army career seemed at an end, when he was seriously wounded and invalided out of the service. Four decades later, however, as commander of 14th Army, he won the greatest land victory the allies achieved over the Japanese in the Second World War.

Unlike the majority of his fellow professionals, Slim's training for his military career was unconventional. He did not attend a military academy; he was commissioned while a lance-corporal in the Territorial army, shortly after the outbreak of the First World War. He was critically wounded during the Dardanelles campaign, but, within a year, by means he never divulged, he was back in the war, fighting in Mesopotamia, where he won the Military Cross. He transferred to the Indian army in 1919, and was commissioned into the Gurkha Rifles. His Second World War service started in East Africa, where he led the Indian army's 10th Brigade (part of the 5th Indian Division) in the campaign against the Italian garrison in Eritrea. In it, he showed considerable personal bravery, breaking the deadlock before Gallabat by leading the assault that captured the town, riding in a Bren gun carrier. Wounded again, he returned to command 10th Indian Division in Iraq, Syria and Persia.

The "forgotten army"

During March 1942, Slim was posted to the Far East to command 1st Burma Corps, which was being attacked by Japanese 15th Army. Throughout April and May he conducted a skilful fighting retreat back to Tiddim, across the Chindwin and to Imphal, the gateway to India. In October 1943, he was appointed commander of 14th Army. Slim had already begun to plan the reconquest of Burma, though, aware of British weakness, he did not believe that a major offensive could be launched before the dry season of 1944. There were, however, small operations that could be mounted; as early as December 1943, he struck into the Arakan with two divisions, which the Japanese separated and surrounded the following February. Here, Slim showed his determination. Instead of authorizing a retreat, he supplied the encircled formations by air, while moving up more troops to surround the Japanese. The enemy was destroyed.

During March and April 1944, the main Japanese army in Burma launched an all-out offensive to capture the key positions of Kohima and Imphal as a prerequisite for an attack into India. After bitter defensive fighting, the enemy was held and then forced back towards the Chindwin valley. Now plentifully supplied with the approaching end of the war in Europe, Slim was able to undertake amphibious operations, launch ambitious air drops and deploy armor on a scale that he and his army had hitherto been unable to contemplate. Accordingly, he increased

JUNGLE GENERAL Slim transformed allied land fortunes against the Japanese in his triumphant Burma campaign.

the scale and scope of his operations.

One bold plan involved the use of faked wireless traffic to bluff the Japanese into attacking what they thought to be an isolated formation; when the Japanese were deeply committed, Slim slipped his main force around their flank to encircle the 15th and 33rd Armies and defeat them. The process culminated with the capture of Rangoon on 2 May 1945, when the Burma campaign closed. Through a combination of rapid movement, the use of unconventional forces, such as the Chindits, and by the extensive use of air supply, Slim and his 14th Army, which had begun the campaign weakened by a long and hard retreat and had then contained a series of bitter enemy offensives, had recovered to inflict the greatest defeat of the war on the Japanese army. After the withdrawal from Burma, starved of supplies and at the bottom of the priority list as far as war priorities were concerned, the soldiers of 14th Army had dubbed themselves the "forgotten army". Slim's triumph in Burma was ample reward for his – and their – efforts.

Slim was an extremely popular commander. His huge frame and determined face bore all the characteristics of a born leader. He refused to live in the relative luxury of a proper headquarters while his men were enduring jungle conditions, locating his battle headquarters as far forward as possible and living on the same rations as his troops.

His insistence on putting his men in the picture by talking to them informally was deeply appreciated, although he spoke to them less to give information on his future plans and more to make himself familiar to them. As he himself said, "I want you to see me, not because I am an oil painting but because you ought to know what the bloke issuing the orders looks like." It was this direct, no-nonsense approach that made Slim such an excellent commander of men, enabled him to establish successful relations with the controversial US general "Vinegar Joe" *Stilwell* and made Slim, in post-war years, a popular Governor-General of Australia.

"Bill" Slim, the man who rose from lance-corporal to field-marshal in 35 years, died in London on 1 December 1970. He is remembered as a man of great personal bravery, an excellent tactician, and a determined fighter in both defensive and offensive battles.

SPAATZ
Carl (1891-1974)
GENERAL (US AIR FORCE)
Second World War

One of the leading theorists of strategic bombing who, during the Second World War, was able to deploy massive air fleets to prove the validity of his theories, was the USAAF general, Carl Spaatz.

Spaatz was born in Pennsylvania on 28 June 1891; and after training at a Flying School in 1915-1916, he flew on active service missions on the Western Front. His forceful personality soon brought him promotion to major and the command of a fighter squadron. During his war-time career, he won two victories in the air.

Belief in bombing

In the post-war years, Spaatz served alternately on squadron and staff duties, the latter chiefly involving training and research. During this period, he worked on the problem of increasing aircraft endurance – this culminated in a non-stop 150-hour flight, made possible by in-flight refueling. As a dedicated professional, Spaatz was also aware of the theories of such advocates of strategic bombing as Mitchell, Douhet and *Harris*. Mitchell's court-martial for publicizing US air weaknesses had as strong an effect on Spaatz as it had upon other forward-thinking airmen, who were convinced that air power would be the decisive factor in any future war.

In 1939 Spaatz was serving on the staff of Air Force Combat Command; in 1940 he was sent to Britain as an official observer during the Battle of Britain. What he saw impressed him greatly and, shortly after his return to the USA, he began to work out heavy bomber tactics and to think out what should constitute priority targets for the bomber force. He understood fully the concept of strategic bombing – that industry is based upon a small number of key products. Destroy the sources of those products

and the enemy war machine is therefore forced to a halt.

Spaatz was not able to introduce his ideas immediately, for his first senior overseas command took him to French North Africa, where allied troops had landed during November 1942. His command abilities, tested there, were further improved in Sicily and in the first weeks of the Italian campaign. Together with the other officers who would lead the allied armies into Europe, Spaatz then returned to Britain, where he stepped up operations by 8th Air Force. Earlier US raids had included attacks upon submarine construction yards and minor industrial targets inside Germany, but nothing of real strategic value. Spaatz began operations by sending the combined 8th and 9th Air Forces against the Romanian oil fields at Ploesti – the Nazi war machine's sole major source of natural oil. In pursuit of his theories on strategic bombing, he then concentrated upon vital strategic targets, such as the Schweinfurt ball-bearing plants.

A round-the-clock air war

During January 1944 Spaatz, now a lieutenant-general, was given command of US Strategic Air Forces – the 8th and 15th Air Forces – based in Britain and Italy respectively. The allied air forces now began their round-the-clock offensive against Germany, with the Americans, flying by day and the RAF by night. Initially, at least, the decision to fly by day cost the Americans dear, for existing escort fighters could only protect the bombers as far as Aachen, on the German frontier. From then on, the bomber streams were unprotected and often suffered severe losses as a result. To reduce these, Spaatz introduced rigorous training methods and improved the tactics used by the so-called "aircraft boxes". In these, layer upon layer of heavy bombers flew in a close-knit formation, which enabled them both to co-ordinate a storm of defensive fire against the Luftwaffe's intercepting fighters and to bomb simultaneously upon the order of the leading aircraft's bombardier.

During what was termed "Big Week" – from 20 to 26 February 1944 – days and nights of co-ordinated strikes by 8th Air Force and RAF's Bomber Command struck at Germany's aircraft factories. During that period, 8th Air Force alone lost 244 heavy bombers and the Luftwaffe 692 fighters. Gradually, Spaatz's strategy and tactics began to take their toll; in the battles for supremacy in German skies, the Luftwaffe lost 2,442 fighters in air battles from March to May. Though the campaign failed in its main objective – many factories were now underground or had been dispersed – the Luftwaffe's losses meant that 8th Air Force now enjoyed air superiority.

Overlord and after

In the run up to *Overlord* – the cross-Channel invasion of France in June 1944 – Spaatz deployed his strategic bombers in a tactical role, using them to cut road and rail communications to isolate the Normandy area from the rest of France; his bomber squadrons maintained their role until the allied breakout from the beachhead had been accomplished. Once proper airfields had been constructed, US fighters were now able to escort the bomber "boxes" to and from their targets. Untroubled by German interception, the bombers could bomb more accurately and, as their raids grew in intensity, German war production at last began to decline dramatically. As an example of the scale of operation, a total of 42,000 missions was flown by all units of the USAAF and RAF during one three-day period in March 1945 alone.

Spaatz's bombers began to run out of strategic objectives as the allied armies overran Germany, so he then unleashed them, as he had done before D-day, to attack tactical targets in order to speed the ground assault. With his task in Europe completed, Spaatz, now a general in rank, moved to the Far East to launch his Strategic Air Forces against Japan. The use of the atomic bomb brought the war to a speedy conclusion.

Like many senior commanders, Spaatz was a gently-spoken man, but concealing beneath his quiet manner a determination and ruthlessness that ensured the success of the plans he initiated. He knew that strategic bombing would work. The policy was correct. It was the strategy and tactics which must be made to fit the policy. Spaatz, the ex-fighter ace with a fine tactical brain, made sure that they did.

SPRUANCE
Raymond A (1886-1969)
US ADMIRAL
Second World War

During the battle of Midway, one of the most decisive sea battles of the Second World War and probably of world history, Rear-Admiral Fletcher was forced to pass control of the US task forces to his subordinate, Admiral Raymond Spruance. By a tactical withdrawal, Spruance gained a major strategic victory over the Japanese.

Spruance was born in Baltimore in July 1886, and commissioned into the navy during 1906. He spent the First World War in the Bureau of Engineering's electrical division; in the post-war years, he studied at the naval war college and served in naval intelligence. In 1938, he was put in command of the battleship *Mississippi*, with the rank of rear-admiral.

After the Japanese attack on Pearl Harbor in December 1941, Spruance, commanding 5th Cruiser Division, was selected to take over command of Admiral Halsey's Carrier Task Force while Halsey was in hospital. This was one of the two carrier task forces that fought the battle of Midway. *Nimitz*, the commander-in-chief of the US Pacific Fleet, divided his carrier force into two task forces – T F 17 under Rear-Admiral Fletcher and T F 16 under Spruance – and positioned them north-east of Midway, which he knew was about to come under Japanese attack. Naval air patrols at dawn on 4 June 1942, discovered Admiral Nagumo's First Air Fleet of four aircraft carriers and smaller vessels steaming towards Midway. Nagumo had

been assured that there were no US carriers in the area and that he had nothing to fear from the heavy units of the US navy, as these were sailing to repel feint attacks upon the Aleutian islands.

Nagumo's bombers were launched to attack the island, while his fighter umbrella defended the carriers against US land-based machines, which had been flown off from Midway. Nagumo was then told that a second strike was needed and prepared his aircraft accordingly. It was then that one of his defensive air patrols reported the presence of Spruance's task force to the north-east. He was now in a very difficult situation. The planes from the first Midway mission were being landed, while others had to be made ready to attack the US carriers. Below decks Japanese fitters were hurriedly changing bomb fuses from fragmentation to naval-action.

The tide turns at Midway

While Nagumo's flight decks were cluttered with aircraft unprepared for battle Spruance's aircraft attacked, but their efforts achieved nothing. The dive-bombers did not find the target and the torpedo bombers, attacking without fighter escort, were shot from the skies. Confident that he had won a victgory Nagumo began to fly off his own aircraft against the US fleet. The operation was under way when the US dive bombers at last found their target and within minutes had hit and set ablaze three of the four Japanese carriers. Planes from the surviving carrier, *Hiryu*, struck and crippled the USS *Yorktown* and Fletcher immediated passed over control of the battle to Spruance. Aircraft from the USS *Enterprise* then found the *Hiryu* and sank her.

Yamamoto, whose fleet was still superior in number to that of the US, concentrated and headed east, intending to lure Spruance into an unequal surface battle. The US admiral, correctly assessing the Japanese commander's intention, withdrew eastwards until, during the night of 5 June, Yamamoto called off the operation. Spruance then altered his own course to pursue the Japanese, but the need to refuel his ships led to the pursuit being broken off, the fleet returning to Pearl Harbor. During the return voyage Fletcher's USS *Yorktown*, which was being towed back to base, was sunk together with her escorting destroyer. These were the only two US naval losses in a battle that had changed the whole strategic picture.

Spruance was promoted to vice-admiral in May 1943, and directed operations in the Gilbert Islands and then against the Marshall Islands. In the battle of the Philippine Sea in June 1944, his carrier aircraft again struck the Japanese fleet, while he also commanded US naval forces in the invasions of Iwo Jima and Okinawa. He succeeded to the command of the Pacific Fleet in November 1945, retired from the navy in 1948 and died in 1969.

Spruance was one of the quiet, dependable, capable commanders upon whom success in naval warfare depends. Logical in thought, fast in both comprehension and decision and resolute in action, he, perhaps more than any other allied leader, can be said to have changed the course of the war in a single day.

STILWELL
Joseph W (1883-1946)
US GENERAL
Second World War

Joseph Stilwell was one of the most controversial US commanders of the Second World War. He was aptly named "Vinegar Joe," for he became notorious for the asperity of his comments upon those whom he considered to be incompetent.

Stillwell was born in Palatka, Florida on 19 March 1883. He graduated from West Point in 1904 and served, firstly, in the Philippines and then as an instructor at the military academy. When the USA entered the First World War, he served in France as a staff officer. His fluency in Chinese led to a three-year posting in that country, Stilwell returning there in 1932 as military attaché in Peking, where he was stationed until 1939.

"VINEGAR JOE" Stilwell understood the Chinese as did few other generals.

Shortly after the USA entered the Second World War, Stilwell returned to China for a third time to take up an appointment as chief of staff to Chiang Kai Shek; he also commanded US forces in the China-Burma-India theater of operations. He thus was responsible to three superiors – the US chief of staff, Chiang Kai Shek and the British commander-in-chief in India. This confused command structure made for poor and often strained relations between Stilwell and his superiors.

Protecting the Burma road

In the first months of 1942, with the Japanese advancing swiftly through Burma, the British commander-in-chief, Alexander, accepted Chiang's offer of help; accordingly, two Chinese armies led by Stilwell arrived at Maymyo, where, together with British troops, they formed a defensive line. The Japanese, however, cut off one Chinese division, which had to be rescued by other allied troops. Then, in April, they attacked again, this time dispersing Chinese 6th Army. Stilwell regrouped his scattered units and, leading them in person, struck back at the Japanese. The enemy pressure was too strong, however; by the end of May, the allied forces had been forced to evacuate their last footholds in Burma.

This was particularly disastrous for the Chinese, since the loss of Burma meant the cutting of the Burma road, their one land link with their allies. Impatient to return to Burma to reopen this vital line of communication, Stilwell began to train the Chinese formations that had escaped from Burma with him; he also put them to work together with local levies, on the construction of the

Ledo road, across the Chin hills in Assam. He was forced to employ part of his force to protect the road builders when, early in 1943, the Japanese attacked the border area of India and northern Burma, but, towards the end of the year, Chiang and Wavell, Alexander's successor, agreed to Stilwell's plan to undertake a two-division offensive to restore the broken land route. Japanese reaction was swift, part of the force being surrounded. Stilwell broke through the Japanese ring and, in a series of fierce counter-attacks, restored his advance's impetus.

Crisis and victory

In January 1944, Stilwell, now deputy supreme allied commander under Mountbatten, led a force of three, later increased to five, divisions in an attempt to capture the north Burma city of Myitkyina and the airfields there before the monsoon broke. His initial operations met heavy Japanese resistance and counter-attacks, but he continued to make slow, steady process. Myitkyina eventually fell and Stilwell then pushed two divisions down the Mongaung Valley, winning a success his superiors had thought impossible to achieve. Reinforced, and with the ground drying out after the monsoon, Stilwell launched five divisions in a further outflanking operation, which opened with great promise. Their success was even more remarkable when it is considered that, compared to Western standards, Stilwell's divisions were ill-equipped and under-strength; each Chinese "division", in fact, had the fighting strength of a weak British brigade.

Far away in east China, however, a crisis had developed. A Japanese offensive had opened there to capture the airfields from which the US General Chennault's 14th Air Force was operating. Chinese resistance to the Japanese offensive faded as the Japanese overran the provinces of Hunau and Kwangsi, but Chiang refused to accept Stilwell's advice on how to make an effective defence. President Roosevelt, believing Stilwell could master the situation, then proposed to the Chinese leader that Stilwell be given command of all Chinese forces. The indignant Chiang replied by demanding Stilwell's recall. On October 1944, he returned to the USA, his active service career at an end.

Stilwell, perhaps aware that his abrasive nature and bitter comments had made him unpopular, did not allow his notebooks, diaries and papers to be published in his lifetime. However, they were published immediately after his death and aroused great controversy. However difficult he may have been to manage as a subordinate, it is clear that Stilwell, like the British commander "Chinese" Gordon before him, understood the minds of his Chinese troops and could inspire them to successes that a lesser general could never have achieved.

His skill in field command and his contribution to the victory in Burma were not appreciated for many years. The building of the Ledo road was visionary and his retreat through the dense jungles of Burma a skilful operation. More impressive still, was the campaign that led to the capture of Myktikyana, for this was a masterly example of strategic planning and tactical execution.

STUDENT
Kurt (1891-1973)
GERMAN GENERAL
Second World War

Certain commanders are able to exploit new methods of warfare – tactically and technologically – in ways that distinguish them from their contemporaries. One such commander was Kurt Student, the creator of the German airborne forces of the Second World War. He is distinguished as the first commander to use paratroops in military operations, though the Russians raised the first paratroop unit.

Student, a landowner's son, was born in 1891 in Prussia, and served throughout the First World War in the Imperial Air Service as a fighter pilot. In the post-war Reichswehr, he applied his active mind and tireless energy to the planning of the new Luftwaffe; from this, he went on to set up the German civil defence organization. It was his involvement with paratroops, however, that made his military reputation.

The first paratroops

When reports reached the Germans that the Soviet army had established an experimental parachute force, Student began to consider whether or not such troops could be of use to the Wehrmacht. He felt that the combination of aircraft and paratroop had opened up a new tactical dimension – the possibility of "vertical envelopment". This involved the transport of troops to an objective behind the enemy line, where they were either landed, or dropped by parachute. Student and his cadre of officers were soon authorized to set up a German airborne force.

The fundamental question was how such a force could be best employed. Were airborne troops best utilized as small sabotage details, or as large units, fighting to gain major objectives? Student formulated what he termed the "drops of oil" tactic, in which small groups would expand the perimeters of their drop zones until these joined to become a battle line. Special equipment for the new force was designed: gliders to carry air-landed units to their objectives; a reliable static line parachute; a robust, reliable machine pistol with a high rate of fire; and energy tablets to overcome exhaustion. Suitable ground tactics and training programs were evolved.

Working at top speed, Student achieved miracles in a very short time. One key factor was the support he was given by Goering, commander-in-chief of the Luftwaffe, since he was only a colonel at the time. In July 1938, however, he was promoted General Officer commanding 7th Parachute Division, though, at this time, the division was still only a skeleton formation. The new force was to be all-volunteer and psychological testing was employed as part of the recruitment vetting process – the first time such tests had been used in any fighting formation. These tests were insisted on by Student. His men were to be truly an élite – both physically and mentally.

PARATROOP PIONEER *Student pioneered the use of paratroops in war, but saw his men decimated in Crete.*

Eben Emael and Crete

No airborne operations were initiated in the 1939 Polish campaign and only a few groups were dropped during the invasions of Denmark and Norway. The key strategic test for Student's new force came at the opening of the blitzkrieg in the west in May 1940. Here, their role was so vital that the entire German timetable of attack was predicated on their success.

A group of paratroop engineers, commanded by Lieutenant Witzig, was to capture the key Belgian fortress of Eben Emael, while other detachments were to seize the river and rail bridges across the Meuse. Though the operations were a complete success, an accident to Student marred the victory. He was wounded accidentally by SS troops while standing at a window in The Hague. The wound was serious enough to keep Student away from duty for several months, but he took advantage of this enforced absence to examine what his paratroops could do in the Mediterranean, the only theater of war in which the British were still conducting land operations. Operation *Sea Lion* had been canceled, so this was the only potential role open for the force.

Student believed his paratroops could take the Suez Canal, using the islands of Crete and Rhodes as stepping stones towards this final objective. The powerful Royal Navy could be ignored – the paratroops would simply fly over the ships. He drew up plans for an airborne attack upon Crete and Goering obtained Hitler's approval for them. The operation, the first major battle fought by airborne troops in the history of warfare, was successful and Crete fell, but it was a Pyrrhic victory, since nearly 25 per cent of the landing force was lost.

From air to ground

The undaunted Student now proposed an airborne operation against Malta, but Hitler would not sanction it at this time – though it was resurrected in 1942, only to be cancelled. The Führer's decision may have been influenced less by the fact that such a scheme might have upset his Italian allies than by the losses in Crete; however, he remained convinced of the paratroop arm's worth and ordered Student to raise new divisions.

Student built these formations around a cadre of experienced battalions or regiments, so that a body of highly-trained men could leaven the recruit mass. Through this technique, Student commanded 11 airborne divisions by the end of the war – a sizeable army of more than 100,000 men. However, except for a few units dropped in Crete, Sicily, at Leros and in the Ardennes, most did not fight in the airborne role for which they had been trained. Instead, they were used as élite infantry, serving in that capacity at Cassino, in Normandy and in western Germany. What soldiers term the "seduction factor" of an élite unit could have raised even more men, but those who failed to meet the high standards that Student maintained until the end of the war were rejected. This demand for excellence led Student and his men to be regarded by the allies as fanatical Nazis and they were treated as such after the war. In a wry sense, this was a compliment to Student, though he was never a fanatic in the political sense. What he fostered was a fiercely loyal unit spirit that still survives, decades after the war, in the German paratroop ex-service organizations.

VLASSOV
Andrei (1900-1946)
SOVIET LIEUTENANT–GENERAL
Second World War

The front page of *Isvestia* for 13 December 1941, carried the photograph of seven generals who had taken a distinctive part in the destruction of the German forces attacking Moscow. Five years later, one of the seven – Andrei Vlassov – had been tried and hanged in Moscow as a traitor to the Soviet people.

Vlassov was born during 1900 near Nimji-Novgorod, the son of a farmer. The young Vlassov's first ambition was to be a priest, but he left the seminary to study agri-culture. Conscripted into a Soviet infantry regiment after the October revolution, he had risen to command a regiment by 1929 and, in the same year, joined the Communist Party. By 1940, he had become one of the youngest generals in the Soviet army and in 1941 was put in command of the 4th Tank Corps in Lemberg.

When Operation *Barbarossa* opened, Vlassov led his corps with such success that in the late summer of 1941, he was given command of 37th Army, positioned around Kiev. His army was one of those threatened with entrapment by German panzer forces. Vlassov, acutely conscious of the threat, asked for permission to withdraw in order to escape the German encirclement. This was refused and he was posted to the Moscow area to take over command of the newly-raised 20th Army. His new command, an élite formation of Siberian units, formed part of the strategic reserve that Stalin had created for the winter counter-offensive.

A Soviet hero

The strategic reserve – 1st Assault Army, 10th Army and 20th Army – was brought into the line, Vlassov being allotted the sector along the Moskva-Volga canal. This was the area in which *Zhukov* had forecast that the main German blow would fall. The untried 20th Army was attacked on 30 November by the 2nd Panzer Division, which overran the field fortifications in front of Krasnaya Polyana and Totshky and, by the end of the day, had advanced to within 18 miles of Moscow.

Vlassov remained undismayed. His first infantry attacks, launched on 4 December, probed the enemy front to find weaknesses which could be exploited when the Soviet armor was committed. When this happened, the tide turned. The next day, the whole of *Koniev*'s Kalinin Front went over to a general counter-offensive. In the battles on Vlassov's sector, his opponent was 4th Panzer Army; within six days of the opening of his assault, he had smashed the 2nd Panzer Division and the 106th Infantry Division and had liberated Solnetshnogorsk.

The rearguard of 4th Panzer Army put up a determined resistance on 15 December, seeking to halt or at least to slow down the pace of Vlassov's advance. The resistance was short-lived. Vlassov had inspired his Siberians, who liberated Istra on 25th. The advance of 20th Army was fiercely contested, for both sides realized the importance of that sector of the front. It was the decisive point. The advance was slow, but irresistible. Ten days into the New Year, Vlassov struck one panzer force at Volokalmsk and then turned to smash again at 4th Panzer Army. In a succession of rapidly delivered blows, he forced the panzer formations into full-scale retreat. By 23 January 1942, the German army had been driven back along the northern approaches to Moscow. The capital had been saved, an operation in which Vlassov's 20th Army had played a vital role.

A traitor to Communism

With Moscow saved, Vlassov was employed on other sectors where a determined and aggressive commander was needed. However, after he fell into German hands during an operation on the Central Front, he became passionately anti-Communist. Realizing that great numbers of Soviet soldiers shared his desire to rid the motherland of Stalin and his party, Vlassov offered to raise an army of Russian prisoners of war for use on the Eastern Front. His plan was accepted by some elements in the German armed forces, but was rejected by others; Hitler was one who saw no advantage to be gained. Some Cossack and infantry divisions were raised, but these saw little or no action as complete units. At the end of the war, Vlassov was handed over to the Soviets by the Americans to whom he had surrendered and was taken to Moscow. There he was tried, condemned and executed for treason.

WAVELL
Archibald (1883-1950)
BRITISH FIELD-MARSHAL
Second World War

Archibald Wavell and his Army of the Nile won Britain's first victories of the Second World War against the Italians in the western desert. Yet, because he fell foul of a political leader, his career ended on a low note, rather than a high one. Because Wavell opposed Churchill's demand for offensive action, he suffered for expressing what were his honest military opinions.

Born on 5 May 1883 in Colchester, Wavell joined his father's old regiment, The Black Watch. After service in the First World War, during which he was wounded several times, his career followed the standard professional pattern of the day, involving service in all parts of the British Empire. One unusual element, however, was a period as military attaché in Russia, where Wavell witnessed a mass air drop by paratroops. He later commented "If I had not seen it for myself, I should not have believed such an enterprise to be possible." In the inter-war years, Wavell showed a great potential for training men and for inspiring them to achieve objectives which they had formerly believed unreachable. His warnings on the menace of a German military build up were ignored, but, shortly before the outbreak of the Second World War, he was appointed to Middle East Command, which embraced a massive area extending from almost up to the borders of India to Egypt.

Desert victory
Italy's declaration of war in 1940 brought hostilities to the left flank of Wavell's vast command area. There, two British divisions, together some 30,000 strong, faced ten times their numbers in an Italian army under *Graziani*. Other attacks from Italian forces in Ethiopia against neighboring British colonies, posed Wavell with additional problems. Slowly, he produced plans to master them, but it was clear that Egypt was the most vital sector of his far-flung command.

In December 1940, Wavell's force attacked Graziani, whose 10th Army had gingerly advanced across the border and was now sheltering in a defensive chain of fortified camps. His Army of the Nile sent the Italians reeling back across the frontier, with General O'Connor, Wavell's field commander, in full pursuit. Only the arrival of Erwin *Rommel* and the Afrika Korps prevented Graziani's complete defeat. In Somaliland and Ethiopia, too, Wavell's operations forced the Italians to surrender.

Quarrel with Churchill
In spring 1941, Wavell was then ordered by Churchill to break off operations in the desert and transfer his best troops to Greece to aid the Greeks against the invading Germans. The number of troops that Wavell could spare were too few to halt the German attack and evacuation promptly followed. Crete then fell to enemy airborne troops, led by General *Student*, while in Iraq and in the Lebanon, Nazi-inspired revolts also drew men away from the critical Egyptian sector.

Churchill never trusted Wavell, who lacked, in Churchill's view, the vital element of aggression. The origins of this mistrust can be traced back to an argument Churchill had had with Wavell, during which the latter had commented bitterly that "a heavy butcher's bill is no proof of generalship." Wavell was removed from command and sent to India as commander-in-chief. There, Wavell was faced with the same problems he had encountered in the desert following the outbreak of war with Japan in December 1941. He had a vast battle front, too few troops, insufficient aircraft and was outnumbered by a courageous, well-led foe. Hastily appointed allied commander in the south-west Pacific, Wavell was unable to halt the Japanese rush of conquest. He was paying the price for years of governmental neglect, but his failure only confirmed Churchill's low opinion of him.

Promoted to the rank of field-marshal, Wavell now became Viceroy of India in June 1943. Since he was a fighting soldier, he was totally suited to troubled times and he earned the reputation of being the finest Viceroy of the century. He served as Viceroy up to February 1947.

Had Wavell not become a soldier, he might have excelled in any other profession, particularly in the literary field. He was a modest man who found pleasure in simple things; yet his powerful personality inspired his soldiers to accomplish the seemingly impossible.

WINGATE
Charles O (1903-1944)
BRITISH GENERAL
Second World War

The most unconventional general in the British army during the Second World War was undoubtedly Charles Wingate. His eccentricity in matters of dress, diet and military operations had caused comment even before the outbreak of war. The various campaigns in which he served during the war served only to accentuate his unusual attitudes.

Wingate was born in Naini Tal, India, on 26 February 1903, the son of a British officer. As a potential artillery officer, Wingate attended the Royal Military Academy at Woolwich and was commissioned in 1923. He became fluent in Arabic and served in the Sudan before being posted, in 1936, to Palestine, which was at that time controlled by the British under a League of Nations mandate.

Wingate's sympathies were pro-Jewish and he was determined to see their settlements defended against Arab attack. For this purpose, he organized Jewish "night patrols", which he led against the Arabs. For many Jews, this was their first experience of combat but they adapted themselves so well, particularly to the unconventional tactics which Wingate had devised, that they had soon forced the Arabs onto the defensive.

Wingate's skill in unconventional warfare did not go unnoticed, and in 1941, holding the temporary rank of lieutenant-colonel, he was selected to undertake operations in Ethiopia. He entered the country, together with the Emperor Haile Selassie, with a force of just under 2,000 men. These formed the nucleus of an army that reduced the Italian garrison's morale to near zero, thus contributing to the liberation of Ethiopia and to the restoration of the emperor to the throne.

Formation of the Chindits

The military disasters that had befallen the British in Burma in 1942 led to a situation where new tactics had to be devised if the Japanese were to be defeated. Wingate convinced his military and civilian superiors that the methods he had employed in Palestine and Ethiopia could be adapted to the conditions of the Burmese jungle. By now a brigadier, he trained 77th Indian Brigade, a force of Burmese, Ghurkas and British soldiers, in jungle warfare and in February 1943, led it on a deep penetration raid behind the enemy lines. His force crossed the Chindwin river and was then split into raiding columns which went on to cut railway lines. Wingate selected the Chinthe, the Burmese dragon-lion motif, as his unit's badge and the term Chindit was to become the distinctive mark of his force of jungle fighters. His rigorous training schedules proved themselves in an operation notorious for the privations suffered by its participants. Such was Chindit ruthlessness – or, given the Japanese attitude to prisoners, realism – that those too badly wounded to make the journey back into India were shot.

The speed of Japanese reaction to the operation forced Wingate to withdraw his Chindits; they retreated during May 1943, having lost 1,000 men, one third of their original strength. Wingate then proposed a deeper penetration by a larger force for a much longer period. The operation had the personal approval of Churchill. Six infantry brigades, grouped together as 3rd Indian Division, were to be employed. Five of them were to be flown in by aircraft and glider to land on jungle airstrips. Acting in accord with a detailed plan of action, the tasks of the brigades, each of which was divided into two columns, would be to disrupt communications to the Japanese troops facing *Stilwell* and *Slim*. Wingate, now a major-general, did not live to see the outcome of the operation for, in April 1944, not long after it had opened, he was killed in an air crash.

Wingate was a ruthless eccentric, as was shown in the treatment of his badly wounded soldiers in his first penetration operation. He was fortunate that such drastic methods would not be needed in the second Chindit expedition, for a proper air-evacuation procedure had now been worked out. In the knowledge of how little could be and actually was achieved through either operation the question has often been raised whether they should have been mounted at all.

Militarily they were not a success, but they did show that British forces could fight and win against the Japanese and that it was possible for a large body of troops, hidden in the jungle, to be supplied by air drop. Wingate may not have been the eccentric military genius some claimed, but he was a successful commander of unconventional forces and should be recognized as a pioneer in that field.

YAMAMOTO
Isoroku (1884-1943)
JAPANESE ADMIRAL
Second World War

Just as Admiral *Togo* dominated the Japanese Navy at the turn of the century, so did Isoroku Yamamoto during the Second World War. His brilliant grasp of naval strategy and tactics enabled his country to establish a vast Pacific empire in a swift campaign – though Yamamoto himself had been against the original decision to commence hostilities against the USA.

Yamamoto was born into a Samurai family at Magako, Honshu, on 4 April 1884. He graduated from the naval academy in 1904, serving as a junior officer on board the battleship *Nissin* at Tsushima the following year. The development of his career was influenced by two factors – the USA and the introduction of aircraft carriers. Yamamoto served as Assistant Naval Attaché and then as Naval Attaché in Washington, postings which enabled him to learn a great deal about US attitudes. As early as 1924, he was an instructor at a naval air station, going on to command an aircraft carrier. He then became head of the aviation branch of the naval general staff and subsequently commander of the 1st Carrier Division. Before starting on his duties as deputy navy minister in 1935, Yamamoto travelled widely, inspecting the major navies in Europe and America. Three years later he was commander-in-chief of 1st Fleet; in August 1941, he was promoted to overall command of the combined Japanese fleets. It was he, therefore, who led the imperial navy at the outbreak of war with the USA.

Strategic priorities

Yamamoto was aware that Japan's island situation made it imperative that the sea lanes were kept open. He was further aware that Japan's maritime position could be challenged by the US Pacific Fleet, particularly by the torpedo-carrying aircraft on its carriers. The overriding strategic objective was therefore the destruction of the US fleet, which, he believed, could be nowhere better achieved than as it lay at anchor in its principal Pacific base – Pearl Harbor.

To begin with, Yamamoto's plan was not accepted. This was because, firstly, it was thought too risky to undertake and, secondly, because it did not fit in with the national strategic aim of striking and seizing the economic prizes of south-east Asia – Malaya, Burma, the Dutch East Indies and the Philippines. As far as the naval supreme command was concerned, the so-called Southern Resources Area was the only objective. This meant operations to the south of the homeland. Yamamoto's proposal would change the direction of the Japanese thrust eastwards into the Pacific and they believed it would be a wasteful side show.

Yamamoto, however, knew US attitudes and US capabilities. The USA would not allow Japan to enlarge its empire at the expense of Britain and Holland and would take positive immediate action to prevent it. The USA would bend all its economic and industrial energies to ensure that Japan's plans did not succeed. If, however, the US fleet in the Pacific could be destroyed, then the Japanese would gain a year or more of precious time to make itself invincible before a new US navy could come back into contention. Yamamoto's force of character and the logic of this argument compelled the supreme command to accept his proposals. The attack upon Pearl Harbor was planned. The Japanese 1st Air Fleet – six aircraft carriers, battleships and smaller vessels, all of them maintaining strict wireless silence – sailed from the Kurile Islands on 26 November 1941; on 7 December, its aircraft attacked the US fleet at anchor. The operation was a brilliant tactical success, but Yamamoto failed to sink the fleet's three aircraft carriers, as these were at sea when the raid was launched. In the light of later events, this was to be an immensely costly failure.

After Pearl Harbor

The success of the Pearl Harbor strike emboldened Yamamoto to exploit his victory. He intended to strike and capture the American-held island of Midway, from which he could attack the principal US bases at Hawaii. The operation involved nothing less than the deployment of all available first-line Japanese naval strength in this one mission. As a result, the remaining naval forces were inadequate to continue with the conquest of the Southern Resources Area and in the ensuing lull the Dutch and British were able to regroup and to reinforce.

The Midway mission was to be carried out by four naval task forces. The Northern Area Force would carry out diversionary operations against Alaska while the main body, sub-divided into three, struck for Midway itself.

However, Yamamoto had based his plan on faulty intelligence. He knew that two US aircraft carriers were operating in the South Pacific – too far away to intervene – but believed that the USA's other carriers had been sunk in the battle of the Coral Sea. Hence, he concluded that his Midway operation would not be opposed by US carrier forces. In reality, his attacks, when launched, were countered by two US carrier task forces and Spruance, the US naval commander, in a brilliant fleet operation destroyed the Japanese carriers opposed to him. Here, the Americans were aided by their naval intelligence, which had broken the Japanese codes and so was able to pinpoint Midway as the object of attack.

This diversion of effort not only cost the Japanese the cream of their carriers; it also allowed the allied navies time to regroup to meet the next challenge in the Solomon Islands. Here, the Japanese conquering advance was finally held. Though the fighting was long and intensive, slowly the Japanese were forced onto the defensive. Yamamoto determined to regain the initiative and reinforced his fleet to launch what he intended to be a devastating blow in the southern Solomons area. To achieve this, he needed to capture the airfield on Guadalcanal – Henderson Field – from which land-based aircraft would be able to support the operations of his carrier-borne squadrons.

Throughout fall 1942, there was furious activity around Guadalcanal. On the ground the US marines defended the northern side of the island against a Japanese invasion force fighting to seize the airfield. At sea, a number of violent, but strategically inconclusive, actions continued until February 1943, when the Japanese land forces were evacuated.

Shot down in flames

During April 1943, in yet another attempt to regain the initiative in the Solomon Islands area, Yamamoto sent in his carrier squadrons to attack allied air bases, but, in exchange for the minor and repairable damage they inflicted, the Japanese suffered heavy naval losses. During the same month, he set out on a tour of inspection, which involved flying from Rabaul to Bougainville. Thanks to decoded Japanese signals, the Americans were aware of Yamamoto's intentions and 16 fighters from Henderson Field intercepted and shot down the two bombers that were carrying the admiral and his staff. The burning machines crashed into dense jungle. On the day on which he died, Yamamoto was promoted to the rank of Admiral of the Fleet.

There is no doubt that Yamamoto was a naval strategist of the highest order, although he was often tempted into diversions from his main plan, with unfortunate results. He reflected all the Samurai characteristics of honor, loyalty and confidence to which he added the personal gifts of a forceful personality and powerful command ability. His death was as serious a defeat for the Japanese as a lost campaign in the field, for his abilities would have proved invaluable in fighting the defensive war into which Japan was eventually forced.

YAMASHITA
Tomoyuki (1885-1946)
JAPANESE GENERAL
Second World War

General Yamashita was one of the leading land commanders produced by Japan in the Second World War. His greatest moment came in 1942, with the capitulation of Singapore; this swift campaign, which, within weeks, had taken him and his forces down the Malayan Peninsula from north to south won him the sobriquet of the "Tiger of Malaya."

Yamashita was born in 1885 into a Samurai family. Though his school reports were unimpressive, once he had entered in the army, he showed a capacity for intellectual effort and won fifth place in the 1908 class at military academy and sixth place in the staff college examinations of 1916. His clarity of mind and a natural flair for staff work were forecasts of a career in which he could expect to achieve high rank. However, Yamashita suffered as a result of his participation in an abortive military coup launched by a group of conservative young officers during 1936. The emperor's disapproval crushed the coup, some conspirators being shot and others committing ritual suicide. Yamashita himself was banished to Korea, but, as part compensation was given command of a brigade. This was a rare chance for a staff officer to gain experience in a field command.

By 1940, Yamashita's natural abilities had ensured that he was brought back into mainstream military life with his appointment as Inspector General of the air force. In that capacity, he led a military mission to Germany where he studied blitzkrieg techniques. His resulting memorandum stressed that Japan should not risk war with Britain or the USA until her own air and tank forces had been enlarged and improved. His advice was ignored, however, and by December 1941, Japan was at war with both powers.

The conquest of Malaya
On the outbreak of war, Yamashita's 25th Army invaded northern Thailand and then advanced into northern Malaya. Anticipating the difficulties of supply in jungle terrain, Yamashita reduced the size of his attack force from five divisions to three, calculating that, both logistically and tactically, this was the largest force which could maintain the coherence and the momentum of the Japanese advance. His soldiers, who would have to fight their way through and live in appalling jungle conditions, would need to be highly trained, first-class fighting men. Accordingly, he selected three élite formations – 5th and 18th Infantry and the Imperial Guard divisions.

Conventional British military thinking believed the jungle to be an impassable barrier and therefore the defence of Malaya was planned only to deal with a seaborne invasion coming out of the south. Yamashita's army, striking out of the north, took the British by sur-

prise, and swiftly drove the confused defenders into what had been considered the impregnable fortress of Singapore. This might have been so if Singapore's formidable defences had not been fixed, pointing to the sea. Taken in the rear with a demoralized native population, short of supplies and with no water sources, the British and Commonwealth garrison, although superior in number to the Japanese, surrendered on 15 February 1942.

This victory, gained so quickly and at such little cost made Yamashita a national hero, much to the chagrin of Prime Minister Tojo, an old and implacable enemy who had Yamashita posted to Manchuria to a training and replacement command. This was demotion, not promotion, but, as Japan's military fortunes declined, his skills were once again in demand. By July 1944, he had been brought back to active service and given control of 14th area army command in the Philippines.

It was clear to Yamashita that no long-term effective defence of the Philippines was possible, but his proposal for a Japanese evacuation was rejected. Deciding not to try to hold Luzon, he established a defence line in the hills outside the city, but, though he withdrew his army units, the naval and marine rearguard he left behind him fought a battle during which atrocities were committed against the civilian population and the city itself almost totally destroyed.

At the war's end Yamashita was tried for war crimes and found guilty on charges relating in the main to the Philippine atrocities. The verdict was never in doubt. He was sentenced to death and was hanged in February 1946.

ZHUKOV
Georgi K (1896-1974)
MARSHAL OF THE SOVIET UNION
Second World War

Of the many Soviet commanders of the Second World War whose battlefield skills won victories on the Eastern Front, one man stands supreme above all others. He was Georgi Zhukov, the architect of Soviet triumph.

Zhukov was born on 2 December 1896, in the village of Strelkovo, near Kaluga; his family was so poor that the young Georgi was forced to go out to work at the age of 11. During the First World War he served in the 10th Novgorod Dragoon regiment, being promoted to the rank of corporal for repeated acts of bravery, which also won him two St George medals and two St George crosses. After the Bolshevik seizure of power in October 1917, he entered the Soviet army, where he fought in the 1st Moscow Cavalry Division.

Relationship with Stalin
From command of the 39th Busulokov cavalry regiment in 1923, Zhukov was sent to Germany to take part in a leadership course run by the Reichswehr; his successful graduation qualified him for entry into the Frunze Mili-

tary Academy. He survived Stalin's bloody purges of the mid-1930s and, in 1939 – nearly two decades after his last battle – led massed Soviet tank units into action against the Japanese on the Kalin Gol river in Manchuria. His success secured the USSR's borders in the Far East. Transferred back to the west in the spring of 1940, Zhukov commanded the Soviet forces that occupied the Romanian province of Bessarabia in June.

Zhukov came to Stalin's special notice as the result of a war game held in January 1941. He was given command of the "western" armies – and was expected to lose. Instead, in a series of short sharp battles, he defeated the "eastern" force, led by the Soviet chief of staff. Infuriated by the latter's incompetence, Stalin dismissed him and appointed Zhukov as his replacement. So began a partnership that was to last for the whole of the Second World War. When, for instance, Stalin had himself proclaimed Generalissimo, he named Zhukov as his deputy. What this promotion meant was that Zhukov was to produce battle-winning plans that Stalin would then issue as his own.

The relationship was not an easy one. Stalin was a dictator who had murdered millions in the past and was to murder millions more in the future. He crushed any opposition with torture and the firing squad. Zhukov was a blunt, outspoken peasant with a reputation for ruthlessness, vindictiveness and viciousness. On one occasion Stalin shouted that a proposal Zhukov had made was rubbish. Zhukov was furious. "If you think that your chief of staff can talk only rubbish," he retorted, "then demote me to a private soldier and let me defend my country with a rifle and a bayonet in my hand."

Fighting the "Hitlerite hordes"
Zhukov first demonstrated his abilities as a commander at Leningrad, where he stabilized the Soviet defence, and then in the battle for Moscow, where he used *Koniev's* West Front to fight Army Group Center to the point of exhaustion. Then, as the enemy offensive faltered, he unleashed upon it fresh Siberian divisions trained and outfitted to meet the harsh winter conditions. Only the superb organization of the German army saved it from complete disintegration as Zhukov's blows fell on it in rapid succession as he switched the point of maximum effort between one sector of the front and another.

Zhukov was now seen as the commander best equipped to deal with crisis. Accordingly, in the fall of 1942, when the Germans seemed on the brink of capturing Stalingrad, he was sent to co-ordinate the Soviet defence of the city and prepare the subsequent counterstroke. He soon realized that the very nature of the German battle-line dispositions had given him the opportunity of winning a splendid victory. While crack German formations were battling their way slowly forward inside the city, their flanks were secured by troops from their satellite allies of substantially less combat efficiency. If those troops could be routed, the 6th Army could be encircled inside Stalingrad. Aided by Hitler's obstinate refusal to recognize the military reality of the situation, Zhukov's

RUTHLESS VICTOR *Zhukov was quick to threaten death or transfer to a penal battalion for command failures.*

scheme worked as planned and in January 1943 the last remnants of Paulus's 6th Army gave themselves up. For the first time in history, a German field marshal had surrendered.

From Kursk to Berlin
Sobered but undeterred, the Germans nevertheless mounted a summer offensive at Kursk. Two panzer armies sought to crush a Soviet salient held by more than 20 Russian armies. Again, Zhukov carefully planned the German defeat; in a two-part operation, he not only smashed their offensive, but also wrested the military initiative from them once and for all. Though Zhukov was to lead the Soviet army to even greater victories, none was more significant. It destroyed the last German hopes of victory in the east. From then on, it was the Soviets who were on the offensive.

The climax of Zhukov's military career came with the battle for Berlin, in which he directed the advance of two Red Army Fronts. In a short battle, he not only captured the Reich's capital, but also raced to the Elbe to prevent the western allies from sharing in the final conquest.

Zhukov was a ruthless general, convinced that subordinates would only be efficient if he ensured that they were. Therefore, he checked and double checked on those whom he commanded, selecting men to lead his armies upon whose ability he could depend absolutely. In pursuit of success, he could and did degrade those who did not carry out orders. But to those whose respect and love he earned, he was the ideal leader – a soldier among soldiers. The subordinates he selected, brilliant though they were, could not eclipse him, for Zhukov was without doubt the most gifted Soviet commander of the war.

1945
to the Present

The detonation of atomic bombs over Hiroshima and Nagasaki in August 1945 brought about a revolution in warfare. At Hiroshima, in less than a second, more than 78,000 Japanese were killed by the combined effects of heat and blast; many survivors were to perish later through the effects of radiation. The nuclear age had begun. By 1949, the USSR had tested its first A-bomb; by 1954, the hydrogen bomb had been produced. In terms of command, what this meant was simple. The A bomb and its more powerful successors – the H and R bombs – changed the nature of war more completely than had the introduction of gunpowder to the battlefield three centuries before.

Atomic power, when used in a bomb is an explosive of fearful and widespread destructive force. Atomic power harnessed and contained is also a fuel which can, in theory, keep submarines and surface ships indefinitely at sea. Thus, even as a fuel, atomic power altered the strategy of war. No longer was it necessary to have overseas bases, coaling stations, the fleet trains and the logistics groups which had once been indispensable to naval operations. No army was needed to garrison a country which could be dominated by long range missiles. As far as the global strategic position was concerned, the existence of nuclear weapons produced a stand-off. The fear of mutual destruction was the deterrent. Nuclear war was something which could not be risked nor, once the possession of such weapons spread, could nuclear powers risk full-scale conventional wars for fear of their escalation.

Nuclear negotiation
Although it was accepted by the

SPECIAL FORCES *In war today, highly-trained specialists play a key role. Here, two US navy SEALS (sea-air-land) pause for a drink in Vietnam.*

nuclear powers that weapons of mass destruction would not be used against areas of mass population, they did accept that tactical nuclear weapons – the so-called "battlefield" type – could be deployed, but there was, at the same time, tacit agreement that, under no circumstances would they be employed. It was considered unlikely that a conventional war would ever escalate through the tactical nuclear stage to an all-out nuclear offensive, since peace negotiations would end hostilities before things had degenerated to that level. However, because battlefield weapons might be used, soldiers needed to be trained in the techniques of fighting

a war in nuclear conditions. Under such conditions, for instance, there would be no place for a formal type of staff system, since a tactical nuclear strike upon a main battle headquarters might destroy the whole command structure, leaving the forces in the field without leadership and bereft of supplies or reinforcements.

A battlefield nuclear war would demand the dispersal of staffs over a vast area, in which case communications would be of critical importance. Even during the Second World War, one soldier in five in the German army was in the communications branch, but, to meet the challenges of an atomic battle, the numbers on both sides would need to increase to a ratio of one in four, or even one in three. There would also need to be two or more identical staff systems, in the event of one being knocked out. However, acknowledging that the possession of nuclear arms by both sides is a mutual deterrent and that battlefield nuclear weapons are unlikely to be used, armies are today still trained to fight conventional wars in which the formal military hierarchical structure is maintained.

Special forces
There have also emerged since the Second World War special commando units, whose successes then ensured that such bodies now form part of standard military forces. Thus, the British SAS, which began as a small raiding group in the desert, is now a specialized detachment, whose members are able to fight in any terrain. It is to be expected that, in war, such special detachments would be used on sabotage missions, in raiding enemy military headquarters, or even in

political assassination. A staff system would not be required for such groups, for they are the equivalent of the independent battle groups which proliferated in the German army during the latter part of the Second World War.

Propaganda and terrorism

War, in fact, is not necessarily a matter of uniformed, fighting units, though this fact is only slowly being appreciated in the west. Propaganda plays an important role in this, its military extension being the wide-world network of urban guerrilla groups, which set out to dominate or discredit governments through the indiscriminate bombing of "soft" targets, or by assassination. To fight such terrorist groups requires a highly flexible command structure and a constant flow of up-to-date intelligence. The British army is the only western force with experience of full-scale urban guerrilla warfare, as a result of its involvement in Northern Ireland, and it is often not appreciated in what a difficult situation its troops are placed. They are restricted by political considerations as to what steps they can take to combat terrorists and so have been reduced to the role of an armed police, or frontier defence militia. The army command and the troops are condemned to fight a defensive, not an offensive war, reacting to the attacks of the guerrillas.

The future of command

Should, as seems likely, the pattern of future wars be that of urban, or rural, guerrilla operations conducted in any continent, then the day of the great captains may well be over. Strategic targets will be political and will be chosen not by generals, but by politicians and their party advisers. The commander's role will be limited to control of small groups and warfare will become a series of "subalterns' battles," fought, at their highest level, on the ground by nobody higher in rank than a divisional commander. Strategy, insofar as it exists, will not be military, but political in its orientation.

BATTLE TODAY *Nuclear weapons may make old-style battle a thing of the past, with smaller forces, such as the company, replacing larger ones.*

It is a widely held belief that statesmen are likely to be more responsible when it comes to matters of war or peace than soldiers are. Clemenceau's comment "War is too serious a business to be left to soldiers" has been accorded the status of gospel. Yet Hitler, Mussolini and Stalin were all statesmen, were all aggressors and were also incompetent military commanders. It was a great commander, the Duke of Wellington, who best expressed the truth of the soldiers' trade when he commented that "The melancholy sight of a battlefield on which a victory has been won can only be surpassed by one on which a defeat has been sustained."

The Nuclear Age

On 16 July 1945, a nuclear device codenamed *Trinity* was exploded at Alamogordo, in New Mexico. Its explosion changed not only the whole nature of warfare, but the course of human history.

Scientific theory does not develop in isolation. The knowledge gained as a result of Rutherford's experiments in splitting the atom gave physicists in all the countries of the developed world the potential to create a nuclear explosion. Quite early in the Second World War, British scientists were sent to the USA for fear that the results of their research should fall into enemy hands if there was a German invasion of Britain. In Germany, progress in the production of a nuclear bomb was certainly made; until the destruction of the German heavy water producing facility in Norway, there seemed the real danger the Germans would be first with a bomb. Luckily, there was little co-ordination of the German nuclear effort and Speer, Hitler's armaments minister, eventually used Germany's stock of uranium for armaments purposes. The Anglo-American effort, however, was massive.

From theory to practice

Once it had been shown that a nuclear detonation was practical, the decision as to whether the bomb should be used against the Japanese became a political consideration. There were those who considered that the use of such a weapon was immoral and that Japan was, in any case, close to defeat. The opposite view was expressed by those who saw the decision as being one of military necessity. Before the war could be ended, the Japanese homeland would have to be invaded and then conquered. The Japanese people – soldiers and civilians alike – had already demonstrated their resolute determination to fight to the death. How much more staunchly would they fight when defending the sacred soil of their motherland? Estimates were that a campaign to conquer Japan would take a minimum of two, but more likely four years to be completed. Allied casualties would be at least 1,000,000, but might rise to three times this figure. The choice was clear-cut. Do we use the bomb and kill thousands of the enemy, or do we not use it and accept the probable casualty figures? The employment of the atomic bomb would, it was argued, shorten the war and thereby save countless lives.

Hiroshima and Nagasaki

An allied ultimatum was sent to Japan via the Soviet government, which did not relay Japan's answer. In the absence of Japanese acceptance of the ultimatum, President Truman authorized the use of the A-bomb, the first target selected being the military headquarters and supply bases located in the city of Hiroshima. The bomb was dropped on 6 August 1945 and killed in excess of 78,000 people as well as destroying two-thirds

AFTER THE BOMB *The ruins of Hiroshima after the dropping of the first atomic bomb. Within a second, a thriving city was reduced to rubble and more than 78,000 perished.*

of the city. Three days later, on 9 August, a second device was exploded over the industrial sea port of Nagasaki. Half of the city was destroyed and more than 40,000 people were killed. The Japanese government sued for peace on the following day.

The nuclear arms race

The realization that mankind now had the power to destroy itself caused the three nations possessing the atomic secret – Britain, Canada and the United States – to offer to share their information on nuclear energy with the other members of the United Nations. They had forgotten the dictum that power shared is power lost; in 1947, Soviet Russia detonated its first atomic device, following this with the explosion of a hydrogen bomb in August 1953. Other nations – notably Britain, France, China and India – also developed their own A-weapons and tested them, usually on remote Pacific islands or, when the storms of protest became too strong to ignore, underground. A nuclear arms race had begun, with the creation of even more potent weapons of destruction as its logical consequence.

At a military level, the nuclear age has produced a revolution. For the first time in history, it is not policy or strategy that determines the weapon, but the weapon that dictates policy. The fitting of nuclear warheads to rockets gave the great powers the ability to send missiles over thousands of miles to strike a target. The certainty of mutual nuclear destruction has produced the situation where it is unlikely such weapons can even be used – at least by any responsible government.

Just as strategic nuclear warfare is unlikely, so is the employment of nuclear weapons at tactical level, though currently they are deployed. The fear that a conventional war could degenerate into a situation where tactical nuclear weapons would be employed and which would then escalate into a full nuclear war is, on the basis of past evidence, an unlikely scenario. It can even be argued that the existence of nuclear weapons has produced over 40 years of armed peace in Europe, although there are still conventional wars being fought in the Middle East, Asia and South America.

THE ULTIMATE DETERRENT

"Little Boy" (left) was the code name given to the atomic bomb dropped on Hiroshima in 1945. With a destructive power equivalent to 20,000 tons of conventional explosive, the bomb destroyed two-thirds of the city, but today it is regarded as a primitive weapon – modern H bombs are graded in megatons. Nuclear fission has transformed other aspects of warfare as well; nuclear-powered hunter-killer submarines (above) are able to travel at high underwater speeds and remain submerged for months, as opposed to the slow speed and limited endurance of diesel equivalents.

DAYAN
Moshe (1915-)
ISRAELI GENERAL
Arab-Israeli Wars

Moshe Dayan is arguably the most successful Israeli commander since the foundation of the state of Israel, but he is undoubtedly the most charismatic. Instantly recognizable through his black eye-patch – he wears this to cover the socket of the eye he lost in the 1941 Syrian campaign – Dayan is still modern Israel's best-known soldier.

Dayan was born on 20 May 1915, at Daganyah in Palestine, which was at that time a province of the Ottoman Empire. The Turks had allowed a certain amount of Jewish settlement and Daganyah was the first to be created. Defeat in the First World War meant the end of Turkish rule and substitution of British control, under the terms of a League of Nations mandate. Bound by the terms of the Balfour Declaration of 1916, which recognized the right of the Jews to a national homeland, the British at first did not discourage Jewish immigration, but this policy caused bitter resentment among Palestinian Arabs. The response was a bitter series of armed raids upon Jewish settlements in an effort to expel the immigrants. The attacks produced a Jewish response with the setting up of *Haganah*, a self-defence organization which the British, trying to hold the reins, soon declared illegal.

The guerrilla warrior

This, then, was the atmosphere in which the young Dayan grew to manhood. In 1929 he joined *Haganah* and soon had formulated tactics he used to counter the Arab raids and then taught to other *Haganah* guerrillas. A strange alliance was then formed. Charles Orde *Wingate*, a British officer who had been posted to Palestine, sympathized with the Jewish cause and formed defence squads to attack the Arab villages from which the raids had been mounted. Dayan was a junior commander in Wingate's so-called "night patrols," from which he learned tactics and the skills of man management. Both were to be of use to him in later years.

In 1939, with the outbreak of the Second World War, British tolerance ended. *Haganah* went underground, but Dayan was caught in a police raid and sentenced to five years imprisonment, from which he was released in 1941. He joined the British army in the same year and served with it in the Syrian campaign to overthrow the pro-German Vichy administration and to install a Free French pro-Allied government.

Israel's general

With the end of the war, *Haganah* renewed its activities – this time directing them primarily against the British in an attempt to force the issue of Jewish independence. In 1948 the British withdrew, but a bitter war between the Arabs and the Jews was the immediate result. The declared intention of the new state's Arab neighbors was

ISRAEL'S SAVIOR *Dayan's guerrilla ruthlessness stood him in good stead against Israel's Arab enemies.*

to drive the Jews into the sea by force of arms and their armies accordingly prepared to invade. Israel had no regular standing army, but *Haganah* was by this time a force of about 30,000 men with an excellent command organization and reserves. In addition, there were local defence groups in each settlement.

This invasion of northern Israel by Syrian and Lebanese forces was quickly halted, with Dayan – now a major commanding a battalion on the Syrian front – playing a prominent part in halting the enemy attack launched across the frontier at Degana. He then drove the Arabs back in a series of successful engagements.

From then on, Dayan's rise was speedy. In 1953, he was selected as chief of staff of the Israeli army. As such, he was deeply involved in the Suez campaign, launched by Britain, France and Israel in November 1956 against Egypt. In it, Dayan deployed an all-arms force of six infantry, three armored and one parachute brigades in the southern sector of Israel, with six others located in the country's central and northern sectors. Taking the offensive without formally declaring war, Israel had beaten the Egyptians within eight days.

Political pressure forced the Israelis to give up their gains and two years later Dayan left the army, entering politics as a Labor Party member of the Israeli parliament. In time he became Minister of Agriculture but, dissatisfied with government policies, then helped to form a splinter group. However, when a government of national unity was formed shortly before the outbreak of the Six Days' War in June 1967, Dayan agreed to serve as Minister of Defence.

The Six Days' War

In reply to Egypt's campaign of provocation the Israeli government produced a document laying out what would be considered *causi belli* between the two nations. Very soon Egypt had breached each of them and Dayan accordingly prepared for war. He had under his command an air force which, though heavily outnumbered, was better trained and superior in fighting spirit to its adversaries. The same numerical inferiority was evident in tanks, guns and men. The Israeli forces, however, were more flexible than the Arab ones, had a firm battle plan and were better prepared. Also, Dayan was prepared to take the offensive without waiting to be attacked.

In a pre-emptive air strike on 5 June 1967, the Egyptian air force was almost totally eliminated on the ground. Over 200 Egyptian aircraft were destroyed for the loss of only 19 Israeli machines. That blow was followed by a series of armored thrusts which penetrated deep into the Egyptian positions. For these, three divisions were deployed, fielding a total of 700 tanks between them and supported by mechanized infantry and artillery. The plan was to strike hard in north and central Sinai and drive hard to seize the key routes to the Mitla Pass and the Suez

Canal to cut the Egyptian front-line forces off from their bases. The three Israeli divisions, led by Israel Tal, Avraham Yoffe and Ariel Sharon respectively, faced seven Egyptian infantry divisions.

Dayan's armor maintained its pressure throughout the second day of battle and into the third when the Israelis faced their only crisis of the campaign. One armored brigade ran out of fuel and ammunition and was surrounded, but another column soon broke through with supplies to relieve it and the advance continued. By 7 June, the Egyptians were in full retreat and the Sinai was in Israeli hands; 15,000 Egyptians were taken prisoner.

The campaign elsewhere was also a success. On the northern front, Egypt's allies, Jordan and Syria, had also been attacked. Jerusalem was captured and the West Bank of the Jordan occupied, while, on the Syrian front, the strategically important Golan heights were taken.

This was Dayan's greatest campaign. In it, he fought against three Arab armies and had won the victory within six days. The significance of this – and the other wars which Moshe Dayan fought – is that he was not the product of a great military academy or of long formal staff training. Such military education as he had received in the pre-war *Haganah* might have been considered better suited to producing a first class guerrilla leader. Instead, in Dayan, it produced a commander of great tactical ability and strategic gifts.

ISRAELI BLITZKRIEG *Israeli troops in action near Ismaila during the Six Days' War. Dayan's dynamic leadership was a major factor in Israel's quick victory.*

VO NGUYAN GIAP
(1912-   )
VIETNAMESE GENERAL
Vietnamese Wars

The Vietnamese Communist general, Vo Nguyan Giap, is universally recognized as one of the masters of modern guerrilla warfare. He used it successfully against the Japanese, French the US and his own people.

Born in 1912, Giap worked as a schoolmaster until his revolutionary activities led to his imprisonment by the French colonial administration. Giap then fled to China, where he studied irregular warfare methods under Mao Tse Tung. Upon his return to French Indo-China, he raised and led guerrilla groups, which, with allied aid, operated against the Vichy French forces as well as against the Japanese army of occupation.

During the Second World War, it was obviously allied policy to supply arms to resistance groups in enemy-occupied territory. So, ironically, it was the US government that encouraged the expansion of Ho Chi Minh's revolutionary *Viet Minh* organization and Giap to increase the scope of his military operations. Both men were fully prepared to fill the power vacuum that the withdrawal of the Japanese during August 1945 and the recall of the French colonial officials who had supported Vichy left waiting to be filled. When the French returned, they found a military regime in power – Giap himself was Minister of Defence and commander-in-chief of the army – which they refused to recognize. As a consequence, the *Viet Minh* promptly returned underground to fight them.

Struggle against the French

The *Viet Minh* had two military forces – the skeleton command structure of a regular army and an active guerrilla force, the *Viet Cong*. Giap's guerrilla operations were successful because he was leading well-trained *Viet Cong* veterans against a conventional army with no counter-insurgency experience. Perhaps this engendered an overconfidence that led Giap to disregard one of the basic rules of unconventional warfare – never to fight a set-piece battle against a better-armed foe – with his decision to launch the Red River delta offensive in 1951. This was a series of attacks launched by the *Viet Minh* against French positions around Haiphong and Hanoi. Having suffered major defeats at Cao Bang and Lang Son, in which isolated French garrisons had been over-whelmed, the French had now retreated to the so-called De Lattre line – named after their commander, General Jean de Lattre de Tassigny – in the delta. This, however, was still under construction and, to Giap, victory must have seemed inevitable.

De Lattre, however, had other ideas. By deploying loyal Vietnamese forces in front line positions, so leaving the bulk of his French units to act as a mobile reserve, he believed he could take on Giap and beat him. The French

GUERRILLA LEADER *Over more than 20 years of fighting, Giap beat two western powers – France and the USA.*

were also operating on internal lines of communication and were backed by strong artillery and air firepower. The offensive started in January and, by June, Giap had had enough.

His troops suffered a 50 per cent casualty rate. However, Giap restored his men's morale and his own reputation in the drawn-out battle for Dien Bien Phu. In November 1953, the French high command air-dropped a military force into a jungle area near the border with Laos, with the task of establishing a complex of nine interconnecting and mutually supporting fortresses with two central airstrips to bring in supplies and to evacuate the sick. Dien Bien Phu was deliberately chosen by the French to force Giap into another set-piece battle, but what they in fact created was the almost classic guerrilla scenario of an immobile enemy in fixed positions, who could only be directed, supplied or reinforced by air from bases far removed from the battlefield.

Giap was not inactive, although the French thought him so. He set his troops, four divisions strong, tunneling their way towards the French "boxes". *Viet Cong* artillery was hauled by hand into position and then opened a sustained and heavy barrage. The tactic was simple. Each "box" was to be attacked in sequence. After one had been bombarded for days, the *Viet Cong* infantry stormed out of the tunnel exits, which were often within the French barbed wire, to storm and overrun the position.

One after the other, the "boxes" fell. Giap's artillery made the landing strips unuseable and attempts to supply or reinforce the garrison by air-drop failed. In May, the French survivors surrendered. The French will to resist crumbled and they evacuated the country, which was divided between the Communist *Viet Minh* north and the non-Communist south.

The USA intervenes

In 1959, Giap's North Vietnamese army and the *Viet Cong* invaded South Vietnam; in 1961, the USA sent in troops to support the anti-Communist regime. The ensuing conflict was one of extreme contrasts. US troops, armed with sophisticated weapons and with total command of the air, faced an irregular force, which lacked both those advantages. However, Giap's logistical ability and powers of organization created a supply route from North Vietnam to *Viet Cong* units in the south – the so-called Ho Chi Minh trail – while, in the guerrilla workshops he established, battlefield debris was recycled to produce bombs and shells for the *Viet Cong*. The chain of supply and reinforcement was never broken, except for the briefest periods, throughout the entire war.

The Giap policy was to win by attrition, a wasteful method of warfare, but one which would guarantee victory because the *Viet Cong* had numbers on its side. A political campaign ran in tandem with the military one. In that tactic, revolutionary organizations world wide exploited every media avenue to attack the US involvement. Through a well-orchestrated propaganda campaign, the US intervention was portrayed as cynical neo-colonial aggression.

The Tet offensive

Once again, however, Giap miscalculated the military situation. In 1968, convinced that he was now strong enough to undertake conventional warfare, that the US and South Vietnamese forces were demoralized and also anticipating support from the South Vietnamese civilian population, he launched the Tet offensive. Its short-term military objective was to break the military stalemate; its long-term political aim was to demonstrate the popular support that the *Viet Cong* enjoyed, thus causing both the collapse of the South Vietnamese government and US withdrawal from the country.

On 31 January 1968, Giap's offensive opened. More than 80,000 soldiers of the regular North Vietnamese army and *Viet Cong*, attacked 100 of South Vietnam's principal cities. However, the civilian population did not react as Giap had expected. Nor were the South Vietnamese and US troops demoralized by the offensive, but fought the Communists to a standstill. Giap's troops suffered tremendous casualties and were forced onto the defensive. One US theory was that the Tet offensive was launched deliberately to lead to heavy losses for the *Viet Cong*. According to this theory, Giap's guerrilla operations had been too successful, arousing the jealousy of the senior commanders of the North Vietnamese army. Tet was thus intended to weaken Giap's personal position; Ho Chi Minh, who also feared Giap's popularity, was party to the plot.

At the same time as Tet was being planned, North Vietnamese regulars attacked the Khe Sanh combat base to divert US and South Vietnamese attention from the forthcoming guerrilla offensive. In this siege, which lasted for 77 days from 21 January 1968, around 6,000 US marines and South Vietnamese rangers held Khe Sanh against an estimated 20,000 North Vietnamese regulars. Giap had hoped for a new Dien Bien Phu, but he was to be thwarted by two factors – the full use of American firepower and airmobility.

Towards victory

Khe Sanh, close to the Laotian border and dominating Route 9, the main road to the coast, was the western anchor of a line of so-called combat bases the US had set up to block any sudden enemy troop movements. At the time of the North Vietnamese attack, it was held by four marine battalions, plus the South Vietnamese 37th Rangers, with substantial artillery and air support. Air power, indeed, was to be one of the keys to the battlefield; US commanders had planned Operation *Niagara* as a deliberate counter-move to any North Vietnamese threat. In this, all available air power was to be used to create "a cascade of shells and bombs" to block any North Vietnamese advance. The Americans had also learned from the fate of the French at Dien Bien Phu, concentrating their ground forces on the peaks of the hills surrounding the main position, being determined to keep its vital airstrip open.

Attacks came thick and fast – first from the north, then from along Route 9 in the south and finally from the east. Khe Sanh itself was under almost constant artillery or rocket fire; this reached a peak on 23 February, when 1,307 shells hit the base. By this time, Khe Sanh's garrison depended totally on parachute drops or helicopter missions for supplies and evacuation of wounded. Nevertheless, the garrison held on grimly until, on 1 April, Operation *Pegasus* was successfully launched to relieve the base. By 7 April, the siege had been lifted.

However, although Giap, the *Viet Cong* and the North Vietnamese regulars had suffered two military defeats, they had won the long-term political objective, the USA indicating that it would withdraw, provided the security of the south could be guaranteed. Despite this accord, Giap's forces, together with the North Vietnamese army, invaded South Vietnam in April 1975 and in a series of bloody battles forcibly unified north and south under Communist rule. The process started with a series of attacks launched in the Central Highlands; quickly realizing that their South Vietnamese opponents were badly deployed and ill-equipped, due to lack of US support, the attacks expanded, reaching a peak with a drive to the coast and the capture of Ban Me Thuot. This split South Vietnam in two. The government panicked, the South Vietnamese army disintegrated and Saigon fell to Giap's triumphant forces in June.

Giap was not to enjoy the fruits of victory. The strain of continual fighting for more than two decades, the stress of command decisions and the constant struggle against the intrigues of his party comrades, caused his health to fail. He retired that same year.

INDEX

ACKNOWLEDGEMENTS

The Paul Press would like to thank the following organizations for the use of their pictures:

11 Bridgeman Art Library; 15, 16, 17 Mary Evans; 17 Peter Newark's Historical Pictures; 19, 21, 23 Mary Evans; 25 Peter Newark's Historical Pictures; 27, 29 Mary Evans; 30 Bridgeman Art Library; 31, 32, 33 Mary Evans; 36 Bridgeman Art Library; 38, 39, 41, 42, 43, 45, 46, 47 Mary Evans; 48 Topham; 49,50 Mary Evans; 51 Bridgeman Art Library; 53 Mary Evans; 54 Bridgeman Art Library; 59 Topham; 61 Mary Evans; 63, 65 Peter Newark's Historical Pictures; 66, 68 Bridgeman Art Library; 70 Mary Evans; 72 Bridgeman Art Library; 73, 75, 76 Mary Evans; 77 Topham; 80, 81 Bridgeman Art Library; 83, 84, 85, 86, 89, 90, 91, 92, 93 Mary Evans; 95, 96, 97, 98 Bridgeman Art Library; 100, 101, 102, 103 Peter Newark's Historical Pictures; 111, 116 The Illustrated London News; 117 Peter Newark's Western Americana; 119 The Trustees of the Imperial War Museum; 121 Bridgeman Art Library; 122 The Trustees of the Imperial War Museum; 124, 127(tl) Topham; 127(br) The Illustrated London News; 129 Topham; 130 The Trustees of the Imperial War Museum; 132 The Illustrated London News; 133 Topham; 135 Peter Newark's Historical Pictures; 137 Topham; 139 Popperfoto; 141, 143 Peter Newark's Historical Pictures; 147 Hulton Picture Library; 149 The Trustees of the Imperial War Museum; 151 Topham; 153, 155 The Trustees of the Imperial War Museum; 157 Hulton Picture Library; 159, 161, 164, 167 Topham; 169 Novosti; 170, 172, 173 The Trustees of the Imperial War Museum; 174 The RAF Museum; 175(tl) Peter Newark's Historical Pictures; 175(tr), 176, 177 The Trustees of the Imperial War Museum; 178, 179 RAC Tank Museum; 180 (top) The Trustees of the Imperial War Museum; 180 (bottom) RAC Tank Museum; 181 Peter Newark's Historical Pictures; 192 The Trustees of the Imperial War Museum; 195 Topham; 196 Novosti; 202, 205 The Trustees of the Imperial War Museum; 206, 209 Topham; 212 Novosti; 213, 218 Topham; 220 The Trustees of the Imperial War Museum; 222 Topham; 224 Novosti; 225 The Trustees of the Imperial War Museum; 227 Novosti; 231 The Trustees of the Imperial War Museum; 234 Topham; 235 The Trustees of the Imperial War Museum; 241 Novosti; 242 Peter Newark's Western Americana; 243 Barnaby's Picture Library; 244, 245 The Trustees of the Imperial War Museum; 246, 247, 248 Topham.

	DATE DUE		